J. M. BEATTIE

Crime and the Courts in England
1660–1800

CLARENDON PRESS · OXFORD

This book has been printed digitally and produced in a standard specification
in order to ensure its continuing availability

OXFORD
UNIVERSITY PRESS

Great Clarendon Street, Oxford OX2 6DP

Oxford University Press is a department of the University of Oxford.
It furthers the University's objective of excellence in research, scholarship,
and education by publishing worldwide in

Oxford New York

Auckland Bangkok Buenos Aires Cape Town Chennai
Dar es Salaam Delhi Hong Kong Istanbul Karachi Kolkata
Kuala Lumpur Madrid Melbourne Mexico City Mumbai Nairobi
São Paulo Shanghai Singapore Taipei Tokyo Toronto

with an associated company in Berlin

Oxford is a registered trade mark of Oxford University Press
in the UK and in certain other countries

Published in the United States
by Oxford University Press Inc., New York

© 1986 by Princeton University Press

The moral rights of the author have been asserted

Database right Oxford University Press (maker)

Reprinted 2002

ISBN 0-19-820057-9

CRIME AND THE COURTS IN ENGLAND
1660–1800

WITHDRAWN

FOR SUSAN

CONTENTS

TABLES

ILLUSTRATIONS

FIGURES

SHORT TITLES OF PRINTED SOURCES

Works frequently cited in the notes have been identified by the following short titles. Others have been fully cited at the first occurrence in each chapter. The place of publication is London unless otherwise noted.

Blackstone, *Commentaries*, vol. 4

William Blackstone, *Commentaries on the Laws of England*, vol. 4, *Of Public Wrongs* (1769)

Brewer and Styles, eds., *An Ungovernable People*

John Brewer and John Styles, eds., *An Ungovernable People: The English and Their Law in the Seventeenth and Eighteenth Centuries* (1980)

Burn, *Justice of the Peace*

Richard Burn, *The Justice of the Peace and Parish Officer*, 1st ed., 2 vols. (1755); 24th ed., 5 vols. (1825)

Cal. H. O. Papers

Joseph Redington and R. A. Roberts, eds., *Calendar of Home Office Papers of the Reign of George III, 1760–1775*, 4 vols. (1878–99)

Cal. S. P. Dom.

R. Lemon et al., eds., *Calendar of State Papers Domestic*, 91 vols. (1856–1964)

Chitty, *Criminal Law*

Joseph Chitty, *A Practical Treatise on the Criminal Law*, 4 vols. (1816)

Clerk of Assize

The Office of the Clerk of Assize: containing the Form and Method of the Proceedings at the Assizes . . . Together with the Office of the Clerk of the Peace, 1st ed. (1676); 2nd ed. (1682)

Cockburn, *Assize Records: Introduction*

J. S. Cockburn, *Calendar of Assize Records, Home Circuit Indictments, Elizabeth I and James I, Introduction* (1985)

Cockburn, *History of English Assizes*   J. S. Cockburn, *A History of English Assizes, 1558–1714* (1972)

Cockburn, ed., *Crime in England*   J. S. Cockburn, ed., *Crime in England, 1550–1800* (Princeton, 1977)

Colquhoun, *Police of the Metropolis*   Patrick Colquhoun, *A Treatise on the Police of the Metropolis, Explaining the Various Crimes and Misdemeanors Which at present are felt as a Pressure upon the Community; and Suggesting Remedies for their Prevention*, 2nd ed. (1796)

Deposition Book of Richard Wyatt   Elizabeth Silverthorne, ed., *Deposition Book of Richard Wyatt, J.P., 1767–1776*, Surrey Record Society, vol. 30 (Guildford, 1978)

East, *Pleas of the Crown*   Sir E. H. East, *A Treatise of the Pleas of the Crown*, 2 vols. (1803)

Eng. Rep.   *The English Reports*, 176 vols. (1900–30)

Fielding, *Increase of Robbers*   Henry Fielding, *An Enquiry into the Causes of the Late Increase of Robbers with some Proposals for Remedying this Growing Evil* (1751)

Foster, *Reports*   Sir Michael Foster, *A Report of Some Proceedings on the Commission of Oyer and Terminer and Gaol Delivery for the Trial of the Rebels in the Year 1746 in the County of Surry and of other Crown Cases. To which are added Discourses upon a few Branches of the Crown Law* (Oxford, 1762)

Gatrell, Lenman, and Parker, eds., *Crime and the Law*   V.A.C. Gatrell, Bruce Lenman, and Geoffrey Parker, eds., *Crime and the Law: The Social History of Crime in Western Europe since 1500* (1980)

G. M.

Gentleman's Magazine

Hale, *Pleas of the Crown*

Sir Matthew Hale, *Historia Placitorum Coronae; the History of the Pleas of the Crown, with notes by Sollom Emlyn* [1676], 2 vols. (1736)

Hawkins, *Pleas of the Crown*

William Hawkins, *A Treatise of the Pleas of the Crown*, 2 vols. (1716–21)

Hay, "Crime, Authority and the Criminal Law"

Douglas Hay, "Crime, Authority and the Criminal Law: Staffordshire 1750–1800" (Ph.D. thesis, University of Warwick, 1975)

Hay, Linebaugh, and Thompson, eds., *Albion's Fatal Tree*

Douglas Hay, Peter Linebaugh, and E. P. Thompson, eds., *Albion's Fatal Tree: Crime and Society in Eighteenth-Century England* (1975)

Holdsworth, *History of English Law*

Sir William Holdsworth, *A History of English Law*, 16 vols. (1922–64)

J.H.C.

Journals of the House of Commons

J.H.L.

Journals of the House of Lords

Kelyng, *Reports*

A Report of Divers Cases in Pleas of the Crown . . . in the Reign of the late King Charles II . . . collected by Sir John Kelyng . . . to which is added the Reports of Three Modern Cases (1708)

Lambert, *Sessional Papers*

Sheila Lambert, ed., *The House of Commons Sessional Papers of the Eighteenth Century*. Section I: 1715–60, 19 vols. (Wilmington, 1975); Section II: 1761–1800, 126 vols. (Wilmington, 1976)

Langbein, "Criminal Trial before the Lawyers"

John H. Langbein, "The Criminal Trial before the Lawyers," *University of Chicago Law Review* 45 (1978), pp. 263–316

Langbein, "Shaping the Eighteenth-Century Criminal Trial"
John H. Langbein, "Shaping the Eighteenth-Century Trial: A View from the Ryder Sources," *University of Chicago Law Review* 50 (1983), pp. 1–136

Leach, *Reports*
Thomas Leach, *Cases in Crown Law, determined by the Twelve Judges; by the Court of King's Bench; and by the Commissioners of Oyer and Terminer, and General Gaol Delivery*, 4th ed., 2 vols. (1815)

OBSP
Old Bailey Sessions Papers

Radzinowicz, *History*
Sir Leon Radzinowicz, *History of English Criminal Law and Its Administration from 1750*, 4 vols. to date (1948–68)

Report on Criminal Laws (1819)
House of Commons. *Report from the Select Committee on Criminal Laws*, Parliamentary Papers (1819), vol. 8

Ryder Notebook
Notes made by Dudley Ryder on cases at the Old Bailey, 1754-56 (see bibliography)

Ryder Assize Diary
Notes mady by Ryder on cases at the Home Circuit assizes, 1754-55 (see bibliography)

S.A.P.
Surrey Assize Proceedings

Smith, *Colonists in Bondage*
Abbott E. Smith, *Colonists in Bondage: White Servitude and Convict Labor in America, 1607–1776* (1947; repr. Gloucester, Mass., 1965)

Stephen, *History of the Criminal Law*
Sir James Fitzjames Stephen, *History of the Criminal Law of England*, 3 vols. (1883)

Strange, *Reports*
Sir John Strange, *Reports of Adjudged Cases in Courts of Chancery, King's Bench, Common Pleas and Exchequer*, 2 vols. (1755)

Surrey Quarter Sessions Records Dorothy L. Powell and Hilary Jenkin-
son, eds., *Surrey Quarter Sessions
Records. Order Book and Sessions
Rolls, 1659–1661*, Surrey County
Council, vol. 6 (Kingston upon
Thames, 1934); idem, *Order Book
and Sessions Rolls, 1661–1663*,
vol. 7 (1935); idem, *Order Books
and Session Rolls, 1663–1666*,
Surrey Record Society, vol. 16,
no. 39 (1938); Dorothy L. Pow-
ell, ed., *Order Book and Sessions
Rolls, 1666–1668*, Surrey County
Council, vol. 9 (1951)

Thompson, *Whigs and
Hunters* E. P. Thompson, *Whigs and Hunters:
The Origin of the Black Act* (1975)

Webb and Webb, *The Par-
ish and the County* Sidney Webb and Beatrice Webb, *The
Parish and the County: English Lo-
cal Government*, vol. 1 (1906;
repr. 1963)

PREFACE

In writing this book I have had the help of a great many people, and it is a pleasure to be able to thank them. I must first acknowledge the financial support of the Canada Council, the Social Sciences and Humanities Research Council of Canada, and the Research Board of the University of Toronto. Their generosity made possible the archival work upon which the book largely rests and also enabled me to analyze much of the data by computer. At a crucial stage in the writing I was fortunate to be awarded a Killam Senior Fellowship, which relieved me from teaching duties, and I am pleased to record my thanks to the Killam Research Programme of the Canada Council.

I owe a considerable debt of gratitude to a large number of librarians and archivists in England and Canada. It is a great pleasure to thank Dr. David Robinson, the county archivist of Surrey, and the staff of the County Record Office for their cheerful and efficient help. I am particularly grateful to Elizabeth Stazicker and Anne McCormack, who have forwarded my work in numerous ways over many years. I remember with gratitude, too, the late Miss Marguerite Gollancz, who was the county archivist when I first worked in Surrey and whose interest and encouragement meant a great deal to me. I am also grateful to the archivists at the Guildford Muniment Room and to Mr. J. R. More-Molyneux for permission of quote from the Loseley Mss., which he has so generously put on deposit there. I would like to express my thanks to the staffs of the Public Record Office, the British Library, the Cambridge University Library, the East and West Sussex Record Offices, the Wiltshire Record Office, and the Robarts Library, University of Toronto. I am particularly grateful for numerous kindnesses to Roy Hunnisett of the Public Record office and to Mary McTavish and Merrill Distad of the Robarts Library.

I have been fortunate to have had the help of a number of research assistants in the collection of evidence, the coding of data for computer analysis, and the running of computer programs. I would like especially to thank Linda Distad, whose skill and enthusiasm I depended on over a long period in the early stages of the research, and Peter Munsche, David Clark, Christine Cook, and Georgina Wyman. I wish to thank Chris Grounds of the Geography Department, University of Toronto, for preparing the maps, and Constance Craig for the figures.

A large number of friends and colleagues have helped me over the years by sending references and by reading and commenting on parts or all of the manuscript in its various drafts. I am of course responsible for the errors and shortcomings that remain, but I have been saved from numerous mistakes and have benefited in countless ways from their suggestions and criticisms. It is a pleasure to have this opportunity to thank Donna Andrew, David Flaherty, Arie Freiberg, Martin Friedland, Thomas Green, Peter King, Norma Landau, Peter Lawson, Peter Linebaugh, Robert Malcolmson, Peter Munsche, and John Styles. I owe a particular debt of gratitude to James Cockburn, whose knowledge of the records of the assize courts and whose advice I have depended on over many years; to John Langbein, who has generously provided me with a great deal of information and who subjected an early version of the manuscript to a particularly thorough and helpful reading; to Douglas Hay, who helped me plan the quantitative aspects of the work at the beginning of my research and who has continued over the years to give me the benefit of his advice on this and other subjects; and to Joanna Innes, who has been the most generous of friends and has shared unstintingly the results of her own work and offered a great deal of valuable advice.

It is also a pleasure to record my gratitude to my colleagues in the Centre of Criminology at the University of Toronto. I have drawn heavily on their resources for typing and computer analysis in recent years, and while the main financial support of my work came from the Canada Council and the Social Sciences and Humanities Research Council of Canada, I must also acknowledge the help of the Ministry of the Solicitor General of Canada through the Contributions grant made to the Centre of Criminology. I am grateful to the staff of the Centre, particularly to Rita Donelan, Marie Pearce who typed the final manuscript, Janet Chan who gave me a great deal of help with data analysis, and Catherine Matthews and the staff of the library. I have benefited not only from the physical resources of the Centre, but also from the criticism, advice, and interest of members of its research and teaching staff, especially Patricia Baranek, Richard Ericson, Clifford Shearing, and Philip Stenning. I feel a particular debt of gratitude to John Edwards, the founder and first Director of the Centre, and to Tony Doob, his successor: their interest in my work and their generous support have meant a great deal.

I wish to thank the editorial staff of Princeton University Press, and particularly Barbara Stump for her skill and patience in editing the manuscript.

Finally, I am grateful to my family: to my children who have helped me in many ways; and above all to my wife, who has taken part in the research and read and criticized every draft of the manuscript. She has contributed greatly to this book from its inception, and it is a particular pleasure to dedicate it to her.

J. M. Beattie

Toronto
January 1985

CRIME AND THE COURTS IN ENGLAND
1660–1800

CHAPTER I

INTRODUCTION

The central concern in this book is the way the English courts dealt with crime in a period in which the foundations of modern forms of judicial administration were laid. It is organized in two sections. The first, a group of four chapters, deals with the process of prosecution, the major offenses brought to court, and the suspects who were charged. The second section consists of five chapters concerned with the character of the criminal trial, the patterns of jury verdicts, and the nature of punishment. Although these matters are laid out in separate sections, my aim is to attempt to uncover the links between them, particularly the links between forms and levels of prosecuted crime on the one hand and the criminal law and the machinery of administration on the other, and to place changes in both over the late seventeenth and eighteenth centuries in a broad social context.

THEMES AND ARGUMENTS

There has been a growing interest in recent years in the history of criminal law and the administration of justice, and in the study of the offenses that societies at different times and places choose to prosecute and punish. Crime has been an attractive subject to social historians because it promises to provide some insight into the behavior of ordinary men and women who have left few records of their lives and attitudes; and the means adopted to deal with crime promise in turn to reveal something of the mentality of the classes who made the law and ran the courts, and to reflect shifts in the distribution of power in society. There has been little agreement as yet among English historians about what the study of "crime" entails. Some would want to include the whole range of unlawful acts that might result in the imposition of a penalty by any court or any official exercising lawful jurisdiction. Others would take a narrower view of the offenses that ought to be lumped together, while continuing to define crime by legal criteria. Still others would be tempted to move away from the constraints of the law altogether and establish the boundaries of the subject in shifting public attitudes toward particular forms of behavior.[1] When one adds the range of meanings that contemporaries brought to the category "crime," it would seem best if we could simply abandon that word entirely in favor of a term that did not seem so obviously self-defining—"offenses," for example. But "crime" is too common and too handy to be given up so easily, and thus I take it as my first task in a book with that word in the title to establish what I mean by it. I can do that best by explaining the title and by setting out the argument I want to present.

By "crime and the courts" I mean to indicate a concern with the character and social meaning of prosecuted offenses (within limits I shall draw presently) and with the way those accused of committing them were dealt with by the courts. The choice of the period 1660 to 1800 was dictated partly by the survival of court records in the county of Surrey (which I wished particularly to examine for reasons I will discuss in a moment) and partly because this was clearly a period in which significant changes were taking place in the criminal law and the system of criminal administration.[2] I wanted a period that would be long enough to provide some sense of the chronology and pattern of those changes and yet that was short enough to be manageable. The latter point is of some importance since there are no ready-made returns of crimes charged and punishments handed out before the nineteenth century—the government made no effort to collect such information before 1810—and it is necessary to gather the evidence from the records of the courts themselves, case by case from the indictment files and the books made up by the clerks that summarized the business of the court sessions.[3] There were two criminal courts of

---

[1] For various approaches to the scope and meaning of crime in England see Hay, Linebaugh, and Thompson, eds., *Albion's Fatal Tree*, pp. 13–15; Thompson, *Whigs and Hunters*, pp. 193–95, 207; J. A. Sharpe, "Crime and Delinquency in an Essex Parish, 1600–1640," in Cockburn, ed., *Crime in England*, pp. 90–109; Gatrell, Lenman, and Parker, eds., *Crime and the Law*, introduction; Kai Erikson, *Wayward Puritans: A Study in the Sociology of Deviance* (New York, 1966); Timothy Curtis, "Explaining Crime in Early Modern England," *Criminal Justice History* 1 (1980), pp. 117–37. For discussions of recent writings on the history of crime in England see Douglas Hay, "Crime and Justice in Eighteenth- and Nineteenth-Century England," *Crime and Justice: An Annual Review of Research* 2 (1980), pp. 45–84; J. A. Sharpe, "The History of Crime in Late Medieval and Early Modern England: A Review of the Field," *Social History* 7 (1982), pp. 187–203; and David Jones, *Crime, Protest, Community and Police in Nineteenth-Century Britain* (1982), chap. 1.

[2] The Restoration seemed a reasonable point to begin in any case, but that starting date was also determined by the fact that the quarter sessions rolls have only survived in Surrey from 1660. I chose to end on the eve of large-scale changes in the criminal law, police, prisons, punishment, and other aspects of judicial administration because they require much more extensive treatment than could be managed in this book.

[3] These records are described in the appendix. There is one source of collected and printed evidence about prosecutions and punishment in the eighteenth century: the report of the parlia-

importance in this period, the quarter sessions and assizes: the latter were held by judges of the high courts who came into each county on circuit twice a year; the former by the justices of the peace of the county four times a year. Both dealt with countywide business at each session, and the county is thus the most useful and natural geographical unit of study if the work of the criminal courts is to be the central focus. This study is based largely on the records of those courts in the county of Surrey, with some supplementary evidence from Sussex.

The offenses dealt with by the assizes and quarter sessions can be divided into several broad categories. There was in the first place a range of offenses that were regarded as particularly serious and that were subject to capital punishment at common law. These included several forms of treason, including offenses against the coinage and the "petty treason" that was committed when a servant murdered his master or a wife her husband, both in the eyes of the law having killed their natural superiors. The most common of the serious offenses were felonies, which included all other homicides, infanticide, rape, robbery, burglary, larceny, and arson. All were triable mainly at the assizes, where they accounted for the largest part of the court's criminal work.

The courts of quarter sessions, both the county sessions and those that met in boroughs, were mainly concerned with a range of lesser offenses. They had ceased to deal with capital offenses by the early seventeenth century;[4] and although they continued to hear cases in which a victim could claim to have been harmed in his person or property, they confined themselves on the whole to matters of lesser seriousness than those that preoccupied the assize courts. The magistrates in quarter sessions were particularly concerned with such matters as assault, riot, petty larceny, fraud, and embezzlement, though in the second half of the eighteenth century they were beginning to take on an increasing proportion of the grand larceny cases arising in some counties. The quarter sessions also had to deal with a large number of offenses without specific victims and others that involved a failure to abide by some form of local obligation or an economic or other regulation. The magistrates, for example, heard com-

---

mentary committee that examined the administration of the criminal law in 1819 (*Report on Criminal Laws* [1819]). Sir Leon Radzinowicz used that data extensively in his discussion of the changing incidence of capital punishment over the eighteenth and early nineteenth centuries (*History*, vol. 1, chap. 5). Douglas Hay has reexamined these figures and is critical of Radzinowicz's conclusions. His preliminary findings can be found in his thesis ("Crime, Authority and the Criminal Law," pp. 511–26). He is preparing for publication a fuller version of the argument presented there.

⁴ Cockburn, *History of English Assizes*, pp. 90–97; John H. Langbein, *Prosecuting Crime in the Renaissance: England, Germany, France* (Cambridge, Mass., 1974), pp. 105–18.

plaints brought forward by constables and local juries against men accused of failing to work on the roads or refusing to act as night watchmen, or men charged with some harmful and prohibited conduct such as keeping an unlicensed alehouse or blocking the highways. In the seventeenth century the quarter sessions were busier dealing with matters of this kind than with cases prosecuted by a victim who thought himself personally harmed. Two-thirds of the charges that went forward from the parish of Terling in Essex between 1560 and 1699 were what Wrightson and Levine call "obligation reinforcement" and "regulative prosecutions," and only a third were more private complaints, "interpersonal disputes" as they call them.[5] This includes cases at both the quarter sessions and the assizes, but it is clear that the bulk of those aimed at the regulation of conduct would have been heard by the justices of the peace rather than the assize judges. That remained true in the eighteenth century.

From one point of view it would be possible to regard all such offenses, and indeed the disputes dealt with at ecclesiastical and manor courts, too, as the proper subject matter for the historian of crime.[6] But to lump all those offenses together would seem to me to lead to confusion, and I believe we will have a clearer understanding of both contemporary views and the character and functioning of the law and the courts if we deal with categories that have some broad internal coherence. That is my justification for concentrating on offenses in which some real harm was done to a specific victim who then generally made the complaint and carried on the prosecution. Within that broad category I will concentrate further on the most serious charges, those that alleged an offense against property—robbery, burglary, and larceny—or against the person, especially homicide, infanticide, and rape. Together they provided the bulk of the criminal work of the assizes and, along with assault cases, the majority of "interpersonal" charges at the quarter sessions. Such offenses against the person and property made up the everyday business of the criminal courts, certainly of the most important of those courts, the assizes.

These "mainstream" offenses have been the subject of some recent work on crime in England in the early modern period.[7] But many recent

---

[5] Keith Wrightson and David Levine, *Poverty and Piety in an English Village: Terling, 1525–1700* (New York, 1979), pp. 116–18.

[6] Sharpe, "Crime and Delinquency in an Essex Parish."

[7] J. S. Cockburn, "The Nature and Incidence of Crime in England, 1559–1625: A Preliminary Survey," in Cockburn, ed., *Crime in England*, pp. 49–71; J. A. Sharpe, *Crime in Seventeenth-Century England: A County Study* (Cambridge, 1983); Douglas Hay, "War, Dearth and Theft in the Eighteenth Century: The Record of the English Courts," *Past and Present* 95 (1982), pp. 117–60; J. M. Beattie, "The Pattern of Crime in England, 1660–1800," *Past and Present* 62 (1974), pp. 47–95; J. M. Beattie, "The Criminality of Women in Eighteenth-Century England," *Journal of Social History* 8 (1975), pp. 80–116; Alan Macfarlane, *The Justice and the Mare's Ale:*

studies have been concerned with offenses like smuggling, poaching, coining, and riot, the kinds of offenses that are sometimes called "social crimes" because, unlike murder, rape, and most ordinary theft, they were not universally regarded as "criminal" and were often carried out with the active approval of the local community.[8] Such offenses have been the subject of some excellent work, much of it in the form of case studies, for which they are peculiarly suited since what is required to make them intelligible is the detailed reconstruction of the social, economic, and political circumstances in which they occurred.[9] In dealing with the large number of offenses included within the property and violence categories over a century and a half, I cannot hope to achieve the level of detail that distinguishes many of these case studies and helps to make them so illuminating. But the "mainstream" offenses have the great advantage of being the offenses that contemporaries generally had in mind when they talked about "crime"; when they complained that crime was rising out of control they meant

---

Law and Disorder in Seventeenth-Century England (1981). Several theses completed in recent years have dealt with crime in the early modern period; for three concerned with the eighteenth century, and which one looks forward to seeing in print very soon, see Douglas Hay, "Crime, Authority and the Criminal Law"; Peter Linebaugh, "Tyburn: A Study of Crime and the Labouring Poor in London during the First Half of the Eighteenth Century" (Ph.D. thesis, University of Warwick, 1975); and Peter King, "Crime, Law and Society in Essex, 1740–1820" (Ph.D. thesis, University of Cambridge, 1984). Property offenses and violence in the nineteenth century have been studied by David Philips, *Crime and Authority in Victorian England: The Black Country, 1835–1860* (1977); J. J. Tobias, *Crime and Industrial Society in the Nineteenth Century* (1967); V.A.C. Gatrell and T. B. Hadden, "Criminal Statistics and Their Interpretation," in E. A. Wrigley, ed., *Nineteenth-Century Society: Essays in the Use of Quantitative Methods for the Study of Social Data* (Cambridge, 1972); V.A.C. Gatrell, "The Decline of Theft and Violence in Victorian and Edwardian England," in Gatrell, Lenman, and Parker, eds., *Crime and the Law*; Jennifer Davis, "The London Garotting Panic of 1862: A Moral Panic and the Creation of a Criminal Class in Mid-Victorian England," in ibid.; David Jones, *Crime, Protest, Community and Police in Nineteenth-Century Britain* (1982); Ted Robert Gurr, Peter N. Grabosky, and Richard C. Hula, *The Politics of Crime and Conflict: A Comparative History of Four Cities* (Los Angeles, 1977). For the study of violence see in particular Ted Robert Gurr, "Historical Trends in Violent Crime: A Critical Review of the Evidence," *Crime and Justice: An Annual Review of Research* 3 (1981), pp. 295–353; and Lawrence Stone, "Interpersonal Violence in English Society, 1300–1980," *Past and Present* 101 (1983).

[8] For the notion of "social crime" and its difficulties see J. G. Rule, "Social Crime in the Rural South in the Eighteenth and Early Nineteenth Centuries," *Southern History* 1 (1979), pp. 135–53; Hay, Linebaugh, and Thompson, eds., *Albion's Fatal Tree*, pp. 13–14; John Styles, " 'Our Traitorous Money Makers': The Yorkshire Coiners and the Law, 1760–83," in Brewer and Styles, eds., *An Ungovernable People*, pp. 245–49.

[9] Excellent examples of work of this kind are to be found in several volumes of essays, including Hay, Linebaugh, and Thompson, eds., *Albion's Fatal Tree*; Cockburn, ed., *Crime in England*; and Brewer and Styles, eds., *An Ungovernable People*. Two first-rate books have been devoted to particular offenses and the way the law concerning them was constructed, interpreted, and enforced: Thompson, *Whigs and Hunters*; and P. B. Munsche, *Gentlemen and Poachers: The English Game Laws, 1671–1831* (Cambridge, 1981).

violence and theft, and particularly the offenses in which they were combined—burglary and robbery. For this reason, and because they made up
the bulk of the day-to-day business of the criminal courts, they are of
particular importance to me. The ordinary mainstream offenses embodied
the most serious and persistent threats to the peace and stability of the
society, and it was in dealing with them in this period that pretrial
procedures were elaborated, the criminal trial itself was transformed, and
the main elements of the system of punishment underwent remarkable
changes.

My aim in the chapters on property offenses and serious violence that
make up Part I is to establish something of the character of these offenses
and of the behavior that typically lay behind them. I will also examine
variations in the level of prosecutions over time and attempt to identify
(as far as is possible) those brought to court as suspects. An important
question, however, arises at the outset: How did cases come to be prosecuted; how did these suspects get drawn into the system? That is clearly
a crucial issue that reveals a great deal about the law as a social institution,
about the significance of the number and kinds of offenses indicted, and
about the public's attitudes toward the criminal law. It is crucial in this
regard that prosecution was left very much to the victim. Cases were
initiated for the most part only when the victim complained to a magistrate. And in the small-scale society of the village a prosecution may not
have been the most effective way to deal with petty violence and theft.
Demanding an apology and a promise not to repeat the offense, perhaps
with some monetary or other satisfaction, may have been a more natural
as well as a more effective response to such an offense, or perhaps simple
revenge, directly taken.

The decision to prosecute or not was likely to have been influenced
by the personal relationship of the victim and the accused and their place
in the village, by the victim's view of the law and the courts, and by the
effects on the harmony of the community that an appeal to the outside
authority of the king's courts might be expected to have. In a small
community the informal sanctions that might be invoked could easily have
been as effective as a full-scale court case, especially given the crucial
importance of character and reputation to an individual's and a family's
standing in the society. In these circumstances an appeal to a magistrate
might well be a last resort or the result of one too many offenses, or might
perhaps be reserved for an accused who was an outsider with no standing
in the village that could be threatened by the alternative means of coercion.
A number of studies, drawing on a range of intersecting sources at the
parish level, have shown how the threat of prosecution could work as an
element in the exercise of authority and have made it abundantly clear

that there was nothing automatic in this period about the registering of complaints before the local magistrates and the pressing of criminal charges, even when it was obvious that an offense had been committed and a suspect was readily at hand.[10]

It is thus important to know how crimes were prosecuted—and how that process changed over time—if we are going to judge the possible relationship between the cases brought to court and that larger unknown world of acts that might have led to charges being laid if only the offense and the offender had been discovered and the victim had chosen to complain to the authorities. Equally important is the identity of the prosecutors, who were generally the victims of property offenses and of most of the violence (except of course homicide). To discover who came forward with a complaint, who chose to use the courts, provides some evidence (though it may not be entirely unambiguous) of the way the law and its administration was regarded by the classes of men who had little influence on the way the law developed as well as by those who had. I will examine aspects of the process of prosecution in chapter two and the factors that might have influenced a victim to exercise his discretion either to press a complaint forward to trial or to let it drop. I will be concerned here with the costs and burdens of prosecution—for it fell to the victim himself to pay the charges incurred and, for the most part, to carry the prosecution in court—and with the possible effects of a variety of stimulants devised by parliament to encourage the apprehension and prosecution of serious offenders. Such an investigation makes plain how much of a burden it must have been for many victims of property offenses to take on the costs of a prosecution—to find the ready money and to take the time away from work it would require. The system of private prosecution obviously worked to the disadvantage of everyone but the well-to-do. And yet, as we shall see when we examine the character of property crime in chapter four, the prosecutors who brought cases to the quarter sessions at least were drawn overwhelmingly from the middle ranks of society and included a significant number of artisans and laborers. Men of all conditions are to be found going to a great deal of trouble to pursue thieves and bring them to justice. We will need to explore the implications of this at some length. But it would seem on the face of it that, however constrained in practice access

[10] See, for example, Wrightson and Levine, *Poverty and Piety in an English Village*, chap. 5; M. J. Ingram, "Communities and Courts: Law and Disorder in Early-Seventeenth-Century Wiltshire," in Cockburn, ed., *Crime in England*; T. C. Curtis, "Quarter Sessions Appearances and Their Background: A Seventeenth-Century Regional Study," in ibid.; J. A. Sharpe, "Enforcing the Law in the Seventeenth-Century English Village," in Gatrell, Lenman, and Parker, eds., *Crime and the Law*; Cynthia Herrup, "The Common Peace: Legal Structure and Legal Substance in East Sussex, 1594–1640" (Ph.D. thesis, Northwestern University, 1982), chap. 3.

to the courts must have been for the poorer victims of theft and other property offenses, there was no profound division in society over the legitimacy of the criminal law and the system of judicial administration.

The possible significance of changing levels of indictments for homicide and other violent offenses is dealt with in chapter three and for property offenses in chapter five. It will not be argued in those chapters that the cases brought to court reflected in any simple way the range of unlawful behavior that might have been prosecuted, or that there is a direct relationship between the one and the other. Emphasis will be placed rather on indictments as the outcome of a process in which some acts were translated into the categories of offenses provided by the criminal law and some were not.[11] That process involved the interaction of several considerations that were each constantly changing: the number of "events" that might have given rise to a prosecution; the determination of the victim to press charges; and the attitudes and efficiency of the authorities. We will frequently be concerned with the implications of this in the chapters dealing with the patterns of prosecution, particularly in chapter five, in which the long-term and short-term fluctuations of prosecutions for property offenses are examined in some detail. My conclusion about the fluctuating levels of indictments is that while they do not provide a straightforward guide to crime levels, they do reveal the direction of change of those levels at particular times and under particular circumstances and thus provide evidence of the character of property crime—and evidence in addition of crucial elements in the lives and experiences of the working population.

Several features of the patterns of prosecution of property offenses emerge with particular clarity. Perhaps the most significant is the difference apparent in the levels of charges brought in two parts of the county of

[11] This subject is further discussed in chapter 5, but it may be worth remarking that the absence of modern police forces in the eighteenth century is likely to have made the relationship between behavior and indictment slightly different then from what it was to become. The interactionist criminologists' formulation, as adopted by Philips for his nineteenth-century studies, that prosecuted crime represents the "end result of the process of interaction between the authorities and the lawbreakers and can be used to give a picture of that process in action" (Philips, *Crime and Authority*, p. 45) does not fit the eighteenth-century situation, in which there is much less of a barrier or filter between the victim of a felony and the court. On the whole, magistrates merely processed the accusations of felony that came before them. And what police forces that did exist were responsible for very few prosecutions. They certainly did not take it upon themselves to decide which of the cases brought by individual victims would go forward to prosecution and which would not. The decision rested fundamentally with the private prosecutor, and as Douglas Hay has pointed out, the "indictment levels in the eighteenth century are therefore less likely to be distorted by influences which today express themselves in police practice" ("War, Dearth and Theft," p. 151).

Surrey: in the Borough of Southwark and a number of neighboring parishes in the northeastern corner of the county that were largely within the metropolis of London on the one hand, and the rural parishes and market towns of the remainder of the county on the other. Over both the short and long term there were different patterns of prosecution in each. In "rural" Surrey, for example, as well as in the county of Sussex, there was a long-term downward trend in indictments in property cases from the 1660s into the middle of the eighteenth century, when the level of charges began to rise noticeably. The first part of this pattern appears to fit closely the trend of prosecutions for property crime that J. A. Sharpe has uncovered for the county of Essex in the seventeenth century. Sharpe has shown that after a period of high levels of prosecutions in the early decades of the century, a long decline ensued. Indictments in property cases were running in the 1660s at about a third of the level they had been in the years 1625–34, and they fell even further thereafter.[12] The Surrey and Sussex evidence confirms that trend in rural parishes and suggests that it continued well into the middle of the eighteenth century. In the metropolis of London, on the other hand (if the Surrey evidence is any guide), prosecutions ran at a higher and broadly rising level over the whole period; and in addition, they showed from time to time much larger and more striking annual fluctuations than in the rural parishes of Surrey or in Sussex. In several periods, prosecutions in the more urban parishes of Surrey rose to what contemporaries described as crisis levels.

These patterns of prosecution offer clues, I will argue, to the meaning and character of property offenses. But they also bear on other issues, especially on the question of the nature and timing of changes in the criminal law and in the administration of justice that will occupy us in the chapters that make up Part II. These are concerned with the forms of trial, especially the trial of serious offenses at the assizes, with the verdicts of juries, and with the changing patterns of punishment. The section begins with a discussion in chapter six of aspects of pretrial procedure and the conditions under which the accused were held in jail for trial. This is followed in chapter seven by a study of the main characteristics of criminal trials in the eighteenth century that investigates such matters as the role and nature of the juries, the relationship of juries and judges, the role of the defendant at his trial, and the way juries deliberated and the options open to them as they reached their verdicts. We will also be concerned with the first introduction of lawyers into criminal trials as both defense

---

[12] Sharpe, *Crime in Seventeenth-Century England*, p. 188. On the pattern of prosecutions for crimes against property in three counties on the Home Circuit in the reigns of Elizabeth and James I, see Cockburn, "The Nature and Incidence of Crime in England, 1559–1625," pp. 49–71.

and prosecution counsel in the second quarter of the eighteenth century, and the far-reaching influence that that was to have.[13]

The verdicts of grand juries and trial juries in Surrey, and the exercise of the judges' right to reprieve condemned prisoners and of the royal power of pardon, are taken up in chapter eight. In explaining the decisions reached by juries and judges it is crucial to examine the forms of punishment available to the courts, for the range of penal options must have significantly affected the way they exercised their discretionary powers. In dealing with punishment in this period we will be concerned with two broad problems. The first and most obvious question is how the courts administered the capital laws, since so many of the accused at the assizes were in danger of being hanged and the image of the gallows so pervaded and dominated the courtroom. It is clear that the threat of capital punishment had a powerful influence on the decisions being made by prosecutors, jurors, and judges, and that it determined the way the central government administered the king's prerogative of pardon. But a second theme is equally important: the development in this period of two noncapital punishments—transportation and imprisonment—that the courts were able to impose on convicted felons. The emergence of these sanctions is important from several points of view. Not the least was the influence they were to have on the way capital punishment was administered by the courts, but their main importance was the striking alteration they brought to the punishment of noncapital felonies. We will examine the emergence and the influence of these sanctions in chapters nine and ten, which conclude Part II.[14]

---

[13] The criminal trial in the early modern period has only recently been studied in some detail. For the eighteenth century see in particular two pioneering articles by John H. Langbein: "The Criminal Trial before the Laywers," and "Shaping the Eighteenth-Century Criminal Trial." For the sixteenth and seventeenth centuries see Cockburn, *History of English Assizes*, chap. 6. See also J. M. Beattie, "Crime and the Courts in Surrey, 1736–1753," in Cockburn, ed., *Crime in England*, pp. 156–86, which sketches some of the matters dealt with a little more fully in chapter 7 below. For the changing role of the jury over the medieval and early modern periods see the masterful study by Thomas A. Green, *Verdict According to Conscience: Perspectives on the English Criminal Trial Jury, 1200–1800* (Chicago, 1985).

[14] For recent work on the history of English punishment in this period see below, chapters 9 and 10. I have been particularly helped by Sir Leon Radzinowicz's monumental study *A History of English Criminal Law and Its Administration since 1750*, vol. 1 (1948); Smith, *Colonists in Bondage*; Michael Ignatieff, *A Just Measure of Pain: The Penitentiary in the Industrial Revolution, 1750–1850* (New York, 1978); Robin Evans, *The Fabrication of Virtue: English Prison Architecture, 1750–1840* (Cambridge, 1982); and two unpublished conference papers by Joanna Innes: "Imprisonment and Punishment in Early Modern England" (International Association of Crime and Criminal Justice Conference, Washington D.C., Sept. 1980), and "English Houses of Correction and 'Labour Discipline' c. 1600–1780: A Critical Examination" (Conference on the History of Law, Labour and Crime, University of Warwick, Sept. 1983).

One broad conclusion that emerges from these chapters on trial and punishment is that significant changes took place in the administration of the criminal law over this period. Men accused of committing a felony in 1800 had more opportunity to defend themselves at their examination before a magistrate and to question the grounds on which they were to be committed to trial than they would have had a century and a half earlier. In addition, if they were committed, and if they could afford it, they would have been allowed in 1800 to engage a lawyer to help them present their case at their trial. They had no such right in 1660. The prison they would be held in as they awaited their trial in 1800 was likely to have been at least marginally cleaner and healthier than it might have been in the seventeenth century. And the punishment they would have been subjected to if convicted of a felony would have been very different indeed—not necessarily more advantageous to them, but certainly different. These changes were in full flood by the end of the eighteenth century, but it is important to emphasize that they had been taking place over much of the period we are dealing with. They did not result from a sudden concerted attack by reform-minded men alerted for the first time to the cruelty and inefficiency of the criminal law and its institutions by the writings of Beccaria and John Howard in the 1760s and 1770s—a view that seemed quite natural looking back from the nineteenth century and that is perpetuated in studies of the late eighteenth century as the beginning of the "age of reform" or the "age of improvement." Changes were indeed more consciously advocated and were conceived as "reforms" in the last decades of the eighteenth century. Campaigns mounted intermittently over the last quarter of the century and in the early decades of the nineteenth resulted in a fundamental restructuring of the criminal law by Sir Robert Peel in the 1820s and in major changes in the way the law was administered. But we need to resist the notion that significant changes only occurred after 1770 and that before that there had been a jumble of inflexible, archaic, and unchanging institutions and practices—indeed an "old regime" in need of reform. It seems to me rather that we will better understand the more rapid and more concerted developments of the late eighteenth and early nineteenth centuries if we recognize the importance of the changes that had occurred over the previous century, changes that laid down lines that continued to be followed and shaped the form new schemes were to take.

The advantage of recognizing that so many aspects of the law and its administration were very different indeed in the middle of the eighteenth century than they had been at the Restoration is not simply that it gets the chronology right and clarifies the character of the earlier period. It also bears on the question of how changes in the law and the machinery of justice are to be explained. It is not likely, of course, that all such changes sprang from the same source. Although there were links and interrelationships among the criminal law, the character of trial, the forms of punishment, the state of the prisons, and so on, each was also in many ways autonomous and had its own history. But one stimulant of change seems to have been particularly influential: increases in crime, especially in property offenses, for they were both a signal of moral decay and a threat to the security and stability of society. An apparent increase of such offenses was likely to find a response in the courts, in the verdicts returned and the sentences handed down, and possibly a longer-term response in the questioning of the efficacy of the law and the established means of punishment.

It is here that the patterns of crime in London may be of particular importance. Sharpe has noted the puzzling fact that the well-known broadening of the scope of capital punishment after 1689 came when prosecutions for property offenses had been declining for fifty years and more.[15] But while that may have been true of the country, it seems not to have been the experience of the metropolis of London. Prosecutions in Southwark and neighboring urban parishes in Surrey did not fall away in the later seventeenth century, as we will see. In the 1690s the capital presented a scene of deepening immorality, of persistent and pervasive theft, of occasional outbursts of violent crime. The metropolis was unlike the rest of the country. Targets and temptations were more abundant there, and the informal controls that could diminish the levels and the importance of property crime in the smaller-scale community could not work there as effectively. Above all, poverty pressed with particular urgency in London, especially when the large population of men and women who lived at the margins of security suffered from shortages of work. On the other side, London contained the largest concentration of men who were likely to be concerned about crime and the loose habits of the working poor. There were clearly great disparities of income within the enlarging ranks of artisans and small masters in the diversity of trades and crafts the metropolis supported, and among the increasing numbers of shopkeepers, professional men, merchants, traders, and financiers. There were, no doubt, sharp differences of opinion over a range of issues within that broad middling segment of society. But it seems reasonable to think that there was a good deal of agreement about the harmfulness of crime that threatened life and property and disrupted commerce and trade.

It seems to me significant that London was experiencing levels and

[15] Sharpe, *Crime in Seventeenth-Century England*, p. 188. For the capital statutes passed after 1689 see Radzinowicz, *History*, vol. 1, chaps. 1–2 and app. 1.

forms of crime in the late seventeenth century and in the early decades of the eighteenth that were not duplicated in quite the same way in other parts of the country until the 1770s and 1780s, when the renewed growth of the population and the greater concentration of the work force began to create similar social and economic circumstances elsewhere. The dissatisfaction that is expressed in the second half of the eighteenth century about the criminal law and the way it was being administered was not merely encouraged by its failure to prevent crime. But that was one sign that the law was in need of reform. It seems to me that it was exactly that same view, though perhaps more narrowly focused on London, that lay behind the piecemeal changes that had been transforming the system of criminal administration for a hundred years and more before the concerted reform efforts of the late eighteenth century.

In studying the criminal law and its administration one is not merely studying the way that men and women confronted crime narrowly conceived. The administration of the criminal laws, as of the poor laws, facilitated the broader exercise of authority at several levels, and the law had a larger significance and a larger role than as a simple defense against criminals.[16] But the principal purpose of the criminal law was to maintain order and to protect property; and in seeking to understand the way the law was administered and the forces making for change in the chapters on procedure and punishment in Part II, it is necessary to begin with the offenses and the offenders that the authorities were particularly anxious to control.

SOURCES AND EVIDENCE

The range and character of the judicial evidence upon which the book is largely based is discussed in detail in the appendix. The value of this material and the special difficulties it raises will also be discussed in the text where those matters are most at issue. The central core of evidence comes from the Surrey assizes and quarter sessions, but a considerable body of material has also been drawn from the courts of Sussex, and that will be brought in to supplement and extend the Surrey data at particular points throughout the book. Evidence from other counties and other courts, especially the Old Bailey, will also be referred to occasionally; and the

[16] For that theme and the general subject of the criminal law as ideology see Douglas Hay, "Property, Authority and the Criminal Law," in Hay, Linebaugh, and Thompson, eds., *Albion's Fatal Tree*; Thompson, *Whigs and Hunters*, chap. 10; and Brewer and Styles, eds., *An Ungovernable People*, introduction. For a view that challenges Hay's approach and conclusions see John H. Langbein, "Albion's Fatal Flaws," *Past and Present* 98 (1983), pp. 96–120.

papers of the secretaries of state (the State Papers Domestic), which include reports from judges to the king and the cabinet on capital cases and the correspondence between the secretaries and the judges on penal questions in general, are frequently drawn on. Since the issues discussed are normally of national and not merely of local importance, I have not restricted myself in using this evidence to Surrey or Sussex cases. But the main evidence on which all sections of this book rest is derived from the work of the criminal courts in Surrey and, to a much lesser extent, in Sussex.

The courts of quarter sessions and assizes together dealt with virtually all criminal charges brought to trial. Broadly speaking, the assize court heard all the serious cases; certainly by 1660 the county justices of the peace who held the quarter sessions four times a year were leaving most felony charges, and particularly all capital cases, to the assize judges who came into the county twice a year with the king's commission to clear the jails and to deal with all outstanding business.[17] The assize judges were mainly judges of the superior courts, or at the least men of considerable standing in the legal profession. On the Home Circuit, of which Surrey and Sussex were part, along with Hertfordshire, Essex, and Kent, they normally held the Lent or Spring assizes in March and the Summer session in July or August. The assizes and county quarter sessions shared jurisdiction to some extent with borough quarter sessions, for some boroughs had been granted the right by their charter to hold sessions, and in some cases their jurisdiction was extensive and excluded both the county magistrates and the assize judges. And in boroughs with a recorder, a legal official who was always a lawyer, his presence on the bench enabled the court to deal with felonies and even capital offenses.

Most commonly, however, the jurisdiction of borough courts ran concurrently with the county sessions, and in practice at least, most seem to have left serious matters to others. In Surrey, borough sessions were held at Guildford, Kingston-upon-Thames, and Southwark. The first two dealt mainly with nuisances and administrative disputes. But in Southwark the borough sessions were held by the mayor and aldermen of London, as an aspect of jurisdiction they had long claimed in Southwark (which formed in fact a city ward, Bridge Ward Without), and from time to time it was a very active court.[18] They dealt regularly with assaults and petty larceny

---

[17] For an excellent introduction to the jurisdiction of the various criminal courts see J. H. Baker, "Criminal Courts and Procedure at Common Law, 1550–1800," in Cockburn, ed., *Crime in England*, pp. 25–32; and for the assizes, Cockburn, *History of English Assizes*, chap. 6.

[18] On the administrative relationship between the city and Southwark and in particular the significance of the rights claimed by the corporation to appoint a Southwark magistrate—the justice of the Bridge Yard, as he was called—see David J. Johnson, *Southwark and the City* (1969), chap. 12.

and, when the Recorder of London was present, with more serious matters. I have taken the work of the Southwark sessions into account to the extent that the records make it possible.[19] In Sussex, several borough courts had extensive jurisdiction, but in practice it appears that they did not have a great deal of serious crime to deal with.[20]

The possibility that some offenders who might have appeared before the county quarter sessions or the assizes faced charges instead at a borough sessions whose records survive erratically complicates matters slightly. There is a further problem that the summary jurisdiction of magistrates was enlarged in the course of the century and a half after 1660 to include offenses on the borderland of larceny, and the evidence of the charges thus dealt with by justices of the peace acting alone has not survived in Surrey. Fortunately, the summary powers of magistrates were not in this period enlarged in such a way that a great deal of ordinary criminal business was removed from the courts. Justices of the peace acquired or assumed the right to deal with game offenses, and by the early eighteenth century cases that might earlier have been tried by way of indictment before the quarter sessions or even the assizes were being dealt with by one or two justices without a jury.[21] Magistrates were also being called upon in the eighteenth century to punish a variety of customary practices in the countryside that were coming to be deplored by the propertied classes. Wood-gathering and gleaning, for example, came increasingly to be opposed by farmers and larger property owners as detrimental to good farming practices or harmful to the wise management of resources, and magistrates acting alone were more likely than the courts to be called upon to prevent them. The

[19] Unfortunately, the records of the Southwark quarter sessions in the Corporation of London Record Office are not complete for the period 1660–1800. I have taken account of the cases dealt with by the court when the surviving records made that possible. In the case of crimes against property this has meant the addition of 179 indictments, distributed over the following years: 1690–93, 1753–58, 1762–70, 1780–84. I have not, however, included the Southwark Borough sessions cases in the graph that reports the changing level of prosecutions for property crime in the urban parishes of Surrey (figure 5.4), since the addition of some years and not others would have distorted the pattern represented there, if only slightly. It was possible for the Southwark Borough sessions to deal with capital cases when the Recorder of London was present; he had virtually the standing of a high-court judge since he sat regularly at the Old Bailey. In practice, however, they left the bulk of even minor matters to the county sessions and the assizes.

[20] The Cinque Ports had jurisdiction independent of both the quarter sessions and the assizes. The records of Rye, in the East Sussex record office, suggest that they did not have much occasion to exercise it. In West Sussex, the Borough of Chichester held a court that dealt with serious offenses. It is a weakness of the Sussex evidence that for the most part the records of these courts have not survived, but it likely that few prosecutions of consequence were undertaken before them every year.

[21] P. B. Munsche, *Gentlemen and Poachers*, esp. chap. 4; and his "The Game Laws in Wiltshire, 1750–1800," in Cockburn, ed., *Crime in England*, pp. 210–28.

jurisdiction of magistrates was also extended in the course of the century by statutes that made the "theft" of turnips and other vegetables from the fields a criminal offense and gave the justices authority to deal summarily with such cases.[22] And finally, at some points over this period, and in some areas, it appears that magistrates may have used their summary powers under the poor laws and vagrancy legislation to commit men and women suspected of theft to brief periods of hard labor in houses of correction. The calendars of the Southwark house of correction list inmates in the early decades of the eighteenth century who had been committed for being not only "idle and disorderly" but also "pilfering persons," and other men and women were being held for actually pilfering a named object from a named victim. It is unclear whether any of these inmates of the houses of correction had actually been charged with a petty theft and might thus have been indicted and tried before a jury, though that seems likely, at least in the case of those who were said to have pilfered from a particular victim. It is also unclear when this practice began in Surrey because the house of correction calendars do not survive for any period before the early eighteenth century. What is clear is that the practice fell off sharply in the second quarter of the century, and such commitments are rare thereafter. It is thus possible that some minor thefts were being diverted from the courts over part of this period, but I think one can say with some confidence that neither this form of summary procedure nor the more established summary powers of the justices resulted in large classes of indictable offenses being transferred to the adjudication of magistrates from trial by jury, as was to happen in the nineteenth century.[23]

It is also worth noting that the court of King's Bench, one of the central common law courts at Westminster, did not in practice deal with ordinary criminal business. It had unlimited jurisdiction and exercised an

[22] For the summary powers of magistrates in general see Norma Landau, *The Justices of the Peace, 1679–1760* (Berkeley, 1984); and for magistrates in rural society see Robert W. Malcolmson, *Life and Labour in England, 1700–1780* (1981), chap. 5; and below, chap. 4. For the extent to which magistrates' summary powers were extended to include the "embezzlement" by outworkers in domestic industries, particularly textiles, see John Rule, *The Experience of Labour in 18th-Century Industry* (1981), chap. 5; Peter Linebaugh's contribution to the discussion of "Distinctions between Socio-Political and Other Forms of Crime," *Bulletin of the Society of Labour History* (Fall 1972), pp. 11–15; and the reservations and cautions expressed by John Styles, "Controlling the Outworker: The Embezzlement Laws and Industrial Outwork in Eighteenth-Century England," in Maxine Berg, Pat Hudson, and Michael Sonenscher, eds., *Manufacture in Town and Country before the Factory* (Cambridge, 1983).

[23] In the 1840s and 1850s a large number of offenses were removed by parliament from the courts in which they had been triable only by indictment and before a jury, and placed within the summary jurisdiction of magistrates. This included both assaults and simple larcenies. See Stephen, *History of the Criminal Law*, vol. 1, pp. 122–26; and Philips, *Crime and Authority*, pp. 22–23, 97–98, 132–34.

important supervisory function over all inferior courts through the writ of certiorari. But few original cases were heard at King's Bench other than riotous offenses and treason, both of which were on the fringes of the criminal activity I am concerned with.[24] I have not added King's Bench material to the evidence derived from the Surrey and Sussex quarter sessions and assizes.

The main record of those courts was the indictment, the formal charge against the prisoner that was normally drawn up by a clerk of the court, written on parchment (until 1733 in Latin, thereafter in English), and read in summary form in court when the prisoner was arraigned. The indictment contained the name of the accused and his occupation and residence, and it stated the date, place, and nature of the crime and the name of the victim when that was appropriate. By the seventeenth century the clerks were listing on the back of the bill the names of witnesses sworn in court. On the reverse side is also to be found the verdict of the grand jury, which either sent the accused to trial (by a finding of "true bill") or discharged him on the grounds that there was no case to be answered (by recording the verdict "ignoramus" or, in the English period, "we do not know" or "no true bill"). The indictments at the assizes also included the clerk's shortform version of other decisions made in court: the prisoner's plea, the verdict of the trial jury, and the sentence handed down by the judge.

The indictments provide the central core of evidence used in this book. Because of the pattern of survival of the assize files, that evidence is much fuller for the second half of the period than the first. The quarter sessions rolls are substantially complete in both counties for every year between 1660 and 1800, as are the assize files after 1730. Unfortunately, the assize records are spotty between 1660 and 1730. In some years no files have survived; in others just one. I have only collected data for complete years, that is, for years in which all four quarter sessions rolls and both assize files are available. By these criteria there are close to a hundred complete years of data over the period I am concerned with. From these I have collected four files, which I use for different purposes. The main body of data upon which most of the analysis is based consists of evidence from sixty-one years of the assizes and quarter sessions of Surrey, drawn unevenly from over the period. This will be referred to as the

[24] Baker, "Criminal Courts and Procedure," pp. 26–27. Douglas Hay has analyzed the records of King's Bench in the eighteenth century and has confirmed that the importance of the court lies in areas other than ordinary matters of serious personal violence and property offenses. I am grateful to him for sharing these findings with me in advance of their publication.

"Sample."[25] In addition, in order to get a sense of the changing level of prosecutions of one or two particular offenses over time, I have made a simple count of indictments in other years for which complete data are available so that with these and the sample years together I have indictment totals in a number of categories of offenses, particularly crimes against property. This set of data I will call the indictment "Count."[26] Because there are relatively few cases of homicide, I have collected a separate file, "Homicide Count," consisting of evidence from all the charges made in the ninety-five years of complete records.

Most of the analysis of the work of the courts will be based on the "Sample" of sixty-one years of indictment evidence. We will be concerned from time to time with the character of that evidence, but some general observations can be made at the outset about its strengths and weaknesses, about other judicial evidence that can be brought to bear, and about the questions that this evidence makes it reasonable to address.

There are good reasons for thinking that while much of the information in the indictment itself is accurate and reliable, some cannot be taken at face value. The names of the accused and the victim are not open to doubt, for example; nor is the parish in which the offense was alleged to have taken place. But it has been demonstrated conclusively that the indictments preferred before the Elizabethan and Jacobean assize courts invariably contained a good deal of "fictitious" information, and that remained true in the eighteenth century.[27] One of the serious problems from the point of view of the social history of crime is the fact that the most consistently and thoroughly misleading entries are those purporting to give the status or occupation of the accused and his place of residence. These are simply not to be trusted in felony indictments—not because the clerks were indifferent or because they did not pay attention to proper

[25] In Surrey the years included are as follows: 1663–65, 1674–77, 1690–94, 1708, 1710, 1714–15, 1722–24, 1736–42, 1747–58, 1762–70, 1780–84, 1795–1802. They differ only slightly in Sussex. For further explanation of the sources and the various samples used, see the appendix.

[26] I have also made a study of all capital convictions in these ninety-five years and attempted to discover who among those condemned to death had been pardoned and who actually executed. I will refer to this as the "Hanged Count."

[27] For the character of assize records in general and indictments in particular see two articles by J. S. Cockburn that deal specifically with the late sixteenth and early seventeenth centuries but form a useful introduction to the later period, too: "Early-Modern Assize Records as Historical Evidence," *Journal of the Society of Archivists* 5 (1975), pp. 215–31; "Trial by the Book? Fact and Theory in the Criminal Process, 1558–1625," in J. H. Baker, ed., *Legal Records and the Historian* (Royal Historical Society, 1978), pp. 60–79. The fullest and most thorough discussion of the character of assize records is Cockburn's *Introduction* to his series of *Calendars of Assize Records* (H.M.S.O., 1985).

form but, on the contrary, because they wanted to ensure that the indictment would not be rejected by the court as being improperly drawn up. When it came to describing the accused man's "estate or degree, or mystery, and . . . the towns and hamlets . . . of which [he was] . . . conversant," as a statute of 1413 required (1 Hen V, c. 5), the clerks opted for the forms that had been found acceptable over decades of trial and error. In the case of felony indictments, that meant that they described virtually every defendant as a "labourer," using a broad status designation rather than a more precise occupation; and they invariably listed his place of residence as the parish in which the crime had taken place. Such categories conformed to the requirements laid down in numerous decisions of the court of King's Bench that the description of the prisoner be "certain" and "precise." They continued to be used in the eighteenth century because they ensured that an indictment so drawn would not be thrown out for insufficiency. As a result, one simply cannot rely on felony indictments to provide real evidence about those on trial.

Other elements in the indictment are less consistently fictitious but are nonetheless problematic. The date on which the offense is said to have occurred cannot always be trusted, for example. But perhaps the most important difficulty concerns the way the offense is described, and that in turn relates to the character and the function of the indictment itself and the way it was drawn up. As we will see, the indictment charged a defendant with a particular offense as defined by the common or statute law—with murder or rape or assault or larceny, and so on. It did not set out to describe what had happened, but what the legal consequences were of the evidence to be presented in court; information not essential to that was excluded. The offense is thus very broadly described in the indictment and is essentially impossible to penetrate. In addition, the form that the charge took was not necessarily the result of a simple and neutral reporting of a set of events, but the result rather of a deliberate choice made by the prosecutor, or perhaps the clerk who drew the bill, about how the offense would be framed. Prosecutors had a wide discretion at this stage, in particular to "downcharge" by reporting the offense in such a way that it fitted into a noncapital rather than a capital category.

There are a number of reasons, then, for thinking that indictments do not reveal a great deal about the offenses being charged. The indictment evidence can be supplemented, however, by several other classes of judicial records. Among the most useful are the depositions made by victims of offenses and their witnesses and the examinations of the accused, all of which were taken in writing by the magistrate who conducted the preliminary hearing required by law. Recognizances are also useful: these bound men to fulfill some stated obligation—to appear in court to answer a charge, to prosecute a named accused, to give evidence in a trial—on pain of forfeiture of a specified sum. Depositions and examinations vary greatly in length and quality, partly because magistrates had different views of what was required: some clearly pushed for more evidence than others. At their fullest, such documents can reveal a great deal of what lay behind the charge being made, what relationship there might have been between the accused and the prosecutor, the way the offense had been discovered, and the way the defendant had been apprehended. In general, they can present the event as it was described by the complainant and responded to by the man charged, before it had been labeled by the clerks and fitted into a legal niche. The recognizances also occasionally add details about the offense not found in the indictment, and when the defendant was bound over rather than committed to jail, his recognizance normally describes his occupation and residence more precisely than the indictment.[28]

The depositions, examinations, and recognizances taken by the magistrate were supposed to be sent to the appropriate court so that the evidence they provided could be referred to during the trial if necessary and so that the recognizances of those who failed to appear could be estreated. Unfortunately, these documents were not retained by the clerks of the Home Circuit assizes once the court session was completed. The written depositions were not part of the formal record. Recognizances might have been regarded as of more permanent value, but they too were being jettisoned by the clerks on the Home Circuit as early as Elizabeth's reign, except in Hertfordshire and Sussex—significantly the counties with the most modest calendars of prisoners to be tried.[29]

The quarter sessions records in Sussex and Surrey are much richer in such evidence. The Surrey quarter sessions rolls contain recognizances after 1660, and beginning in the early eighteenth century a set of records now called "quarter sessions papers" include depositions and examinations as well as jail calendars and a variety of other documents.[30] Of course, the quarter sessions materials relate only to the cases tried in that court, that is to say only to the least serious among those I am concerned with. They provide nonetheless useful illustrative evidence, and they help to illuminate a number of matters, including, for example, the identity of prosecutors, the way suspects were apprehended, the work of magistrates, and the availability and uses of discretion at several stages in the administrative

---

[28] For the view that in an earlier period recognizances are also more accurate in some respects than indictments, see Cockburn, "Early-Modern Assize Records as Historical Evidence," p. 224.

[29] This is clear from the calendars of the Home Circuit assize files edited by J. S. Cockburn.

[30] QS 2/6. For the Sussex records in the seventeenth century see the excellent use made of depositions and other nonindictment evidence by Herrup, "The Common Peace."

process before trial. They make it clear how invaluable a parallel series of assize depositions would be. But even if they had been available, the central document of this study would have remained the indictment. Despite the difficulties that surround some of the evidence they provide, the indictments have the virtue of being consistent over the 140 years we are dealing with and, where the files have survived, of giving us a record of all the criminal cases tried before a jury in a county in a year. For the matters I am particularly concerned with, these are considerable virtues indeed.

The court records do not provide us with straightforward evidence about the offenses actually being committed in the community. They are much less problematic, however, when we turn in Part II to ask what happened to those accused before the quarter sessions and assizes, how the courts worked, what the rates of conviction and acquittal were, and what punishments were imposed for particular offenses. It is in respect to questions of that kind that the judicial records, especially the indictments, come into their own, since they provide us with a full record of jury verdicts (including on the Home Circuit the verdicts of the grand jury as well as the trial jury) and the sentences that followed.

Along with the patterns of jury verdicts and the changing forms of punishment, we will also be concerned with pretrial process and the nature of the criminal trial itself. In dealing with this latter subject we are fortunate to have available a number of "reports" of trials conducted at the Surrey assizes spanning roughly a hundred years from the 1670s that were produced for commercial reasons and essentially as entertainment but that nonetheless tell us a good deal about the characteristics of the criminal trial in a period in which other evidence is difficult to come by. These reports were published in the form of pamphlets under a variety of titles, mainly variants of "The Proceedings at the Assizes of the Peace, Oyer and Terminer and General Gaol-Delivery for the County of Surrey." I have chosen to call them simply "Surrey Assize Proceedings," abbreviated as S.A.P. Reports of thirty-five sessions have come to light so far, including a complete run—one for each of the ten sessions—for the five years 1738–42. There are good reasons to suppose that more were published.[31] But

---

[31] The earliest is for the session Lent 1678, and the latest Lent 1774. More than half fall in the period 1738–59. The majority of the Surrey pamphlets are in the British Library, including those for 1738–42. That core has been supplemented by examples from the Minet Library in Lambeth, the Guildhall Library, the library of the Greater London Record Office, the Bodleian Library, and the Library of Lincoln's Inn. For the complete list see the bibliography. It seems certain that more were published than I have found so far. By the 1750s the cases included were numbered consecutively for the whole year, which suggests that it was the publisher's intention to issue one for each session of the court. The pamphlet for the Summer 1751 assize begins, for

it is doubtful that they were issued as regularly as the pamphlets they so closely resemble that reported the trials at the Old Bailey, and that also began in the 1670s and ran for more than two centuries in a series that is substantially complete from the beginning, and entirely complete— eight sessions of the court being covered every year—from 1729 on.[32]

Like the Old Bailey reports, the Surrey pamphlets consisted at first simply of brief summaries of the offenses charged against the prisoners and a note of the verdict and sentence in each case. By the early decades of the eighteenth century, however, while routine thefts continued to be given only a few lines (perhaps for the sake of completeness, which the publisher of the "Old Bailey Sessions Papers" was striving to achieve by the 1740s),[33] several of the more interesting cases in each session tended to be reported more fully and with some of the evidence given for and against the prisoner. The pamphlets became longer and more elaborate no doubt as it was revealed that the public wanted to read as much as possible of the actual testimony given in court, particularly when the prisoner was convicted and sentenced to death,[34] and perhaps especially in murder and rape cases, which occasionally revealed intimate details of the lives of the principals involved and presented opportunities for a delicious mixture of prurience and moral outrage. The richness of the detail was made possible by the reporters' use of shorthand. By the mid-eighteenth century the pamphlets were running to twenty and more double-columned pages a session, and some of the trials were reported at considerable length.

These pamphlets never became formal trial reports, and much of the procedural detail that would have been merely tedious to the contemporary reader, however valuable to lawyers and legal historians, was naturally omitted. Nonetheless, a good deal can be learned from them about the way trials were conducted, and despite their shortcomings, they provide us with evidence that the State Trials series by its nature (its concentration on treason and large show trials) cannot give of the day-to-day work of

example, with case number thirty-eight; I have not been able to find a copy of the Lent pamphlet that must have contained the first thirty-seven.

[32] For their publishing history see Michael Harris, "Trials and Criminal Biographies: A Case Study in Distribution," in Robin Myers and Michael Harris, eds., *Sale and Distribution of Books from* 1700 (1982), pp. 1–15. And for the value and limitations of this exceptionally rich source of evidence for the legal historian see the two important articles by John H. Langbein: "Criminal Trial before the Lawyers," and "Shaping the Eighteenth-Century Criminal Trial." The pamphlets were generally referred to in the eighteenth century as the "Old Bailey Sessions Papers," though that was not their actual title. I have followed Langbein in abbreviating this to OBSP.

[33] Langbein, "Criminal Trial before the Lawyers," p. 269, n. 23.

[34] An advertisement for a series of Home Circuit trial reports in May 1774 emphasized that "these numbers contain the trials of no less than thirty-two prisoners who were capitally convicted" (OBSP, May 1774, p. 240; I owe this reference to John Langbein).

the assizes. It is possible that similar pamphlets will be found for other counties,[35] but the present evidence suggests that no other county had a sufficiently large and concentrated audience to attract the commercial interest of publishers. With respect to the provincial assizes we can perhaps say of these Surrey pamphlets what Langbein says of the Old Bailey reports: that they "are probably the best accounts we shall ever have of what transpired in ordinary English criminal courts before the later eighteenth century."[36]

THE COUNTY OF SURREY

The value of the Surrey Assize Proceedings is such that even if other considerations had not done so, they would have tilted the balance in this study toward the Surrey evidence, for they not only tell us a good deal about trial procedure but also provide considerable detail about particular cases. But Surrey evidence also presses forward and occupies the center of the discussion because more offenses were committed there than in Sussex, and particularly more of those regarded as especially serious because they threatened life as well as property. The court calendars at both quarter sessions and assizes in Surrey were always longer and more dramatic, and like the Old Bailey, the court that dealt with the major offenses in the City of London and Middlesex, the Surrey assizes frequently confronted

[35] Langbein notes one for an Essex session in 1680 ("Criminal Trial before the Lawyers," p. 272, n. 29). The entire Home Circuit was reported in one pamphlet in the spring of 1688 and again in the spring of 1739 (see bibliography), but that was apparently not repeated thereafter. The proceedings on the special commission under which the smugglers who murdered two excisemen in Sussex in 1748 were tried were reported at length in *The Whole Proceedings on the Special Commission . . . for the County of Sussex . . .* (1749). That was clearly a special case. The Lent session at the Kent assizes in 1750 was reported. The man who had reported the Old Bailey trials for some years, Joseph Gurney, published separate accounts of the trials in at least four of the Home Circuit counties in the spring of 1774 (Hertford, Essex, Kent, and Surrey). He advertised the publication of these in the OBSP in February (p. 148) as well as May (p. 240): "All taken down in Short Hand by Joseph Gurney and published by Permission of the Judges." If this was a flier to test the commercial possibilities of a regular series of Home Circuit reports to parallel the Old Bailey pamphlets (in a period in which property crime in London seems to have been running at a moderately high level for some years) the results were apparently discouraging, for no further pamphlets seem to have been published. (For Gurney see Langbein, "Shaping the Eighteenth-Century Criminal Trial," p. 12.) In the same period, the trials at the Yorkshire assizes were reported in a series of pamphlets published between 1775 (Lent) and 1778 (Lent), under the title *The Trials at Large of the Felons in the Castle of York. . . .* Copies of these pamphlets can be found in the York City Reference Library (I owe my knowledge of these to John Styles).

[36] Langbein, "Criminal Trial before the Lawyers," p. 271.

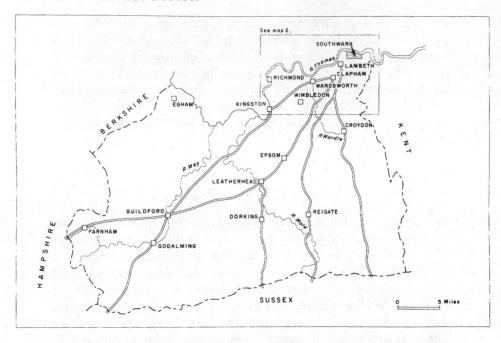

Map 1   Surrey in the Eighteenth Century.

the kinds of offenses and offenders who were at the center of public
discussions of crime when it was particularly alarming. It did so because
Surrey included an urban population of considerable size that was part of
the larger metropolis of London. And that made Surrey a county of significant contrasts—contrasts that are reflected in criminal prosecutions and
that make it a particularly useful area in which to study both the patterns
of indictments over time and the shifting responses of the courts.

    We will make a good deal in the course of the book of the distinction
between the "urban" area of Surrey and the remainder of the county, the
rural parishes and market towns that I will summarize as "rural" Surrey.
But it is well to recognize that there is something artificial and arbitrary
in such a division. It is a distinction full of difficulties, not least because
the line dividing one from the other is unclear and changes over time. I
should make clear that what I will describe as urban Surrey consists of
two areas: one that was firmly within the metropolis in 1660; the other,
the environs of the capital that were gradually being absorbed over the
period we are concerned with and that even in 1660 felt the influence of
the large concentrated population in its economy, as well as in the migration of gentry and city merchants to build villas within convenient

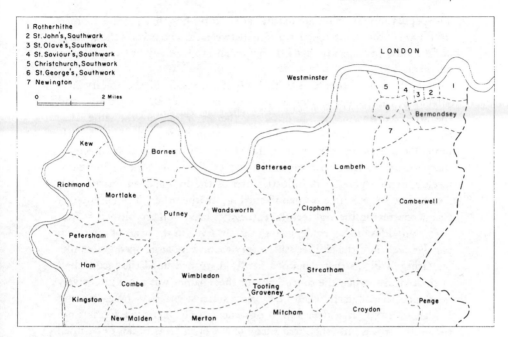

1 Rotherhithe
2 St. John's, Southwark
3 St. Olave's, Southwark
4 St. Saviour's, Southwark
5 Christchurch, Southwark
6 St. George's, Southwark
7 Newington

Map 2   Northeastern Surrey.

reach of the city.[37] In the first category there was mainly the Borough of
Southwark, but it also seems reasonable to add to the urban area four
neighboring parishes that were within the Bills of Mortality: Rotherhithe,
Newington, Bermondsey, and Lambeth. In the outer ring of environs I
have included the remaining parishes of the Hundred of Brixton, running
from Mortlake and Wimbledon in the west to Merton, Streatham, and
Camberwell in the south, and including the parishes along the river,
Battersea, Wandsworth, and Putney. The heart of the urban area, thus
defined, remains Southwark and its neighboring parishes. They contained
the bulk of the population and were the scene of the vast majority of
prosecutions for property crimes and violence. But to take some of the
expansion of the metropolis into account over the period 1660 to 1800
and its growing influence in the county, I have counted a changing proportion of the population of the parishes in the environs in the urban total.

[37] For Surrey in this period I have relied largely on the following: *The Victoria County History
of England: Surrey*, 4 vols. (1902–12); D. Lysons, *The Environs of London*, 2nd ed. (1811); Owen
Manning and William Bray, *History and Antiquities of the County of Surrey*, 3 vols. (1804–14);
Thomas Allen, *History of the Counties of Surrey and Sussex*, 2 vols. (1829–30); Sir Walter Besant,
South London (1899); O.H.K. Spate, "The Growth of London, 1660–1800," in H. C. Darby,
ed., *The Historical Geography of England before 1800* (1936).

The population estimates are hardly satisfactory, but they provide a broad indication of the changing relationship between the two parts of the county, and I should perhaps say that I do not intend to base any fine calculations on them.[38]

A number of problems arise from the division of the county into urban and rural spheres. One is the implication that all the parishes and the market towns that get lumped together as "rural" are the same, that there are no distinctions worth making among them; I shall say a little more about that in a moment. Another is that the division implies a sharpness of contrast that might be too extreme: an entirely built-up, faceless, densely populated, industrial area on the one hand; an agricultural, face-to-face society, free of manufacturing, on the other. The falseness of such a contrast in the eighteenth century has been well established.[39] And Surrey provides further evidence for caution. Even in the heart of the urban parishes well into the eighteenth century there were large open spaces like St. George's Fields that remained hardly disturbed until the second half of the century, when the south bank of the Thames was more intensively developed, particularly when new bridges across the river (Westminster Bridge in 1750, Blackfriars in 1769) enormously increased access from the north. It was only then that many of the open areas began to be filled with roads and buildings. A parish like Bermondsey, which had grown in population from the late seventeenth century, retained nonetheless something of a rural character even toward the end of the eighteenth. It still

[38] I arrived at the following population estimates by working back from the parish populations in the census of 1801 on the basis of the total county population given for a number of points in time by Phyllis Deane and W. A. Cole, *British Economic Growth, 1688–1959*, 2nd ed. (Cambridge, 1969), p. 103. In addition I accepted Wrigley's view that the population of London continued to grow between 1660 and 1760 ("A Simple Model of London's Importance in Changing English Society and Economy, 1650–1750," *Past and Present* 37 [1967], pp. 44–46); and I have assumed further that the rural population of Surrey contributed through migration to the growing urban area and that it stagnated through the late seventeenth century and declined slightly in the early eighteenth—as the population of Sussex apparently did. Both parts of Surrey as well as Sussex grew rapidly after 1760. As a result of these guesses I estimate the populations of the areas I am mainly concerned with to have changed roughly as follows over this period:

	Urban Surrey Parishes	Rural Surrey Parishes	Sussex
1660	60,000	60,000	97,000
1700	68,000	60,000	97,000
1750	80,500	55,000	94,000
1801	177,000	101,000	165,000

[39] On the location of industry, for example, and the character of rural life see John Rule, *The Experience of Labour in Eighteenth-Century Industry* (1981); and Robert W. Malcolmson, *Life and Labour in England, 1700–1780* (1981).

included large market gardens, for example, and pasture on which dairy cattle were kept. Similarly, in Lambeth buildings and roads came to occupy half the parish in the eighteenth century but market-gardening and cow-keeping continued to flourish. Newington also had extensive market gardens and pasture at the end of the eighteenth century. As for the wider ring of parishes that were being gradually influenced by and absorbed into the metropolis, they retained much of their rural character, though there was a good deal of building in many. By the middle of the century Camberwell contained numerous houses of merchants and other citizens of London, many of whom chose to live there and travel into the city precisely because it *was* rural. Clapham remained a village, as did Putney, though both also included numerous villas of the London gentry.

What we will identify as urban Surrey was thus by no means an area of continuously built-up houses; nor was it entirely given over to manufacturing and commerce. And on the other side, although Surrey was not a large center of domestic industry, there were important manufacturing and other enterprises outside the capital. For ten or more miles along the river Wandle at the end of the eighteenth century, for example, some forty mills sustained a variety of industries, especially calico-printing and paper-making.

There is also some danger in the contrast of urban and rural areas of exaggerating the extent to which society in the city is conceived as entirely fluid and anonymous, and without the means of social control available to the smaller, stable world of the countryside in which parents, parsons, gentry, and magistrates maintained a close surveillance over village society and exercised a tight discipline—on the one side a society sustained by natural authority, on the other a society without a source of cohesion and held together only by the compulsions of law and policing. There is a particular danger in this of exaggerating the anonymity of London and of missing the stable communities that were at the heart of many of its parishes, the ranks of middling tradesmen and artisans and other local notables who acted as constables and overseers and churchwardens, and gave continuity and permanence in the midst of change.

When all the necessary qualifications have been made, one can still acknowledge, however, that there were contrasts of great significance between the conditions of life of the majority of the working population in the urban parishes and of those who lived in the countryside or in Reigate, Farnham, Guildford, or the other market towns of the county. The south side of the Thames was one of the most active centers of manufacturing in London—itself by far the largest industrial center in England, and indeed in Europe. A number of offensive and dirty, though crucial, trades had been centered there, safely away from the city itself. Tanning, a particularly noxious process, was perhaps the chief industry south of the river. It was carried on extensively in Southwark and Bermondsey, and it had encouraged a number of associated trades there and in Rotherhithe and other waterside parishes: a large wool-stapling trade, for example, and currying, leather-dressing, and glue-making. Breweries and distilleries, including vinegar distilleries, were also numerous in Southwark and Lambeth. There was in addition felt-making and hat-making on the south bank, and enough weavers to cause considerable disturbances in 1676 over the introduction of a new "engine-loom" that threatened work practices and employment. Dying and bleaching and other textile trades were also being carried on there in the late seventeenth century. Glass was made in these northern parishes of Surrey, and half a dozen potteries (including Doulton's) made Lambeth an important center of English ceramics. Lambeth also had extensive timber yards.

Much of this economic activity depended on the river, and a large number of other jobs derived directly from ship-building and rope works and from the numerous docks in Rotherhithe and in Southwark. The waterside parishes were a jumble of barge-builders and small foundries and other activities associated with the river—as well as taverns and lodging houses catering especially to seamen and river workers—along with other enterprises like soap-making and sugar-boiling. In the middle of the eighteenth century Rotherhithe was said to be "inhabited mostly by seafaring people and watermen."[40] And much of the economic life of Southwark and of the more western parishes along the Thames was heavily dependent on the river.

The urban parishes sustained a large working population in these industries and services as well as in domestic and the newer forms of service in shops, and in the market gardens and other agricultural pursuits farther afield. The work attracted young people to the city,[41] and yet much of it was precarious, seasonal, or casual, and subject to circumstances that could change rapidly. Underemployment and casual labor were not confined to the urban economy, but the conditions under which the laboring population lived and worked in these urban parishes was significantly different from those they would have experienced in a rural parish or small market town. It is a difference that is reflected in the offenses prosecuted before the courts, and it reveals much, I will argue, about the character of property crime especially.

The urban and rural differences in Surrey are not the only axis upon

[40] "A Description of the County of Surrey," *The Universal Magazine* 25 (1759), p. 114.
[41] E. A. Wrigley, "A Simple Model of London's Importance in Changing England's Society and Economy, 1650–1750," *Past and Present* 37 (1967), pp. 44–70.

which the discussion will turn, but they are sufficiently striking and revealing that they will be frequently brought forward in our analysis of the offenses before the courts. There are some drawbacks in such an approach, for there is a tendency to aggregate the rural parishes and overlook differences among them. A proper analysis of crime in Surrey would require that distinction be made between regions in which geology and soil conditions made for different patterns of settlement and land use. The offenses prosecuted in downland parishes could be contrasted, for example, with those arising from the Weald or the hilly country in the southwest corner of the county or the sandy soils of the northwest. Other characteristics of rural parishes could be equally significant. It undoubtedly made a difference to the "reality" of crime within a parish or market town, and certainly to the offenses brought forward to the courts, what the patterns of land-ownership were and patterns of authority, whether there was a resident and active magistrate, whether it was on a busy route or was isolated, what form of agriculture was practiced, whether it was a thinly populated or a populous parish, and what by-employments were available.

In discussing forms of prosecuted offenses I will from time to time distinguish aspects of rural Surrey that seemed to have been particularly crucial: the development of the road system; the growing number of city merchants who built houses beyond the outer ring of metropolitan parishes in places like Epsom and on Banstead Downs; and the importance of the large stretches of heathland in the west of the county, the "sandy deserts," as Defoe called them, of Bagshot and neighboring parishes. But I have not in this book been able to do justice to the variety of regions in Surrey, not to speak of the large county of Sussex. I am conscious of how unsatisfactory for some purposes it is to group together all the parishes of what I will call rural Surrey and to deal with Sussex as a single unit; and also of how much might be gained by parish-level analysis. Yet there are advantages in isolating the case of London and underlining the character and levels of offenses prosecuted there. In particular, it is useful to study the offenses that caused the greatest public anxiety about crime and that were relatively more common, or more commonly prosecuted, in the metropolis than elsewhere over much of this period. It is useful too to deal with London from the middle of the seventeenth century, when for a hundred years or more many aspects of the crime found in the capital were not yet causing deep anxieties elsewhere. It was in the capital that the threat to social order and the threat of social indiscipline and immorality were particularly acute. And it was those anxieties and the solutions they encouraged that formed the leading edge of change in the law and its administration, and that made possible the even more fundamental "reforms" that were called for when these same problems became more insistent and more national in scope after 1780. Surrey provides evidence over a long period of the interrelationship of "crime" and the changing means adopted to deal with it. This is the theme I am concerned to explore.

PART I

OFFENSES AND OFFENDERS BEFORE THE COURTS

CHAPTER 2

PROSECUTION

When Henry Fielding enquired in 1751 into a recent increase in crime in London, he identified several general causes. On the one hand, he thought the poor were becoming increasingly immoral as their habits of life were undermined by the growth of commerce and the consequent enlargement of the pleasures of the capital. On the other, he thought that the courts were failing to deter men from turning to crime, that the law was being administered so spinelessly that the experience of the few men put on trial was more likely to encourage offenses than to prevent them. But what seemed particularly serious to Fielding, as a London magistrate, was the apparent reluctance of victims of property crimes to bring offenders to justice, even when they could identify their assailants and have them apprehended. Victims were discouraged from bringing prosecutions, he thought, by the costs and the trouble involved and by an altogether misplaced tenderness that made some men reluctant to see offenders hanged for minor offenses. The weak-kneed responses of victims and the courts were together, he was certain, undermining the deterrent capacities of the law.[1]

Whatever the shortcomings of Fielding's analysis of that particular crisis, he was undoubtedly right about the crucial role of private prosecution in the administration of the criminal law. Until the state assumed the management of crime in the nineteenth century and professional police forces took over the pursuit and apprehension of suspects, the gathering of evidence, and the preparation of cases—and indeed began to decide which cases would be taken to trial and which would not—these matters were left largely to the private initiative of the victim. If he wanted to bring an offender to justice in the eighteenth century, the victim himself (or his agent) had to take on the burden and the expense of the prosecution, not only bringing the offense to the attention of the authorities but also preparing himself unaided for the trial, assembling witnesses, and taking the lead in laying out the evidence in court. Only in rare cases did the law officers of the crown or local constables actively prosecute offenses against property or the person. It was becoming more common in the

[1] Fielding, *Increase of Robbers*, pp. 106–10.

eighteenth century for prosecutors to hire counsel to take the lead in court, but this did not alter the fundamental point that virtually all prosecutions in cases involving personal violence or the loss of property were still initiated and carried forward by the enterprise and at the expense of the victim.[2]

Victims of theft or violence who were sufficiently outraged to want to bring the offender to justice, or sufficiently anxious to recover their property, had first to bring the suspect before a magistrate. The justices of the peace formed the essential link between the victim and the courts. As we will see, it was their duty to bring the parties in conflict before them, to take depositions of the complainant and his witnesses, to examine the accused, and to ensure that they all appeared at the next sitting of the appropriate court. In the course of fulfilling this duty, most magistrates felt little obligation to do more than deal with the evidence brought before them and to leave the main work of detecting and apprehending the suspect to the victim. The victim might get a magistrate's warrant to authorize a constable to search for missing goods within his parish or to bring in a suspect for questioning, but in most ordinary cases of theft or violence the authorities were not likely to take the initiative to pursue an accused and secure him.

It is not possible to discover how each suspect brought before the Surrey courts had been discovered and apprehended, but depositions in the quarter sessions records and the printed accounts of assize trials provide numerous examples of the wide variety of ways that detection and arrest could take place, as well as of the continuing engagement in this of the victim himself. This evidence makes it clear that, as one would expect, many property cases came to court because a thief had been caught red-handed, immediately delivered to a constable, and taken by him before a magistrate who committed him for trial. Men who had snatched something from the window of a shop, for example, and who had been pursued and taken by the shopkeeper in the street were brought before the courts in Surrey every year. Very often pursuit had been taken up by people in the crowd. Certainly the impression formed from many depositions is that the "hue and cry"—the ancient requirement that the men of a hundred go in pursuit of a felon once the "hue and cry" was raised by a constable—was still working if only in an attenuated form, and that in the streets of towns and the metropolis bystanders responded readily to the cry "stop thief."[3]

---

[2] Douglas Hay, "Controlling the English Prosecutor," *Osgoode Hall Law Journal* 21 (1983), pp. 167–80.

[3] The experience of one Jonathan Weeden, a porter, was typical of a number of cases that could be cited from the Surrey quarter sessions depositions. While carrying a load in Tooley Street in Southwark in 1772 his pocket was picked of a silk handkerchief; he cried out "Stop

Help in apprehending an offender was especially likely when only one suspect was involved, rather than a gang. But even groups of more dangerous and threatening offenders—street robbers and highwaymen, for example—were occasionally taken by men who happened to be in the vicinity of an offense and joined in the chase.[4] Some of this enthusiasm for stopping suspected robbers and thieves may have been encouraged by the hope of a reward, a subject we will take up presently. Certainly some victims of street crime got help in pursuing their attackers apparently by the promise of money. But the hue and cry had depended at least in part on a broad public acceptance of the criminal law, and it seems likely that a similar broad agreement about the law and about the wickedness of theft or robbery helps to explain the spontaneous character of many arrests in the eighteenth century and the willingness of large numbers of ordinary people to lend a hand in apprehending those accused of property offenses.

Many of those brought to trial had been taken at the scene of the crime by the victim, aided perhaps by his family or employees or passersby. Others had been arrested soon afterwards because they acted suspiciously or were unable to explain sudden wealth, or because they had offended before and had been let off with a warning, or simply because they had a reputation for dishonesty.[5] But of course many victims of property crimes had no idea at all who had broken into their house, stolen from their shop, picked their pocket, held them up on the highway, or taken their horse. No doubt most did little to find out, or at least did

---

thief" and pointed to the fleeing suspect, who was stopped within a few yards by a waterman (QS 2/6, Mids. 1772, 26).

[4] Again, many examples of this could be cited. One case was reported in great detail in the printed accounts of the Surrey assizes in 1742 because one of the pursuers had been killed by a highwayman who was on trial for murder. It is clear that numerous men had given chase when the victim—who had not actually been robbed, merely threatened—rode quickly ahead of his two assailants to the town of Ripley crying out all the way "Highwaymen, highwaymen." Two men found horses and took up the chase, one armed with a brace of pistols, and they followed the suspects to the green in Ripley, where a cricket match was in progress, also crying out as they went "Stop thief, highwaymen." The robbers found themselves in the midst of the cricket match and were surrounded by the players; one got away, but the other was knocked to the ground by a "brick-bat," and the players advanced on him to the general cry "Knock him down, knock him down." At this point the cornered man shot and killed one of the players with his pistol and was then overpowered by the others. A constable was called and took him into custody. The other suspect was taken in another part of Ripley, for as was said in court, "The town being alarmed, [he was] beset on all sides" (S.A.P., Summer 1742, pp. 2–9).

[5] In at least one case in the Surrey assizes, as late as 1753, a man whose alehouse had been burglarized was said to have gone to "a cunning man" for assistance in discovering who had done it; this man showed him the prisoner's face "in a glass," and he had him arrested (S.A.P., Lent 1753, p. 19). For "cunning men" and their use in the detection of offenders in the sixteenth and seventeenth centuries, see Keith Thomas, *Religion and the Decline of Magic* (1971), pp. 212–22.

not take the matter further if they did discover their assailant. But in virtually every session of the courts men were on trial because the victim of their alleged offense had made an effort to find them and to get them arrested. Some of those efforts had been time-consuming and complex, and had taken men around the likely pawnbrokers and shops to find their stolen goods and in some cases back and forth across the countryside tracking down the thief, identifying their belongings, finding witnesses, and in other ways organizing the case.[6]

As we will see, the possibilities of tracing suspects were increased in the eighteenth century by a considerable improvement in communication made possible by the development of the London and provincial newspaper press and the emergence of an effective postal system. The newspapers were particularly important. They enabled the news of offenses to be widely circulated, rewards for information to be advertised, and the descriptions of suspects to be broadcast.[7] The offer of rewards became more common in the eighteenth century, at least partly because of the facilities offered by newspapers. And rewards helped to encourage the tracing and arrest of suspects, and indeed encouraged the mobilization of more "professional" policing, of both a private and a more official kind, especially in the capital. We will deal with some aspects of these eighteenth-century developments. Important as they were, however, they did not relieve the victim of the burden of pursuing the suspect and organizing his prosecution; they were meant to encourage, not replace, the private prosecutor.

Because the victim remained the central agent in criminal prosecutions, responsible for instituting the case and carrying it through its various stages, he also inevitably retained a great deal of discretionary power that was not easily controlled by the authorities.[8] The victim of a property

---

[6] A servant to Lord Winterton lost a pair of shoes from a stable on his estate and (to give just one example of the kind of trouble some men went to) walked several miles to Godalming in search of a man who had passed through some days earlier. He found him in the "cage" at Godalming, having been apprehended as a vagrant. He was indeed wearing the shoes in question. The complainant then walked to North Chappell in Sussex and managed to persuade the shoemaker who had made the shoes to come with him to Godalming to identify them. In the meantime the vagrant had been transferred to the Guildford house of correction, but the two men trudged on there. The shoemaker duly identified the shoes, and the vagrant confessed (QS 2/6, Mich. 1761, 31).

[7] For the importance of newspapers and of the creation of an effective information network about offenses and offenders in the second half of the eighteenth century, see in particular John Styles, "Sir John Fielding and the Problem of Criminal Investigation in Eighteenth-Century England," *Transactions of the Royal Historical Society*, 5th ser., 33 (1983), pp. 127–49.

[8] This included the power to lay false and malicious charges as a means of furthering a private dispute, or earning a reward if one was available, or for a variety of other motives. Prosecutions were undoubtedly undertaken in the criminal courts in the seventeenth and eighteenth centuries out of malice or greed, though they were more likely to be for an alleged assault or trespass than

offense, for example, could choose to report the circumstances surrounding the offense and the value of the goods stolen in ways that would determine whether the accused was charged with a capital or a noncapital crime, or whether a simple theft would amount to grand or petty larceny. The victim could also initiate a case and then in effect bring it to a halt by not appearing in court to give evidence, though in doing so he risked having his recognizance estreated. The victim's most important option, then as now, was simply not to report the offense in the first place. Unless the crime had been committed in public and the offender had been apprehended by a crowd and turned over to the authorities—in which case he might well have no choice but to carry on the prosecution—the victim could let it pass, perhaps extracting an apology or some compensation, but not in any event invoking the law.

Informal means of dealing with offenders, including direct and immediate physical punishment, must often have been preferred to a formal and troublesome prosecution, especially in a small community in which a court case might well be disruptive of social relationships.[9] In trespass or assault cases in which the public interest was not thought to be deeply engaged, magistrates were themselves encouraged to arrange agreements that would settle the issue privately and keep it out of the courts. Such private arrangements were illegal when the alleged offense amounted to a felony, but they were clearly common. Paying for the return of stolen goods under the pretense that the money was a reward for their recovery and with "no questions asked" (and thus no threat of prosecution) was perhaps the most common form that such compounding took. That was part of the "service" that Jonathan Wild offered in George I's reign. And despite the Act of 1717 that made it a capital offense to take a reward for the return of stolen goods and the Act of 1752 that imposed a fine of fifty

a felony. For the circumstances under which such prosecutions might occur see M. J. Ingram, "Communities and Courts: Law and Disorder in Early Seventeenth-Century Wiltshire," in Cockburn, ed., *Crime in England*, pp. 120–22; and especially Hay, "Crime, Authority and the Criminal Law," pp. 449–71.

9 See Keith Wrightson, "Two Concepts of Order: Justices, Constables and Jurymen in Seventeenth-Century England," in Brewer and Styles, eds., *An Ungovernable People*, pp. 30–31; M. J. Ingram, "Communities and Courts," pp. 116–18, 127–34. For the range of available informal sanctions see J. A. Sharpe, "Enforcing the Law in the Seventeenth-Century English Village," in Gatrell, Lenman, and Parker, eds., *Crime and the Law*, pp. 111–17. Numerous examples can be found of offenders being beaten by a crowd and then released rather than prosecuted. The *Gentleman's Magazine* reported a typical case in 1784 when "a gentleman gazing at a printshop in the Strand, had his pocket picked of his purse, in which were bank notes to the amount of £1700. A poor woman that stood by observed the transaction, gave notice, and the fellow was pursued and taken, and the purse recovered. The fellow, after being rolled in the kennel, and had undergone the discipline of the mob, was permitted to escape; and the woman who discovered the theft rewarded with five guineas" (54 [1784], p. 635).

pounds on the advertiser and the printer of such a reward (both passed when property crimes were particularly common in London), such mutually satisfactory arrangements were also facilitated in the eighteenth century by the development of newspapers, for their advertisement columns provided a ready means of communication between the thief and his victim.[10] In some circumstances a prosecution might be the only way the victim could establish his ownership of the goods at issue and get them returned,[11] but there might well be a great advantage in compounding, where that was possible. It seems clear, too, that some victims were bought off by agreeing to take some form of compensation in return for not pressing charges.[12] Other considerations might also discourage a victim from making an official complaint: fear of retaliation, for example, or dislike of a law that might put the accused's life at risk for a minor offense. Undoubtedly many of those who might have pressed charges for such offenses as theft or assault chose not to do so.[13]

In seeking to uncover some of the forces that determined whether suspects would be apprehended and prosecuted in the eighteenth century, we should thus begin with the victim and ask what factors might have influenced him as he thought about laying charges. A number of impulses may well have tugged him one way and another, but it is likely that of great immediate importance to many men was the realization that a prosecution would involve a good deal of trouble and expense. The potential cost may well have been of overriding importance, for while criminal cases were carried on in the name of the king and were organized in their initial stages by magistrates, the fees and other charges were paid by the private prosecutor. The need for ready money and the prospect of having to lay out more as the case unfolded, as well of course as the trouble it involved and the inevitable loss of time from work it would require, must have played an important part in a victim's decision to prosecute or not. It is

[10] On Wild see Gerald Howson, *The Thief-Taker General: The Rise and Fall of Jonathan Wild* (1970), pp. 74–80. The statutes referred to are 3 Geo I, c. 11 (1717), and 25 Geo II, c. 36 (1752). For the law relating to the compounding of felonies and the main forms that such compounding took in the eighteenth century see Radzinowicz, *History*, vol. 2, pp. 313–18.

[11] Blackstone, *Commentaries*, 12th ed. (1795), pp. 362–63.

[12] There is inevitably not a great deal of evidence about compensation being paid in return for not pressing charges. Allegations were made in court from time to time that such an accommodation had been offered by the prosecutor, and it was also frequently charged that constables and other peace officers as well as the unofficial "thief-takers" were easily bought off (S.A.P., Summer 1743, p. 13 [Scate]; Radzinowicz, *History*, vol. 1, pp. 117ff.).

[13] For the discretion available to prosecutors see Hay, "Controlling the English Prosecutor," pp. 168–71; his "Crime, Authority and the Criminal Law," pp. 399–415; and Peter King, "Decision-Makers and Decision-Making in the English Criminal Law, 1750–1800," *Historical Journal* 27 (1984), p. 27.

thus worth considering what the costs of mounting a prosecution were in ordinary criminal cases in the eighteenth century, at least after the suspect was in custody or had been identified, before going on in this and subsequent chapters to enquire into other factors that determined the number and the character of offenders brought before the courts.

COSTS OF PROSECUTION

The costs of a case began as soon as the victim took his complaint to a magistrate, for if his witnesses and the suspect were not also present he might have to pay for subpoenas to have the witnesses summoned and a warrant to have the accused brought in to be examined. He would also have to pay fees for the recognizances in which he and his witnesses would be bound over to give evidence if the magistrate committed the accused to trial. When the case reached the court, more fees would be required: to the clerk of the peace or the clerk of assize for drawing the indictment; to the officer who swore the witnesses in court; to the doorkeeper in the courtroom; to the cryer; and to the bailiff who took the prosecutor from the court to the grand jury room with his bill of accusation. The total cost would depend on the number of witnesses sworn and on the court of trial, but in a felony or assault case it would likely be at least ten shillings to a pound.[14]

Two other, and less predictable, sources of expense could push the costs well beyond that. The most serious for some prosecutors was likely to be the costs of attending the court. If they were far from home they might have to stay over several days between their appearance before the grand jury and the time the case actually came to trial, and they would have to pay not only their own expenses for food and lodging but those of their witnesses too. Some prosecutors may well have also found it necessary to compensate those witnesses for their trouble and loss of time at work. Especially in the second half of the eighteenth century, the prosecutor might also have felt obliged to engage a solicitor to prepare the case and counsel to present it in court. That remained in 1800 the

---

[14] Richard Wyatt, a Surrey magistrate, records fees of a shilling for a warrant, 2s. 4d. for each recognizance, and six pence for a warrant to raise a hue and cry (*Deposition Book of Richard Wyatt*, p. 1). In the same period the following fees were paid at the Surrey quarter sessions: to the clerk for the bill of indictment 2s. 0d. in assault; 3s. 4d. in the case of felonies, 2s. 0d. for swearing witnesses; 1s. 0d. to the doorkeeper; and 1s. 0d. for each warrant (QS 2/6, Ep. 1758, 2). If subpoenas had to be issued for witnesses, fees had to be paid for the documents and to the officer who served them, and in addition each witness had to be given a shilling (SP 35/63, f. 258). Such fees were higher at the assizes (PP 1836, 27, pp. 15–17).

choice of a minority of prosecutors, as we will see, but many men were in fact assuming that extra expense by then.

Total costs obviously varied considerably from case to case, but we can perhaps get some sense of a minimum level from the compensation awards that were paid by the courts to some prosecutors in the second half of the century. These arose from legislation of 1752 and 1754 recommended by a committee of the House of Commons investigating the crime wave that hit London in the years following the peace of Aix-la-Chapelle in 1748. The committee accepted a notion frequently asserted in the past, by Hale among others, and vigorously restated in 1751 by Henry Fielding, that the costs of prosecution were bound to discourage victims of theft from taking the thief to court even when they could identify him and have him apprehended. Fielding thought that the fees were modest but that other costs were crippling and likely to discourage prosecutions. When one considered, he said,

> the Expence of Attendance, generally with several Witnesses, sometimes during several Days together, and often at a great Distance from the Prosecutor's Home; I say, when these Articles are summed up, and the Loss of Time added to the Account, the whole amounts to an Expence which a very poor Person, already plundered by the Thief, must look on with such Horrour (if he should not be absolutely incapable of the Expence) that he must be a Miracle of Public Spirit if he doth not rather choose to conceal the Felony. . . .[15]

The committee took this long-standing criticism seriously and in an Act passed in 1752, aimed primarily at the control of crime in London by the regulation of "disorderly houses" and places of public entertainment, accepted the principle that the system of private prosecution could not work unless the state paid some of the costs.[16] The Act gave power to the bench to order the treasurer of the county to pay the prosecutor his charges, including "a reasonable allowance for his time and trouble therein," taking his "circumstances" into account. Costs were to be paid only in the case of conviction (to discourage prosecutions from being brought simply for the purpose of generating an inflated list of expenses), and only in felonies. The 1754 legislation allowed the court to meet the costs of "poor persons" bound over to give evidence for the prosecution.[17]

These statutes were initially interpreted strictly by the judges. At

---

[15] Fielding, *Increase of Robbers*, p. 110.
[16] 25 Geo II, c. 36, s. 11 (1752).
[17] 27 Geo II, c. 3, s. 3 (1754).

the Surrey Summer assizes in 1753, when the first awards of costs are recorded, eight prosecutions for larceny and other felonies resulted in convictions, but only three of the prosecutors were given an allowance of costs. Two guineas went to two of them and £1.5.4 to the other—the first two payments clearly a rough and ready calculation and the third apparently related to a bill of costs submitted by the prosecutor.[18] At the following Lent assizes in 1754 twenty-two convictions were returned, but the judge awarded costs to only one prosecutor (£2.0.8) and divided £2.11.6 among five witnesses who had given evidence in a case of shop-lifting.[19] Dudley Ryder's practice on the Home Circuit in 1754–55 was to award a payment for costs and for time and trouble to those who appeared to him to be poor, the judges "having construed the Act," as he was told by the clerk of assize, "to mean only poor persons." He determined this largely by their appearance. When he was petitioned for costs by four prosecutors at the Essex Summer assizes in 1754, he denied them to an innkeeper "of considerable figure" but "settled the costs of three others who appeared to be poor . . . without any affidavit of their poverty and without affidavit of their charges. . . ."[20] At the Surrey Summer assizes that year, he again denied costs "to an innkeeper of substance" and allowed them to "an alehouse keeper not seeming to be in very good circumstances." He had also by then adopted the practice of awarding five shillings a day for compensation for time and trouble besides fees and other court charges.[21]

Within a few years the judges were interpreting the rules more generously than Ryder had done, and in deciding who might be given costs they began to pay less attention to the apparent condition of the prosecutor. In the 1760s, for example, costs were awarded at the Surrey assizes to several "shopkeepers," and while the mere title tells nothing about their circumstances, the fact that one had lost goods worth thirty pounds in the theft suggests that he at least was not desperately poor. Costs were also awarded to the owner of a warehouse and the owner of a whitening ground, and to a merchant, John Heathcote, Esq., when he prosecuted a man for stealing lead from his bargehouse.[22] The number of

[18] ASSI 31/3, p. 174.

[19] ASSI 31/4, p. 34. Perhaps only fifteen of the twenty-two were eligible according to the rules the judges appear to have worked under initially, for Dudley Ryder said that the judges decided not to pay costs in cases in which parliamentary awards applied. Rewards will be dealt with in a later section of this chapter.

[20] Ryder Assize Diary, p. 7.

[21] Ryder Assize Diary, pp. 13, 16.

[22] ASSI 31/8, pp. 57, 149; ASSI 31/9, pp. 40, 109. Nor was the early rule that prohibited costs from being paid to those eligible for a statutory reward enforced: several prosecutors of robbers and burglars were granted costs in this same period.

prosecutors applying for and being granted costs thus expanded soon after the Acts were passed and after the first few years of practice. In the 1760s about a third of the prosecutors (and their witnesses) in felonies that ended in convictions were awarded costs at the Surrey assizes (table 2.1). It seems reasonable to think that men who appeared to have few resources were given preference, and in fact Peter King has demonstrated that at the quarter sessions men described as laborers were granted costs more readily than tradesmen, craftsmen, and other middling men.[23] But it is also clear that at the Surrey assizes (as at the Essex quarter sessions investigated by Mr. King), within a few years of the legislation the judges were allowing costs to more than the very poor.

The assize judges had also enlarged the scope of the legislation in other ways by then. In the years 1766–71, for which the evidence is complete but for one session, the judges at the Surrey assizes not only awarded costs in thirty-five per cent of the cases that resulted in convictions but also allowed costs in eighteen cases in which the accused had been acquitted, perhaps because they disagreed with the verdict or at least thought that the prosecutors deserved to be rewarded for bringing charges. This went squarely against the legislation, and it was presumably the prevalence of such practices that led to the recognition in a statute of 1778 of the continuing discouragement to prosecution when costs were only paid in the case of conviction. This Act (18 Geo III, c. 19, ss. 7–8) authorized the courts to pay any prosecutor and his witnesses their expenses and an allowance to those "in poor circumstances" for their time and trouble whether the accused was convicted or not. The payment of costs broadened considerably under this encouragement in the 1780s and after. In the three years 1792 to 1794, to take another period by way of example,

TABLE 2.1

Costs Allowed at the Surrey Assizes

Period	Eligible Cases	Costs Allowed in Eligible Cases		Costs Allowed in Apparently Ineligible Cases	
		No.	%	Defendant Acquitted	Bill Not Found
1766–71	168	59	35.1	18	0
1792–94	190	123	64.7	0	10

SOURCE: ASSI 31/8–10, 17.

[23] King, "Decision-Makers and Decision-Making," pp. 32–33.

the judges at the Surrey assizes awarded costs to the prosecutors and witnesses in two-thirds of the 190 felony trials that took place. They also extended the meaning of the Act in yet another direction by ordering compensation to ten prosecutors whose bills had been turned back by the grand jury and who had thus not been able to get their cases into court (table 2.1).

The actual value of the awards remained roughly steady over the second half of the century, though the proportion of prosecutors granted them expanded considerably. Just over a quarter of the awards fell between one and two pounds and another quarter between two and three, so that (with the handful below a pound) close to sixty per cent of the costs granted were less than three pounds (table 2.2). Another quarter were between three and five pounds and the remainder between five and ten. Only four grants in thirty-seven sessions of the court over the second half of the century were for amounts over ten pounds.

It is difficult to tell how closely these awards approximated the actual costs that prosecutors and their witnesses had been put to, and thus whether they can be thought to provide a guide to the expenses that a victim of a felony who was contemplating bringing a charge might have reasonably anticipated. They were clearly not meant to cover every expense prosecutors had incurred. They did not, for example, cover the costs at the magistrate's hearing or the expenses connected with the apprehension of the accused.

TABLE 2.2

Costs Awarded at the Surrey Assizes, 1755–1794

Award	Number of Cases	Percentage of Cases
Less than £1	13	2.9
£1–£1.19.11	123	27.4
£2–£2.19.11	120	26.7
£3–£4.19.11	124	27.6
£5–£10	65	14.5
More than £10	4	.9
Total	449	100.0
SUMMARY		
Under £3	256	57.0
£3–£5	124	27.6
Over £5	69	15.4

SOURCE: ASSI 31/4–17 (37 sessions altogether in the years 1755–57, 1766–73, 1780–84, and 1792–94).

It is also unlikely that many would have included the fees of solicitors or prosecuting counsel, so some of the settlements probably fell far short of actual costs. But counsel were still in 1800 likely to be engaged by those wealthy enough not to request costs or who at least were not granted costs. Perhaps the most important thing to note about these figures, if we hope to get some sense of the level of actual expenses, is that they were the total allowed to both the prosecutor and the witnesses, and that they included an allowance to some for "time and trouble," an allowance that in the 1750s had been five shillings for each day's attendance at the court. This was paid mainly to those who successfully pleaded poverty, and it is unclear how commonly such an award was made.[24] If we assume that the addition for time and trouble was not very commonly paid and that most of these costs awarded at the assizes were for out-of-pocket expenses (fees, traveling charges, food, and lodging for both prosecutor and witnesses), it would appear that most prosecutors were faced with minimum expenses of between one and three pounds.

At the quarter sessions the payments of costs suggest that the expense of bringing a case there was much lower than at the assizes—as one would expect, not only because the fees were lower but also because the court met more frequently in Southwark and provided much easier access for a large number of prosecutors. While the majority of allowances paid at the assizes ran between one and three pounds, those at the quarter sessions were half that and less. The evidence is not as full for the lower court, but in 1767, for example, no allowance at the Surrey quarter sessions exceeded a guinea, and two men were given costs of seven and ten shillings.[25]

In the end we are left with no more than a rough indication of the possible costs of undertaking a prosecution in the second half of the eighteenth century. It is likely that the county allowances did not fully meet the expenses that most prosecutors had to bear, especially those who had difficulty finding the suspect or organizing the evidence upon which the prosecution would rest.[26] In many cases, the costs must have been much

[24] That this compensation was not paid to all prosecutors and witnesses is suggested by the request of a magistrate to the clerk of the Norfolk assize circuit in 1776 on behalf of a man bringing a case before the court that the charges of this man's witnesses be allowed because they were "in low circumstances" (ASSI 39/7, loose correspondence).

[25] QS 2/6, Ep. 1768, 27. In 1741 a bill presented to the magistrates by a lawyer who had prosecuted on their behalf a man charged with rescuing someone from the house of correction gives some sense of costs. He took two witnesses from London to the session at Reigate and provided their food and lodging for an unspecified number of days at a cost of £1.14.6; he paid 5s. 4d. for court fees; his own expenses and fee came to £1.12.8 (QS 2/6, Ep. 1741, 1).

[26] Better evidence of actual costs may emerge from the detailed work now underway on the activities of prosecution associations because they commonly undertook to make up for their members the difference between their outlays and the allowances made by the court.

higher than the sums awarded by the judge because some prosecutors had engaged in elaborate searches for the suspect and others (in increasing numbers) took on the services of a solicitor and barrister, and these expenses were not likely to be covered in the county allowance. If the minimum costs were on the order of a pound or two at the quarter sessions, and perhaps double that at the assizes, this might not in itself have provided a serious financial barrier to a reasonably well placed tradesman or crafts-man. For shopkeepers and merchants the immediate costs of prosecution were not in any case likely to have been as serious a disincentive as the time they and their employees would lose in making a complaint and then attending the court, waiting perhaps several days for the case to come on. [27]

Such concerns were commonly voiced in the century, and the House of Commons committee investigating the administration of the criminal law in 1819 heard evidence that among tradesmen and merchants in London there was "a great disposition to avoid prosecution on account of the waste of time, not of the expense, because that is not great, unless they employ counsel; but the attendance is very inconvenient."[28] But for a laboring man costs of a pound or two were obviously substantial, and the prospect of getting some of it back from the county treasurer, even with an allowance for his time and trouble, could not have helped the man crippled by a lack of ready money to pay for warrants, recognizances, and so on, except possibly as an aid to borrowing the necessary cash. It is indeed surprising just how many men described as laborers in fact undertook prosecutions despite the costs involved. As we will see, some-thing on the order of a fifth of those bringing cases at the quarter sessions were apparently laboring men. It seems reasonable to assume that poor men must have had to be moved very strongly to bring a prosecution against someone who had assaulted them or stolen from them. But they did so, and in large enough numbers to make it clear that the system was not entirely closed to men of modest means and that the laboring popu-lation did not regard the criminal courts as merely the province of the rich. [29]

[27] A glass manufacturer in Vauxhall asked the clerk of the peace in 1726, for example, to get a case brought on early because the workman he had sent to give evidence against a man he was prosecuting for theft was "very much wanted in our glass works" (QS 2/6, Mids. 1726, 7).

[28] *Report on Criminal Laws* (1819), p. 83.

[29] That is not to say that numerous men and women did not find prosecutions a crippling burden. In the case of Joseph Cooper and his mother, for example, a magistrate asked the clerk of the peace to give their case "what dispatch you can, they are poor people and cannot afford to keep their witnesses and themselves too at a country sessions one night" (QS 2/6, Mids. 1719, 64); or the two men for whom Lord Palmerston asked that they be sworn "as soon as the court sits, that they may go to the grand jury and be dispatched" (QS 2/6, Ep. 1730, 96); or the man

It was said after 1818, when by Bennet's Act the terms under which costs were awarded were enlarged, that there had been an increase of malicious prosecutions, including prosecutions by constables, because of the size of the payments being awarded.[30] There is no evidence that the payment of costs had had a similar effect in the eighteenth century. Whether the legislation had even encouraged significant numbers of legitimate prosecutions that would otherwise not have been undertaken is unclear. Perhaps the prospect of getting some of the costs back tilted the balance for some victims of property crimes. But I would guess that these payments did not make a great deal of difference at the moment of decision to those contemplating a prosecution in that they did not remove many of the problems that most sharply discouraged prosecutors, whether it was the lack of ready money or the prospect of its taking a great deal of time and trouble. As an actual incentive to prosecution the payment of costs is likely to have been of marginal importance.

PROSECUTION ASSOCIATIONS

The costs of mounting a court case, especially if it was thought necessary to engage a solicitor and counsel, must have nonetheless worked as a disincentive to prosecution. This is one reason it became common in the second half of the eighteenth century for propertied men to join together in associations to share the costs of catching and prosecuting thieves. Associations for the prosecution of felons can be found in some form in the late seventeenth century, but they were not numerous until after 1760 or 1770, when they were found all over the country. They were typically formed from among the middling property owners of a town or parish or group of parishes. They were perhaps encouraged by moments of acute anxiety about the level of crime, especially in the 1780s, and by the increasing conviction that crime was being encouraged by the uncertainty of punishment and the failure of victims to prosecute. By promising both the determined pursuit and the prosecution of everyone who offended against their members, and by sharing the costs of such a policy, they had a natural appeal to those who thought their property increasingly at risk. Over the late decades of the eighteenth century and into the middle

---

said to be so poor that he was "not able to prosecute the person that robbed him" and who wanted to drop the case and have his recognizance canceled (QS 2/6, Mich. 1760, 43).

  [30] Radzinowicz, *History*, vol. 2, pp. 74–82; Hay, "Controlling the English Prosecutor," pp. 170–74.

of the nineteenth, a great many local associations, often short-lived, sprang up in both towns and rural parishes.[31]

Associations for the prosecution of felons were of several types, but they all undertook to help their members in two general ways: in return for an annual subscription, a member who had been the victim of a felony was helped both to find and apprehend the offender and then to mount a prosecution. Most restricted this help to the subscribers, but a few took a broader view and aimed at more general deterrence by extending these benefits to all residents of their parish or town. The association formed in the Surrey parish of Mortlake in 1784, in a period of considerable anxiety about property crime, was one such society. It undertook to pay rewards for evidence that would lead to the conviction of anyone who stole within the parish, whether from a member or not, and to pay the costs of those victims of theft too poor to undertake a prosecution. Forty-five residents of the parish pledged total annual contributions of more than five hundred pounds. It was presumably the wide-ranging help they offered that explains why that association seems not to have lasted more than a decade.[32]

The association formed in Godalming Hundred in Surrey in 1796 was perhaps more typical in that it undertook to advertise only those offenses committed against its members, offering rewards in handbills and newspaper advertisements for information that would convict the offender.[33] The society's treasury also made up any difference there might be between the actual costs of prosecutions undertaken by members and the compensation ordered by the courts. At the meeting of January 1797, for example, it was agreed that "if David Speere shall not be allowed the whole of his charges and expenses and for his time in prosecuting John Collyer for bee stealing by the judge, he shall be allowed such reasonable sum out of the stock of the society to make good the deficiency."[34] The

[31] Adrian Shubert, "Private Initiative in Law Enforcement: Associations for the Prosecution of Felons, 1744–1856," in Victor Bailey, ed., *Policing and Punishment in Nineteenth-Century Britain* (1981), pp. 25–41; Hay, "Crime, Authority and the Criminal Law," pp. 355–94; Peter King, "Prosecution Associations, Courts and Community Concerns in Essex, 1740–1800"; David Philips, "Good Men to Associate and Bad Men to Conspire: Associations for the Prosecution of Felons in England, 1770–1860" (the King and Philips papers were both presented to the Conference on the History of Law, Labour and Crime, University of Warwick, Sept. 1983).

[32] Surrey RO 2414/8/1–4. What was in effect a countywide association was proposed by the Surrey magistrates in July 1785. A schedule of rewards, to be paid from a privately subscribed fund, was published (Guildford Muniment Room, Ms. 85/2/4/1). Besides the association formed in Godalming, evidence survives for associations also having been established in Guildford and the Hundred of Blackheath (Guildford Muniment Room, Ms. 85/2/4, no. 166; Ms. 129/29/40).

[33] Surrey RO 2133/15/1 (minutes, Apr. 1797).

[34] Ibid., Jan. 1797. It is interesting as a comment on the previous discussion of the relationship between actual expenses and the costs awarded by the court that there seems to be an assumption here that Speere might or might not have been seriously out of pocket when the case was over.

Godalming association had restricted aims. On one occasion, however, it did pay for the prosecution of offenses committed in the parish against nonmembers of the association who were judged not to be "in circumstances to prosecute him for themselves," though the suspect in this case was also charged with an offense against one of the subscribers.[35]

Some societies also maintained patrols in their parishes to prevent crime and to pick up anyone who looked suspicious; others required that their members (or a paid substitute) turn out to conduct searches for stolen goods. At the trial stage, a number of societies engaged a solicitor to prepare the case and to brief counsel.[36] It seems likely that prosecution associations were responsible for the detection and arrest of offenders who would otherwise not have been caught, and that they encouraged prosecutions that would otherwise not have been undertaken. And they not only countered some of the disinclination to prosecute, but in parts of the country, especially in the first half of the nineteenth century, they provided forms of private policing that foreshadowed and perhaps encouraged the adoption of the "new police" in the decades after 1830. But whether they made a significant difference to the number of cases that came to trial is more doubtful. Those who have examined the impact of associations on prosecutions are inclined to conclude that they did not have a major effect on the number of offenders brought to trial before the quarter sessions and assizes.[37] In Surrey, associations do not seem to have been sufficiently active in the parishes in which most property offenses were committed to have had a broad impact on the administration of the law, especially in anything more than the short term.

REWARDS

It was a fundamental part of the strategy of the associations to advertise when an offense was committed and to offer a reward for evidence that would lead to the arrest and conviction of the offender. Such payments were encouragements to the public to take on functions that the official agents of law enforcement in the parish would be unlikely to perform. A man anxious to discover who had stolen his horse or burglarized his house would normally get little help from a justice of the peace or his parish constable. They would not be likely to make enquiries for him, chase after

[35] Surrey RO 2253/15/1 (Nov. 1799).

[36] Shubert, "Private Initiative in Law Enforcement," pp. 31–33; Philips, "Good Men to Associate," pp. 20–21.

[37] King, "Prosecution Associations," pp. 13–19; Philips, "Good Men to Associate," pp. 26–27.

clues, follow suspects across the country, or in other ways compile evidence and make arrests. Some magistrates in the eighteenth century did conduct vigorous campaigns against offenders in their neighborhoods and entered into correspondence with like-minded men elsewhere.[38] But they were distinctly unusual. Neither magistrates nor constables were likely to do more than respond to the complaints brought to them The point of offering a reward was to encourage initiative in just these areas of investigation and prosecution, on the part of both the victim and others. The rewards offered by the associations were in fact by no means unusual, for by the middle of the eighteenth century rewards for evidence that would convict offenders were commonplace. Parliament had long before taken the lead in enlisting in this way the pecuniary self-interest of the public in the administration of the criminal law.

Rewards had been offered in the seventeenth century. Soon after the Restoration, royal proclamations promised ten pounds to anyone whose information led to the apprehension of a robber or burglar, and offered a pardon to offenders who gave evidence against their accomplices. Other ad hoc rewards were offered over the next three decades.[39] But it was only after 1689 that rewards emerged as a fundamental aspect of public policy and an established element in the system of criminal administration. The significant extension of the scope of capital punishment by the removal of benefit of clergy from numerous offenses in the reigns of William III and Anne was accompanied by the establishment of statutory and extremely valuable rewards and other inducements for the conviction of certain kinds of offenders.

The alteration of the criminal law and the creation of statutory rewards both give evidence of the dissatisfaction in parliament and in the courts in the late seventeenth and early eighteenth centuries with the law and its administration and with the available punishments, especially for crimes against property. As we will see, several expedients were tried after 1689 to stiffen the administration of the law and the consequences of conviction. These did not proceed from a coherent plan or well thought out principles, but from an intermittent anxiety to bolster the forces of order and social defense. The removal of clergy from a range of offenses was intended to enlarge the terrors of the law and to increase its deterrent capacities. Similarly, the rewards established by statute (and the offer of a pardon that was so often linked to the reward) aimed to exert the greatest pressure on offenders by a massive appeal to the self-interest of those who could

[38] John Styles, "An Eighteenth-Century Magistrate as Detective: Samuel Lister of Little Horton," *The Bradford Antiquary*, new ser., 47 (1982), pp. 98–117.

[39] SP 29/49, f. 237; SP 44/1, p. 29; Radzinowicz, *History*, vol. 2, pp. 84–88.

turn others in. Along with a variety of other measures, these statutory rewards were the product of a period determined to wage a fierce war on what was clearly thought to be a serious problem of crime and immorality.

The first statute to establish a permanent reward, passed in 1692, promised the considerable sum of forty pounds (and the offender's horse, arms, and money if they were not stolen property) for the apprehension and conviction of highway robbers, including those who robbed in the streets of the metropolis or other towns.[40] Rewards were added in William's reign for convictions in cases of counterfeiting and shoplifting; in Anne's for burglary, housebreaking, and horse-theft; and later in the century for sheep-stealing and cattle-theft (in 1741 and 1742) and unlawfully returning from transportation (1743). The reward for convicting a horse thief was a so-called Tyburn ticket, a certificate issued by the assize judge that granted a lifelong exemption from parish office and that might be sold (depending on the parish to which it applied) for as much as twenty-five pounds.[41]

In addition to these statutory rewards the government continued to offer further sums by proclamation from time to time in response to particularly shocking offenses—a murder, for example—or to encourage the conviction and punishment of offenders when crime seemed to be especially prevalent. Many such proclamations related to violent offenses in London. They typically offered huge rewards for a limited period of time beyond those established by statute. In 1720, for example, a royal proclamation added one hundred pounds, to be paid by the Treasury, to the forty pounds already available for the prosecution and conviction of street robbers in the cities of London and Westminster and within a radius of five miles.[42] It ran for a year and was renewed for several brief periods over the next thirty years, whenever street robbery caused a panic. It was said in 1732 that the government would never again offer fixed additional bounties since it had been discovered that such massive sums encouraged malicious prosecutions and, even worse, encouraged men to lead others into committing offenses so that they might be "discovered" and profitably convicted. It was also feared that juries were reluctant to convict genuine

---

[40] 4 Wm and M, c. 8, s. 2 (1692). For rewards in general see Radzinowicz, *History*, vol. 2, chaps. 3–6.

[41] The relevant statutes after 1692, some of which amplified previous ones, are: 6 and 7 Wm and M, c. 17, s. 9 (1695); 10 and 11 Wm III, c. 23, s. 2 (1699); 5 Anne, c. 31, s. 1 (1706); 6 Geo I, c. 23, s. 8 (1719); 14 Geo II, c. 6, s. 2 (1741); 15 Geo II, c. 34 (1742); 16 Geo II, c. 16, s. 3 (1743).

[42] For royal proclamations I have relied on the list in *Bibliotheca Lindesiana*, vol. 8, *Handlist of Proclamations, 1714–1910* (Wigan, 1913); and SP 37/15, ff. 491–98 (proclamations on crime and related matters, 1689–1753).

offenders when so much money was at stake because of their suspicion of prosecutors' and witnesses' motives. Instead it was thought that the government might simply allow the judges to order extra payments at their discretion when they thought them deserved.[43] But in fact the old policy was revived in 1735, when for a year one hundred pounds was offered for the conviction of street robbers in London. The policy was renewed in 1744 for six months, and again in 1749 and 1750, when crime in and around the metropolis increased sharply. The rewards were gratefully received. In 1748 and 1749, for example, the Treasury paid out two hundred and six hundred pounds respectively for statutory and other rewards; in the following two years payments under the bounty proclamation reached £4600 and then £6500.[44]

It is unclear whether it was the financial burden or the disquieting side-effects of the policy that persuaded the government that these large rewards were not in the public interest, but that conclusion had certainly been reached by the early 1750s. The offer of a huge extra reward—and what would amount to £140 for the conviction of a single highwayman or street robber, £280 for a pair—was never renewed thereafter. The policy was terminated even before the public outrage arose from the trials between 1754 and 1756 of Stephen Macdaniel and his associates, who had enticed men into crime in order to prosecute them and who had been responsible for the conviction of a young man hanged at Tyburn in 1754.[45]

The policy of rewarding those responsible for the conviction of offenders was not abandoned, however. Rewards remained an important cornerstone in the administration of the criminal law. Although statutory rewards were not extended to other offenses in the second half of the century and huge extra bounties were no longer paid for whole classes of offenders, rewards were offered for the apprehension and conviction of offenders in specific cases, for particular offenses. They were offered by government departments, local authorities, groups of merchants and residents, insurance companies, associations for the prosecution of felons, and frequently by individuals. They were advertised in newspapers—the growth of the press in the eighteenth century provided the crucial mechanism for the elaboration of both public and private rewards—and by handbills. If the offense had been particularly heinous the reward might be enlarged by the promise of a royal pardon to any of the offenders who would turn king's evidence, in which case the reward money might enable

[13] *G. M.* 2 (1732), p. 1029.

[44] SP 36/153, f. 16.

[45] On the Macdaniel scandal see Radzinowicz, *History*, vol. 2, pp. 326–32; Langbein, "Shaping the Eighteenth-Century Criminal Trial," pp. 110–14; Foster, *Reports*, pp. 121–32.

him to leave the district to avoid the possible revenge of the condemned men's friends.[46]

The rewards given under statute were paid by the sheriff following a settlement among the various claimants made by the judge at the conclusion of the session.[47] Occasionally the claims were made in court,[48] but for the most part the business of parceling out the "blood money" (a term increasingly used as disapproval mounted in the late eighteenth century— often inaccurately since by no means were all the convicted offenders actually hanged) was settled in private. If the parties with a claim reached an agreement among themselves judges appear to have largely accepted it,[49] and as a result some of the settlements made fine discriminations among a large number of claimants. In the case of the conviction of three highway robbers in 1785 that produced a total of £120 in reward money,

[46] As examples of ad hoc rewards and of the offer of a royal pardon: in a case of arson in 1738, a royal pardon was offered, along with twenty pounds from the landlord whose barn was burned down (*London Evening Post*, 10–12 Jan. 1738); when the parish church of Egham was robbed, five guineas were offered by the churchwardens for the conviction of any of the offenders (ibid., 15–17 Aug. 1738); after a vicious murder of a woman in Surrey, the lords justices offered fifty pounds' reward for the conviction of the murderer and the parish of St. Saviour's, in which the woman lived, offered twenty pounds, advertised in the *Gazette* (S.A.P., Lent 1749, p. 10); and a weaver in Sussex, having lost close to thirty pounds by theft and the suspect having escaped before trial, offered a one-guinea reward and "all reasonable charges" to anyone who apprehended him (*Sussex Weekly Advertiser*, 5 May 1750). For numerous examples of rewards in all these categories see Radzinowicz, *History*, vol. 2, chaps. 4–5 and apps. 2–3.

[47] By 3 Geo I, c. 15, s. 4 (1716), the sheriff was able to apply directly to the Treasury for repayment rather than claiming what could be substantial sums in his cravings. For payments made to sheriffs see the series (P.R.O.) T 53. At T 53/31, p. 60, for example, there is an account of the money paid to the sheriff of Surrey to cover his disbursement of rewards in ten cases in 1724.

[48] S.A.P., Lent 1738, p. 5; Lent 1741, p. 14.

[49] When he was first called upon to make such a division, Dudley Ryder noted that he

> signed several certificates for the distribution of the rewards, vizt. £40 for burglary, and certificates to discharge from parish offices by giving it to those who were agreed between the several person, witnesses to have it [*sic*], the clerk of the assizes showing me in one instance an agreement under their hands, in the other only saying it was agreed between them. But I think I should not do that so easily without the parties witnesses [*sic*] would agree in writing or come to me and acknowledge it. (Ryder Assize Diary, p. 7)

On another occasion "where the parties did not settle it among themselves" he divided "the rewards of £40 among the prosecutors and the witnesses concerned in apprehending or discovering in such proportion as seemed right" (ibid., p. 16). But for the most part the various claimants seem mainly to have come to their own arrangement well ahead, and the judge merely sanctioned it and signed the certificates they would take to the sheriff for payment. Such was the system at the Old Bailey in the early nineteenth century (H. C. Committee on the Police of the Metropolis [1817], p. 417).

for example, the victim-prosecutor got sixty pounds and a Tyburn ticket and his wife got twenty pounds. Three men who had a hand in appre-hending the robbers were given twenty, twelve, and five pounds, and three witnesses received one pound each. In another case at that same session, six claimants each received an equal share of the eighty-pound reward for the conviction of a pair of highway robbers. Another six shared a similar sum in amounts that ranged from two to fifty-eight pounds. In the following session twelve men divided the eighty pounds derived from the conviction of two burglars in finely graded amounts, with the pros-ecutor taking thirty pounds and the others receiving sums between £2.8.0 and ten pounds.[50] Twelve was an unusually large number of claimants, but four, five, and six were common, and most often the sharing of rewards was carefully worked out.

THIEF-TAKERS

It seems likely that rewards frequently had the effect they were meant to have and encouraged victims to give chase and to get others to join them in tracking down a robber or burglar. There are strong suggestions in the circumstances of their apprehension that some of those brought to trial at the Surrey assizes had been pursued quite simply for the reward money.[51] The shadowy group of men known as "thief-takers" in London in the first half of the century were at least in part in the business of detecting and apprehending offenders whose conviction would pay a reward. There is some confusion surrounding the term "thief-taker," in part because it was applied to a number of different activities. It was used, for example, of Jonathan Wild, the "Thief-Taker General," who attempted to control thieves and profit from offenses by negotiating the return of stolen goods for a price, and who exercised control over offenders by "bringing them

---

[50] ASSI 34/43, unpaginated.

[51] "Was not the hope of having part of a reward for taking highwaymen the inducement that made you go in pursuit of him?" a judge asked one witness in 1753 after he had given evidence that he had recognized the suspect from the description given by the victim and had seized him at his lodgings in Godstone. "To be sure it was," the man replied, and then in case that honesty did not meet with approval, he added, "and for the sake of justice" (S.A.P., Lent 1753, p. 10). Some men were undoubtedly especially conscious of the possibilities and were ever on the lookout for an opportunity to collect reward money. Gentlemen's servants, for example—especially those who traveled frequently in and around the capital with their masters—were surely aware of the huge rewards to be earned. When an accused highwayman was acquitted of a charge of robbing Sir Edward Lawrence, one of his accomplices said that that had "balked the expectations of Sir Edward's footmen who took him" (Ralph Wilson, *An Account of Robberies committed with John Hawkins* [1722], p. 16).

to justice" when it suited his purpose.[52] Thief-takers were also commonly accused of being thief-makers, like Stephen Macdaniel and his associates, who enticed naive young thieves into committing offenses in order to prosecute them and collect the reward money. One man who had been apprehended by thief-takers and was then impeached by his accomplice in a robbery claimed that such "thief-takers bail out thieves, and take in such wretches as I; then they go upon such a lay, as soon as they can get us to go along with them; they do the facts themselves, and our lives are taken away for the reward."[53]

In the middle of the century, when the blood-money conspiracies of Macdaniel and others were in the forefront of public discussion, John Fielding was at pains to distinguish these men from another group, the "real and useful thieftakers" associated with the Bow Street magistrates' office who earned rewards by tracking down offenders in a spirit of public service.[54] The distinction may not have been entirely deserved, but there were indeed men acting as freelance detectives and bounty hunters, and even before the Fieldings organized their small force of constables. Several appeared regularly at the Surrey assizes in the 1730s and 1740s, often giving evidence about the way a prisoner had been tracked down and apprehended or adding other details to the case against the accused, upon whose conviction their share of the reward money depended.

It is clear that these men were well enough known (at least by the late 1730s, for which there is a run of assize trial accounts in Surrey) to be sought out and hired by victims. In other cases, the thief-takers offered their services to the victim when the offense was reported in the press; in still others, they clearly "discovered" an offender first, by means not always clear and occasionally suspect, and then made contact with the victim to press him into prosecuting. In one case in the Surrey reports, a servant who had been robbed and beaten on London Bridge was approached by one William Rice to whom he described the two robbers. Rice thought he knew these two "loose fellows" and with two other men, Mitchell and Holderness, went after them. One got away, but they seized the other. They got the victim to identify him and then took him before Sir John Lade, a Southwark magistrate, who committed him for trial on the prosecutor's positive identification. The prisoner made little defense except to denounce Mitchell as an old thief who had "hang'd many a man [and who]

---

[52] See Charles Hitchin, *A True Discovery of the Conduct of Receivers and Thief Takers in and about the City of London* (1718); Howson, *Thief-Taker General*, pp. 81–90.

[53] S.A.P., Summer 1751, pp. 29–30 (Brian).

[54] John Fielding, *A Plan for Preventing Robberies within twenty miles of London with an account of the rise and establishment of the real thieftakers* (1755), p. i.

makes it his common practice to take people for the sake of the reward." He was convicted and sentenced to be hanged.[55]

Ralph Mitchell was indeed well known as a thief-taker. He would appear in 1756 in Joseph Cox's account of the Macdaniel scandal as "a man eminent in the thief-taking way," who, though friendly with Macdaniel (and associated with him on occasion), was not himself accused of entrapping young men into committing offenses that produced statutory rewards for convictions.[56] At the same session of the court in which he helped prosecute the servant's assailant, he gave evidence in the trials of two other highwaymen who had clearly been jockeyed into confessing, each believing that they would be allowed to turn king's evidence. The first had been arrested by Lamorock Maynard, a long-serving Southwark constable who had taken three men with him when he got word that a man with a brace of pistols in his great-coat pocket had put up at a Southwark inn. The prisoner had confessed and impeached his partner, who was then taken by Mitchell. Again both prisoners tried to use the common distaste for thief-takers in their defense. "These people swear my life away for the sake of the reward," one said, while the other appealed to the good sense of the judge: "My Lord," he said at his trial, "is it probable that I should confess a Robbery to a common Thief-catcher?" One was acquitted, but the other, identified by a witness to the robbery, was convicted.[57] Two years later Mitchell was again in court helping to convict two more highwaymen. He and two others, including Holderness again, had been hired by the victim to find the men who had attacked him. They had traced them through a pawnbroker and taken them after a battle with pistols and cutlasses.[58] Mitchell and Holderness appeared regularly at the Surrey assizes in the 1740s and 1750s, and there may well have been other thief-takers whose names I do not recognize.[59]

[55] S.A.P., Summer 1738, p. 11 (Kilburn).

[56] Joseph Cox, *A Faithful Narrative of the most Wicked and Inhuman Transactions of that Bloody-Minded Gang of Thief-takers alias Thief-makers Macdaniel, Berry, Salmon, Eagan alias Gahagen . . .* (1756), p. 9.

[57] S.A.P., Summer 1738, p. 17 (Cooper and Bird).

[58] S.A.P., Summer 1740, pp. 3–4 (Hooper).

[59] Holderness gave the evidence that convicted a man in 1741 for receiving, and two years later he was instrumental in the conviction of a man for returning prematurely from transportation—within months of that offense's becoming eligible for reward money. He clearly had a considerable knowledge of the underworld on the south side of the river, and had known for some time that this man had returned from America and where he could be found (S.A.P., Summer 1743, pp. 7–8). Along with Mitchell, Holderness testified in the successful prosecution of a burglar in 1744 and of a gang of highwaymen in the following year. Mitchell was also active on his own, for in 1748 he gave evidence in an assault case (presumably for a fee), and he was involved in the trials of at least four robbery cases (S.A.P., Lent 1745, pp. 3–9; Summer 1751, pp. 25–26; ASSI 35/181/8/62 [R vs. Mineer]; ASSI 35/184/7/7 [R vs. Millist]; ASSI 35/185/

Holderness and Mitchell may or may not have worked on both sides of the law. But in some of their guises they were forerunners of the Bow Street officers recruited by the Fieldings, and of the other groups of constables who gathered around the "rotation offices" even before their small forces of detectives were authorized in 1792.[60] The system of rewards encouraged the development of forms of policing that provided a foundation for the more fully regularized police established in London in 1829. But rewards had debilitating side-effects, too. That had been revealed most glaringly by the malicious conspiracies that had accompanied the payment of massive bounties for the conviction of street robbers. But the payment of ordinary and more modest rewards also had unfortunate side-effects (or at least their weaknesses became more revealed over the late eighteenth century), particularly the suspicions that could be aroused in the minds of trial jurors when the prosecutor and witnesses in a case all stood to gain financially from the conviction of a man on trial. These suspicions were exploited by defense counsel, who, as we will see, were admitted into the criminal courts in the eighteenth century and were employed by a substantial proportion of defendants by 1800.

The House of Commons committee investigating the "police of the metropolis" in 1817 heard a great deal of evidence about the way the payment of blood money had undermined the credit of peace officers in the courts.[61] Their conclusion, urged by many witnesses, was that rewards were seriously weakening the administration of justice and that they ought to be abolished in their present form. A bill to accomplish that was passed by parliament in 1818. Under Bennet's Act, as it was known, after the chairman of the committee who introduced it, standing rewards were replaced by payments that were in effect generous costs. They were paid at a level to be decided by the judge and would cover more of the costs of a prosecution, including the costs associated with apprehending offenders and bringing a case to the grand jury, than had been compensated for earlier by the courts.[62] This perhaps recognized that most ordinary victims of property offenses were more discouraged from bringing a prosecution by the costs involved than they were encouraged by the hope of a reward.

7/18 [R vs. Gibs et al.]; ASSI 35/188/8/18 [R vs. Bernado]; ASSI 35/190/8/9 [R vs. Vincent and Lewis]). Joanna Innes informs me that Mitchell can be found giving evidence in three cases at the Old Bailey in 1740, 1751, and 1752, and that he is mentioned in payments for reward money on three occasions between 1746 and 1754.

60 For Henry and John Fielding and the development of the Bow Street police office see Radzinowicz, *History*, vol. 2, pp. 26ff., 177ff.; vol. 3, pp. 29–62; R. Leslie Melville, *The Life and Work of Sir John Fielding* (1934); Styles, "Sir John Fielding and the Problem of Criminal Investigation"; and Langbein, "Shaping the Eighteenth-Century Criminal Trial," pp. 55–76.

61 "Report of the Committee on the Police of the Metropolis," *Parliamentary Papers* (1817), vol. 7, pp. 417, 427, 522.

62 58 Geo III, c. 70, s. 4 (1818); and see Radzinowicz, *History*, vol. 2, pp. 74–82.

But mainly the Act recognized that the payment of rewards was now seriously crippling the force of detective police officers they had helped to create. The assumption of the committee of 1817 and of those who took part in the debate over the bill in 1818 was that rewards were mainly important in stimulating police officers to greater exertions. Bennet's Act aimed to strengthen that force in the face of the massive increase of offenses that followed the peace in 1815 by compensating officers fully for their efforts, without tainting the arrests they made and the evidence they gave in court as the product mainly of a greedy desire to increase their "blood money."

MAGISTRATES

It is clear that many victims of attacks on their person or property were discouraged by the costs and the trouble from taking their complaint to a justice of the peace and beginning the process that would bring the offender to trial. Many sought private compensation or more likely did nothing. But a number were sufficiently outraged to think of bringing the offender to justice. Whether they did so or not must have been significantly influenced by one further consideration: the ease with which they could find a magistrate.

Magistrates were not distributed evenly around the country, since the men who qualified for inclusion in the commission of the peace by social standing or wealth were not themselves to be found in every corner of every county. But even if they had been, the government (in whose hands, through the Lord Chancellor, the appointment rested) could not have arranged an adequate distribution of justices because those named to the commission could decide whether they would act or not. A newly appointed magistrate had to take oaths of allegiance and supremacy and an oath of office that was in turn authorized by his taking out a writ of *dedimus potestatem*.[63] Not everyone named in a commission chose to do so, for some sought inclusion merely for the honor it provided or the confirmation of their local prestige. Inclusion in the commission of the peace gave men "credit and title in their county," in Lord Cowper's words, and for many that was sufficient, "without giving themselves," as Cowper went on to say, "the trouble of doing the Duty. . . ." Governments had long recognized the problems that this often created. But little could be done.[64]

---

[63] Lionel K. J. Glassey, *Politics and the Appointment of Justices of the Peace, 1675–1720* (Oxford, 1979), p. 21; Norma Landau, *The Justices of the Peace, 1679–1760* (Berkeley, 1984), pp. 81–82.

[64] Quoted by Glassey, *Politics and the Appointment of Justices*, p. 24. Clarendon warned in 1665 that a man ignoring the king's commission might be proceeded against. But when Hardwicke

The problem of finding active magistrates was seriously complicated by political considerations in the late seventeenth century and the first half of the eighteenth, for it is clear that over at least two generations from the 1670s the membership of the commissions of the peace was determined as much by party affiliation as administrative needs. The influence that judicial office might give a man in local electoral contests, as well as the prestige that it conferred, sharply increased the anxiety of men to be included in the county's commission in this highly competitive age. The advantages of removing their enemies and placing their supporters in such positions of influence was obvious to all administrations, and in the period of intense party conflict after 1680 the commissions were regularly remodeled and reissued as the balance of power shifted in Westminster.[65] One result was that they grew inexorably in size. In Surrey, the eighty-eight men named to the commission for the county in 1680 (excluding the Borough of Southwark) had increased to 150 by Anne's reign, to over two hundred by George I's, to 345 when Walpole left office in 1742, and to close to five hundred by 1761.[66] Not many counties experienced that rate of growth, but everywhere the commissions were substantially larger in the middle of the eighteenth century than they had been at the Restoration.

Even with the number of potential justices increasing substantially, however, there was a serious shortage of active magistrates in the eighteenth century. A sharply declining proportion of those named to the commissions took out a *dedimus*, and even of those who qualified themselves to act, fewer and fewer actually did so. In Kent, about three-quarters of the justices in the commission took out a *dedimus* in 1714; by 1760 fewer than half did so. Over the same period the proportion who actually engaged in judicial business—as measured by their attendance at meetings of the quarter sessions and assizes as well as their involvement with criminal and

---

made a similarly vague threat almost a century later it is clear that the problem had only worsened. Hardwicke urged the judges in the king's name as they were going on circuit in 1754 to "exhort and encourage the gentlemen of the several counties, who are in the Commission of the Peace, to act as Justices of the Peace." And, he went on:

In this there is a great abuse. Gentlemen are apt to be very pressing to get into the Commission of the Peace, and when they are appointed, to be very backward in acting. 'Tis a common complaint in many counties, that, tho' great numbers are in the Commission, yet there are not acting justices enough to do the ordinary business of the country. You will teach them their duty better, and let them know what the law says. . . . (Add Mss. 35870, f. 242)

[65] Glassey, *Politics and the Appointment of Justices*, passim; Landau, *Justices of the Peace*, chap. 3.
[66] Landau, *Justices of the Peace*, app. A. Separate commissions were issued for Southwark; see, for example, C 231/7, p. 265 (1665).

administrative matters in their own parishes—fell from two-thirds of the commission to about forty per cent.[67] That experience was being repeated all over the country. In Surrey, one measure of the same concentration of judicial business in fewer hands may be seen in the way the distribution of recognizances relating to offenses against the person and property returned into quarter sessions by justices changed in the century after the Restoration (table 2.3). The return of recognizances does not account for all magisterial activity, of course; this is not a measure of the number of justices engaged in county business. But dealing with criminal matters like assault and larceny was such a crucial aspect of the work of magistrates

TABLE 2.3

Recognizances Returned to the Surrey Quarter Sessions

Period	Number of J.P.'s	Number of Recognizances	Percentage of Total
1661–63	1	92	17.8
	1	85	16.5
	1	80	15.5
	3	20–29	14.2
	5	10–19	11.1
	13	5–9	14.5
	27	1–4	10.5
Total	51	516	100.1
1738–39	1	89	26.9
	1	52	15.7
	1	25	7.6
	5	10–19	18.7
	7	5–9	13.0
	32	1–4	18.1
Total	47	331	100.0
1751–52	1	130	38.4
	1	79	23.3
	1	32	9.4
	3	10–19	12.1
	3	5–9	6.2
	17	1–4	10.6
Total	26	339	100.0

SOURCE: Offenses against property and the person, quarter sessions rolls: *Surrey Quarter Sessions Records* (1661–63); QS 2/5 (1738–39, 1751–52).

[67] Landau, *Justices of the Peace*, p. 322.

that if a magistrate was active at all, the chances are reasonably strong that at least one such case would have come his way over a two-year period and required that he bind the complainant over in recognizances to appear and carry on a prosecution.

The returns in the table do suggest that the concentration of business in few hands and the disinclination to act that Dr. Landau found elsewhere is mirrored in Surrey. Half the recognizances returned into the quarter sessions in 1661–63 had been taken by three magistrates whose activities centered in Southwark and neighboring parishes; the remainder were sent in by another forty-eight men from around the county. In a two-year period in the middle of the eighteenth century, only twenty-six magistrates returned recognizances, though the commission of the peace had increased more than fivefold over the preceding century. By then, too, an even larger proportion of the work was being carried by three magistrates in the Southwark area, one of whom accounted for close to forty per cent of all the recognizances returned in the county in those two years. Those were particularly busy years for magistrates in the urban parishes of Surrey, but the distribution of work that these figures reveal was mainly the result of the fact that the business of dealing with criminal prosecutions in the county was concentrated in very few hands.

Men might have declined to act as justices for a variety of reasons. The trouble and expense of going to quarter sessions and assizes and to the local petty sessions and committee meetings were no doubt sufficiently discouraging for some. But perhaps the most obvious discouragements arose from the bother involved in dealing in their parlors with the disputes of their neighbors and with the administrative concerns and criminal matters over which single justices had jurisdiction. The number of issues that magistrates could deal with summarily increased sharply in the eighteenth century, and Blackstone blamed this particularly for the reluctance of gentlemen to take up the burdens of the office.[68] The shortage of rural justices was to some extent compensated for by the inclusion of increasing numbers of clergymen in the commission—men whose status was rising in the course of the century and who had the time and education to act as justices of the peace, particularly in rural parishes and small towns. Clerical magistrates had not been unknown in the seventeenth century, but it was only in the middle of the eighteenth that they were created in

---

[68] *Commentaries*, vol. 4, p. 279. The tendency of rural justices to withdraw from active supervision of their communities is one aspect perhaps of a more general withdrawal of landed gentlemen from the communities in which they lived and of a growing social distance between these men of natural authority in the countryside and their more plebeian neighbors; see E. P. Thompson, "Eighteenth-Century Society: Class Struggle without Class?" *Social History* 3 (1978), pp. 133–65.

significant numbers. In Surrey, they made up ten per cent of the county commission in 1761. By the end of the century clergymen accounted for as much as a quarter or a third of the magistracy, and in many places they were among the most active and most effective of the justices.[69] Clerical magistrates clearly helped to solve some of the problems in rural Surrey caused by the disinclination of many gentlemen to take on the burdens of judicial office, but one can only assume that in some parts of the county an active magistrate was not easy to find.

If the returns of recognizances and commitments to jail suggest that there was less change in the activity of magistrates in the urban parishes of Surrey over the first half of the century, it was because judicial business there was already concentrated in few hands at the Restoration. In South-wark and in other more heavily populated parishes along the river, the heavy load of judicial business—what John Evelyn called "the perpetual trouble" that magistrates in those places were put to[70]—had for some time discouraged many men from acting who might have been qualified to take on the office. The work was left to a few who by being willing to do it attracted a great deal of business to themselves. In the 1660s the load was carried by three men who were recognized by the government and by the public as the magistrates most likely to be available to issue warrants and deal with disputes.[71] A core of two or three active men remained the norm over the next century and more. They included merchants and brewers, some of whom, such as Sir John Lade and William Hammond, one of the most active Southwark magistrates of the mid-eighteenth century, were also sometime M.P.'s. And if they were not all men of secure wealth and standing, Surrey nonetheless escaped the worst examples of the "trading justice," men of "mean degree" found in significant numbers north of the river who were often accused of taking bribes and bringing unnecessary charges, and of inflaming rather than composing quarrels in order to increase their fees.[72]

But in fact not many magistrates in the metropolis, outside West-

[69] For clerical magistrates see Landau, *Justices of the Peace*, pp. 141–43; Webb and Webb, *The Parish and the County*, pp. 350–60; Eric J. Evans, "Some Reasons for the Growth of English Rural Anti-Clericalism, 1750–1830," *Past and Present* 66 (1975), p. 101.

[70] John Evelyn, *Diary*, ed. E. S. de Beer, 6 vols. (1955), vol. 3, pp. 433–34.

[71] When Secretary Bennet asked the lord chief justice in 1663 to suggest some Southwark magistrates to attend to the release of Quakers from jail, he was given the names of Sir John Lenthall and Sir John Bromfield, who both lived in the Borough, and George Moore, who lived nearby. These were the three men who appear in table 2.3 as returning three quarters of the recognizances from the urban parishes into the quarter sessions in 1661–63 and who indeed accounted for almost half of the county's total (*Cal. S. P. Dom.*, 1662–63, p. 2).

[72] On trading justices see Webb and Webb, *The Parish and the County*, pp. 326–37; Radzinowicz, *History*, vol. 3, pp. 32–33; Landau, *Justices of the Peace*, pp. 184–90, 200–4.

minster and the urban parishes of Middlesex, were men of this type. Dr. Landau found no conclusive evidence of "trading justices" in Kent in the first half of the eighteenth century, at a time when several Middlesex magistrates were expelled from the commission for turning their houses into "shops of litigation."[73] And while one cannot rule out the possibility that some of the Surrey magistrates were corrupt in these ways, "trading justices" were certainly not prominent among the men who acted in Southwark and neighboring parishes. A man who complained in 1782 about the corruption of the Middlesex bench, and who blamed the method of their appointment, offered as proof the fact that "Surrey though the adjoining county has no such complaints."[74] Nor do there seem to have been many earlier in the century.

Those willing to take on the burdens of the urban magistracy must have found that their work grew increasingly onerous, especially in the second half of the eighteenth century. Some aspects of their administrative work increased in both amount and complexity, in part because the population of Southwark and the wider metropolis of London grew rapidly, and in part because the quarter sessions took on more tasks and assigned them largely to the magistrates on the spot. The justices in the Southwark area became increasingly concerned, for example, with the county jail, located as it was in the parish of St. George, in the Borough, to take just one area of new or enlarged work. Other administrative tasks assigned to the petty sessions—there had been a weekly meeting of magistrates in Southwark to deal with poor law and other administrative matters at least since the Restoration—became increasingly burdensome.

On the criminal side, too, the active magistrates in the northern tier of urban parishes in Surrey found their work enlarging significantly toward the middle of the century. Two justices took two hundred recognizances for the quarter sessions merely for cases involving theft and assaults in 1751–52, and committed between them almost a hundred accused offenders to the county jail and houses of correction at the same time. They did so because a great many complaints were coming to their doors, for in some years in particular, as we will see, the criminal business arising in the urban parishes of Surrey rose to substantial heights, compared with the average level for the century. In these years the magistrates not only had to take on a much larger number of preliminary examinations but also had to face significantly increased business at the quarter sessions, for much of the business previously dealt with by the judges of assize was turned back to the lower courts in the second half of the century. Much

[73] Landau, *Justices of the Peace*, p. 185.
[74] SP 37/15, ff. 499–500.

of this increased work fell on the shoulders of the active urban magistrates, since the busiest meetings of the quarter sessions were invariably those held in Southwark.

There were thus some significant increases in the criminal work of magistrates in the metropolis in the course of the eighteenth century. One response to this can be seen in efforts to regularize the hours at which magistrates would be available to the public, both as a way of encouraging victims to report offenses and as a way of sharing the burden among the active justices. The mayor of London and the aldermen who acted as justices of the peace for the City decided as early as 1737 to take turns sitting daily at the Guildhall from 11:00 a.m. to 2:00 p.m. to deal with judicial business.[75] At the same time, a form of public office developed in Westminster when Thomas de Veil moved to Bow Street in 1739 and made his house a center of magisterial activity, a beginning that was expanded upon after 1748 by his successors, Henry Fielding and his half-brother John. The Bow Street office became a model for similar developments elsewhere. Particularly under John Fielding, after Henry's poor health forced his retirement in 1754, it became the source of a great number of innovations that undoubtedly strengthened law enforcement and policing in London and indeed throughout the country. Of particular importance was the emergence of Bow Street as a center of information about offenses and offenders, and the source of the regular advertisement of recent offenses in the *Public Advertiser*. Equally important for the future was the organization around the Bow Street office of a group of more "professional" constables who, though they depended fundamentally on earning rewards, were retained by a small stipend and were available for the variety of tasks that this more permanent force attracted—both protection and detection, and outside London as well as within the metropolis.[76]

Of particular importance for Surrey was the example of the public office at which magistrates kept regular hours for the conduct of business. At Sir John Fielding's urging, two more public offices were established in Westminster in 1763,[77] and soon thereafter the Surrey bench established a similar "rotation office" at St. Margaret's Hill in Southwark. As in the offices north of the river, the Southwark magistrates gathered around them

[75] *G. M.* 7 (1737), p. 763; Langbein, "Shaping the Eighteenth-Century Criminal Trial," pp. 76–81.

[76] For the development of the Bow Street office see the sources cited in note 60 above.

[77] *G. M.* 33 (1763), p. 256. Fielding submitted a plan to the government in 1761 that envisaged a network of public offices, centering on Bow Street, at which salaried magistrates would act without fee or reward; the plan also called for an extensive foot-patrol to be organized from those offices, a mounted patrol to guard the turnpikes, and a full system of advertising of offenses. See Leslie Melville, *Life and Work of Sir John Fielding*, pp. 137–40.

a small force of "thief-taking" constables who were "employed by the magistrates," as one man said in 1770, "to go in pursuit of . . . dangerous rogues who through the fear or ignorance of peace officers were likely to escape justice."[78] The establishment of the rotation office in Southwark at which a small group of magistrates sat daily in turns did not prevent other magistrates living in the vicinity from issuing warrants, conducting preliminary hearings, and handling other aspects of the criminal business of the justice's office. But undoubtedly it further concentrated the burden of that work and perhaps also further encouraged business for those willing to serve their turn.

The urge to improve policing and to encourage prosecutions, of which the rotation (or, as they were later to be known, "police") offices were a product, arose particularly in periods in which crimes against property, especially violent offenses like robbery and burglary, increased in London to unusually high levels. As we will see, such crime waves came invariably in years immediately following the conclusion of wars and provoked widespread feelings of anxiety and even panic. Anxious concern about crime in the metropolis was evident in the early 1750s and again after 1763, when the Fieldings' innovations were supported by subventions from the government, and when other groups of magistrates in London sought ways to encourage the apprehension and prosecution of the most dangerous offenders. At another moment of deep anxiety following the end of the American war in 1782, when the criminal courts in the London area were as busy as they had ever been in the century and the Home Office (as it had just become) was being bombarded with requests for help from around the country and suggestions about what ought to be done, an even more fundamental reorganization of magistrates' criminal work in the metropolis was proposed by the Pitt administration in a bill introduced into parliament in 1785 by the Solicitor General. This "London and Westminster Police Bill" represented a departure from the principle of local autonomy, for its central intention was to create a single "District of the Metropolis" that would include the City of London, Westminster, a number of Middlesex parishes, the Borough of Southwark, and the neighboring Surrey parishes of Lambeth, Bermondsey, Newington, and Rotherhithe, within which all established authority for the maintenance of the peace was to be put into the hands of three commissioners of police. Under these men the metropolis was to be divided into nine divisions in which all criminal matters were to be dealt with only at a "public office" by stipendiary magistrates.

The bill was vigorously opposed by the City of London and by the quarter sessions of Middlesex and Surrey, who all sought to retain their

[78] QS 2/6, Ep. 1770, 36.

autonomy and professed to find no reason to change the present arrangements, though in that very year they were all dealing with more offenders in their courts than any magistrate could have remembered. The opposition of the City was particularly telling, but the bill was also defeated because it aroused the hostility of men inside and outside parliament who were opposed to what seemed to be a French-style police and a serious enlargement of government power that threatened the rights and liberties Englishmen held dearest: their freedom from arbitrary authority.[79]

It was no doubt because a modest bill put forward in 1792 attacked neither the privileges of the City nor proposed a commission to direct all magisterial and police activity within the metropolis that it was found acceptable. (Perhaps too the strengthening of authority in the capital that it proposed was welcomed because of the violent turn that the Revolution had taken in France in 1792 and the emergence in England of working-class political organizations that seemed to many men of property to threaten a similar violent overthrow of the constitution at home.) This Act "for the more effectual administration of the office of a justice of the peace in such parts of the Counties of Middlesex and Surrey as lie in and near the metropolis" regularized and extended the public "rotation offices" established in the 1750s and 1760s in the metropolitan area.[80] It authorized seven such offices besides Bow Street (including one in Southwark) at which three magistrates were to be appointed to deal with all the criminal business that arose in that district. The magistrates were to have stipends and were forbidden to take fees. Each office was to have a detachment of up to six constables who were also to be paid a weekly stipend and expenses, though they continued to depend for the bulk of their income on statutory and private rewards.

THE WATCH

By the end of the century the London area was served by magistrates' courts at which a sitting magistrate could always be found. Whether the existence of the rotation office in Southwark from the 1760s had made it easier for victims of offenses in the urban parishes of Surrey to begin a prosecution is difficult to say, though it seems likely that the regularity

[79] For the Bill and the opposition see Radzinowicz, *History*, vol. 3, pp. 108–21; and David Philips, " 'A New Engine of Power and Authority': The Institutionalization of Law-Enforcement in England, 1780–1830," in Gatrell, Lenman, and Parker, eds., *Crime and the Law*, pp. 165–71.

[80] 32 Geo III, c. 53. For the provisions and significance of the Act see Radzinowicz, *History*, vol. 3, pp. 122–37.

of the court's hours would have had that effect. In addition, the constables associated with them no doubt increased the likelihood that offenders would be discovered and prosecuted, though such constables were still apt to pursue only the most serious offenders because of the reward system.

Of greater importance to the general policing of the metropolis was the parallel development in the century of better street lighting and a more effective system of preventative surveillance mounted by watchmen in the metropolis. Changes in both areas have been perhaps too little noticed or too lightly dismissed by those who see the force created by Sir Robert Peel in the 1820s as the first effective police in the capital.[81] The same concerns about the prevalence of crime and disorder that convinced groups of magistrates in the capital to establish public offices also led numerous parishes in the London area to improve their street lighting and to strengthen the watch that patrolled their streets at night, commonly by getting the authority of an Act of parliament to raise the necessary rates. Hitherto the parish watch had depended on the requirement established by the Statute of Winchester in 1285 that every householder take his turn at least during the summer months to patrol his own neighborhood, a duty that had been mainly fulfilled by the householder himself finding a substitute or more often paying a fine with which the parish authorities hired watchmen (in default of which he was liable to be presented at the quarter sessions for "not watching"). How the old watch was actually recruited and how well or badly it functioned remains to be investigated. But that it was found wanting by many parishes in London by the early decades of the eighteenth century is clear. In the mid-1720s a group of magistrates in Westminster and Middlesex requested new regulations for the nightly watch in a representation to Lord Townshend, the secretary of state, as part of a plan to combat crime in the streets.[82] The Westminster magistrate, Nathaniel Blackerby, the author of a justices' handbook, explained to an undersecretary what they had in mind. He suggested that

> a regular nightly watch be provided by Act of Parliament, and
> that such a pound rate be made as shall be sufficient to pay such
> a number of watchmen as that their stands be in sight of each

---

[81] For the structure of the parish constabulary and watch in London see Radzinowicz, *History*, vol. 2, chap. 7; and for changes in the watch in the first half of the eighteenth century see Peter Linebaugh, "Tyburn: A Study of Crime and the Labouring Poor in London during the First Half of the Eighteenth Century" (Ph.D. thesis, University of Warwick, 1975), pp. 80–82, and especially J. J. Tobias, *Crime and the Police in England, 1700–1900* (1979), chap. 2.

[82] SP 35/67, f. 14.

other or at least in hearing and that no person above the age of 50 be employed as a watchman.

That the watchmen be obliged to go their walks at least every half hour. . . .

That after twelve a clock at night they be obliged to examine all persons walking for fire arms, loaden sticks or implements for breaking houses, and if they find such like things about them or bundles or other goods suspected to be stolen that they carry such persons before and put [them] into the custody of the constable of the night in order to their examination before a justice of the peace.[83]

No general act of parliament was forthcoming, but within a few years such improvements in the watch were being made on a piecemeal basis. In 1734, for example, the vestry of the fashionable parish of St. George's, Hanover Square, in Westminster, procured the right by a local Act of parliament to remove the obligations on the inhabitants imposed by the Statute of Winchester in exchange for the payment of a rate that would maintain a permanent force of watchmen in the parish.[84] The responsibilities of these men did not change much under the new system of financing. They were to report for their evening's duty at the parish watchhouse and, as they had earlier, go from there to their appointed streets, where they took their place in a watch-box and patrolled their beat every half-hour through the night. But Tobias has found that there was a much greater concern among the officials of St. George's parish with the effectiveness of the system after the new force was established—with the siting of boxes, the laying-out of patrol areas, the hiring of suitable men, and the provision of equipment, and so on—and it is clear that the vestry paid a good deal of attention thereafter to the surveillance of the parish.

The City of London and many other parishes in the metropolis followed this lead over the next few years, and certainly over the following decades the watch was regulated in many places, often facilitated by the raising of a rate. By the same means the lighting of the streets, clearly an associated measure, was greatly improved in the middle decades of the century.[85] These were matters very much in the public mind in this period. A burglary in Bermondsey Street, Southwark, in 1739 drew the comment in the newspaper report that it was "not surprising to men who know the

[83] SP 35/61, f. 121.
[84] Tobias, *Crime and the Police*, pp. 36–43.
[85] Malcolm Falkus, "Lighting in the Dark Ages of English Economic History: Town Streets before the Industrial Revolution," in D. C. Coleman and A. H. John, eds., *Trade, Government and Economy in Pre-Industrial England: Essays Presented to F. J. Fisher* (1976), pp. 187–211.

place, for that street is sadly watch'd and worse lighted"; and another a little later in Red Cross Street in the Borough was similarly "not to be wondered at . . . there being scarce either Watch or Lights in that Part."[86] It was this persuasion that lack of surveillance had permitted property crime to flourish that encouraged the City to reorganize its watches in 1737 on the Westminster model, and it explains why, by Tobias's reckoning, "most of the metropolis had a watch on the revised pattern by 1740."[87] Within a short time the urge to light the streets and to improve surveillance over them had reached the more outlying parts of the wider metropolitan area. The inhabitants of the villages of Camberwell and Peckham in Surrey established trustees by an Act of 1776, for example, to collect a rate that would make it possible to light some of their streets and to support a foot patrol to watch the road from Peckham over the fields to Blackman Street in Southwark.[88] Other agencies of local improvement, such as the commissioners of pavements, were also authorized by statute to employ forces of watchmen.[89]

One need not exaggerate the effectiveness of the enlarging peacekeeping forces in the capital nor overlook the continuing deficiencies of these uncoordinated parish watchmen to recognize that the policing of the capital as well as the work of the magistrates changed significantly in the course of the eighteenth century, beginning in the 1730s or perhaps a little before.[90] It is likely that there had been parallel developments in the office of constable, particularly perhaps in Southwark and in the parishes close to the metropolis. It has recently been persuasively argued that constables in the seventeenth century were more effective in carrying out their administrative duties and in helping to administer the criminal laws than has been generally believed.[91] Their deficiencies in the eighteenth century may also have been exaggerated, and the ways in which they adapted to new tasks overlooked. Much remains to be discovered about

---

[86] *London Evening Post*, 26 Aug. and 12 Oct. 1738.

[87] Tobias, *Crime and the Police*, p. 42.

[88] 16 Geo III, c. 26 (1776).

[89] QS 2/6, Ep. 1792, 131. For the resulting welter of separate authorities by the early nineteenth century see Radzinowicz, *History*, vol. 2, pp. 171–201.

[90] A House of Commons committee appointed in 1772 to enquire into burglary and robbery in London and Westminster heard a good deal of evidence about the defects of the Westminster watch. See the "Report on the Nightly Watch and Police of the Metropolis," *Parliamentary Papers* (1812), vol. 2, pp. 95ff.

[91] J. A. Sharpe, "Enforcing the Law in the Seventeenth-Century English Village," in Gatrell, Lenman, and Parker, eds., *Crime and the Law*; J. A. Sharpe, "Policing the Parish in Early Modern England," Past and Present Colloquium on Police and Policing, Oxford, 1983. Joan Kent provides a useful discussion of the office and a persuasive argument that constables were men of higher social standing than has frequently been assumed in "The English Village Constable, 1580–1642: The Nature and Dilemmas of the Office," *Journal of British Studies* 20 (1981), pp. 26–49.

eighteenth-century constables, but it seems certain that they were more
active, more numerous, and more experienced by the end of the century
than they would have been a hundred years earlier and that, along with
a variety of other official and quasi-official agencies and officers, they had
contributed substantially to an improvement in the forces of order, especially in the capital.

That these changes were still insufficiently far-reaching to cope with
the problems of crime and disorder that multiplied toward the end of the
eighteenth century and especially in the early decades of the nineteenth
should not lead us to write those changes off as insignificant. If the
eighteenth century did not abandon the ancient system of parish constables
and watchmen in favor of more fully professional and more centralized
police forces as they were to develop in the new circumstances of the
nineteenth century, the more piecemeal solutions were nonetheless very
important. Certainly one gets the impression from the printed accounts
of trials at the Surrey assizes and from the informations returned into the
quarter sessions by magistrates that watchmen were providing more effective surveillance in the second half of the century than they had earlier
and that they were responsible for apprehending more suspected offenders
in the streets of Southwark and other urban parishes south of the river
than accounts of the watch as decrepit and ineffectual bumblers are likely
to lead one to expect. This evidence is too fragmentary to make possible
a comparison of arrests made by the watch over time, but it does at least
make it clear that not all watchmen spent every evening "fuddling in the
watch-house or sleeping in their stands," as was said of the old force in
one of the Southwark parishes, and that they did not run at the first sign
of trouble.[92]

No doubt the availability of rewards helps to explain why watchmen
might be more inclined than earlier to stop and question men they were
suspicious of late at night, or why they might come to the aid of the
victim of a mugging. In a case that came to the Surrey assizes in 1739
in which the prosecutor and a companion, attacked by four men one night
in Southwark, had called out "Watch, Murder," the prosecutor testified
that several watchmen "came to our assistance as soon as could be."[93] But
rewards cannot explain entirely why by the middle decades of the century
numerous examples of watchmen apprehending men who were then taken
before a magistrate for questioning can be found in the examinations and
informations returned into the quarter sessions. In the returns for just one
session in 1768, for example, a beadle in Southwark apprehended a man

[92] *London Evening Post*, 7 Nov. 1738; and see Daniel Defoe, *Street Robberies Considered* (1728),
p. 59.
[93] S.A.P., Lent 1739, p. 21 (Brooks). For other arrests made by watchmen in cases that came
to the assizes see S.A.P., Lent 1738, p. 17 (Tudman); Lent 1753, p. 12 (Hays and Brown).

at 3:00 a.m. who was trying to sell a cheese in the street; a watchman in St. Saviour's parish stopped a man at 2:00 a.m. with a sack of coals on his back; a Bermondsey watchman brought in a man he arrested at 4:00 a.m. on suspicion of stealing; two Lambeth watchmen took a man into custody early one morning who could not give them a satisfactory account of how he came by the hen and three ducks he was carrying on his back; and two others who patrolled Blackman Street in Southwark arrested two women they suspected of theft. These watchmen had all been on patrol, and on beats short enough that they were able to call others if necessary. One man described how he had been able to get help in arresting two men on suspicion of theft, giving "the signal by blowing a horn to the other watchmen."[94]

The impression that such reports give is that the watchmen in the streets of Southwark and in the neighboring parishes within the wider metropolis of London were much more active and more effective than they had been in the 1720s and earlier. It is possible that some of this is merely a reflection of the increased number of informations and examinations preserved in the quarter sessions papers from the second half of the century. But it is not merely that. There had clearly been a genuine improvement in the lighting of the streets and in the forces patrolling them. There is also evidence that thieves were conscious in the later period of the dangers these watchmen presented: one man explained that he and his accomplices had hidden overnight in a loft in Tooley Street in the Borough after snatching a hat from a man in the street because they were afraid "the watchmen might apprehend them."[95]

If this impression is in fact a correct one, the improvement in the policing of the streets must have had some effect, however modest, on the number of prosecutions reaching the Surrey courts. But these changes were also surely significant in another way. If they were unable in the end to contain the problems created by the enlarging population and changing economic circumstances at the end of the eighteenth century or to provide security against the crime and the disorders and political challenges from below that followed the peace in 1815, they may well have extended the public's expectations about policing and patrolling the streets of the capital and helped to create a felt need for the "new" police, the more centralized and professional force that came to seem an essential bulwark of authority and property in the 1820s. The system that then gave way had already changed over the previous hundred years, and despite the complaints of police reformers like Patrick Colquhoun, London was being far more effectively policed in 1800 than it had been at the Restoration.

[94] QS 2/6, Ep. 1768, 45, 47, 64, 65, 80; Ep. 1769, 49.
[95] QS 2/6, Mids. 1770, 39.

CONCLUSION

It is impossible to say with confidence whether changes in the magistracy and in peace-keeping arrangements made much difference to the number of offenders charged in Surrey with crimes against property and violent offenses against the person. It is likely that the more ready availability of magistrates in the Southwark area encouraged some prosecutors to institute proceedings; the possibility of recovering some of the costs of the trial may also have had an effect. What one can say with certainty is that at the end of the eighteenth century the responsibility for prosecution still lay largely with the victim of the offense. No police force was as yet interposed between him and the court to decide what would and would not be charged. And in this system of private prosecution it remained open to the victim to deal with the accused in some private way, perhaps coming to an arrangement for the return of his goods with no questions asked or agreeing to some appropriate compensation. I have suggested that the decision to prosecute or not must have been influenced by a number of broad incentives and discouragements that changed over the period. But other considerations could also have been crucial in particular cases. The character of the offense itself was likely to have been decisive. There was no general attitude toward "crime" or "the law," either among the propertied or the poor, but rather attitudes toward particular offenses with particular sanctions attached to them. Sharp distinctions were likely to be made, not only between offenses like smuggling and poaching on the one side—that is, offenses essentially without victims and often enjoying a measure of public approval—and murder and robbery on the other, but also within the broad categories of crimes against property and the person. Some forms of theft were much more likely to be prosecuted than others. But the decision to prosecute would also depend on who the suspected offender was, and perhaps on what was thought to be the general state of crime. The level and the character of the indictments before the courts are thus not likely to be a simple reflection of the acts that might have led to criminal charges. In examining in the following three chapters the cases of property crime and violence brought before the Surrey assizes and quarter sessions over the period 1660 to 1800, we must keep in mind that they arose from a changing propensity to prosecute acting upon the changing reality of criminal behavior in the society; and that the study of the offenses before the courts is thus as much a study of that process of prosecution as of the behavior of those accused of breaking the law.

CHAPTER 3

VIOLENT OFFENSES

Violent physical conflict brought men and women to court charged with a wide variety of offenses against the person that had differed in the violence employed and in their motives and consequences, and that differed in the way they were regarded by society and the courts. Prosecutions that arose from some form of personal violence have some common charactistics, for usually a real victim suffered some harm. But murder, manslaughter, infanticide, rape, assault, and riot (which in some of its forms belongs here) were so fundamentally different that they simply do not form themselves into a neat and coherent subject. A more serious difficulty arises from the fact that the view of violence from the courts is inevitably very limited. Most confrontations in which physical force or intimidation was used in the resolution of conflicts did not give rise to legal actions, and it is clear that the character and the full extent of violence in society cannot adequately be judged from the small number of prosecutions that were undertaken.

There is good reason to think that violent physical conflict and physical abuse were commonly experienced in seventeenth- and eighteenth-century society. The family was the scene of much of it, for family discipline was commonly maintained by physical force. With society's concurrence, men controlled their wives and children by beating them for their transgressions. Children at school and young adults in service were similarly subject to what was widely accepted as the necessary persuasion of the rod. Physical intimidation within the household was matched and sustained by a broader acceptance of violence in society, and by the expectation that disagreements among men might reasonably be solved by physical means, or an insult redressed by fighting. On the whole such matters would have been regarded as private, not something that should normally engage the attention of the authorities. Men and women in the eighteenth century were not repelled by all forms of cruelty or violence in everyday life. That is plainly revealed by the large number of popular recreations and sports in which physical damage was either the consequence or indeed the point.[1]

Perhaps even more revealing of the general attitude toward violence and of the violent temper of the society is the use of terror and physical

---

[1] R. W. Malcolmson, *Popular Recreations in English Society, 1700–1850* (1973), chap. 3.

intimidation by the State in combating crime. What has been called "judicial violence" was at the heart of the system of criminal justice.[2] Hangings and burnings and floggings were witnessed by crowds of thousands, of all ages, all over England. In London, the sessions at the Old Bailey produced a crop of victims for the gallows at Tyburn eight times a year; and in most counties throughout England there were hangings twice a year following the Spring and Summer assizes. Occasionally, a woman who had killed her husband or a man convicted of treason provided the crowds with the yet more terrible spectacle of the traitor's death: the woman burned; the man hanged, drawn, and quartered. Men and women were regularly set on the pillory, where they were taunted and occasionally physically abused by the crowd. Between the assizes, the courts of quarter sessions, meeting more often and in more places, produced a regular flow of convicted offenders to be whipped in public, often stripped to the waist and flogged through the streets on a market day to attract the largest possible audience. Perhaps even more common was the sight of a vagrant being taken to the house of correction, where he would be made to labor and perhaps be whipped several times before being released to go on his way. Few children in the eighteenth century could have avoided physical punishment at home or at school, in service, or as apprentices; and few adults could have failed at least to witness physical violence.

There was clearly a high tolerance of violent behavior in eighteenth-century society. Not all violence was acceptable: murder was universally condemned and likely to be reported to the authorities. But many other forms of violence were not reported and not prosecuted, either because they were not thought to be illegal or because, even if they might have sustained a criminal charge, men would be more likely to depend on themselves or their friends or relatives to extract revenge. The most serious offenses might be reasonably well represented by the cases that came to court, but it is clear that the minor ones were not. The level of indictments thus cannot be taken to reflect the actual level of violent confrontations in society, nor their full range and character. And while other judicial records and reports in newspapers and other "literary" evidence can help to illuminate some of the characteristics of violent offenses, it is necessary to acknowledge the obvious limitations of indictments as guides to levels and fluctuations of offenses against the person, let alone actual violence in society.

This is particularly true of prosecutions for assault, by far the most common form of violence brought before the courts. Assault charges could arise from such a wide variety of events and behavior that they do not

---

[2] Pieter Spierenburg, *Judicial Violence in the Dutch Republic: Corporal Punishment, Executions and Torture in Amsterdam, 1650–1750* (Ph.D. thesis, University of Amsterdam, 1978).

form a category of offense that can be usefully analyzed from the court records. Even with reasonably complete and detailed depositions and examinations, it is unlikely that judicial evidence alone would enable us very often to reconstruct the circumstances in which charges of assault arose. It is also the case that magistrates and the courts commonly treated a complaint of assault as though it were a civil action between two disputing parties rather than as a breach of the peace that engaged the public interest; and they were as likely to try to arrange a settlement of the conflict satisfactory to both sides as they were to insist that the accused be brought to trial and punished if found guilty. Of course individual cases of assault can illuminate contemporaries' experience of violence, but assault indictments taken as a whole do not disclose very much about the place of violence in eighteenth-century society.

That same opaqueness of the judicial records applies as emphatically to the conflicts indicted as riots, for "riot" is a legal category, not a description of behavior. A riot occurred when an unlawful deed was done with force and violence or even when a lawful act was performed in a violent and tumultuous manner. If a display of force by three or more men alarmed even one person a riot could be said to be in progress, and indeed any apparent threat to disturb the peace by such a group could lead to a charge of riotous behavior. The vagueness of the offense meant that it was applied to a wide range of activities. The vast majority of the four hundred or so riots prosecuted in the Surrey courts in the sixty-one years sampled had involved no more than six people altogether and had been apparently as personal in motivation as any assault case. At the other end of the riot spectrum were large-scale "risings of the people" in demonstrations and protests. These popular disturbances have been the subject of a great deal of recent work and have provided a revealing avenue into the study of the laboring population.[3] But if one general conclusion has emerged from that work it is that if crowd actions are to be made intelligible the circumstances that gave rise to them—the targets chosen, the form they took, what was said and done and by whom—all have to be uncovered in their particularity. That local context generally cannot be reconstructed from the court records.

It is for these reasons that I have not attempted to analyze either assault or riot indictments in this chapter. I have chosen instead to concentrate on the more serious forms of violence prosecuted as homicide, infanticide, and rape. In these offenses the matters at issue are reasonably clear, and frequently there is a good deal of information available about individual cases in the courts' records, particularly in the printed accounts of trials at the Surrey assizes. These offenses are also interesting from the

[3] See below, n. 126.

point of view of trial procedure, and in dealing with them I will anticipate some of the issues that will be of particular concern in the second part of the book. At the end of the chapter, I will return briefly to the more general question of the place of violence in eighteenth-century society and discuss the possibility that both the level of violent behavior and attitudes toward it were changing over the period we are dealing with, for that question too has an important bearing on some of the main themes of the book, particularly on the development of penal ideas and practice.

HOMICIDE

Attitudes toward many offenses and the punishments they are thought to deserve have changed strikingly since the eighteenth century. An extraordinary transformation in penal ideas and practice took place in the period we are concerned with and in the first half of the nineteenth century and has created a mental gulf between a society in which men and women were liable to be executed for what we would regard as trivial offenses, especially involving property, and one in which capital punishment has been essentially abandoned. Only in the case of murder does there remain strong sentiment in favor of capital punishment. In this area opinion has perhaps changed least in penal matters since the eighteenth century. Certainly there was no significant opposition then to the death penalty for deliberate killing, even among those who campaigned vigorously for its abolition for lesser offenses. Despite the common experience of death, given the high mortality rate of young children and the frequency with which adults succumbed to accidents and disease, there was no indifference to murder. It terrified and fascinated eighteenth-century society as it does our own, and in the trial and execution of the murderer the shared moral values of the society found their strongest expression. In the printed accounts of the Surrey assizes the murder trials often occupied the bulk of the space, partly no doubt because they were longer and more elaborate than those for run-of-the-mill property offenses, but mainly because the commercial purposes of the Surrey Assize Proceedings would be best served if they contained as many of the details of the bloody deed as possible.

The significance of murder is also reflected in the way it was punished. It was the first offense from which benefit of clergy was withdrawn by statute.[4] That was in cases in which "malice aforethought" was clear or could be construed. As we will see, benefit of clergy still applied in

---

[4] Petty treason was removed from clergy by 12 Hen VII, c. 7 (1597); murder was withdrawn by 1 Ed VI, c. 12, s. 10 (1547); accessories to murder were denied clergy by 4 and 5 P and M, c. 4 (1557).

manslaughter and continued to save convicted men and women from the gallows. But when deliberate killing could be proved the convicted prisoner was invariably hanged. Indeed there were many suggestions after 1700 for making the punishment of murder even more terrifying. This was presumably because so many other felonies had been removed from clergy by then that mere hanging was thought (by those doing the hanging) to be commonplace and insufficiently distinctive and frightening. It was also perhaps encouraged by the association of murder and robbery. Killing in the furtherance of another felony was indeed regarded as one of the "grosser" forms of murder,[5] and there was always the danger that a robber, especially when armed, would kill his victim. Few did, but the clear possibility that they might sustained the conviction that when robberies were common, murders were common too.

In the midst of one such crisis of crime, after 1748, a parliamentary committee was established to "consider on amending the laws against the vices of the lower people, which were increased to a degree of robbery and murder beyond example."[6] One result was the so-called Murder Act of 1752 (25 Geo II, c. 37), which aimed, according to the preamble, to add "some further Terror and peculiar Mark of Infamy" to the punishment of death for murder because it had been "more frequently perpetrated than formerly and particularly in and near the Metropolis." This it did by ordering that the convicted murderer be executed within two days, and that his body be "dissected and anatomized" by surgeons, a powerful mark of infamy.[7] Even more terrible punishments were frequently proposed. Breaking on the wheel and similar forms of pain were favored, especially in the first half of the century (prompted perhaps by Continental practices).[8] By the 1750s they were giving way to suggestions more in step with the march of science. Part of the point of the added punishment of dissection was that it provided the surgeons and schools of anatomy with cadavers for experimentation and teaching. In 1755 a suggestion was made, apparently seriously, that would have even more neatly combined science and terror when a correspondent to the *Gentleman's Magazine* proposed that convicted murderers not be hanged but be turned over immediately to the surgeons, for "such experiments as can only be made upon a living subject."[9] Only traitors suffered more terribly than convicted murderers after

[5] East, *Pleas of the Crown*, vol. 1, p. 215.

[6] On this see chap. 10.

[7] For the significance of this see Peter Linebaugh, "The Tyburn Riot against the Surgeons," in Hay, Linebaugh, and Thompson, eds., *Albion's Fatal Tree*, pp. 65–117.

[8] John H. Langbein, *Torture and the Law of Proof* (Chicago, 1977), pp. 27-28.

[9] *G. M.* 25 (1755), p. 295.

1752.[10] There is no question that murder retained its hold over the public imagination.

On the other hand, few men and women were in fact convicted of murder in which the deliberate intent was clear; and, far from increasing, the number if anything declined over the century. Blackstone defined murder, following Coke, as occurring "when a person of sound memory and discretion unlawfully killeth any reasonable creature . . . with malice aforethought, either express or implied."[11] The main business of the trial for murder was to discover whether the killing had indeed been malicious and what degree of responsibility the accused ought to bear. Malice was the crucial issue, and the law developed around it, ever more refined by decisions in reported cases and by judges' discussions of particularly knotty points.[12] Some clear distinctions and several established mitigations had emerged by the eighteenth century. For example, the killing could be found to have been justified, as in the case of someone resisting arrest who was killed by an officer having proper authority and using proper means. Or it might be found to have been excusable. Such a finding would include self-defense, as well as deaths caused by accidents when the act that had occasioned it was itself lawful. Or the offense might be adjudged to be manslaughter rather than murder, a distinction that had emerged in the early sixteenth century in statutes and legal writings and that remained of fundamental importance in the eighteenth century because manslaughter was clergyable, and thus noncapital.[13] Manslaughter was killing without

---

[10] Men convicted of treason, including coining, were cut down from the gallows while still alive, disembowelled, and quartered; women were burned alive, including those who committed the petty treason of killing their husbands. Killing one's husband and the killing of a master by a servant were species of treason because they were committed "against a Subject, between whom and the Offender, the Law presumes there is a special Obedience and Subjection" (Sir James Ansty, *General Charge to all Grand Juries* [1725], p. 58). This punishment was thought to be a mitigation in the case of women, "the decency due to their sex" forbidding, as Blackstone said, "the exposing and publicly mangling their bodies"; he did have the sense to add that to be burned alive was "as terrible to sensation as the other" (*Commentaries*, vol. 4, p. 92). It was generally believed in the eighteenth century that as an act of mercy executioners strangled women ordered to be burned alive and thus rendered them insensible before the bonfire was lit.

[11] Blackstone, *Commentaries*, vol. 4, p. 195.

[12] See Foster's "discourse" on homicide in his *Reports*, pp. 255–337. Several judges' conferences at Serjeants' Inn on homicide cases are referred to in Strange's *Reports* (vol. 1, pp. 499–502; vol. 2, pp. 766–75, 882–88) and especially in Leach's *Reports* (vol. 1, pp. 6–7, 96–97, 112–14, 137–38, 360–62, 388–90, 457–60; vol. 2, pp. 569–72). For the judges' discussions in general see John Baker, "The Refinement of English Criminal Jurisprudence, 1500–1848," in Louis A. Knafla, ed., *Crime and Criminal Justice in Europe and Canada* (Waterloo, 1981), pp. 29–32.

[13] On this see J. M. Kaye, "The Early History of Murder and Manslaughter," *Law Quarterly Review* 83 (1967), pp. 365–95, 569–601 (pts. 1 and 2); John Baker, ed., *The Reports of Sir John Spelman*, Seldon Society, 2 vols. (1978), vol. 2, pp. 303–16; and two important articles by Thomas A. Green: "Societal Concepts of Criminal Liability for Homicide in Medieval England,"

premeditation, as, for example, in the course of a quarrel, in the heat of passion, or as the result of sufficient provocation. It could also be charged when an unlawful act resulted accidentally in someone's death, such as in prizefighting or the playing of a prohibited game like cock-throwing ("always dangerous to by-standers," according to one law writer).[14] By the eighteenth century manslaughter was also charged occasionally in the case of accidents caused by a failure to take sufficient care.

There were thus many possible variations in homicide cases, and as a law writer observed, "The shades between some of these are in many instances very faint."[15] Discriminating among them was very much the business of the trial. The coroner's inquest, the investigation of deaths caused by violence or apparently unnatural means by the coroner's jury, resulted in a finding that became the basis of the indictment.[16] The indictment was not, however, necessarily shaped by the coroner's verdict. An acquittal at the inquest might still lead to a suspect's indictment for murder, and a finding of a manslaughter verdict by the coroner's jury did not mean that the indictment would repeat that charge. Whereas homicides are today categorized before trial by the police according to the evidence at hand, there was no equivalent screening in the eighteenth century. The categorization was in fact done by the jury at the trial on the basis of the evidence presented in court. Whatever the verdict of the coroner's jury, the indictment in a homicide would virtually always allege murder against the defendant, even when it was clear that the victim's death had been accidental or at least that the accused would most likely be convicted of manslaughter. The most serious offense was charged so that the defendant would be in the position of having to explain the circumstances that had led to the victim's death. He was thus assumed to have killed deliberately, and it was left to him to provide the jury with the evidence that could allow them to convict him for an offense short of murder. It was a general rule, Blackstone said,

> that all homicide is malicious, and of course [i.e., as a matter of course] amounts to murder, unless where *justified* by the command or permission of the law; *excused* on a principle of accident or self-preservation; or *alleviated* into manslaughter.

Speculum 47 (1972), pp. 669–94, and "The Jury and the English Law of Homicide, 1200–1600," *Michigan Law Review* 74 (1976), pp. 413–99.

[14] East, *Pleas of the Crown*, vol. 1, pp. 270–71.

[15] Ibid., p. 214.

[16] For the work of coroners in the eighteenth century see R. F. Hunnisett, ed., *Wiltshire Coroners' Bills, 1752–1796*, Wiltshire Record Society, vol. 36 (Devizes, 1980), introduction; Thomas Rogers Forbes, "Crowner's Quest," *Transactions of the American Philosophical Society* 68, pt. 1 (1978).

. . . And all these circumstances of justification, excuse, or
alleviation, it is incumbent upon the prisoner to make out, to
the satisfaction of the court and jury: the latter of whom are to
decide whether the circumstances alleged be proved to have
actually existed; the former, how far they extend to take away
or mitigate the guilt. For all homicide is presumed to be ma
licious, until the contrary appeareth upon evidence.[17]

Because virtually all indictments in homicide cases charged the accused with murder, whatever the circumstances behind the death of the
victim, they are even less revealing of the real issues than are indictments
in other offenses. Some tell us a little about the events leading to the
victim's death, but to make sense of the charges laid in court it is necessary
to bring other evidence to bear. Occasionally juries explained their verdicts
in such a way as to reveal the circumstances behind the indictment.[18] But
that alas is rare. The coroners' inquests, which often contain details about
the cause of death that are left out of indictments, are frequently to be
found in the assize files. Accounts in newspapers add details about some
of the more sensational events and help to illuminate the general character
of homicide in this period. But perhaps the richest source, at least for
some of the genuine murder cases in Surrey, is the printed reports of assize
trials, for they often contain full accounts of the evidence presented by
both the prosecution and the defense. None of this evidence is complete
or extensive enough to make it possible for us to penetrate behind every
murder indictment, but taking it all together does enable us to make some
distinctions among the cases brought to court and to attempt a preliminary
sketch of murder and other forms of homicide.

EXCUSABLE HOMICIDE AND MANSLAUGHTER

Let us begin by looking at the verdicts of the juries at the Surrey assizes
in the 315 cases dealt with in the ninety-five years between 1660 and

---

[17] Blackstone, *Commentaries*, vol. 4, p. 201.

[18] Between 1687 and 1701 trial juries were occasionally asked (required?) to explain in writing
verdicts of not guilty in homicide cases when the grounds for the verdict were that the death
had been caused by misfortune or by an act of self-defense. Such statements are to be found
(unnumbered) in the following files: ASSI 35/128/6 (two); ASSI 35/129/7; ASSI 35/141/7; ASSI
35/142/8. The Surrey evidence in this period is too fragmentary to reveal how commonly juries
submitted such written explanations of their findings. They date from at least the middle of the
seventeenth century: a jury in 1654 signed a statement that "Wee finde that Will Draper did
by chance accidentally kill Isaacke Axetell with a pronge as they were playing together" (ASSI
35/95/7/37).

1800 in which records for this court are available.[19] The first judgment was made by the grand jury, whose duty it was to assess the evidence brought forward by the prosecutor and either send the case on to trial or throw it out by finding a verdict of "ignoramus" ("we do not know") when in their view there was no case to be answered. They could also reduce the level of the charge to manslaughter, and in the late seventeenth century they did so very occasionally. But it was being argued then that since grand jurors heard only part of the evidence they were in no position to reduce a murder charge to manslaughter and that they should leave this to the trial jury and the judge.[20] This seems to have been indeed the normal practice by the eighteenth century, as Blackstone observed. The grand jury in Surrey did turn back homicide indictments entirely in about fifteen per cent of the cases involving principals between 1660 and 1800, either because there was nothing in the prosecution case that could amount to any form of homicide in law or because no responsibility could be attached to the accused (table 3.1). It was presumably on the former grounds that the grand jury threw out a case against a man accused of murdering a five-year-old girl "by putting the private parts of himself . . . upon, against, and into the private parts of her . . . , giving to her . . . one mortal bruise."[21] But the grounds upon which most grand jury verdicts rested remain obscure.

Most of the homicide charges that came to the assizes were sent to trial unaltered by the grand jury. This could result in one of three verdicts: guilty (which in the case of murder meant capital punishment); not guilty; or guilty of the reduced charge of manslaughter. At the Surrey assizes over the period 1660 to 1800, more than a third of those accused of murder were found not guilty of any offense and discharged (table 3.1).[22] Why they were acquitted is not always clear, but most often it seems that such a verdict arose not from a finding that the accused had not done what was alleged, but rather that what he had done did not amount to either murder or manslaughter. In some cases (the evidence does not allow us to be more precise than that), acquittal was the result of plain signs of insanity in

[19] Because there are few cases every year, I have broadened the homicide study to include the indictments in all the years for which evidence is complete in the Surrey assize files. See the appendix for this "Homicide Count."

[20] Zachary Babington, *Advice to Grand Jurors in Cases of Blood* (1680), pp. 15–16, 62–63, 113.

[21] ASSI 35/204/8 (Balcomb).

[22] This refers to principals only. An even larger proportion of those accused as accessories, of aiding and abetting the principal accused, were acquitted. In addition to those discharged when the principal was acquitted, accessories were also dismissed when the jury found the principal guilty of manslaughter, for there could be no accessories to manslaughter. Of the sixty-seven accessories charged in the years examined whose verdicts are known, the bills of about a third were found ignoramus by the grand jury, and half were acquitted by the trial jury.

TABLE 3.1
Verdicts in Homicide Cases at the Surrey Assizes, 1660–1800

	Accused	Known Verdicts	Grand Jury Verdicts (% of Known Verdicts)			Trial Jury Verdicts (% of Known Verdicts)			At Large	Unknown	Indictments	
			Ig.	T.B.	T.B. Mansl.	N.G.	G.	G. Mansl.			Murd.	Mansl.
Principals												
Men	304	266	12.8	86.1	1.1	38.4	19.6	29.7	24	14		
Women	30	29	34.5	65.5	0	41.4	17.2	6.9	1	0		
Total	334	295	14.9	84.1	1.0	38.6	19.3	27.5	25	14	309[a]	6
Accessories												
Men	72	58	27.6	58.6	13.8	56.9	1.7	13.8	2	12		
Women	9	9	66.7	22.2	11.1	11.1	11.1	11.1	0	0		
Total	81	67	32.8	53.7	13.4	50.8	3.0	13.4	2	12		

SOURCE: Homicide Count.

[a] Includes four under Stabbing Act.

the prisoner. In a case in 1688, for example, the jury found that "Elizabeth Waterman, the prisoner at the Barr being distracted and not of sound mind did kill Mary Waterman, her daughter, with a razor and that she came by her death by no other means."[23] She was acquitted, as was a man some years later who had been indicted for murdering his father and who was found by the jury to be "a Lunatick person and Non Compos Mentis."[24] These prisoners were both discharged, but there was no fixed practice in this. Much depended on whether relatives were willing to take care of the prisoner and guarantee his future behavior. If no such person could be found, the court could send the discharged lunatic back to jail "for the safety of the King's subjects."[25]

Apparent insanity was not necessarily, however, a bar to conviction. Much depended on the circumstances of the case, and probably on the advice and guidance the jury received from the judge. This is made clear in the famous case in 1724 in Surrey in which Edward Arnold was accused of "shooting at" Lord Onslow and pleaded insanity. The case was not in fact a homicide because Onslow did not die. It was instead brought under the recently passed Black Act, which had been designed against the deer hunters and protesters of Waltham Forest and other forest communities near London but which included within its multifarious provisions the now capital offense of shooting *at* someone. It had been passed just in time to catch Arnold, giving the first hint of just how useful its vague and sweeping provisions might be to the authorities in the future.[26] Arnold pleaded that he had not known what he was doing and intended Onslow no harm. But in this case the judge in his summing up led the jury to a strict definition of what a successful defense of insanity would require. It would have to be plain, he said, that the prisoner was an idiot and was permanently and "totally deprived of his understanding and memory, and doth not know what he is doing no more than an infant, than a brute or a wild beast." An idiot "never recovers," he went on to say, but a lunatic "may, and hath his intervals." He pressed the jury to think of Arnold as a lunatic, and to think of his possible state of mind when he shot at

    [23] ASSI 35/129/7/18 (Waterman).

    [24] ASSI 35/142/8/1 (Skinner).

    [25] In a case in Norwich in 1724 a woman was found not guilty on her trial for cutting her child's throat, "being a lunatick," but was ordered to be imprisoned for a year, the presumption being that her madness would have passed over by then (*The Evening Post*, 8–11 Aug. 1724). The Vagrant Act of 1744 clarified this by authorizing two justices to apprehend and secure a lunatic, with chains if necessary. See Blackstone, *Commentaries*, vol. 4, p. 25; Nigel Walker, *Crime and Insanity in England*, vol. 1, *The Historical Perspective* (Edinburgh, 1968), p. 43; Kathleen Jones, *Lunacy, Law and Conscience, 1744–1845* (1955), pp. 26–35.

    [26] E. P. Thompson, *Whigs and Hunters*, pp. 209–10 and passim, on the Act, the circumstances under which it was passed, and the uses to which it was put.

Onslow. No doubt impressed by such clarity of thought in so murky an area, the jury agreed that Arnold knew what he was doing. He was sentenced to death, though he was later pardoned and committed to jail for the rest of his life.[27]

This was an unusual case, for Onslow was a prominent Whig, and he and others were convinced that behind Arnold was some kind of plot against the king. Even without that element, an attack on a nobleman who was so prominent a supporter of the new regime made it, as the judge told the jury, "a great offense," and the court plainly pressed hard to defeat the insanity defense. Such striving was not likely in ordinary cases, and there seem not to have been any established rules and procedures. It is indeed likely that the seriousness with which the plea was treated by the court depended entirely on the nature of the case and the general character of the accused, rather than on any strict evaluation of his state of mind at the time of the offense or even his present state of mind. Women, who were more likely to be acquitted than men anyway, probably had a better chance of successfully pleading insanity, especially in a case in which the jury might well be looking for support for a not guilty verdict. In 1751 a woman accused of murdering her newborn son by cutting his throat—not under the Infanticide Act of 1624 because she was married, but under the common law offense of murder—successfully employed a defense of temporary insanity. She claimed in court not to have known anything about it. After the delivery, which she had managed herself, she had not been in her senses, she said, and that state of mind was testified to by several of her fellow servants. Some supported her; others, including a midwife who attended her later, certainly did not. But her explanation was accepted, and she was acquitted.[28] Such a defense in murder cases was not uncommon by the middle of the eighteenth century. It has been estimated that an insanity plea was entered in perhaps a dozen cases a year throughout England and Wales in the 1750s and that it was successful in about a third of them. And it appears that it was made with increasing frequency after mid-century.[29]

Other acquittals in homicides, indeed most likely the vast majority,

---

[27] Walker, *Crime and Insanity*, vol. 1, pp. 56–57. Arnold died in the Surrey county jail in 1753 or 1754.

[28] S.A.P., Summer 1751, p. 25 (Sturt). In the following year in Surrey another woman, accused of murdering her aunt with a poker, was not tried on her first appearance in court because when "she was brought to the bar to be arraign'd, she discovered such plain signs of lunacy that she was ordered back again as not fit to be tried." She was tried at the following session of the court some months later and acquitted, and it is entirely possible that her mental condition was responsible for that verdict (S.A.P., Lent 1752, p. 22 [Leedum]; ASSI 31/3, p. 115).

[29] Walker, *Crime and Insanity*, vol. 1, pp. 66–72.

followed from the jury's decision to excuse the prisoner on the grounds that the facts of the case did not sustain a charge of murder or even manslaughter. For most of this period, men were rarely charged with a criminal offense when death occurred in accidents. Very few of the homicide cases before the courts arose from death caused by accidents with horses or coaches and wagons—surprisingly few, perhaps, considering how many of these accidents there must have been.[30] In the case of those that were pressed forward (perhaps by the victims' families), the tendency of juries was to find a verdict of death by "misfortune" and to acquit the accused entirely.[31] This was also true of cases involving firearms, even when the act had been imprudent and the defendant might well have been thought to bear some responsibility for the death that had occurred. The likelihood over much of this period was that if the death had clearly not been intended the jury would find a verdict of not guilty.[32]

Other forms of excusable homicide account for several acquittals. A father who killed his child or a master his servant while punishing him for misbehavior was liable to be indicted for murder, and if it was found at the trial that he had used immoderate methods of correction—"as if a cudgel . . . be of large size, or if a child be thrown down and stamped upon"[33]—he might be convicted of that charge. That did not happen often, but juries did occasionally insist on convicting a father of the murder of his child under such circumstances.[34] Normally a parent or master who used "moderate" methods and a "reasonable" instrument in chastising those over whom they had natural authority would have been acquitted of both murder and manslaughter.

---

[30] See on this P.E.H. Hair, "Deaths from Violence in Britain: A Tentative Secular Survey," *Population Studies* 25 (1971), pp. 5–24, who stresses the dangers of accidents in early modern England from the very large number of horses. He points out that there were eight thousand private and public coaches in London in the middle of the eighteenth century and obviously many thousands of horses. The earliest reliable survey, in 1840, suggests that there were about a thousand deaths from accidents involving horses and carriages in that year.

[31] Thus John Weaver, whose horse ran away with him in Southwark and knocked a woman down and killed her, was indicted for murder but acquitted by the jury and discharged upon their finding a verdict of death by "misfortune" (ASSI 35/129/7, Summer 1688).

[32] Cases involving firearms were more commonly prosecuted than other accidents. Even when the act had clearly been dangerous, the accused was most often acquitted. In 1742 a man on the deck of a merchant ship in the Thames shot a pistol "to frighten the Bomb-boat Women" (who hawked liquor and other things to sailors and who were often accused of aiding in the pilfering of merchantmen in the river) and killed a man working on a barge nearby. He, too, was found not guilty (S.A.P., Summer 1742, p. 16 [Jewell]).

[33] R vs. Mawgridge: Kelyng, *Reports*, p. 134; *Eng. Rep.*, vol. 84, p. 1114 (1707).

[34] In a case in Kent in 1729 the jury found a man guilty of murder when a child he had beaten died. The judge thought him deserving of a pardon, however, because he had not used an "improper Instrument" (SP 36/11, f. 98).

The courts were also likely over much of this period to excuse a man who killed another in legitimate self-defense. If a defendant could show that he had been attacked and that he had retreated as far as he was able before striking back and killing his assailant, he would in all likelihood be excused by the jury, and acquitted and discharged. It was on these grounds that a man accused of murder at the Surrey assizes was found not guilty when it was shown that he had been driven into a river by a furious attack with a stick and could go no further before he turned on his tormentor and killed him with his sword.[35] Some years later, a Surrey petty jury explained its decision in a similar case in the following terms:

> We find that Capt. Devenish was before Nicholas Leschiers upon the highway near Putney, and that Capt. Hawker was behind and followed the said Nicholas Leschiers then and there. And that a Wall was there on one side of the said Nicholas Leschiers and a pale hedge on the other. Whereupon Capt. Devenish drew his sword upon Nicholas Leschiers and Nicholas Leschiers to avoid the said Capt. Devenish withdrew to the Wall and there in his own defence killed the said Capt. Devenish (the said Leschiers not being able to goe any further to avoid the said Capt. Devenish). So we find that the said Nicholas Leschiers killed the said Devenish se defendo and not otherwise.[36]

In cases of self-defense and in some cases of death by misadventure, the accused prisoner had been subject in a remote period to forfeiture of goods. That threat had, however, been removed by the granting of a pardon and the restitution of goods as a matter of course. Such pardons were still being issued as late as the 1670s. But by the eighteenth century they were no longer thought to be necessary. Blackstone explained that "to prevent this expense [of a pardon], in cases where the death has notoriously happened by misadventure or in self-defence, the judges will usually permit (if not direct) a general verdict of acquittal," allowing the accused to go free.[37]

The distinction between forms of excusable homicide that would lead to an acquittal and a verdict of manslaughter, that is, "the unlawful killing of another, without malice either express or implied," was very fine in

[35] ASSI 35/128/6 (unnumbered).

[36] ASSI 35/141/7. For such statements, signed by the trial jurors, see above, n. 18.

[37] For such a pardon see C 82/2467 (warrants for the Great Seal, June 1675). A pardon was issued to Richard Wetherby when he was indicted for murder in 1674 in the death of a three-year-old child who had been run over by Wetherby's cart in the streets of Southwark. Wetherby was acquitted.

practice.[38] But the consequences of the jury's finding one or the other were considerable, for manslaughter was a felony, and even though it remained clergyable in the eighteenth century and thus in practice noncapital, conviction could lead to some form of punishment. It is true that over most of the period prisoners convicted of manslaughter were granted clergy, burnt in the hand, and discharged. This continued well into the second half of the eighteenth century and well past the point at which the majority of clergyable felonies were dealt with that way. After 1718, when parliament passed the Transportation Act and made it possible for the courts to punish clergied felons by transporting them to America for seven years, that option was taken up in a large way for the punishment of crimes against property.[39] But not for manslaughter. Men and women convicted of manslaughter continued after 1718 to be burned in the hand and discharged, presumably because transportation was thought to be too severe and too blunt a weapon for offenses in which the degree of culpability varied hugely from one case to another.

This pattern of punishment began to change in the 1760s, when imprisonment, as we will see, became well established as a possible sanction in felony. A number of men and women convicted of manslaughter in the last decades of the century were ordered to be imprisoned, presumably becaue they were thought to have been in some way responsible for the victim's death, even though they had not intended it. Imprisonment was not always thought to be appropriate. There was a good deal of anxiety, for example, about sentencing gentlemen to a term in the common jail, and gentlemen were of course more likely to kill than steal. When the Reverend Bennett Allen was convicted of killing a man in a duel in Hyde Park in 1782 and sentenced to be imprisoned in Newgate for six months, the jury that tried him were among many who petitioned to have him excused. The judge thought the sentence justified because the insults that gave rise to the duel were far in the past and the duel had been deliberately sought on both sides. (There had been "nothing unfair in the duel itself"— that is, it had gone according to the rules of honor—and so a manslaughter verdict was acceptable, he thought.) The sentence of six months' imprisonment for a gentleman and clergyman clearly startled the jury. "They never thought," their petition to the king declared, "he would be subjected to so grievous a punishment."[40] It was perhaps that sense of the inappropriateness of imprisonment for certain offenders, as well as the need to impose some penalty on convicted manslaughterers and to find a substitute

---

[38] Blackstone, *Commentaries*, vol. 4, p. 191.
[39] See below, chap. 9.
[40] HO 45/1, ff. 168–69, 228–31.

for the burning in the hand of clergy (which was abolished in 1779), that encouraged the use of fines along with imprisonment by the last decade of the century. Both had the advantage of being infinitely divisible, capable of being doled out in larger or smaller amounts to fit each case and to match the degree of responsibility the prisoner was thought to bear and to match, where it was thought appropriate, the prisoner's social class and circumstances.

The development of these punishments was a crucial aspect of the change in the way the courts dealt with homicides short of murder in the second half of the eighteenth century. But of course punishments emerge to some extent because they are wanted, and it seems likely that men and women convicted of manslaughter were being subjected to punishment essentially for the first time not merely because these more flexible penalties were available, but because jurors and judges were more anxious to extract a penalty on behalf of society than they might have been fifty or a hundred years earlier. A change in attitude toward forms of behavior that might once have been overlooked but were increasingly condemned could also help to explain the long-term tendency for the level of acquittals of men accused of murder to decline over the eighteenth century. The decline was by no means persistent over the period, and it also appears to be tied to a decrease in the number of cases sent to trial by the grand jury (table 3.2). We will take up the question of jury verdicts more fully in a subsequent chapter. What we might note here is the tendency for some of the accused who would earlier have been granted a clergyable discharge to be subjected to some, though not always very severe, punishment. Thus a man indicted in 1791 for killing a woman with his phaeton, which he had been "racing and driving furiously" in Southwark, was convicted of manslaughter and imprisoned for three months. Another man who had killed someone with a sword was also found guilty of manslaughter and fined twenty pounds.[41] If such men had been convicted before 1760 or so (and their conviction, I would guess, would have been less likely then), they would at most have been burnt in the hand and discharged. It must be said that there were few such cases in the late eighteenth century and that the punishments handed out were in some instances hardly more than nominal. Still, there does seem to have been some strengthening of the view that men ought to be held more accountable for actions that led to serious injuries and deaths, even when they did not intend them.

If that sentiment was more evident in the late eighteenth century, it might well have been further encouraged by a growing concern to establish causes of death in doubtful cases more scientifically than before.

[41] ASSI 35/231/8/27; ASSI 35/234/8/26.

TABLE 3.2

Homicide Cases over Time at the Surrey Assizes: Men Accused of Murder

Period	Years	Indictments	Individuals	Known Verdicts and Sentences	Grand Jury Verdicts (% of known Verdicts)			Trial Jury Verdicts (% of Known Verdicts)		
					Ig.	T.B.	T.B. Mansl.	N.G.	G.	G. Mansl.
1660–1679	7	53	47	46	2.7	84.8	6.5	47.8	10.9	32.6
1680–1699	12	74	72	57	7.0	93.0	0	52.6	22.8	17.5
1700–1719	6	27	27	23	8.7	91.3	0	60.9	4.4ª	30.4
1720–1739	10	26	23	22	9.1	90.9	0	40.9	13.6	36.4
1740–1759	17	40	38	35	8.6	91.4	0	8.6	40.0	42.9
1760–1779	20	49	47	40	17.5	82.5	0	20.0	27.5	35.0
1780–1802	23	45	50	43	28.0	72.1	0	37.2	11.6	23.3

Sentences
(% of Known Verdicts)

Period	Sentenced to Death	Pardoned	Hanged	Clergy/Discharged	Imprisoned	Fined	At large or unknown
1660–1679	10.9	0	10.9	32.6	0	0	1
1680–1699	22.8	3.5	19.3	17.5	0	0	15
1700–1719	4.4	4.4	0	26.1	0	0	4
1720–1739	13.6	4.6	9.0	36.4	0	0	1
1740–1759	40.0	5.7	34.3	42.9	0	0	3
1760–1779	27.5	0	27.5	27.5	7.5	0	7
1780–1802	11.6	0	11.6	0	9.3	14.0	7

SOURCE: Homicide Count.

ª One man was denied clergy, sentenced to death, and subsequently pardoned.

This concern is clear in the increasing use of expert medical testimony at inquests and, after 1816 in any event, in the reliance placed for the first time by coroners' juries on evidence derived from autopsies. Medical jurisprudence became firmly established in the last two decades of the eighteenth century and in the early years of the nineteenth.[42] While medical evidence does not in itself lead to a heightened determination to establish responsibility for death caused by accidents, the concern for a better and more scientific understanding of the relationships between disease and injury and death, of which these developments in forensic medicine and the transformations in the inquest give evidence, must have strengthened the court's and the layman's willingness to think that when dangerous actions led to serious injuries and death the perpetrator ought to pay a penalty. Both the science and the availability of penalties that made it possible for judges to award punishments that were serious without being necessarily devastating facilitated the emergence and strengthening of a tougher attitude in the courts toward carelessness that led to death and an anxiety to condemn forms of violence that earlier might have been entirely excused.

MANSLAUGHTER AND MURDER:
THE QUESTION OF PROVOCATION

The distinction between excusable homicide and manslaughter was perhaps becoming less clear in the eighteenth century. The main forms of manslaughter, however, had long been homicides that resulted either from unlawful acts or from sudden, heated quarrels in which there had been no long-established malicious intention to cause death. This question of intention was at the root of the distinction between murder and manslaughter, between a killing that was planned and deliberate and one that had resulted from a spontaneous outburst. By the end of the eighteenth century it was becoming more common, with the establishment perhaps of the more moderate punishments, for some of the accused actually to be charged with manslaughter (there were six examples in Surrey, mainly around 1800). For the most part, however, and certainly over most of the period we are concerned with, it had been left to the accused to persuade the jury that he had not intended to cause the victim's death, and that if he was to be convicted at all it should be for a reduced charge of manslaughter.

In several murder cases in Surrey that ended with such a verdict, the victim had met his death in a boxing match. Such contests seem to have

---

[42] Forbes, "Crowner's Quest," pp. 42-45.

been common. They provided a means by which men could settle their differences, a sort of popular duel, though a duel that normally did not have lethal results. These were not matches in the sporting sense; when young men fought for recreation and as a way of showing their courage and skill, they would probably wrestle.[43] Nor were they simply brawls, but rather controlled and apparently well-ordered contests that would result in a settlement that both could accept with honor. A visitor to London noticed that men with "a disagreement that they cannot end up amicably" commonly

> retire into some quiet place and strip from their waists upwards. Everyone who sees them preparing for a fight surrounds them, not in order to separate them, but on the contrary to enjoy the fight, for it is great sport to the lookers-on, and they judge the blows and also help to enforce certain rules in use for this mode of warfare. The spectators sometimes get so interested that they lay bets on the combatants and form a big circle around them. The two champions shake hands before commencing, and then attack each other courageously with their fists, and sometimes also with their heads, which they use like rams. Should one of the men fall, his opponent may, according to the rules, give him a blow with his fist, but those who have laid their bets on the fallen man generally encourage him to continue till one of the combatants is quite knocked up and says that he has had enough.[44]

Although such fights were governed by rules and conventions, men were occasionally seriously hurt in them and even killed. They gave rise to several of the prosecutions for murder at the Surrey assizes. In one, in 1726, a young man was indicted for "mortally bruising" the deceased "in a Boxing-Match, of which bruises he died in half an hour." The defendant told the following story in court:

> I and the Deceas'd were playing a Match at Cricket, and the Deceas'd doing some things which I did not like, together with my being in a fair Way to lose, ruffled my Temper; whereupon I went up to the Deceas'd and desir'd him to be easy, otherwise I would knock him on the head with my Bat. The Deceas'd

---

[43] Malcolmson, *Recreations*, pp. 43, 55. In an account of a dispute between two men in 1746 that ended in tragedy, it was said that after their first quarrel one of them "and another of the Company [present] Wrestled by way of Diversion and to show their Skill and Manhood" (SP 36/82, f. 249).

[44] *A Foreign View of England in the Reigns of George I and George II: The Letters of Monsieur César de Saussure to his Family*, ed. Madame van Muyden (1902), p. 180, quoted in Malcolmson, *Recreations*, p. 42.

still persisting to provoke me, I challeng'd him to Box, but he refusing . . . [because he had been bound over to keep the peace] I was easy, and all was quiet.

A short while later, however, as they were separating, the deceased challenged him to fight, and he, "not willing to be thought a Coward," went back. He went on to tell the court how they

> stripp'd, and went into a Pound, where we fought some time, till he allow'd me to be the best Man. The Pound being lock'd, we were both oblig'd to get over the Rails, and he, in all Appearances got over as well as I.[45]

William Yates, the defendant in this case, was found guilty of manslaughter, burnt in the hand, and discharged. Several other manslaughter convictions in the years we have studied arose from similar kinds of semi-formal fights in which two quarreling men agreed to settle their differences by fighting under some general rules of combat. It is impossible to say how many of the seventy-eight men who were convicted on the reduced charge of manslaughter by the jury had fought in this way, for the indictment never discloses the circumstances under which the blows alleged to have caused the death were delivered. We know about the Yates case because it came in one of the sessions of the Surrey assizes for which printed trial accounts are available. There are one or two others in the thirty-five Surrey Assize Proceedings discovered so far, which suggests that they were not uncommon. Another came to court in 1742 when William Gray was indicted for causing the death of a young man with whom he had quarreled in a public house in Walton-on-Thames. They had exchanged hot words, but were first calmed by the landlord, who said he would have no quarreling in his house. They were quiet for a while, until, as a witness deposed,

> they began arguing again, and at last agreed to go out into the Yard and Fight, and went out by themselves in the Dark. It was about 12 at Night. They call'd for a Candle, and the Landlord carried one, for fear they should fall into a Well. I followed the Landlord, and saw them both stript to the Skin. The Prisoner ran his Head against the Deceased's Belly, and catching hold of both his Hands, pitch'd him upon his Shoulders and Neck.[46]

He was brought in and laid on chairs until his father came about 3:00, when he and the publican "wheel'd him home in a Wheelbarrow." He died the next afternoon. Again the verdict was manslaughter, and Gray was allowed his clergy.

[45] S.A.P., Lent 1726, p. 3 (Yates).
[46] S.A.P., Summer 1742, pp. 10–12 (Gray).

Not unexpectedly, many of the fights that ended this way took place in taverns and alehouses and when men were in their cups. Nor is it surprising that many occurred at work. In these cases, perhaps because men might have known each other over a long period and might be thought to have built up resentments and harbored grudges, the bench seems to have been especially anxious to discover whether the accused had acted with a malicious intent and had really been sufficiently provoked to rule out murder. This was always an issue in homicide, and even in tavern brawls men often made a point of saying that they had acted spontaneously: a gardener who killed a soldier with a long knife in a Surrey alehouse insisted at his trial that he "never saw the Man 'till the Day before, and had no Malice in my Heart."[47] But it was more obviously a point to be investigated when men had known each other, and when they worked together. Thus when in 1740 a coal porter was indicted for killing his fellow worker on board a ship in the Thames, the judge made a point of questioning the witnesses about the provocation. They had quarreled about who would go down into the hold, and threw their bushel baskets at each other until the accused beat the other man with a broomstick, of which blows he died within a few minutes. There was no autopsy to discover the real cause of death; the assumption was that the blows with the broomstick had been sufficient in themselves, and it was left to the jury to determine whether it was murder or manslaughter. Had the accused been determined to kill him and picked a quarrel? So the judge asked the principal witnesses: "Who made the first assault?" "Was there any provocation?" "Do you imagine the prisoner bore any malice to the deceased?" The answers were all negative; it was a "hasty quarrel." The master of the ship said that the accused was "a peaceable, quiet working man," and the court was satisfied to find him guilty of manslaughter and to allow him to plead his clergy and go free.[48]

In another argument in the workplace, though perhaps with a more elevated tone, two pewterers "quarrelled about their workmanship." One called the other a son of a bitch, the other returned that he was a double son of a bitch, and the first then struck the other on the head with an iron and killed him. The accused said in court that "he had no ill Will to the prisoner [i.e., the deceased], and was sorry that he gave that unfortunate Blow," and witnesses deposed that the dead man had said as he languished in hospital that he was sure the prisoner had not intended him any harm. Again the verdict was manslaughter.[49]

[47] S.A.P., Summer 1742, pp. 2–3 (Rosse and Smith).
[48] S.A.P., Lent 1740, pp. 11–12 (Prate).
[49] S.A.P., Lent 1749, p. 5 (Butler).

In determining the question of provocation, the courts in the eighteenth century applied a number of well-established rules. For one thing it was clear that mere words by themselves, however aggravating they might be, provided insufficient provocation to justify a manslaughter verdict. Normally blows had to be struck.[50] In addition, the assaulted man had to retaliate immediately. The courts would not be likely to find a manslaughter verdict if after a quarrel in which blows were exchanged an interval of time passed sufficient to cool tempers and then one struck a blow killing the other. If he had not acted in a passion and in heat of blood the slayer would be found guilty of murder.[51] There were some exceptions to the provocation-by-blows rule. It was considered sufficiently provoking, for example, for a man to find his wife in bed with another—such adultery being, Kelyng said, "the highest invasion of property." When a corkcutter in London returned home to find his wife and lodger in bed together and then killed the man in a rage and surrendered himself to a magistrate, he was convicted of manslaughter and ordered by the judge to be burnt "gently" in the hand "because there could be no greater provocation."[52] The vast majority of manslaughter verdicts, however, were found in cases in which men had quarreled and blows had been struck.

The rules of manslaughter had developed in general and rough accordance with the community's sense of just deserts.[53] The common sense of what was proper continued to shape the law, since the trial juries made the crucial decisions and their verdicts sprang to a considerable extent from their assessment of the responsibility of the accused for the victim's death. In the abstract, the roles of the judge and jury were clear: the jury, Blackstone said, was "to decide whether the circumstances alleged are proven to have actually existed," and the judge then decided "how far they extend to take away or mitigate the guilt."[54] But there was the possibility of serious tension in this apparently simple and clear relationship, room for conflicts that could turn on differing "judicial and social concepts of liability."[55]

No doubt in the vast majority of cases juries accepted the judge's view of the evidence. After Bushel's case in 1670, however, they could

---

[50] In Bristol in 1729, for example, a man was convicted of murder for killing someone who had taunted him in the street. He was provoked beyond control, he claimed (unsuccessfully), "by having snow balls throwed at me because they thought I was an Irishman, having the Irish arms upon my Coat" (SP 36/14, f. 175).

[51] For the judges' discussion of this in Oneby's case (1727), see Strange, *Reports*, vol. 2, pp. 766–75; *Eng. Rep.*, vol. 93, pp. 835–40.

[52] *G. M.* 26 (1756), p. 203.

[53] Green, "The Jury and the English Law of Homicide," pp. 487–99.

[54] Blackstone, *Commentaries*, vol. 4, p. 201.

[55] Green, "The Jury and the English Law of Homicide," p. 499.

no longer be bludgeoned into accepting it, and occasionally in the eighteenth century a jury stood out against the judge's plain direction.[56] In the case mentioned earlier of the man in Kent convicted of murdering his son by beating and whipping him, the jury ignored the judge's guidance, delivered in his summing up, that the father had not exceeded the force the law allowed him in punishing his child, nor had he used an "improper instrument." They also ignored his further suggestion that since the child had had a fever at the time of the beating that must have been the real cause of death. Perhaps it was the inhumanity of beating a child while he was ill with a fever that brought the jury to ignore the judge's view of the legalities. In any event, they brushed the judge's direction aside and convicted the man of murder. (It was within the judge's power to stay his execution, however, and to apply to the king for a pardon, as he did in this case.)[57] At the Exeter Lent assizes in 1728 two men were similarly convicted of murder against the specific recommendations of the judge.[58] And some years later, in Warwickshire, a man who was indicted for killing another in a "boxing match" provoked by a quarrel was found guilty of murder, again in the face of the judge's explanation that the offense amounted to manslaughter in law.[59] The judge (ironically in this case Mr. Justice Page, "the Hanging Judge," who had a reputation for harshness) could only save this man from the gallows by reprieving him and recommending him to the king for a full pardon. It is possible that there was behind such incidents some local knowledge of the previous relationship between the deceased and the defendant that might not alter the legalities of the actual moment of conflict at issue in the trial but that by a common-sense view of justice fixed a much more serious responsibility for what had happened upon the prisoner.

VERDICTS IN HOMICIDE CASES

Of the 334 individuals charged as principals in homicide cases at the Surrey assizes in the years sampled, more than half were either not indicted by the grand jury (fifteen per cent) or acquitted by the trial jury (thirty-

[56] Green has found that "jury tracts after 1670 frequently supported their contentions with the argument that, in cases of homicide, the jury had an unbridled right to decide whether the slaying was murder, manslaughter, or a form of excusable homicide" (ibid., p. 497, n. 304; and see his *Verdict According to Conscience: Perspectives on the English Criminal Trial Jury, 1200–1800* [Chicago, 1985], chap. 6).

[57] SP 36/11, f. 98.

[58] SP 36/5, ff. 7, 78–83.

[59] SP 36/47, f. 227.

eight per cent), on the grounds that the evidence did not convict them of the offense, that the death was accidental, or that the defendant had been justified in acting as he had (table 3.1). Another quarter were convicted not of murder but of the reduced charge of manslaughter. Some of those so convicted, especially toward the end of the eighteenth century, were held to have caused someone's death in what clearly was an accident, but an accident in which their behavior was thought to have been so imprudent and careless that they deserved some punishment. But most of the manslaughter verdicts were found by the jury in cases in which a death had occurred as a result of a fight or sudden quarrel. It is hardly surprising, in view of that, that virtually all involved men: only two women were among the eighty prisoners convicted of manslaughter as principals (after being indicted for murder), and only one of the nine so convicted who had been charged as accessories, aiding and abetting the main protagonist. (Another seven men—no women—were actually charged with manslaughter, of whom three were convicted.) This dominance of men simply reflects differences in patterns of life. Men were much more likely than women to be in taverns, to drink too much, to think their courage slighted, and to feel compelled to give and accept challenges to fight. They were also more likely to be carrying weapons or a knife or tool of some kind.

In general, many fewer women were involved in homicides than men. Of the principals indicted at the Surrey assizes, nine per cent were women (thirty of the 334 accused) and eleven per cent of the accessories charged were women (table 3.1). Few of these women were convicted of manslaughter, as we have seen. They were also much more likely than men to be discharged by the grand jury and acquitted by the trial jury: more than seventy-five per cent of the accused women were discharged by the juries, compared with half the men. But in one respect women, though fewer in number, were represented in the same proportion as men, that is in convictions for willful murder. About a fifth of both men and women accused were actually convicted of murder (or in the case of one of the women who had killed her husband, petty treason) and sentenced to be executed. This is explained in part by the fact that the murderer and the victim were likely to have been on intimate terms.

Convictions for murder were common in two types of cases: slayings committed in the course of a serious crime like robbery and burglary, and cases in which malice and deliberation were clear. The second were by far the most common. There was also the possibility of a murder conviction arising from some other unlawful action, like dueling, but such convictions were rare. None of those executed in Surrey in the ninety-five years sampled had apparently fought duels, though of course it is not always clear, especially simply from the indictment, whether a particular homicide had occurred in a duel or not. Duels were certainly still common in the late seventeenth century and were not unusual in the eighteenth. And it is perhaps a reasonable assumption that the six cases in which a gentleman or an esquire was accused of killing another man with a sword or a gun (and that were not under the Stabbing Act, which applied only when the victim had been unarmed) were duels. Five of these men had killed with swords, between 1660 and 1708, and the sixth, in 1793, had used a pistol. None was convicted of murder. Three of the swordsmen were acquitted, one was convicted of manslaughter, and the fifth was at large when his trial came on; the man accused of killing with a pistol was acquitted. If these men had been engaged in duels they had benefited from the leniency of juries in all such cases, for it was well established and well known in the eighteenth century that juries would not find murder convictions so long as the "rules of honour" had been obeyed.[60]

Murder cases were fascinating no doubt in part because they so frequently revealed intimate details of others' lives and circumstances and emotions. But the murders that occurred during robberies and burglaries more terrified than fascinated. Again, I do not have enough information to be certain how many of those hanged in Surrey had in fact murdered in the course of committing another felony, but at least nine of the forty-seven men executed in the ninety-five years examined had done so. Some of their victims had discovered a burglar in their house or shop; some had resisted being robbed or had tried to prevent a robber from escaping. One all-night customer in a bawdy house was killed when he objected to being robbed by the owner of the house and the women he had been sleeping with, who threw him from the second-story window when he called for help.[61] Another man, a sailor from North Carolina, killed his landlord, a publican in Rotherhithe who was sixty-two years old, and his wife, seventy-three, strangling the man as he lay asleep and bludgeoning his wife. He took clothes, silver plate, and a little money, crossed the river, and spent most of the money in a night house. He drank until noon the next day and was caught as he went down the river to get away, having been identified and described by servants who had worked for the dead man and woman. The callousness of the offense and the age of the victims made this American sailor famous. The jail in which he was kept for trial was so besieged by crowds trying to see him that "it was difficult to get in or out of the Prison after Nine o'Clock in the Morning, till its being locked

---

60 Donna Andrew, "The Code of Honour and Its Critics: The Opposition to Duelling in England, 1700–1850," *Social History* 5 (1980), pp. 412–13.

61 S.A.P., Summer 1743, pp. 2–7 (Day et al.).

up," and on the day of his execution a crowd of "upwards of 20,000" gathered at the gallows on Kennington Common.[62]

EVIDENCE OF MURDER IN THE SURREY ASSIZE PROCEEDINGS

Such murders as this, or the torture and killing of customs officers some years earlier by smugglers in Sussex, which was very widely reported, stirred the public deeply and cast a long shadow.[63] It took very few to convince people that murder went hand in hand with robbery and burglary, and that all such wickedness was increasing out of hand. The evidence of the murder trials in Surrey is not conclusive in this area, for many more such murders may have been committed than can be identified from the indictments alone; and of course many certainly occurred without a suspect being arrested. So the fact that there were only something on the order of two a decade in Surrey in the eighteenth century does not mean that that is all that were committed or all that people heard about. But it does appear that killings in the course of robbery and burglary were less common than contemporary opinion might lead one to suspect.

They were also certainly less common than murder by relatives or friends of the victim. The essential character and quality of the legal offense of murder was a malicious intention to kill. Almost by definition this meant that most murderers and their victims would have known each other very well, for such an extreme of malice must have proceeded most often from deep hatreds and jealousies built up over time. My rough guess from the indictments is that in half of the cases resulting in a murder conviction the accused and victim had been closely related or intimately involved with each other. The indictments do not always make such relationships clear, but that proportion is essentially confirmed by the much more detailed and satisfactory information available in the small sample of cases contained in the Surrey Assize Proceedings. The surviving published accounts of Surrey trials include only thirteen cases (involving twenty-two accused) in which the jury returned convictions for murder.[64]

---

[62] *The Genuine Account of the Trial, Confession and Dying Words of William Corbett* (1764), p. 4; *The Public Advertiser*, 5 Apr. 1764.

[63] *The Whole Proceedings of the Special Commissions . . . for the County of Sussex . . . January*, 1748/9 (1749). This is the only published account of a Sussex trial in this period that I have been able to find. See also Cal Winslow, "Sussex Smugglers," in Hay, Linebaugh, and Thompson, eds., *Albion's Fatal Tree*.

[64] S.A.P., Lent 1678, pp. 3–5; Lent 1683, p. 1; Lent 1688, p. 3; Summer 1711, p. 3; Lent 1726, pp. 1–2; Lent 1738, pp. 8–16; Lent 1740, pp. 7–9; Summer 1742, pp. 2–10; Summer 1743, pp. 2–7; Lent 1749, pp. 7–12; Lent 1753, pp. 3–6; Lent 1759, pp. 4–9.

In six the murder had been committed within the family: two by wives of their husbands; two by husbands of their wives; one son convicted of killing his mother; and the last a young girl who brutally murdered her aunt.

The printed trial accounts support the less certain evidence of the indictments that a considerable proportion of the homicides the juries judged to have been malicious and deliberate had taken place within the family; they also reveal something of the hatreds and jealousies that so commonly lay behind them. The two women convicted of killing their husbands both made what must often have been on the face of it a plausible plea of self-defense. One, in 1678, claimed that her husband had beaten her with a frying pan and that he had then "accidentally" run against the scissors she was holding, the wound from which it was judged he died some days later. But her neighbors testified that she had "often threatened to do his business." There was further damning evidence from a woman who had seen the victim lying bleeding after he had been stabbed, and asked the accused "if her husband were in a swoon; to which she replied surlily, bidding her meddle with her own business. . . ."[65] The jury found her guilty. She was convicted of petty treason, an aggravated degree of murder defined by the Treason Act of 1351 as the killing of a master by his servant, of a husband by his wife, or an ecclesiastical superior by a man in orders—the murder being a breach, as Blackstone said, "both of natural and civil relations," since such offenders owed their masters faith and obedience.[66] To be convicted the accused had to be proved to have killed "traitorously," with malice aforethought, and as a species of treason a conviction ought to have required the evidence of two witnesses. The punishment was also distinguished from that of ordinary murder, for the woman was to suffer the female traitor's death of being burned at the stake. The second wife convicted of killing her husband (in 1738) also claimed that he had attacked her and that while he was dragging her about the room and beating her "the knife stuck in his leg unknown to me." Again the evidence of the neighbors was decisive. Their fellow lodgers in a house in Southwark had heard them in a violent quarrel over the husband's wanting to bring another woman, who had offered to provide a "penny's worth of gin," into their room overnight. This had ended with a loud crash and the neighbors had gone up to find the man bleeding to death. Remarkably enough, she too was convicted of petty treason, which as a form of murder ought to have required evidence of premeditation, rather than manslaughter, and she was also ordered to be burned to death.[67]

[65] S.A.P., Lent 1678, pp. 3–5.
[66] Blackstone, *Commentaries*, vol. 4, p. 203.
[67] S.A.P., Lent 1738, pp. 15–16 (Goodson).

Another woman whose trial is included in the printed assize accounts was alleged to have poisoned her husband with laudanum because he was spending all her money. After an unusually long trial of thirteen hours she was acquitted, even though persuasive evidence had been presented that he had indeed been poisoned and that she had bought laudanum.[68] Poisoning has been thought to be more typical of women's murder than the fragments of Surrey evidence makes clear. It is of course natural that it should be, not because women are secretive by nature or that their crimes are necessarily masked to a greater degree than men's,[69] but because they had abundant opportunities to doctor food and drink and because poisoning was clearly much safer especially against a husband than some more open method. But the murders committed by women in Surrey, as revealed by the indictment evidence and by cases reported in the press as well as in the Proceedings, make it clear that not all women who killed did so by stealth and indirection. Some of the most vicious murders before the Surrey assizes were by women on young children, including for example the case of the inappropriately named Mercy Etherton who attacked her eighteen-month-old son with a shredding knife in 1665 and "cut off his head."[70] A few women also killed adults by main force. Among the women charged with murder in Surrey, one, for example, had taken advantage of her husband's drunken stupor to beat him to death; the young girl who killed her aunt, whose case was mentioned earlier among those included in the printed trials, had beaten her with a poker and cut her throat; another woman killed her daughter-in-law with a smoothing iron; and a case was reported in 1774 of a woman committed to jail in Southwark

> for the murder of a man with whom she had cohabited for nineteen years, and had bore him eleven children. She cut his throat in a fit of jealousy, and that not putting an immediate end to his life, she dashed out his brains with a poker. Her resentment was so strong, and she was so far from denying the fact, on her examination, that she owned, if the deed could be recalled, she would again repeat it.[71]

Such burning resentments and jealousies had also driven many of the men who came before the Surrey assizes charged with murder within the family, although in many cases the death they had caused seems to have been as much a result of cruelty as deliberate intent to kill— a final beating in a catalogue of abuse and mistreatment. That would seem to explain the

---

[68] S.A.P., Lent 1732, pp. 2–8 (Longley).
[69] Otto Pollock, *The Criminality of Women* (New York, 1950), esp. chap. 3.
[70] ASSI 35/106/7/17, 27.
[71] S.A.P., Lent 1759, pp. 4–9 (Edmondson); Lent 1683, p. 1 (Tymon); G. M. 44 (1774), p. 233.

death of a woman in Surrey in 1683 whose husband was indicted for murder. The brief account of his trial revealed that he kept cows in Lambeth and his wife carried the milk around for sale, and that he had forced her to resume her rounds soon after she had been delivered of a child and "before she was in a condition to rise." He had also "kick'd and abus'd her" for selling a calf for less than he thought it worth. She had died some days later. A midwife at his trial gave it as her opinion "that the Blows he had given her, and the unseemly forcing her to work, was the cause of her Death," and the jury were satisfied with that, though that seems to have been the extent of the medical evidence submitted. He was convicted and hanged.[72] In other family murder cases a man was alleged to have killed his brother because he was "a favourite of his parents," and a seventy-two-year old man his niece because she treated his son unkindly.[73]

Motives in such murders are often reasonably clear. In other Surrey cases, greed, or as they might have seen it necessity, drove some men to kill relatives, including a young man who killed his mother in a quarrel over money[74] and—in a case with a modern ring—a man who killed his wife in order to collect her life insurance. The man was an apothecary so hard pressed by his creditors that he was obliged to live separately from his wife. He saw her as a way he might recover his fortune. "Accordingly," the prosecution at his trial alleged,

> he goes to the London Insurance Office, and I think, by Order of the Company, Mr. Fletcher and Mr. Robinson are ordered to receive his Proposals, and report it to the Committee. He asked Mr. Fletcher the Nature of it, and told him if he could insure his Wife's Life it would be of the utmost Convenience and Service to him, for she would be of Age in a Month's Time, and then he could come at her Fortune, which was very considerable. I think Mr. Fletcher told him he must see the Person whose Life they were to insure, before they could have an Order for the Policy. The Prisoner said his Wife was a modest young Woman, and did not care to expose herself any where; however he would bring her to the King's Arms Tavern on Ludgate-Hill, and hinted to Mr. Robinson, that there would be no Occasion to let his Wife know the cause of their Meeting. They met at the King's Arms Tavern, on Ludgate Hill, they saw she was a healthy young woman, in full Vigour and Strength of

[72] S.A.P., Lent 1683, p. 1 (Evans).
[73] *Mr. Noble's Speech . . . at Kingstone Assizes* (1713), p. 3; *The Public Advertiser*, 31 Jan. 1764; *G. M.* 29 (1759), p. 390; 36 (1766), p. 388.
[74] S.A.P., Lent 1679, p. 5.

Life, so on the 14th or 15th of October, he got the Policy; I think he paid 10 s. per Hundred for one Kalendar Month, so if she died by any Means whatsoever within a Kalendar Month from the Date of the Policy, he would be intitled to the sum insured for, which was £200.

In fact his wife was nineteen and not an heiress. After a month had gone by, her husband renewed the policy for another month and then took her one night into St. George's Fields in Southwark and stabbed her to death. He bungled it badly, for even before the insurance company had an opportunity to become suspicious, he was identified by several people who had seen him taking his wife across the Fields that night and who came forward after her body was taken to St. George's workhouse and "exposed to public view." The jury took only a few moments to convict him, and he was hanged.[75]

Inevitably, motives in many murders were not so clear, or at least they did not emerge during the trial. The bitterness of past injustices and of wrongs done loom behind some without ever becoming clear. The case of Thomas Quick, who was hanged for killing his infant son is a striking example. His story is most directly told in the printed report of his very brief trial in 1711, at which he made no defense:

It appear'd that the Prisoner lived in the Parish of Staines, and having got the Woman who afterwards became his Wife, with Child, he was by the Church Wardens oblig'd to Marry her; after which she was deliver'd of a Boy, which was Christen'd after the Father's Name; soon after he had been Married, his Wife died, not without suspicion of his having Poison'd her, for she died in a very odd manner. The Child was therefore put to Nurse, and the Nurse depos'd, on the Date aforesaid, the Prisoner came to her House to see the Child, and after some Talk, desir'd her to go and fetch a Pot of Drink, and gave her Money for it, and whilst she was gone he had waken'd the Child, which before lay in the Cradle asleep, and it's suppos'd had given it something; but soon after she came in again, he said to her, God be wi'ye, and went away. He was no sooner gone, but the Child fell a Vomiting of ugly Stuff, which the Dog licking up, he died quickly after, and the Child continued very sick a little longer, and then died. The Apothecary, a Quaker, declar'd, that he came to him the same time, and bought some Poison, but he did not Examine what it was for. He was ask'd

[75] S.A.P., Lent 1738, pp. 8–15 (Smith).

what he had to say for himself, but he made no defence; and being told of the heinousness of the Fact, he was ask'd what induc'd him to it, but he gave no Answer. The Judge askt him if he could say his Prayers, but he said, his Parents had never taught it him. The Fact being plainly prov'd, the Jury found him guilty of the Murther.[76]

Apart from the six cases of murder within the family, the surviving printed Proceedings for Surrey contain accounts of two cases in which the victims had been killed by robbers; one in which a thief-taker had been murdered by a gang of six men, all of whom were sentenced to death; and another in which the charge of murder had followed the death of a woman who had been raped, and in which the man convicted and hanged was discovered two years later to have been entirely innocent.[77] In three other cases, the issue and motive remain unclear from the brief account of the evidence given at the trial.

These are murders as defined by the trial jury, the cases included in the Surrey Proceedings in which the accused was convicted of premeditated killing and sentenced to death. But since at least some of the evidence that was heard in court is included in the printed report (though often very briefly indeed), it is possible to make some independent assessment of the character of the homicide cases contained in the surviving Surrey pamphlets and to classify them in a way that is simply not possible from the indictment alone. That general categorization (table 3.3) is of course entirely fanciful since many of the accused listed there as having committed "murder" were in fact acquitted by the jury or convicted merely of manslaughter. And there are, in any event, too few cases (a total of thirty-nine) to sustain confident general conclusions about the nature of homicide charges in this period. But these cases reported in the Proceedings do suggest some possible characteristics of homicide.

Inevitably, cases that appear on the evidence to have amounted gen-

---

[76] S.A.P., Summer 1711, p. 3 (Quick).

[77] This murder had raised considerable passion because of its brutality. It had occurred as the woman crossed St. George's Fields in the dark (she was returning from the annual bean feast given for his workers by her employer, a rug-maker in Southwark), and the attack by three men was vicious in the extreme. She got to St. Thomas's Hospital "torn in a most barbarous manner" and died some weeks later when her wounds mortified. A man who had been seen to leave the tavern with her where the party had taken place was arrested; despite his denials, and despite the testimony of two witnesses who swore to his being with them, and despite there being no real proof of his guilt, he was convicted by a jury that discussed the evidence for two minutes without leaving the court. The horror of the case seems to have required a victim. Two years after this man had been hanged his innocence became clear when another man confessed to the rape, and he and another were tried, convicted, and hanged (S.A.P., Lent 1749, pp. 7–12 [Coleman]; Summer 1751, pp. 33–37 [Welch and Jones]).

TABLE 3.3

Categories of Homicides in the Surrey Assize Proceedings,
1678–1774 (32 Sessions)

Category	Number of Indictments	Percentage of Total Indictments	Number of Individuals Accused		Percentage of Total Accused	
			Men	Women	Men	Women
Murder						
In family	14	35.9	6	9	14.6	81.8
During course of crime	5	12.8	10	2	24.4	18.2
Other	3	7.7	8	0	19.5	0
Total	22	56.4	24	11	58.5	100.0
Accidental death	5	12.8	5	0	12.2	0
Manslaughter (quarrel)	9	23.1	9	0	22.0	0
Justifiable homicide	1	2.6	1	0	2.4	0
Unclear	2	5.1	2	0	4.9	0
Total	39	100.0	41	11	100.0	100.0

SOURCE: S.A.P.

uinely to murder occupy a more prominent place when homicides are classified in this way than when one depends on the verdicts of the juries. More than half of the cases were at least presented as premeditated killings. Within that group the trial evidence confirms that the family was by far the most common setting for such murders: close to two-thirds of the allegations that seem to amount to "actual" murder, killing with malice aforethought, involved accused and victims who were related by blood or marriage, and those cases accounted for about a third of all homicide charges. (That is in terms of numbers of cases. The proportions are different when one considers the number of accused who were charged, for in some cases, for example in those committed in the course of another crime, several offenders were more likely to be involved than in family murders or in quarrels or in accidental deaths. When proportions are looked at that way, the proportion of "family" murders falls to under thirty per cent [table 3.3].) Whether the circumstances behind these murders—the stories of breakdown and deprivation, of jealousy and hatred—tell one anything about the quality of family life in this period is to be doubted.[78]

[78] The possibility that the proportion of homicides committed within and outside the family might throw some light on the quality of family relationships in the past has been raised in an essay by J. A. Sharpe, "Domestic Homicide in Early Modern England," *Historical Journal* 24 (1981), pp. 29–48. Dr. Sharpe has studied indictments for homicide laid before the Essex assizes

The much wider evidence of violence within the family contained in other criminal charges and other court records, including recognizances binding over to keep the peace, is undoubtedly more informative on this subject.

One other characteristic of homicide in this period underlined by the evidence from the Surrey Assize Proceedings is the narrow range of women's offenses. Women accounted for sixty per cent of the charges involving family deaths, but only two of the remaining thirty-seven defendants were women. This may be one area, however, in which this small sample of homicides is not entirely trustworthy, for it looks as though these overall proportions exaggerate the involvement of women in homicides over the period 1660 to 1800. What is undoubtedly a truer measure of that emerges from the much larger sample represented by the indictments laid before the Surrey assizes in the ninety-five years for which data are complete. As we have seen (table 3.1), 334 individuals were charged as principals in homicides, of whom ninety-one per cent were men and nine per cent women. (Another eighty-one were indicted as accessories, in roughly the same proportions of men and women.) The indictments confirm in other ways the spheres within which women's offenses took place, for of the fourteen victims of women's homicide in the indictment sample whose relationship to the accused seems clear, all but one was either a member of her family or a close acquaintance, and the other was the client of two prostitutes who had tried to rob him. Both the smaller sample from the printed trials and the indictments over the ninety-five years confirm that men were much more likely than women to commit an offense or to be involved in an event that would result in a manslaughter verdict—offenses arising from quarrels, for example, or from accidents at work or in the streets. Even in the urban parishes of Surrey women did not often become involved in incidents outside the family that would lead to homicide charges.[79]

---

in the period 1560–1709 and raises as a central issue the fact that whereas in modern England something on the order of half the murders committed are domestic, in sixteenth- and seventeenth-century Essex the proportion was about half that. He wonders whether this is significant evidence of a difference in the quality of family life and the character of domestic relationships in the early modern period as against the modern. It seems to me that the basis of comparison is false, that analogous samples are not being compared. Dr. Sharpe is comparing the early modern category of homicide, which included a wide range of offenses—excusable and justifiable homicide as well as murder—with the narrower modern category "murder" (as analyzed by Terence Morris and Louis Blom-Cooper, *A Calendar of Murder: Criminal Homicide in England since 1957* [1964]). If he had tried to extract from the seventeenth-century indictments only those cases that would be counted as murder in modern statistics, the differences would be much diminished, at least on the evidence of the Surrey assizes in the period 1660–1800.

[79] The urban and rural distribution of homicide cases in Surrey (in the cases in which the location of the offense is clear) is as follows:

HOMICIDE OVER TIME

The larger sample of homicide cases from the indictments also enables us to enquire into a possible pattern of change over time. In fact the simple numbers of charges show a straightforward decline over the period. This cannot be charted in fine detail since there are few cases in any one year and it seems wise to aggregate them into twenty-year periods. But even this rough measure shows an unmistakable decline in Surrey over the late seventeenth century and into the second quarter of the eighteenth, followed by some leveling off until the very end of the century, when the decline in the number of indictments was once again renewed (table 3.4). This pattern is much more obvious if one takes the changing population into account since it roughly doubled over the period we are dealing with. Rates of offenses cannot be fully depended on, of course, when the numbers are small and when the size of the population has to be guessed at. But the rate per 100,000 population shown in table 3.4 is likely to be in roughly the right order of magnitude. It suggests just how significantly the level of homicide prosecutions fell in the county: from an average rate of six indictments per 100,000 in the two decades after the Restoration to under four in the early eighteenth century and to steadily lower rates thereafter. By the early years of the nineteenth century, I would estimate that prosecutions for homicide were under one a year per 100,000 of the Surrey population.

It is worth noting that this was not the result of a change in one part of the county. It was most decidedly, for example, not merely a rural phenomenon. The decline of prosecutions was indeed even more striking in Southwark and the London area than in the rest of the county, partly because the rates were much higher there in the late seventeenth century. The levels fell together in both parts of the county—though the rural rate made a brief modest recovery in the middle decades of the eighteenth

	Men	Women
Urban parishes	63%	73.1%
Rural parishes	37%	26.9%
N	297	26

Much of the difference between the indictment of men in urban and rural parishes is explained by population patterns, for close to sixty per cent of the county's population over the period lived in Southwark and the surrounding urban parishes. In the case of women the sample seems too small to make anything of; even though women might tend to become more frequently involved in affairs that led to homicide charges in urban over rural parishes, there were still very few in either place.

TABLE 3.4

Homicide Indictments in Urban and Rural
Parishes of Surrey and in Sussex, 1660–1800

| Period | Years | | Indictments per Year | | | | Approx. Rate per 100,000 Population | | | |
| | Surrey | Sussex | Surrey | | | Sussex | Surrey | | | Sussex |
			Urban	Rural	Total		Urban	Rural	Total	
1660–1679	7	8	5.0	2.6	7.6	2.5	8.1	4.3	6.2	2.6
1680–1699	12	5	3.3	2.8	6.1	1.8	5.0	4.7	4.9	1.9
1700–1719	6	5	2.8	1.7	4.5	1.2	3.9	2.9	3.5	1.2
1720–1739	10	6	2.1	.5	2.6	1.0	2.8	.9	2.0	1.1
1740–1759	17	15	1.6	.9	2.5	1.8	2.0	1.6	1.8	1.9
1760–1779	20	9	1.8	.8	2.6	.6	1.7	1.1	1.4	.5
1780–1802	23	13	1.3	.8	2.1	.9	.9	.9	.9	.6

SOURCE: Surrey, Homicide Count; Sussex, Sample.

century—until by 1800 both had reached the same low point. A similar
pattern was followed in the county of Sussex. The rate of prosecutions for
homicide in Sussex was generally lower than in Surrey, even in the rural
parishes of Surrey, and the level in the late seventeenth century appears
to have been particularly lower (table 3.4). The decline was thus not as
sharp in Sussex, but it nonetheless followed the same contours, including
the slight recovery in the middle of the eighteenth century. In both
counties, and in the urban as well as the rural parishes of Surrey, the rate
of indictments and even the absolute number of indictments per year were
distinctly lower in 1800 than they had been a century earlier.

Two explanations of this seem reasonable: one is that there was a
change over the period in the events reported and prosecuted as homicide;
the other, that there was a decline in the number of offenses. It seems to
me likely that both were operating in this period, that on the one hand
cases were appearing on the court record in the late seventeenth century
that would probably not have been proceeded with by the end of the
eighteenth, and on the other that there were by then fewer cases to be
reported. Neither of these assertions is capable of being proved conclusively, but there is evidence for both. It seems to me likely that the first
helps particularly to explain the sharp decline in homicide prosecutions
from the late seventeenth century into the early decades of the eighteenth.

The argument for an administrative explanation rests principally on the fact that many types of murder cases that appear in the court record in the late seventeenth century largely disappear in the eighteenth. It is perhaps worth saying that this does not include causing death by witchcraft, which would be an obvious example of the way certain kinds of prosecutions fell from favor if there had been more of them in our sample. In fact there is only one case of this in the years examined after the Restoration. Two other categories of offense contributed much more obviously to a possible inflation of charges in one period over the other. In the first place there are a number of cases in the late seventeenth century in which the defendant named is clearly fictitious. No doubt someone had died in suspicious circumstances; the coroner's jury found a verdict of murder, but no suspect was to be found. In some years (but why in some and not in others is unclear) this resulted in a bill of indictment being drawn up and presented to the grand jury, and very often endorsed true by them, but then going no further because there was no such person as had been named in the bill. This at least seems to be the best explanation of why on at least five occasions between 1688 and 1692 indictments for murder were drawn against John Whitecoat, John Redcoat, John Greycoat (twice), and John Greencoat, against none of whom a verdict was recorded. Three accomplices in another case in 1687 in which the principal was at large when the trial came on were named as John and Thomas Greycoat and Henry Blewcoat.[80] There were perhaps not enough of these fictitious defendants to make a great difference to the numbers of charges being laid, but the fact that there were even a few such indictments suggests something about the character and quality of administration in the late seventeenth century, and the possibilities for significant inflation in the numbers of charges appearing on the court record. It is possible that there were fictitious defendants after 1700 lurking under more plausible names, but that does not appear to have been the case.

Charges that invited an ignoramus verdict or an acquittal by the trial jury because the case being made was obviously weak seem to have been more commonly pressed forward in the late seventeenth century than a hundred years later. A striking example of that was the indictment of a man for murder in 1663 seven months after he was alleged to have assaulted the victim.[81] It is possible of course that the victim in this case had lingered near death all this while, but it seems more likely that there was little connection between the assault and the death and that the indictment was either malicious or proceeded simply from only a weak understanding of what might have caused her death. In another case a man who had beaten

[80] ASSI 35/128/6/1; ASSI 35/129/6/1; ASSI 35/131/7/27; ASSI 35/133/8/1, 3.
[81] ASSI 35/104/12 (Bassnett).

someone and thrown him to the ground in June 1695 was indicted when this victim died six months later.[82] In both cases the grand jury refused to find the bills, and it seems to me a reasonable assumption that they did so because of the tenuousness of the connection between the assault and the victim's death. Several other murder charges arose from punches and kicks and throwings to the ground that were followed several weeks or months later by the death of the person assaulted. Many of those resulted in acquittals by the trial jury.

This can be no more than impressionistic, but there is a suggestion in some of these examples that cases were being pressed forward to trial in the late seventeenth century that were not well founded. That might help to explain—though it is not necessarily the whole explanation—why so many not guilty verdicts were recorded by the trial jury at the Restoration and into the first decades of the eighteenth century (table 3.2). And if, as appears simply from the indictments, fewer such apparently weak charges were being made by the second quarter of the new century—and the falling away in the level of acquittals adds some support to that—it would help to explain why fewer homicide indictments were being prosecuted. One other indication that the practice of the courts with regard to such indictments changed in the late seventeenth century and in the early years of the eighteenth is to be found in the treatment of accessories. In the forty years after 1660 accessories in homicide were commonly added to the indictment of the principal, particularly when the victim had been killed in a fight, struck on the head with a staff or bargepole or heavy stick—to name some of the occasions on which as many as five, seven, or eight men were named in the indictment as having aided and abetted the accused who actually delivered the blow. Altogether, in twenty years examined between 1663 and 1700, sixty-seven accessories were indicted. Few of them were in fact convicted, and this might help to explain why, beginning apparently in the earliest years of the eighteenth century, the habit of bringing such men into court fell into disfavor. The difference can be seen in the fact that in the fifteen years examined between 1701 and 1739 only nine were named, and in the following sixty years only five. Not a single woman was named as an accessory in the eighteenth century.

Why this change in style occurred is not at all clear. It is possible that there was a significant change in substance, that brawls were rare thereafter and that there was never more than one man present when men were killed in fights in the streets or in taverns. That seems unlikely. Rather it was surely the case that the coroners' juries ceased to name crowds

---

[82] ASSI 35/127/8/7 (Browning).

of aiders and abettors and they ceased to be arrested, and it is possible that this and the more careful formulation of charges in general reflects changing views about what might be reasonably charged as homicide, as well as a clearer understanding of the causes of death.[83] But there is reason to think that there was also a real decline in the number of violent deaths to be reported and prosecuted as murder. Again it is not possible to be certain, but I take the verdicts of trial juries over the period as providing some support for this, since the number and the rate of guilty verdicts, combining those guilty of both murder and manslaughter, also went down over the period, at a time when juries were likely to be more rather than less concerned to fix responsibility and to impose a penalty on those who caused deaths that were not entirely and purely accidental (table 3.5). As we have seen, there is some evidence of an increasing sensitivity in the eighteenth century to human culpability in accidents. At least juries were not more lax in such matters then than earlier, or generally more lax in regard to all violent confrontations that resulted in deaths. A fall in the rate of guilty verdicts from roughly two a year per 100,000 population in the late seventeenth century to less than one over much of the next hundred years and to an average by 1800 of only one conviction every three years or so thus seems likely to have proceeded from a real reduction in the incidence of such offenses rather than simply from changes in the juries' definitions of what constituted a reasonable homicide charge.

The pattern of prosecutions suggests that there was a reduction over the century and a half following the Restoration in the number of deaths

---

[83] Over the long term, improving medical knowledge and a more scientific understanding of the causes of death undoubtedly encouraged the more careful formulation of murder indictments. It seems unlikely, however, that they played any part in the falling away of the weaker homicide indictments in the late seventeenth century and the early years of the eighteenth. The effects of advances in medical knowledge were mainly felt perhaps toward the end of the eighteenth century, when efforts were being made to bring medical expertise to bear on the investigation of homicide. The coroner appointed by the Corporation to act for the City of London and the Borough of Southwark was very active—between 1788 and 1829, for example, he performed more than six thousand inquests—and he was clearly attentive to the causes of death in the cases he did investigate (Forbes, "Crowner's Quest," pp. 8, 42-45). It is most unlikely that advances in forensic medicine can explain changes in the way murder indictments were constructed in the late seventeenth and early eighteenth centuries. The chronology is surely wrong, apart from anything else. But improvements in medical knowledge and greater expertise among coroners perhaps reinforced over the period the tendency toward the more careful drawing of homicide indictments. Of course such expertise might well have also had the effect of uncovering cases of homicide that might earlier have gone undetected; or on the other side advancing medical skill might have saved some wounded men from dying and thus forestalled murder charges that might otherwise have been brought to court. But it seems reasonable to think that advances in medical knowledge worked particularly to decrease the number of homicide prosecutions in which the connection between the action complained of and the death of the victim was not demonstrable.

TABLE 3.5

Guilty Verdicts in Homicide Cases in Surrey, 1660–1800

Period	Years	Accused Found Guilty			Guilty Verdicts Per Year	Approx. Rate per 100,000 Population
		Murder	Manslaughter	Total		
1660–1679	7	6	15	21	3.0	2.5
1680–1699	12	12	11	23	1.9	1.5
1700–1719	6	0	16	16	2.7	2.1
1720–1739	10	4	8	12	1.2	.9
1740–1759	17	17	16	33	1.9	1.4
1760–1779	20	11	15	26	1.3	.7
1780–1802	23	5	13	18	.8	.3

SOURCE: Homicide Count.

in quarrels, of murder in the furtherance of robbery, and of deliberate and planned killing. Men and women would seem to have become more controlled, less likely to strike out when annoyed or challenged, less likely to settle an argument or assert their will by recourse to a knife or their fists, a pistol, or a sword. The court record suggests that other ways of resolving conflicts became increasingly favored and that men became more prepared to negotiate and to talk out their differences. This supposes a developing civility, expressed perhaps in a more highly developed politeness of manner and a concern not to offend or to take offense, and an enlarged sensitivity toward some forms of cruelty and pain. Such an explanation would further suppose that these changing sentiments were experienced well beyond a narrow band of upper-class society, or even among the commercial and professional middle class—that they had a substantial effect on the outlook and the behavior of at least the broad ranks of the artisans, tradesmen, and shopkeepers. If changes in attitudes toward violence and in behavior lie behind the apparent decline in homicide, they would have to have taken place through a large part of the society.

Before enquiring further into the possible truth of such an explanation, it is perhaps wise to see if homicide cases are unique. There are, after all, very few of them, and they are in many cases distinguished from other indictable offenses only by the victim's death. It seems worth investigating other forms of violence prosecuted before the courts to see if the patterns of prosecution of those offenses throw light on a possible change in the level of violence in society.

INFANTICIDE

Women were involved in many fewer violent incidents than men and were less frequently prosecuted. The number of women before the courts on homicide charges in our period is more than tripled, however, when one takes into account infanticide, the killing of a baby at or very soon after birth, an offense for which men were only very rarely indicted.[84] In law, the offense took two forms. If a married woman (or a man) was prosecuted for killing a newborn child, the charge would be the common law offense of murder, and a conviction could only be obtained if there was evidence that the child had been born alive and that the accused had deliberately killed it. The mother would be presumed innocent—as much as anyone was in the eighteenth century—until the evidence proved her guilty. There might also be charges against others as accessories. But if the woman involved was not married, the case fell under a statute of 1624 that altered the matter entirely, for that legislation laid it down that an unmarried woman who gave birth to a child subsequently found dead, the birth of which she had concealed, would be presumed to have killed it unless she could prove by the testimony of at least one witness that the child had in fact been born dead.[85] The charge to be proved under this statute was not murder, but merely concealing the birth. The penalty was death. The Act seems to have been aimed as much against immoral behavior as against the killing of children. It sought to discourage fornication by making it more difficult for unmarried women to escape the results of their immorality; it was aimed, one seventeenth-century commentator said, "against

[84] I have counted the killing of children older than a few weeks in the previous section among the homicides. Unfortunately, this makes my data not directly comparable with that of Peter C. Hoffer and N.E.H. Hull in their recent book *Murdering Mothers: Infanticide in England and New England, 1558–1803* (New York, 1981). They decided to include the killing of all children up to the age of nine years as infanticide, because such children were considered to be infants in law, including (despite the title of their book) the killing of children by strangers, even in street accidents, when they gave rise to indictments for homicide. This all-inclusive definition removes a good deal of the analytical precision and force of the category "infanticide," it seems to me, as well as flying in the face of the common meaning of the word. Apart from this recent book, the fullest discussion of the offense is to be found in the excellent article by R. W. Malcolmson, "Infanticide in the Eighteenth Century," in Cockburn, ed., *Crime in England*, pp. 187–209. See also Walker, *Crime and Insanity*, vol. 1, chap. 7; Keith Wrightson, "Infanticide in Earlier Seventeenth-Century England," *Local Population Studies* 15 (1975); and idem, "Infanticide in European History," *Criminal Justice History* 3 (1982), pp. 1–20.

[85] 21 Jas I, c. 27. For the courts' and contemporaries' views of this Act over the seventeenth and eighteenth centuries see Radzinowicz, *History*, vol. 1, pp. 430–36.

lewd whores, who having committed one sin, to avoid their shame, and the charge of a bastard . . . privately destroy the infant."[86]

It is hardly surprising that the vast majority of infanticide charges were brought under this statute. Between 1660 and the end of the eighteenth century the Surrey assizes dealt with one infanticide case every eighteen months on average: there were sixty-two indictments in our ninety-five-year sample (table 3.6). Of these, forty-seven were against unmarried women and three were against widows. The remaining twelve accused were married, all but one, women; only one man was charged with infanticide, a laborer accused in 1698 of strangling an infant born to his wife, and his case was thrown out by the grand jury. One of the women charged under the statute of 1624 had been married but was no longer living with her husband. The evidence against her was very strong, and indeed one witness claimed that she had confessed, but the court ruled that as she was married "it could not be supposed that the Child was a Bastard as the Indictment sets forth" and she was acquitted.[87]

Not only were three-quarters of those accused of infanticide spinsters, they were spinsters of a particular kind. Far from being the "lewd whores" the statute had been directed against, most of the women in court had a good character and were in trouble because of their efforts and their desperation to maintain it. As Mandeville said, "Common whores, whom all the world knows to be such, hardly ever destroy their children . . . because they have lost their modesty to a greater degree, and the fear of shame makes hardly an impression on them."[88] But the shame and loss of character could be cataclysmic for some women, especially for those living in as servants. Vast numbers of young women in their early child-bearing years lived with families as domestic or farm servants. For them pregnancy was a disaster. A servant had little hope of keeping both her job and her child, and it is hardly surprising that a very large number of women charged under the statute of 1624—perhaps as many as two-thirds at the Surrey assizes—were servants.[89] Such women were vulnerable on several counts, for they were in constant and close contact with men, their fellow servants and their master and his sons, some of whom could offer inducements for sexual favors or threaten retaliation for their refusal.

---

[86] Zachary Babington, *Advice to Grand Jurors* (1680), p. 174. For the origins of the statute see Hoffer and Hull, *Murdering Mothers*, chap. 3.

[87] S.A.P., Summer 1740, p. 9 (Powell).

[88] Bernard Mandeville, *The Fable of the Bees*, ed. P. Harth (1970), pp. 108–9, quoted by Malcolmson, "Infanticide," pp. 205–6.

[89] Malcolmson found that approximately seventy per cent of the women indicted for infanticide before the Old Bailey between 1730 and 1774 whose occupations are known were servants ("Infanticide," p. 202).

TABLE 3.6

Indictments for Infanticide at the Surrey Assizes, 1660–1800

Period	Years	Indictments				Status of Accused					
		Urban	Rural	Total	Per Year	Spinster	Wife	Widow	Male	Total	Accessories
1660–1679	7	3	6	9	1.3	8	1	0	0	9	1
1680–1699	12	8	6	14	1.2	9	3	1	1	14	3
1700–1719	6	2	2	4	.7	3	1	0	0	4	1
1720–1739	10	3	5	8	.8	5	3	0	0	8	0
1740–1759	17	4	4	8	.5	5	2	1	0	8	0
1760–1779	20	1	7	8	.4	8	0	0	0	8	1
1780–1802	23	2	9	11	.5	9	1	1	0	11	1
Total	95	23	39	62	.7	47	11	3	1	62	7
		= 37.1%	= 62.9%	= 100.0%		= 75.8%	= 17.7%	= 4.8%	= 1.6%	= 100.0%	

SOURCE: Homicide Count.

TABLE 3.6 (*cont.*)

Indictments for Infanticide at the Surrey Assizes, 1660–1800

Period	Years	Grand Jury Verdicts		Trial Jury Verdicts		Sentences			Verdict / Sentence Unknown
		Ig.	T.B.	N.G.	G.	Sentenced to Death	Pardoned	Hanged	
1660–1679	7	1	8	5	3	3	2	1	0
1680–1699	12	6	8	4	3	3	3	0	1
1700–1719	6	1	3	1	2	2	0	2	0
1720–1739	10	0	8	8	0	0	0	0	0
1740–1759	17	1	7	7	0	0	0	0	0
1760–1779	20	3	5	4	0	0	0	0	1
1780–1802	23	5	6	5	1	1	0	1	0
Total	95	17	45	34	9	9	5	4	2
		= 27.4%	= 72.6%	= 79.1%	= 20.9%		= 55.6%	= 44.4%	

That many servants became pregnant and then tried to hide it and deliver their child unknown to others—and perhaps to do away with it, or at least abandon it—is understandable. The women who came to court charged under the statute had succeeded in delivering their babies themselves, most often under appalling circumstances in fields and outhouses and under stairs, and the babies had either been stillborn or had died by accident or by design. Some women claimed in court, plausibly enough, that when they were delivered they had fainted and the child had fallen or strangled without their knowing. One young woman said that she had known "nothing of the Matter, the Child dropt from me, and I was taken with a fainting Fit, and fell down." She put the dead child into her box ("until I could inform my Mother"), where it was discovered by her fellow servants.[90] Others claimed that the child had come unexpectedly and prematurely while they were in the fields or sitting in the necessary house.[91] Why these women were prosecuted is usually impossible to discover. But it seems reasonable to think that many more might have been, for it was surely difficult for a servant to keep her pregnancy secret from her employer and fellow servants. Even if she had, and had managed in addition to deliver the child herself, it was obviously difficult to avoid all suspicion and to remove all signs of the birth. Many of the women ended up in court because a dead infant was found in a river or a well or a necessary house and someone remembered that she had had a difficult night some time before, and perhaps had cried out in pain and was concerned (malicious?) enough to report it.[92]

There was a distinct shift of opinion about infanticide in the early years of the eighteenth century. Zachary Babington's view seems typical of the late seventeenth century. He had no doubts at all that the statute of 1624 was wise and just: women had been able to "destroy the Infant, and yet avoid the danger of the Law" even though "really and in truth" they had killed it. He approved the requirement that the accused woman produce evidence that the child was born dead, for, he announced, "Honest and innocent Women . . . always desire help in their Labour. . . ."[93] This unambiguous view of the law was clearly shared by jurors and judges at

[90] S.A.P., Lent 1739, pp. 17–18 (Mills).

[91] S.A.P., Lent 1759, pp. 16–17 (Holmes).

[92] In 1678, for example, a servant was accused of infanticide when a dead child was found, and the girl's mistress recalled that she had heard her "groan and make a great noise in the night" but "thinking it common sickness, took no notice of it" (S.A.P., Lent 1679, p. 6). Another servant who was also heard to cry out in the night and who answered enquiries by saying she had an ache was suspected when the body of a newborn baby that had been strangled was subsequently found (S.A.P., Lent 1679, p. 4).

[93] Babington, *Advice to Grand Jurors*, pp. 174–75.

least into the early years of the eighteenth century, for until then women were frequently convicted under the statute of 1624 and hanged. Twenty-seven women were indicted in the twenty-five years for which records are complete between 1660 and 1720. Eight were convicted, of whom seven were spinsters charged under the Jacobean statute (table 3.6). Three of these women were pardoned, but five appear to have been hanged. These conviction rates did not quite match the level of ferocity of the courts in the decades immediately after the passing of the Act, when in Essex, for example, almost sixty per cent of those accused were convicted.[94] But at both the county assizes and the Old Bailey it is clear that into the very early years of the eighteenth century jurors were not unwilling to convict under the statute and judges were not unwilling to see convicted women hanged. Between 1684 and 1714 at the Essex assizes as many as eleven of the twenty-three women indicted were convicted; over a three-year period at the Old Bailey in the 1680s six of nine women on trial were also found guilty.[95]

The view of these women and of the law that lies behind these figures is reflected in the unwillingness of Mr. Serjeant Comyns to give any benefit of doubt to an eighteen-year-old girl convicted before him in Newcastle in 1728. He sentenced her to be hanged and when her family ("a family of some substance") and "many people of quality" petitioned the king to pardon her, he resisted. She had been convicted because she had been delivered of a child "in the middle of the night on the stair head," and to prevent it crying out had put a rag around its neck; when an hour later she found that it had died she "put it in a closet" and told no one. The case under the statute was clear. But so was the case for a reprieve and an appeal for a pardon, for as Comyns acknowledged, she had been debauched by a sailor and she was "slow and dull and stupid" at her trial. None of this made an impression on the jury or on Comyns himself, however, and it was only when great pressure built up from "people of quality" that he relented and recommended that her life be spared.[96] This is all of a piece with a conviction rate of a third or more of those on trial.

By then, however, a striking change in attitudes had occurred. The spottiness of the Surrey records over the first quarter of the century makes it impossible to establish a decisive moment in that county, but what evidence there is, and the experience of the Old Bailey, suggests that by the middle of the 1720s at least the courts were taking a softer line with women on trial for infanticide, and especially perhaps women being tried

[94] Hoffer and Hull, *Murdering Mothers*, p. 24.
[95] Malcolmson, "Infanticide," p. 337, n. 30; Hoffer and Hull, *Murdering Mothers*, pp. 67–68.
[96] SP 36/9, ff. 11, 13.

under the statute of 1624. In Surrey, thirty-five women were indicted for infanticide between 1722 and 1802. With the exception of a widow convicted in 1795, they were either discharged by the grand jury (about a quarter) or acquitted by the trial jury (table 3.6). The change is also clear in the conduct of trials. Compare, for example, the trial of Anne Henriout in 1711 with the trial of women a generation and more later. Anne Henriout was "a weeder to Sir Charles Cox" in Clapham who was charged under the statute of 1624 when she confessed that an infant found dead in a field was hers. She said that it had been born dead, but had no witnesses to prove that. She was shown little pity, "being told [in court] that tho' the Child was Still born, as she said, yet if she had not proof of it, nor provided for it's Birth, yet it was nevertheless Death by the Law. To which she had very little to say, and the Jury considering the matter, found her guilty of the Murther."[97]

The next surviving printed account of a trial of a woman for infanticide dates from 1739. This was the servant who claimed that the child had suddenly dropped from her and that she had put it into her box so that she could ask her mother what to do. It would appear from the brief account of the trial that she was treated with some solicitude and that the court went out of its way to find evidence that would enable them to acquit her. A surgeon's testimony was mixed. On the one hand, there were no marks of violence on the child; on the other, when he "took out the Lungs, and put them in a Pail of Water . . . they Swam." This was a test frequently employed that supposedly showed whether the infant had ever breathed: if the lungs sank, it was taken to prove that the child had been stillborn. In this case, the lungs floated. But that was brushed aside by the jury in favor of evidence that she had made preparation for the birth. She proved this by producing a few scraps of linen in court. Whether she had collected these in preparation for the birth or the trial was not enquired into, and she was acquitted.[98]

This seems to have been typical of the way that women were in fact treated in court during the remainder of the century. The validity of the lung test was increasingly challenged on medical grounds. By 1771 a doctor could say that the notion that such a test provided decisive evidence of whether a baby had been born alive or dead was now "exploded."[99] It continued to be used and to all appearances taken seriously,[100] but it is clear that it never provided evidence strong enough to override the inten-

[97] S.A.P., Summer 1711, p. 3 (Henriout).
[98] S.A.P., Lent 1759, pp. 17–18 (Mills), and see Hoffer and Hull, *Murdering Mothers*, pp. 68–69.
[99] Quoted in Malcolmson, "Infanticide," p. 200.
[100] Forbes, "Crowner's Quest," pp. 41, 200.

tion of the courts to acquit most of the women charged with infanticide, certainly those charged under the statute of 1624. The legal and human doubts seem clearly to have preceded the medical doubts.

The kind of evidence that came increasingly to the fore concerned the woman's intentions. If she had confessed her pregnancy and sought assistance in her labor, there would have been no case to answer. Apart from that, the decisive evidence of intention that the courts sought, and frequently found, was evidence of preparation for the birth. If she had collected linen or prepared a bed, this was proof that she had intended to care for the baby and must not then have killed it. That this was all beside the point—the statutory offense was concealing the birth—made little difference, for the courts intended to acquit, and this provided an apparently acceptable way of doing so in the vast majority of cases that came to trial. Most women accused of infanticide in the second half of the eighteenth century were thus in effect tried for murder. It was increasingly necessary for the prosecution to prove that the woman had actually killed the child and had intended to. Evidence of preparation was taken as telling decisively against that.

By the time Ann Seabrook was indicted in 1756 this line of argument was fully established. She was a servant suspected by several people of being pregnant and when the body of an infant was found on the bank of a river near where she lived she was immediately questioned. She confessed to a midwife that the child was hers, but claimed that it had been stillborn. She had "kept it to her warme for two hours, but during that Time it never stird a Limb nor open'd its Eyes, whereupon she threw it into the River in hopes the Tide would have carry'd it away and this she did in order to hide the shame from the Eyes of the World." A surgeon reported that the lungs swam and that it was his opinion that "the Child had breath'd in open air." More decisive, however, was her evidence of preparation. A fellow servant deposed that he had several times "seen her making little Shirts and Caps," and instead of this being taken as evidence of her guilt under the statute (and plainly she was guilty, having concealed the birth), it was taken as proof positive that she had not intended to kill the child and had not therefore done so. As the reporter recorded the outcome, "The Murder not appearing plainly it having been prov'd that she . . . had been seen making Preparations for a Child, the Jury without going out of Court brought her in not Guilty." The judge gave the prisoner "a severe and proper Reprimand"; he might also have reprimanded the jury, to whom he must surely have explained the 1624 statute.[101]

Medical evidence became less rather than more important in eight-

[101] S.A.P., Summer 1756, pp. 17–18 (Seabrook).

eenth-century infanticide cases, for in itself it could not generally prove that a mother had murdered her newborn child. Or rather, it became important only for defense. The testimony of surgeons and midwives carried weight when it supported an acquittal; and in those circumstances it was decisive, even when unsubstantiated, or when its validity was clearly questionable at best. A woman tried in 1759 was acquitted when a midwife testified at her trial that she had examined the body of the infant and declared that it had been born dead "for want of assistance." By way of explanation, the midwife went on to say that "it often happens, that children are born in *appearance* dead, which by outward application might recover, but I believe it was inevitable then." In the present case she was sure that "if the child was not born dead, it died in the birth." Despite the statute, the prisoner was clearly being tried here for the common law offense of murder, and she was acquitted, even though she had plainly concealed the birth of the child and was guilty under the statute. Another woman at the same session of the court was also acquitted, though she too had hidden her pregnancy and delivery. She was helped apparently by the testimony of a surgeon that the child found in the "boghouse" had been born dead because the lungs sank in the water test.[102]

The anxiety of the courts to acquit women charged with infanticide is further illustrated by two other Surrey trials. In one, a defense of not guilty by reason of temporary insanity was successful.[103] In another, the accused said nothing in her own defense, but two witnesses reported that they had heard her deny that she had given birth to a child. Upon this, Willes, the lord chief justice, announced a rule that was not commonly insisted on in trials of women for picking pockets or shoplifting or any offense against property. "As the confession of a Prisoner is made use of to convict them," he said in his summing up, "so if they own anything which may be in their Favour, it ought to have some Weight at their Trial." Her denial as remembered by two witnesses was, with this encouragement, sufficient to get her acquitted.[104]

---

[102] S.A.P., Lent 1759, p. 11 (Martin), pp. 16–17 (Holmes).

[103] This was a case of murder rather than a case under the statute, for the accused was married. There was a great deal of damaging evidence: the baby was found with its throat cut, and a bloody knife was discovered among the accused's possessions. Since she was married and since the evidence against her was powerful, evidence of her preparations could not have saved her. Instead her defense, presented by counsel, was that immediately following delivery she had not been in her senses and knew nothing about what happened. One witness who had nursed her after the delivery testified that she had had "no sense in her for four or five days, I was forced to guide what she took in that time (which was but about half a biscuit) to her mouth." This was sufficient to enable the jury to find a verdict of not guilty (S.A.P., Summer 1751, p. 25 [Sturt]).

[104] S.A.P., Summer 1741, pp. 5–6 (Scott).

Women may have been executed in some counties for infanticide in the second half of the eighteenth century,[105] but not in Surrey. By then the provisions of the statute of 1624 were being entirely ignored, and Blackstone was surely reflecting the opinion of Surrey assize jurors when he said that the law "savours pretty strongly of severity." Blackstone also went on to confirm that "it has of late years been usual . . . to require some sort of presumptive evidence that the child was born alive, before the other constrained presumption (that the child, whose death is concealed, was therefore killed by its parent) is admitted to convict the prisoner."[106] This explains why there was only one conviction in Surrey under the statute after 1715—and after 1735 the court records are complete. It also helps to explain why there were fewer prosecutions by the end of the eighteenth century than there had been a hundred years earlier. There had never been very many cases before the Surrey assizes, but the average of one every two years over the second half of the century was distinctly lower than the level in the decades after the Restoration, when an average of more than one infanticide case had come before the county assizes every year. The decline is even clearer when one remembers that the population of the county rose strongly after the mid-century.

It is striking, too, that the falling away of infanticide charges was particularly noticeable in the urban parishes of the county. Before 1715 the Surrey cases came equally from the rural and urban parts of the county; there was some thought in the seventeenth century that infanticide was a particularly urban problem.[107] In the eighteenth century the urban cases diminished in number even more significantly than the rural. Indeed over the last forty years only three cases came to the Surrey assizes from the now much larger population of Southwark, Rotherhithe, Bermondsey, Lambeth, and the other populous districts within the metropolis, while

[105] In Wiltshire, for example, there is evidence that as many as seven women, all of them spinsters, were convicted of infanticide between 1752 and 1796; one was pardoned but the other six may have been hanged (Hunnisett, *Wiltshire Coroners' Bills*, nos. 195, 530, 760, 933, 1346, 2773).

[106] Blackstone, *Commentaries*, vol. 4, pp. 197–98: the first edition was dated 1769. See on the statute East, *Pleas of the Crown*, vol. 1, pp. 228–29. The 1624 statute was so repulsive that it was one of the first of the "bloody code" to be repealed. This was recommended by a Commons committee in 1770, partly on the grounds that it was so cruel the courts could not enforce it, and partly on the grounds that the law was brought into disrepute when statutes that had lapsed in practice were retained on the books. There was sufficient opposition to defeat the motion on that occasion. After several further attempts it was repealed in 1803 and was replaced by a statute that removed the provision that concealment of the birth of a bastard subsequently found dead was to be taken as evidence that the mother had killed it (Radzinowicz, *History*, vol. 1, pp. 430–36).

[107] Ivy Pinchbeck and Margaret Hewitt, *Children in English Society* (1969), vol. 1, p. 209.

sixteen came from rural parishes (table 3.6). Does this offer some clue to the falling away of both prosecutions and convictions for infanticide?

It seems reasonable to think that part of that decline—and perhaps a very considerable part—reflects changing attitudes toward the law that are revealed by the way the courts transformed the statutory offense in practice and by the obvious reluctance of juries to convict. The change in attitude was not perhaps toward the killing of babies at their birth. But the way the law was couched came to be thought cruel and harsh. It seems likely that magistrates and coroners shared the views of judges and jurors. The Surrey magistrate Richard Wyatt clearly had no notion of sending to trial an infanticide case that came before him in 1774. It involved a young woman who was a cook to a family in his neighborhood and who had confessed to having given birth to a child without her mistress or her fellow servants knowing. They had suspected, however, and when the body of the baby was fished out of the necessary house, she was charged and confessed. She maintained that it had been born dead; she also produced some linen, prepared, she said, against the lying-in. There were no signs of violence on the body, and Wyatt discharged her.[108] Wyatt was simply anticipating the court's verdict, since a conviction would require proof that the child had been born alive and that the mother had murdered it.

Perhaps there was a real decline in the number of babies that died soon after birth by design or deliberate accident. I have no evidence of that. It is possible that the establishment of the Foundling Hospital by the middle of the eighteenth century[109] encouraged some unmarried women in London to abandon their babies where they might have some chance of being taken into the Foundling rather than abandoning them in a way that meant certain death. But it seems to me that the real significance of the foundation of such hospitals, and even more of the wide range of charitable institutions established particularly in the capital in the 1750s that set out to provide better maternity care (maternity hospitals and lying-in charities), was the change in attitude they proclaimed toward the unmarried mother.[110] For some of the charities were willing to help the unmarried mother through her pregnancy and delivery, and while such women were hardly approved of, that seems a very different attitude from that which considered them simply as "lewd whores."

It is that change of attitude that is most clearly being charted in the declining rate of prosecutions, especially those under the statute of 1624.

[108] *Deposition Book of Richard Wyatt*, pp. 48–49.

[109] Ruth K. McClure, *Coram's Children: The London Foundling Hospital in the Eighteenth Century* (New Haven, 1981).

[110] Donna T. Andrew, "London Charity in the Eighteenth Century" (Ph.D. thesis, University of Toronto, 1977), chap. 3.

Perhaps infanticide was in fact less common in the eighteenth than in the previous century, but it seems likely that what is being measured in the court record is a change in sentiment about the appropriateness of the way the offense was formulated and punished. Over the course of the eighteenth century the view gradually strengthened that it was wrong to threaten the death of the mother when direct proof of her killing her baby was not available, even though some who had undoubtedly caused the death of their infants escaped punishment. The decline of prosecutions for infanticide thus seems to me to be further evidence of the growing sensitivity to cruelty and to violence that lies behind the changing patterns of homicide generally. Perhaps these changing sentiments also discouraged the killing of the newly born too, though so difficult was the act to discover and prove that court records can hardly speak to that at all. But the records speak directly to the numbers reported and the numbers convicted and punished. The rejection of the crudity of the Jacobean statute seems clear in Surrey, certainly among magistrates and those who served on juries, and that would seem to fit with the apparently increasing willingness of this very broad segment of the society to look for other ways of dealing with problems besides direct and damaging violence.

RAPE

There is no doubt that few violent encounters gave rise to a court case in the eighteenth century. Only rarely did a servant or apprentice thrashed by their masters beyond a level acceptable to society, a wife beaten by her husband, or a man assaulted in the streets or in a tavern complain to a magistrate and institute a prosecution. Most incidents of physical abuse and violent conflict were ignored or revenged privately, or at least settled without an appeal to the courts. Violent offenses short of those that caused very serious injury or death must have been massively underreported. It would surely not have occurred to many of those who might have had a case in law actually to undertake a prosecution. Apart from anything else, the trouble and the expense involved in going to a magistrate to make the complaint and then, several weeks or months later, traveling with witnesses to appear before the quarter sessions or assizes must have discouraged all but the most determined prosecutors.

In the case of rape, there was a further discouragement to prosecution, one that continues to influence the number of cases made public. Those who complained to a magistrate and went forward to trial opened themselves inevitably to publicity and to the embarrassment and pain of having to prove in court that an attack had taken place and that it was indeed a rape, that the accused had had carnal knowledge of her "forcibly and against her will." To get a conviction it was necessary to prove that the rape had actually been accomplished, that there had been penetration. Elizabeth Hewet, who was attacked by a soldier near Farnham, told the court at his trial that he had thrown her to the ground and "lay with me, and entered his————into my————. I cried out murder as long as ever I was able; he stopt my mouth with my apron; I had hardly breath, and was near almost gone. He hurt me very much." The editor of the printed account of the trial, from which this comes, then added, "This witness fully proved every minute circumstance necessary in the sense of the law, to constitute a rape," which "for the sake of common decency" he thought they were "obliged to conceal from the public."[111] The insistence by the men who made the laws and administered justice that "every minute circumstance" be proved did not arise from prurience or from a lack of regard for the seriousness of the offense. Rape had been excluded from benefit of clergy in 1576, and men continued to be hanged for it in the eighteenth century. Their circumspection arose from the view that the charge of rape was more easily made than disproved. The courts were highly sensitive to the ease with which a malicious accusation could be made. In his brief discussion of the offense, Blackstone quoted Hale's caution that

> "rape is a most detestable crime, and therefore ought severely
> and impartially to be punished with death; but it must be
> remembered, that it is an accusation easy to be made, hard to
> be proved, but harder to be defended by the party accused,
> though innocent." He then relates [Blackstone goes on] two
> very extraordinary cases of malicious prosecution for this crime,
> that had happened within his own observation; and concludes
> thus; "I mention these instances, that we may be the more
> cautious upon trials of offences of this nature, wherein the court
> and jury may with so much ease be imposed upon, without
> great care and vigilance; the heinousness of the offence many
> times transporting the judge and jury with so much indignation,
> that they are over-hastily carried to the conviction of the person
> accused thereof, by the confident testimony of sometimes false
> and malicious witnesses."[112]

Perjury was acknowledged to be a serious and fundamental problem, and especially of course in capital cases. But there was an unusually high

---

[111] S.A.P., Lent 1759, pp. 9–11 (Tibbs).
[112] Blackstone, *Commentaries*, vol. 4, p. 215.

level of concern in rape, and the result was that a woman bringing a charge and giving evidence in court opened herself to an investigation into her life, for if the defense could show that she was not of good character, doubt might be thrown on the accusation. In addition the courts were likely to discount her testimony if it could be shown that she had not reported the attack immediately, or had not at least told someone about it. It was also taken to be a weakness in the case if during the attack she made no attempt to cry out for help (this is the significance of the evidence given by the woman in Farnham that her apron was stuffed into her mouth). All of these possible weaknesses in the case could be examined in court.

Some women were indeed perhaps tempted to accuse men falsely, and trials did on occasion turn up evidence that at the least complicated the accusation sufficiently to win the accused man an acquittal. John Harris, who was accused of raping a married woman in St. George's Fields with whom he had spent most of the day and as he was escorting her home at night, proved in court that they had shared a bottle of wine together after their sexual relations. This, along with the suggestion that the woman needed a story to tell her husband to explain her lateness, threw sufficient doubt on the charge to get him acquitted.[113]

The character of the accused and defendant was a matter of routine interest in all trials in this period, especially when the defendant's life was at stake. "One excellence of the trial by jury," Blackstone said, "is that the jury are triers of the credit of the witnesses, as well as of the truth of the facts."[114] In rape trials it was especially the case that the credit of the witnesses and particularly of the woman who brought the charge was very often the leading issue in the trial. Even without the kind of organized defense that counsel might provide (and few defendants yet had counsel), the court looked for evidence of the victim's character and past life, and any doubts raised by this were often sufficient to overthrow the charge. The brief report of the trial of a Lambeth victualler accused of raping his servant girl states simply that he was acquitted when it appeared "that she had not the best of characters."[115]

It is thus hardly surprising that only a few women brought rape charges to court. As we will see, over the period 1660 to 1800 a case came before the Surrey assizes on average once every year and a half and before the Sussex courts only once every four years. And if one can judge from the dozen or so cases contained in the printed accounts of Surrey assize trials in the eighteenth century, the cases that most commonly did

[113] S.A.P., Lent 1726, p. 1 (Harris).
[114] Blackstone, *Commentaries*, vol. 4, p. 214.
[115] S.A.P., Lent 1745, p. 13 (Highfield).

come forward had a particular character: either the woman had been so seriously injured that this not only provided evidence of the attack but also brought it to the attention of others who might have encouraged her to report and prosecute; or the rape had actually been interrupted by witnesses who not only encouraged the prosecution but also provided evidence. A man who raped a girl of sixteen on Abinger Common was seized in the middle of the attack by a farmer and his son who took him to a magistrate and gave evidence that she was gagged and moaning in pain. There was thus no question about her unwillingness, and he was tried, convicted, and hanged.[116] In another case a destitute woman, "very big with child," had applied "for assistance at a public house" in Croydon where three men were drinking. Under pretense of helping her find a lodging for the night, they took her in fact to a hay loft "where all severally lay with her." They were caught because the landlord wondered why they had not returned and went in search of them. It was presumably his reporting of the offense that brought them before the assizes.[117]

Other cases came before the Surrey assizes, it would seem, because the woman had to seek medical attention and the story came out that way; very often in these cases the prosecution was encouraged by others. The woman attacked by the soldier at Farnham did not report the rape immediately. She did not live at home, but "with an old woman," and it was only when she became ill "with the foul disease" and had to seek the help of a surgeon and an apothecary that the story came out, her family became involved, and she was taken by her brother to the army camp near Farnham, where she identified the soldier. He too was convicted and hanged.[118]

This handful of cases in the Surrey Assize Proceedings suggests that few women on their own reported rape to a magistrate. Indeed in many of the cases involving a sexual attack that did come to court the victim was not an adult woman but a child. The same statute of 1576 that removed benefit of clergy from rape also made the offense of carnally knowing and abusing a girl under ten years of age a capital crime. Five of the dozen cases involving sexual attacks by men on women included in the printed Surrey reports were under that provision, and it is clear from other evidence that such cases quite often came before magistrates.

Some of the cases in Surrey involved children as young as two and three years of age. In one, Samuel Ravenscroft, an attorney's clerk in Southwark, was accused of an "assault with an intent to ravish" his master's

[116] S.A.P., Summer 1718, p. 5 (Yeowell).
[117] S.A.P., Summer 1764, p. 8 (Banister et al.); *G. M.* 33 (1763), p. 612.
[118] S.A.P., Lent 1759, pp. 9–11 (Tibbs).

daughter of three, with whom he shared a bed in his master's house. The child had been found "inflam'd and excoriated" and was discovered to have the clap. Ravenscroft had blamed it on a ten-year-old boy who also slept with them, but a doctor testified that it was "not possible such a Youth should contract the foul Disease and give it to a child." The clerk had left his master's house when the accusation was made and negotiations about what might be done proceeded between them. It was only because Ravenscroft and his family would not accept the attorney's demands that it came to trial at all. The young man had begged in a revealing letter that "the troublesome affair might be made an End of and neither he nor his Parents expos'd to the *Vox Populi*," and he offered to "make satisfaction for the Injury done to him and his." For his part the attorney was unwilling to accept mere monetary satisfaction and insisted on punishment: he wanted Ravenscroft's father to transport his son "for he could not bear to see or hear of a Person that had done such an Injury to his Child." The father's unwillingness to do this led to the charge being laid. Ravenscroft was convicted of an assault with intent and sentenced to a year in jail.[119] The cases that got prosecuted had often come to light, like this one, because the child got venereal disease and the parents extracted a story from her of how a lodger or a servant or a neighbor had, as one child said, "put a rabbit under her petticoat." It was common for adults and children to share beds, and it is thus hardly surprising that such cases came forward with some regularity.[120]

Not many complaints of this kind were pressed forward to trial, in part because of the difficulties surrounding the evidence of a very young child especially in a capital case. The courts were as anxious as in rape cases that men not be falsely convicted, and that could make for a hostile atmosphere.[121] The families of these children were as reluctant to prosecute

---

[119] S.A.P., Summer 1738, pp. 17–18 (Ravenscroft).

[120] For depositions in several such cases over a three-year period in the 1760s in Surrey see QS 2/6, Xmas 1764, 41; Mich. 1764, 34; Xmas 1766, 84; Ea. 1767, 43.

[121] There was clearly some confusion in the eighteenth century about the validity of children's evidence. In a case at the Surrey assizes in 1726 the evidence of a seven-year-old girl was disallowed (after a good deal of argument and brandishing of authorities) on the grounds that she was under the age of discretion, that is, twelve (R vs. Travers: Strange, *Reports*, vol. 1, pp. 700–1; *Eng. Rep.* vol. 93, pp. 793–94 [1726]). Hale had thought that children under twelve could be sworn if it appeared to the court that they understood what an oath meant, and that even if she was not sworn, a girl under twelve who was the alleged victim of a sexual crime should be allowed to tell her story in court (*Pleas of the Crown*, vol. 1, p. 634). In the eighteenth century many children were in fact sworn in court and their testimony taken; in addition, the courts often accepted as evidence what the child had told her parents. A ten-year-old girl was allowed to give evidence against her mother's seventeen-year-old apprentice after this exchange with the judge:

as women who had been raped. Some agreed to forego trial and accept compensation instead. In the Ravenscroft case the accused man himself wrote to make an offer to the victim's father. On other occasions magistrates acted as intermediaries, as in an ordinary assault case. Similar agreements clearly kept a number of more straightforward rape cases out of the courts. A Kent magistrate records two instances in 1773 and 1780 of a man "making satisfaction" to a woman he had attacked. In one, the magistrate took the evidence of both parties when the woman complained of being "misused" and recommended that they "settle the matter" by the man paying her a guinea; in the other, the "satisfaction" was made in an unspecified amount.[122]

Many women who did press on to trial charged their attacker simply with attempted rape, which was a misdemeanor and not therefore a capital offense, in order no doubt to avoid the unpleasantness that a rape trial would entail. Blackstone thought that indictments for attempts were "much more usual, than for the absolute perpetration of the facts themselves, on account of the difficulty of proof."[123] It was not necessary to prove in attempted rape that penetration had occurred, but simply that that was what the attacker had had in mind, and it is clear that many women who might have succesfully pressed charges of rape swore only to an assault and attempt. The pregnant woman who was attacked by the three men in Croydon "from a great tenderness and Delicacy natural to

---

JUDGE: You are going to swear upon the bible; do you know what is the consequence of taking an oath if you speak falsely?

CHILD: I shall go to the naughty man?

JUDGE: What do you mean by going to the naughty man?

CHILD: Going to the devil.

JUDGE: Suppose you should speak the truth?

CHILD: I shall go to God Almighty.

She went on to tell what Robert Newberry had done to her. Her evidence, and the fact that she had the clap (as did he), condemned him, and he was sentenced to death (S.A.P., Lent 1759, p. 15). But some children simply could not give evidence in what must have been extremely frightening circumstances. It did not help when the judge barked at one terrified child under ten who simply could not speak, "Why don't you tell the truth, child? What is the matter?" The judges in Brazier's Case in 1779 settled that "no hearsay evidence can be given of the declarations of a child who hath not capacity to be sworn, nor can such a child be examined in court without oath: and that there is no determinate age at which the oath of a child ought either to be admitted or rejected" (Blackstone, *Commentaries*, 12th ed. [1795], vol. 4, p. 214). For Hale's views see Langbein, "Criminal Trial before the Lawyers," p. 294, n. 87.

   [122] Add Mss. 42599, ff. 77, 83.
   [123] Blackstone, *Commentaries*, vol. 4, pp. 216–17.

her, would not swear to the Rape, so that the Prisoners were acquitted of that Charge, and again indicted for an assault only." They were convicted of that, but only sentenced to be imprisoned for four months, since they had been in jail already for eight months awaiting trial.[124]

A further advantage of charging intent was that the lesser offense could be tried at the quarter sessions, which was certainly less expensive and for most prosecutors probably more convenient than attendance at the assizes. Along with the likelihood that a woman would not be exposed in such a trial to a searching cross-examination, that explains why attempt became the most common charge by the eighteenth century. Blackstone was right about the numbers of cases, at least in Surrey, where twice as many women pressed charges of attempted rape as of rape itself—eighty-six, compared with forty-two in our sixty-one-year sample (table 3.7). It is perhaps significant that more of the rape charges arose in rural than in urban parishes. It seems likely that that reflects the crucial role of family and close friends in the prosecution of a rape case. Women were more likely to be living on their own in the urban parishes in and around London than in villages and small towns, and without encouragement and support and the indignation of relatives, women were perhaps more anxious to press prosecutions for rape mainly in the form of assault with intent. In Sussex, where many fewer cases were reported even than in Surrey, the charge was brought as often in its full form as in the lesser (table 3.8).

Although the numbers involved are very small indeed, there is a noticeable increase in Surrey in the level of reported cases over time, particularly in prosecutions for attempted rape. It seems reasonable to think that this reflects mainly an increasing willingness to prosecute. A decided reluctance seems very clear indeed in the seventeenth century, when not even one case a year was prosecuted on average and when charges that alleged something less than rape itself appear to have been subsumed under indictments for common assault. A gradual change is apparent over the first half of the eighteenth century. Some of the increase, particularly after 1750, can be explained by the increasing population, but it seems apparent that women became more willing in the century to prosecute sexual attacks on them than they had been a hundred years earlier, though it needs of course to be emphasized that the number who did so was still very small, no more than four a year on average at its highest, of rape and attempts together.

If there had been some increased willingness to come forward, it may

---

[124] S.A.P., Summer 1764, p. 8. It was also possible for a judge to sentence a convicted man to stand on the pillory in such cases, and several men were indeed ordered to that extremely unpleasant, even dangerous, form of punishment.

TABLE 3.7

Indictments for Rape and Attempted Rape in Surrey and Sussex

Period	Surrey					Sussex				
	Rape	Attempt	Total	Years	Ind./Year	Rape	Attempt	Total	Years	Ind./Year
1660–1699	8	1	9	12	.75	5	0	5	13	.4
1700–1739	5	15	20	11	1.8	2	3	5	11	.5
1740–1779	16	47	63	25	2.5	5	9	14	25	.6
1780–1802	13	23	36	13	2.8	5	7	12	13	.9
Total	42	86	128	61	2.1	17	19	36	62	.6
	= 32.8%	= 67.2%	= 100.0%			= 47.2%	= 52.8%	= 100.0%		

SOURCE: Sample.

TABLE 3.8

Indictments for Rape and Attempted Rape
in Urban and Rural Surrey

Place	Rape (No.)	Attempt (No.)	Total	Rape (%)	Attempt (%)
Urban parishes	19	53	72	26.4	73.6
Rural parishes	23	33	56	41.1	58.9
Total	42	86	128		
Urban parishes (%)	45.2	61.6			
Rural parishes (%)	54.8	38.4			

SOURCE: Sample.

have derived in part from women's perceptions of the court as slightly
more sympathetic to their plight, slightly more willing to consider women
as victims than earlier views of women as sensuous and morally dangerous
beings might have allowed. A similar shift in perspective and sentiment
seems to lie behind the undermining of the offense of infanticide as defined
by the statute of 1624. It is also apparent that there was a heightened
sensitivity and anxiety about violence in all of its forms over the second
half of the eighteenth century, and that must also have helped to increase
public disapproval of offenses like rape that had earlier been largely hidden.
It is these changing views of violence and of women who had been assaulted
that are likely to be reflected in increasing prosecutions, rather than the
level of rape itself, on which these court cases can throw little light.

CHANGING LEVELS OF VIOLENCE, CHANGING ATTITUDES
TOWARD VIOLENCE?

The level of violence in society is a particularly elusive subject, as indeed
are attitudes toward violence. Such matters can only be partially illumi-
nated by the records of the courts, but they are nonetheless worth enquiring
into briefly in the period we are dealing with because there are suggestions
that changes of some significance were in fact taking place in both violent
behavior and the way it was regarded.[125]

[125] For very helpful discussions of trends in violent crime over the long term see Ted Robert
Gurr, "Historical Trends in Violent Crime: A Critical Review of the Evidence, *Crime and Justice:
An Annual Review of Research* 3 (1981), pp. 295–353; and Lawrence Stone, "Interpersonal Violence
in English Society, 1300–1980," *Past and Present* 101 (1983), pp. 22–33.

One indication of attitudes toward violence is to be found in the behavior of crowds, a concern that has been the subject of a great deal of recent work on riots in both rural and urban settings.[126] Much of the work on food riots and other protests and demonstrations in early modern England has been at pains to emphasize that rioting crowds were not invariably violent and destructive, that they were not made up of rampaging hooligans. Emphasis has been placed rather on the self-discipline of protesters and on their tendency to attack property rather than people. But crowds did in fact turn on individuals on occasion, and they were certainly capable of treating their enemies very harshly indeed. It seems reasonable to think that successful protests depended on the threat of such violence and on the widespread acceptance of its legitimacy in certain circumstances—that the power and persuasiveness of a crowd came from its willingness to exercise physical force not only to wreck houses or mills or Dissenters' chapels but also to deal harshly with individuals. It also seems reasonable to think that the crowd's willingness to act violently was not acquired for the occasion, or was simply made palatable by the safety of numbers, but that it arose from a general view of the acceptability of certain kinds of violence. And it must have been acceptable to more than a violent fringe, for large-scale demonstrations depended on mobilizing opinion and getting ordinary men and women to take part.

These thoughts about contemporaries' attitudes toward violence are prompted not so much by the well-known examples of large-scale protests in the eighteenth century as by the activities of other, more spontaneous crowds of men and women especially in the streets of London, crowds whose behavior is likely to have reflected, and to have depended, on broadly shared attitudes and standards. I am thinking, for example, of the engagement of crowds in the punishment of a criminal sentenced to stand on the pillory, an experience that was determined entirely by the crowd that came to watch. On the one hand, they might applaud and take up a collection for a man who was thought to have been unjustly convicted, or whose offense was not regarded as criminal. On the other hand, the crowds at the pillory occasionally treated prisoners with vicious brutality, taunting and pelting them with dirt and stones. Men who had committed

---

[126] See in particular E. P. Thompson, "The Moral Economy of the English Crowd in the 18th Century," *Past and Present* 50 (1971); George Rudé, *Wilkes and Liberty* (1962); the essays of George Rudé collected in *Paris and London in the Eighteenth Century* (1970); George Rudé and E. J. Hobsbawm, *Captain Swing* (1973); Nicholas Rogers, "Popular Protest in Early Hanoverian London," *Past and Present* 79 (1978); W. J. Shelton, *English Hunger and Industrial Disorders* (1973); John Stevenson, *Popular Disturbances in England, 1700–1870* (1979); R. W. Malcolmson, *Life and Labour in England, 1700–1780* (1981), chap. 5; and Geoffrey Holmes, "The Sacheverell Riots," *Past and Present* 72 (1976).

crimes that were especially repulsive, such as sexual crimes against children, were often dealt with harshly by large groups of people, and were even on occasion killed by crowds too strong to be controlled by the authorities, or at least not controlled by the authorities.[127]

Crowds often dealt roughly with other individuals whose behavior was thought to be beyond morally acceptable bounds. Informers were hated, for example, especially those who profited by reporting tradesmen who infringed regulations regarded as unjust. There were many crowd actions against informers when the Gin Act of 1736 presented them with thousands of targets by making it an offense punishable by the stiff fine of ten pounds (half of which went to the informer) or two months in the house of correction to sell gin by retail in amounts under two gallons without a prohibitively expensive license. The point was to reduce the consumption of gin by eliminating the gin shops and small drinking places that had multiplied in London over the previous several decades.[128] The public's hostility toward the law was expressed in a number of disturbances when the Act came into force, but even when these diminished the law continued to be resisted by the deep popular hostility toward those who alone could put it into practice: informers. It is clear that there was no shortage of men and perhaps especially women who were tempted to inform by the handsome rewards; nor should this be surprising considering the difficulties that many people faced in the city and particularly if they were living alone or with small children. The rewards of informing must have been very tempting. But the risks were great, for a powerful counter-regulation existed in the crowds that seemed to form rapidly whenever an informer was identified. The ease and the speed with which the crowd could be gathered is indeed striking, as is the unanimity of their views about what should be done. This makes it clear that the treatment meted out in London to so many informers against gin sellers was widely condoned and was not simply the work of groups that might be thought to have had a special interest in seeing the law repealed. Crowds of ordinary men and women in London felt fully justified in punishing with considerable violence those "idle persons," as a London paper called them in 1738, who "for lucre . . . will never scruple to take any oath right or wrong."[129]

Dozens of examples of the crowd's instant justice were reported in the London press. In 1738, for example, a woman accused of being an informer was surrounded by a crowd who "used her with such severity by beating, kicking and cramming dirt into her mouth" that she was reported

---

[127] On the pillory see below, chap. 9.

[128] Rudé, " 'Mother Gin' and the London Riots of 1736," in *Paris and London in the Eighteenth Century*; Dorothy George, *London Life in the Eighteenth Century* (1925), pp. 40–41.

[129] *London Evening Post*, 4–7 Feb. 1738.

to have died subsequently. In the same week another "enrag'd mob" beat several informers, two of whom, a man and a woman, were thought to have been killed and a third, "used with severe discipline," was expected to die from the blows he had received. Three others were carried away "half-dead" in search of a place where they might hide and recuperate, not being able to find any house "public or private" that would "give them sanctuary."[130] It was also reported that a soldier who had informed

> fell into the hands of the Mob, who pelted him, and dragg'd him through several Horse-Ponds, Channels etc., so that 'tis thought he cannot recover [from] the Treatment he met with. The Mob was so vastly great that all Monmouth-street was almost fill'd with them, and many of the inhabitants were forc'd to shut up Shop; the Soldier liv'd in a Cellar there, where he got in; but the Mob dragg'd him out, tho' his Wife, with his Bayonet, stabb'd two or three of them.[131]

Some of the crowds that surrounded informers were very large, like this one, and not easily dispersed. But large or small, they frequently acted decisively and violently and were often beyond the control of the authorities. Indeed magistrates and constables were often themselves attacked when they were examining informers or conveying gin sellers to jail.[132] These were in no sense bought or manipulated crowds, not specially rounded-up gangs of thugs, but rather groups of ordinary men and women in the London streets who were apparently willing to thrash and even to kill those who violated deeply felt community values. This seems to me to illuminate the high tolerance in the middle of the eighteenth century of physical violence itself. Limits were no doubt drawn in popular belief as well as in law, but the limits were still very wide.

It is an important question whether those limits were changing in significant ways over this period. The court record does not provide a reliable guide to actual behavior, as we have seen. But there are hints in homicide prosecutions and in the courts' treatment of murder and manslaughter, of some change in society's attitudes toward violence, and perhaps in the level of actual violence itself. And there is also a good deal of other evidence of a growing antipathy toward cruelty and extreme physical violence. One can see that on one level in the growing hostility toward violent sports, particularly blood sports like bull-baiting and throwing at cocks, and cruelty to animals in general. There are signs of that before

[130] Ibid., 3–5 Jan., 7–11 Jan., 4–7 Feb. 1738.
[131] Ibid., 9–11 Feb.
[132] Ibid., 21 Jan., 14, 25 Feb., 20 May 1738; S.A.P., Summer 1738, pp. 19–20; *Memoirs of the Life and Times of Sir Thomas Deveil* (1748), p. 40.

1750, but it was particularly strong in the last two decades of the eighteenth century and into the nineteenth.[133] This was surely linked in turn with the more broadly developing sentiment antipathetic to cruelty of other kinds that helped to encourage opposition to the slave trade or support for prison reform or the abolition of capital punishment, all of which emerged toward the end of the century.

A parallel shift of attitudes has been detected in changes taking place over the eighteenth century in the family and in domestic relations. There has been some dispute whether the stimulus for that came from the urban middle class and the gentry or from the aristocracy, but the changes that created a heightened sense of domesticity within marriage and more loving relationships between husbands and wives and between parents and children seem clear by the second half of the eighteenth century. This could not fail to have had a profound effect on what were thought to be acceptable methods of discipline and control. If the image of the husband and father as master of the household did not disappear, the legitimacy of his imposing his will by physical means was to some extent undermined by a growing hostility toward excessive violence and the vicious beating of wives, children, and servants.[134]

These broadly changing ideas about violence, within the family and without, are reflected in stiffening penalties imposed by the courts after the middle of the eighteenth century for wife-beating and the abuse of children, and in the increasing willingness of the courts to establish clearer criminal responsibility in deaths caused by accidents and other manslaughter. Such changes proceeded not in response to legislation, but from a shift in attitude on the part of jurors and judges and from what was at bottom a growing hostility toward forms of physical violence that had been readily accepted a hundred years earlier. One does not have to think that men had earlier been entirely indifferent to violence to accept that there was a quickening of concern about physical abuse and suffering in the second half of the century. Such changes perhaps developed initially among those who had the most profound interest in the establishment of regularity and order in life, particularly merchants, tradesmen, professional men, and manufacturers, whose social views demanded discipline in the working population and an ordered conformity to the needs and demands

[133] Malcolmson, *Popular Recreations*, chap. 7; Keith Thomas, *Man and the Natural World: Changing Attitudes in England, 1500–1800* (1983), esp. chap. 4.

[134] Lawrence Stone, *The Family, Sex and Marriage in England, 1500–1800* (1977), esp. chaps. 6–9; Randolph Trumbach, *The Rise of the Egalitarian Family: Aristocratic Kinship and Domestic Relations in Eighteenth-Century England* (New York, 1978); J. H. Plumb, "The New World of Children in Eighteenth-Century England," *Past and Present* 67 (1975), pp. 64–95.

of commerce and the market in the population in general.[135] But by 1800 such views were widely shared.

It was widely believed by then that a shift in behavior had also taken place. The view was frequently expressed in the early nineteenth century that a considerable change in manners and behavior had occurred over the previous generation or two, particularly in London, which many men remembered as having once been a place of danger and violence. Francis Place collected a great deal of evidence to support and illuminate his conviction that the quality of life in London had been transformed over the last three decades of the eighteenth century and into the nineteenth, and that the result was a considerable decline of brutality, of roughness and violent behavior.[136] For Place the change was a product of the expansion of trade and industry, and with it of greater wealth and better education. It was his view that

> the progress made in refinement of manners and morals seems
> to have gone on simultaneously with the improvement in arts,
> manufactures, and commerce. It moved slowly at first, but has
> been constantly increasing in velocity. Some say we have refined
> away all our simplicity, and have become artificial, hypocritical,
> and on the whole worse than we were half a century ago. This
> is a common belief, but it is a false one, we are a much better
> people than we were then, better instructed, more sincere and
> kind-hearted, less gross and brutal, and have fewer of the con-
> comitant vices of a less civilized state.[137]

There is further evidence of a real change in behavior in the apparent decline of violent forms of property crime in this period, particularly robbery. We will examine this in more detail in the next chapter, but it is worth noting here the decline of prosecutions for such violent property crimes because it seems improbable that the falling away of cases could be fully explained by changes in sentiment. Robbery remained a deeply disliked offense, and even the growing objections to capital punishment in the late eighteenth century are unlikely to explain its decline. Many

---

[135] "Commerce and manufactures gradually introduced order and good government, and with them, the liberty and security of individuals, among the inhabitants of the country, who had before lived almost in a continual state of war with their neighbours, and of servile dependency upon their superiors" (Adam Smith, *Wealth of Nations*, ed. Edwin Cannan [Chicago, 1976], vol. 1, p. 437, quoted in Alan Macfarlane, *The Justice and the Mare's Ale* [1981], p. 2).

[136] See, for example, Add Mss. 27823, a volume of extracts from eighteenth-century newspapers and other sources illustrating what Place called the "grossness and immorality" of the 1780s and before, and demonstrating the changes that he was convinced had occurred by the 1820s. See also *The Autobiography of Francis Place*, ed. Mary Thrale (Cambridge, 1972), pp. 14–16, 74–82.

[137] Place, *Autobiography*, p. 82.

contemporaries thought that violent property crimes were diminishing. The most extensive evidence of this comes from the parliamentary committees that looked into the police of the metropolis and investigated the criminal law in the first three decades of the nineteenth century. In 1816, for example, several police officers with experience of London crime spoke about changes they thought had taken place in their lifetimes. One who had been a constable at Bow Street since about 1780 said that "with respect to cruelty in robbery, such desperate things as we had formerly, there is not a thing [now] to be compared to." He went on to say "there are no footpad robberies or road robberies now, but merely jostling you in the streets. They used to be ready to pop at a man as soon as he let down his glass; that was by bandittis. . . ." Another man who had been at Bow Street at the time of the Gordon Riots, recalling how years before large gangs had terrorized people in the streets of the city, said that an officer "could not walk in Duck-lane, Gravel-lane, or Cock-lane, without a party of five or six men along with him, they would have cut him to pieces if he was alone." That kind of gang, he added, no longer existed.[138] Of course these men were anxious to show that the new police offices established by the 1792 Act and the constables attached to them had had a profound effect on "the manners and morals" of the lower classes. But many men besides police officers told this committee that while crime against property was as extensive as ever, it was much less "atrocious" than it had been a generation earlier.[139]

Attitudes toward violence and the character of violence itself both appear to have changed in some significant ways in the later eighteenth century, each no doubt encouraged by the other. It suggests that this period may be an important point in what was clearly a very long term transformation of the place of violence in society, from a period in the late Middle Ages when violence was less restrained by either the state or men's attitudes, to what has come to be the broad disapproval and control of private violence in the modern world. That such a long transition took place in England has recently been denied,[140] but it seems to me that the evidence both of prosecutions and of contemporary opinion supports the view that there were indeed changes in violent behavior in the late eighteenth century, that there was some shifting of the line dividing acceptable from unacceptable conduct and a strengthening of feelings of shame, guilt, and repugnance about acts that had once raised no eyebrows.

Perhaps the clearest indication of such a movement of opinion comes

---

[138] *Parliamentary Papers* (1816), vol. 5, pp. 143, 144, 212.
[139] Ibid., pp. 73–74, 185, 223.
[140] Macfarlane, *The Justice and the Mare's Ale*, pp. 185–99.

from the way the law was administered. It is in the State's attitude toward violence that the new sensibilities are most evident. In the first half of the eighteenth century few questioned the rightness of the massive physical terror deployed by the State to punish convicted criminals and to discourage others. By the early nineteenth century, as we will see, all physical punishments—hanging, public flogging, the pillory—were being widely questioned. The criticism was spurred by their apparent "failure" to prevent crime. But more fundamental surely was the movement of opinion, the unwillingness to accept their legitimacy. The State's violence changed character as the opinion changed upon which it depended for its effectiveness. And it seems likely that such a change of opinion would not have emerged so clearly had there not also been some significant change in actual behavior, in the character of serious violence over the eighteenth century, and if England, and perhaps especially the metropolis of London, had not been a less violent and dangerous place in 1800 than it had been at the Restoration of Charles II.

CHAPTER 4

PROPERTY OFFENSES
AND OFFENDERS

Of the serious offenses prosecuted before the Surrey courts, those involving the taking of property were by far the most common. At the assizes the occasional murder trial or an infanticide or rape case might capture more attention and would almost certainly be reported more fully in any printed account of the session. But the assize court would not have met often or for long if such forms of personal violence had been its only concern. Day in and day out its main work was provided by the wide variety of offenses in which men alleged that someone had taken something of value from them. Until the mid-eighteenth century such property cases were less commonly dealt with at the quarter sessions, where the calendar was more likely to be crowded with assaults and misdemeanors and with cases involving economic or administrative irregularities. This balance changed in Surrey in the 1750s, as we will see. In the second half of the century both criminal courts in Surrey were largely concerned with property offenses, and allegations of theft, robbery, and burglary formed then an even larger proportion of all cases being tried in the county by way of indictment.

Crimes against property varied enormously. They differed most obviously in the nature and value of the goods stolen, for the category "property crime" accommodated on the one hand the burglary in which the Archbishop of Canterbury lost twelve hundred pounds' worth of plate and other valuables, and on the other the loss of a pile of rags valued at two pence. The value of the goods taken was indeed crucial to the definition of the offense in a number of respects, the most important being the fundamental distinction long made in the criminal law between grand and petty larceny: the theft of goods valued at a shilling or more was grand larceny and a capital felony at common law, while thefts of under a shilling were petty larceny and noncapital. Beyond that, the question of the value of the goods stolen came to play a crucial role in another aspect of the definition of offenses, for it helped to shape the rules governing the application of benefit of clergy; and the way that fiction was applied in 1660 and its changing scope thereafter largely determined the character of the criminal law over the period we are dealing with. Benefit of clergy and the consequences that followed from it changed in significant ways in the century and a half after the Restoration, but whether an offense was within clergy or had been excluded from its privileges continued to be the most significant determinant of the way it was regarded by the public and the way it was treated by the courts.

BENEFIT OF CLERGY AND OFFENSES AGAINST PROPERTY

Originally, benefit of clergy had arisen from the claims of churchmen to be subject only to the jurisdiction of the ecclesiastical courts, even for secular offenses, and which had resulted in a compromise by which clerks were to be indicted and tried in the king's court but if convicted were to be allowed to claim the benefit of their clergy and be delivered to the ordinary to be punished.[1] That was the practice at least by the fourteenth century, but by then, too, the original and narrow meaning of the privilege had been broadened both in practice and in statute to take in others than ordained clerks, and it was this broadening of the scope of clergy that made it so fundamental a determinant of the shape and character of the criminal law over the early modern period. The history of clergy is complex, and its evolution cannot be followed here in detail. But its main outlines need to be sketched, especially changes in the law relating to clergy from the sixteenth through the eighteenth centuries, to enable us to follow the way the main offenses against property were categorized by the courts in the period 1660 to 1800. Changes in two related aspects of the subject need to be followed in particular: offenders to whom clergy was allowed, and the offenses to which it applied.

We may begin with eligibility. The original intention was that it would be confined to the ordained clergy, but by the fourteenth century the courts were accepting as proof of clerical status a test that was to act over several centuries as a means by which benefit of clergy was extended to a larger and larger circle of claimants. This was the proof of literacy, the demonstration of which usually took place in the court just before sentence was to be pronounced by the prisoner being asked to read a verse from the Psalms. That was to be the means by which clergy became a massive fiction that tempered in practice the harshness of the common law rule that virtually all felonies were capital offenses. With the estab-

[1] On the history of benefit of clergy see John Baker, ed., *The Reports of Sir John Spelman*, Seldon Society, 2 vols. (1978), vol. 2, pp. 327–34; Stephen, *History of the Criminal Law*, vol. 1, pp. 457–73; Langbein, "Shaping the Eighteenth-Century Criminal Trial," pp. 37–41.

lishment of the rule that literacy brought benefit of clergy and thus fore-stalled the death sentence, the way was open for laymen who could read to save themselves from the gallows and, more to the point, for the courts to grant clergy to those deemed to have read. Clergy was broadened by these means over the fourteenth and fifteenth centuries. A statute of 1487, indeed, enacted that those not actually in orders would be allowed clergy once only and, to ensure that it would be denied them on their second conviction, laid it down that murderers granted clergy would be branded in court with an *M* on the brawn of the thumb and those convicted of theft with a *T*.[2] The rule forbidding clergy to second offenders was not being applied with any consistency by Elizabeth's reign (if it ever had been), and it simply added another element to the discretionary authority of the judges.[3] The link with the ecclesiastical courts was also entirely broken in 1576, when the requirement that the clergied offender be turned over to the ordinary to undergo purgation was abolished.[4] Henceforth, the successful pleading of clergy was to be followed by immediate dis-charge. The statute authorized the judge to imprison a clergied prisoner for up to a year if he thought fit, but in fact that was rarely insisted on, then or later. Benefit of clergy retained for some time thereafter one reminder of its roots in that it was not until 1623 that it was made available to women in a limited way and not until seventy years later that women were allowed to plead the privilege on the same footing as men.[5]

The situation in 1660 was thus that with some significant exceptions, as we will see, men convicted of offenses to which clergy applied were likely to be granted it whether they could read or not, and women who came within the provisions of the statute of 1623 were allowed its benefits without any literacy test. By the end of the seventeenth century, the point of the test was sufficiently obscure and its usefulness sufficiently diminished (and perhaps the newly created anomaly of its applying to men and not women sufficiently clear) that it could be abolished by statute. In 1706, in an Act that introduced a number of changes in the law, the reading test was abandoned.[6] Thereafter, the fate of convicted felons would rest not on their sex or status (as signaled by their ability to read) but on the crime they had committed. It remained the rule that clergy was to be

---

[2] 4 Hen VII, c. 13 (1487).

[3] Cockburn, *Assize Records: Introduction*, chap. 9.

[4] 18 Eliz I, c. 7, ss. 2, 3 (1576).

[5] By 21 Jas I, c. 6 (1623), women convicted of theft under ten shillings were allowed to plead benefits similar to those of clergy and would be saved from the sentence of death that would otherwise be passed upon them. The full rights to the privilege on the same terms as men were conferred on women by 3 and 4 Wm and M, c. 9, s. 6 (1691).

[6] 5 Anne, c. 6, s. 6 (1706).

available to an offender once only; proof of a prior clergied conviction disqualified him from further benefit. That was disregarded in practice, however, and after 1706 a clear distinction emerged for the first time between capital and noncapital offenses as the distinction between those who might or might not qualify for clergy disappeared. It is worth noting that in a century in which the criminal law was to become increasingly bloody, the 1706 Act saved numerous illiterate men from the threat of capital punishment who earlier had to depend on the courts' overlooking the fact that they did not strictly qualify for clergy.

Although benefit of clergy was thus expanding, another transformation was working in the other direction to restrict the offenses to which it applied. In 1485, with very minor exceptions, clergy was available in all felonies. But as more and more men came within its qualifications, and perhaps as the number of serious offenses appeared to increase, the government in the sixteenth century sought to stiffen the penalties for particularly heinous crimes by excluding them from clergy and thus making them capital for all offenders, literate or not. The first such removal came in 1497 when men convicted of petty treason (killing their "lord, master, or sovereign immediate") were deprived of the right to plead their clergy upon conviction because, the statute announced, such murders had been encouragd by the offenders' belief that clergy would save them from hanging.[7] In 1512 and 1531 certain other forms of murder and robbery were excluded from clergy, and a major statute in 1547 added several other offenses thought to be both prevalent and dangerous. Clergy was removed by this Act from murder, housebreaking (when there was someone in the house who was "put in fear"), highway robbery, horse-stealing, and theft from churches. In Elizabeth's reign pocket-picking was added in 1565 and burglary in 1576.[8]

By the end of the sixteenth century, then, several of the more threatening crimes had been made capital for all convicted offenders by being excluded from clergy. The list included the most serious offenses against the person—murder and rape—and property crimes that threatened violence against the victim: highway robbery, burglary, and some forms of breaking and entering. One or two larcenies had also been made capital in this way, presumably because of the value of the object stolen (as in the case of horse-theft) or the difficulty of preventing the offense (picking pockets). But on the whole larceny remained clergyable, and most of those convicted of theft were not in fact hanged.

Thus things stood at the Restoration. There had been few changes

---

[7] 12 Hen VII, c. 7 (1497).

[8] 1 Ed VI, c. 2, s. 10 (1547); 8 Eliz I, c. 4, s. 2 (1565); 18 Eliz I, c. 7 (1576).

in the scope of clergy since 1600, with the important exception of the inclusion of women convicted of thefts of less than ten shillings in 1623, and indeed few changes were to be made in the next thirty years.[9] There was in this period, however, an evident dissatisfaction in the courts with the sanctions available for the punishment of clergyable offenses and an anxiety to create stiffer alternatives than mere branding on the thumb. It was perhaps one consequence of the failure to find such alternatives that the scope of benefit of clergy was much further narrowed than it had been in the sixteenth century.

This second wave of restrictions on clergy began soon after the Revolution of 1689 in a period in which there was a good deal of concern about the moral health of society and what seemed to many men an alarming increase in the level of crime. Indeed it was only one of a number of responses. It was in the 1690s, for example, that rewards for the apprehension and conviction of certain offenders were first offered by statute. And for a few years in this period (1699 to 1706) the courts were authorized to brand a clergied offender on the cheek rather than the thumb in an attempt, clearly, to stiffen the consequences of a successful plea of clergy. But the main effort to increase the terrors of the criminal law was by way of a return to the Tudor policy of enlarging the effective scope of the death penalty by removing particular offenses from the clergyable category. This began again in a major way soon after the Revolution. During the reigns of William and Anne a number of property crimes were excluded from clergy: these included taking goods from a house when the owner was present and put in fear, and breaking into houses, shops, and warehouses and stealing to the value of five shillings (1691); shoplifting to the value of five shillings and thefts to the same value from stables and warehouses (1699); and theft from a house or outhouse to the value of forty shillings, even without breaking in and even if no one was present (1713).[10]

These post-Revolution statutes that removed clergy from a number of larcenies defined in terms of the place and value of the theft established a pattern that was to be repeated in other statutes in the following century. Unlike the Tudor statutes, these eighteenth-century restrictions on clergy tended to be aimed at essentially trivial offenses that appeared (to someone) to be increasing. They proceeded from a habit of mind that thought of the gallows as the only real deterrent, and they proliferated in part because momentary and sudden anxieties could be much more easily translated

---

[9] A statute of 1670—22 Chas II, c. 5—did remove from clergy the theft of cloth from racks during the process of manufacture, although it also made it possible for the judge to reprieve a condemned offender and to order that he be transported for seven years (s. 4).

[10] 3 and 4 Wm and M, c. 9 (1691); 10 and 11 Wm III, c. 23 (1699); 12 Anne, c. 7 (1713).

into legislation now that parliament was meeting regularly for the first time. It remains unclear how much of this legislation originated as government business and how much simply from the efforts of interested groups inside and outside parliament. The latter seem on the face of it to have been more important. Blackstone was to complain that the reshaping of the criminal law was left "as a matter of indifference to the passions or interests of a few, who upon temporary motives may prefer or support such a bill." Certainly at least one statute removing clergy from a form of larceny, the Sheep-stealing Act of 1741, seems clearly to have arisen simply in response to the complaints of a number of farmers and to have been treated as a species of local business.[11]

Most of the statutes restricting the scope of benefit of clergy after 1689 appear to have been passed without much debate or much investigation into their implications. They were not part of any larger view of the criminal law and its administration. Nor did they proceed from any particular political persuasion. They were not imposed upon the country as part of a new Whig social and economic vision or as an aspect of the oligarchic political stability established after 1714. The scope of capital punishment had been enlarged significantly before the Hanoverian succession; and indeed two of the major statutes that provided for the withdrawal of clergy from forms of larceny were passed in 1699 and 1713 by parliaments dominated by country and Tory sensibilities. The statutes of William's and Anne's reigns provided models for further restrictions of clergy in the eighteenth century: not only was sheep-stealing removed in 1741, but also cattle-theft (1742), theft from a bleaching ground of linen or cotton cloth worth ten shillings or more (1731, 1745), theft from a ship in a navigable river or from a wharf goods valued at forty shillings or more (1751), theft from the mails (1765), and other offenses.[12]

Apart from the changes introduced by the restrictions on benefit of clergy, the criminal law was also enlarged in the eighteenth century by another stream of enactments that extended the scope of existing offenses or created new offenses, some as felonies without benefit of clergy. The most striking single piece of such legislation was the notorious Black Act of 1723, which both removed dozens of felonies from clergy and created others, and which made it a capital offense to appear armed and disguised (with the face blackened) in a public place, or maliciously to shoot at someone, to attack deer, to steal conies and hares from warrens, to break down the heads of fishponds, or to cut down or damage trees.[13] In numerous

---

[11] Blackstone, *Commentaries*, vol. 4, p. 4. For the Sheep-stealing Act see below, text at n. 63.

[12] For these statutes, and more generally for the changes in the law in the eighteenth century, see Radzinowicz, *History*, vol, 1, app. 1.

[13] On the Black Act see Thompson, *Whigs and Hunters*.

other ways, in both statutes and judicial decisions, the boundaries of other offenses were also extended. The definition of larceny was widened in the course of the century, for example, to take in objects that earlier, as it were, had not been capable of being stolen: objects affixed to buildings or to the soil, or things of a "base nature" such as dogs or ferrets, as well as animals *ferae naturae* like hares, conies, and fish. A series of enactments also extended the law against forgery of specific documents, supplementing a general statute of 1729 that had removed forgery from benefit of clergy. Further enactments extended the borderland of larceny by clarifying the criminal character of obtaining goods by false pretenses and fraud and embezzlement by servants and employers.[14]

Offenses against property thus came before the courts in the eighteenth century in several broad categories, and the discussion in this chapter will deal with each in turn. An alternative might have been to organize the discussion of property crimes around the nature of the objects stolen, an approach that would perhaps more effectively establish the context of offenses and help to place them within the framework of the local economy.[15] I have adopted such an approach in dealing with some aspects of clergyable larceny. But the distinctions established in the law remain the basis of our discussion, in large part because they are crucial to the themes we take up in the second part of the book. The most important distinction from the court's point of view was that between clergyable and nonclergyable felonies, which effectively separated noncapital from capital crimes. But within each group, and within the second in particular, some offenses were regarded with special distaste by the public and the courts, and it seems wise for us to recognize those distinctions in our study of the offenses brought before the courts. Thus we will deal first with a group of crimes widely regarded as particularly serious because they not only involved the loss of property but also threatened physical violence, notably robbery and burglary. They had been among the first removed from clergy in the sixteenth century, and they continued in the eighteenth to account for the largest number of convicted property offenders executed, indeed for the largest number of all offenders executed. In Surrey, well over two-thirds of the men hanged between 1660 and 1800 had been convicted of either robbery or burglary.[16] It seems reasonable then to consider these violent offenses separately from other nonclergyable property crimes, which were

---

[14] For the statutes see Chitty, *Criminal Law*, vol. 3, pp. 929–34; and Hawkins, *Pleas of the Crown*, 8th ed. (1824), vol. 1, pp. 142–212. And for their significance see Jerome Hall, *Theft, Law and Society* (New York, 1935; repr. 1952), chaps. 2–3; and Stephen, *History of the Criminal Law*, vol. 3, pp. 121–76.

[15] For such an approach see Hay, "Crime, Authority and the Criminal Law," chap. 2.

[16] See chaps. 9–10.

mainly varieties of larceny. The third group of offenses we will examine will be the clergyable larcenies, which formed by far the largest category of property crimes before the courts. We will also examine briefly the handful of offenses that can be categorized as fraud or cheating, but our principal effort will be concentrated on the major property crimes.

The numbers of indictments for offenses in these three categories in the years sampled in Surrey and Sussex are set out in table 4.1. In dealing with these various forms of property crime, my intention will be to break these categories down further and to recover as much as possible the realities that lie behind the terse language of the indictments. By examining evidence in recognizances, trial reports, petitions for pardons, newspaper accounts of offenses, and similar sources, I hope to be able to suggest the range of behavior that was subsumed under these legal categories and to learn something more than can be recovered from the indictment itself about the character of the victims who brought prosecutions and the prisoners they accused, and about the relationship of property offenses and the local economy. In the course of the discussion the numbers of indict-

TABLE 4.1

Indictments for Crimes against Property in Surrey
and Sussex Courts, 1660–1800

Offense	Surrey		Sussex	
	No.	*%*	*No.*	*%*
Robbery	487	7.6	74	4.1
Burglary	463	7.2	149	8.3
Housebreaking	144	2.2	117	6.5
Nonclergyable larcenies				
Theft from house	191	3.0	29	1.6
Theft from shop	79	1.2	11	.6
Theft from warehouse	33	.5	6	.3
Theft from ship, etc.	27	.4	1	.1
Theft from manufactory	29	.5	0	0
Pocket-picking	92	1.4	3	.2
Sheep-stealing	73	1.1	43	2.4
Cattle-theft	3	.1	3	.2
Horse-theft	227	3.5	111	6.2
Simple grand larceny	3514	54.6	769	42.7
Petty larceny	855	13.3	454	25.2
Fraud	220	3.4	33	1.8
Total	6437	100.0	1803	100.2

SOURCE: Sample.

ments prosecuted under these heads will be considered, but the broader question of the general level of property offenses and the fluctuation of prosecutions over time will be reserved for separate treatment in the following chapter, in which the character of property crime will be more fully considered.

ROBBERY

In examining the principles that should govern the punishment of convicted offenders, William Paley concluded in 1785 that three forms of aggravation justified the harshest sanctions: "repetition, cruelty, combination." The most serious crimes were violent offenses committed repeatedly by men in gangs, which were particularly to be condemned because "they endanger life and safety, as well as property: and . . . render the condition of society wretched, by a sense of personal insecurity."[17] Paley went on to illustrate this by the example of burglary which had certainly long been feared and condemned. The act of breaking into a house while the inhabitants were asleep and defenseless had from a very early day been regarded as especially reprehensible, and it was among the first offenses to be removed from clergy. It was also perhaps becoming more common when Paley wrote. For most of the eighteenth century, however, the offense that caused the greatest anxiety was robbery, which always involved the direct confrontation of victim and offender and which all too often in fact led to serious physical violence.

Robbery on the king's highways was particularly feared and had long been regarded as one of the most heinous offenses, no doubt because it threatened not only the safety of individuals but also freedom of travel and commerce, and involved violence in a place especially protected by the king's peace. It was "a great obstruction to trade," a group of Bristol merchants complained in 1723 when offenses were common.[18] Highway robbery was one of the earliest offenses to be removed from benefit of clergy (1531), and it remained long thereafter an offense for which the courts were likely to impose the death penalty. By the late seventeenth century there was clearly a good deal of public disquiet about robbery, particularly perhaps in London, and not only were all forms of robbery excluded from clergy in 1692 but robberies were also the first offenses for which rewards were offered by statute for the apprehension and conviction of offenders.[19]

[17] William Paley, *The Principles of Moral and Political Philosophy* (1785), pp. 536–37.
[18] SP 44/81, p. 91.
[19] 23 Hen VIII, c. 1, s. 3 (1531); 1 Ed VI, c. 12, s. 10 (1547); 3 and 4 Wm and M, c. 9, s. 1 (1691). For rewards see above, chap. 2.

Robbery seems to have acted in many ways as an indicator of the state of "crime" in general, and over much of this period any apparent increase in crime was most likely to be discussed in terms of the increased dangers to life and property posed by the "banditti" who were thought so often to be infesting the roads, particularly the roads around London and the streets of the capital itself. Thus the author of an early-eighteenth-century tract who thought violent crime such a serious problem that only punishments more terrifying than hanging would discourage it spoke of highway robbery as so commonplace that "we shall shortly not dare to travel in England unless, as in the Deserts of Arabia, it be in large Companies, and Arm'd."[20] Robbery was by no means confined to London, but the metropolis and its hinterland seem to have provided conditions by the early eighteenth century in which it flourished: a vast built-up area provided victims as well as cover, and was surrounded by an ever-expanding suburban belt in which the rich and middling classes built their villas and added tempting targets to the flow of traffic constantly moving along the main roads in and out of the capital.

Much of the danger of robbery in the metropolis arose south of the river in Surrey—in the Borough of Southwark and in neighboring urban parishes and particularly along the main roads to the south and southwest that cut through the county. Attacks on traffic along these roads and in the streets of the metropolis were more common in some periods than in others. They tended to diminish during wars, for example, as we will see, and to increase sharply when peace and the demobilized soldiers and sailors returned. The sharpness of the transition played its part in creating the sense of panic that invariably ensued. But what was particularly alarming was the fact that so many of the reported offenses were by gangs of armed and violent men.[21] To judge simply from the number of indictments for robberies brought before the Surrey assizes one would think that the panic that invariably arose at such times was seriously misplaced, since the assize juries were asked to deal with a mere eight cases a year on average between 1660 and 1800. But of course these figures mean very little, for they must have represented a tiny fraction of the offenses committed. Sir John Fielding's rhetorical estimate that "not one in a hundred of these robbers are taken in the fact" may well have been close to the mark in some years.[22] And of course even when men were taken and charged, many of the offenses they might have committed would not appear on the record. The number of offenders indicted does not mean a great deal. One man or a gang could

---

[20] *Hanging, Not Punishment Enough, for Murtherers, High-way Men, and House-breakers. Offered to the Consideration of the two Houses of Parliament* (1701; repr. 1812 by Basil Montagu), p. 8.

[21] On gangs and on the transition from war to peace see below, chap. 5.

[22] Sir John Fielding, *A Plan for Preventing Robberies within Twenty Miles of London* (1755), p. 7.

terrorize a neighborhood for weeks or months, and it would only take a few groups of men operating at the same time, even over a wide area, to create the sense of intense danger that pervades so much of the commentary on crime, especially in the first half of the eighteenth century. The sense of deep anxiety was no doubt exacerbated by the weakness of the forces that could be ranged against groups of armed men. But the sense of alarm and foreboding probably arose mainly from the violence that these men employed. Whether this was in fact "much worse than in former ages," as one man said, it was widely believed to be so, probably because offenses were so much more widely publicized. The newspapers established in London over the first decades of the century and the monthlies like the *Gentleman's Magazine* (1731) reported violent crimes in detail. When one adds the accounts of London trials being published eight times a year by the 1720s and the numerous "lives and dying speeches" of convicts hanged at Tyburn, it is clear that crime formed one of the staple items before the reading public.[23] Then as now, crime fascinated, and violent crime fascinated particularly.

There was also without doubt a good deal of violence to be reported. The likelihood that a victim would be beaten during a robbery differed of course from case to case. But there seems to have been a broad distinction in this regard between street and highway robberies. The main contrast between these was not so much, as was often said, a sharp social difference between the mounted highwayman and the footpad—though many highwaymen at least claimed to be gentlemen and few footpads were, as we will see—but rather the difference that being on horseback or being on foot produced in the relationship between the robber and his victim and the amount of violence that each thought it necessary to use. Certainly most of the horror stories reported in the newspapers arose from attacks by footpads.

Some victims put up a fight and were beaten for that reason, but it is usually difficult to tell from accounts in the press or from printed trial reports why some robbers thought it necessary to deal harshly with their victims. One man told the Surrey assizes in 1726 that he and his mother had been attacked by footpads as they crossed Putney Common between seven and eight at night. He had become alarmed, he said, when he saw two men running after them, but his mother had "encouraged" him "by saying they were working men, and were going home to their families (it being Saturday night)." But one had in fact approached them and "beat

[23] For the Old Bailey Sessions Papers see above, chap. 1, n. 32; and for the Ordinaries' "Account" see Peter Linebaugh, "The Ordinary of Newgate and His 'Account,' " in Cockburn, ed., *Crime in England*, pp. 246–69.

my mother about the head with a pistol," and robbed them of some clothes and five shillings.[24] Presumably many footpads thought it necessary to disable their victims to give themselves time to get away. That seems to be the point of the attack on John Gotobed, an apprentice to a pastry cook who was stopped by two men in St. George's Fields in Southwark in 1738. He told the court at the trial of one of these men that

> on the 13th of May, between 11 and 12 at Night, I was coming from Cuper's-Gardens to my master's on London-Bridge, where I serv'd my time, to work. When I had got half way over the Fields [St. George's Fields], between the Blue-Bell and the Cow-House, the prisoner at the bar (and one Edwards, as I am since inform'd) came up to me, and the prisoner presented a pistol and demanded my money.

> *Court:* What did he say?

> *Gotobed:* He bid me deliver, or I was a dead Man. I had a Link [a torch] in my hand, and saw him before he came up for the Space of 6 Yards. He rifled my Coat-Pockets, and then my breeches, and took the things mentioned in the Indictment [a watch, pair of silver shoe buckles, silver stock buckle, a penknife, a cork screw, a good halfpenny and a bad one]. Then the other Man came behind me, and snatch'd the Link from me, and flung it away, so I could not see his Face so plain as I did the Prisoner's. When they had robb'd me, they ask'd me, if I was a Master or a Servant. I told them, only a Servant; so they bid me go on, and think myself well off, and as I was going away, they beat me very much over the Head with their Sticks, and I bled so much that I could not work: They then went off; but which Way I cannot tell.[25]

The implication is that a master would have been beaten even more seriously, but the servant was sufficiently disabled to prevent his giving an effective alarm. Beatings were in any event common enough that street robbers were the most feared of criminals. London newspapers reported their brutalities regularly. The story of the attack on a man near Ludgate Hill in 1738 by three footpads who cut him with a sword ("so that his teeth and jaw-bone could be seen"), knocked him down "to stop him crying out," and then got a shilling from his pocket and ran off was

[24] S.A.P., Lent 1726, p. 4 (Blackborn).
[25] S.A.P., Summer 1738, pp. 10–11 (Kilburn)

familiar enough in all its essential details to the readers of London newspapers throughout the century.[26]

Such treatment of their victims by footpads contrasted in the public mind and to a considerable extent in reality with the more courteous business of mounted robbery on the highway. Highwaymen were not of course invariably polite and gentle. Victims who resisted or who complained too volubly might well be beaten, and highwaymen whose escape was threatened or whose identity was in danger of being revealed could be as nasty as any street mugger. It was reported in 1722, to take a striking example, that after three highwaymen had robbed a stagecoach, a peddlar woman standing nearby "cried out to the people that she knew the rogues," at which "they turned back and cut her tongue out."[27] And some victims were indeed killed. But there is no doubt that mounted highwaymen were much less in danger of immediate capture and that the circumstances surrounding their robberies allowed them to indulge in a form of polite interchange with their victims that no street robber could have had time for. Courtesy cushioned the experience for both victim and robber and encouraged the pretense that violence was not being threatened. Perhaps highway robbery was for that reason the crime that a gentleman in trouble might naturally turn to since it made such politeness possible and gave room for honorable behavior; it also brought other gentlemanly virtues and accomplishments—horsemanship, daring, skill with weapons—into play.

Whether born to it or not, the tradition was powerful enough to encourage men taking to the road to ape the manners of the polite world. An ironic "letter" in the press from Mr. Maclean, "Esquire and Highwayman," to Ned Slinker, "Footpad, Pick-pocket, and House-breaker," written when they were both in jail "to point out the differences between

[26] *London Evening Post*, 28 Feb. 1738. A few months before, they had read how "Mr. Shenton of the Bank was robbed on the road to Hackney by two footpads who knocked him into a ditch where he lay some hours before he recovered" (28 Jan. 1738), and about a man going at night from Camberwell to Blackman Street who was beaten by two footpads and left for dead because he put up some resistance (19 Aug. 1738). In November of the same year it was reported that Anthony Silk of Peckham, Surrey, was attacked by two street robbers, cut on the face with a sword, severely beaten, and shot at with a pistol (11 Nov. 1738). When they turned from newspapers to the monthly magazines, similar stories kept readers conscious of the violence of the streets in and around London. The *Gentleman's Magazine* for August 1742, to take just one month's reports, listed six robberies in the metropolis in which the victims had been physically assaulted (p. 443).

[27] *Weekly Journal or British Gazeteer*, 25 Apr. 1722. That was sufficiently shocking behavior that when Ralph Wilson published his account of his career as a highwayman and of the doings of the Hawkins gang, he thought it necessary to deny that they had done it (*A Full and Impartial Account of all the Robberies committed by John Hawkins, George Sympson . . . and their Companions* [1722], p. 26).

them" caught the pretensions of the highwayman exactly. Maclean was presumably meant to be James Maclean, a parson's son who indulged in such elaborate courtesies in the course of robbing victims on the roads around London in the middle of the century that he was known as the "gentleman highwayman." He could take comfort, he said

> that I cannot reproach myself with doing any Thing unbecoming a Gentleman. When the scanty Allowance of five Hundred a Year that I had from that Old Gripe my Father was gone, having always entertain'd a just Contempt for the Pedantry of Study, and being above any mechanic Employment, I embraced the only Scheme left for a Man of Spirit, and commenced a *Gentleman of the Shade*; in which Occupation I have acquitted myself with equal Courage, Honour and Genius. There has not been for some years an Instance in the Papers of Generosity, Compliance to Ladies, or Dexterity of Contrivance, that I cannot justly claim the Honour of. . . .[28]

Examples indeed abound in the eighteenth century of highwaymen being excessively polite, especially to women: not pointing their guns, returning some favored object, not searching them. Courteous and amusing repartee was also frequently reported, even pacts of honor into which highwaymen and their victims entered for their mutual advantage, as when a man, robbed of his watch, persuaded the highwayman to accompany him to his house without risk so that he might exchange the watch for two guineas.[29] Frequent reports of such behavior and of the daring and bravado and insouciance of so many men helped to surround the highwayman with an attractive and even heroic aura. The exploits of some became well known, especially when their biographies and "true lives" were published as they came to the gallows. The daring of a Dick Turpin and the astonishing exploits of Jack Sheppard extended the tradition well established by the late seventeenth century of the highwayman as romantic

---

[28] *The Public Advertiser*, 29 Feb. 1764.

[29] *The Public Advertiser*, 1 Mar. 1764. For examples of politeness see *The Weekly Journal or Saturday's Post*, 17 Aug. 1723; S.A.P., Summer 1738, pp. 3–6; *The Universal Spy*, 2 Sept. 1732; SP 36/116, f. 137. For repartee, *G. M.* 33 (1763), p. 200, which reports that a man robbing around London in that year assured his victims that he was heir to a considerable fortune and that he would repay them when he came into it. Another man, having taken a large sum of money from a clergyman, gave him back a guinea "to bear his charges" but refused him his watch, which he begged for because, the highwayman told him, "he was at present without one himself, and as he often wanted to know how Time passed away, he could not oblige him with it" (*London Evening Post*, 23 Feb. 1738). Another told his victims in a stagecoach in 1751 that he needed the money in order to go into mourning for the recently dead Prince of Wales (S.A.P., Summer 1751, p. 31 [Keys]).

figure, a tradition that continued to flourish in the eighteenth century and perhaps especially in the nineteenth, when the highwayman disappeared from the roads and could be more safely romanticized in fiction.[30] The reality of the eighteenth century was that while highwaymen were indeed able to behave differently from those who robbed on foot, the menace that was always just beneath the surface often in fact led to a violent attack on the victim when things went wrong. On the other side, too, it might be noted, highwaymen were occasionally seriously wounded by their intended victims or by armed men riding as guards on stagecoaches.[31]

Another element in the heroic highwayman tradition was his reputed unwillingness to rob the poor and his selection of victims from those who could afford to contribute to his well-being—a view, that is, of the highwayman in some sense as a dispenser of rough justice, if not exactly a Robin Hood, at least not a man of injustice. In his dispute with Ned Slinker, Maclean laid claim to that mantle by revealing that he had "obliged a couple of sneaking foot-pads to refund the week's wages they had taken from a poor labourer."[32] But again the main difference between the mounted highwayman and the street robber in this regard was no doubt that the street robber simply did not have the same opportunity to be discerning about his victims. In London he might be able to attack a rich victim on foot or in a coach, and even on the highways outside the capital footpads in gangs did occasionally attack coaches and men on horseback. But most of their victims were on foot and many of them turned out to be servants and working men and women. In several of the robberies tried at the Surrey assizes the victims had been peddlars, people out in the early morning to buy provisions, or men going to work, or on one occasion a "poor milk woman." This was not the stuff of legends.[33]

Highwaymen, well mounted and armed with a brace of pistols, did not normally find it necessary to relieve such victims of their pennies. They were after larger game: the coaches of the rich, farmers returning from market, or stagecoaches and the mail service. Such targets multiplied

---

[30] For this theme see Keith Hollingsworth, *The Newgate Novel, 1830–1847* (Detroit, 1963).

[31] This did not happen as frequently as some would have liked. When a young highwayman was shot dead on Putney Heath "by a servant behind the coach of a gentleman whom he had just robbed," the *Gentleman's Magazine* thought that a few more "instances of this kind would in all likelihood have a better effect in suppressing robberies than 100 executions" (24 [1754], p. 242). And although highwaymen were shot in Surrey in 1766 and 1779, it was believed by some at least that the gentry were losing their ability or their willingness to defend themselves on the highways. *The Public Advertiser* in 1764 (18 Jan.) linked both this weakness and the spread of insubordination to a loss of martial spirit.

[32] *The Public Advertiser*, 29 Feb. 1764.

[33] S.A.P., Summer 1738, pp. 10–11; Lent 1739, pp. 18–19; Lent 1741, p. 6; Summer 1741, pp. 9–10; Lent 1752, p. 23; Summer 1764, pp. 2–3.

in the course of this period as roads were improved. In the second half of the eighteenth century most of the major roads between London and provincial centers had been turnpiked and were carrying an increasing traffic of coaches and wagons. By the end of the century, for example, several dozen stagecoaches a day left London for Manchester, Bristol, Edinburgh, and numerous other places.[34] In time, and in association with the extension of the built-up area and the improvement of policing, the turnpikes probably did as much as anything to make highway robbery increasingly risky. But for much of the century the balance of advantage from the improved roads probably favored the highwaymen, particularly the rapidity of escape they made possible and the ease of access to London. The improved roads also increased the number of valuable targets in the counties near London.

Surrey, for example, was traversed by several major roads from London to the south and west that were vastly improved in the century and that came to bear a considerably increased load of traffic. The road to Portsmouth ran through Vauxhall to Kingston, Esher, and Guildford (and branches ran from there to Farnham and to Chichester on the south coast). Several other roads ran through the county to the Sussex coast: one went to Brighton via Croydon, Godstone, and East Grinstead; another went from Southwark across Clapham Common through Reigate and Cuckfield; yet another started along the same route and branched off through Epsom, Leatherhead, and Dorking to Horsham and beyond. In addition, the main road to Winchester and the southwest crossed the Thames at Staines after leaving London north of the river and ran for several miles across the northwest corner of Surrey from Egham across Bagshot Heath.[35] Large stretches of these roads south of the capital ran over heaths and commons that provided ideal conditions for the mounted robber. Bagshot Heath was especially notorious as a favorite haunt of highwaymen, and a significant number of the robberies reported in the press and of those prosecuted in the Surrey courts had taken place on the long, lonely stretch of road that ran over that sandy and virtually deserted corner of the county. Reports like the following were common:

> Monday last between the hours of three and four in the afternoon, the Exeter Stage Coach was stopped upon Bagshot Heath on its way to London, and several passengers in it robbed of considerable sums, by a single highwayman, viz. a stout well-made

[34] William Albert, *The Turnpike Road System in England, 1663–1840* (1972), p. 188; Philip S. Bagwell, *The Transport Revolution from 1770* (1974), pp. 41, 43.
[35] Daniel Paterson, *A New and Accurate Description of all the Direct Principal Cross Roads in England and Wales* . . . , 14th ed. (1808).

young man, of middle stature, dressed in a blue surtout coat, brown cut wig, a black crepe mask over his face, mounted on a bright bay gelding. . . .[36]

The roads in and around the capital provided rich possibilities for the enterprising highwayman. The individual traveler might not carry large amounts of money, but those who traveled in coaches could be counted on for a reasonable purse and for watches, silver buckles, and similar valuables. But the targets that increased most temptingly for the determined and daring highwayman were the postboys who carried the mail around the country. A postal system was established by 1660, with postboys carrying the mail along six major routes from London and on a number of cross- and by-routes. This was much extended in the eighteenth century, especially when Ralph Allen managed the cross-road and by-letter system under contract from the Post Office between 1720 and 1762.[37] The mail was tempting because of the promise of bank bills and other negotiable paper, and several of the highwaymen brought before the Surrey assizes had waylaid a postboy and rifled his bags. But it was also a risky business. This was partly because of the suspicions that might be aroused when they tried to pass off the stolen notes and bills: certainly two men who had stopped a postboy on Bagshot Heath carrying the Western and Portsmouth mails were discovered for this reason.[38] It was also chancy because it brought in the government. It might lead to the dispatch of the secretary of state's messengers to investigate, but more certainly and more seriously it would be followed by the offer of a huge reward by the Post Office for the apprehension and conviction of any one of the offenders—rewards of two hundred pounds over and above the forty pounds available by statute were not uncommon—and the offer of a royal pardon to any of them who turned king's evidence.[39]

The effectiveness of such vigorous pursuit and of such large rewards from the government's point of view was revealed by the experience of the Hawkins gang in the 1720s. According to Ralph Wilson, who committed numerous robberies in and around London in company with John Hawkins and George Simpson and others, they were never in danger of being apprehended until they "meddled with the mails." In his account of their

[36] The Public Advertiser, 4 Jan. 1764.
[37] Howard Robinson, The British Post Office: A History (1948); Benjamin Boyce, The Benevolent Man: A Life of Ralph Allen of Bath (1967), pp. 12, 52, 96.
[38] S.A.P., Summer 1740, pp. 2–3; G. M. 10 (1740), pp. 198, 260.
[39] For such rewards see G. M. 10 (1740), p. 198; 16 (1746), p. 437; 25 (1755), p. 153; London Evening Post, 21–23 Feb. 1748, 14–17 Jan. 1749.

robberies, Wilson claims to have warned his confederates of the dangers of attacking the post boys:

> I endeavoured all I could to hinder this Attempt. I told them, that the Nature of our circumstances were such, that of necessity we were firmly attached to one another's Interest, as being all impeached together, which hindered any one designing Person amongst us injuring the other two. That that Union would be dissolved when a Promise of the King's Pardon should be published after such a Robbery, with a Reward as usual. I told them, that the Post-House was indefatigable in their Searches after Men who had robbed them; and lastly, that we should get nothing by it but a Gibbet.[40]

What Wilson described as their "league of friendship" was indeed dissolved when they were hotly pursued by agents of the Post Office after they stole from the mails, and when he was examined before the Post Master General and accepted a pardon and a reward in return for impeaching Hawkins and Simpson.

Before they "meddled with the mails," the three of them and a variety of companions had intermittently over several years committed robberies in the London area. Wilson's account of their mode of operation points to several broad characteristics that appear to have been typical of the activities of mounted highwaymen in this period. One is the obvious point that one gang of men could commit a very large number of offenses over a short period of time. Wilson recalled their making several attacks an evening, two or three times a week for a month or so, followed by a period of lying low. They mainly worked the roads around London, up to about five miles outside, though they also attacked coaches in the built-up area itself. For one period in 1721, when they had a secure connection with a livery stable keeper who lent them horses and took a cut ("his snack") as payment, they were able to get horses safely at any time of the night and so were able to get out of town early enough to prey on the morning stagecoaches. Over a brief period, Wilson claims with probable exaggeration, they "harrass'd" in turn all the coaches leaving London:

> One Morning we robb'd the *Cirencester*, the *Worcester*, the *Glocester*, the *Oxford*, and *Bristol* Stage-Coaches, all together; the next

---

[40] Wilson, *Account of the Robberies*, pp. 19–20. William Hawkins published a reply to Wilson's pamphlet, to defend his brother's character and conduct, entitled *A Full, True and Impartial Account of all the Robberies Committed in City, Town and Country for several Years Past by William Hawkins in Company with Wilson, Wright, Butler Fox and others* (1722). It is a much less interesting account of the London "underworld" than Wilson's.

morning the *Ipswich* and *Colchester*, and a third morning perhaps
the *Portsmouth* Coach. The *Bury* Coach has been our constant
Customer; I think we have touch'd that Coach ten times.[41]

Similar levels of activity by both individuals and gangs of men can be
found over shorter and longer periods of time in the eighteenth century:
confessions of five or ten-year careers in robbery were not uncommon.
When such robbers were finally taken (if they were), a number of victims
might come forward and thus they might face two or three or even more
indictments, each relating to a separate event. But even when highwaymen
were apprehended and charged, the number of indictments they faced bore
little relationship to the offenses they are likely to have committed, and
in robbery especially (since one man could commit so many in a brief
period) the level of indictments provides no meaningful guide to the likely
level of activity.

Over the whole period 1660 to 1800 so few indictments for robbery
were laid before the Surrey assizes on average that little is to be drawn
from their short-term fluctuation. The fact that the offenses prosecuted
had taken place overwhelmingly in the northeastern corner of the county
is perhaps more reliable evidence of the pattern of robbery in Surrey. The
Borough of Southwark was itself the scene of close to a fifth of the county's
robberies, and most of the remainder had taken place in its environs: in
Lambeth and Camberwell in particular, but also in Rotherhithe, Newington, Clapham, and Deptford. This metropolitan area accounted for
fifty-seven percent of all the prosecuted robberies. Another significant
number, about twelve per cent, were alleged to have taken place in parishes
just beyond that ring in Putney, Wimbledon, Kingston, and Croydon, a
little more distant from the capital but clearly within its orbit and within
the range of mounted highwaymen operating from the city. Beyond that,
the parishes of Windlesham and Egham (where the main road to the
southwest crossed Bagshot Heath) were the scene of another five per cent
of the robbery cases brought to the assizes (table 4.2). Altogether, close
to three-quarters of the robberies prosecuted had taken place in the northern
band of the county where the traffic to and from the capital passed and
repassed. The influence of the city is likely indeed to have been even more
pervasive, for many other parts of the county were easily accessible to well-
mounted men.[42]

---

[41] Wilson, *Account of the Robberies*, p. 17.

[42] This perhaps helps to explain why the "rural" parishes of Surrey—those not in the immediate
environs of the city—had a slightly higher level of robbery indictments than the neighboring
county of Sussex. The numbers are too small to make much of this difference, but the parishes
removed from the immediate "urban" influence in Surrey provided 154 prosecutions for robbery
(2.5/an.), while Sussex, with a larger population, had a total over the same 61 years sampled of
74 (1.2/an.).

TABLE 4.2

Robbery in Surrey, 1660–1800

Place	Number of Indictments	Percentage of Total
Southwark and environs	333	68.4
Rural parishes	154	31.6
Total	487	100.0
Boroughs or parishes with ten or more indictments for robbery		
Southwark	86	17.7
Lambeth	77	15.8
Camberwell	52	10.7
Putney	21	4.3
Croydon	14	2.9
Rotherhithe	14	2.9
Clapham	13	2.7
Kingston	12	2.5
Wimbledon	12	2.5
Windlesham	12	2.5
Deptford	11	2.3
Newington	11	2.3
Egham	10	2.1

SOURCE: Sample.

County towns and entirely rural parishes did see an occasional robbery; farmers returning from market, traders attending a fair, and the occasional stagecoach or private coach were held up by mounted highwaymen deep in the Surrey countryside, and even footpads occasionally robbed well away from London. But the distribution of the offenders prosecuted makes it clear that robbery flourished much more naturally in an urban environment. There is no reason to think that it was more difficult to detect and apprehend an offender in a rural parish; on the contrary, it is likely that the indictments understate urban offenses even more than rural. And the pattern that the prosecutions suggest is amply confirmed by a great deal of other evidence, including Ralph Wilson's account of the activities of the Hawkins gang. The conclusion that seems to emerge from this evidence is that in the eighteenth century conditions in and around London were especially conducive to robbery.

In addition to targets, the city provided a network of "safe" public houses and lodging houses, receivers, and liverymen and stable-keepers who would hire out horses without asking too many questions. It was a constant theme of those who thought about the high level of crime in the metropolis in the eighteenth century that much of the blame was to be placed on the weakness of regulation over the large numbers of taverns, pawnbrokers, stable-keepers, and the like; and the solution of increased surveillance and control was as constantly urged. The Fieldings were particularly active in bringing forward such schemes, many specifically aimed at the highwaymen who sheltered in London and pillaged on its outskirts. In designing a plan to discourage robberies on the highways around the capital in the middle of the century, John Fielding based his scheme on "the following facts":

> 1st, That those persons who rob upon the highway, within twenty miles of London, set out from thence for that purpose; 2ndly, That they ride hired horses; 3rdly, That they retire thither for shelter; 4thly, That they are generally taken in town. . . .[43]

And his "plan" rested largely on an appeal to the public to report offenses to Bow Street so that they might be advertised with a description of the offender and the goods stolen, and on rewards that might encourage publicans, pawnbrokers, and stable-keepers to report suspicious characters to the magistrates.

A combination of circumstances made the northern band of Surrey attractive for highway robbery. Some of these circumstances were changing significantly by the early nineteenth century. Mounted police patrols in the highways around the capital and a much extended system of more "professional" constables organized around the stipendiary magistrates' offices improved both the preventative and the detective police and, in conjunction with the advertising of offenses and the system of rewards, made highway robbery a little more risky than it had been. An important further element in this was the very growth of the city itself, particularly after 1780, when the population rose strongly and the built-up area was extended rapidly. One consequence was the disappearance of large parts of the open space so close to the central urban area. St. George's Fields and the open areas in parishes like Clapham, Lambeth, and Putney were much diminished by the early decades of the nineteenth century. So rapidly had such developments taken place that a newspaper in 1810 reminded its readers in some wonder that only a generation earlier "from Blackfriars Bridge to the Elephant and Castle" in Newington (an area then largely built over) "there were not, including both sides of the road, fifty habitations." As an aspect of what it said had been an astonishing transfor-

---

[43] Fielding, *A Plan for Preventing Robberies*, p. 9.

mation, the report went on to the further reminder that "it is not forty years since highway robberies were frequent in St. George's Fields. . . ."[44]

The collection of materials made by Francis Place, of which this newspaper report is part, provides a great deal of evidence along the same lines, evidence that he assembled to illustrate the dramatic change that had taken place in his lifetime in manners and behavior in London, including forms of crime and levels of violence. The diminution of highway robbery was one element in that transformation in London life. Place even remembered people waiting at the "Dog and Duck" and other notorious public houses in St. George's Fields to see the highwaymen mount up at dusk and say farewell to their "flashy women."[45] This memory may be an aspect of the romantic haze in which highwaymen were enveloped in the early nineteenth century, in which the brutality and menace tended to be forgotten and the courage, skill, and freedom of the life magnified. But there had undoubtedly been some significant changes in the generation after 1785.

The patterns of prosecution do not provide a reliable guide to the chronology of that change, partly because so few offenders were brought to court at any time that it is dangerous to draw conclusions about variations in the figures. It is also impossible to tell merely from the indictment whether an attack had been made on foot or by mounted men. Nonetheless, it is worth noting that while the actual number of robbery prosecutions rose very slightly in the last decades of the eighteenth century, measured as a rate of the population the incidence of charges of robbery made between 1780 and 1802 was lower than in any comparable period since 1660 (table 4.3). Street robbery was probably less affected by the building up of London and the development of the police and other changes that helped to discourage robbery on the highway. The latter did in fact rapidly disappear, for Dr. Gatrell has revealed that the last mounted highway robbery was recorded in 1831.[46]

BURGLARY

One other offense caused as much anxiety as robbery and was as harshly dealt with by the courts: burglary, the breaking into a house at night,

---

[44] Add Mss. 27826 (Place collection), clipping from an unidentified newspaper of 1810.

[45] Add Mss. 27826, f. 189; and see Dorothy George, *London Life in the Eighteenth Century* (1925), p. 305. The landlord of the "Dog and Duck" was prosecuted at the quarter sessions in 1776 for encouraging "disorderly women and other persons assembling together by keeping an organ for their entertainment" (QS 2/6, Ea. 1776, 6).

[46] V.A.C. Gatrell, "The Decline of Theft and Violence in Victorian and Edwardian England," in Gatrell, Lenman, and Parker, eds., *Crime and the Law*, p. 317.

TABLE 4.3

Indictments for Robbery over Time in Surrey and Sussex

		Surrey				Sussex		
Period	Years	Total Indictments	Per Year	Rate Per 100,000 Pop.ᵃ	Years	Total Indictments	Per Year	Rate per 100,000 Pop.
1660–1699	12	75	6.25	5.0	13	10	.8	.8
1700–1739	11	95	8.6	6.6	11	7	.6	.6
1740–1779	25	191	7.6	5.0	25	35	1.4	1.4
1780–1802	13	126	9.7	4.1	13	22	1.7	1.2

SOURCE: Sample.

ᵃ The rate is based on an estimate of the population in the middle year of each period.

which was particularly condemned because it violated the privacy and protection of the home and put the inhabitants at risk of being physically assaulted under circumstances in which they could do little to defend themselves. Burglary had been one of the first offenses removed from clergy in the sixteenth century. Other forms of breaking and entering were also made capital in this way under the Tudors: housebreaking during the daylight hours when there was someone at home who was "put in fear," for example; and (at the end of Elizabeth's reign) housebreaking even if there was no one present if goods were stolen of more than five shillings in value.[47]

Clergy was to be much further restricted after the Restoration. An Act of 1691 consolidated earlier legislation and added to the nonclergyable list breaking and entering shops and warehouses connected with a dwelling house.[48] Other buildings and other circumstances were added thereafter, by statute and judicial interpretation (of which there was inevitably a great deal). The result was that the law became increasingly complex in the eighteenth century. It was "apt to create some confusion," Blackstone observed; and William Eden thought that no more than ten men in England "exclusive of those who are obliged by their profession to be conversant in the niceties of the law" understood its provisions.[49] But, simply put, it was a nonclergyable offense in the eighteenth century to

[47] The most important statutes had been 23 Hen VIII, c. 1, s. 3 (1531); 1 Ed VI, c. 12, s. 10 (1547); 5 and 6 Ed VI, c. 9, s. 4 (1552); 18 Eliz I, c. 7 (1576); 39 Eliz I, c. 15, s. 2 (1597).

[48] 3 and 4 Wm and M, c. 9, s. 1 (1691).

[49] Blackstone, Commentaries, vol. 4, p. 240; William Eden, Principles of Penal Law (1771), p. 265.

break into a house at night with the intention of committing a felony or during the day if someone was put in fear, or to break into a house and a variety of other buildings during the day if goods were stolen to the value of five shillings, even if there was no one present whose safety was threatened.

As in the case of robbery, offenses indicted as burglary and house-breaking covered a wide range of unlawful acts. Whether a particular set of facts amounted to a nonclergyable offense was frequently a matter of judicial discussion.[50] Apart from that, even if the law was interpreted strictly, the range of acts covered was very broad, and the variation in seriousness even wider than in robbery. A spur-of-the-moment snatch-and-run of a few shillings' value might technically qualify as a house-breaking or a burglary and thus be a capital offense, while at the other end of the spectrum were large-scale, carefully planned attacks on houses and shops that brought gangs of men considerable returns. The level of violence threatened and used also varied considerably. Most break-and-enter offenses were probably conducted without the owner's knowing he was being burglarized, and that was clearly the ideal most of the time. But some turned out to be more like robberies in that the victim was confronted and threatened, sometimes inadvertently when he awoke during the course of a burglary, sometimes deliberately, especially when large enough numbers of men took part to overawe the inhabitants.[51]

However the operation was conducted, burglary and housebreaking could bring in considerable returns. That is not to say that poor households were not also victimized: they were, some with devastating consequences, according to the stories told in court.[52] But burglary particularly attracted

---

[50] Hawkins, *Pleas of the Crown*, vol. 1, pp. 129–37, 207–11; East, *Pleas of the Crown*, vol. 2, pp. 481–523.

[51] The Gregory gang, for example, with whom Dick Turpin was associated, forced their way into numerous houses of rich farmers in Essex, Kent, and Surrey in 1735, overpowered the inhabitants, robbed them, and carried off their valuables. See *G. M.* 5 (1735), pp. 50, 106; Derek Barlow, *Dick Turpin and the Gregory Gang* (1973), pp. 43–99.

[52] At the trial in 1739 of John Blundall for breaking and entering the house of Thomas Blake in Lambeth and stealing clothes and money, Blake, the prosecutor, told the court:

> My House was broke open the 8th of June. He got in at the Window. I lost every Thing, my Lord. I had a Sash Window, and the very Window Curtains were gone. All my poor Wife's Smocks were gone, my Child's Frocks, all my Handkerchiefs—every Thing was stole—nay, and out of six Shirts, I lost five; and if I had not had one on my Back, that would have been gone too. Indeed, I lost every Thing that I had in the World. Fourteen Shillings and Sixpence that was in a Box, and that was taken away. (S.A.P., Lent 1739, p. 21 [Blundall])

Some years later, at the trial of a man for breaking into Mary Eslander's house at Linfield, she testified that she had gone out early in the morning to go hop-picking and came home at night

committed and organized gangs of men, especially in London, because of the promise of large rewards. The burglary that brought in close to twelve hundred pounds in silverplate from the Archibishop of Canterbury's palace in 1788 was out of the ordinary in every way, but other large hauls were reported in the press, and several burglaries involving losses of hundreds of pounds were brought to trial at the Surrey assizes over the century and a half after 1660. The values reported in court suggest that burglaries were more profitable than robberies—as might be expected since few men carried vast sums of money around the country, and highwaymen or street robbers normally could not hope to carry off a large cargo of even valuable objects. Burglars had more time, especially if the house was empty or if a gang of men overpowered the inhabitants, and more opportunity to arrange for transportation; under the right circumstances they could virtually clean out a house or a shop.[53] Like robberies, the break-and-enter offenses ranged across a wide spectrum, but while fully a quarter of the robberies prosecuted in the Surrey assizes had involved sums of under ten shillings, only about fourteen percent of the burglaries fell into that category. Conversely, fewer than one in ten of the street and highway muggings netted the offender more than ten pounds, while a quarter of the reported burglaries did so (table 4.4).

Large-scale burglary was likely to have been committed by gangs of habitual offenders who could call on men skillful enough to break into well-locked houses and men in sufficient numbers to provide lookouts and transportation. In addition, a successful raid that netted a considerable haul of silver or valuable clothes or furniture or other distinctive goods would require a safe place to store the goods and, above all, a fence who could handle a large number of valuable and easily identifiable objects, who could get them out of the country, perhaps to Holland (a common destination for stolen property), or otherwise dispose of them. Contacts with trustworthy landlords and with receivers who could deal with more than a watch or two or a few pieces of iron and clothing were on the whole likely to be available mainly to those regularly involved in illegal activities and to some extent committed to it and organized for it. Gangs of such men did indeed operate in London in the eighteenth century, as we will see. And while some perhaps practiced street or highway robbery exclu-

---

to find that her house had been broken into and that she had lost from a locked box "7 guineas and two half crowns, and other small pieces my mother left me for my daughter" (S.A.P., Lent 1752, p. 15 [Patrick]).

[53] In one case in 1745 a gang of five men had broken into a linen-draper's house/shop at one in the morning, locked the only inhabitant into the cellar, and spent the remainder of the night removing the shop's contents. The woman was released in the morning to discover losses of about £1,250 in money and goods (S.A.P., Lent 1745, pp. 3–7 [Cavenaugh et al.]).

Table 4.4

Value of Goods Taken in Robbery
and Burglary in Surrey, 1660–1800

Value	Percentage of Indictments	
	Robbery	*Burglary*
Under 10s.	24.7	13.6
10s.–£2	24.9	27.4
£2–£10	40.9	33.8
Over £10	9.5	25.2
	100.0	100.0

Source: Sample.
Note: $N = 462$ for robbery and 405 for burglary. The value of
goods taken was not recorded in the case of 25 robbery indictments
and 58 burglary indictments.

sively, the more skillful probably concentrated on the kind of burglaries
that took some planning and a reasonably elaborate system of support
afterwards, or at least combined this with robbery. Some men within
loosely organized gangs specialized in particular offenses. In his account
of his criminal activities in the London area in the 1720s (as he reported
them to a magistrate after his conviction at the Old Bailey), Edward
Burnworth listed forty-one burglaries of shops and houses he remembered
committing with a variety of accomplices (never more than two others at
once, but with a total of ten men altogether) and nine street robberies
committed in shifting combinations with seven different companions. Only
one man (and he only once) joined Burnworth in both robbery and
burglary.[54]

   Because they were largely the work of men like Burnworth and because
most of the attractive targets were in the metropolis, the burglaries prosecuted at the Surrey assizes were particularly concentrated in Southwark
and the more populous parishes in the northeast of the county. There were
attractive targets outside London, but there was not the same need for
burglars to range far afield as for highwaymen, and indeed there were good
logistical reasons why they should not. It is of course impossible to know
how the cases that were prosecuted mirror the reality of "actual" offenses
committed, though it is likely that the ten burglary and housebreaking

[54] SP 35/61, ff. 193–97. For Burnworth see Gerald Howson, *Thief-Taker General* (1970), pp.
190–94, 202–3; and for further discussion of gangs see chap. 5.

indictments that came to the Surrey courts on average every year between 1660 and 1800 (table 4.1) represent the merest fraction of those committed. Roughly seventy per cent of prosecuted offenses had taken place in Southwark or in the immediately adjacent ring of urban parishes (table 4.5). In terms of simple numbers of indictments, more breaking offenses arose from the rural parishes than did charges of robbery; that is surely because many acts that could be charged as the capital offense of housebreaking or even burglary were in fact very minor. And while they were almost certainly severely underreported for this reason or quietly transformed by the victim or the examining magistrate into simple larceny and thus removed from the capital category, they were likely to have been much more common than robberies. The Surrey experience in this regard is rather confused by the long reach of the city into the countryside, but the pattern of prosecutions in the neighboring rural county of Sussex, far from the influence of the capital, is perhaps more revealing. In Sussex, robbery indictments averaged merely one a year over the period 1660-1800, while prosecutions for break-and-enter offenses, including burglary, ran at about four a year. In addition, a higher proportion of them than in the rural parishes of Surrey took the generally less serious form of housebreaking (table 4.5).

If few of the offenses that might have been prosecuted actually came to court (a circumstance that was probably exaggerated in the case of burglary and housebreaking by the difficulty of catching the most serious offenders and the reluctance to prosecute the most minor), the long-term pattern of indictments cannot provide a reliable guide to changes in the behavior of offenders over this period. There is no long-term trend of note,

TABLE 4.5

Indictments for Burglary and Housebreaking in Surrey and Sussex

	Surrey					
Offense	Southwark and Environs (No.)	Rural Parishes (No.)	Total	Southwark and Environs (%)	Rural Parishes (%)	Sussex (No.)
Burglary	330	133	463	71.3	28.7	149
House-breaking	82	62	144	56.9	43.1	117
Total	412	195	607			266
Burglary (%)	80.1	68.2	76.3			56.0
House-breaking (%)	19.9	31.8	23.7			44.0

SOURCE: Sample.

though, as in the case of robbery, the rate of these offenses as measured against the population of the county clearly diminished toward the end of the eighteenth century. Unlike certain forms of robbery, however, burglary was not squeezed out by changes in the environment or by heightened surveillance and the increased level of policing in the nineteenth century. Indeed over the long term, as targets became increasingly attractive burglary became more than ever the offense that the more "professional" criminal was likely to turn to. Prosecutions for burglary and breaking and entering did not fall away in the nineteenth century as they did for robbery, and by the first decade of the twentieth the gap between these two forms of violent property crime that had been prosecuted at roughly the same level in Surrey in the eighteenth century had grown massively in favor of the breaking offenses.[55]

HORSE-THEFT

It is apparent from the way the courts dealt with robbery and burglary that these offenses continued to be regarded throughout the eighteenth century as by far the most serious of the crimes against property. The largest numbers of indictments for property offenses, however, were for larceny, taking property without the threat of violence. The law relating to larceny changed substantially in the period we are concerned with, shaped by two broad movements: the enlarging scope of larceny, and particularly the exclusion by statute of a variety of forms of larceny from benefit of clergy. Most of these nonclergyable larcenies were not prosecuted in large numbers, however: in Surrey they averaged about fourteen indictments a year, once the main post-Revolution additions had been made, and in Sussex there were even fewer (table 4.6). To some extent these figures reflect the reluctance of victims to prosecute men and women for offenses that were often trivial when the consequences might be that they would be hanged. This was particularly noticeable in the last few decades of the eighteenth century, when confidence in the justice and effectiveness of capital punishment was eroding more generally. By the last quarter of the century prosecutions in Surrey for some of the nonclergyable larcenies like shoplifting, picking pockets, and stealing from a warehouse had virtually ceased altogether.

Some of these offenses continued to be charged in significant numbers, however. In the case of horse-theft—surely the most serious of them in the public's estimation and one of the first offenses of any kind to be

---

[55] Gatrell, "Decline of Theft and Violence," pp. 317–21.

TABLE 4.6

Indictments for Nonclergyable (Capital) Larcenies in Surrey and Sussex, 1660–1800

| | Surrey | | | | | Sussex | | | | |
| | | Annual Average | | | | | Annual Average | | | |
Offense	Total	1660–1699	1700–1739	1740–1779	1780–1802	Total	1660–1699	1700–1739	1740–1779	1780–1802
Theft from										
Dwelling										
house	191	0	4.9	3.9	3.1	29	0	.6	.6	.5
Shop	79	0	3.4	1.3	.8	11	0	.1	.3	.2
Warehouse	33	0	.6	1.0	.1	6	0	.1	.2	.2
Ship	27	0	0	.3	1.5	1	0	0	0	.1
Manu-										
factory	29	0	.1	.8	.7	0	0	0	0	0
Pockets	92	.4	3.5	1.7	.5	3	0	0	0	.2
Theft of										
Sheep	73	0	0	1.4	2.9	43	0	0	1.0	1.4
Cattle	3	0	0	.1	.1	3	0	0	.1	0
Horses	227	6.4	2.0	2.6	4.9	111	1.6	1.9	1.6	2.2
Total	754	6.8	14.5	13.0	14.5	207	1.6	2.6	3.9	4.6
(N =)		(82)	(159)	(325)	(188)		(21)	(29)	(97)	(60)

SOURCE: Sample.

removed from clergy by the Tudors,[56] presumably because horses were both valuable and easy to steal—the level of prosecutions was probably more significantly affected by the difficulty of catching the thieves than reluctance to see them hanged. Of course in practice horse-theft covered a broad range of acts. Some of the cases that came to court had apparently merely involved joy-riding or a slightly ambivalent "borrowing."[57]

The thefts that were of particular concern, and not just to the very

[56] 37 Hen VIII, c. 8, s. 2 (1545).

[57] A boy told the Surrey assizes that he had ridden the horse he was accused of stealing "for pleasure," a plausible enough story except that when the pleasure ended he tried to sell the horse for twenty-five shillings and was arrested; he was convicted and sentenced to death, though subsequently pardoned and transported (S.A.P, Lent 1739, p. 16 [Trigg]). Another man thought that his need for a horse might excuse his borrowing it for a while. He was going "a great way into the Country," he told the court, "and having neither Shoes nor Stockings on his Feet, and seeing a Horse in a Yard, and he being very weary, took it to ride a little Way, in order to ease himself." He did not offer it for sale, but he was nonetheless convicted of horse-theft (S.A.P., Lent 1726, p. 3 [Swainman]).

rich, were the work of the more deliberate and more organized horse-thieves who operated around the county and the country within a network of safe inns, stables, and reliable receivers, and who were difficult to trace and apprehend. There were criminal gangs in the eighteenth century,[58] and although little detailed evidence about their horse-stealing in Surrey emerges from the court record, it was frequently asserted in newspapers that much of the horse-theft in the county was the work of men organized for it. In the years of peace following 1763, for example, when a good deal of property crime was reported in the London area, the arrest in Surrey of several habitual horse-thieves was announced in the press, and a gang was broken that was said to have "lately infected the County of Surrey" and "been the terror of the Country People for some Months past."[59] Horse-theft by such men was very difficult to prevent. There were thousands of horses in paddocks and fields, and they of course provided their own means of rapid movement out of the district and into parts of the country where they might be disposed of without much risk if the right contacts could be made.

Casual and amateur efforts were more easily detected. It was clearly dangerous to try to sell a stolen horse too close to home or too soon after stealing it, both faults that the casual thief was likely to fall into. One man was arrested because the farmer who lost a mare out of his stable picked up the thief's trail easily and found him at the horse fair in the parish of Chertsey "on the back of his mare" looking to sell it.[60] But the better-organized thieves moved quickly and got their horses out of the county. One gang that stole horses successfully for some years sold in the north of England what they stole in the south, and vice versa.[61] Examples can be found of Surrey thieves being stopped in neighboring counties and of men being charged at the assizes with a series of thefts of horses in widely separated parishes.[62] But it seems likely that serious horse-thieves in Surrey and in other counties close to London could in fact dispose of their stolen animals relatively safely in the capital, that the city provided an attractive outlet for horses as it did for other property: the fast roads in Surrey and the other Home Counties all led to London anyway. The

[58] See below, chap. 5.

[59] *The Public Advertiser*, 11, 12, 27 Jan., 3 Feb, 1764.

[60] *Deposition Book of Richard Wyatt*, p. 3.

[61] This was the Poulter gang, on whom see chap. 5. For another gang that followed the same pattern see *G. M.* 39 (1769), p. 165.

[62] For two Surrey horse-thieves stopped in Kent in 1719 see Add Mss. 42598, f. 160v. An example of a man tried at the Surrey assizes for stealing in various parts of the county is provided by John Hunt, who was charged in 1722 with five indictments for horse-theft in different and widely separated parishes (ASSI 35/212/7/16).

227 indictments for horse-theft brought before the Surrey assizes in the sixty-one years sampled, and the 111 cases in Sussex in the same period, must surely represent a small fraction of the charges that might have been laid if the thieves had been easier to catch. There seems to have been in any event little weakening of the persuasion that horse-thieves deserved to be hanged and thus, unlike other capital larcenies, little reluctance to bring prosecutions. Horse-theft remained at the end of the eighteenth century an offense for which men were executed.

SHEEP-STEALING

Although the theft of sheep and cattle also became capital offenses in the eighteenth century, they were never regarded with the same seriousness as horse-stealing. This was perhaps because sheep and cattle were less valuable, more difficult to dispose of, and certainly more difficult to move around in large numbers, and thus did not attract gang enterprise. Cattle-theft seems to have been very rare, and certainly prosecutions were few and far between. Sheep-stealing was much more common, but it was likely to be the work of local men rather than a marauding gang, and the sheep were likely to be taken for consumption rather than for the money they might bring. The circumstances under which the theft of sheep was removed from clergy in 1741 and the pattern of prosecution thereafter tend to confirm that characteristic of the offense.

The act making sheep-stealing a capital offense was passed in 1741 at a moment of serious rural distress. The harvests of 1740 and 1741 were both poor, and after several years of abundance and stable prices, the price of wheat rose sharply. As we will see in the following chapter, there was an increase in the number of prosecutions for theft in these years that almost certainly reflects an increase in offenses, especially in rural parishes—offenses that it seems plausible to think were committed to relieve some of the distress brought on by the shortage of agricultural work and the increasing price of necessities.[63] One of the offenses apparently being committed more frequently in the London area was sheep-stealing. In 1740 the Surrey assizes dealt with twelve cases involving the theft of sheep compared with an average over the century of two cases a year. It was by far the highest number of prosecutions in any of the years sampled in the century. Complaints about the theft of sheep in the Home Counties were received by members of parliament in sufficient number that in January 1741 the House appointed a committee to look into it and suggest a

[63] See chap. 5.

remedy. The result could have been predicted. As so often in the century, an apparent increase in an offense was countered by its withdrawal from clergy. An Act making sheep-stealing nonclergyable became law two months after the committee was appointed.[64]

There are too few indictments thereafter (a mere seventy-three in the years sampled through the remainder of the century, and forty-three in Sussex) to speak with certainty about their trends and patterns, but it is perhaps suggestive that the only years in which the number of prosecutions rose significantly above the annual average (of about two) were years in which the price of provisions was unusually high: 1800 and 1802. Sheep-stealing might well have been a more significant problem in Surrey if the large flocks on the Downs had been much closer to the capital. As it was, they were probably far enough removed from the London market to make the large-scale theft of sheep an unattractive proposition, since moving large amounts of meat or driving the animals could not be easily accomplished without arousing suspicion. There may have been some killing of sheep to supply not so much the mutton and lamb markets in London as the market for other parts of the animal. The skin was valuable, though it might be tricky to dispose of because of the possibility of identification. But the fat, the tallow, was both valuable and easy to sell. There were numerous reports of sheep killed in the fields and butchered not for their meat but for the several pounds of tallow that would find a ready buyer among the tallow chandlers of London. Farmers around London were particularly hit by raids of this kind. A bag of tallow would not rouse the same suspicions as a large quantity of meat, particularly since it was common for men to go around collecting it legitimately from farmers.[65]

Most of the sheep-stealing in Surrey was probably the work of local men, perhaps one or two working together, tempted by the significant supplement that half a sheep would make to the budget of a hungry family. Even without the occasional sharp provocation of a steep rise in the price of necessities, the prospect of a number of good dinners must have made sheep-stealing a temptation even at the best of times. It was certainly one of the offenses that local men with bad reputations were suspected of. Unlike horse-theft, it was as likely to be suffered by the small cottager or laborer, who might well have a beast or two on the

---

[64] 14 Geo II, c. 6 (1741). *J.H.C.* 23 (1737–41), pp. 572, 586–88, 690. Although there had been few complaints about the theft of cattle, they were also included in this Act, and a subsequent statute made it absolutely clear that bulls, cows, oxen, and lambs were to be protected by the threat of the gallows (15 Geo II, c. 34 [1742]).

[65] A farmer near Kensington had fifteen sheep and twenty-seven lambs killed one night, their throats cut and their fat taken away, which, it was alleged, was sold to a tallow chandler in Southwark (S.A.P., Lent 1745, pp. 10–12 [Chettle]).

common, as by a large farmer, and as in the case of the widow who lost two sheep out of the churchyard at Mitcham, it could be a significant loss for them.[66] But while the two indictments prosecuted on average every year in the Surrey courts provide no useful indication of either its incidence or its significance, sheep-stealing clearly did not bring on the sense of anxiety or dismay that burglary or even horse-theft aroused.

THEFT FROM BLEACHING GROUNDS

Other larcenies that were similarly related to the structure and the circumstances of the local economy had been made capital by parliament. The theft of various forms of cloth in the process of manufacture, which had been withdrawn from clergy by several statutes beginning in 1670,[67] was of importance in Surrey because of the extensive bleaching and calico-printing industry that developed from the late seventeenth century along the River Wandle. Along the ten miles of this river from the parish of Carshalton through Merton and Mitcham to Wandsworth and the Thames, bleaching grounds and printing mills were common by the first decades of the eighteenth century. The racks and tenters on which the cloth was stretched must have provided a standing temptation to thieves: the grounds were extensive and obviously difficult to watch carefully, especially at night. And although a good deal of cotton or linen would have to be taken to make a theft of substantial value, two or three thieves could carry away enough to raise a significant sum. Two men and a woman took 168 yards of Irish linen in 1775, for example, which the owners valued at sixteen guineas (though how much they got from a receiver is another matter). The bleaching grounds do not seem to have attracted the more committed criminal gangs of the capital, however, but instead more occasional and local thieves like William Good, a Wandsworth blacksmith, who was seen with three other men spreading out a piece of white cloth in a field behind the workhouse the morning after the theft of three pieces of cotton from a whitester's ground in the parish.[68] The fact that some of the most vigorous complaints came at times of distress in the rural community (one man talked in 1741 of being robbed hourly)[69] supports that view.

Owners adopted aggressive methods of defense from time to time (at least one company employed a man armed with a gun to watch their

---

[66] S.A.P., Lent 1742, p. 4 (Gunnell).

[67] 22 Chas II, c. 5 (1670); 4 Geo II, c. 16 (1731); 18 Geo II, c. 27 (1745).

[68] QS 2/6, Ep. 1762, 22–24, 29.

[69] S.A.P., Lent 1741, p. 4 (Forster).

grounds at night in the 1770s),[70] but it was undoubtedly difficult to apprehend thieves, given the size of the grounds to be patrolled. And it may well have appeared to the owners not to be worth their while to prosecute a lone offender even when they caught him because it would have meant sending an employee for several days to the assizes in Kingston or Guildford. A warning might well have seemed as effective, especially if the offender was a local man. These considerations help to explain why only twenty-nine prosecutions for such offenses came before the Surrey courts in the years I have sampled, barely one every two years on average. It seems probable, too, that there was not a persistently significant problem of theft from these places of manufacture.

THEFT FROM HOUSES

In the case of these textile offenses, clergy had been removed for the theft of a particular object from particular places (bleaching grounds and tenter racks). They share this latter characteristic with another group of thefts that made it a capital offense to steal goods over a certain value from houses, shops, and warehouses and from ships on navigable rivers. The first of these, theft from a dwelling-house of goods valued at more than forty shillings, was removed from clergy in the reign of Queen Anne. This was aimed directly at domestic servants, whose pilfering, the preamble to the bill declared, had been encouraged by the Act of 1706 making clergy available to everyone regardless of literacy: "Divers wicked and ill-disposed servants, and other persons, are encouraged to commit robberies in houses by the privilege, as the law now is, of demanding the benefit of clergy. . . ."[71] Just over two hundred men and women were charged in Surrey under that statute in the forty-seven years sampled between the passage of the Act and the end of the century. It is clear, however, that prosecutors were reluctant to invoke the extreme penalty it imposed to punish the petty pilfering of those they knew well. It is a reasonable assumption that few employers in any case went to the trouble and expense of taking their servants to court when they might deal with them more effectively themselves or simply dismiss them. But many more servants were taken to court by their employers than prosecutions under this statute would suggest, for apart from the victims' reluctance to hang men and women for minor offenses, the courts construed the Act very narrowly (as they did in the case of all nonclergyable larcenies), and in any case many thefts by

[70] S.A.P., Lent 1774, p. 17 (Morris).
[71] 12 Anne, c. 7 (1713).

employees were under forty shillings. If we are to investigate thefts by servants to the limited extent it is possible from the court record, we must broaden our enquiry beyond the prosecutions brought under this Act.

There is evidence that a considerable number of larceny charges tried at the assizes and quarter sessions in fact involved employees. It is also clear that this was an area in which a good deal of misunderstanding and malice could operate. Some misunderstanding was the result of disagreement about what servants and employees might or might not take as part of their legitimate payment: certainly some of those accused of theft claimed that the object they had "stolen" was in their view their rightful perquisite.[72] Such disputes could only have become more common in the course of a period in which customary forms of payment were giving way to more regularized wages. But most prosecutions seem to have been the outcome of more straightforward disputes between masters and workers. A journeyman shoemaker charged with stealing two pairs of shoes from his master claimed in court, for example, that he took them because he had not been paid fully for his work; and another man accused of stealing from his employer charged in turn (though the court did not accept his story) that the accusation was made only after he had lent his master five pounds and had had to threaten him with a suit to get it back. The larceny charge was a malicious prosecution, as he saw it, designed to get him to call off the bailiffs.[73] Several other cases before the courts were also said by the defendant to be malicious or vindictive.[74]

It is a fair presumption that the real level of servants' pilfering was at a much higher level than the numbers of charges made under this statute or the more general charge of simple larceny involving employees would lead one to suppose. The few who were brought to court were prosecuted on the whole not by the rich and socially prominent, who perhaps had more effective informal ways of punishing thefts by servants, but by men and women of more middling status. Most of those who used the courts in this way were farmers or tradesmen or craftsmen who had domestic servants, servants in husbandry, apprentices, and journeymen living in or working in their houses. Occasionally a substantial sum was alleged to have been stolen, but generally even the thefts brought to court were very

[72] A carpenter accused of stealing wood from his master thought that it was a cutting he was entitled to by long custom; a domestic servant prosecuted for stealing a bottle of Madeira valued at two shillings had told him she thought it was "small beer," which presumably they agreed she was entitled to (SP 35/67, f. 57; QS 2/6, Ea. 1755, 20).

[73] S.A.P., Lent 1774, p. 141 (Mowney).

[74] A young woman charged with theft claimed, for example, that her master had given her a present to "lie with her" and had only accused her when she refused (S.A.P., Summer 1740, p. 10 [Floodgate]).

minor indeed. The evidence often suggests that what is being charged is merely the last of a series of offenses or suspected offenses, and that this case came to court because the master or mistress was sufficiently harmed or outraged to go to a magistrate to get this breach of trust punished severely—perhaps as much as anything as a warning to others.[75]

Pilfering by servants was undoubtedly encouraged in London by the fact that it was easy to pawn or sell goods in the capital without much fear that enquiries would be made into their ownership, as contemporaries concerned with the increase of crime never tired of complaining. That perhaps helps to explain why four out of five of the accused prosecuted under the statute that made theft from a house a nonclergyable offense lived in Southwark or in a parish within the environs of the metropolis. It was also simply a matter of numbers: in the more densely populated parishes in the northeast of Surrey there was a greater concentration of domestic servants, apprentices, and journeymen working in the shops and houses of tradesmen and craftsmen. If the indictments can be thought to reflect a real difference of behavior, it is likely that the difference can be explained by the temptations surrounding servants in the city, and the greater variety of entertainments available to them and thus the greater need for spare cash. The relatively low level of prosecutions in the rural parishes of Surrey was matched by the similar experience of the neighboring county of Sussex, for there as in rural Surrey prosecutions were rare under the 1713 Act, amounting in each case to hardly more than one every other year (table 4.6).

THEFT FROM SHIPS

The statute had removed clergy not from servants caught stealing but from the act of a stealing from a house. It made theft from a particular place a capital offense. Other places came to be similarly protected. The theft of goods worth more than forty shillings from a ship on a navigable river or from a wharf was made nonclergyable in 1751, for example, by a statute that applied not simply to theft on the Thames but that was clearly stimulated by it.

London was by far the largest port in the country, and merchants had long complained about losses from their ships in the river and from

---

[75] For a blacksmith complaining about a series of thefts by a journeyman who lived with him and a staymaker complaining for the same reason about his apprentice, see their depositions at QS 2/6, Ea. 1764, 26, and Ep. 1767, 60. A woman was tried at the assizes in 1741 for systematic theft of linen from her employers, who ran a laundry business (S.A.P., Lent 1741, pp. 10–11 [Smith]).

its quays and docks. Hundreds of ships from all over the world provided an enormous concentration of valuable goods, particularly the East Indiamen and the ships of the North American and West Indian merchants. By the end of the century, Patrick Colquhoun estimated, the value of goods passing through London exceeded sixty-five million pounds, taking imports and exports together, and that more than thirteen thousand ships used the river in the course of a year.[76] This was after a period of striking growth, but London had handled a massive volume of goods for well over a century, and merchants' complaints about their losses through the depredations of laborers and lightermen and the army of other workers engaged in the complicated process of unloading the ships were as old.[77] Many of these thefts were thought to take place on the south bank of the river, along the extensive wharves in Southwark and Rotherhithe.

Ships on the Thames were vulnerable because they had to be unloaded from anchorages in the middle of the river, their cargo being transferred to lighters and brought to the customs' quays for inspection and weighing and storage in warehouses.[78] Dozens of pairs of hands moved the goods, and the unloading and checking, the customs inspection, and the transfer to storage could take months. Some goods stuck. At numerous points there were opportunities for hogsheads of tobacco or sugar or rice to be dipped into or for "spillage" to occur or for some goods to be dropped overboard. The issue of "theft" is not, however, as simple as it might seem, or as it seemed to merchants, the judiciary, or interested commentators like Patrick Colquhoun. As with a great deal of other "theft" in the workplace, there was something of a double vision of what taking goods on the river meant. To the merchant the issue was straightforward—and perhaps became increasingly clarified over time: taking his goods was theft. But to the sailors, lightermen, and porters who worked on the river and unloaded the ships, taking some goods was a right and an integral part of their legitimate remuneration. This included in particular the right to "sockings" and "spillage," the sweepings left over in the hold or on the decks.[79] What the merchants of course suspected was that at all stages of the unloading process spillage was helped along, hogsheads were broken open, and sugar and tobacco simply creamed off that did not fall legitimately within the claimed perquisites. As the volume of traffic increased and the river became ever more crowded and the plunder, as they thought, threatened to get out of control, the merchants with help from the state

[76] Colquhoun, *Police of the Metropolis*, preface, chap. 3.
[77] Radzinowicz, *History*, vol. 2, pp. 349–57.
[78] Peter Linebaugh, "Socking, Tobacco Porters, the Hogshead, and Excise," in his *Crime and the Wage in the Eighteenth Century* (forthcoming).
[79] Linebaugh, "Socking."

and the criminal law made an effort to cut down their losses by bringing the labor force under control. At the beginning of the nineteenth century this led to the building of extensive and enclosed dock facilities and to the creation of a force of river police.[80] But the struggle had gone on for long before that. An important part of the eighteenth-century effort had been the statute of 1751 making thefts on the river of more than two pounds a capital offense.

There are few hints in the printed reports of men tried at the Surrey assizes for theft from ships of a defense being based on the "custom" of the river, though that is not to say that some of them had not felt justified at the time.[81] And many of the offenses brought to court were clearly unambiguous. The vast wealth of the river attracted numerous straightforward thieves like two men convicted in 1739 of stealing coal from lighters, a practice they had allegedly carried on for a number of years and for which they regularly hired a boat at four shillings a week.[82] In addition, as on the land, much of the theft was suffered not by the rich or by the East India Company, who might be thought to be able to afford it, but by men who almost certainly could not. The watermen at Fountain Stairs in Rotherhithe found it necessary to organize their own nightly watch—"a custom agreed on among the Watermen at several Stairs," one of them explained, "to take it by turns to prevent their Goods being lost, and their Boats taken away."[83] The statute removing theft from ships was passed at the request of merchants in 1751 (at the high point, as we will see, of what seems to have been a period of high property crime), which strongly suggests that the river crime they were seeking to deter by bringing to bear the terror and the deterrent power of the gallows was not theft covered by the claims of customary right but the attacks on ships from the outside, as it were.

What is striking is that even though complaints about river theft were of course to continue, the victims of these outrages did not find it necessary or possible to invoke this statute very often. Indeed in Surrey only one indictment a year on average was prosecuted at the assizes under it in the second half of the century. Of course the value of the statute to the merchants and shipowners was not to be measured in the number of

---

[80] Radzinowicz, *History*, vol. 2, chaps. 12–13.

[81] One man did say in his own defense that he had not thought the theft a felony because his accomplices had persuaded him "they had an Authority for doing it," but he could hardly have thought it some form of legitimate perquisite since they had rowed out to an East Indiaman at night, broken into the hold, and removed eight hundred pounds of saltpeter worth thirty-three pounds and taken it immediately to a receiver (S.A.P., Lent 1741, p. 12 [Carr]).

[82] S.A.P., Lent 1739, p. 20 (Crucherford and Wells).

[83] *Account of the Trial, Confession, and Dying Words of William Corbett* (1764), p. 7.

times it led to men being hanged: the occasional example and the general threat over those tempted to steal from a ship was justification enough for its passage. It is also likely that it was particularly difficult to detect and apprehend river thieves and that some who were caught continued to be charged with simple larceny, because the theft did not amount to the forty shillings necessary to bring it under the statute or the place of theft would be difficult to prove in court or the victim simply chose to report it as a noncapital offense. Nonetheless, even taking these considerations into account, if theft on the river had been as serious a matter as some thought— Colquhoun called it an "immense plunder and pillage" in the 1790s[84]— it is surprising that so few prosecutions were mounted under a statute that had been sought to stamp it out.

SHOPLIFTING

However unrepresentative these few cases might be thought to be of the full extent of river theft, in one respect they were likely to reflect it accurately enough: that is the extent to which the charges were brought exclusively against men. Women did not work on the river, and they were much less likely than men to board a ship at night to steal from its hold or cabins. Women were much more involved, however, in another of the larcenies removed from clergy in the eighteenth century: shoplifting. The offense of "privately stealing" goods from a shop to the value of five shillings had been excluded from clergy in the statute of 1699 that had also made theft from a warehouse or stable a capital offense.[85] It was obviously seriously underreported, at least in the form that would bring a case under this statute, for in the roughly fifty years sampled of the Surrey assizes in the eighteenth century not even two offenders a year were charged with this capital offense, even though it seems clear from the complaints of shopkeepers and the reports in the press that shoplifting was very common. Complaints arose from all the towns of any size in the country—from Guildford, Croydon, and Kingston—but of course the greatest outcry came from the metropolis, including the Borough of Southwark, where shops multiplied in the course of the century and displayed larger amounts of consumer goods and food more invitingly. It is hardly surprising that more than ninety per cent of the shoplifting charges brought to the Surrey courts had been committed in these urban parishes within the larger metropolis of London.

The reasons for the underreporting are not far to seek. It is likely in

[84] Colquhoun, *Police of the Metropolis*, p. 57.
[85] 10 and 11 Wm III, c. 23 (1699).

the first place that shopkeepers were as discouraged as anyone from going to the trouble and expense of prosecuting, especially if they had caught the thief red-handed and got their goods back. It was also not likely to be good for business, especially if the prosecution ended with a petty thief going to the gallows. By the early nineteenth century at least, it was clear that merchants and shopkeepers in London were unwilling to take that chance,[86] and the number of prosecutions undertaken in Surrey suggests that this view had prevailed for a long time (table 4.6). Part of this reluctance clearly stemmed from the fact that shoplifting was in the main a petty offense, and that while some shoplifters (particularly women) were regulars, on the whole most were not only small-time but also very occasional offenders. A House of Commons committee was told in 1819 that some shoplifters were "in the habitual practice of it" but that many were "not persons who are regular traders in thieving, but are persons in better circumstances, particularly the women."[87] Nor was it an offense that required gang organization, though shoplifters often worked in pairs so that one could distract the attention of the shopkeeper while the other lifted something, and the newspapers occasionally conjured up visions of larger shoplifting gangs being formed in London, especially of young boys.[88] In the main, it never took a form that persuaded the public or the courts that it was sufficiently ominous to require the vigorous use of the death penalty. As we will see, very few shoplifters were hanged in the eighteenth century despite the statute.

[86] *Report on Criminal Laws* (1819), pp. 8–9, 11–12, and passim.

[87] Ibid., p. 27. In 1764 a newspaper reported the apprehension of "a very notorious woman shop-lifter" who had "in company with another female (proficient in that science) for about six months past, obtained from different shops (chiefly in the City of London or in the Borough of Southwark) jewels, rings, muslins, gauzes, linens, etc. to a very considerable amount" (*The Public Advertiser*, 18 Jan. 1764). In the same year three women were apprehended, and numerous victims came forward to prosecute them. The *Gentleman's Magazine* claimed that one of them, Sarah McCabe, alias Sarah Flood, alias Ridgely, alias Clarke, alias Brewit, had "for upwards of twenty years, carried on the practice of shop-lifting." She had been transported for seven years in 1748, according to this report, but had returned in four and "immediately resumed her former practices, and was again apprehended and tried at the Old Bailey; but no person proving her to be the same who had been before transported, and she being tried by a different name, she was acquitted." Now, however, she and her companions were examined several times before the magistrates "for the conveniency of the Tradesmen in general seeing them," and several came forward to press charges (*G. M.* 34 [1764], p. 144; *The Public Advertiser*, 3 Mar. 1764). It was widely believed that many women engaged regularly in shoplifting in London. The recorder opposed the petition of a female shoplifter to be excused transportation in 1735 because, as he told the secretary of state, when "such people are set at liberty . . . they generally return to the same practices" (SP 36/37, f. 23).

[88] *London Evening Post*, 7–9 Mar. 1738, 1–3 June 1738. For two women working together see QS 2/6, 1712, 46; Ep. 1767, 59.

PICKING POCKETS

Shoplifting was clearly a great deal more common than prosecutions might suggest. This was true of another offense that had been among the first to be removed from clergy in the sixteenth century, presumably because it was thought to be both common and difficult to prevent. This was picking pockets, stealing "privately" from the person. To judge by newspaper reports and by the insistent warnings to travelers and to those who attended fairs and race-meetings or who stood in the crowds at Tyburn or elsewhere, it was widely prevalent in the eighteenth century.[89] But in the sixty-one years examined in Surrey, a mere ninety-two indictments for picking pockets were laid before the Surrey assizes, involving 112 individual offenders. In fact, prosecutions for actual picking of pockets in the streets may have been even less frequently undertaken than this suggests, for one of the commonest forms of the offense in the courts qualified as pocket-picking in only a technical sense. This was theft by prostitutes from their clients, who were often asleep or so drunk or otherwise engaged that they did not notice that their watch or purse was being taken. Not many such men complained to the courts, for obvious reasons, but some did and it seems likely that cases of this kind help to explain why women charged with picking pockets in Surrey outnumbered men two to one and also to explain why the courts dealt relatively leniently with pickpockets, especially women, for judges commonly made it clear that they thought the victims of such crimes not worth much sympathy.

Theft from the person in its more straightforward form was only rarely prosecuted. This was partly simply a reflection of the difficulty of catching skilled pickpockets at work and the further difficulty of apprehending them, especially if they had accomplices, as they often had. Perhaps, too, the possibility that the convicted man would be hanged discouraged some who might have been willing otherwise to try to take them in. A more common response in London, a newspaper implied in 1738, was to pay them "with a few blows" there in the street, and let them go.[90] Picking pockets was also a reasonably specialized offense. It may have been troublesome in certain parts of London, where neighborhoods like Covent Garden or Drury Lane or around the Exchange were

[89] See, for example, the *Gentleman's Magazine* warning in 1795 about the danger of "expert genteelly-dressed men and women pickpockets [who] constantly make it their business to attend at every fair, race, or encampment, of the least celebrity, for the express purpose of plundering the spectators of their watches, purses, and pocket-books" (65 [1795], p. 657).

[90] *London Evening Post*, 27 June 1738.

said from time to time to be "infested" by gangs of pickpockets, and whenever large crowds gathered elsewhere. But it seems not to have been regarded as sufficiently serious and threatening to prosecutors or indeed to the courts to overcome an apparent reluctance to put men and women in danger of being hanged for offenses that were mainly very trivial.

GRAND AND PETTY LARCENY

Few of the larcenies we have been dealing with that had been removed from clergy and thus made capital were prosecuted in large numbers in Surrey (still fewer were brought to the Sussex assizes), and of those that were only horse-theft and to a much lesser extent sheep-stealing were in practice likely to bring offenders to the gallows in significant numbers. One can tell very little about the "reality" of such offenses from the numbers of indictments when the public was reluctant to prosecute, particularly since the reluctance increased over time. The larcenies made nonclergyable by statute after 1689 were prosecuted most vigorously in Surrey in the first decades of the eighteenth century, immediately following the passage of the bulk of the statutes. In the years sampled between 1700 and 1739 they formed 14.4 per cent of all property charges in both courts together. Over the middle decades they fell back gradually from that level and then shrank ever further in the last twenty years of the century, to a mere six per cent of all property indictments laid before the Surrey courts (table 4.7).

The most likely explanation of this falling away of prosecutions for offenses made capital after 1689 is that offered by numerous witnesses before the House of Commons committee that investigated the administration of the criminal law in 1819, that is, that victims were reluctant to prosecute because of the harshness of the law. That reluctance took two forms: most victims probably refused to prosecute at all; others seem to have reported the crime and charged the offender but without revealing the circumstances that brought the offense under a capital statute—not specifying at the time the indictment was drawn, for example, where the theft had taken place, or reducing the value of the goods stolen below the critical level. In that case the indictment would be drawn simply for larceny, which remained through the eighteenth century a clergyable felony and in practice noncapital. There was thus a broad tendency over the eighteenth century—after an initial decline in its early decades when the nonclergyable larcenies were mainly introduced—for the simple larceny category to become proportionately larger. It was always by far the most numerous of the property offenses: by the end of the century three out of

TABLE 4.7

Indictments for Crimes against Property
over Time in Surrey

Offense	Indictments	Percentage of N			
		1660–1699	1700–1739	1740–1779	1780–1802
Robbery, burglary, housebreaking, and horse-theft	1,321	30.7	27.9	17.9	17.7
Other nonclergyable larcenies (mainly post-1689)	527	.6	14.4	11.1	6.2
Simple grand larceny and petty larceny	4,370	68.7	57.7	71.0	76.1
(N=)		(905)	(952)	(2,346)	(2,015)

SOURCE: Sample.

four indictments involving the loss of property brought to the Surrey courts were for clergyable grand larceny or petty larceny (table 4.7).

At common law a sharp distinction had been drawn between grand and petty larceny, that is between thefts of goods worth a shilling or more and those worth less than a shilling. While grand larceny had been a felony punishable by death (though subject to clergy), petty larceny had always been regarded as a noncapital felony, punished mainly by whipping. In the eighteenth century the crucial differences between them were largely eliminated, particularly when the right to benefit of clergy was extended to all convicted offenders in 1706, and the crimes to which it applied, including simple larceny, thus became in practice noncapital; and when, further, the Transportation Act of 1718 authorized the courts to sentence both grand and petty larcenists to a period of exile in the colonies.[91] In practice, petty larceny continued to be punished largely by whipping, though some offenders were transported, and most convicted grand larcenists were sent to America. But the sharp differences of the past no longer applied. Few crucial distinctions remained, and it seems wise for us to treat grand and petty larceny together as simple theft.

The offenses that constituted this largest category of indictable crime varied enormously in the kinds of goods stolen and in their value. For the

[91] See below, chap. 9.

most part they tended to involve modest sums. It is unclear how the values stated in the indictments were arrived at and how accurate they were, and it is entirely likely that they were the result of a good deal of rough estimation and in some cases certainly of deliberate undervaluation. Some of the reported petty larcenies were flagrantly fictional.[92] For a number of years in the middle of the eighteenth century, as we will see, every indictment for larceny tried at the Surrey quarter sessions carried an automatic valuation of the stolen goods of ten pence—even when the objects stolen were several half-crowns. And there may have been similar fictions in many grand larceny indictments. But since the value of the goods reported would not have affected the punishment a convicted offender received, so long as the manner of the offense or the object stolen or some other circumstance did not remove it from clergy, there is no reason to think that the indictments are likely to have been systematically biased. There must have been much guesswork behind the stated value of a pillow case or a pair of old sheets or a piece of scrap metal, but the impression one gets from the precise figures that are so commonly put upon each object listed in indictments is that thought was being given much of the time to getting it at least roughly right. Without thinking that the values of thefts were necessarily very accurately reported, we might take them as indicating in an approximate way the general levels of prosecuted theft. In Surrey, by this measure, most of the simple grand larcenies were very modest indeed, for half had involved goods valued between one and five shillings and another thirty per cent fell between five shillings and two pounds (table 4.8). Only a fifth of the reported grand larcenies were over two pounds in value, and only a very small number of those (less than two per cent of the total) involved objects valued by their owner at more than twenty-five pounds.

This broad pattern held for thefts prosecuted in the Borough of Southwark and the other parishes within the metropolis as well as for those reported from the rural parishes and market towns of the county. There were some differences at the extremes. More of the rural thefts were for very small amounts: among the grand larceny cases roughly forty-seven per cent in the urban parishes were fixed below five shillings in value, for example, as against fifty-six per cent from the small towns and rural parishes. At the other end of the scale almost twenty-three per cent of

---

[92] Few were as flagrant as a case at the Sussex quarter sessions in 1693 in which a woman was indicted for stealing sixty-one yards of bone lace valued by the prosecutor at eight pence so that, with a silk girdle valued at two pence, the indictment could be kept within petty larceny and the accused kept entirely out of danger of being hanged. Some years earlier twenty-five yards of bone lace had been valued at forty-one pounds at the Surrey assizes (QR/E 256, QS Roll, Apr. 1693; ASSI 35/104/7/1).

urban thefts were over two pounds in value, as against fifteen per cent
rural; and over the period we have been dealing with almost fifty larcenies
in the Surrey metropolitan area were valued at more than twenty-five
pounds (including ten over a hundred pounds), while only four similar
thefts, all about twenty-five pounds, were reported from rural Surrey (table
4.8).

There was also a real difference in the level of offenses prosecuted in
the "rural" and "urban" parts of the country. Fully three-quarters of the
larceny cases before the Surrey quarter sessions and assizes came from
Southwark and its neighboring parishes; and if the charges that had been
dealt with by the Southwark Borough quarter sessions (the court presided
over by the mayor and aldermen of London) could be fully recovered and
taken into account, the imbalance in prosecutions for larceny would be
even greater. Part of the difference is of course explained simply by the
number of people involved: the population of Southwark and surrounding
parishes rose more strongly than the rest of the county over the period we
are dealing with, and from a position of being roughly equal in population
in 1660 the "urban" area contained something on the order of sixty-four
per cent by the end of the eighteenth century.[93] It is also possible that
there was a greater reluctance in rural parishes to prosecute someone well
known in the community, and in any case more effective informal sanctions
could be brought to bear against offenders there. We will explore these

TABLE 4.8

Value of Goods Stolen in Simple Grand Larceny
Indictments in Surrey, 1660–1800

Value	Percentage of N		
	Southwark and Environs	Rural Surrey	Total Surrey
Less than 5s.	46.5	56.3	49.1
5s.–£2	30.9	28.3	30.2
£2–£5	11.2	9.4	10.7
£5–£25	9.2	5.4	8.2
Over £25	2.2	.5	1.8
Total	100.0	99.9	100.0
(N =)	(2,123)	(773)	(2,896)

SOURCE: Sample.

[93] See chap. 1, n. 38.

possibilities more fully in a later chapter when we examine patterns of prosecutions more generally, particularly contrasts in the prosecution of men and women. The argument will be made that, taking population into account and the other imponderables like differences in attitudes toward the courts and in access to magistrates, there were nonetheless real differences in the level of property crime in the urban and rural parishes that sprang from real differences in the circumstances of life and work.

Certainly on the face of it the pattern of prosecution for simple larceny suggests strikingly different experiences. More than two-thirds of the parishes of the county reported a larceny (taking petty and grand larceny together) that went on to be tried in the courts only once every five years on average. This is true of the whole range of rural parishes in the southern two-thirds of the county, of parishes large and small, on the Downs and in the Weald. As might be expected, parishes with market towns reported more cases than those without substantial central settlements. Croydon, Farnham, Dorking, and Reigate reported a case every year or two; and more than one larceny was prosecuted every year on average in Epsom, which attracted visitors to the spa and the races on the Downs. Some of the parishes along the main roads also reported a slightly higher number of cases than other rural parishes. But with these few exceptions it was only in the northern tier of the county, particularly the more populous parishes within the larger metropolis of London, that more than the merest handful of larcenies arose over the century and a half after 1660. Only eight parishes altogether reported an average of more than two larceny cases a year to the Surrey assizes or quarter sessions: four were in the Borough of Southwark and the others were Newington, Rotherhithe, Bermondsey, and Lambeth. (One gets some confirmation of this picture from Sussex, where there was no large urban population at all. Outside Lewes and Brighton and Chichester, and one or two modest towns in the county, no parishes reported more than a handful of larcenies to the county quarter sessions or the assizes.)

There is evidence, too, in the nature of the objects stolen, as well as in the number and value, that there were real differences in the character of larceny in the urban and rural parishes of Surrey. It is difficult to calculate the frequency with which particular kinds of goods were stolen, since one indictment might include a large number and the next one only one or two. I have adopted the rather crude method of counting stolen goods by types, defined in very broad categories, and making one entry for each (up to three in every indictment), regardless of how many examples of that category the indictment contained. This is almost certain to undervalue the most frequently stolen goods and to exaggerate somewhat the proportions assigned to those less commonly taken. But it provides a rough and ready guide to stolen goods. The results are listed in table 4.9, which includes the most common categories. These account for more than eighty per cent of the objects reported stolen in Surrey and Sussex in the years sampled; the remainder consisted of many other things in very small numbers.

In Surrey, clothes form by far the largest category of stolen goods, clothes in large and small amounts, new and used, valuable and virtually worthless. They are followed at some distance by household goods including furniture and linens, objects made of worked metal, food (included in just about nine per cent of the indictments, and fourteen per cent if one includes the theft of pigs and chickens and geese and other fowl), money, silver dishes and plate and cutlery, and watches and jewelry. If one compares indictments from rural and urban parishes, clothes head the list decisively in the parishes in and immediately around the metropolis, but in the rural areas they are displaced by the theft of foodstuffs and fowl together. There are equally significant differences further down the list. The leading categories of stolen goods in Southwark and its neighborhood were clothes, household goods, worked metal goods, food, money, silver, and watches. Many of the goods taken were likely sold or in other ways dealt away, though it is of course unclear, as we have said, whether clothes, household goods, and food taken especially in modest quantities were sold or used and consumed. It seems likely that the valuables in the list were mainly pawned or sold. In the countryside the leading category was food (including fowl), followed by clothes and household goods and then by a list ordered differently and with different proportions from that of the urban parishes of Surrey. The fourth category in the rural parishes was tools, which figured in about seven per cent of indictments as against four per cent in urban. The place of valuables was also different, for in rural Surrey watches, money, and silver made up eleven per cent of the stolen goods as against about eighteen per cent in the county's more urban parishes (table 4.9).

These differences are broadly confirmed by the experience of the county of Sussex, where the ordering of the categories of goods stolen in simple larcenies is virtually identical with that of the rural parishes of Surrey, beginning with food and moving down as in Surrey to clothes and household goods. Such differences are of course entirely to be expected, since the character of theft must surely have been related to the opportunities available—both for stealing and for disposing of goods through receivers—as well as to the structure of the local economy. Several features of these patterns of simple theft in Surrey suggest as much. Perhaps the most obvious is the large place occupied in rural parishes by the theft of

Table 4.9

Categories of Goods Stolen in Petty and Grand Larceny
(Ranked by Percentage of Total)

Surrey		Southwark and Environs		Rural Parishes of Surrey		Sussex	
1. Clothes	23.7%	1. Clothes	27.1%	1. Food	26.5%	1. Food	29.2%
2. Food	14.0	2. Household goods	14.4	2. Clothes	21.4	2. Clothes	22.8
3. Household goods	12.0	3. Worked metal	13.2	3. Household goods	9.5	3. Household goods	10.1
4. Worked metal	10.6	4. Food	11.4	4. Tools	7.4	4. Worked metal	8.1
5. Money	7.3	5. Money	9.2	5. Worked metal	6.6	5. Tools	6.5
6. Silver	3.8	6. Silver	4.7	6. Crops	5.8	6. Money	5.5
7. Watches/jewelry	3.1	7. Tools	3.9	7. Money	5.8	7. Crops	4.0
8. Crops	2.8	8. Watches/jewelry	3.8	8. Silver	2.6	8. Fuel	2.4
9. Tools	1.9	9. Timber	1.9	9. Watches/jewelry	2.6	9. Silver	2.0
10. Timber	1.7	10. Crops	1.5	10. Timber	2.2	10. Watches/jewelry	1.5
11. Fuel	1.0	11. Fuel	1.1	11. Fuel	1.7	11. Timber	1.5

SOURCE: Sample.
NOTE: "Food" includes fowl.

foodstuffs in general including the theft of hens, geese, and ducks.[94] It is clear that some of these were the work of men who engaged in it regularly, partly to enrich the family diet, partly as a way of raising a little extra money. There were receivers in the countryside who could dispose of stolen fowl, and a well-established network, however modest, obviously encouraged some men to engage in thievery regularly.[95] But such thefts were more likely to have arisen from necessity, allied with opportunity. In urban parishes too, and particularly those parishes in the environs of London accessible to men from the city, much of the theft of foodstuffs and of fowl from farmyards and backyards were at levels that also suggest consumption rather than sale as a motive. But the concentration of food in the city in shops and warehouses and in the extensive market gardens that ringed London meant that there were more opportunities there than in the countryside for substantial thefts of food that might be sold to a dealer. More than a fifth of the food thefts in the urban parishes of Surrey were valued by the victim at more than two pounds, well over twice the proportion of the countryside.

The concentration of goods and people in the metropolis shaped the characteristic forms and targets of larceny there in numerous ways. It helps to account for the greater prominence of valuables (silver, watches and money) in the table of stolen goods, for one thing because there were more public places where strangers might meet, where coats and other belongings might be left lying around. Taverns and alehouses were found of course all over the country, but it was presumably easier to steal from them in the city than in a village or small town. The evidence of newspapers and depositions and published trials suggests that a significant number of the larcenies that came to the Surrey courts had arisen in public houses, especially in and around Southwark, and were thefts both of customers' and of publicans' belongings, including from time to time thefts of silver tankards. Several such cases came to trial in Surrey involving pots worth four, five, or six pounds. If, as these cases suggest, the customers of public houses were commonly served their beer in valuable tankards it makes one wonder why there were not even more trials of men like Richard Cole, alias Black Waistcoat Dick, who took a pint pot valued at fifty shillings from a Southwark house in 1738, or two women who took silver mugs worth thirty shillings and six pounds in the following year, also from

---

[94] For an excellent discussion of the theft of fowl within a broader discussion of the relationship of theft and a local economy, see Hay, "Crime, Authority and the Criminal Law," pp. 62–66.

[95] Several of Lord Onslow's servants were prosecuted in 1758 and 1760, for example, for stealing fowl, some of which they had sold (QS 2/6, Ep. 1758, 36; Ep. 1760, 10, 13). For the trade in game in the eighteenth century see P. B. Munsche, *Gentlemen and Poachers: The English Game Laws, 1671–1831* (1981), pp. 55–62.

public houses in Southwark.[96] The costs of prosecution and the trouble it entailed must have discouraged prosecutions, especially when the missing tankard had been recovered. But it is also possible that it was in fact merely an occasional problem, that few customers were tempted to steal in public houses, even when the tankard they were given was worth several hundred times the beer they were drinking.

There was also perhaps encouraged in the metropolis by the ease with which almost any object could find a buyer or be pawned. A piece of soap, an old blanket, a pewter plate, candle ends, rags, a few scraps of paper or iron—virtually anything could be turned to account, and it seems clear that many shopkeepers and publicans as well as pawnbrokers and street traders were willing to accept goods without asking too many questions. Depositions in Surrey speak of such transactions again and again: a man accused of stealing a shirt and selling it to a publican; a woman of stealing books from her master's house and selling them to a cheesemonger for waste paper; another of stealing the feathers from the bed in her lodgings and selling them to a man who kept an old iron shop.[97] It was a common view throughout the century that receivers contributed massively to the prevalence of crime in the capital and that they operated virtually with impunity, both the major receivers who provided capital and support and a fencing network for the large-scale criminal confederacies, and the shopkeepers and merchants who simply failed to enquire closely into the ownership of goods offered to them for sale.[98] At the end of the century Patrick Colquhoun thought that there were no more than fifty or sixty men in the first category (and only ten who had the capital to engage in receiving on a large scale) but "several thousand" dealers who received stolen goods in a small way either knowingly or carelessly.[99]

Like Henry Fielding and others before him, Colquhoun thought that much of the blame for the freedom with which receiving was conducted could be placed on defects in the law and the lack of controls over pawnbrokers and other dealers. There is no doubt that it was difficult to convict a receiver. Receiving was not a felony at common law; indeed it was not until 1691 that it was in some measure effectively punished. By a statute of that year a person who received goods knowing them to be stolen was deemed to be an accessory to the felony.[100] To convict a receiver under

---

[96] S.A.P., Lent 1738, p. 19 (Cole); Lent 1739, p. 16 (Bullock); Summer 1739, p. 10 (Marsh).

[97] QS 2/6, Ep. 1767, 55; QS 2/6, Mich. 1790, 40; *Whitehall Evening Post*, 29 Mar. 1783.

[98] See, for example, *Hanging Not Punishment Enough* (1701; repr. 1812), p. 15; Henry Fielding, *An Enquiry into the Causes of the Late Increase of Robbers*, pp. 68–75; and Colquhoun, *Police of the Metropolis*, pp. 187–209.

[99] Colquhoun, *Police of the Metropolis*, pp. 189–92.

[100] 3 and 4 Wm and M, c. 9.

this statute it was first necessary, however, to convict the thief, and to convict him of a felony: if the charge was petty larceny, or if it was reduced to petty larceny by the jury, the receiver could not be convicted, for there could be no accessories in the noncapital offense of theft of under a shilling. The law was broadened in Anne's reign to make it possible for a receiver to be charged with a misdemeanor if the principal felon could not be taken, and in 1718 it was further made possible for the courts to transport for fourteen years a receiver convicted of being an accessory to a felony. But it clearly remained difficult to prosecute receivers successfully because it was normally necessary first to convict the thief who sold him the goods and then to bring evidence independent of the thief's testimony that he had received the goods knowing them to be stolen.[101] Colquhoun was not the first to see in the difficulties of getting convictions of receivers much of the reason for widespread theft in the metropolis nor the first to advocate changes in the law, but it may be doubted whether even a more effective law against receiving would have made a substantial difference at least to minor offenses in London, given the opportunities for disposing of even the most insignificant object.

How much property crime there actually was in the urban and rural parishes of Surrey and in Sussex and what the relationship was between prosecutions and offenses is impossible to say. It is a safe assumption that the offenses that were prosecuted represent only a very small fraction of the total that might have given rise to a charge. In light of that (as well as the costs of mounting a prosecution), it is striking how minor most of the larceny charges were that came before the courts. In Surrey only about a fifth of the indictments involved goods worth more than two pounds, and half of the grand larceny indictments were for less than five shillings (table 4.8).

It is true that a number of other crimes against property increased the level of prosecutions, though only slightly. Indictments were laid

---

[101] On the law see Radzinowicz, *History*, vol. 1, pp. 575, 682–84; Jerome Hall, *Theft, Law and Society*, 2nd ed. (1952), pp. 52–58. Several other statutes modified the law with regard to receiving particular kinds of goods over the eighteenth century; they are listed and briefly described in Colquhoun, *Police of the Metropolis*, pp. 193–200. Receiving was made a substantive felony in 1827 by 7 and 8 Geo IV, c. 29. The difficulty of convicting a receiver is illustrated by the case of Samuel Chettle, a tallow chandler of Southwark, who was accused of receiving the fat of several sheep and lambs after a man had been convicted and hanged for killing the beasts. The convicted man had named Chettle as the receiver, and his wife gave evidence at Chettle's subsequent trial that she had gone with her husband to deliver the fat to him. The question was, Should the tallow chandler have known that the fat was stolen? Much of the evidence at his trial, given by butchers and other experts, turned on this point. On the one side it was alleged that since the fat was not entirely clean Chettle would have known it had not been taken honestly ("for whilst the skins are warm, the guts come away very well"); but other testimony contradicted this point, and Chettle was acquitted (S.A.P., Lent 1745, pp. 10–12).

against men and women for obtaining goods by fraud, an offense that included, for example, inducing a gullible stranger to play a rigged card or shell game, or pretending to be a servant or employee sent to collect goods from a shop or warehouse. Not all of the two hundred or so allegations of fraud that led to an indictment in the Surrey courts involved the unlawful obtaining of property, but that was the commonest reason for the complaint being made and the prosecution undertaken, and they have been included in table 4.1 as property offenses. On the other hand, several others that have some claim to being considered property offenses have been excluded, forgery and coining being the most important. They have been excluded partly because they were very often without specific victims, but mainly because they are so complex that the connections between the prosecuted offenses and the realities that lie behind them seem to be even more attenuated than in the mainstream property crimes. They require much more thorough and specific investigation than I am able to give them.[102]

Prosecutions tell one nothing about the possible level of coining going on. Slight variations in the level of prosecutions, most clearly in the 1690s at the time of the recoinage, presumably derive more from official efforts to discourage business than from the amount being conducted. Even less revealing of the reality that lies behind indictments is the handful of prosecutions for forgery: fewer than three dozen indictments alleging some form of forgery were brought to the Surrey assizes in the sixty-one years sampled. It was an offense widely regarded in the abstract as posing a serious threat to the heart of the commercial economy, and members of parliament were apparently easily persuaded that the forgery of particular documents and instruments should be added to the list of nonclergyable felonies.[103] But to judge from the prosecutions undertaken and the evidence given before the parliamentary committee investigating the criminal law in 1819, the law was always regarded in practice as too harsh. The committee was told about merchants and bankers who had overlooked repeated forgeries because they could not face the prospect of condemning a man to death for such an offense, an attitude presumably encouraged in many

---

[102] Counterfeiting gold and silver coins was included in the statute of 1351 as a species of treason. It remained so in the eighteenth century, but the offense had been also considerably extended by statutes of the sixteenth century and of the reign of William III, passed at the time of the great recoinage, which together brought a variety of acts under the offense of coining: counterfeiting, clipping, coloring, or in other ways altering the coinage, possessing coining implements, and uttering. One can tell little about the world of coining associations from the two hundred prosecutions for the variety of coining offenses prosecuted in the Surrey courts in the years sampled. On coining see in particular John Styles, " 'Our Traitorous Money Makers,' " in Brewer and Styles, eds., *An Ungovernable People*, pp. 172–249.

[103] Radzinowicz, *History*, vol. 1, pp. 642–50, 684–86.

cases by the social class and evident respectability of the offender.[104] Even had all such offenses been included in our count—the two hundred coining cases and the mere thirty forgeries in the years sampled—it would have made little difference to the level of indicted property offenses prosecuted in the Surrey courts over the period 1660 to 1800.

PROSECUTORS

There are many reasons to think that the level of indictments reveals little about the number of offenses actually being committed that might have sustained similar charges. But something of the character of these offenses has perhaps been revealed by some of the evidence surrounding the trial of the offenses that did come to court, and that investigation can be taken a step further by looking at those who brought the prosecutions, the victims who used the courts to bring charges.

Who they were is not easy to discover. Information about the victim, who was in the vast majority of cases also the prosecutor,[105] is not normally included in the indictment, where he or she is merely identified by name. Recognizances are more helpful because this bond, which obliged the victim to prosecute and into which he entered when the magistrate committed the accused to trial, normally included the victim's status or occupation. Unfortunately, recognizances survive only for the quarter sessions in Surrey and Sussex: the clerks of assize had not been in the habit of keeping the circuit's recognizances at least since the sixteenth century.[106] In their absence there is no systematic way of identifying prosecutors in the higher court. The printed reports of Surrey assize trials identify some of the victims of offenses tried in that court, but they do not invariably do so and it seems likely that a sample of victims mentioned in those accounts would be biased toward the rich and socially prominent, if only because the editors gave most space to the major offenses, particularly burglary and robbery.

Systematic evidence about prosecutors in the Surrey courts can only be derived from the quarter sessions recognizances (and thus for cases of

[104] *Report on Criminal Laws* (1819), pp. 13–16.

[105] I have not calculated precisely the number of cases prosecuted by constables or other officials or by agents on behalf of the victim of the offense, but it was clearly a very small proportion of the total number of property cases. Douglas Hay has calculated that only 13.6 per cent of the cases of theft in Staffordshire in the second half of the eighteenth century were prosecuted by someone other than the victim of the offense ("Crime, Authority and the Criminal Law," p. 340, n. 1). For Essex in the same period see Peter King, "Decision-Makers and Decision-Making in the English Criminal Law," *Historical Journal* 27 (1984), pp. 27–34.

[106] Cockburn, *Assize Records: Introduction*.

simple larceny). I have examined, as a sample, the recognizances of those bound over to prosecute in property cases in the years 1743–53, the period in which such cases first became numerous at the Surrey quarter sessions along with those in the first year of each of the following four decades. They provide evidence of the occupations or status of 438 victims of property offenses who chose to prosecute. Of course a man's stated occupation provides no guide to his wealth and circumstances, since he might be a successful master employing apprentices and journeymen, or merely an apprentice or a journeyman himself. He might also be unemployed. The evidence of the recognizances can only take us so far, therefore, but it offers a few clues to the identity of those who used the courts to prosecute property crime in the eighteenth century.

One striking characteristic of these quarter sessions prosecutors is that few of them were gentlemen or members of the old social elite (table 4.10). That is mainly to be accounted for perhaps by the minor character of most of these offenses, certainly by the absence of robberies, burglaries, horse-theft, and other capital crimes. (The victims of such offenses included a much higher proportion of gentlemen and esquires than the five per cent of quarter sessions prosecutors given such status.)[107] Some of those de-

TABLE 4.10

Status and Occupation of Prosecutors in Property Cases at the Surrey Quarter Sessions, 1743–1790

Status/Occupation	Number	Percentage
Knight, esquire, gentleman	29	6.6
Farmer, yeoman	37	8.5
Merchant, manufacturer, tradesman, shopkeeper	105	24.0
Craftsman, artisan	114	26.0
Victualler, publican	64	14.6
Laborer, servant, sailor, waterman, other unskilled	62	14.2
Widow, spinster	27	6.2
Total	438	100.1

SOURCE: Recognizances to prosecute in QS 2/5 (1743–53, 1760, 1770, 1780, 1790).

[107] In the printed accounts of the Surrey assizes in 1738 and 1739, to take two years as a sample, forty-five victims are identified by occupation or status. Of those, ten were named as knights, esquires, or gentlemen, or as the wives and daughters of such men.

scribed as yeomen or farmers or even gardeners—twenty-two altogether—
may have been landowners of some substance. Certainly the man who
reported the loss of a vast quantity of asparagus from his market garden
was growing on a large scale for the London market. But mainly they
were clearly not very large landowners, nor men of high status.

Merchants, manufacturers, tradesmen, and shopkeepers accounted for
a large proportion of quarter sessions prosecutions. The character of the
thefts they complained about suggests that many may have been very small
dealers. But the men described as "merchants" (eleven of the sixty-one in
this group) and several of the manufacturers were men (or companies) of
substance: they included a substantial coal merchant, two vintners, a
worsted company, and six brewers, including Ralph Thrale, whose Southwark brewery prosecuted on three occasions during these years for thefts
of barrels, rope, and other tackle. The frequency of thefts from taverns
and alehouses is further suggested by the prominence of victuallers among
the prosecutors.

The largest group of prosecutors at the quarter sessions were craftsmen,
114 altogether, a quarter of our sample. They were led by sixteen carpenters, seven shoemakers, six weavers, and included smaller numbers of
other craftsmen—more than forty trades were represented altogether. As
I have said, there is no way of telling merely from this description what
the actual situation of the prosecutor was, nor from the indictment what
his relationship was with the accused, or why he had taken his complaint
to a magistrate. The evidence of depositions (the statement that the victim
gave the examining magistrate that was signed by him and sent into the
court) helps to fill this out a little, however. They suggest in the first
place that many of the craftsmen who brought prosecutions for a minor
theft were men of modest means. Some were small masters prosecuting
employees for theft on the job. Typical of these allegations was that of a
carpenter in 1764 that he

> lost three saws and a turkey stone out of one of the houses now
> building in Bermondsey and he believes the prisoner William
> Perkins stole them for that he has been employed by this in-
> formant and left his work soon after the robbery had been com-
> mitted and was there seen at an unusual time that morning.[108]

Another man, a brushmaker in Southwark, complained to a magistrate
about a journeyman who had worked for him and had stolen a saw that
he had found by making the rounds of the pawnbrokers' shops.[109] Many

[108] QS 2/6, Mich. 1764, 42.
[109] QS 2/6, Ea. 1752, 4.

complaints were brought by journeymen and by men whose depositions, often signed by a mark, suggest that they were not likely to have been able to afford the costs of prosecution very easily. The two shipwrights who charged a man with stealing their saws in the yard of Edward Harris in Southwark were presumably merely employed there, and numbers of other examples are to be found in the depositions of workmen prosecuting others for taking their tools at work: a wheel-maker, a carpenter, and a sawyer, for example. Other artisans brought prosecutions against men and women who they charged had stolen from their lodgings.[110]

In addition, a significant number of prosecutors were unskilled men. Thirty-three described themselves in their recognizances as laborers and another twenty-nine as servants, sailors, lightermen, or watermen. Altogether they accounted for some fourteen per cent of those bound over to prosecute at the quarter sessions for a minor property crime. Included among them was a waterman who charged two women who rented a room in his house with stealing from him "a bar of iron, a white waistcoat, a linen sheet and a copper saucepan," all of which he found at a pawnbroker's in Wandsworth; and the underostler of the Bush Inn in Farnham who brought a complaint against "a lame fellow . . . who used to lurk about the Bush Inn yard" for taking his spurs and selling them in a shop in Farnham.[111] At both the assizes and the quarter sessions cases were brought by men and women who, according to their depositions or their testimony in court, were in circumstances in which the costs of prosecution must have been a significant concern. It is possible that in some of these cases the costs were being borne by an employer. That seems entirely likely, for example, in the case of domestic servants or servants in husbandry who brought charges against a fellow employee. A man like Joseph Legg, "servant to Robert Albury, farmer of St. Marthas on the Hill," who lost most of his clothes when a fellow servant broke into his box (in a room in which seven of them slept) and then left suddenly, was undoubtedly encouraged to go after him by the farmer and perhaps also helped with the costs of prosecution.[112] Several servants prosecuted others for similar

[110] QS 2/6, Ep. 1745, 19; Ea. 1752, 5; Ep. 1764, 37. A journeyman baker who lodged in a widow's house in Rotherhithe charged a woman who lived in the same house with stealing the £6.8.0 he had "saved and got together" and that he kept in a locked box in his room when he found the box broken open, and this woman some days later "got new cloaths of different sorts" that she could not account for (QS 2/6, Mich. 1767, 34). For other examples: a cordwainer prosecuted a man for stealing his watch from his room (QS 2/6, Ep. 1759, 27); a blacksmith complained to a magistrate about his loss of a hen, valued at 1s.6d. (QS 2/6, Ep. 1759, 30); a carpenter prosecuted a man for stealing a teakettle from his workshop in Southwark (QS 2/6, Ep. 1785, 16).

[111] QS 2/6, Ea. 1752, 2a; Ep. 1760, 22.

[112] QS 2/6, Ea. 1772, 48.

thefts in these years at the quarter sessions. Some had lost the few pounds they had saved up after months and years of work, and they must have needed little encouragement to complain to a magistrate if that was the only way to get their money back. It is not inconceivable, in addition, that some wanted to get revenge for the loss of the money that, as one woman said, they had worked hard for.[113]

It is impossible to say how many of the artisans and laborers or watermen or servants who prosecuted for property offenses at the assizes or quarter sessions were encouraged and helped to do so by employers: there is no reliable evidence on this point. The payment of prosecution expenses after 1752 perhaps encouraged some men to bring a complaint forward who might not have done so earlier, but even before that a significant number of apparently poor men and women thought it necessary to bring someone to court for stealing from them. Why those who would have found it financially difficult began such prosecutions is something of a puzzle. We might presume, as seems to have been so often the case generally, the charge was brought only after repeated losses or other provocation,[114] and that many such cases were not as straightforward as they seem on the surface. It is also possible that prosecution fees were occasionally waived, though I should emphasize that I have no evidence of that. It seems wisest to assume, in the absence of other evidence, that poor men went to a great deal of trouble to pursue those who stole from them and to bring the charge to a magistrate and to the courts for the same reasons that richer men did. They were outraged by the theft, wanted their goods back, and thought the thief deserved to be punished.

One does not have to think that the legitimacy of the criminal law was accepted in its entirety throughout society to acknowledge that when it came to straightforward crimes against property—to robbery, housebreaking, and theft—there was no sharp class disagreement between rich men of large property and the large majority of the working population. When it came to mainstream property crime, virtually everyone in the society was propertied. Of course the particular form of the criminal law was determined by those whose interests were represented directly in parliament; and obviously the rich had, as always, greater access to the courts. But the trials at the quarter sessions and assizes did not range the rich on one side and the poor on the other. Artisans and laboring men were simply not as unconcerned about theft, as hostile to the criminal law, nor as shut out from the courts by poverty and ignorance as such a

[113] S.A.P., Lent 1752, p. 15 (Langsden).
[114] As in the case of the Southwark clothworker who charged a woman with taking an apron from his house, having "lost divers things out of his house" before (QS 2/6, Ep. 1752, 32).

view of the eighteenth-century courtroom would suggest. The evidence about those who brought prosecution in the eighteenth century casts great doubt on that, evidence not only from Surrey but also from the quarter sessions in Essex in which Peter King found unskilled men and women bringing prosecutions in significant numbers.[115]

There can be no doubt that poor men would not have found it an easy matter to appeal to the courts. But it is important that we not overemphasize the remoteness of magistrates or the courts to the ordinary man in the eighteenth century or assume and exaggerate his inarticulateness. Englishmen at all levels shared a powerful awareness of the rights and liberties they had inherited from the struggles of the seventeenth century and that were guaranteed by the constitution and the common law in the eighteenth. The rights of free-born Englishmen were frequently invoked, particularly freedom from arbitrary arrest and the right to be tried by a jury. It seems implausible that such rights would have been so widely celebrated had ordinary men thought of the courts as fundamentally closed to their interests and as oppressive institutions. It seems on the contrary that the English courts were accessible to the ordinary man (though of course the costs of prosecution, even after the legislation allowing the courts to repay most of them, must obviously have discouraged many from bringing a case) and that the criminal law relating to the mainstream property offenses of burglary, robbery, and larceny rested on values widely shared throughout the society.

Who then, one might ask, committed offenses, and what was the fundamental character of property crime in the eighteenth century? There is, of course, no single or simple answer to such questions, for undoubtedly

[115] King, "Decision-Makers and Decision-Making," pp. 25–58. King found that about a third of those bound over to prosecute in felonies at the Essex quarter sessions between 1760 and 1800 were farmers or yeomen, another third were "tradesmen and artisans" (i.e., my categories three and four together), 17.8 per cent were laborers, and 3.4 per cent were of "maritime occupations" (p. 29, table 1a). On the basis of depositions and other evidence, as well as these recognizances, King concludes that a "broad group of farmers, tradesmen and artisans . . . dominated quarter sessions prosecutions," but he also remarks on the number of laboring men who brought charges and argues that they too "made extensive use of the courts for their own purposes" (pp. 32–33). David Philips also found a significant number of working men amongst prosecutors in the Black Country in the middle decades of the nineteenth century (*Crime and Authority*, p. 128). And in Staffordshire in the previous century, Hay concluded that close to a fifth of prosecutions were "brought by, or on behalf of, labouring men" ("Crime, Authority and the Criminal Law," p. 396, and table 7.4). But elsewhere Hay has urged caution in interpreting such findings, emphasizing particularly (in a comment stimulated by Philips' work) that "without knowing the circumstances of each case brought by a poor prosecutor, it is difficult to know whether they represent personal disputes, malice, or have other meanings beyond the prosecution of 'crime' " ("Crime and Justice in Eighteenth- and Nineteenth-Century England," *Crime and Justice: An Annual Review of Research* 2 [1980], pp. 73–74).

offenses and offenders ranged over a wide variety of types, from the spur-of-the-moment grab by a hungry boy to the carefully thought out operations of groups of committed robbers and burglars. But if, as we have suggested, the forms of prosecuted offenses can be seen to relate to local economic and social structures in the sense that they defined opportunities for certain kinds of crimes and created the circumstances of control and surveillance in which offenses might be inhibited or encouraged, one might also expect those economic and social contexts to determine the character of crime in deeper and more fundamental ways. That is the subject of the following chapter, in which we will explore further the character of property crime in the eighteenth century. In so doing we will confront an explanation of crime that became increasingly compelling to contemporaries at the end of the eighteenth century and into the nineteenth—that is, that crime was very largely the work of an alienated fringe population living in idleness, immorality, and depravity, in fact a criminal, and a dangerous, class that congregated particularly in London and the enlarging cities. In challenging this view of property offenses, we will investigate in the first place the fluctuations of prosecutions over time and particularly their differing patterns in urban and rural parishes, and go on to analyze the limited evidence that can be uncovered in the eighteenth century of the identity of those brought to trial. My intention is to investigate further the way that the range and pattern of prosecutions derived from local economic and social relationships and the immediate circumstances of life and labor of the working population, and to continue to investigate the extent to which prosecutions can be thought to reflect the patterns of crime "actually" committed.

CHAPTER 5

PATTERNS OF PROSECUTION AND THE
CHARACTER OF PROPERTY CRIME

The property offenses brought to the quarter sessions and assizes resulted from a process of prosecution that depended on the willingness of victims to press charges and the acquiescence and cooperation of magistrates, constables, and the grand jury. Undoubtedly the decision of prosecutors to report offenses and of officials to send them to trial was influenced by what each took the state of crime to be—just as, as we will see, the willingness of juries to convict the accused varied with the number and the seriousness of offenses before the court. The crucial question for the study of crime in the judicial records is whether indictments mainly reflect such opinion, or can be taken on the other hand to mirror to some degree the changing reality of law-breaking. It is certain that the offenses brought to court represent merely a fraction of the "offenses" that might have been charged, of the occasions on which someone thought that the law had been broken: the rest had gone undetected or unreported by the victim or had not come to indictment because the accused could not be found or arrested or because the evidence was too weak. And since the relation between the sample of crime that was recorded in the court record and the larger number of events is unknown, and unknowable, the indictments at any session of the court or those prosecuted in any particular period cannot provide us directly with a guide to the reality of property crime in the community, either its character or its level.

Few people would dispute that fundamental point. That does not mean, however, that indictments do not reveal anything at all about the reality of crime. If the extent of the offenses actually committed were reflected even to *some* degree in the indictments brought to court, then fluctuations in the aggregate level of cases over time—session to session, year to year, decade to decade—might suggest very broadly some of the circumstances under which property offenses increased or diminished and thus provide some evidence of their character in this period. That of course is the central question: whether there is any such relationship at all. A variety of views have been expressed on that in recent years. Some historians (particularly of course those who have centered their work on the indictment files) have remained optimistic that prosecutions are likely to mirror the changing reality of crime; others (working often at the level of the parish) have insisted on the problematic character of indictments and have emphasized the extent to which judicial records are likely to reflect the process of prosecution.[1]

I want to argue in this chapter that the fluctuations of indictments are likely to reflect both the changing reality of crime and changing attitudes toward it. It is impossible to specify precisely the various effects on prosecution of the movement of opinion and the reality of offenses. But the evidence seems to me to suggest that over the short term and with regard to property offenses (though not for victimless crimes like drunkenness, prostitution, and gambling) the formation of opinion largely followed the changing level of offenses, at least as those levels were suggested by reports in the press and by the length of court calendars. Over the longer term changing attitudes toward crime and changes in the law and administration are likely to have had a substantial effect on the number of cases prosecuted. Such developments in the eighteenth century, for example, as the authorities' encouragement of prosecution by offering

[1] In the former group I would place J. S. Cockburn, "The Nature and Incidence of Crime in England, 1559–1625," in Cockburn, ed., *Crime in England*, pp. 49–71; and my own previous work, especially "The Pattern of Crime in England, 1660–1800," *Past and Present* 62 (1974), pp. 47–95, and "The Criminality of Women in Eighteenth-Century England," *Journal of Social History* 8 (1975), pp. 80–116. Doubts about the usefulness of that approach were expressed by John Styles in a paper to the Social History Society Annual Conference in 1977; see a brief report of his paper in "18th-Century English Criminal Records," *Social History Society Newsletter* 2, no. 1 (Spring 1977). And other historians have developed other lines of criticism by investigating the process of prosecution and revealing the layers of discretion that attended the origins of indictments. The result has been some excellent detailed work on the considerations that might lie behind the decision to prosecute. See in particular Keith Wrightson and David Levine, *Poverty and Piety in an English Village: Terling, 1525–1700* (1979), chap. 5; M. J. Ingram, "Communities and Courts: Law and Disorder in Early-Seventeenth-Century Wiltshire," in Cockburn, ed., *Crime in England*, pp. 110–34; and the essays in the same volume by T. C. Curtis, "Quarter Sessions Appearances and Their Background: A Seventeenth-Century Regional Study," and J. A. Sharpe, "Crime and Delinquency in an Essex Parish." See also Sharpe's essay "Enforcing the Law in the Seventeenth-Century English Village," in Gatrell, Lenman, and Parker, eds., *Crime and the Law*, pp. 97–119; his *Crime in Seventeenth-Century England: A County Study* (Cambridge, 1983); Peter King, "Decision-Makers and Decision-Making in the English Criminal Law, 1750–1800," *Historical Journal* 27 (1984), pp. 25–58; and Cynthia Herrup, "The Common Peace: Legal Structure and Legal Substance in East Sussex, 1594–1640" (Ph.D. thesis, Northwestern University, 1982), esp. chaps. 3–4. For an analysis of this question, including an effective criticism of the most extreme version of the view that indictments can only be taken to reflect the decisions of prosecutors and officials, see the masterful essay by Douglas Hay, "War, Dearth and Theft in the Eighteenth Century: The Record of the English Courts," *Past and Present* 95 (1982), pp. 117–60, in which the meaning of indictments is effectively examined and judicial data for Staffordshire in the second half of the eighteenth century are subjected to a sophisticated and revealing analysis. It will be clear in this chapter that I have learned a great deal from this important piece of work.

rewards for conviction and by paying some court costs, the increasing availability of magistrates (at least in and around London in the second half of the century), the improvement in the watch and policing, the increased use of newspaper advertising, are all likely to have enlarged the proportion of offenses that resulted in a prosecution. On the other hand, there is some reason to think that victims of property crimes were in creasingly discouraged from prosecuting a charge in the same period by a dislike for the law, and particularly by a growing distaste for the capital punishment that threatened so many thieves and robbers. The effects of these contradictory forces are impossible to measure, but it is certain that they make it unlikely that trends in prosecutions provide us with a precise guide to the changing levels of "real" crime over the long term.

Over the short term, however, and particularly from year to year, those considerations are not as likely to have influenced the proportion of offenses brought to court. Momentary anxiety about the crime level, or lack of concern in other circumstances, might have affected the victims' willingness to prosecute; but if such shifts in attitude followed from real changes in the levels of offenses (as I believe they did) rather than operating independently of them, they would not invalidate the study of short-term fluctuations as guides to shifting crime levels. We must also remember, though, that we are dealing with very small numbers of cases—about a hundred a year in Surrey, a third of that in Sussex—and that, as John Styles has pointed out, in such circumstances it would not take much of a change in "the propensity of victims to prosecute," a change that might be induced by official encouragements or by attitudes toward the law or by current views of the state of crime, to produce "considerable proportional changes in annual totals of indictments."[2] We will do well to keep that problem in mind especially when annual fluctuations of indictments appear to be particularly striking.

I will take the view in this chapter, then, that indictments arise at the intersection of property crime, which is itself the product of decision-making by those who committed it, and the shifting determination of its victims and those responsible for the administration of justice to discourage and diminish it. I follow Douglas Hay in thinking that we need to explore both in order to assess the meaning of the judicial record.[3] I will not argue that indictments really do after all provide a means by which crime can be measured, nor that changes over time in the level of cases in court reveal the dimensions of changes in offenses. But in the course of examining short-term changes in property indictments in the first part of this chapter,

[2] Styles, "18th-Century Criminal Records."
[3] Hay, "War, Dearth and Theft," pp. 158–60.

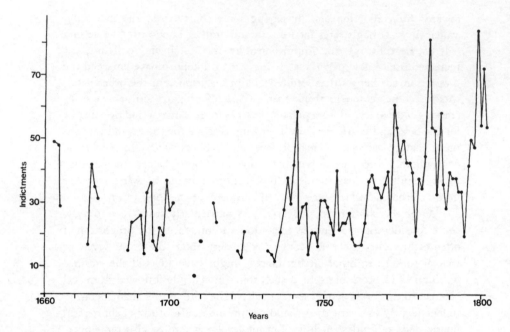

Figure 5.1   Indictments for Crimes against Property: Rural Parishes of Surrey.

and in attempting to relate them to changes in social and economic circumstances, I hope to show that while the movement of opinion about
the state of crime had an effect on the level of indictments, these fluctuations derive ultimately from changes in real offenses and that the patterns of prosecutions can thus provide clues to the nature of property crime
in this period. That general subject will then be carried forward in the
remainder of the chapter in a study of those accused of property offenses—
sex differences will be considered, for example, and, as much as the evidence
allows, the ages and occupations of defendants and the extent to which
they had been organized in criminal gangs.

FOOD PRICES AND PROPERTY CRIME

The indictments laid annually for property offenses arising in the rural
parishes and the market towns of Surrey in the years for which the data
are complete are presented in figure 5.1, and the sample drawn from Sussex
in figure 5.2. (The rather different pattern of prosecutions in the urban
parishes of Surrey will be considered in a later section of this chapter.)[4]

[4] To take some account of the shifting boundary between the urban and rural parts of Surrey
over the century and a half we are dealing with, I have divided the county into three parts—

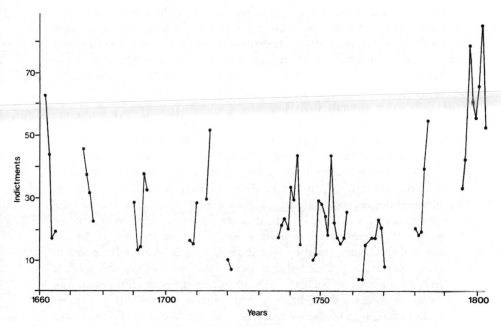

Figure 5.2   Indictments for Crimes against Property: Sussex.

In all cases the indictments included are those prosecuted before the quarter sessions and assizes for property offenses—robbery, burglary, and larcency—with which I have included the few cases of fraud that came to trial on the grounds that they are likely to have been motivated by reasons similar to those behind larceny. Although I have counted the indictments tried in the court sessions of each calendar year, the offenses date very roughly (because of the timing of the meetings of the assize courts and the quarter sessions) from the late summer of one year to the late summer of the year in question—a "court year" rather than strictly a calendar year.[5]

the Borough of Southwark and those neighboring parishes that were clearly within the metropolis of London even in 1660; the ring of parishes around that area that were within the environs of London; and the rural parishes and market towns of the county—and then counted a shifting proportion of the "environs" as being drawn into the "urban" area over the course of the period and a shifting proportion of the indictments arising there as being "urban" rather than "rural." In the period before 1750 I have counted arbitrarily a quarter of the indictments and a quarter of the population in the parishes that I have called the "environs" of London as being "urban"; thereafter, I have counted half the indictments and population as being within the city. It should perhaps be said that this adjustment does not greatly alter the fundamental differences between patterns of prosecution in the urban and rural parishes of Surrey. Those differences would remain decisive even if the urban area was taken to consist only of the Borough of Southwark and its neighboring parishes within the Bills of Mortality.

[5] Since the assizes met generally in March and August (or July) and the quarter sessions in

Because I will be particularly concerned here with the patterns of annual fluctuations, the indictments are given in these graphs without concern for the changing populations of Surrey and Sussex. If that were taken into account, as far as those numbers can be estimated, the result would be to flatten the late-eighteenth-century increase considerably since the population was relatively stable from the mid-seventeenth to the mid-eighteenth and increased strongly thereafter.

Despite the obvious problems posed by long-term fluctuations, we might note at the outset the broad similarity between the movement of prosecutions in the rural parishes of Surrey and in Sussex. The long-run trends in both appear to move broadly together, without being identical. Over the first half of the period there is clearly some danger that the picture of decline they both suggest is an accident of record-survival, since the data are very patchy. But the downward trend appears to be genuine enough. It matches and continues a trend from the 1630s into the late seventeenth century noted by Sharpe for Essex.[6] In the rural parishes of Surrey, prosecutions averaged over forty a year in 1663–65 and seem to have fallen from that point through the late seventeenth century and into the fourth decade of the eighteenth. Apart from an unusually large number of cases brought to the Surrey courts in 1740–41, the level of indictments appears to have held reasonably steady from the 1730s into the 1760s, when a new upward trend set in and with it a new pattern of much sharper annual fluctuations than had been the case earlier. The general increase is largely explained by the rise in the population, but the fluctuations are not of course diminished by taking that into account. They bring a change to what had been the expected pattern of rural prosecutions. In Sussex, the decline from mid-seventeenth-century levels is both clearer than in rural Surrey and longer maintained when one considers how much lower

January, April, July, and October, the effect of basing the annual count on the calendar year is to include offenses prosecuted roughly from September to August at the assizes and October to September at the quarter sessions. There would be some slight advantage in creating a different "court year" by substituting the previous year's Michaelmas (October) quarter session for the calendar year's, so that the indictments counted for, say, 1750 would consist of those presented at the October 1749 and January, April, and July 1750 quarter sessions along with the two assize sessions for 1750. In that way the indictments would run from September to August at the assizes and roughly August to July at the quarter sessions, and that might be a slightly better fit not only of one court with the other but also of both with "harvest year." Douglas Hay has adopted such a method of calculating annual indictments ("War, Dearth and Theft," p. 122, n. 12). I have opted here simply to use the calendar year, mainly on the grounds of convenience and because the difference is likely to be only very slight indeed. So dominant are the Lent assizes and the January quarter sessions that it is reasonable to say that very broadly the indictments in figures 5.1, 5.2, and 5.4 are those tried in Surrey and Sussex over the twelve months beginning in the late summer or early fall of the year before the one in question.

   [6] Sharpe, *Crime in Seventeenth-Century England*, p. 189, fig. 2.

the levels of prosecutions were in the 1760s than they had been a hundred years earlier. As in Surrey, prosecutions then increased over the last three decades of the century, fluctuating often strongly from year to year and no doubt, despite the simultaneous growth of the county's population, giving contemporaries a sharp sense in some years that crime was increasing dangerously. The rate of prosecutions may not have gone up much in rural Surrey and in Sussex in the 1780s and 1790s, but the level and the pattern of charges, especially over the last decade of the century, were entirely different from the experience of the previous century and more.

Apart from this general conformity between Sussex and the rural parishes of Surrey over the long run, the more revealing pattern in these graphs may be the way in which charges frequently moved together over shorter periods, even from year to year. The correspondence is rarely exact in either its dimensions or its timing. But it seems clear simply from the visual evidence that prosecutions in Sussex and in rural Surrey often increased and diminished together, as though in response to a common and changing circumstance. Recent investigations of the movement of indictments over the short term have sought part of the explanation for their fluctuations in the changing price of food and in other indicators of the economic well-being of the working population. That effort has been considerably clarified and extended in Douglas Hay's work on Staffordshire, in which, as one aspect of a more complex analysis, he shows that in some periods at least there was a close correlation between thefts on the one hand and wheat prices and more general consumer prices on the other.[7] One measure of those changing prices, the Schumpeter-Gilboy price index, represented in figure 5.3, suggests that the same relationship existed at some of the moments of decisive fluctuation in the rural parishes of Surrey and in Sussex.

There is abundant evidence that the standard of life of the vast majority of the working population in early modern England was subject to sharp variations. Wrigley and Schofield have recently reminded us that by the sixteenth century "a significant section of the population [was]

---

[7] Hay, "War, Dearth and Theft," pp. 124–35; and see also Hay, "Crime, Authority and the Criminal Law." The latter is by far the most thorough work of this kind yet attempted in both the manipulation of the quantitative evidence and the discussion of the meaning of the patterns uncovered. For earlier discussions of the relations of the prosecution of property offenses and economic circumstances, see Beattie, "The Pattern of Crime," and "The Criminality of Women in Eighteenth-Century England"; Cockburn, "The Nature and Incidence of Crime in England"; Philips, *Crime and Authority in Victorian England*; V.A.C. Gatrell and T. B. Hadden, "Criminal Statistics and Their Interpretation," in E. A. Wrigley, ed., *Nineteenth-Century Society: Essays in the Use of Quantitative Methods for the Study of Social Data* (Cambridge, 1972), pp. 336–96; V.A.C. Gatrell, "The Decline of Theft and Violence in Victorian and Edwardian England," in Gatrell, Lenman, and Parker, eds., *Crime and the Law*, pp. 238–337.

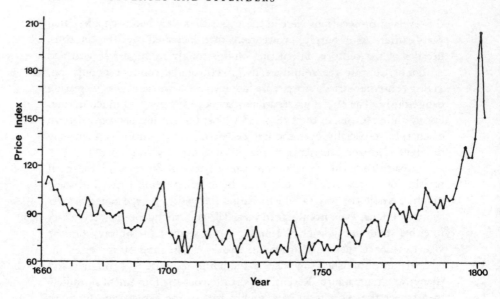

Figure 5.3   The Schumpeter-Gilboy Price Index.

dependent on the market for the satisfaction of all or most of its food requirements" and that the character of the harvest was thus a matter of the greatest consequence "since expenditure on food comprised a large proportion of the budgets of ordinary people." In addition, the proportion of the population who would be adversely affected by a poor harvest and an increase in food prices was growing over the early modern period with "the increasing prevalence of wage labour in agriculture and the growth of the non-agricultural sector of the economy."[8] There were presumably many among the lesser freeholders and farmers and artisans who were sufficiently close to the line that they too could easily find themselves destitute if the harvests failed or, in some cases, if the demand for labor diminished.[9]

In the century following the Restoration the trend of prices was very broadly in favor of the consumer, particularly in the first half of the eighteenth century when a combination of good harvests (especially in the 1730s and 1740s) and a stable population helped to keep wheat prices low

[8] E. A. Wrigley and R. S. Schofield, *The Population History of England, 1541–1871: A Reconstruction* (1981), pp. 305, 313.

[9] For an attempt to estimate the distress that the rising price of food was likely to have caused in Staffordshire in the second half of the eighteenth century on the basis of estimates of the distribution of income made by Joseph Massie in 1760 and by Patrick Colquhoun, see Hay, "War, Dearth and Theft," pp. 131–32. His conclusion is that in a very bad year as much as forty-five per cent of the population could be thrown into destitution.

despite substantial exports of grain, encouraged by subsidies. Even in this period of bounty, however, harvests failed from time to time and brought savage periods of difficulty. In the late seventeenth century wheat prices had risen quickly in response to dearths in 1662, 1675, and 1678, and over much of the last decade of the century, particularly between 1694 and 1699; in the first half of the eighteenth century the harvests failed in 1709–10, 1728–29, and 1740–41. These periods of difficulty for those who depended on the grain market for the bulk of their food are revealed in the available series of wheat prices and in consumer price indexes constructed with wheat as a main component.[10] These measures also reveal

[10] Wheat prices paid at Exeter, Eton, and Winchester over this period are printed in B. R. Mitchell and Phyllis Deane, *Abstract of British Historical Statistics* (Cambridge, 1962), pp. 484–87. They are based on material collected by Sir William Beveridge, *Prices and Wages in England from the Twelfth to the Nineteenth Century* (1939), vol. 1, which also forms the basis of the price indexes constructed by Elizabeth Schumpeter and Elizabeth Gilboy that almost exactly cover the period we are concerned with (Gilboy, "The Cost of Living and Real Wages in Eighteenth-Century England," *Review of Economic Statistics* 18 [1936], pp. 134–43; Schumpeter, "English Prices and Public Finance, 1660–1822," ibid., 20 [1938], pp. 21–37). Gilboy and Schumpeter collaborated in this work but produced two different indexes because Gilboy's was weighted according to budgets of the late eighteenth century published by Eden and Davis. As Peter Linebaugh has pointed out, the indexes reproduced in Mitchell and Deane, *Abstract*, pp. 468–69, are the unweighted series compiled by Schumpeter. He suggests that changes in the standard of living of the laboring population are best represented by the weighted series ("Tyburn: A Study of Crime and the Labouring Poor in London during the First Half of the Eighteenth Century" [Ph.D. thesis, University of Warwick, 1975], p. 87, n. 1). I have followed Hay (in "War, Dearth and Theft"), however, in opting to use the Schumpeter-Gilboy index reproduced by Mitchell and Deane. The advantage of this index (in both versions) is that it is based not on a calendar year but on a "harvest year," Michaelmas to Michaelmas, and thus closely approximates the "court year" for which I have counted indictments. The disadvantage of the index is that it is based on prices paid by institutions, and it is thus not as sensitive as one might wish to short-term changes in consumers' prices. But I am not looking to make finely grained correlations between, let us say, monthly or even quarterly shifts in prices and indictments)—the indictments seem to me to be too few in number to make that worthwhile. My purpose is simply to see if there is some very general relationship between the level of prosecutions and changes in the standard of life, and for that, annual aggregates of indictments and the annual price-index number are satisfactory enough. The Schumpeter-Gilboy index parallels the other index of prices that covers this period in the course of dealing with a much longer run of years: the Phelps Brown-Hopkins index of price changes based on a "basket" of consumer commodities, for which see E. H. Phelps Brown and Sheila V. Hopkins, "Seven Centuries of the Price of Consumables, Compared with Builders' Wage-Rates," *Economica*, n.s., 23 (1956), pp. 296–314. M. W. Flinn has noted that the Schumpeter-Gilboy index has been used by other historians: by Phyllis Deane and W. A. Cole (*British Economic Growth, 1688–1959* [1967]), as he says, "with only a moderate show of reluctance for the eighteenth century," and by John Burnett (*A History of the Cost of Living* [1969]), "with some degree of approval." See Flinn, "Trends in Real Wages, 1750–1850," *Economic History Review*, 2nd ser., 27 (1974), pp. 400–1. For an excellent analysis of the weaknesses of price and wage indexes based on the available contemporary data, see Wrigley and Schofield, *The Population History of England*, pp. 312–13, 638–41.

that the general run of good harvests and low prices was reversed soon after the middle of the century. Prices tended to rise after 1760. There were in addition at least half a dozen periods of dearth in the second half of the century, some of them several years in duration: 1756–57, 1766–68, 1772–74, 1782–84, 1795–96, 1800–01. In these last two periods, in which the effects of several disastrous harvests were exacerbated by the expensive war against France, the century ended in near famine and great hardship with inflation far beyond anything previously experienced.[11]

There were thus a dozen or more periods over the century and a half following the Restoration in which a large proportion of the population, particularly those wage-earners who were entirely dependent on the market for their food, faced a sharp fall in their standard of living. Was it in fact at such times of distress that the periodic increases in prosecutions for theft and other offenses against property occurred in the rural parishes of Surrey and in Sussex? The answer is a qualified yes: yes, but not invariably. In some periods food prices and prosecutions for theft did indeed advance closely together. This was clear, for example, in many years over the last two decades of the eighteenth century, when both prosecutions and prices often moved sharply from year to year. But a particularly good example is provided by the years 1740–42, in which the price of grain rose suddenly and strongly and then as suddenly returned to low levels. These years of dearth came at the heart of what has been called the "agricultural depression" of the 1730s and 1740s, a period of great difficulty for landowners and farmers arising from the abundance of the harvests and the low prices of grain and other foodstuffs, and during which farmers were hardly able to cover their costs and rents were substantially in arrears in many parts of the country.[12]

Food prices had been low in the early 1730s, and they remained moderate until the winter of 1739–40, when the weather was exceptionally severe. This was followed by a summer of unusual drought and then by

[11] For short-term fluctuations in harvests and food prices see in particular T. S. Ashton, *Economic Fluctuations in England, 1700–1800* (Oxford, 1959), chap. 2. For food prices and the course of agriculture more broadly see T. S. Ashton, *An Economic History of England: The 18th century* (1955); A. H. John, "Agricultural Productivity and Economic Growth in England, 1700–1760," *Journal of Economic History* 25 (1965), reprinted in E. L. Jones, ed., *Agriculture and Economic Growth in England, 1650–1815* (1967); A. H. John, "The Course of Agricultural Change, 1660–1760," in L. S. Pressnell, ed., *Studies in the Industrial Revolution* (1960); D.E.C. Eversley, "The Home Market and Economic Growth in England, 1750–1780," in E. L. Jones and G. E. Mingay, eds., *Land, Labour and Population in the Industrial Revolution* (1967); John Burnett, *A History of the Cost of Living*; J. D. Chambers and G. E. Mingay, *The Agricultural Revolution, 1750–1880* (1966); and G. E. Mingay, "The Agricultural Depression, 1730–1750," *Economic History Review*, 2nd ser., 8 (1956), reprinted in E. M. Carus-Wilson, ed., *Essays in Economic History* (1962), vol. 2.

[12] Mingay, "The Agricultural Depression."

another difficult winter: the combination was disastrous for two harvests in succession, and the results are to be seen in the prices of wheat and other food. According to the prices reported in the *Gentleman's Magazine*, wheat had been selling at Bear Quay in London for five years fairly steadily at under thirty shillings a quarter. Through much of 1739 it was at twenty-seven shillings. In the summer of 1740 it leapt suddenly to fifty-four shillings a quarter, and although there was some moderation from those heights after August 1740 the price remained generally well over forty shillings until the summer of 1741, when it became clear that the harvest of that year would be reasonably abundant. Prices fell again from that point and were again below thirty shillings in 1742 and often below twenty in the year following. Wheat prices in other markets and those paid by institutions show a similar sharp rise in 1740 from the generally low levels prevailing for many years before. Eton College, for example, had paid twenty-nine shillings a quarter on average for wheat over the 1730s; in 1740 the average cost was almost forty-nine shillings. At Winchester, from an average over the previous ten years of under twenty-eight shillings a quarter, the price rose to more than fifty in 1740.

The cold also affected other crops and other sources of food and necessities, and prevented men from doing their normal work. It was so cold in the winter of 1739–40 that it was said cattle died in their stalls or were so starved that they were unable to produce calves.[13] William Stout recorded that "sheep starved, the ground being covered with frozen snow a month together" and that "many trades men [were] frozen out of their trades and imploy, and starved for want of fire; coles and turfs being at double prices." Another man said that the dearth and the cold had killed "many poor People who wanted Heat and Victuals." Fuel was indeed in short supply. In London, the Thames froze in the winter of 1739–40 and so entirely prevented coal from being brought from the Tyne that the price rose from the twenty-five shillings a chaldron that had ruled in early 1739 to seventy shillings a year later. The broad increase in the cost of all provisions "grew hard upon the poor," as William Stout said. It is reflected in the Schumpeter-Gilboy price indexes, which after being for a decade at the lowest levels of the century moved up in 1740 to the highest point in thirty years, in fact since the great harvest failures of 1709–10.[14]

In such circumstances of sudden shortage and savage inflation, a great many people were plunged into destitution. Not only were the prices of necessities extraordinarily high, but work was in such short supply that

[13] Ashton, *Fluctuations*, p. 19.

[14] J. D. Marshall, ed., *The Autobiography of William Stout of Lancaster, 1665–1752* (Manchester, 1967), p. 227; William Ellis, *Modern Husbandman* (1750), vol. 6, p. 141 (I owe this reference to Robert Malcolmson); Ashton, *Fluctuations*, p. 5.

family incomes must have been seriously curtailed. That may have been more damaging than the increase in prices. There is a good deal of evidence of suffering, and even of starvation, in Surrey and Sussex. Pedlars reported being unable to make money at Bletchingly fair in the summer of 1740, for example, because "the Country People had none to spare." More ominous than reports of that kind were the grim statistics of the Bills of Mortality in London, which recorded unusually large numbers of deaths over births in these years. The mortality was indeed so heavy in the country as a whole that the year beginning September 1741 saw one of highest rates of mortality in the entire early modern period, one of very few years placed by Wrigley and Schofield in a category of mortality crises of the highest degree of severity. The year following was not too far behind. As an indication of what could happen under the circumstances then prevailing, an unusually large number of prisoners died in the Surrey county jail in 1740 and 1741. Their allowance from the county of one penny a day for bread had brought less and less as prices rose steeply. It had been raised belatedly to three half-pence in January 1741 and to two pence in April. But by then several dozen prisoners had died, many of whom the magistrates themselves thought had starved to death.[15]

It is certain that a considerable proportion of the population of Surrey and Sussex went hungry and suffered a variety of privations in those years. It looks as though many more of them than would normally have done so closed some of the gap between what they could earn or grow and what was necessary to sustain life by stealing. That seems to be the most satisfactory explanation of the sharp rise in prosecutions for theft in 1740 and 1741, especially in the latter year, when after months of difficulties life must have been becoming desperate for many. Over the 1730s prosecutions for property offenses from the rural parishes of Surrey averaged just over twenty-two a year. In 1740 this rose to forty-two, and in 1741 to fifty-nine. These are not massive numbers in themselves, but the increase is perhaps put best into perspective when it is realized that in about a hundred years examined between 1660 and 1800 that total from rural Surrey was exceeded only three times and those three years came at the end of the eighteenth century, when the population had grown considerably over its 1740 level and when prices were astronomically high. In Sussex, the increase of prosecutions was neither as immediate nor as large, but after averaging about twenty-one cases a year from 1736 to 1739, the annual totals rose to thirty-four and thirty-nine in 1740 and 1741 and

[15] S.A.P., Summer 1740, p. 8; Dorothy George, *London Life in the Eighteenth Century* (1925), pp. 26–27; Wrigley and Schofield, *Population History*, pp. 332–36; QS 2/6, Mids. 1741, 21a–b. For the deaths in the Surrey jail see chap. 6.

then to forty-four in the following year before falling back to lower levels. In both Surrey and Sussex, prosecutions for property offenses were at unusually low levels by the middle of the 1740s.

It seems reasonable to suppose that the increase in prosecutions in these years derived from an increased number of thefts. Some contemporaries were certain that there was much more crime than usual, including a sufficient number of farmers in the Home Counties complaining about the sheep they were losing to move the House of Commons to make sheep-stealing a capital offense in 1741.[16] It is possible that part, or even all, of the increase in prosecutions was the result more of the anxiety and apprehension of men of property than the behavior of those facing starvation. But that seems unlikely; indeed, if the attitudes of jurors are any guide to the opinion of the public in general, the dominant view was much more forgiving than perhaps a farmer who had lost a sheep could manage to be. A smaller proportion of those who came to trial from the rural community were convicted in 1740 and 1741 than was usual, and the difference was striking.[17] If the outlook of the jurors mirrored the views being commonly expressed in the towns and villages they came from, the number of prosecutions undertaken must very seriously under-represent the actual number of thefts taking place. In any event, increases in prosecutions in 1740 and 1741 did not apparently proceed from anxiety about crime in rural society. Rather it seems likely that they reflected a real increase in the numbers of men and women who stole necessities (including sheep) or some object that could easily be turned into cash, and that the attitudes of the public worked to diminish rather than to enlarge the proportion of cases brought to court.

On the evidence of figures 5.1–5.3 the annual levels of indictments in rural Surrey and in Sussex appear to fluctuate in a general way with the movements of prices as they are reflected in the index constructed by Schumpeter and Gilboy. There are too few runs of complete data before 1732 to make that relationship clear, but thereafter, when the indictments are complete year after year, prosecutions and prices seem broadly to move together more often than not. The relationship can be expressed more precisely in statistical terms by the calculation of correlation coefficients. A regression analysis correlating the indictments in the rural parishes of Surrey and in Sussex with the Schumpeter-Gilboy price index reveals a positive relationship between fluctuations in prosecutions and the price of food in this period. As one way of stating the strength of that relationship it is possible to calculate from the results of the regression analysis the

---

[16] See above, chap. 4.

[17] Hay, "War, Dearth and Theft," pp. 154–56; and see below, chap. 8.

degree to which the fluctuation of one variable, say indictments, could be predicted by knowing the fluctuation in the other, prices. In the case of rural Surrey, it can be said that the relationship between prosecutions for property offenses and the fluctuating prices that are represented in the Schumpeter-Gilboy index numbers is such that thirty per cent of the variation in indictments over time could be predicted from the index. In Sussex the comparable level is fifty-two per cent.[18]

We will consider those results more fully in a moment. We should first, however, investigate another factor that seems strongly to influence the levels of indictments: the alternation of periods of war and peace. Douglas Hay has shown that correlations between prices and prosecutions for theft in Staffordshire in the second half of the eighteenth century were markedly different in periods of war and peace.[19] Such differences are also clear in Surrey and Sussex. They emerge both in tests of correlation[20] and in a more general way in the graphs presented in figures 5.1–5.3. In the rural parishes of Surrey and in Sussex the influence of the international situation is suggested by the fact that the only periods in which significant changes in the price index were not matched in the graphs by some shift in the level of prosecutions (1693–98, 1756–57, 1793–95) were years of war. There is a hint here that wartime may have provided some cushioning effects against rising prices. But the pattern of prosecutions for property offenses was even more decisively marked by alternating periods of war and peace in the urban parishes of Surrey. There the match between fluctuations in indictments and the passage from peace to war and back to peace was so close that the possible influences of war on the level of crime, or on the propensity of victims to prosecute, clearly requires investigation.

[18] The indictments included in the calculation were those for offenses against property in the ninety-eight years included in the "Count" in Surrey and in the sixty-one years of the Sussex "Sample" (see appendix). The linear trends in both series and in the price index were removed, and regressions were then performed on the detrended series to determine the coefficient of multiple determination (R^2). The results were as follows: in all Surrey parishes together, $R^2 = 0.413$; in Surrey rural parishes alone, $R^2 = 0.301$; in Surrey urban parishes alone, $R^2 = 0.300$; in Sussex, $R^2 = 0.524$. The value for R^2 can be interpreted as a percentage, the percentage of one variable that can be predicted by knowing the value of the other, by shifting the decimal place two points to the right.

[19] Hay, "War, Dearth and Theft," pp. 124–28, nn. 19, 20, 22.

[20] The results are not quite as clear, however, as Hay found for Staffordshire. In the urban parishes of Surrey and in Sussex the correlations of indictments and the price index were higher in wartime than in peacetime, as Hay also found in Staffs. But the reverse was the case in the rural parishes of Surrey. The results of a regression of indictments on prices were as follows: in Surrey urban parishes, wartime: $R^2 = 0.659$, peacetime: $R^2 = 0.277$; in Surrey rural parishes, wartime: $R^2 = 0.275$, peacetime: $R^2 = 0.433$; in Sussex, wartime: $R^2 = 0.592$, peacetime: $R^2 = 0.384$.

WAR AND PROPERTY CRIME

A decisive pattern emerges from the prosecutions for property offenses in Southwark and its neighboring Surrey parishes within the ambit of the metropolis of London (figure 5.4). After 1732, when the judicial records are complete year after year, the simple number of indictments shows a steadily rising trend particularly over the second half of the eighteenth century that is largely accounted for by the increase in population. Of course, what contemporaries were aware of was not the "rate" of prosecutions but the number of reports of offenses and trials in the press and magazines and pamphlets. At many points in the second half of the century it might well have seemed to those who paid attention to such things that the society was in some danger of being overwhelmed by crime.

We should not allow the size of the fluctuations to exaggerate the level of prosecutions: even at their highest the numbers involved are modest by modern standards. But (apart from the fact that reports of offenses were always more numerous than trials) it seems to me well to recognize that several factors combined to make some of these increases in prosecutions seem ominous to men in eighteenth-century London. One is that the institutions and the machinery that dealt with crime were limited in size and resources: jails were tiny, courtrooms easily crowded, and the number of active magistrates, constables, and other officials modest. A rapid increase in the number of men and women committed for trial would quickly stretch resources and impress the seriousness of the crisis on the authorities and those they came into contact with. A second factor that increased the sense of panic from time to time was that year-to-year fluctuations were often relatively substantial, as one can see in the graphs. The passage from a low point to the highest could be very sudden indeed. In the third place we must remember that we are dealing here with a fragment—a sixth perhaps—of a large urban population that mainly centered across the Thames in the City of London, in Westminster, and in a number of heavily populated parishes in Middlesex. The larger metropolis of London experienced fluctuations of prosecutions on a similar order,[21] so that contemporaries' knowledge and experience of crime was formed by many more reports of incidents and of cases than those taking place in Surrey and tried in the Surrey courts.

It was also the case that when prosecutions (and the reports of offenses) were at their most numerous, the most violent and alarming offenses

---

[21] Linebaugh, "Tyburn," chap. 1.

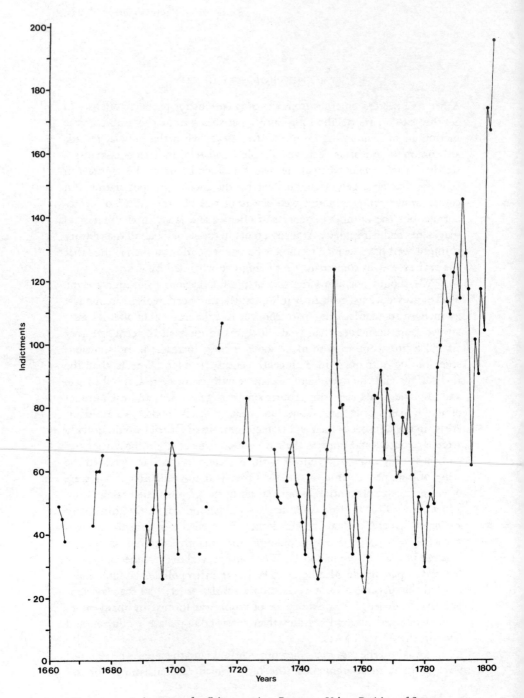

Figure 5.4 Indictments for Crimes against Property: Urban Parishes of Surrey.

committed by gangs also tended to be common. That was associated in the public mind with one further factor that much inflamed opinion and that is clearly revealed by the short-run fluctuations of prosecutions in figure 5.4: after 1732 indicted offenses in the urban parishes of Surrey fell into a pattern of remarkably similar configurations—a series of four troughs separated by four peaks or high plateaus. And what is immediately apparent and significant about that is its close conformity with periods of war and peace over the last two thirds of the eighteenth century.[22] The four troughs all came in the course of the wars that followed each other over that period (in 1739–48, 1756–63, 1776–82, and 1793–1815), and with the exception of the 1790s, the sharp upturn in prosecutions began again as the wars came to a close. The making of peace was invariably followed by a strong increase in prosecutions for property crimes that then tended to run roughly at that higher level until another war intervened and diminished the number of charges being laid in the courts. That is clear, for example, in a comparison of the rates of prosecution for property offenses in these urban parishes of Surrey in years of war and peace over the period 1660 to 1800 (table 5.1). The median rate over that period was seventy-four indictments per 100,000 population.[23] Three-quarters of the years

TABLE 5.1

Indictments for Property Offenses in Urban
Parishes of Surrey, 1660–1800
(Median = 74 Indictments per 100,000 Population)

	Below Median		*At Median*		*Above Median*		*Total*	
	No.	*%*	*No.*	*%*	*No.*	*%*	*No.*	*%*
Years of peace	12	21.4	2	3.6	42	75.0	56	100.0
Years of war	35	83.3	1	2.4	6	14.3	42	100.0
Total	47		3		48		98	
Years of peace (%)	25.5		66.7		87.5			
Years of war (%)	74.5		33.3		12.5			

SOURCES: Count and Sample.

[22] I have adopted a simple if mechanical test for deciding whether to count a year as one of war or peace by taking as decisive the situation on January 1. If the country was at peace as the year opened I have counted it as a year of peace, even when, as in 1793, war was declared soon thereafter.

[23] The Surrey population figures used in these calculations are of course estimates, but even if they are seriously deficient, their deficiencies should not affect a comparison of alternating periods of war and peace.

below the median were years of war, while almost ninety per cent of those above were years of peace. That result is even more striking when one considers that four of the six war years that saw prosecutions above seventy-four per 100,000 were 1794, a year of serious dearth, and 1800–02, when the price of food rose to heights never before remotely experienced. But not even discounting those distinctly untypical war years, it is clear that the common experience in London over this period had been that peacetime saw the heaviest levels of prosecution for property offenses and that war reduced them significantly.

It is difficult to make much of the judicial records in Surrey over the late seventeenth century and the early decades of the eighteenth, since the indictments have survived in complete runs for only a few years. But over the half century from the Revolution of 1689 to the 1730s the pattern of prosecutions seems to conform roughly to the picture outlined above. There was not a great deal of fluctuation in prosecutions in the 1690s, and nothing much can be made of the fact that the lowest levels of prosecution came in years of war or that the high point came in the year after peace was declared. Similarly, the fragments of data in Anne's reign produce a piecemeal picture, though they do seem to fit the pattern of the later eighteenth century. Certainly few cases were prosecuted in 1708, in the middle of the war of Spanish Succession, for example; and there was a striking increase in the immediate postwar period, for the rate of prosecution in 1714–15 was close to being the highest of the eighteenth century. Although prosecutions diminished from that peak in succeeding years, the few years of complete data in the 1720s and the evidence of the 1730s suggest that the general level of indictments for property offenses remained at a relatively high level over the quarter century of peace between the Treaty of Utrecht in 1713 and the outbreak of the war with Spain in 1739. Contemporaries thought that crime was a serious problem in London in these years, particularly in the 1720s. It is true that in the first half of that decade the activities of Jonathan Wild, who built up a protection and thief-taking business in London, drew attention to the existence of criminal gangs and perhaps magnified the problems of crime in the capital and encouraged prosecutions. But it is more likely that Wild's activities were made possible by the level of existing crime and the opportunities it presented for control and manipulation than that there was an appearance of crime being created by his racket.[24]

A great deal of concern was expressed through the 1720s in pamphlets and in the press and by the authorities about the extent of crime in the capital. The London newspapers seem to have carried an unusually large

---

[24] On Wild see Gerald Howson, *Thief-Taker General: The Rise and Fall of Jonathan Wild* (1970).

number of reports of robberies and violent offenses in the early 1720s: in some issues in 1722, for example, there were lists of incidents reported over the previous few days. "So many . . . robberies happen daily that 'tis almost incredible," one paper said in its preface to an account of seven robberies in February 1722, a month in which another said that the road and footpaths running from the city out to Clapham were "so infested with free Booters" that several robberies had been committed among them for ten nights in a row. In the same period it was said that property offenses were indeed so common in all parts of the country that jails were more crowded than they had ever been.[25] The government obviously took all of this seriously, for massive rewards were offered by royal proclamations over and above those payable by statute for the apprehension and conviction of men who committed robberies in the streets of the capital and within a radius of five miles, and little mercy was shown to the numerous offenders convicted of violent property crimes. In 1722–24 an unusually high proportion of convicted offenders were hanged.[26]

There are no years of complete evidence for Surrey in the second half of the 1720s, but crime appears to have continued to be a serious problem in London. The royal proclamation offering one hundred pounds for the conviction of street robbers was renewed in 1727 and 1728, for example; and Daniel Defoe clearly thought crime a matter of widespread public concern, since he published a series of pamphlets over the second half of the decade on the problems of maintaining order and morality in a society "ripened up to crime to a dreadful height."[27] When the Surrey records are again complete in the 1730s there had been some diminution from the levels of 1722 and 1723, but prosecutions of property offenses were still nonetheless at a moderately high level; and in 1738 and 1739, on the eve of the war with Spain, a large proportion of the accused on trial for capital crimes were being convicted and executed. Crime was sufficiently serious in those years that a bookseller thought it worth his while (quite unusually) in March 1739 to publish an account not merely of the trials held at the Surrey assizes that spring, but of those in all the counties of the Home Circuit. He underlined both the current concern with dangerous offenders and the commercial character of the Proceedings by informing prospective readers on the title page that the pamphlet contained

[25] *Applebee's Original Weekly Journal*, 24 Feb., 3 Mar. 1722; *The Weekly Journal or Saturday's Post*, 10 Feb. 1722.

[26] For the levels of conviction and execution in this period see chap. 9.

[27] *Conjugal Lewdness: or Matrimonial Whoredom* (1727); *Street-Robberies Consider'd: the Reason of their being so Frequent* (1728); *An Effectual Scheme for the Immediate Prevention of Street Robberies and Suppressing of all other Disorders of the Night* (1730).

"the trials of twenty-nine persons who were capitally convicted at the . . . Assizes, and received sentence of death."[28]

Of course it might be said that someone can always be found who thinks that crime is increasing, and even a small number of incidents reported in the press can create an impression of extreme danger. But in fact in the eighteenth century, while crime was of course constantly being reported and commented on, it seems clear that public alarm and panic about London offenses moved in distinctive waves and were largely concentrated in the same years in which the Surrey courts were at their busiest. It is not possible to demonstrate that clearly over the late seventeenth century and the first three decades of the eighteenth because the court records are so spotty, but the connection becomes much clearer when complete indictment information is available and when over the remainder of the century four well-defined waves of prosecution were separated by the four wars that followed each other in succession. Each of these moments of apparently increasing crime was accompanied by an outburst of public discussion of the state of the criminal law and the machinery of justice, the failures of punishment to deter the wicked, and the growing immorality of the people. And in each there was particular emphasis placed on the problems caused by the demobilization of the armed forces. Both the character of this discussion and the pattern of indictments seem to me to throw a great deal of light on the nature of crime in the eighteenth century.

It remains a question, of course, whether the levels of prosecution are a reflection of real events in the world—a real increase in theft and robberies and burglaries—or simply a reflection of public anxiety, of the changing propensity of victims of offenses to report and prosecute and of the authorities to encourage them. It could be both. But the bulk of the evidence seems to me to suggest that when prosecutions declined during wars it was because the number of offenses actually had gone down, rather than that prosecutors chose for some reason not to bring offenders to justice in the courts, and that when they rose with the peace it was because the number of offenses had increased. There are a number of reasons for thinking this. Some relate to the types of crimes prosecuted during and after wars, a point we will return to. But the strongest evidence for the view that the pattern of indictments mirrors in a broad way changes in the actual incidence of property offenses is to be found in the conjunction of prosecutions and the opinion of contemporaries. It seems to me in particular that expressions of concern and anxiety at apparent increases of crime were too broad and too complex to be the product merely of some version of a "moral panic." There is abundant evidence of such reactions in the years

[28] *The Genuine Proceedings at the Assizes on the Home Circuit held in March 1739 . . .* (1739).

of peace after 1748, 1763, and 1782 (and, though we will not pursue it, strikingly after 1815).

Soon after peace was declared in 1748 reports of offenses in the metropolis became increasingly frequent. The newspapers and monthly magazines over the next several years published numerous examples of the dangers to be met with in the streets of London and on the roads leading into the capital, of the prevalence of burglary, the frequency of shoplifting and theft on the river, and all other forms of property crime. What seemed particularly frightening was the number of gangs and the apparent inability of the authorities to do much about them. The *London Magazine* set the tone in 1748 when it reported that "not only pickpockets but street-robbers and highwaymen, are grown to a great pitch of insolence at this time, robbing in gangs, defying authority, and often rescuing their companions and carrying them off in triumph." Such reports continued for several years, including numerous examples from south of the Thames. At one point it was reported that travelers between London and places in northern Surrey like Putney and Richmond were being stopped so frequently by highwaymen that some began to meet in groups so that they could go home "in companies." Nor were such reports confined to public commentators. Horace Walpole, who was perhaps particularly sensitive to the prevalence of robbery after being held up in Hyde Park, wrote in the winter of 1749–50 of there being "little news from England, but of robberies" and that "one is forced to travel, even at noon, as if one were going to battle."[29]

The administration responded to what it took to be a considerable increase in violent property offenses by once again offering rewards for convictions, both the general offer of an additional sum above the statutory amount paid for robberies committed in the metropolis and particular rewards in individual cases. The king's speeches opening parliament reminded members of the need to "suppress those audacious crimes of robbery and violence which are now become so frequent, especially about this great capital." Parliament also responded to the anxieties of the merchants of London about the level of theft on the Thames by removing such offenses from benefit of clergy. Enlarging the terror of the law was a well-established parliamentary response to a momentary increase in a particular offense. But parliament took a novel step in these years by setting up a committee in 1750 to investigate the criminal law and to find ways of suppressing offenses "which were increased to a degree of robbery and murder beyond

[29] Horace Walpole, *Correspondence with Sir Horace Mann*, ed. W. S. Lewis, Warren Hunting Smith, and George L. Lam, 6 vols. (New Haven, 1960), vol. 4, p. 111; F. Homes Dudden, *Henry Fielding: His Life, Works and Times*, 2 vols. (Oxford, 1952), vol. 2, pp. 759–60; G. M. 21 (1751), p. 423.

example." Their recommendations for changes in the law and the administration of justice paralleled many of those made at the same time by Henry Fielding in his *Enquiry into the Causes of the Late Increase of Robbers*, published in 1751, which offered an explanation of the causes and a set of remedies based on his experience as a magistrate at Bow Street over the previous several years.[30]

As much as attention was concentrated on the capital in these years, there was concern at the same time about the increase in property crime all over the country. In February 1754 the bishops were called together to consider what recommendations they would make to counter the alarming extent of immorality; and a week later the judges who were about to go on their assize circuits were called before the king (most unusually) and were read a speech by Lord Chancellor Hardwicke to urge them to encourage magistrates around the country to do their duty and suppress crime in their neighborhoods.[31] In Surrey, where prosecutions rose in 1751 to their highest level in at least a century, the effect of the great increase in business was felt both in the mortality rate in the county jail and very clearly in the way the courts did their business, for the number of cases to be tried and the crowding in prison forced the quarter sessions to relieve the pressure by taking on cases that it had earlier left to the assize judges. The result, as we will see, was a considerable reorganization of the work of the courts.

It is inconceivable that this variety of reactions over several years could have been stimulated by the mere threat of offenses following the war that ended in 1748. Similarly, the decline in prosecutions that followed the onset of the Seven Years' War in 1756 seems quite clearly to have mirrored a real decline in offenses. It is possible that some of the falling away of indictments that occurred in the urban area of Surrey during the war represented decisions not to prosecute by victims of offenses who might have complained to a magistrate when public alarm was at its greatest; it is also possible that some accused offenders were allowed to escape the serious punishment that the courts might impose by agreeing to enlist in the army or navy rather than being sent to trial. It is likely

---

[30] For rewards see, for example, *G. M.* 19 (1749), p. 88; 20 (1750), pp. 41–42, 569. For the king's speeches and the parliamentary committee of 1751 see Radzinowicz, *History*, vol. 1, pp. 399–424; and below, chap. 2. Henry Fielding said in 1751 that robberies had increased so seriously "within these few years" that the streets and roads in and around London would "shortly be impassable without the utmost Hazard" (*Increase of Robbers*, p. 1). For other contemporary comment on the level of street robberies in this period, see Saunders Welch, *Letter on the Subject of Robberies* (1758).

[31] For the bishops' recommendations see SP 36/125, ff. 272–75; and for Hardwicke's speech, Add Mss. 35870, ff. 240–43.

indeed that when offenses were apparently less threatening than they had
been over several years the number of indictments would be further reduced
in these ways. But it seems hardly possible that the availability of an
alternative and informal means of punishment could explain the precipi-
tousness of the fall in indictments.[32]

It is of course true, we need to remind ourselves once again, that the
numbers are very small by modern standards. At the peak of 1751 a mere
171 indictments were prosecuted in the Surrey courts for felonies against
property in urban parishes; at the low point ten years later there were
almost exactly one hundred fewer. It is a proportionately massive decline,
but the actual number of cases is not huge. Nonetheless it seems clear
that the fall in indictments followed, without in any sense necessarily
measuring, the diminution in incidents that might have supported a charge
of theft, robbery, or burglary. If it was merely that prosecutors had forgiven
or overlooked offenses during the war or found alternative means of punishing them without the expense and trouble of a court case, one would
surely expect that they would be more inclined to have done so with regard
to petty crimes rather than the more serious offenses—the theft of chickens
rather than highway robbery, or, broadly, clergyable larceny as against
capital felonies. In that case the number of capital offenses would not have
been much affected and indeed ought to have increased as a proportion of
the whole. In fact all forms of property crime declined sharply during this
war as during all others. Highway robbery and burglary and horse-theft
fell off as much as petty larceny and simple grand larceny, and indeed in
the urban parishes of Surrey there was if anything a slight decline in the
proportion of capital offenses in the relation to all property crimes
indicted.[33]

The evidence of the London papers and the monthly magazines is
also decisive. If the stagecoaches had been held up as frequently during
the war as they had been in the early 1750s and if street robbers had been
as active, it is likely that that would have been reported. As it is, the
weight of comment, in the *Gentleman's Magazine* for example, emphasizes

[32] For the use of the army to get rid of "undesirables," and the example of one man allowed
by a magistrate to enlist who might have been prosecuted for assault with intent to rape, see
Arthur N. Gilbert, "Army Impressment during the War of the Spanish Succession," *The Historian*
38 (1976), pp. 696–97, 700. For the suggestion that accused men might have been diverted
from the courts to the army during wars, see King, "Decision-Makers and Decision-Making,"
p. 27, and Radzinowicz, *History*, vol. 4, pp. 96–97; neither provides much evidence.

[33] In 1749–56 in the urban parishes of Surrey, capital property offenses accounted for about
26 per cent of all property crimes brought to trial; during the Seven Years' War they ran at the
same level (24.5 per cent). It was John Brown's view in 1757 that "Street Robberies hath been
almost wholly suppressed"; he attributed this to the police reforms of the Fieldings (*An Estimate
of the Manners and the Principles of the Times* [1757], p. 219).

the relative infrequency of crime, the absence of business before the courts, and in particular the remarkable fact that for several years on end few convicts were hanged—in London as well as in other parts of the country.[34] That was certainly the case in Surrey and Sussex, as we will see. The level of executions for property offenses presented a startling contrast during the war with the numbers hanged in the early 1750s. And the contrast was striking enough all across the metropolis that Stephen Janssen was able to illustrate it vividly by pointing out, as he did in a broadsheet in 1772, how many men and women had been hanged at Tyburn every year since 1749. He made the explicit contrast between years of war and peace and showed how the patterns of executions had formed a distinct U-shape over the previous two decades, when the high levels of the early 1750s (when as many as eighty-five men and women were executed at Tyburn each year) gave way to the comparatively modest numbers during the ensuing war and then had increased again sharply with the coming of the peace in 1763.[35]

In Surrey, too, the Peace of Paris brought another increase in indictments. Neither the levels of prosecutions nor the tone of contemporary comment quite matched the levels and the intensity of the years after 1748, though there is no doubt that contemporaries were again conscious of danger in the streets of London and offenses were once again reported in the press with great frequency.[36] And there was to be a great deal of anxiety about public order in this decade of Wilkite riots and of the coalheavers' and sailors' disturbances in the capital. It was partly no doubt those matters that encouraged the efforts made after 1763 to strengthen the magistracy in London and also the policing of the capital, though the numbers of offenses being reported were perhaps encouragement enough.[37] At another level entirely, the capacity of the law and the administrative

[34] In 1760, for example, the magazine reported that only one man was executed in the five counties that made up the Home Circuit following the Summer assizes (G. M. 30 [1760], p. 391). Similar reports were published following most of the assize sessions during the war.

[35] Tables of Death Sentences (1772), published originally as a broadsheet, of which there is a copy in the Guildhall Library. It was republished in the 4th edition of John Howard, The State of the Prisons in England and Wales (Warrington, 1792). And see Radzinowicz, History, vol. 1, pp. 145–46.

[36] The quarter sessions held in Southwark in January 1764 were confidently reported to be the "largest session that has been in Southwark for these Fifty Years past" (The Public Advertiser, 11 Jan. 1764), and the same newspaper said in February that the upcoming Home Circuit assizes would be dealing with a "greater number [of felons] than was ever known before" (4 Feb. 1764). In the following months the press was full of reports of offenses on both sides of the Thames. "In Horslydown, Rotherhith and parts contiguous [in Surrey], there is not a night passes but houses are broke open and robbed" (11 Feb.; and see 19 Apr. for a similar observation).

[37] Radzinowicz, History, vol. 3, chaps. 1–3.

system to deal with crime and social disorder became in this decade a subject of wider concern and discussion than had been apparent earlier. The discussion was undoubtedly encouraged by the publication in 1767 of an English translation of Beccaria's tract *Of Crimes and Punishments*, in which the basis of the established system, in England as elsewhere, was called into question. But the debate was carried forward in print and in parliament—by Blackstone, Eden, and others and by the investigations of another parliamentary committee in 1770—because the questions being raised were of crucial significance when the evidence of the courts and in the press was that crime in London was a serious problem that the penal system was unable to check.

There was perhaps less anxiety in the 1760s about crime in the metropolis than there had been a decade earlier. At least the tone of newspaper and other comment seems to have been less apocalyptic, the fears less extreme. But the anxiety of the propertied was to return in double measure in the 1780s, when after another interruption of the peacetime indictment level by the American war between 1776 and 1782 (during which London was again relatively peaceful and the courts relatively untroubled by serious offenses), the levels of prosecutions once again rose strongly with the peace. They were to rise in absolute terms to levels much above those of the 1760s and even of the mid-century peak; and that, and the violent character of so much of the crime being reported and the fact that it seemed now to be occurring in serious proportions well beyond London, led to levels of hysteria and anxiety that were also beyond the reactions even of the early 1750s.

Undoubtedly one of the reasons why magistrates and other officials responded particularly anxiously to the rapid increase in offenses after 1782 was that for fifty years and more they had been able to reduce the populations of their jails at times of crowding by sending convicted felons to America. But transportation had come to an end in 1776, and in the years of renewed crime when the war was over, the loss of what had become the most common form of punishment for property offenders was felt immediately and keenly. Jails all over the country filled up not only with the accused awaiting trial but now with the convicted too, and the Home Office (as it had just become) was inundated by urgent requests from many counties for help in getting rid of some of these men, either to the hulks (the prison ships that had been established in the Thames as the war began) or to some renewed form of transportation.[38]

The overflowing of the jails may have been partly responsible for the astonishing level that capital punishment was to reach in the mid-1780s

---

[38] See chap. 10.

in what was to be in effect the last large-scale effort of terror to prevent men from robbing and stealing. As we will see in a later chapter, there was a huge number of hangings particularly from 1783 to 1786 in Surrey and across the Thames at Tyburn, and at Newgate after the place of execution was moved there in 1784. It was clearly the conviction that crime had not only reached unexampled heights but that criminals were more desperate and more violent than ever before that encouraged this counterviolence of the State. It also brought an unusually large number of schemes and suggestions to the Home Secretary about how the crisis should be dealt with. One of his most active correspondents was Sampson Wright, the Bow Street magistrate, who followed suggestions made by his predecessors, Henry and Sir John Fielding, in urging that more active measures be taken to control receivers and stable-keepers in the capital. Another magistrate wanted carbines and pistols to be lent out of the Tower to associations of householders who would patrol the streets in vigilante groups to counter the increasing violence. Still another urged that executions be staged in a more awe-inspiring and frightening way: he told the secretary that in his view crime was then, in September 1782, the main topic of interest to the "middling people" of London, certainly of more importance to them than the "fate of Gibraltar or the event of our arms."[39]

Two themes emerged particularly strongly in this period: the sense that serious levels of crime were being experienced in parts of the country that had not been thought to suffer from the kind of pervasive criminality and widely spreading immorality that afflicted the capital; and the conviction that there were large numbers of dangerous offenders robbing on the highways and breaking into houses. A strong sense of anxiety about the threat of violent crime emerged in the daily press, in the magazines, in correspondence to the Home Office, and in pamphlets on the inadequacies of the police or other weaknesses in the administration of the law.[40] In Surrey the magistrates who met at the quarter sessions in the summer of 1785 resolved that a new plan was necessary to counter the wanton and deliberate cruelty of some of the gangs of burglars and robbers and their

---

[39] HO 42/1, ff. 290–93, 333, 337.

[40] The *Gentleman's Magazine* said in 1784 that the number and the character of the offenders convicted at the Old Bailey "must make every man tremble for his safety, who is under the necessity of frequently visiting the metropolis" (54 [1784], p. 712). A number of pamphlets were published in these years on the state of policing and surveillance in the capital. See, for example, William Blizzard, *An Essay on the Means of Preventing Crime* (1785); and William Man Godschall, *A General Plan of Parochial and Provincial Police* (1787). Godschall was a Surrey magistrate. See also Henry Zouch, *Hints Respecting Public Police* (1786). There was a great deal of discussion of this question in the debate over and rejection of the Westminster Police Bill in 1785, another manifestation of the crisis in the capital (see chap. 2).

more frequent use of weapons. It was necessary, they said, because of "the several daring Burglaries, Robberies and other Felonies that have lately been either attempted or committed in this County, with a Force which few private Families were equal to resist, and an appearance of System and Contrivance not easy to be disconcerted or defeated. . . ." They went on to order constables to be vigilant in the control of vagrants and alehouses, of gambling and drunkenness; and they established new rewards for the conviction of a variety of offenders against property, with burglary, interestingly enough, paying the handsomest return (fifteen pounds), followed by highway robbery (ten pounds) and so on down to petty larceny at two pounds. These rewards were to be paid out of a fund maintained by public subscription; in effect the magistrates established a countywide society for the prosecution of felons.[41]

The mayor and aldermen of London, petitioning the king on the seriousness of crime in the capital in 1786, linked the violence of the gangs of burglars and others with the ending of transportation and the "great numbers of experienced and well-practised thieves now in the kingdom. . . ."[42] It was a central element in arguments then being made for a return to some form of transportation that if such men were not sent abroad or hanged they would eventually be turned back upon society where they would form a large and dangerous criminal class. The notion that "old offenders" were likely to be dangerous was not new in this period: one of the justifications of capital punishment had clearly been the view that those who committed the most serious offenses, especially violent offenses, had lost all moral sense and would be likely to go on to commit further and greater outrages. But the fear that "practised thieves" were being allowed to remain in the kingdom to spread terror among a largely defenseless populace was undoubtedly magnified by the ending of transportation. It merged powerfully with another and related source of anxiety that had been felt as previous wars came to an end in the century but now seemed more serious than ever, that is, the fearful prospect of the return of the armed forces and the demobilization of tens of thousands of soldiers and sailors.

It had long been recognized that the conclusion of wars in the eighteenth century brought "a great harvest of crime," as was said in 1819,[43] and the reason, most commentators would have said, was not far to seek.

[41] QS 2/1/26, p. 395; and Guildford Muniment Room, Ms. 85/2/4/1. For further resolutions of the Surrey magistrates to counter robberies and burglaries and to promote the objectives of the Royal Proclamation for the Encouragement of Piety and Virtue, see Godschall, *General Plan*, pp. 107ff.

[42] *G. M.* 56 (1786), p. 263.

[43] Samuel Favell, *A Speech on the Propriety of Revising the Criminal Laws* (1819), pp. 4–5.

The peace brought back to England large numbers of disreputable men who had spent several years being further brutalized by service in the armed forces, without any provision being made for their re-entry into the work force. The same complaint was voiced after every war. As early as 1701, for example, the author of a pamphlet on the causes of the violent crime then being experienced in London thought that the disbanding of the army after the Treaty of Ryswick in 1697 had simply brought large numbers of dangerous men into the country and thus increased the numbers of robbers and burglars:

> We need not go far for Reasons of the great numbers and increase of these Vermin: for tho' no times have been without them, yet we may now reasonably believe, that after so many Thousands of Soldiers disbanded, and Mariners discharged, many of them are driven upon necessity, and having been used to an idle way of living, care not to work, and many (I fear) cannot, if they would.[44]

By the second half of the century the coming of peace was greeted with apprehension, and if anything, the fears increased as war succeeded war over the second half of the century.[45] When Horace Walpole told Mann in January 1750 that "you will hear little news from England, but of robberies," he added by way of explanation, "The numbers of disbanded soldiers and sailors have all taken to the road, or rather to the street." Smollett observed of the same period that "all the gaols in England were filled with the refuse of the army and navy, which having been dismissed at the peace [of 1748], and either averse to labour, or excluded from employment, had naturally preyed upon the commonwealth." Again after 1763 the same explanations were offered: "Robberies, frauds, and thieveries were never more practised than at present," the Gentleman's Magazine commented in May of that year, "most of them committed by Irish

---

[44] Hanging Not Punishment Enough (1701; reprinted by Basil Montagu, 1812), p. 24.

[45] Accounts of the number of sailors borne and the number of men voted for the army gathered together in Parliamentary Papers (1868–69), vol. 35, pp. 693–704 (and summarized in Ashton, Fluctuations, p. 189, table 8) suggest the following order of magnitude of men demobilized from the forces after wars in this period: in 1698–99: 106,000; in 1713–14: 157,000; in 1749–50: 79,000; in 1764–65: 155,000; in 1784–85: 160,000. For slightly different estimates following the conclusion of the War of Austrian Succession, the Seven Years' War, and the American War, and for work on the army and navy from which such estimates can be derived, see Hay, "War, Dearth and Theft," p. 139, n. 51. To the sources cited there might be added Stephen Gradish, The Manning of the British Navy during the Seven Years' War (1980); H.C.B. Rogers, The British Standing Army of the Eighteenth Century (1977); and for the reigns of William III and Anne, John Ehrman, The Navy in the War of William III, 1689–1697 (1953), and R. E. Scoullar, The Armies of Queen Anne (1966).

disbanded soldiers or discharged seamen." And when Stephen Janssen, the lord mayor of London, published in 1772 his statistical analysis of convictions and executions in the capital over the period 1749 to 1771 and arranged it so that the contrast between years of war and peace would be clearly apparent, he added the following explanation:

> The conclusion of a War, thro' very bad Policy; when we turn adrift so many thousand Men, great Numbers fall heedlessly to thieving as soon as their Pockets are empty, and are at once brought to the Gallows; The Wiser ones survive a while by listing with experienced Associates, by which means in a few Years, those numerous and desperate Gangs of Murderers, House-breakers, and Highway-Men have been formed, which have of late struck such a Terror within the Metropolis and 20 Miles around.[46]

The fears expressed by so many contemporaries about the numbers of soldiers and sailors engaged in robbery and burglary and other property offenses sprang particularly from the methods that such men used. They had spent many years learning skills as useful to the robber as the dragoon: how to wield a cutlass, ride a horse, and shoot a pistol, as well as comradeship and courage. It is hardly to be wondered at that some might employ these same skills at home if it seemed necessary. It was the power of such men in gangs—their determination, their arms, their support for one another—and, on the other side, the weakness of the civil authorities that frightened so many commentators. That was a central theme of Henry Fielding's analysis of London crime in 1751, and it is what particularly alarmed the authorities in London, including Surrey, after 1782, when dozens and dozens of incidents involving groups of armed men who seemed clearly to be discharged soldiers or sailors were being reported in the press.[47] The anxiety in the 1780s about crime becoming more common

---

[46] Walpole, *Correspondence with Sir Horace Mann*, vol. 4, p. 111; Tobias Smollett, *The History of England from the Revolution to the Death of George II* (1814), p. 294, quoted by Linebaugh, "Tyburn," p. 658; *G. M.* 33 (1763), p. 256. For Janssen see above, n. 35.

[47] The ease with which such men escaped justice, Fielding thought, was a great encouragement of crime, and they escaped by superior power and their willingness to use it. Have not some highwaymen, he asked, "committed Robberies in open Daylight, in the Sight of many People, and have afterward rode solemnly and triumphantly through the neighbouring Towns without any Danger or Molestation? This happens to every Rogue who is become eminent for his Audaciousness, and is thought to be desperate; and is in a more particular Manner the case of great and numerous Gangs, many of which have for a long time committed the most open Outrages in Defiance of the Law" (*Increase of Robbers*, p. 94). The following are just a few of the numerous instances in the 1780s: a woman "who kept the mills at Dorking in Surrey" was attacked by five men with cutlasses and pistols; two men "dressed like marines, and armed with cutlasses

throughout the country was reflected in similar reports of depredations by disbanded troops well beyond London. A provincial paper reported in October 1783 that "a great number of disbanded militia-men, who are too idle to return to their farming business, are robbing in all parts of the country; in Oxfordshire and Berkshire the highways are particularly infested with them."[48]

That soldiers were "too idle" to work is another common theme. They were not ony brutalized by war, but became unaccustomed to ordinary labor and were unwilling to take it up again when they came home. Occasionally, as one sees in the anonymous author of *Hanging Not Punishment Enough* or in Smollett's remarks quoted earlier, contemporaries acknowledged the appalling difficulties that thousands of these disbanded men found themselves in because they were not able to *find* work. They were demobilized with their back pay, and the sailors, their prize money (if they were lucky). Even if they received that on time and did not spend it quickly on drink and gambling or lose it to a prostitute,[49] demobilized soldiers and seamen needed to find work. Soldiers were perhaps especially hard pressed at the peace, for some seamen would presumably have been able to find work on merchantmen (how many would have depended on the state of trade in the early years of peace, and that varied from one period to another). If trade was depressed, the demobilization of the navy would be as hard on seamen as on soldiers, and the minor concessions that parliament might make, such as allowing them to work at certain trades without having completed the required apprenticeship,[50] was not likely to be fundamentally helpful. Sailors had the advantage of organization, solidarity, and numbers, of being able to assemble crowds of several hundred to press their rights to their back pay or their prize money, or to ensure that any work on merchantmen went to one of their number rather than to either "landsmen" or foreign sailors.[51]

---

and pistols" robbed a higler; two footpads "in soldiers clothes" and four "dressed like sailors" robbed several victims in Chelsea; sailors put their expert knowledge to work on the Thames in November when ten men "armed with cutlasses and pistols, in two boats, boarded a vessel near Union Stairs, Wapping, bound for St. Sabastian, about two this morning, and stole thereabout two bales of woollens" (*Whitehall Evening Post*, 2 Jan., 1 Mar., 17 May 1783; *G. M.* 52 [1782], p. 450; 53 [1783], p. 973).

[48] *Salisbury Journal*, 6 Oct. 1783 (I owe this reference to Peter Munsche).

[49] One sailor claimed to have had £59.12 stolen by a prostitute in Southwark in 1749 (S.A.P., Lent 1749, p. 4 [Ward]).

[50] See Hay "War, Dearth and Theft," p. 140.

[51] It was reported in the *Whitehall Evening Post* on 19 April 1783 that "about 600–700" sailors met at the Admiralty to demand the payment of their prize money and that "the same day the sailors unrigged ships outward-bound, which were ready to sail down the river to proceed on their voyage, declaring that neither landsmen nor foreigners should be employed whilst there was such a number of able seamen out of employment."

For soldiers, disbandment always made alternative work immediately necessary.[52] And especially if they were looking in London they had to compete with thousands of others for jobs that might be shrinking in number rather than expanding as the war came to an end. It is the problem of structural unemployment and underemployment that demobilization exposed so clearly and devastatingly; it brought a jarring and rapid return to normal peacetime circumstances in the labor market of the capital, which had been temporarily relieved by the boon of the war.

In the absence of a detailed study of London trades, it is impossible to be precise about the patterns and changing levels of employment in the capital and the effect of war and the transition back to peace on the supply of work. But it is clear that, as was generally true in the country as a whole though in London for particular reasons, a considerable proportion of the work force depended on casual labor that was irregular in supply, to some extent seasonal, always capricious. Even at the best of times, many of those employed regularly in London trades were only seasonally employed, for many depended on the custom of upper-class families who were in the capital only for the season and on the court, which regularly moved to the country (if not to Hanover) every summer, often against the petitions of those whose livelihood would be harmed. A guide to the trades of London of the mid-century made it clear that many craftsmen and laborers were idle for at least part of every year.[53] Beyond that form of irregularity, the significant numbers of workers in textiles—silk particularly, but also other branches of textiles like calico-printing—might be sharply affected by interruptions in the export trades as would the large number of workers whose employment revolved around the port, perhaps as many as a quarter of the work force at the beginning of the century.[54] A considerable part of the remainder of the working population of London depended on even more casual work in the market gardens that ringed the capital, in carting or general laboring, on hawking and other trades

---

[52] This was why Elizabeth Skelton was so exercised in 1718 when her husband's regiment was to be stood down. She saw it as certain ruin for them: "God damn King George," she was accused of saying, "he is a Hanoverian Son of the Bitch [and] had given orders for disbanding all the Soldiers which would oblige her husband to goe on the highway or goe a begging" (Middlesex RO, M/SP/1718/Feb/63, quoted by Nicholas Rogers, "London Politics from Walpole to Pitt: Patriotism and Independency in an Era of Commercial Imperialism, 1738–63" [Ph.D. thesis, University of Toronto, 1974], p. 563).

[53] R. Campbell, *The London Tradesman* (1747), pp. 104, 118, 159, 160, 163, 193. On the irregularity of work see Robert W. Malcolmson, *Life and Labour in England, 1700–1780* (1981), chap. 2; John Rule, *The Experience of Labour in Eighteenth-Century Industry* (1981), chap. 2; D. C. Coleman, "Labour in the English Economy of the Seventeenth Century," *Economic History Review*, 2nd ser., 8 (1956).

[54] E. A. Wrigley, "A Simple Model of London's Importance in Changing English Society and Economy, 1650–1750," *Past and Present* 37 (1967), p. 65.

that were poorly paid, usually overstocked with workers, and always liable to sudden interruption as well as the common seasonal layoffs. Many workers in London thus lived in perilous circumstances and could be plunged into the most desperate straits if work failed, especially families with children when the work of husband and wife was interrupted simultaneously. It seems likely that a large proportion of the working population of London faced more serious difficulties than a mere shortage of food brought on by rising prices. The loss of work could mean utter destitution. The poor law authorities might have helped those with a legal claim to parish relief, charity might have been available from the parish church, and begging perhaps offered a hope. But theft must have been a great temptation for many of those in desperate straits.

Although war may have been a mixed blessing to the English economy as a whole, to the working population of London it brought some clear benefits.[55] It meant in the first place that some of the surplus labor force was drained off by the recruitment of the army and navy. On the other side, for those who remained, the war effort stimulated some industrial activity and provided other work for craftsmen and laborers. The war brought work to the dockyards and to a large number of trades that supplied the other needs of the armed forces—some branches of textiles for uniforms, sails, and the like, and those trades engaged in provisioning the army (a large part of which was frequently camped near London) and the navy and supplying the forces abroad. In addition, the export and reexport trades flourished in several of the wars against France in the eighteenth century, especially when British naval power was sufficiently well established to provide protection for merchantmen. And the closing of some sources of imported goods, silks for example, had a stimulating effect on domestic industry. Some of these circumstances began to change in the American war, when many markets for British goods were closed, and there was a serious trade depression when the war began against Revolutionary France in 1793. But throughout the century, wars undoubtedly had a broadly beneficial effect for the working population in London.

It was noted in 1747 that some trades in London that had been seriously overstocked were "thinned" during war, in part by the activities of press gangs.[56] And it is clear that in the textile trades women found it easier to get work during wars, even in the better paid branches of the

---

[55] This section is based largely on Ashton, *Fluctuations*, chaps. 3–4; A. H. John, "War and the English Economy, 1700–1763," *Economic History Review*, 2nd ser., 7 (1955), pp. 329–44; and George, *London Life*.

[56] Campbell, *London Tradesman*, p. 226.

industry from which they were normally excluded.[57] There seems also to have been a shortage of agricultural labor in the farming districts around London in wartime. In 1745 farmers in Middlesex were having such difficulty getting sufficient labor to bring in the hay harvest that several of them put an advertisement in the *Northampton Mercury* to ensure laborers that they were protected by statute against impressment between mid-May and mid-October if they came down to work in the harvests. It is possible that the price of agricultural labor rose sharply in wartime, as Arthur Young was to say later in the century, because so many young men became apprentices to avoid the press. But whatever the reason, it would seem that more work than usual was available during wars on farms and in market gardens within reach of the capital.[58]

The circumstances that favored the working population of the capital were on the whole reversed at the peace. It is true that exports ran at a high level after some wars in the century—after 1748 for example, and in the 1780s—but when they did not they compounded the very great difficulties that arose from the closing down of the industries that had been geared up to supply the troops in the field and the ships at sea. It is likely that the demobilized men found work hard to come by. And while the brief period immediately following the peace may have been particularly difficult in this regard, as the wartime work ended and the competition for jobs was especially fierce before some men drifted from the capital, it was not simply the transition from war to peace that caused the problem but peace itself: the return to normal conditions of significant levels of underemployment in which many men and women merely scratched a living and were always close to destitution.

It is the return to such circumstances of life and labor that is reflected, it seems to me, in the patterns of prosecution for theft in the capital. The variations they exhibit are more extreme than those in the rural parishes of Surrey and in Sussex, mainly, I would argue, because for many in London there were fewer cushions against serious adversity than in the countryside. In circumstances in which the worker and his family had no access to the produce of a garden, no right to relief from the parish, and perhaps little neighborly support, unemployment was devastating—much more devastating than the adjustments that a rise in the price of food would force on everyone who depended on the market. There were no doubt other reasons why prosecutions of theft would be more likely in an urban parish as against a rural parish or a small town: the availability in

[57] George, *London Life*, p. 182; and see Ivy Pinchbeck, *Women Workers and the Industrial Revolution, 1750–1850* (1930; repr. 1969), pp. 168–69.

[58] *Northampton Mercury*, 27 May 1745; Arthur Young, *Six Months Tour through the North of England*, 4 vols. (1771), vol, 2, p. 155 (I owe this reference to Robert Malcolmson).

the latter of more effective informal means of controlling the behavior of the offending party, for one thing. But I would say that there were more prosecutions in the urban parishes because there were more offenses, and more per capita, because the conditions in which a significant number of workers lived could quickly throw them into desperate need. When the rural poulation also increased strongly toward the end of the eighteenth century and rural poverty increased in the southeast, unemployment—particularly perhaps of women in agriculture—seriously reduced family incomes.[59] Spreading destitution in the countryside was mirrored in the poor rates and also in prosecutions for property offenses, which came to resemble the urban pattern more closely. One can see this beginning in the 1780s and 1790s, and by the early decades of the nineteenth century increases in crime in "the agricultural districts" had become a subject of serious concern.[60]

The fluctuations of prosecutions for theft and robbery and burglary and other offenses against property in both rural and urban parishes suggest that the level of such offenses was directly influenced by economic circumstances—that on the whole men who could support themselves and their families by working did so, and that when they could not find work and to a lesser extent when they suffered a sharp drop in their real wages they might then help to alleviate their desperation by theft. That would not explain all offenses. But that seems to me the leading characteristic of at least a significant proportion of the thefts taking place. The alternation

---

[59] K.D.M. Snell, "Agricultural Seasonal Unemployment, the Standard of Living, and Women's Work in the South and East, 1690–1860," *Economic History Review*, 2nd ser., 34 (1981), pp. 407–37; E. J. Hobsbawm and George Rudé, *Captain Swing* (1969), chap. 4; Dorothy Marshall, *The English Poor in the Eighteenth Century* (1926; repr. 1969), chap. 4.

[60] *Parliamentary Papers* (1826–27), vol, 6, pp. 5–70. Another indication of the effect of war on employment is provided by the fluctuation of commitments made under the poor laws and vagrancy statutes. To take just one period of contrast as an example, the Surrey houses of correction were full to overflowing in the early and mid-1750s with men and women who were not working and who had been taken up by constables and committed by magistrates to be chastised and returned to their parishes of legal settlement. There had been so many after the peace in 1748 and so expensive had it been to deal with them that the quarter sessions contracted with a man to take over the business of conducting them out of the county. By 1752 he was complaining about the numbers of vagrants he had to take care of and the consequent lack of profit under his contract (QS 2/6, Mids. 1753, 58; calendars of the houses of correction and accounts submitted by the contractor of vagrants are among the quarter sessions papers). On the other hand, during the Seven Years' War, even in the depths of the winter, few inmates were reported in the houses of correction. The keeper of the Guildford house listed no one in custody in his report in January 1759 except a woman who was "a lunatick"; a year later the calendar of the county's main house of correction in Southwark contained only three names. Again, with the peace the contrast with these years could not be clearer: the houses of correction in the county in 1763 and 1764 and after were once again jammed with men and women who had taken to the roads to find work.

of the experience of war and peace years in London points to this and particularly the falling away of prosecutions during the wars (at least until the 1790s, when even the advantages of fuller employment were overwhelmed by the sharp rise in the price of food). Previous wars had seen low levels of offenses that got if anything lower as the war effort mounted and the size of the army and navy increased.

Contemporary commentators regularly remarked on the striking differences in the levels of offenses in war and peace, and many identified a connection between crime and unemployment. Most were likely to explain unemployment and crime in exclusively moral terms and to abstract the offender (and the vagrant) from his real material circumstances. The Surrey magistrate, William Man Godschall, denied that the great increase in offenses in the 1780s followed from the conclusion of the American war. Rather, he thought they were the product of "a diffused depravity in the minds of the offenders, and a general aversion to honest employment of any kind."[61] But some observers were more sympathetic, especially to the disbanded troops. One man acknowledged in 1748 that

> the approach of peace, amidst all the joy which that has naturally produced, has raised not only compassion, but terror in many private gentlemen, and no less, I suppose, to those in publick stations, who consider well the consequences of discharging so many men from their occupations in the army, the fleet, and the yards for building and repairing the navy. As one half of these poor men will not be able to get employment, there is great, and just apprehension, that necessity will compel them to seize by violence, what they can see no method to attain by honest labour. . . .[62]

A few years later, on the publication of Henry Fielding's tract on the recent increase in crime in which he blamed the growing immorality of the poor and urged better administration of the criminal law, a Tory critic said that what was needed was not new laws and tighter enforcement but jobs "for those who are willing to work, but are destitute of Employment." Crime would be reduced, he thought, if there was public provision for those out of work, "to give them decent, temporary subsistence . . . to save many from falling when tempted by idleness or oppressed by want."[63] A similar point was made in the *Gentleman's Magazine* in 1763 in an

[61] *General Plan of Police* (1787), pp. 2–3.
[62] *G. M.* 18 (1748), p. 293.
[63] *The True Briton*, 6 Mar. 1751.

"Address to the Public in favour of disbanded Soldiers," and again after later wars.[64]

The accused added their own testimony. Many of their pleas of poverty and dire necessity should no doubt be discounted as the desperate arguments of men and women who had nothing else to urge on their own behalf. But many also have an authentic ring, and occasionally they were to some extent corroborated. Three men who were convicted of robbing on the highway between Kennington and Clapham in 1723 and who in pleading for pardons said that it had been "Occasion'd through want and necessity as having been reduc'd by misfortune in Trade, and destitute of Friends and Employment" were supported in their appeal by their victims, who had made enquiries and were convinced that the men had robbed because of their "extreme poverty" and their inability "to maintain their Families."[65] Similar claims were made at times of particular economic difficulty. A man who stole cloth in Carshalton in 1741 when food prices were high claimed that he needed the money to support his wife and six children, "provisions being very dear, and his wife ready to lye in."[66] Another man in London in the same period of bad weather and failed harvests excused his illegally appropriating the works of a watch from his employer by a plea of necessity: the prosecutor, he said, had "wanted him to work for little or nothing, and wanting money in the hard frost, he pawn'd the inside of the watch to buy him victuals and a little drink."[67]

Examples could be added from other times and places. Piling them up would not in itself make a case, but they illustrate and add particularity to the case that emerges clearly from the changing levels of prosecution. Over the period we have been dealing with, indictments for property offenses fluctuated around a reasonably stable per capita rate of cases but

[64] The demobilized veteran, it was said in 1763, "must return to some vocation which he had forgot, or which is engrossed by others in his absence; he must sue for hard labour, or he may starve. If human nature cannot submit to that, cannot he lie down in a ditch and die. If this disbanded brave man should vainly think that he has some right to share in the wealth of his country which he has defended, secured, or increased, he may seize a small portion of it by force—and to be hanged" (G. M. 33 [1763], pp. 119–20). Even men whose conclusions about the nature of crime led them to advocate better policing or tougher laws as a solution to social disorder acknowledged the part played by unemployment, as did, for example, Patrick Colquhoun after 1815 when he told the Commons committee on the criminal law that "one of the chief causes of the increase of crimes" at that time "may fairly be attributed to the demand for labour being much less than the supply" (Report on Criminal Laws [1819], p. 67). The Society for Prison Discipline acknowledged that the massive levels of prosecuted offenses "arose from the numbers who have been thrown out of employment" (Add Mss. 27826, f. 206, unidentified newspaper clipping of 2 June 1824).

[65] SP 35/42, ff. 414, 418.

[66] SP 36/56, f. 210.

[67] S.A.P., Summer 1740, p. 10 (Lyon).

displayed a recurring and persistent pattern of short-term movement. Both the nature of that movement and all the other evidence that can be adduced suggest that property crimes had a particular character in that society. The conclusion this points to is not that all offenses were motivated by necessity or that all starving men stole but that offenses increased and decreased—and on some occasions increased sufficiently to produce a sense of social crisis largely when unfavorable economic circumstances made it more difficult than usual for large numbers of the working poor to support themselves.

CRIME AND ECONOMIC CONDITIONS

Prosecutions for property offenses thus seem to have varied with changes in the availability of work and the price of necessities. It seems reasonable to suppose that the influence of these factors operated in different ways as they were variously combined—that increases in prices, for example, would have been felt more sharply in periods of high unemployment and less seriously when work was readily available. As we have seen, correlations of indictments and prices do reveal some differences in periods of war and peace. The results are mixed in that in rural Surrey they are different from those in urban Surrey or Sussex, and in that some periods of war and peace show correlations distinctly different from others.[68] The differing effects of high prices on the level of indictments in periods of war and peace may

[68] Regression of detrended Schumpeter-Gilboy index on detrended series of indictments in urban and rural parishes of Surrey and in Sussex in particular periods of war and peace result in the following correlation coefficients:

	Surrey Urban Parishes (R^2)	Surrey Rural Parishes (R^2)	Sussex (R^2)
Periods of war:			
1690–1697	0.085	−0.006	0.265
1740–1748	0.280	0.632	0.435
1757–1763	0.219	0.730	0.707
1777–1782	0.821	0.078	−0.750
1794–1802	0.479	0.253	0.325
Periods of peace:			
1698–1701	0.806	−0.001	—
1736–1739	0.704	0.261	0.697
1749–1756	−0.114	0.046	0.072
1763–1776	0.002	0.497	0.068
1783–1793	−0.078	0.303	—

be more clearly demonstrated by a method that is less demanding and less powerful than regression analysis but in this instance perhaps more revealing. Table 5.2 represents the results of this alternative approach. The linear trends in the price index and in the indictment series have been calculated, and in each case years have been grouped into "high" and "low" categories, that is, years in which prices and indictments were above or below these trends. The number of years in which indictments and prices were "high" or "low" are compared with each other in table 5.2, taking into account in addition the fact of war and peace. The result is a matrix in which four sets of circumstances are compared. On the one hand there is what I think can be assumed to be the "worst case" for the working population, that is, peace and high prices—high levels of unemployment combined with high food prices. The "best case" would be the reverse: war and low prices. Between those two extremes are the mixed situations of war with high prices and peace with low prices.

Against these four sets of circumstances I have simply counted the number of years in which indictments in the rural and urban parishes of Surrey and in Sussex were above and below their trends. The result confirms the significance both of war and peace (and, I would argue, of variations in employment opportunities) and of prices. In combination they had a decisive effect on prosecutions in Surrey and Sussex. When both conditions

TABLE 5.2

Economic Circumstances and Indictments for Offenses against Property, 1660–1800

Circumstances	Place	Years of "High" Indictments	Years of "Low" Indictments
War and low prices	Urban Surrey	1	24
	Rural Surrey	7	19
	Sussex	4	13
War and high prices	Urban Surrey	10	6
	Rural Surrey	9	7
	Sussex	10	0
Peace and low prices	Urban Surrey	22	16
	Rural Surrey	12	26
	Sussex	2	17
Peace and high prices	Urban Surrey	16	1
	Rural Surrey	13	3
	Sussex	6	3

SOURCES: Count and Sample.

were favorable indictments were strikingly at their lowest, particularly in the urban parishes of Surrey, where in only one year of the twenty-five in which war and low prices came together were indictments above the trend. On the other hand, peace and high prices were much more likely to produce a year of "high" indictments and, again, particularly in the urban parishes of Surrey. The mixed circumstances produced mixed results. When prices were high during wars indictments were more likely to be above the trend than below it, though that result is perhaps a little misleading since seven of the years of high indictments fell between 1795 and 1802, when food prices were frequently so high that they must have overwhelmed any advantage accruing from increased employment during the war. In years of low prices in peacetime the differing experiences of urban Surrey on the one hand and rural Surrey and Sussex on the other seem to confirm the view expressed earlier that price levels were likely to be a more important factor in rural parishes and the competition for work more important in the metropolis. In general it seems to me that the broad result of the pattern of indictments in table 5.2 is to underline the influence of economic circumstances on property offenses in the seventeenth and eighteenth centuries.

WOMEN OFFENDERS

The character of property crime might be more fully revealed if we could uncover in some detail the circumstances in which the accused were living at the time of the alleged offense. Unfortunately, the judicial records of Surrey and Sussex do not give us a great deal of help in this regard. As we have seen, indictments do not provide accurate information about the residence and the occupation of those accused of felonies. And because they were mainly committed to jail to await trial, few of the accused were bound over in recognizances that might conceivably have been a source of such evidence. We can distinguish the accused by sex, however, and it is worth asking whether that provides any further clues to the nature of property crime; and as we will see, there are one or two small pools of evidence that enable us to learn a little about the ages and occupations of those charged at the assizes toward the end of the eighteenth century. All of this adds further support for the view of property crime that, it has been argued, emerges from the study of the changing levels of prosecution. Let us begin with sex differences, and in particular with the prosecution of women.

Of roughly seven thousand individuals accused of property offenses before the Surrey courts in sixty-one years sampled between 1660 and

1800, over three-quarters were men (table 5.3).[69] In Sussex, eighty-seven per cent of the accused were men. In addition, as we saw in the previous chapter, women were much less likely than men to be charged with the more aggressive and violent forms of property crime. Few women confronted their victims—certainly not as directly as Elizabeth Smith, who greeted a man in St. George's Fields one evening in 1779 with "How do you do, daddy," clapped him on the shoulder, stole his watch, and ran off.[70] In Surrey, robbery and burglary accounted for about a fifth of men's offenses (nineteen per cent) but only eight per cent of women's; on the other hand, simple larceny made up three-quarters of the charges against women and sixty-five per cent of those against men.

Some of these differences arose no doubt from the greater reluctance of victims to charge women than men. The rule that a married woman could not be held responsible for illegal acts done in the company of her husband (unless he could be shown to be blameless) may also have discouraged some prosecutions.[71] But underreporting is not likely to explain differences in the types of offenses men and women were charged with, particularly because serious capital crimes made up a much smaller proportion of women's prosecuted offenses than men's. More broadly, underreporting is not likely to have been so massive as to cast serious doubt on the main conclusion the pattern of indictments points to: in Surrey women committed something like one offense for three by men, and that in Sussex they committed even fewer.

What is particularly interesting about the prosecution of women in Surrey is not so much the contrast it forms with men's offenses, but

---

[69] A fuller version of the following paragraphs on women's property crime can be found in Beattie, "The Criminality of Women." The data used here are slightly different in some particulars from those printed in that essay, largely because the years included in each differ slightly and because I have altered the crime categories a little. But the main conclusions and the main points of argument are the same. It should perhaps be said that the "individuals" counted are those charged at any one session. Thus a man or woman accused of three similar offenses and indicted three times at one session of the court is counted once; if they appeared at a subsequent session they would be counted again.

[70] QS 2/6, Mich. 1779, 30.

[71] A married woman continued into the eighteenth century to be regarded as being subject to her husband's will, and it was thus assumed that in his company she must have acted under coercion. This led to a number of married women being discharged by the courts. This rule did not, however, mean that a woman arrested with her husband would not be indicted at all. Because her husband might in fact be acquitted, in which case she would be liable to be convicted and held responsible, married women were often indicted with their husbands, and they can be found being convicted following their husband's discharge. The more common experience, of which many examples could be cited in this period, was for a wife to be discharged after her husband was found guilty, on the grounds that she must have acted under his direction. See below, chap. 8, nn. 25–26, and the evidence cited there.

TABLE 5.3
Gender of Accused in Property Offenses, 1660–1800

Offense	Surrey Male (%)	Surrey Female (%)	Surrey N	Urban Surrey Male (%)	Urban Surrey Female (%)	Urban Surrey N	Rural Surrey Male (%)	Rural Surrey Female (%)	Rural Surrey N	Sussex Male (%)	Sussex Female (%)	Sussex N
Robbery	91.5	8.5	531	86.6	13.4	305	98.2	1.8	226	97.8	2.2	90
Burglary	85.9	14.1	623	83.9	16.1	434	90.5	9.5	189	87.3	12.7	173
Housebreaking	65.7	34.3	204	59.8	40.2	122	74.4	25.6	82	81.0	19.0	100
Nonclergyable larceny	73.9	26.1	808	64.5	35.5	515	90.4	9.6	293	94.2	5.8	226
Simple grand larceny	74.4	25.6	3,870	70.7	29.3	2,745	83.5	16.5	1,125	88.4	11.6	753
Petty larceny	71.3	28.7	812	66.2	33.8	524	80.6	19.4	288	80.6	19.4	480
Fraud	72.8	27.2	213	70.9	29.1	172	80.5	19.5	41	82.6	17.4	23
All property offenses	76.0	24.0	7,061	71.5	28.5	4,817	85.7	14.3	2,244	87.0	13.0	1,845

SOURCE: Sample (excluding Borough of Southwark sessions).

TABLE 5.4

Gender of Accused in Property Offenses, 1660–1800

| | Surrey | | | | Percentage in Surrey | |
	Urban	Rural	Total	Sussex	Urban	Rural
Men	3,442	1,923	5,365	1,605	64.2	35.8
Women	1,375	321	1,696	240	81.1	18.9
Total	4,817	2,244	7,061	1,845		
Men	71.5%	85.7%		87.0%		
Women	28.5%	14.3%		13.0%		

SOURCE: Sample

differences between the prosecution of women in urban and rural parishes. Some differences are to be expected from the more general urban-rural patterns discussed earlier. But the differences were significantly greater for women than for men (table 5.4). While two-thirds of the men indicted in Surrey were accused of committing property offenses in Southwark and parishes within the metropolis and a third in the remaining rural parishes and small towns of the county, well over eighty per cent of the women so accused were prosecuted in the capital. The contrast is equally clear when one considers how women contributed to the charges laid in each area: in the city they accounted for twenty-nine per cent of the total accused, in the countryside fourteen per cent. This latter figure is revealingly matched in Sussex, where women formed about thirteen per cent of the prisoners brought for these offenses before the quarter sessions and assizes.

Part of this difference in urban and rural prosecutions of women is no doubt explained by the likelihood that informal sanctions would have been more effective and would have been used more readily as an alternative to a court case in the smaller-scale society of the countryside. The ease of access to a sessions court in a borough seems also to have encouraged the prosecution of the kinds of minor offenses typically committed by women: at least Peter King has found that in Essex, towns with a borough sessions court saw a much higher proportion of women charged with property offenses than those in which a woman defendant would have to be taken to the county quarter sessions or the assizes.[72] It is possible that the urban-

[72] Peter King, "Crime, Law and Society in Essex, 1740–1820" (Ph.D. thesis, University of Cambridge, 1984), chap. 3, table 12.

rural differences in prosecutions in Surrey were shaped by such considerations. Certainly the few years of complete data from the Southwark
Borough Sessions, the court held once a year by the mayor of London, do
suggest that women were more likely to be prosecuted when there was a
court close at hand that handed out more modest penalties than the senior
courts: close to forty per cent of the defendants in property cases before
that court were women.[73] These cases are not included in the data in tables
5.3 and 5.4; but the fact that the county quarter sessions met for its
busiest session (in January) in Southwark and that the adjourned sessions
were often held there makes it at least possible that some of the differences
in the prosecution of women in the urban and rural parts of the county
are reflections of the comparative ease of access to that court. But that is
not likely to be a major factor. The pattern of meetings certainly made
the county quarter sessions more accessible to prosecutors in Southwark
and neighboring parishes, but by the middle of the eighteenth century
the quarter sessions were likely to deal harshly with simple larceny—and
almost as harshly as the assizes—and there was by then no certainty that
a woman prosecuted before the sessions for a relatively trivial crime would
be treated lightly.

A more fundamental explanation of differences in the prosecution of
women in urban and rural parishes of Surrey is that this pattern reflects
real differences in the levels of offenses being committed, and that these
in turn derive from differences in the circumstances in which women lived
and worked in the city as against the countryside. It is true that men
would also have found life in a populous parish very different from that
of a village or small market town. Rural life was likely to be more restrictive
for all; community pressures on those whose conduct threatened to disrupt
village life were likely to be insistent and authority immediate, personal,
and formidable. The more densely populated parishes, on the other hand,
encouraged and allowed a relatively freer life for the working population.
Indeed this was identified by many upper-class observers as the main
corrupting influence of the city. The urban environment was seen as enlarging consciousness of self, encouraging unnatural desires for clothes and
entertainment that would lead inevitably to social disorder, rebelliousness,
idleness, and crime. It was particularly the freedom that city life made
possible, the lack of controls over the working population and especially
the young, that seemed to many to be the center of the problem.[74] Such
arguments rest on a central truth that life in the city did allow the poor
greater license to come and go at will, to dress like their betters, to

[73] For Southwark Borough sessions see above, chap. 1.
[74] For one such explanation of crime see Fielding, *Increase of Robbers*, pp. 3–30.

entertain themselves as they chose at the thousands of taverns that catered
to them.

But the relative freedom of the city must have been even greater for
women than men. In rural society women were particularly hedged in by
restraints, both in growing up and after marriage, and were limited in
their range of social contacts and permitted behavior. Rural women contributed importantly to the family economy, but they were normally
limited to work in and around the house—in spinning or similar tasks,
managing a small plot of land, keeping a beast or two, and supplementing
the whole with work at harvest time—though even at this work women
were losing rather than gaining opportunities for employment as wheat
increasingly dominated agriculture in the southeast over the seventeenth
and eighteenth centuries.[75] The circles within which even married women
moved in rural society were more circumscribed than their husbands',
whose work took them out more regularly into the world and who could
engage more freely in the social and recreational life of the village.

The "liberating" effects of the city must have arisen in part from the
greater demand there for women's labor, in the textile and clothing trades
in particular, but also in the intensive agriculture carried on in its immediate environs in which many women found intermittent employment
as weeders and carters. Large numbers were also employed in a variety of
service jobs, domestic service most prominently, but also in shops and the
like. Others scratched a living as hawkers, ballad singers, and street sellers,
by taking in washing and doing odd jobs, including work of the most
menial kind.[76] It was these opportunities that attracted young women to
the capital and kept single women there; they also provided work for
married women who could thus make a larger contribution to the family
income in the city. But in providing opportunities the city also created
considerable difficulties for many women. This was partly because their
wages were a fraction of men's. The clothing trades, which employed so
many, were overstocked and poorly paid, especially for women: their wages
were assumed to be supplementary, and they were fortunate to receive half
the man's rate for the same work. The irregularity of employment in these
trades thus hit women even harder than men. Many of the other jobs they
did in the city were seasonal or subject to huge swings of demand, and
in such circumstances many women, perhaps especially single women,
were often in a precarious position. Like other immigrants to the capital,

[75] Snell, "Agricultural Seasonal Unemployment," pp. 410–13, 421–22.
[76] Campbell, *London Tradesman*; George, *London Life*, chap. 4; Pinchbeck, *Women Workers*, pp.
287–90.

those who had neither legal residence nor friends and family to turn to in their troubles could easily find themselves destitute.

It is the precariousness of life that women experienced from time to time in the capital that is likely to explain why they were prosecuted so much more frequently for theft and similar offenses than those who remained in the smaller world of the village and the countryside, and why indictments against women in urban parishes fluctuated much more clearly with changing economic circumstances than did those brought against women in rural parishes.[77] Women in London were more likely to be on their own, more in contact with the wider society, more engaged in the world of work and dependent on wages, and thus more vulnerable to economic fluctuations. Many obviously turned to prostitution, particularly perhaps when conditions were extremely harsh and work difficult to find. But some also turned at such times to theft. The prosecution of women in Surrey thus seems to me to reinforce the picture of crime that emerges from the broader pattern of indictments: that a considerable proportion of offenses against property were committed by men and women feeling the pinch of economic necessity.

AGES AND OCCUPATIONS OF OFFENDERS

Two further fragments of evidence help to clarify the character of property crime by providing for a few years a little more information than is generally available about the accused brought before the assize courts on the Home Circuit. For the most part in the eighteenth century the accused offender was not asked his age at any point in the administrative process, either at his commitment to jail or at his trial—or at least such information was not recorded. In 1776, however, the prisoner's age became a matter of some importance when the American war brought an end to transportation and filled the jails with convicted men who had to be punished by some alternative method. The judges had several choices, but broadly they had to decide whether to send the convict to a spell of hard labor in the hulks moored in the Thames or to a term in the county jail or a house of correction.[78] It seems likely that it was as an aid in sentencing that judges began in 1776 to enquire and the clerk of assize to record the ages of convicted prisoners.[79] For some years only the ages of those who had been found guilty are recorded, but for some reason (perhaps it is simply a

[77] See graphs IA–C in Beattie, "The Criminality of Women," pp. 104–5.
[78] See chap. 10.
[79] In the Agenda Book of the Home Circuit, ASSI 31/12 and subsequent volumes for 1776 and after.

reflection of the point at which the question was asked) the ages of all of those who came to trial were recorded over a six-year period between 1782 and 1787. Records are thereafter incomplete again until 1799–1800, when the age of virtually every man and woman on trial was recorded in the Home Circuit Agenda Book in three successive sessions of the court. These runs of complete information, particularly 1782 to 1787, provide us with the most satisfactory guide to the ages of prisoners charged with property offenses, and it is that evidence that we will analyze briefly here.[80]

It is as well to begin by recognizing that this evidence has some distinct limitations and possible biases. Since it is from the assize court, it is heavily weighted toward the more serious property offenses committed in the county and is thus possibly biased toward older offenders. Peter King, who has studied some quarter sessions evidence in another county, thinks that it is not, but the possibility exists that data from the court that dealt with the more petty thefts, particularly perhaps in Southwark and other parts of the metropolis, would reveal a larger number of very young offenders on trial than were brought to the assizes. In the second place, the ages recorded were those reported by the accused themselves, whose knowledge in this matter might or might not have been accurate and who might in any case have thought it to their advantage to fudge it just a little, in particular to present themselves as a little younger than they really were in the hopes of getting a lighter sentence.[81] The figures are thus not to be trusted in fine detail, but they give us a broadly accurate picture of the ages of all those accused of robbery and burglary and theft in the most important court dealing with such offenses. It is at least unlikely that wildly incorrect statements of age would have been accepted by the court.

The age distribution of the accused in Surrey and Sussex from 1782 to 1787, the longest run of complete data, is presented in table 5.5: the first part (A) is arranged in five-year groups, along with the proportion of the population in the country as a whole in each age bracket; and the second part (B) is in three groups that separate in broad terms very young offenders from those in their late teenage years and early twenties, and

---

[80] King has analyzed the ages of the accused in all five counties of the Home Circuit in the years 1782–87; my sample represents roughly forty per cent of his and essentially duplicates his findings ("Decision-Makers and Decision-Making," pp. 34–42).

[81] King has found in the larger sample of all five counties of the Home Circuit a tendency for prisoners to avoid reporting their age as twenty-one. That may also have been the case in Surrey, and it certainly appears to have been true in Sussex. They did so presumably because they thought that it marked the beginning of adulthood and perhaps feared to be dealt with more harshly than if they could pass for twenty. Mr. King also finds older prisoners tending to round off their ages to thirty or forty and so on. See "Decision-Makers and Decision-Making," p. 35.

TABLE 5.5

Ages of the Accused in Property Offenses at the
Surrey and Sussex Assizes, 1782–1787

	Percentage of the Accused		Percentage of Population over
Age Group	Surrey	Sussex	10 Years in Age Group
A:			
10–14	1.7	0	14.1
15–19	20.6	17.4	12.6
20–24	30.5	30.3	11.3
25–29	18.6	23.9	10.0
30–34	11.3	9.2	9.6
35–39	6.1	2.8	8.3
40–49	6.3	11.0	13.5
50–59	4.3	4.7	10.1
60 and over	.7	.9	10.6
B:			
10–17	6.7	5.7	
18–25	51.1	50.0	
26 and over	42.2	44.3	
(N) =	(462)	(109)	

SOURCE: ASSI 31/13–15.

both of those from older accused men and women who were likely to be
married and with families.[82] In both Surrey and Sussex men and women
in their late teens and twenties were overrepresented in the indictment
column, compared, that is, to their proportion in the population (table
5.5A). In both counties the highest rate of prosecution was in the age

---

[82] In table 5.5 I have followed the age groups adopted by King to make my data comparable
with his fuller information ("Decision-Makers and Decision-Making," p. 36, table 2). I also owe
the population data in table 5.5 to him; he in turn obtained them from the Cambridge Group,
and I quote them with his and their permission. The figures in table 5.5 are for male and female
accused together. Men were on the whole a little younger than women (in Surrey), as can be
seen in the following age distribution, but the differences do not seem to be very significant:

Age Group	Men (%)	Women (%)
10–24	53.5	47.0
25–39	35.5	39.4
40+	11.0	13.6
N	400	66

group twenty to twenty-four. In Surrey and on the Home Circuit as a whole, though not in Sussex, men and women continued to be prosecuted into their thirties more freqently than their share of the population would warrant.

Surrey offenders tended to be slightly younger than those in Sussex, in part no doubt because Southwark and the metropolis in general attracted so many young people looking for work, and because Sussex was one of the counties from which many of them would have come. But it is worth noting that even the Surrey age distribution contrasts sharply with modern English experience, in which the highest rates of conviction for indictable offenses are in the age group fourteen to seventeen.[83] Eighteenth-century offenders, or at least accused offenders, were older than that; indeed, less than seven per cent of those charged before the Surrey and Sussex assizes were under eighteen (table 5.5B).[84] Prosecution patterns do not necessarily reflect the real world of offenses committed. It is likely that young children caught stealing would have been frequently dealt with informally—cuffed and whipped on the spot perhaps rather than being sent to trial. The absence of the very young from the courts is nonetheless striking when compared with modern experience and indeed compared with nineteenth-century experience, for then the problem of young offenders was at least thought by many observers to be especially serious, and specialized institutions were developed to cope with it. It would be unwise perhaps to exaggerate the contrast. The activities of young thieves were often remarked on in the eighteenth century, particularly when they were organized into gangs and appeared to be directed by an adult who acted as their receiver.[85] Many London pickpockets were said to be very young, and gangs of burglars and housebreakers were occasionally thought to recruit children because they could gain entry into places a grown man would have difficulty penetrating. But the conviction that juveniles were responsible for a great deal of crime seems clearly to have intensified in the early decades of the nineteenth century, particularly when the level of prosecutions rose sharply in the years of peace after 1815. The parliamentary Committee on the Police of the Metropolis in 1816–17 heard evidence on this point and reported on the wisdom of establishing a penitentiary system for juvenile

[83] F. H. McClintock and N. Howard Avison, *Crime in England and Wales* (1968), p. 165.

[84] Even in 1799–1800, when a large number of men in their twenties were in the army and navy (and when perhaps men were sent to the forces instead of being prosecuted) and the average age of the accused went up sharply, the proportion of those under eighteen did not change: it was still about six per cent in Surrey (ASSI 31/18).

[85] For examples of such gangs of young boys in London picking pockets and stealing from shops under the direction of an adult see *G. M.* 35 (1765), p. 145; *The Public Advertiser*, 30 Jan. 1765.

offenders in the metropolis.[86] Young offenders did not appear in the eighteenth-century courts in the numbers that were to become common in the nineteenth, nor were they as isolated as they were to be then as a separate and crucially important criminal group.[87]

The majority of accused offenders prosecuted before the Surrey and Sussex assizes in 1782–87 were aged between eighteen and their mid twenties. Both men and women were still normally unmarried at that stage of their lives in the eighteenth century and were employed as servants (as domestics or as servants in husbandry) or were completing an apprenticeship. In his analysis of the age structure of offenders in property cases on the Home Circuit in this period, Peter King has drawn attention to the circumstances in the lives of especially the young men in this age group that might have contributed both to their propensity to steal from their masters and to their being prosecuted for doing so—particularly the temptations they were surrounded by, and the constraints and controls under which they lived until well into their twenties.[88] It is true that servants and employees were prosecuted regularly in the Surrey courts, as we have seen. But in Southwark and the parishes within the metropolis of London that so dominate the Surrey figures, it is likely that it was as much the lack of employment and the irregularity of employment that explains the prosecution of relatively large numbers of men and women in their late teens and early twenties, particularly in the years after 1782, when the army and navy that had fought the American war was demobilized. Some hint of the effects of war on patterns of prosecution in Surrey is provided by the complete age data in 1799–1800, for in those years of war the proportion of accused in the eighteen-to-twenty-five age group fell from the fifty per cent of the 1780s to thirty-six per cent. Six out of ten men and women on trial at the assizes for property offenses were older than that. This may reflect the possibility that young men accused of crimes during the war were forced to enlist as an alternative to being prosecuted. But that possibility would not have been confined to men in their early twenties, and the more likely explanation is that the war brought

---

[86] "Second Report of the Committee on the Police of the Metropolis,"*Parliamentary Papers* (1817), vol. 7, pp. 327–33. See also Margaret May, "Innocence and Experience: The Evolution of the Concept of Juvenile Delinquency in the Mid-Nineteenth Century," *Victorian Studies* 17 (1973), pp. 7–29; and Susan Magarey, "The Invention of Juvenile Delinquency in Early-Nineteenth-Century England," *Labour History* 34 (1978), pp. 11–27.

[87] In the middle decades of the nineteenth century fifteen to twenty per cent of the accused in the courts in the Black Country (depending on the year) were under the age of eighteen (Philips, *Crime and Authority*, p. 162).

[88] King, "Crime, Law and Society in Essex," chap. 4.

work for young men, both at home and in the armed forces, and diminished their temptation to steal.

These years at the very end of the eighteenth century were undoubtedly unusual, not only because they were years of war but also because 1800 in particular saw very high food prices that must have brought numerous families under serious threat of destitution. This no doubt helps to explain why close to sixty per cent of those charged with property offenses before the Surrey assizes in those years were over twenty-five. But even in the 1780s forty per cent and more in both Surrey and Sussex were in that age group, a proportion that David Philips found duplicated in the criminal courts of the Black Country in the second quarter of the nineteenth century.[89] Such figures suggest that a significant number of the accused were adults who were likely to have been married and with families—which lends support to the view of property crime that emerges from the patterns of fluctuating prosecutions over time, that is that a significant proportion of such offenses was committed by a working population facing difficult times. Philips can add further evidence because he has data over a long enough period that he is able to discover the age group particularly affected when prosecutions for property crime increased sharply during periods of economic depression. What he found was that the increase came strikingly among men aged between twenty-six and forty, and his conclusion was that

> if this does indeed reflect an increase in criminal activity during
> the period of distress (as, it has been argued, it does—even if
> at a distance), then it is an increase in adult crime, carried out
> by people in their late twenties and thirties. It was not only
> juveniles who might find themselves suddenly out of work, or
> unable to cope, turning to illegal activity to supplement their
> incomes in times when jobs and money were short; in depression
> years in the Black Country many adults found themselves in
> this position.[90]

The limited information about the ages of those on trial on the Home Circuit in the 1780s suggests that a similar explanation would hold good for Surrey and Sussex.

One other piece of information in the Home Circuit Agenda Book in this period adds a fragment of further evidence about the identity of the accused. In two of the years in which the ages of those on trial were recorded, the clerk also noted the occupations they had followed, or said

[89] Philips, *Crime and Authority*, p. 162.
[90] Ibid., pp. 163–64.

they had followed. This arose presumably from the same need that had encouraged the clerks to record the ages of the accused: particular difficulties surrounding sentencing in the 1780s, when transportation had been cut off and there seemed to be large numbers of dangerous men to be dealt with by the courts. In those circumstances it is likely that the judges were especially anxious to ensure that the right men found their way to the hulks, and the prisoner's occupation was one of several pieces of information that could help the bench to get a sense of his "character" and so determine his placement.[91] Thus in 1786–87 the clerks on the Home Circuit recorded the occupations as well as the ages of all those accused of property offenses before the assizes. In the following years only those apparently being considered for transportation were asked their occupation, but for two years all prisoners had been, and it is this information that is summarized in table 5.6.

The fact that a man claimed to follow a particular occupation does not tell us a great deal about his circumstances. He might be an apprentice or might have completed an apprenticeship years before and not worked at that trade since; he might be a master or a journeyman; he might be prosperous or poor, employed or unemployed.[92] Without further evidence these occupational designations have only a limited value. Yet they are suggestive, particularly in light of the ages of prisoners before the assizes in this period and the patterns of fluctuations of charges.

There is a certain amount of arbitrariness about the divisions established in table 5.6, but a central point emerges with some clarity: half the men on trial in Surrey claimed to have worked at a trade that had required training and skill. Of course it is impossible to know whether the four butchers who are included in the first group were in the wholesale or retail trade and what positions they occupied, just as it is unclear whether the fifty-eight artisans in group two had recently followed their trades and with what success. The kind of detailed reconstruction of their biographies that might make this clear is not possible in the case of most of them. Only when they were convicted and hanged was it likely that something of their life would be revealed in the form of their "Confession and Dying Words," and in Surrey that kind of account was by no means as common

[91] For sentencing in the 1780s see chap. 10.

[92] It is possible that some of the claims being made were entirely fictitious—an attempt to achieve a kind of respectability that the prisoner might have thought would help him in court. It seems unlikely, however, that that was being done on a large scale in view of Peter Linebaugh's discovery that statements about occupations given by convicts hanged at Tyburn to the Ordinaries of Newgate and included by them in their "Accounts" tended to be confirmed by other evidence ("The Ordinary of Newgate and His 'Account,' " in Cockburn, ed., *Crime in England*, pp. 263–64).

TABLE 5.6

Occupations of Men Accused of Property Offenses at the
Surrey and Sussex Assizes, 1786–1787

Stated Occupation	Surrey		Sussex	
	No.	%	No.	%
Tradesmen				
Butcher	4		—	
Barber	2		1	
Horsedealer	2		—	
Fishmonger, stationer,				
chandler, vuctualler	4		—	
Total	12	8.6	1	2.2
Artisans in				
Textile and clothing trades	26		1	
Building trades	9		—	
Metal trades	7		3	
Ship-building and related	5		1	
Printing trades	4		1	
Food trades	3		1	
Wood-working and miscellaneous	4		2	
Total	58	41.4	9	19.6
Unskilled				
Laborer	38		31	
Other unskilled	8			
Total	46	32.9	31	67.4
Other				
Sailor	10		4	
Soldier	1		—	
Waterman	10		—	
Other	3		1	
Total	24	17.1	5	10.9
Total	140	100.0	46	100.0

SOURCE: ASSI 31/14–15.

as it was north of the Thames, where they were regularly published by
the ordinaries of Newgate. It would further be necessary to investigate
the circumstances of each of the London trades to explain why in 1786–
87, for example, the only occupations represented by more than one or
two men were weavers and shoemakers, with seven each, and tailors with
five. Failing those detailed reconstructions, we are left merely to speculate
about the meaning of these elusive occupational designations.

In those terms, it seems to me significant that half the accused in a
county in which there was a great deal of manufacturing described themselves as tradesmen and artisans. A large majority of the accused in Surrey
were from the Borough of Southwark and the urban parishes nearby, and
the occupations they reported to the court make them look very much
like a cross section of a working population that, in London especially,
included a wide range of trades. The dominance of the capital is also
reflected in the fourth division, which consists mainly of ten sailors and
ten watermen, along with a soldier, two fishermen, and a "musician."
The thirty-eight laborers may or may not have worked in agriculture,
along with the three gardeners whom I have also included among the
"unskilled." I would not say that this is a cross section in the sense that
it perfectly replicates the occupational structure of the county of Surrey,
but it does seem to reflect something of the complexity of an economy
dominated by the large urban population in its northeast corner. It also
forms a striking contrast to the occupations reported by the accused in
the largely agricultural county of Sussex, two-thirds of whom listed themselves—or were listed—as laborers.

If any inferences can be drawn from these occupations, they would
seem to reinforce the picture of property crime that emerges from the
pattern of prosecutions and the ages of those on trial that the accused
were largely working people. At least the claim of significant numbers
that they had had experience in skilled trades suggests similarities between
those who got into trouble and the generality of the ordinary working
population, and in so doing questions contemporaries' explanations of
crime that would have emphasized (in the case of serious offenses certainly)
distinctions within the larger body of the poor. In the eighteenth century
emphasis tended to be placed on moral explanations of crime, on the
inevitable progress of a man in immorality if once he stepped from the
path of hard work and obedience: a man who neglected his religious duties,
who failed to go regularly to church, who fell into idleness, would, it was
thought, slide into dissipation and self-indulgence, begin to commit petty
offenses and end inevitably on the gallows. Such an explanation assumed
a division between an "industrious" (and subordinate) working class on
the one hand and the "idle" (and rebellious) on the other—a view that

could easily harden into the more sinister and increasingly familiar categories that distinguished the "respectable" working class from a "criminal" class that could be assumed to be responsible for the bulk of offenses committed.

That view of property crime as the product of a separate group, whether morally or politically defined, fits ill with the evidence of the court records, particularly with the changing patterns of prosecutions and with what can be learned about the identity of those charged. On the other hand, the existence of gangs of criminals who were committed to a life of crime and who appear to have been responsible for large numbers of the most serious and violent offenses does seem to confirm on the face of it that there were significant distinctions between property offenders and the bulk of the ordinary working population. They look very much like a criminal class if ever there was one, and a study of property crime in the eighteenth century, particularly in London, requires some investigation into the structure and the character of these gangs and some assessment of their significance.

CRIMINAL GANGS

Even if one could show that economic circumstances and conditions played a large part in stimulating property crime it would not follow that all the accused before the courts at any time had acted from similar motives, that everyone who stole had been feeling the pinch of necessity. There was in fact considerable variety among the men and women charged with property crime. Several broad distinctions can be made, though of course the categories are not rigid and exclusive. At one end of the spectrum were those who had stolen out of immediate and pressing need, impulsively and on their own. Others pilfered not because they were out of work but because their work provided the opportunity, some of which pilfering may have been at the disputed edge of customary payments and the wage.

Most suspects who came to court were probably not in either of those categories but had set out deliberately to steal, probably from a stranger. They varied hugely in both their modes of operation and their dependence on such crime. They could be said to include petty but habitual thieves, among whom were women who shoplifted occasionally or youths for whom robbing was something of a lark. Shoplifters and pickpockets and skillful offenders of that kind obviously must have differed quite considerably from one to the other in their dependence on crime, and particular individuals are likely to have stolen more or less often depending on circumstances, including their ability to find work. Not all such thieves were necessarily regular practitioners, but they clearly shaded into those who were fully committed and dependent on crime at least for the time being. Some of those may have operated alone, but generally speaking those offenders needed the support of others. The most notorious were those organized in the gangs of burglars, highwaymen, and street robbers who were so feared.

It was undoubtedly easier to sustain a criminal career of any type in London, where victims and receivers were more plentiful and surveillance less obtrusive and intense. But "notorious" thieves, especially of a minor variety, were not unknown in the countryside—men who raided henroosts, took a sheep occasionally, stole grain or wood. Some managed to support themselves fully in this way for a time. A man accused of stealing hens in various parishes of Surrey over a long period claimed to earn his living driving hogs, but a woman who had "kept him company" for a year confessed that she "did not know he had any way of living but by theft."[93] Some of those who came eventually to court faced a battery of indictments alleging thefts over long periods. One Surrey man confessed to making a practice of walking with his father and brother-in-law into distant parts of the county or into Kent to break into "summer houses" to steal what furniture and household goods they could carry, which they then took to a "broker" in London.[94] A variety of other men, and a few women, acquired bad reputations in rural parishes because they worked irregularly and were consequently suspected of stealing or poaching or smuggling, and who often compounded this by going off from time to time and leaving their families to be taken care of by the parish or by an independence of manner that enraged the local notables. It was the fact that Edmund Plaw's wife and children had cost the parish of Cranley more than twenty-three pounds over the previous two years because he was in the habit of "running away" and leaving them that made him the subject of a report to the quarter sessions when he was in the house of correction awaiting their judgment. But it clearly did not help him that he had been suspected of smuggling, convicted and punished for theft, and accused of highway robbery over this same period and had resisted all efforts to have him sent to the army; nor that he promised that if he was in the army he would "come when he pleased and beget children for the Parish to keep" and announced when sent to the house of correction on the last occasion that "he would be damn'd if he work'd for any of them."[95]

A variety of forms of criminality can be found in rural parishes,

[93] QS 2/6, Ea. 1765, 96–97.
[94] QS 2/6, Ep. 1770, 49–50.
[95] QS 2/6, Mich. 1773, 5.

though few men sustaining full-fledged criminal careers—at least in their
own parishes. A number of gangs operated in the countryside in the
eighteenth century (with some contacts in the city for fencing purposes),
but like the men who on the smaller scale walked around Surrey looking
for business, they were very largely itinerant. They were also likely to
engage in a wide variety of offenses rather than specializing rigidly. These
characteristics are at least suggested by the activities of the rural gangs
about which a good deal is known: the group around John Poulter, whose
"Discoveries" provide an account of their operations over several years;
and the so-called Coventry gang who were pursued and prosecuted by the
unusually active magistrate John Hewitt and then described and publicized
in his account of his life.[96] Both moved around a great deal. Poulter's
gang committed offenses over a large part of the Midlands and the North
in the late 1740s and early 1750s, at race meetings, fairs, cockfights, and
other large gatherings. They stole from inns, broke into houses and shops,
conducted for a while a trade in stolen horses that involved selling in the
north what they had stolen in the south and vice versa, and particularly
engaged in confidence tricks and cheating at cards.

Some of the variety of offenses that Poulter describes may have been
included for literary effect, to avoid tedium in his account of their doings
and to provide opportunities for the widest possible use of canting expressions: they went "on the sneak" and on "the sharping lay"; they "jumped
the glass of a gentleman's lay." His account begins to sound like something
written to appeal to those who knew what to expect from their "rogue
literature." But the Coventry gang also engaged in a range of offenses that
included theft from inns and picking pockets, and they too depended
heavily on fraud and confidence tricks. They also moved around a great
deal, across a network of "safe" inns and public houses run by landlords
they could trust who might hide stolen goods or act as a receiver.[97]

Such gangs obviously found it possible to operate sucessfully for a
number of years by moving around the country, but London provided the
most conducive conditions for men who intended to band together in
criminal activities because it offered both the richest targets and a denser
network of "flash houses" and receivers and other "underworld" connections

---

[96] *The Discoveries of John Poulter* (1753); John Hewitt, *A Journal of the Proceedings of J. Hewitt*
(1790). Both gangs have been extensively analyzed in Hay, "Crime, Authority and the Criminal
Law." My account touches only briefly on one or two aspects of their activities.

[97] There is a valuable account of the notorious Gregory gang, who moved around Essex and
others of the Home Counties in the 1730s, going on from deer-stealing to housebreaking and
robbery (and with whom Dick Turpin was for a while associated), in Derek Barlow, *Dick Turpin
and the Gregory Gang* (Chichester, 1973). Barlow reproduces a great deal of contemporary evidence
from the press and from government and private sources.

that enabled men to live irregularly without necessarily drawing suspicion upon themselves.[98] The capital did not provide fully segregated criminal areas, for there was no district that could not be penetrated by some means and no house that was entirely "safe." But there were parts of London where numerous "flash houses" provided meeting places and a base to which a group of robbers or burglars might return in relative security, as well as providing entertainment—gambling, drinking, prostitution—and contact with receivers and other support necessary to the conduct of a sustained criminal enterprise. Wilson and Hawkins centered their activities for a while on a "most convenient house" near London Wall that, Wilson said, was a "Nest for Highwaymen."[99] There were such houses in all parts of the metropolis, but they were concentrated north of the river in several heavily populated districts and centered on a number of notorious courts and alleys like Chick Lane, Field Lane, and Black Boy Alley—"Republics of Thieves," as William Blizzard described them in 1785.[100] These were not sanctuaries like the Mint in Southwark, where until it was closed in 1723 debtors could find shelter because within its boundaries bailiffs were not able to serve writs: such sanctuaries did not harbor felons, in large part because it was clear that their pretended privileges would have been abolished much earlier had they attempted to do so. Rather these were simply crowded areas that afforded some protection and that in some cases—the Irish districts for example—added the protection of national and religious solidarity.

On the south side of the Thames, Southwark, Bermondsey, Lambeth, and other parishes along the river had their share of such districts and flash houses, some of them licensed, some not. The charge against easy-going public houses was summed up in the indictment of a man at the Surrey assizes in 1751 (one of the moments at which crime seemed to be

---

[98] Accounts of gangs in London emerge from trial evidence at the Surrey assizes and from the brief biographies ("the behaviour, confessions and dying words") of men executed for robbery and burglary. See, for example, *A Genuine Account of the Behaviour, Confessions, and Dying Words of the Six Malefactors . . . who were executed at Guildford. . . .* (1742). Several accounts of other groups of "malefactors" were published by the Ordinaries of the Surrey county jail, but not as regularly as the pamphlets produced by the Ordinaries of Newgate dealing with the lives of the men and women executed at Tyburn, for which see Linebaugh, "The Ordinary of Newgate," pp. 246–69. Some of the characteristics of the London gangs also emerge clearly from an account of one that operated in Surrey as well as north of the Thames and referred to earlier: Ralph Wilson, *A Full and Impartial Account of all the Robberies committed by John Hawkins, George Simpson . . . and their Companions* (1722). For the gangs of the 1720s see Howson, *Thief-Taker General*.

[99] Wilson, *Account of the Robberies*, pp. 16–17.

[100] See, for example, "A List of Houses of Resort for Thieves of every Description" (1815), in HO 42/146, discussed by Radzinowicz, *History*, vol. 2, pp. 299–304; William Blizzard, *Desultory Reflections on Police* (1785), pp. 30–31.

alarmingly extensive and threatening in London) for "keeping a disorderly house, permitting loose and disorderly men and women to frequent and come together, tippling, drinking, dancing, scolding, cursing, swearing, and otherwise misbehaving themselves."[101] The "Dog and Duck" in St. George's Fields had the reputation, as we have seen, for being a rendezvous for highwaymen, and not just among magistrates and constables.

As well as "safe" houses, London also provided convenient access to receivers, both small-scale dealers and pawnbrokers who might take in a watch or two with no questions asked and some who had sufficient capital and sufficient expertise to handle a large amount of stolen property. Colquhoun thought that there were fifty or sixty receivers of consequence in the capital in the 1790s, of whom ten were "persons of property, who can raise money to purchase articles of value."[102] It was frequently alleged that the biggest receivers were accessories before as well as after the crime, that they provided support and information and tools—a point that was being made in court when John Hood was indicted for receiving, in Surrey, in 1764. He was alleged to have rented a house in Southwark where stolen plate, linen, and clothes to the value of three hundred pounds were found and also "a great number of Picklock Keys . . . that would open almost any Lock whatever."[103]

Gangs of highwaymen and burglars did operate in London and from the metropolis along the roads that reached out into the surrounding countryside. And they were undoubtedly supported and perhaps stimulated by a social network of sympathetic publicans and pawnbrokers and stable-keepers and the like. But we should not exaggerate the extent of the "underworld" nor its coherence and impenetrability. Some contemporaries undoubtedly did so, particularly men like the Fieldings, Blizzard, Colquhoun, and Saunders Welch, who tended to argue that London required police forces because the old parish watch was ineffectual in the face of the dark and threatening power of the criminal gangs. We should be careful not to accept their views too uncritically, especially since many of the most alarmed accounts date from periods in which prosecutions— and, I would argue, offenses—were at their height. At least it is necessary to investigate the character of the gangs. What that suggests is that many of them were not permanent and highly organized groups of skilled and sophisticated thieves. They were "professional" criminals in the straight-forward and limited sense that they were fully dependent, for the time

[101] ASSI 35/191/8/46 (Joyce).
[102] Colquhoun, *Police of the Metropolis*, pp. 189–90.
[103] S.A.P., Summer 1764, pp. 5–6 (Hood).

being, on crime for their income.[104] But the gangs appear not to have been longlasting, nor to have had certain and fixed membership. It is true, of course, that this is an impression formed from the evidence of those that failed, from trials and confessions and criminal biographies, and at the outset it is worth emphasizing the tentative character of an account that is the most preliminary investigation of a complex phenomenon.

The most detailed study of the underworld at one moment in the eighteenth century found several large gangs dominating the London scene in the early 1720s before Jonathan Wild effectively eliminated them: Spiggott's gang of highwaymen, with eight members; Hawkins' gang, described by Wilson, of six men; Shaw's gang of footpads with thirteen known members; and Carrick's gang of about fifteen that, Gerald Howson says, was loosely allied with three other groups, one with a dozen footpads and two with six.[105] Such a range is compatible with estimates later in the century when, to mention at random a few examples reported in the press in the 1750s and 1760s, a gang of fourteen was said to be operating in Essex, a group of fourteen street robbers was reported in London, a dozen men who specialized in river offenses were placed in Southwark, and sixteen pickpockets were said to be operating as a gang in London.[106] Occasionally a group of ten or even a dozen actually took part in a particular crime, but that was rare and it seems clear that even if gangs were in fact the size that contemporaries guessed they might be (exaggerating a little on occasion for effect perhaps), groups of twelve or fifteen men would not normally find it profitable to work together on the kind of job they were most often involved in.

The effective operating size may have been a group of four or five, and there are suggestions that the larger gangs were associations of several smaller groups. Saunders Welch observed that gangs of fourteen or sixteen street robbers working in London in the 1750s "divide into parties to rob" and only come together to assist the escape of any member taken into custody.[107] There is a great deal of evidence to confirm that. Two highwaymen apprehended in 1723 confessed to belonging to a gang of sixteen who were all out that night in different parties. Another member of a gang of footpads described a similar pattern of operation but added that the whole gang shared the proceeds equally: everything was divided, "let who would get it first; for we went sometimes more or less out, and by

---

[104] This is the sense of that term adopted by Mary McIntosh, *The Organization of Crime* (1975), p. 12.

[105] Howson, *Thief-Taker General*, pp. 171–72, 190.

[106] *G. M.* 20 (1750), p. 377; 29 (1759), p. 91; 33 (1763), p. 411; *Public Advertiser*, 10 Jan. 1764.

[107] *A Letter on the Subject of Robberies* (1758), p. 61.

two's and three's, different ways."[108] Such sharing may have been unusual. Edward Burnworth (who was mentioned in the previous chapter and who was said by Howson to have led a gang of a dozen or so men)[109] confessed in 1726 to having committed forty-one burglaries over the previous year with a total of ten different accomplices, never more than two at one time; and to nine robberies with seven other companions in various combinations. There is no evidence of the proceeds having been shared beyond those who took part.[110]

A wide variety of structures and forms of operating seem to have existed, but loose rather that tight organization predominated, and shifting combinations of forces were common. The looseness of structure was perhaps made possible by the circuit of taverns and flash houses. Contacts could be made there and alliances formed among those who earned their membership in this unstable criminal subculture by deeds and reputation, perhaps by their familiarity with the canting language or by sporting an alias: Cocky-my-Chance, Kiddy Baker, Black Sam, Irish Ned, Jemmy the Shuffler, Cocky Wager, Country Dick, Black Waistcoat Dick, Cock-ey'd Jack, and the Parson were all tried at the Surrey assizes in the eighteenth century for committing robberies in gangs. Ralph Wilson met John Hawkins at a tavern—at a time when the latter was in hiding and "not daring to appear where he was known, except at such houses as he could confide in"—and drank with him and "took much pleasure hearing him speak of his merry Pranks and many Robberies." Hawkins thus drew him in, and they agreed to take to the highway together, along with a third man, a survivor of one of Hawkins' earlier gangs. They formed a "league of friendship" and (it was reported in the press when they were eventually apprehended) swore "the most solemn oaths and obligations."[111] Trust was indeed the essential binding force of these alliances. "If you can trust one another," a man said later in the century, there was no difficulty in stealing successfully from ships in the river at night.[112]

As the temptations to betrayal were enlarged by the government and by private interests in the eighteenth century in the form of rewards and

[108] *The Weekly Journal*, 12 Oct. 1723.

[109] Howson, *Thief-Taker General*, p. 314.

[110] SP 35/61, ff. 193–98. There is a good deal of other evidence of groups loosely associated into larger gangs, in some cases perhaps simply by being so labeled by a contemporary observer. Hewitt described the Coventry gang as variously between twenty-five and a hundred in number and made up of several wings and divisions centered on different places in the North and Midlands; and Poulter at one point described a gang of twelve going into the West from Bath, but "in three setts," two of which took money from farmers "at the unlawful game of pricking in the belt" (*Journal of Proceedings*, pp. 150, 154, 192; *Discoveries of John Poulter*, p. 18).

[111] Wilson, *Account of the Robberies*, pp. 6–7; *Weekly Journal or British Gazeteer*, 5 May 1722.

[112] S.A.P., Lent 1741, p. 13 (Carr and Fletcher).

pardons for turning king's evidence, trust was increasingly important and insisted on, and such oaths of loyalty and friendship as Wilson and Hawkins swore to each other were common. If Wilson's discomfort in explaining why he eventually gave evidence against his companions is any guide, these oaths were taken as seriously in the flash houses as they were in the courts at Westminster. He protested that after they were apprehended for a mail robbery (partly by the extraordinary efforts of officials at the Post Office and the interest of the secretary of state) he had no intention of turning king's evidence until he heard, from his interrogators, that another member of the gang was himself ready to come forward, and since the first man to turn evidence was likely to get a pardon and no others the threat had the effect intended, as it must have in dozens of other cases. It was a powerful solvent of even the most determined of friendships and obligations. Wilson's explanation is full of self-justification. He saw a letter said to be from his accomplice, Simpson, in which he offered to confess:

> As soon as I read it, I knew it to be Sympson's Letter, so that without any more Words I made a Discovery, and I am of opinion any Man in England would have done the same. That League of Friendship which was between us, was certainly dissolved by this Design against me. As for they who talk of solemn Oaths and Protestations, I can assure them that there never were any such amongst us; and if there had, no Oath is binding, the keeping whereof is a greater Sin than the breaking of it: An Oath is always administer'd for some laudable Purpose, but such Oaths tend to nothing but the Destruction of our Country.[113]

The vulnerability of gangs to being impeached by one of their members, who would thereby earn a pardon (or immunity from prosecution) and a handsome reward though he was as guilty as the rest, is evident in the emphasis that was put on oath-taking. Another group in the 1780s was reported to have sworn that "who ever should prosecute, or appear as evidence against any of the gang, should be marked for vengeance; and these rules every member binds himself by the most infernal oaths to observe, and never to 'peach, but to die *mute*."[114] But in fact a large number did impeach their colleagues, most often when they were apprehended, at which point men were readily persuaded in the eighteenth century to save their own skins by informing on their accomplices and giving the evidence that would convict them.[115]

[113] Wilson, *Account of the Robberies*, p. 24.
[114] *G. M.* 54 (1784), p. 710.
[115] See chap. 6.

Apart from the threat to gangs posed by such inducements, the huge rewards also encouraged private thief-takers to fish around in this world for bountiful victims. They were in turn able to find some of the more valuable offenders precisely because the underworld was sustained by flash houses and receivers. Where thieves congregate they can be found, and the "safe" houses were never in fact entirely safe. When the Hawkins gang robbed the mails—against Wilson's advice, he said, because he feared that the government would spare no effort or expense to catch them and that their "union would be dissolved when a promise of a King's pardon should be published after such a Robbery, with a Reward as usual"—Wilson noticed soon after that "two or three Men whose Countenances I did not like" began to frequent their usual drinking place. They were indeed the agents who seized him in the end.[116]

It is remarkable, perhaps, given this vulnerability, that the gangs did not more frequently shore up their oath-taking by arranging for revenge against those who saved themselves by turning king's evidence. Such threats were made, and it was partly to diminish fears of vengeance that accomplices who impeached their colleagues were given a reward as well as a pardon, for that would enable them to leave the area and set up elsewhere. And there were indeed some examples in the century of men murdered or intimidated by gangs to prevent them from giving evidence. At least one thief-taker was murdered in Surrey—by Edward Burnworth who was convicted and hanged with five other members of his gang; they also tried to kill the man who gave the crucial evidence that sent them to the gallows.[117] But there appears to have been less of that kind of intimidation and enforced silence than one might have imagined gangs operating in a reasonably small and self-contained underworld would have managed. It points to what seems to me to have been the essential fragility of the gangs of highwaymen, street robbers, and burglars, even given the weakness of the official agencies of control, the magistrates and unpaid and untrained constables.

The ease with which the gangs could be penetrated and undermined by one of their members looking out for his own interests underlines their lack of internal cohesion and lack of effective leadership. And it accounts for what seems to have been their essentially transient nature. When the whistle blew, gangs did not apparently hold together to face the threat and to silence the evidence or eliminate the witness who threatened them: they dispersed as every man thought to protect himself. When the dust settled, the survivors re-formed or found other partners and other groups,

---

[116] Wilson, *Account of the Robberies*, p. 20.
[117] S.A.P., Lent 1726, pp. 1–2 (Blewet et al.); Howson, *Thief-Taker General*, pp. 290–91.

or they drifted out of London entirely. Gangs formed, splintered, and re-formed, apparently quite readily, and individuals did not necessarily spend many years associated with the same men. This is suggested for example by John Hawkins' career as it is described by Wilson, which seems to be typical in its essentials. He began, Wilson said, as a single highwayman a little before 1720 but soon found it convenient to join with four others with whom he committed robberies on Bagshot Heath in Surrey and also on the north side of the Thames. This continued for two years until his companions were apprehended in Guildford on one occasion when he was not with them; they were all convicted at the Surrey assizes and Hawkins went into hiding. He "engaged with a fresh gang" some months later, but one of its members was soon taken and impeached the rest, so that that gang also dispersed, "some to Ireland, others to Wales." Hawkins again went into hiding, and it was at that point that Wilson joined him. With another man and then with Hawkins' brother, they committed a series of robberies on stagecoaches around London. Again they were dispersed by the arrest of their third member. To their surprise he did not impeach them (the man "of the greatest Fidelity to his Companions I ever knew in a Highwayman") and he was acquitted, but they were further alarmed when Hawkins' brother was arrested and they again had to go into hiding. They emerged from that to engage with yet another partner, George Simpson, with whom they committed the offenses that finally brought Hawkins to the gallows.[118]

There was undoubtedly a wider variety in forms of gangs and greater differences in their degree of cohesion and longevity than this account is suggesting. But it does seem that the gangs that were particularly prominent in the eighteenth century—those who were responsible for much of the burglary and the robbery in and around London—were less well organized and shorter-lived than some of smaller groups of men and women who engaged reasonably regularly in other forms of property crime that required some training and skill. Some shoplifters and pickpockets sustained long careers because they *were* skillful and because they committed offenses that were less threatening and drew less attention to themselves. Their skills were no doubt passed on in families or were learned in a form of apprenticeship. But the large and prominent gangs of urban bandits did not require much training at all. They could expand rapidly. They were "professional" and "organized" in the sense that they depended on crime for their income and set out to commit offenses that would bring it in. But at a deeper level many of them were disorganized amateurs,

---

[118] Wilson, *Account of the Robberies*. On Hawkins' gang and on the structure of gangs in general see Howson, *Thief-Taker General*, pp. 172–85.

without internal cohesion and without particular criminal skills. They engaged in offenses that relied on courage and violence and the force of numbers. Though by no means all such offenses in the years of crisis after wars were committed by demobilized soldiers and sailors—who were not the only ones to suffer from the flooding of the labor market and the closing down of some industries—their experience with weapons and the ability of some to ride well made them natural recruits for gangs of robbers, and such offenses must have seemed the most obvious way to extract a living if they formed gangs of their own.[119]

It is presumably one of the characteristics of fully "professional" thieves that they are not directly affected by changes in the level of economic activity and are not likely to contribute much to either an increase or a diminution of offenses being committed. They have their living to earn, rain or shine. There were undoubtedly some such criminals in eighteenth-century England, men and women who mainly supported themselves by crime over a long period of time and who had perhaps known no other life. But the structure and character of the gangs in eighteenth-century London suggests that few of their members were men of this type or that they had been drawn in by family connections or by training, but rather that they were activated by the same forces that (I have suggested) impelled other individuals who suffered deprivations when times were bad. The gang members for the time being swelled the numbers of full-time and serious offenders, but without being necessarily committed to crime over the long term. Gangs were broken as men were hanged or transported, and then were re-formed and broken again. Their members drifted away, went back to sea, back to Ireland, or off to some part of the country where their criminal connections were not suspected and took up some other line of work, even if later they returned to the city and to another gang.

Peter Linebaugh has shown how commonly in the first half of the eighteenth century men moved back and forth from legitimate to criminal

---

[119] Among the highwaymen convicted in Surrey in 1753 were two men who had been discharged from the *Hound* sloop of war and who took to the road when their money ran out and they were unable to find work (evidence was presented that they had tried). The first man they attacked turned out to be another sailor looking for someone to rob: "I told them," he said later at their trial, "I was one of their own Calling and that we must not rob one another." They agreed to join forces and went to an alehouse and "drank together upon our agreement" (S.A.P., Lent 1753, p. 7). And there is a good deal of other evidence, as we have seen earlier, of demobilized men putting their military skills to work in this way, including one who had learned his "dexterity in horsemanship" in Burgoyne's light-horse and another who had "behaved boldly at the taking of Havannah" (G. M. 32 [1762], p. 44; 35 [1765], p. 391). In the 1780s in particular there were numerous reports of footpads around London using cutlasses, a weapon they perhaps acquired and learned to use effectively in the navy.

enterprises.[120] The more scattered Surrey evidence, as well as accounts in newspapers and magazines, reveal such patterns of life among offenders there too. Ralph Wilson tired, so he said, of the dangerous and "gloomy" life of a highwayman and returned at one point to his home in Yorkshire to make a new start by taking up his mother's business, before his former companions forced him by blackmail to return to London and to the highways. He said too that another of his companions had also left London and taken up honest work before he was caught and convicted.[121] That was a common experience, even of men who committed numerous offenses and over a long period. The *Gentleman's Magazine* reported the case of one Cook, a shoemaker of Stratford, who was committed to trial in 1741 for what were thought to be more than a hundred robberies in and around London over several years. In the middle of this run of offenses, however, he had gone off to Birmingham, where under the name Stevens he "set up a Shoemaker's shop, and lived for some time in Credit."[122]

CONCLUSION

Indictments are a fragile guide to criminality. Prosecutions arose from a complex of interacting forces and from a series of decisions made by a number of men. There was certainly nothing automatic about the process that would ensure that even serious offenses would result in a charge being laid, even when the evidence against a suspect was powerful and he could be readily apprehended. Self-interest and community-interest frequently suggested a better alternative. Similarly, economic difficulties did not turn everyone who was suffering deprivation of some kind into a thief, even those brought to the brink of starvation by the lack of work or the high price of necessities. Some took a chance and stole, others clearly chose not to. It is also true that numerous property offenses were committed by men and women who were not in fact in such dire straits but who were providing or supplementing their income by illegal means. It is normally impossible to uncover with any kind of certainty the motives that might lead a man or woman to steal or break into a house, or to discover why a prosecution was undertaken—what set of social relations and what history of previous conflict might lie behind a decision to take this particular offense to a magistrate. Some of that evidence can be recovered by a close investigation of the society in which the conflict occurred, and a great deal can be learned

[120] Linebaugh, "Tyburn," pt. 3.
[121] Wilson, *Account of the Robberies*, pp. 9, 14–15.
[122] *G. M.* 11 (1741), pp. 356, 441, 498.

in this way about the context and the meaning of the huge variety of behavior that is squeezed and manipulated and edited to fit the legal categories the court dealt in. It seems to me that there is value in observing the trends in prosecutions at the county level and attempting to discern what circumstances might explain the patterns that emerge. What is being observed is a crude reflection of two intersecting factors: the number of offenses actually being committed, and the determination of those who thought themselves victims (and of the authorities) to punish them. The indictments that resulted from that complex process do not provide in any sense a *measure* of either crime or prosecutorial zeal. But changes in the level of offenses over the short term do reflect one or the other, or both. And I would argue that the evidence we have examined in this chapter strongly suggests that what is being principally reflected in the changing level of indictments from year to year (though not necessarily over the very long term) is the changing pool of offenses. It is that that makes most intelligible the patterns of prosecutions in rural Surrey and Sussex and, most particularly perhaps, in the urban parishes of Surrey, and that most satisfactorily explains the way particular offenses change over time.

The impression that the court records suggest is that most men given the opportunity to work and support themselves would do so, and that when employment was available and prices were moderate property crime was likely to be at a low level. But of course what contemporaries thought was true was crucially important to the way they responded to increases in offenses, and particularly helps to explain why crime and public order were to be such major issues in the century after 1750, when the population increased rapidly and so many men and women in the agricultural south and from time to time in the industrializing north were engulfed by poverty. What men thought caused property offenses bore directly on their views of the criminal law and the way it was being administered. From that point of view, it matters little whether the patterns of prosecutions we have been describing reflected a reality of crime or not. There is no doubt that it was at those moments when the accused filled the jails to overflowing and the gallows and whipping posts were at their busiest that contemporaries expressed their concerns about the state of crime and the criminal law, about the effectiveness of judicial administration and the system of punishment. Inevitably these matters were all related, and we will not entirely leave behind the question of the apparent character of crime when we turn now to ask how this society dealt with those charged with offenses—how, in particular, trials were conducted and how the convicted were punished.

PART II
THE ADMINISTRATION OF JUSTICE

CHAPTER 6

COMING TO TRIAL

We have been concerned to this point to investigate the behavior that typically led to prosecution for crimes of violence and crimes against property, and to suggest how the level of prosecutions might be related to the number of offenses actually committed. It is some relief to turn from questions that the court records can illuminate only indirectly to those for which they present concrete, direct, and (where they are complete) reliable evidence; that is, to the question of what happened to those who were prosecuted. We will be concerned with that in the remainder of the book. In this chapter we will deal with aspects of the process of prosecution, from the point at which the accused was brought before a magistrate to the beginning of the trial. Principally, we will be concerned with the obligations that magistrates were under as they conducted their examination into the charges laid by a complainant, with the working of the bail laws, and, since most suspects in felony cases were in fact held for trial, with the conditions in the jails in which they were kept. In subsequent chapters we will investigate in turn the character of the trial that followed, the patterns of jury verdicts, and the punishments imposed on those convicted.

It is necessary to separate these matters in order to examine them, but they are of course closely related: how men are treated before trial is shaped by the nature of the trial that is to follow; conditions in jails are affected by the role of imprisonment as a punishment; verdicts are given to some extent in the knowledge of the punishments available to the courts; and the administration of the law in general is affected by the length of the court calendar and, at moments of stress, by the dangers that crime is assumed to be posing for the society. There is the further complication that all these aspects of the process of prosecution, trial, and punishment changed in significant and fundamental ways over the period of almost a century and a half we are dealing with, and change in one inevitably bore some implications for the others. In the course of the following chapters I hope to suggest ways that these elements—crime, judicial procedure, and punishment—were linked and related.

PRETRIAL PROCESS

The prosecution of the kinds of offenses we have been largely concerned with, offenses in which an individual was harmed in some way, depended on the victim's decision to lodge a complaint and to bear the cost and trouble of the case. We have seen that men were likely to have had widely varied motives in pressing charges, and that those who were arrested and proceeded against had been apprehended in a variety of ways, from a simple nabbing at the time of a physical attack or a theft to arrests made only after time-consuming and expensive searches by the victim or someone employed by him. In most cases, unless a magistrate or constable happened to be present, the victim of an assault or a theft had an opportunity to decide whether to prosecute or not, and clearly a number of responses were possible. The most common, especially in the case of minor offenses, was undoubtedly to let the matter rest, perhaps with a warning to the offender or after extracting an apology or a promise not to offend again on pain of prosecution next time, and perhaps with some monetary compensation—in any event, without calling in the machinery of the law.

If a victim wanted to press charges he would normally do so by taking his complaint to a justice of the peace, though he could also go to a sitting court and get an indictment drawn and a bench warrant to secure the accused. A justice's response to an accusation made before him would depend to a considerable extent on the offense being alleged. Assaults and trespasses and other misdemeanors were frequently settled by the justice's mediation: they were clearly encouraged to attempt to reconcile the disputing parties in such cases rather than sending the matter to trial. Dozens of examples of their doing so in the eighteenth century can be found in magistrates' diaries and quarter sessions' papers. When a widow complained to the Surrey magistrate, Richard Wyatt, that she had been assaulted and beaten by a blacksmith in a local public house, to take just one Surrey case, Wyatt brought both parties before him, took their depositions, and made the blacksmith pay her eight shillings, "the assault being proved."[1] "In complaints of this sort, where the injury is but small," the chairman of the Middlesex quarter sessions said in 1780, "the magistrate to whom the complaint is made, cannot better exercise his hu-

---

[1] *Deposition Book of Richard Wyatt*, p. 16, and pp. 7, 18, n. 45. For other examples of such arbitration and reconciliation see Elizabeth Crittall, ed., *The Justicing Notebook of William Hunt, 1744–49*, Wiltshire Record Society, vol. 37 (Devizes, 1982), pp. 29, 30, 39. And for this subject generally see Norma Landau, *Justices of the Peace, 1679–1760* (Berkeley, 1984), pp. 173–75.

manity, and I may add, his wisdom, than by persuading the parties to peace and reconciliation; an expedient which I have seldom known to fail."[2] He was perhaps being overly sanguine about its effectiveness, but there is no doubt that such reconciliation was common.

In a second category of cases in which the public interest was thought to be more fully engaged than in misdemeanors of that kind, magistrates were empowered to dispose of cases by exercising summary jurisdiction, convicting or acquitting the party complained against, and imposing a penalty where that was warranted. Magistrates were empowered to exercise such summary powers on their own in some cases; in others they could act only in pairs or with two other justices.[3] That authority was expanding in the eighteenth century, as magistrates came to deal summarily with such matters as game cases, the embezzlement of materials by employees, wood-theft and hedge-breaking, and offenses under the vagrancy laws. It would seem, too, that in Surrey (and in Middlesex) magistrates were using their summary powers in the early eighteenth century to deal with minor cases of theft. This at least would seem to explain why a number of men and women were incarcerated in the house of correction for brief periods (by the order of single magistrates) as "idle and disorderly and pilfering persons" or in some cases simply as "pilfering persons," or even for pilfering a particular object from a named victim. The accused dealt with in this way were mainly from the urban parishes of Surrey, and it seems reasonably clear that such committals resulted from the magistrates' decision to take advantage of the gray areas on the borderland of larceny and of the vagueness of the vagrancy acts to punish those suspected of small thefts by sending them for a brief period of hard labor and perhaps corporal punishment rather than committing them for trial at the quarter sessions or assizes. When that practice began in Surrey it is impossible to say, since there are neither justices' records nor house of correction calendars for the seventeenth century. But it was common by the early decades of the eighteenth century. It is possible that it was at its height then, and that it was one aspect of the efforts being made in William's reign and in Anne's, particularly in the metropolis of London, to find more effective means of managing and disciplining the poor and to find more effective punishments for petty property offenders. Those efforts had led to a number of experiments in penal practice, as we will see, including the introduction for a brief period of imprisonment at hard labor. The use of the summary powers of magistrates to incarcerate a number of "pilferers" in the houses of correction seems clearly related to that broader effort. The practice di-

[2] Sir John Hawkins, *Charge to the Grand Jury of Middlesex* (1780), pp. 26–27.
[3] Landau, *Justices of the Peace*, chaps. 6–7.

minished over the middle decades of the century and then petered out. It is unclear how many of those who were incarcerated for "pilfering" in the first half of the century (if any) had been diverted from the courts, but over the long term it is clear that there was no shift of property offenses in the eighteenth century from trial by jury to the summary jurisdiction of magistrates. In 1800 the mainstream property offenses (and other felonies) remained firmly the business of the courts.[4]

In dealing with such offenses the magistrates to whom victims brought their complaints had much less discretion and much less room for maneuver than they had when the charge amounted to a misdemeanor. How they were to proceed against accused felons was still largely governed in the eighteenth century by statutes of 1554 and 1555 that together required them to take depositions of the victim and his witnesses in writing and to examine the accused and reduce his statement also to writing.[5] At the conclusion of this enquiry, the magistrate was required to grant the accused bail or to commit him to jail. When the evidence was incomplete, or if the magistrate wanted to get more information from a suspect about his accomplices or perhaps persuade him to become a witness for the crown or encourage other victims to come forward to identify him, he might order him to be held "for further examination," though for no longer than three days.[6] For the most part, magistrates concluded their examinations either by bailing the accused or sending him to prison to await trial. We will look more fully at these options in a moment. In either case, the magistrate was required to ensure that the prisoner would appear for his trial at the quarter sessions or assizes and to ensure that the prosecutor and those who had given evidence would also appear to carry on the prosecution by binding them over.

The depositions and the prisoner's statement were to be returned to the appropriate court. The evidence they contained was not commonly read at the trial, at least in the eighteenth century.[7] The jury was informed by the oral repetition of the evidence, which was shaped by questions from the judge and subject to cross-examination. But if a witness died or perhaps

[4] This paragraph is based upon the house of correction calendars among the quarter sessions papers (QS 2/6), beginning in 1709.

[5] 1 and 2 P and M, c. 13 (1554–55); 2 and 3 P and M, c. 10 (1555). On this see in particular John H. Langbein, *Prosecuting Crime in the Renaissance* (Cambridge, Mass., 1974), pt. 1.

[6] Hale, *Pleas of the Crown*, vol. 2, pp. 120–21.

[7] *The Office of the Clerk of Assize*, however, advised clerks to sort out these documents as the trial began, and in the case of the prisoner's examination "if it be evidence for the king, he readeth it to the jury." Similarly, the witnesses' depositions were to be used "if the evidence for the king falter in his testimony to refresh his memory." The same advice was given to clerks of the peace for the quarter sessions (pp. 48, 157). This does not appear to have been the practice after 1700.

seriously contradicted his earlier testimony, the deposition might be introduced if it was proved to the satisfaction of the court, most effectively by the magistrate who took it or his clerk, that it was authentic.[8] Similarly, a confession made by the accused at his examination might be introduced into court, although, as we will see, by the eighteenth century judges were increasingly concerned about the status as evidence of both confessions and depositions of deceased witnesses.

The examination of the accused was obviously intended in 1554 and 1555 to be a vigorous searching out of the evidence that would lead to a conviction, not a full and rounded enquiry into the circumstances of the case. The Tudor magistrates were not being asked to act impartially or judicially, to investigate and dispose of the case as they thought the facts warranted, committing some accused to trial and discharging others. Indeed they were clearly forbidden to discharge anyone brought before them accused of committing a felony. All suspects were to go on to trial, and the magistrate's task was to ensure that they got there and that the strongest evidence of their guilt would be contained in the depositions and examination that they were required to send in to the court. In the Marian procedure the magistrate was more a policeman than a judge: he was charged to assemble a prosecuting brief that would stiffen and supplement the case presented orally by the victim-prosecutor in court. He was not actually forbidden to report information that was in the prisoner's favor, but nor was he expected to search for such evidence "as maketh against the king," in Michael Dalton's phrase.[9]

The Marian legislation gave the prisoner few rights at this stage of the investigation. He was not to be told precisely what the evidence was against him, nor to be present when the deposition of his accuser was taken. This examination fitted a particular form and conception of trial in which it was believed that the truth would be most clearly revealed if the prisoner was confronted with the evidence only in the courtroom so that the jury could judge the quality of his immediate, unprepared response. What was sought was a trial in which the victim of the offense would present his case in such a way that the issues would be reached quickly and the accused would be forced to reply to them on his own behalf, directly and unaided by a lawyer.[10] The prisoner's ignorance of the evidence was thus not mere indifference to his feelings but an essential element in the staging of the trial as an oral conflict between two unpre-

---

[8] Chitty, *Criminal Law*, vol. 1, pp. 585–89; Hawkins, *Pleas of the Crown*, vol. 2, p. 429.
[9] Michael Dalton, *The Countrey Justice* (1618), p. 265.
[10] See chap. 7.

pared amateurs, one asserting the guilt of the other, the accused proving his innocence to the jury by the force and sincerity of his denials.

This view of the trial remained very much intact in 1660 and into the eighteenth century, and with it a view of the magistrate's examination as a search not for the truth of the charges laid and denied but for the strongest evidence that proved the prisoner's guilt, evidence that he would have his chance to deny and to counter in court. The Marian statutes were intended perhaps primarily to repair weaknesses in local administration and to ensure that magistrates were not intimidated and in other ways deflected from their duty as law-enforcement officials by powerful local interests—the hope being that if the magistrate was obliged to send all charges of felony to be dealt with by the courts, more cases might be prosecuted and actually go to trial.[11] That obligation persisted well past the time when magistrates were likely to be frequently and systematically overawed in such ways. They continued to be advised in guides to magistrates' practice in the seventeenth and early eighteenth centuries merely to process the complaints they received, especially when a felony had clearly been committed and the victim had made an accusation under oath. In his manual originally published in 1618 and reprinted many times in the seventeenth century and as late as 1746, Michael Dalton expressed the view that "even though it shall appear to the Justice that the Prisoner is not guilty" his best and safest course was to commit him, "for it is not fit that a Man once arrested and charged with Felony (or suspicion thereof) should be delivered upon any Man's Discretion, without further Trial." Dalton advised justices to take no chances whatsoever. The evidence might be weak; the witnesses might be inconsistent in their testimony or they might themselves be discredited by having been convicted previously of an offense particularly debilitating to their character and credit; witnesses might even be unable "to inform any material thing against" the prisoner beyond declaring the merest suspicion of him—nonetheless the magistrate would be well advised to take their evidence and commit the accused man for trial.[12] How closely magistrates followed this advice in their actual practice in the seventeenth century is unclear, but the advice itself was repeated and reinforced by Matthew Hale writing after the Restoration and in widely used justices' manuals published by Bond and Nelson.[13]

[11] Langbein, *Prosecuting Crime in the Renaissance*, chap. 1.

[12] Dalton, *Countrey Justice*, p. 260 (1746 ed.), p. 377; and see Langbein, *Prosecuting Crime in the Renaissance*, pp. 7–8.

[13] "If a person be brought before a Justice, if it appears no Felony be committed, he may discharge him; but if a Felony be committed, though it appears not that the party accused is guilty, yet he cannot discharge him, but must commit or bail him" (M. Hale, *Pleas of the Crown: or a Methodical Summary* [1678], p. 98, quoted by Langbein, *Prosecuting Crime in the Renaissance*,

By the early eighteenth century, however, attitudes toward the accused at this stage of criminal procedure were beginning to change, particularly views of the implications of patently weak evidence. Take, for example, the status of depositions as evidence when the witness who had given the statement was dead or was unable for some other reason to attend the trial. In the late seventeenth century general objections were being successfully raised against the admission of written evidence when the witness was available to give that evidence orally and to undergo cross-examination.[14] And by the middle decades of the eighteenth century objections were being raised against the introduction of depositions sworn before magistrates by witnesses who died before the trial, on the grounds that the prisoner would have no opportunity to cross-examine the witness and thus no opportunity to throw doubt on the validity of his evidence. At the Old Bailey in 1739, for example, a defense counsel made such an objection; the judge ruled that the deposition could be read, but that it would not be taken as conclusive if it was not strongly corroborated by other testimony. Ten years later the same point was raised at the Surrey assizes, though, again the deposition was allowed as evidence.[15]

Such matters were plainly at issue by 1750. Well before the end of the century they were being decided in the prisoner's favor and in a significant way, for depositions were being allowed as evidence only when the accused had had an opportunity to cross-examine the deponent as he gave his statement to the magistrate at the pretrial stage. In a murder trial in 1791 the reading in court of a statement made to a magistrate by the victim as she was lingering near death was successfully opposed by defense counsel on the grounds that the accused had not been present when it was taken.[16] This was clearly a crucial point in a murder case in which the dying victim had given evidence damaging to the accused that could not be directly challenged. But by then, or at some point soon after 1790, the principle had been accepted in its most general terms, and it was being argued that the accused ought routinely to be present while

p. 7). For the same advice see J. Bond, *A Compleat Guide for Justices of the Peace*, 2nd ed. (1696), p. 92; and William Nelson, *The Office and Authority of a Justice of Peace*, 4th ed. (1711), p. 272.

[14] John H. Wigmore, "The History of the Hearsay Rule," *Harvard Law Review* 17 (1904), pp. 454ff.

[15] R vs. Westbeer: Leach, *Reports*, vol. 1, pp. 12–15; *Eng. Rep.*, vol. 168, pp. 108–9 (1739); ASSI 34/54, an unpaginated "Precedent Book" kept by the clerks of assize that records a number of decisions of the court presumably thought to be particularly significant. It includes a note on a case of 1749 in which the deposition of a deceased witness had been read in court, even though the prisoner had not been present when it was taken, "nor had any opportunity to contradict the same."

[16] R vs. Dingler: Leach, *Reports*, vol. 2, pp. 561–63; *Eng. Rep.*, vol. 168, pp. 383–84 (1791).

depositions were being taken.[17] It is clear that a remarkable change had come over the magistrate's preliminary hearing.

It is unclear when this process began, but in the course of the eighteenth century the magistrate's examination ceased being simply a means of assembling the best evidence against the prisoner and took on some of the characteristics of a judicial hearing. Magistrates began to feel more obligation to make some assessment of the evidence being presented and to assume more right to dismiss charges when they thought the case too weak to justify a trial. This emerged in practice and in the face of the authorities. Henry Fielding explained in 1752 that

> by the law of England as it now stands, if a larceny be absolutely committed, however slight the suspicion be against the accused, the justice . . . is obliged in strictness to commit the party, especially if he has not sureties for his appearance. . . . Nor will the trifling value of the thing stolen, nor any circumstances of mitigation justify his discharging the prisoner. Nay, Mr. Dalton says, that when the felony is proved to have been done, should the party appear to demonstration innocent, the justice . . . must commit or bail. And however absurd this opinion may appear, my Lord Hale hath thought fit to embrace and transcribe it in his *Pleas of the Crown*.[18]

Fielding refers to Dalton and Hale in order to dismiss their arguments. In his own practice as a magistrate he was not unwilling in certain circumstances to discharge an accused man or woman despite the constraints of the law and the weight of legal opinion. The account of his practice as a magistrate in 1752 drawn up by his clerk in the *Covent-Garden Journal* contains several examples of men being discharged following examination because, as was said of one man implicated in a murder, "he made his innocence appear so evident."[19] I am not certain when such powers were first assumed by magistrates, but it is clear from justices' notebooks that they were being widely exercised at least by the second quarter of the eighteenth century. Henry Norris, the Hackney magistrate, records several cases in the 1730s in which he discharged men and women brought before him on suspicion of theft: one man was dismissed because there was not "sufficient ground to charge him"; another because "nothing appeared sufficient to charge him." The notebook of William Hunt, a Wiltshire justice of the peace, provides similar examples of suspects discharged after

[17] Burn, *Justice of the Peace*, 24th ed. (1825), vol. 1, pp. 1006–7.
[18] *Covent-Garden Journal*, 25 Feb. 1752.
[19] Ibid., 28 Jan. 1752. For Fielding's practice as a magistrate see in particular Langbein, "Shaping the Eighteenth-Century Criminal Trial," pp. 60–67.

being examined because, as Hunt said on one occasion, he had "found nothing material to prove the fact" or, on another, because "he judged the grounds of [the accusation] to be so very little." Richard Wyatt in Surrey was making similar decisions in the 1760s. He felt able, for example, to discharge two chimney sweeps who had been working around northern Surrey and sleeping in barns and who were suspected of burglary in a yeoman's house in Egham when he concluded after examining them that there was "insufficient evidence" to justify their being held for trial.[20]

These cases had one thing in common: the defendant had been brought in on the mere suspicion of having committed the offense. Had they been charged on the oath of the victim with stealing the goods in question it is clear that the magistrates would have felt themselves obliged to send the case on to trial, even though they might have had serious doubts about the evidence. It remained the view of the authorities (and the practice of the justices) that a magistrate could not dismiss a charge that had been sworn to on oath by a respectable prosecutor.[21] But in other circumstances magistrates were thought entitled by the eighteenth century to discharge a man or woman brought before them for examination who was merely suspected of committing an offense and against whom the evidence was weak. It is my impression, though it is not based on a great deal of evidence, that magistrates would not have felt as free to exercise this discretion in even marginal cases in the 1550s or at the Restoration as they did in the middle decades of the eighteenth century, when Blackstone acknowledged them to have the power to dismiss charges if they thought the "suspicion entertained of the prisoner wholly groundless."[22] There was

---

[20] G.L.R.O., "Justice Book of Henry Norris," entries for 21 Mar., 17 Sept. 1731; *The Justicing Notebook of William Hunt*, pp. 40, 42 (I am grateful to John Styles for drawing my attention to these entries); *Deposition Book of Richard Wyatt*, pp. 23–24. Norma Landau tells me that the Kent Justice Paul D'Aranda was discharging suspects in property cases in Anne's reign because of the weakness of the evidence presented against them (D'Aranda's notebook is in the Kent AO, U442/045).

[21] Chitty, *Criminal Law*, vol. 1, p. 89. At the conclusion of his examination into a rape in which "the charge was positive" but that he believed to be so entirely false that the accused man was "sure . . . of being acquitted at his Trial," Fielding did not discharge him but went as far as he clearly thought possible and "ventured" to admit him to bail (*Covent-Garden Journal*, 25 Jan. 1752). Or, to take another case from 1783, when a prisoner charged the guard taking her to jail in a hackney coach with stealing her money the magistrate committed him to jail for trial, though there was no other evidence, because the offense was "positively sworn to" (*G. M.* 53 [1783], p. 890). Magistrates clearly might persuade prosecutors to withdraw charges in such cases. Henry Norris noted a case in which he "discharged the defendant by consent of the prosecutor" (G.L.R.O., "Justice Book of Henry Norris," 5 Oct. 1738). The *Covent-Garden Journal* account of Fielding's practice included several examples of withdrawal of charges; on that see Langbein, "Shaping the Eighteenth-Century Criminal Trial," p. 63, n. 240.

[22] Blackstone, *Commentaries*, vol. 4, p. 293.

clearly a transformation in the magistrates' view of their authority at the pretrial stage over the seventeenth and eighteenth centuries, for there is a world of difference between Dalton's advice to magistrates in 1618, quoted earlier, and the view of a law writer two centuries later that while a direct charge on oath left a magistrate powerless, he was in other circumstances "clearly bound, in the exercise of a sound discretion, not to commit any one unless a *prima facie* case is made out against him by witnesses entitled to a reasonable degree of credit."[23]

These changes in the character and function of the preliminary investigation were accompanied and encouraged by a broadening of what might be loosely called the prisoner's rights, in particular his right to the advice of a lawyer while he was being examined, his right to call the evidence into question upon which his commitment might be based by cross-examining the witnesses for the prosecution, and, if he were committed, his right to know the evidence he would face at his trial. Such matters were still very much in dispute in the first quarter of the nineteenth century. But how much the magistrate's hearings had changed by 1800 is clear from how much had been conceded even by those who wanted to resist further change. In 1802, for example, a number of magistrates in Lancashire sought legal advice on practices that had crept into their preliminary examinations, particularly the attendance of attorneys and the consequences that flowed from that. They explained to five legal authorities, including the solicitor general, whose advice they sought, that in Lancashire

> it frequently occurs upon the examination of persons charged with felony, that attornies are employed on their behalf to attend at their examinations taken before the magistrates previous to their commitments, and have insisted upon doing so, not only where the prisoners have been examined at the public places appointed for doing the business, but even at the dwelling houses of the magistrates, and when the prisoners are upon examination, frequently interrupt the magistrates, and direct the prisoners "to hold their tongues, not to answer any questions, and to say nothing", which prevents the prisoners from the discoveries they might otherwise be inclined to do, and thereby discover their accomplices. . . . The attornies for prisoners also insist upon having copies of the informations taken by the magistrates.[24]

---

[23] Chitty, *Criminal Law*, 2nd ed., 4 vols. (1826), vol. 1, p. 89. For Dalton see above, n. 9.
[24] *Copy of Case and Opinions printed by W. Shelmerdine and Co . . . , Manchester* (Liverpool, 1802), pp. 3–4 (I owe this reference to Joanna Innes).

These intrusions, which "in a great measure rendered nugatory the provisions of 1st and 2nd Phil. and Mary c. 13th" (i.e., the Marian bail legislation), were being resisted by magistrates, and they wanted to know from the authorities whether lawyers had a right to be present at the examination of a suspect, to advise him as he responded to questions, to cross-examine those who gave evidence against him, and to take notes that would better enable the prisoner to defend himself in court if he came to trial. They asked further whether the prisoner had a right to have copies of the prosecution depositions. There are interesting differences in emphasis in the replies, but they broadly agreed that it remained within the discretion of magistrates to allow the prisoner to be accompanied by counsel and to allow him to seek his advice during the examination. They agreed further that the prisoner not only had no right to have copies of the depositions but should positively not have them.

This enquiry and the replies to it make it clear that by the end of the eighteenth century the magistrate's examination was becoming what one of the respondents called an investigation "to ascertain whether there is ground to warrant a commitment of the prisoner for trial."[25] The replies to the Lancashire queries acknowledged that the presence of lawyers (which all respondents were willing to accept in practice, though with different degrees of grace), and particularly their cross-examination of the prosecution witnesses and their taking notes of the evidence given, had produced a new kind of magistrates' hearing. The implications of that were only fully worked out in the nineteenth century, and they were not to be fully registered in law until Jervis's Acts of 1848 made it entirely clear what was to take place was a judicial enquiry that might result in the accused's being bailed or committed to jail for trial or equally in his being discharged.[26] But these changes were becoming well established in practice over the second half of the eighteenth century.

An explanation of this transformation in the magistrate's investigation from the process laid down in the Marian legislation to that described in Victorian statutes must await a more precise fixing of its chronology.[27]

[25] Ibid., p. 17.

[26] On the Jervis Acts see Stephen, *History of the Criminal Law*, vol. 1, pp. 220–21; David Freestone and J. C. Richardson, "The Making of English Criminal Law (7): Sir John Jervis and His Acts," *Criminal Law Review* (Jan. 1980), pp. 5–16; W. Wesley Pue, "The Criminal Twilight Zone: Pretrial Procedures in the 1840s," *Alberta Law Review* 21 (1983), pp. 335–63. This last article is a useful account of the form and purpose of pretrial procedures in the 1840s and argues that the first of Sir John Jervis's Acts (11 and 12 Vict., c. 42 [1848]), which dealt with the duties of justices of the peace out of sessions with respect to persons charged with indictable offenses, merely confirmed the law and practice already in being.

[27] An important recent book by Barbara J. Shapiro makes it clear that such an explanation will also have to take into account the fundamental transformations in intellectual life in the

But it should perhaps be noted that an even more significant transformation was taking place in the criminal trial itself in the eighteenth century, and that that had also followed the introduction of lawyers into the courts. Prosecution and defense counsel were active at the Old Bailey and the provincial assizes by the 1720s and 1730s, and their influence on the conduct of trials and particularly on the rules of evidence was felt soon thereafter. It is unclear when lawyers first began to attend magistrates' pretrial examinations to advise prosecutors or suspects and to take notes of the evidence being given, but it seems reasonable to think that solicitors may well have been engaged for such purposes by those who intended to depend on a lawyer to present their cases or defend them in court.

The extent to which solicitors were engaged to prepare prosecution and defense briefs in the eighteenth century remains unclear. One can presume from the way some cases were presented in court and from the fullness and effectiveness of some defenses that a good deal of preparation had been done ahead of the trial.[28] And if such work was being done by lawyers in even a few cases, and if the timing made it possible, they would presumably have been anxious to attend at the magistrate's hearing at which the depositions would be taken and that would result in the discharge or commitment of their client. Sir Thomas de Veil, the magistrate who preceded Henry Fielding at Bow Street as the "court magistrate" in Westminster between 1729 and 1748, complained in the 1740s about the way "Newgate Solicitors, and other very crafty Persons . . . take all Opportunities to slip into Justices Houses. . . ." They slipped in, he went on to say, to "extricate notorious offenders out of their difficulties, and from the danger of being committed" to trial.[29] Leaving aside his contemptuous characterization of these men (he calls them "Old Bailey Solicitors" elsewhere),[30] de Veil's complaint seems to foreshadow that of the

---

seventeenth century that are the subject of her work. Shapiro analyzes the emergence in the seventeenth century of new conceptions and principles of proof in philosophical, scientific, and religious thinking and argues persuasively that they had an important influence on the way evidence was evaluated in the law courts, and in particular on the standard of proof required for conviction (*Probability and Certainty in Seventeenth-Century England: A Study of the Relationships between Natural Science, Religion, History, Law, and Literature* [Princeton, 1983], chap. 5).

[28] See chap. 7.

[29] Sir Thomas de Veil, *Observations on the Practice of a Justice of the Peace* (1747), pp. 2, 4. For the "court magistrate" in Westminster, de Veil, and especially the Fieldings at Bow Street see Langbein, "Shaping the Eighteenth-Century Criminal Trial," pp. 55–76.

[30] De Veil, *Observations*, p. 3. In a pamphlet published in London in 1728 an anonymous author complained about "the oppressive and dishonest practices of the tribe of solicitors, in prosecutions for felony about this City." They stirred up prosecutions, he thought, for the sake of rewards, and his pamphlet was intended as a guide to encourage victims to undertake prosecutions without the help of this "sharping troop" (*Directions for Prosecuting Thieves without the help of those False Guides, the Newgate Sollicitors* . . . [1728]; I owe this reference to John Langbein).

Lancashire magistrates half a century later and was perhaps a reaction against the beginning of the process that was well advanced by 1800, when the presence of lawyers at the magistrate's hearing was fully accepted.

In the process by which the pretrial hearing was gradually transformed in the eighteenth century it had perhaps been significant that some magistrates had long worked in public, or at least in not entirely private settings. De Veil said that the "solicitors" about whom he complained slipped into justices' houses "with a Croud (which is unavoidable)."[31] It was unavoidable in his own case because he conducted his business in an "office-room" in his house, which was fitted up to some extent like a courtroom—it included a "bar," for example—and in which it seems clear more people were present than merely those immediately concerned with the case he was looking into. The Southwark justice, Sir John Lade, appears to have had a similar arrangement in his house in the same period, and to have conducted his business at least partially in public, for a witness was called in a trial in 1738 to depose what he had heard the prosecutor say at the prisoner's examination before the justice. His testimony makes it clear that it was thought perfectly reasonable for a stranger to be present (and merely out of curiosity) as the justice conducted his examination. He told the court that

> seeing a great Crowd in the Borough, I was enquiring what was the Matter, and was told a Man was going before Justice Lade, so I went there to see what was the Matter, and as I lean'd over the Justice's Hatch, I heard the Prosecutor say he could not swear to the Man.[32]

Public examinations were being conducted at least by the 1730s (and perhaps much earlier) in the City of London, where the lord mayor had for long sat regularly as a magistrate at the Mansion House, and where, by 1737 at least, the aldermen of the city (who constituted the commission of the peace) were taking it in turn to hold daily sittings at the Guildhall to conduct judicial business in public, including the examination of accused felons.[33]

By the 1750s Henry Fielding was taking advantage of the public character of pretrial hearings to make suspects under examination known to those recently robbed or stolen from. He established a public "police office" at Bow Street in which the full range of magisterial business was conducted openly. This practice was carried further by his half-brother,

---

[31] De Veil, *Observations*, p. 2.
[32] S.A.P., Summer 1738, p. 11 (Kilburn).
[33] Langbein, "Shaping the Eighteenth-Century Criminal Trial," pp. 76–81.

Sir John Fielding, and with his encouragement public magistrates' courts—"police" or "rotation" offices—were established in the 1760s in Southwark and in other parts of the metropolis. They were put on a more regular footing in 1792.[34] In these offices magistrates were on duty at stated times to conduct judicial business. Cottu describes examinations of accused offenders taking place in London in 1820 "in a room open to the public." He also found such examinations frequently being conducted by solicitors acting for both the prosecutor and the defendant, with the magistrate (or his clerk) taking down the depositions of the plaintiff and his witnesses, recording the prisoner's statement if he chose to make one, and then deciding whether to commit the accused to trial or to discharge him.[35] The magistrate's investigation was by then well on its way to becoming a judicial hearing in which the magistrate would in the end make a judgment about the strength of the case being presented.

That represents a sharp change from the attitude the magistrate was expected to take under the Marian statutes and from what I have taken their actual practice still to have been in 1660. It seems to me that the agents of that change—as of so much in the trial itself—had been lawyers acting on behalf of defendants threatened with commitment to trial, and that their questions and their concerns had made the character of the prosecution evidence a more important issue at this and at other stages of the judicial process than it had ever been before. It had been at least in part the increasingly public character of the preliminary enquiry that had provided the opportunity for lawyers to be present when their clients were giving evidence or being examined. It need not have become a public occasion: as late as the middle of the nineteenth century it was confirmed in Sir John Jervis's Act dealing with pretrial procedures that the room in which examinations took place was not to be deemed an open court and that magistrates continued to have the right to exclude anyone if they chose to.[36] But the preliminary enquiry had in fact become a public hearing in the eighteenth century, and mainly as a means of strengthening the primary purpose of the committal procedure as it had been laid down in the Marian statute, that is, to ensure that offenders would be effectively prosecuted. One can see this particularly clearly in pretrial practices in the City of London and in the Fieldings' efforts to improve the detective and prosecutorial procedures in Westminster in the middle decades of the century. The public pretrial enquiry also enlarged the possibility that a suspected offender, aided by a lawyer, might challenge the evidence upon

[34] Ibid., pp. 60–76; Radzinowicz, *History*, vol. 1, pp. 188–94; vol. 3, chaps. 2, 5.
[35] M. Cottu, *On the Administration of Criminal Justice in England* (English trans., 1822; originally published as *De l'Administration de la Justice Criminelle en Angleterre* [Paris, 1820]), p. 34.
[36] Pue, "The Criminal Twilight Zone," p. 362.

which his commitment to trial would be based and that he might expose unfounded and malicious charges. As those rights of the accused were established, the purpose of the magistrate's examination was gradually enlarged beyond that for which it was originally conceived.

The changes we have been describing no doubt proceeded unevenly. Practice must have differed from one magistrate to another, perhaps from one part of the country to another. But changes of considerable consequence for accused felons were clearly in process by the second half of the eighteenth century. Perhaps the most immediately important of those consequences for some prisoners was the magistrates' power of discharge. That clearly saved some who had been charged frivolously or against whom the evidence was patently weak (as in the cae of the Egham chimney sweeps) from the possibility of a long stay in jail before they got a chance to establish their innocence. And commitment to jail to await trial was the almost certain prospect of those charged with felonies if the magistrate sent the case to court, even at the end of the eighteenth century. If it was a case for the assizes it could be a long wait indeed, and in unpleasant conditions.

AWAITING TRIAL: THE AVAILABILITY OF BAIL

Whether a prisoner committed for trial was held in jail or allowed bail depended largely on the offense he was charged with. Although statutes concerned with particular offenses might establish rules peculiar to them, the broad regulation laid down in the Statute of Westminster I (1275) and confirmed in the first Marian statute was that bail was not to be allowed in crimes of any seriousness, and certainly not in felonies, except in open court and by two justices acting together.

Generally speaking, bail was available in misdemeanors, to those charged for example with assault and threatening behavior, trespass, forcible entry and detainer, most forms of cheating and extortion, riot (at least when the affair had been "private" or on a small scale), and a wide range of other allegations of this kind. Bail might be denied in a case involving violence if the offense had been particularly vicious. If there was any chance that the victim would die of wounds received in an assault, the accused would probably be denied bail because the charge to be faced would then be murder. When the sister of his maid was committed to trial on an assault charge and there was some danger she would be "halled through the streets by a constable" and held in jail, the Surrey justice, Sir John Lade, protested on the grounds that a surgeon had sworn before the magistrate who had taken the depositions in the case that "there was no danger in the wound."[37] Presumably, some of those held in jail for assault and similar charges were there for such reasons, though it was within a magistrate's discretion to refuse bail in any case if he thought the accused unworthy, or if he thought the offense particularly heinous. Others were denied bail because they could not find suitable men to enter into sureties on their behalf, a problem that must have caused strangers particular difficulty. There were always for these reasons a few men and women in jail awaiting trial for assault and similar offenses, though in the great majority of cases those facing such charges were granted bail and were bound over in recognizances to appear, generally at the next quarter sessions.[38]

It was very different indeed for those accused of a felony. Bail was to be allowed only in restricted circumstances, and justices were encouraged by law writers to be extremely cautious. The example of the Surrey justice who bailed an accused horse-thief in 1745 and was threatened by an assize judge with an information before the King's Bench was referred to by Burn in his section on "granting bail where it ought to be denied."[39] Two justices acting together could bail an accused felon who was merely suspected of committing an offense. But in practice those charged with felonies, simple larceny as well as capital offenses, were committed to jail to await trial. Even in the case of petty larceny magistrates were advised by the eighteenth century that while they might allow bail if they had some doubt about the guilt of the accused, they ought otherwise to deny it: "If such persons be taken with the manner," Hawkins said, "or confess the fact, or their crime be otherwise open and manifest, it seems they ought not to be bailed."[40] Few of those committed to trial for larceny of any kind, even at the quarter sessions, were likely to be bailed. In a sample of five years over the second half of the eighteenth century, twenty-three of the roughly 250 men and women indicted for theft at the Surrey quarter sessions had been bound over rather than committed to jail. All had been accused of minor offenses, and it is clear that the evidence against many of them was weak, since fifteen of them (two-thirds) were discharged by the grand jury or acquitted by the trial jury or, in the case of one man, not prosecuted at all. The eight who were convicted received minimum sentences: seven were whipped and discharged, and the other jailed for two months.[41]

[37] QS 2/6, Mids. 1730, 41.

[38] Calendars of prisoners in the county jail and the houses of correction in Surrey are among the quarter sessions papers, QS 2/6.

[39] Burn, *Justice of the Peace*, 24th ed. (1825), vol. 1, p. 257.

[40] Hawkins, *Pleas of the Crown*, vol. 2, p. 101.

[41] Based on the indictments, jail calendars, and recognizances in the Surrey quarter sessions

The vast majority of men and women accused of even simple larceny were thus held for trial in the county jail or, in the case of a few, in a house of correction. There they joined those charged with robbery and burglary and other capital offenses against property and waited for the next session of the appropriate court.

COURT OF TRIAL: QUARTER SESSIONS OR ASSIZES?

For the most part (certainly in Surrey before 1750), felonies were dealt with by the assize judges on their semiannual circuits. The Surrey courts had arrived at a clear division of work by 1660—and this conformed in a general way to a national pattern—by which the quarter sessions dealt mainly with misdemeanors and left felonies, and certainly capital offenses, to the assize judges. At the Restoration, assault cases and charges of unlawful assembly and riot were dealt with by magistrates in quarter sessions, as were most of the petty larcenies that came to trial in Surrey (table 6.1). But all other property offenses were left for the assizes.[42] This remained the rule in Surrey until the middle of the eighteenth century, when, quite suddenly, the magistrates began dealing in quarter sessions with significant numbers of grand larceny cases. Who suggested that transfer of jurisdiction does not appear. It was undoubtedly legal, since the commission of the peace gave formal authority to the quarter sessions to deal with felonies. And it could be easily accomplished because in Surrey, as we have seen, a large proportion of the pretrial examinations were conducted by two or three justices in Southwark and neighboring parishes, men who lived near one another, who met regularly not only at the quarter sessions but also presumably at petty sessions, and who could

---

records for 1750, 1760, 1770, 1780, and 1790. The magistrates had become more rather than less cautious about granting bail in petty larceny cases over the period we have been dealing with. In the 1660s about seventy per cent of those accused of theft under a shilling were bailed (*Surrey Quarter Sessions Records*, 1662–65). By the 1730s the quarter sessions recognizances reveal that it had been reduced to twenty-five per cent, and by the end of the century only one in ten of those accused of petty larceny were allowed bail.

[42] On the division of work arrived at in the sixteenth and early seventeenth centuries see Cockburn, *History of English Assizes*, pp. 90–97; and Langbein, *Prosecuting Crime in the Renaissance*, chap. 5. At the Restoration, justices of the peace were advised to reserve grand larceny cases for the assizes. A manual dealing with court procedure advised clerks of the peace that if "grand felons" were committed to jail for trial at the quarter sessions the court should indeed proceed to their trial; but it also made it clear that all offenses other than petty larceny should be sent to the assizes, for that was "the proper work and business of his majesty's justices of assize and general gaol delivery" (*The Office of the Clerk of Assize . . . together with the Office of the Clerk of the Peace. . . .* [1682], p. 149).

TABLE 6.1

Court of Trial of Simple Larceny Cases

| | 1660–1749 | | | 1750–1802 | | |
	N	Quarter Sessions %	Assizes %	N	Quarter Sessions %	Assizes %
Surrey						
Grand larceny	1,233	2.3	97.7	2,233	65.5	34.5
Petty larceny	282	88.3	11.7	453	95.6	4.4
All simple larceny	1,515	18.3	81.7	2,686	70.6	29.4
Sussex						
Grand larceny	279	18.6	81.4	494	57.1	42.9
Petty larceny	286	94.4	5.6	182	96.2	3.8
All simple larceny	565	57.0	43.0	676	67.6	32.4

SOURCES: Sample and Count.

themselves transform the workload of the courts by committing some men
to trial at the quarter sessions rather than at the assizes.

Why the transfer of cases from the assizes occurred is unclear, but it
was no doubt in part encouraged by the overcrowding in the county jail
with the increase in prosecutions after the peace signed in 1748. That
such a transfer took place is evident indeed. Before 1748, when the county
quarter sessions concerned itself only with petty larceny among the property
offenses, it was rare for more than one or two such cases to come before
the court every year. This changed suddenly in 1748 and after. In 1749
ten property offenders were taken from the county jail and tried before
the magistrates in quarter sessions. In the next year twenty-one were, and
in the following three years the total rose to 138 (table 6.2).

One striking aspect of this change in the distribution of cases was
that the convention that the quarter sessions dealt with petty larceny and
the assizes with grand larceny and more serious offenses was maintained
for several years by as clear an example of judicial sleight of hand as could
be found in a system that abounded in fiction and pretense. Because the
quarter sessions had only dealt with petty larceny, everyone tried for a
property offense before that court in the years during which the transfer
of jurisdiction was accomplished was indicted for petty larceny, regardless
of the value of the object stolen and of the actual charges against them in
the jail calendar. Thus men who had been committed for thefts from ships,
wharfs, and factories for amounts that should have led to their being

TABLE 6.2
Larceny Cases Tried in Surrey at the County Quarter
Sessions and Assizes, 1747–1757

| Year | *Grand Larceny* | | | *Petty Larceny* | | | *All Simple Larceny* | | |
	N	Quarter Sessions %	Assizes %	N	Quarter Sessions %	Assizes %	N	Quarter Sessions %	Assizes %
1747	20	0	100.0	9	88.9	11.1	29	27.6	72.4
1748	27	0	100.0	20	100.0	0	47	42.6	57.4
1749	22	0	100.0	37	91.9	9.1	59	57.6	42.4
1750	40	0	100.0	45	100.0	0	85	52.9	47.1
1751	31	0	100.0	67	100.0	0	98	68.4	31.6
1752	21	14.3	85.7	63	98.4	1.6	84	77.4	22.6
1753	39	74.4	25.6	33	100.0	0	72	86.1	13.9
1754	69	68.1	31.9	17	94.1	5.9	86	73.3	24.7
1755	44	50.0	50.0	11	90.9	9.1	55	58.2	41.8
1756	37	29.7	70.3	10	90.0	10.0	47	42.6	57.4
1757	36	50.0	50.0	8	100.0	0	44	59.1	40.9

SOURCE: Sample.

charged with noncapital grand larceny were brought before the quarter sessions charged with petty larceny. Indeed, for several years every larceny indictment at the quarter sessions stated the value of the goods stolen as ten pence: the clerk used blank bills with that sum already inserted, and simply made every case fit. Eight bushels of sea coals were declared to be worth ten pence, and in a subsequent indictment at the same session of the court, a chaldron of sea coals (thirty-two bushels) was given the same value. Three silver teaspoons were valued at ten pence; so were twelve pounds of bacon (together with two pounds of sugar) and thirty pounds of cheese. Even more remarkably, the quarter sessions also declared eleven half-crowns to be worth ten pence, and in another case assigned that same value to two and a half guineas, that is, more than fifty-three shillings (or, to make the fiction plain, well over six hundred pence).[43] If a case went to the quarter sessions in these years, it went as a petty larceny. It is unclear—as one minor aspect of a quite extraordinary set of manipulations—how all the prosecutors were persuaded to accept such significant

[43] These cases are drawn from QS 2/5 (Surrey QS Rolls): Ea. 1750 (Phillips and Buckeridge); Mich. 1750 (Pollett and Warren); Ep. 1751 (Till); Ea. 1751 (Clark and three others); Ea. 1752 (Alcraft).

undervaluations, though of course it would have been less costly for most of them to attend at the quarter sessions than at the assizes, and that may be explanation enough.

Charges of petty larceny had clearly been constructed in the past by systematic undervaluation of stolen goods. At the quarter sessions at Lewes in Sussex in April 1694, for example, one can find successive indictments for the theft of a sheep, a ram, four pounds of bacon, and two silver spoons, all of which were valued at ten pence.[44] But the sheer extent of the fiction in Surrey in the early 1750s is striking, as is the effect it had on the subsequent balance of work between the quarter sessions and the assizes. All theft cases at the quarter sessions were treated as petty larcenies for more than two years (in about twenty meetings of the court, including adjournments) until the end of 1752, when for reasons equally unclear the justices began to treat simple larceny cases more or less on their merits. The objects stolen began to be valued at something much closer to their real worth, and quite suddenly the court of quarter sessions in Surrey found itself dealing with a considerable proportion of the grand larceny cases tried in the county, on paper as well as in fact. Perhaps the clerk had used up his supply of blank indictments. Perhaps someone pointed out that it would not make a great deal of difference in practice to the punishments that might be awarded whether an offense was described as petty larceny or grand larceny, since benefit of clergy (which applied to grand larceny) had been made available to all prisoners in 1706 and since both grand and petty larceny were transportable offenses.[45]

Many of the fictional petty larcenists of 1750–52 were indeed punished by transportation, as they would have been had they been convicted of the grand larceny for which they had been committed. It is true that many were ordered to be whipped, which had long been a likely outcome of conviction for petty larceny—and it is almost certainly the case that on the whole these offenders were dealt with differently than they would have been if they had been left to the assizes or tried at the quarter sessions for grand larceny. But it seems unlikely, to say the least, that such considerations explain why the quarter sessions in fact took these cases on. A concern to regulate punishments is an unlikely explanation of this bizarre episode, which seems much more a product of sheer confusion and misunderstanding on the part of the Surrey bench about its powers and authority. One can only wonder whether the magistrates sought the advice

[44] QI/EW7, f. 47.

[45] For transportation see chap. 9. So many of these convicted petty larcenists were ordered to be transported and it was such an unusual outcome that the clerk of the peace had to be authorized in the spring of 1750 to make contracts with merchants and to manage the business on behalf of the county (QS 2/1/18, p. 57).

of the assize judges when they decided to deal with large numbers of the accused felons in the jail as petty larcenists, or whether they simply decided on their own that the safest course was to continue down a known and acceptable path and to bend the facts to fit.

The magistrates had been perhaps encouraged to take on these cases in this period because of the crowded conditions in the jail, a subject that we will consider presently. However, having begun, they continued thereafter to deal with prisoners committed for noncapital felonies, and indeed from then on the quarter sessions dealt with more cases of simple grand larceny than the assizes, roughly two-thirds to one-third over the second half of the century. If one adds petty larceny, the magistrates at the Surrey quarter sessions heard about seventy per cent of all noncapital property cases in the county in the fifty years after 1750 (table 6.1).

It seems reasonably certain that this transference of jurisdiction did not result from a directive from the central government, not certainly as part of a general plan of law enforcement. There was no national plan or pattern. The practice in Sussex, for example, was entirely different from that in Surrey. In Sussex, more than half the larceny cases prosecuted between 1660 and the middle of the eighteenth century involved objects of under a shilling in declared value, as against about twenty per cent in Surrey. Most of those cases were tried at the quarter sessions, as they would have been in Surrey. But in addition the magistrates in Sussex also dealt with about a fifth of the grand larceny cases in the same period, and that was strikingly different from the Surrey practice (table 6.1), as indeed it was from what seems to have been the more common pattern elsewhere from the sixteenth century. One can only speculate that the willingness of the Sussex magistrates to ignore the recommendation of such manuals as *The Clerk of the Peace* and to continue to deal with grand larceny charges at their sessions was encouraged by a generally low level of crime in the county and by a desire in those circumstances to make the trial of minor property cases as inexpensive for prosecutors and as free from trouble as possible.

After 1706, when the literacy qualification for benefit of clergy was abolished and grand larceny was no longer even potentially a capital offense, the sharp distinction between petty and grand larceny was significantly diminished; and it was further reduced when transportation was made available by statute in 1718 as a punishment for both forms of larceny. It was these changes that no doubt had made it possible for the Surrey magistrates to take on grand larceny cases at mid-century when the press of business in the county seemed to require it. Thereafter, the quarter sessions in Surrey and Sussex both dealt with two-thirds and more of the simple larceny prosecutions in their counties. The assize courts were left with the serious felonies, including all capital offenses. The transfer of minor cases to the quarter sessions relieved what would have been a growing burden on the assizes, especially in a county like Surrey in which prosecutions increased inexorably with the growth of population over the second half of the century. Given the essential rigidity of the assize system (which we will examine later in the chapter), this enlargement of the work of the quarter sessions undoubtedly helped to preserve the form and structure of judicial administration until well into the nineteenth century.

THE COUNTY JAIL: SECURITY

It was not a matter of indifference whether a prisoner was tried at the assizes or quarter sessions. It is difficult to know whether any one defendant would have been more readily convicted at one or the other or more harshly punished, though in general the conviction rate tended to be a little higher at the quarter sessions while the assizes tended to order stiffer punishments for the same offense.[46] There was one immediate advantage, however, in being sent to the quarter sessions: the trial was likely to come on more quickly than it would at the assizes, for the sessions met four times a year (and occasionally more often) and the assizes twice. For all but those who would end on the gallows, a speedy trial and a rapid deliverance from jail could only have been an advantage.

The main place of incarceration for those awaiting trial in Surrey was the county jail at Southwark. Some were held in the houses of correction at Southwark, Guildford, and Kingston, and as we will see, these institutions also came to play a significant role in the punishment of felons as well as of the idle and disorderly poor they had been established to deal with. But most prisoners awaited their trials in the county jail. What that experience was like depended a great deal on how crowded it was, though there is no doubt that conditions in the jails and bridewells were frequently offensive and even dangerous, and at those times especially how long a prisoner had to wait for his trial was a matter of considerable significance.

Not a great deal is known in detail about English jails and houses of correction in the eighteenth century, though, perhaps paradoxically, a strong impression has formed of their condition. That is surely because of the work of prisoner reformers in the years after 1770 and especially of John Howard, whose tours in the 1770s and 1780s and whose reports published as *The State of the Prisons in England* (first edition, 1777) provide the foundation of our knowledge of English penal institutions in the last

[46] See chaps. 8–10.

quarter of the century. Howard's enquiries have shaped the subject and remain fundamental to it. It is worth remembering, however, that he collected information on the jails and houses of correction for a purpose: he wanted to reform them. The fullest subsequent account, that of the Webbs, is in the same mold, for they found little of value in any of the institutions of the "old regime."[47] Valuable work has been done recently on prisons and imprisonment between the Restoration and the early nineteenth century, but we still await the systematic and full-scale study that will establish the subject on a foundation not determined by the outlook and attitudes of those who sought fundamentally to condemn the prison system of the eighteenth century.[48]

When the jails and houses of correction of the century before Howard are more carefully investigated, their less attractive characteristics are likely to stand out more starkly than ever. Two were of particular concern to those being held for trial: the generally low level of security, which made for harshness of treatment; and the threat that conditions in the prison from time to time posed to the health of inmates.

Unlike the control exercised by administrators of modern penal institutions (or at least the ideal they would like to achieve), jailers in eighteenth-century prisons had only the loosest influence over the lives of inmates. Prison life went forward to a considerable extent under the slightly detached control of the keeper and his guards, the turnkeys. In Newgate, and it is likely in other jails too, several matters of crucial importance to the prisoners were largely in the hands of trustees, prisoners in some measure elected to maintain aspects of discipline, who also distributed charitable contributions and collected the "garnish" that new prisoners were to pay on entrance and that was used to buy candles, soap, and coal.[49] The keepers controlled directly those aspects of prison life they profited from—and on which indeed they entirely depended for their income, for

[47] John Howard, *The State of the Prisons in England and Wales*, 1st ed. (Warrington, 1777), 4th ed. (Warrington, 1792); Sidney Webb and Beatrice Webb, *English Prisons under Local Government* (1922; repr. 1963).

[48] Michael Ignatieff, *A Just Measure of Pain: The Penitentiary in the Industrial Revolution* (New York, 1978); Robin Evans, *The Fabrication of Virtue: English Prison Architecture, 1750–1840* (Cambridge, 1982); Joanna Innes, "The King's Bench Prison in the Later Eighteenth Century: Law, Authority and Order in a London Debtors' Prison," in Brewer and Styles, eds., *An Ungovernable People*; Peter Linebaugh, "The Ordinary of Newgate and His 'Account,' " in Cockburn, ed., *Crime in England*; W. J. Sheehan, "Finding Solace in 18th-Century Newgate," in ibid.; Sean McConville, *A History of English Prison Administration, 1750–1877* (1981); Eric Stockdale, *A Study of Bedford Prison, 1660–1877* (Bedford, 1977); Margaret Eisenstein DeLacy, "County Prison Administration in Lancashire, 1690–1850" (Ph.D. thesis, Princeton University, 1980).

[49] Sheehan, "Finding Solace in 18th-Century Newgate," p. 234; Evans, *Fabrication of Virtue*, pp. 22–32.

even if they got an allowance from the county it was not until the end of the eighteenth century conceived as providing in itself full compensation for their work. In the 1720s, for example, the fees to be taken by the keeper of a new jail built in Surrey were established by the quarter sessions on the basis of past practice and the custom of other countries at 13s. 4d. from each prisoner committed for felony upon his discharge, 10s. 10d. for a misdemeanor, and 6s. 8d. from a debtor ("and not more under any pretense whatsoever").[50] Beyond that, the keeper might add to his income by providing special accommodation outside the common wards for those prisoners who could afford it (debtors and felons, both before trial and after), in a special wing or perhaps in his own house or apartment. Other fees might be collected from visitors, and perhaps for arranging the sexual commerce inside the prison and between the prison and the outside world. But the largest portion of the keeper's income was likely to have come from the prison taproom, from the sale of beer and liquors and tobacco. When in 1784 taps were abolished by Act of parliament, the keeper of the Surrey county jail estimated that his profit from this source had averaged £228 over the previous five years.[51]

Since the keeper's income came largely from the prisoners—the income from which he paid the salaries of the guards and other servants he employed—he had a natural interest in those aspects of prison life that affected his remuneration. But he was not directed from the outside, by the central government or the judges or the magistrates of the county, to organize the prisoners' day in any particular way. By and large, the prisoners were left to organize it themselves. Broad separations were maintained in the Surrey jails between men and women and between debtors and felons, but the architecture of the prisons before the end of the eighteenth century did not make feasible (even if that had been actively sought) the separation of young or first-time offenders from the experienced, or of those awaiting trial from those already convicted. It was this indiscriminate mixing of prisoners that gave the prisons the reputation of being schools of vice and that encouraged resistance to the notion that confinement (in jail at least) might be a useful punishment. For much of the time, the prisoners were allowed to mix freely in the day-rooms, perhaps in a small courtyard, and in the taproom. At night they were generally locked into their wards—not individual cells—in groups whose size and composition would depend a great deal on the population in the prison at that moment.

Contact with other prisoners was matched by contact with the outside world. Visitors were allowed to come and go during the day (for a fee),

50 QS 2/6, Ep. 1724, 71.
51 QS 2/6, Mids. 1785, 27.

and all of this meant that some prisoners, especially those with friends or family available, and those with funds, might be able to do a great deal to prepare for the trial that was to come. If there were experienced men in the jail who could give advice, the internal arrangements of the prisoners' lives facilitated that advice being sought; and those with money could pay for legal help. Friends and relatives, and particularly an experienced so licitor, could also arrange for the attendance of the witnesses whose testimony would be crucial at the prisoner's trial.

The absence of minute control over the daily lives of the prisoners, the mixing of the prison population, and the relative ease of access from the outside all made for a form of incarceration that enabled those with friends or money to ameliorate their present situation and to prepare for some of the difficulties ahead. But these arrangements also produced problems of security that were not counterbalanced by the buildings that typically served as prisons in the eighteenth century. It was this aspect of the jail business—buildings rather than rules and regulations and internal controls—that mainly engaged the attention of the magistrates, and by the eighteenth century, to judge by the Order Books of the quarter sessions, it engaged them regularly.

In many counties the problem of the jails stemmed from their being in old buildings built for some other purpose.[52] At the Restoration, the Surrey county jail had been in a building for more than a century that had once been an inn, the White Lion on St. Margaret's Hill in Southwark, near the King's Bench prison. The county had in fact only acquired ownership of the land and the buildings on it (which included a house of correction adjoining the jail) in 1654, and by then the fabric was in serious disrepair. The jail had been pulled down by a crowd of London apprentices in 1640, and though it had been rebuilt and was in use at the Restoration, it was in such poor condition by 1681 that the prisoners could no longer be held securely and the county abandoned it. There is evidence that the Surrey magistrates fully intended to sell the site and to build a new jail elsewhere, but for some reason they failed to do so. Instead they entered into an arrangement with the keeper of the Marshalsea, the prison of the king's Palace Court, who took the county's prisoners into his jail in exchange for the use of part of the old White Lion site. (The house of correction continued to function in its old building; and another part of the White Lion was leased to two other men.) For forty years the county was to be without its own jail. It was not unique in thus contracting out its prisoners; other counties did so too. But the broad trend in the late seventeenth century was for counties to move toward gaining control over

[52] Evans, *Fabrication of Virtue*, pp. 22–23.

their jails: having done just that by getting a freehold title to its jail in 1654, Surrey then went against the trend by alienating it less than thirty years later and by entering into an arrangement that could only mean a loss of control over the county's prisoners.[53]

The arrangements with the keeper of the Marshalsea proved not to be a satisfactory solution for long. By 1693 the Surrey magistrates were considering building a new jail and house of correction on the site of the White Lion in Southwark, but they abandoned that plan in view of the expense it would entail.[54] Their concern about the arrangements for keeping the county's prisoners was evidently widely shared in the 1690s. It obviously reached the administration, for the judges were asked to meet in 1696 "and consider what regulations may be proper to be made in relation to prisons and their keepers, in order to oblige those keepers to look better to their prisoners and to prevent escapes. . . ."[55] If Surrey's experience is any guide, the inadequacies of the jails may have been particularly revealed in this period by overcrowding, and there are a number of reasons to think that that problem became especially serious toward the end of the 1690s, at least in the metropolis of London.[56] The inadequacies of the jails were in any event felt sufficiently acutely to lead to the passage of an Act in the 1698–99 session of parliament to encourage the building

[53] I owe to Joanna Innes the information about the extent to which the Surrey arrangements were typical of other counties in this period. For the White Lion jail see Owen Manning and Wiliam Bray, *The History and Antiquities of the County of Surrey*, 3 vols. (1804–14), vol. 3, app., pp. xi–xvi; *The Victoria County History of Surrey*, 4 vols. (1902–12), vol. 4, p. 141; W. H. Hart, "Further Remarks on Some of the Ancient Inns of Southwark," *Surrey Archaeological Collections* (1865), vol. 3, pp. 195–203.

[54] The Surrey bench had complicated the problem of building a new jail by leasing part of the White Lion site for a term of years; it was perhaps the cost of buying up that lease, as well as the cost of the new buildings themselves, that discouraged them from going forward in 1693. They may also have had doubts about their authority to raise the large sums required. In any event, they went no further in 1693. It was recorded in the QS Order Book that "having considered the great charge that must ensue in erecting and building of a new gaol and how difficult it would be to raise and charge the county with so great a sum of money . . . they did rather think fit to treat with Mr. Lowman who hath for diverse years past kept the county prisoners as well debtors as felons in the Marshalsea. . . ." Such arrangement continued to seem "the best expedient" and the scheme "most to the advantage of this County" (QS 2/1/7, pp. 236–37).

[55] *Cal. S. P. Dom.*, 1696, p. 449.

[56] Partly this was a matter of an increased number of prosecutions for clipping and coining and, in the years of dearth at the end of the decade in which also the army and navy were disbanded following the peace of 1697, an increase in prosecutions for property offenses. On the other side, there do seem to have been special difficulties in finding adequate and acceptable means of punishing the guilty in this same period (including difficulties in transportation) that are likely to have resulted in prisoners being kept in jail longer than they might otherwise have been. For these subjects generally see chap. 9.

of new prisons, action that was required according to the preamble because the jails were becoming "prejudicial to the health of prisoners and insufficient for the safe custody of them." The Act gave magistrates authority, following a grand jury presentment of "the insufficiency or inconveniency" of the county jail, to appoint a receiver and raise money to rebuild or enlarge it.[57]

Several counties took advantage of the jail-building Act over the next decade. The Surrey magistrates seem not to have been in a great hurry to do so, and in the early years of the new century the pressures on the county jail clearly eased, in part because prosecutions fell away during the war that began in 1702, in part because that war provided in service in the army and navy a penal option that further helped to clear the jails. In Anne's reign it was the house of correction that came in for most attention because there arose a strong interest in the possibilities of imprisonment at hard labor as a penal weapon, even in the case of minor felons.[58] Thus in 1712, when the county's prisoners were still being kept in the Marshalsea by contract, the Surrey magistrates declared their house of correction at Southwark to be

> ruinous, decaying and very much out of repair and not only
> insufficient for the safe custody of prisoners but very prejudicial
> and destructive to their healths by the dampness and coldness
> of it and that no repairs could make it convenient or render it
> wholesome for prisoners but that it ought to be rebuilt.[59]

Soon thereafter the insufficiency of the arrangements for housing the inmates of both the jail and houses of correction was once again made plain by another sharp increase in prosecutions for property offenses and thus in the number of men and women crushed into the prisons awaiting trial. The numbers may not seem massive to modern observers, but an increase in 1714 and 1715 to about 170 men and women being held for trial on property charges from wartime levels in Anne's reign of forty to eighty represented a significant increase in pressure on the accommodation in what were small buildings. Overcrowding made for discomfort inside the prisons and gradually for discomfort outside, as the fear grew of a mass escape and serious violence or, if not that, of a threat to the health of everyone who came into contact with the prisoners. The inadequacy of the arrangements for dealing with the county's prisoners was brought home with sufficient clarity in 1714 and 1715 for the Surrey magistrates to agree

---

[57] 11 and 12 Wm III, c. 19 (1700).
[58] See chap. 9.
[59] QS 2/1/11, p. 211.

soon thereafter to build not only a new bridewell in Southwark but a new county jail too. They rejected an offer from the keeper of the Marshalsea to build a new jail and house of correction himself (with a little financial help from the county) and to take on the whole business of imprisonment in exchange for a ninety-nine-year lease to the entire White Lion site. The magistrates drew back from what might have been in some respects an attractive offer to create a private prison service for the county in what the keeper of the Marshalsea promised would be a "fitting and convenient House of Correction and a Strong and convenient Gaole." The committee of six justices who recommended against this offer were of the opinion

> that if this proposal was accepted, it would be giving up the county's right in the Lands they had purchased for 99 years, and entailing Gaolers of both Prisons for the same Terme, without any redress. Upon the whole it was thought more adviseable to . . . build on the ground a County Gaol and House of Correction at the county charge, and then it would always be in the Power of the Justices, and Sheriff, to appoint what Gaolers they pleased.[60]

It took some years of further discussion, and perhaps the working out of better arrangements for raising the money in the county,[61] before grand jury presentments in 1719 and 1720 led to a decision by the quarter sessions to build a new prison on the old site, next to the house of correction.[62] Work began toward the end of 1721; and some three years later the New Gaol, as it was called, consisting of a debtor's ward, male and female felons' wards, and a keeper's house, was substantially completed.

Security had clearly been one of the major concerns behind this effort, the fear that the prisoners might break out en masse from a dilapidated

---

[60] QS 2/6, Mids. 1716, 29, 30.

[61] Joanna Innes has suggested to me that improvements in county finances between the Revolution and the 1720s might explain why the reluctance of the magistrates to build a new jail in the 1690s was overcome in the second and third decades of the eighteenth century. Several other counties, she informs me, either built new jails or contemplated new buildings in the 1720s: Suffolk and Bucks, for example. The establishment of an exact pattern of the building of new jails and the enlarging of existing buildings between 1690 and 1730 might cast light on the possibility that changes in county finances, and the ability of the county government to draw more effectively on the wealth of its inhabitants (in a way parallel to the increasing ability of the national government to tap the national wealth more effectively), lies behind the boldness of the magistrates in the 1720s when they had been so apparently timid thirty years earlier.

[62] QS 2/6, Ea. 1719, 67; Mids. 1719, 31; Mids. 1720, 62; QS 2/1/12, pp. 8, 95. A presentment of the grand jury was required by the Gaol Act to authorize the magistrates to raise the money.

building. That concern was not entirely removed, however, even when the prisoners were moved into this purpose-built structure, for the same conditions of prison life continued, the same relative absence of control over the inmates' activities. Within a decade it was reported that the wainscotting in the felons' wards, both male and female, had been pulled down either to be used as firewood (understandably, since the county gave them no fuel allowance) or "by reason of the many attempts the Prisoners have made to get out."[63] The keeper of the jail had had to report the escape of eight felons some years before, and he had petitioned the quarter sessions to take measures to strengthen the fabric of the jail. A committee of justices was asked to

> view the said gaol and to consider what is necessary and fitting
> to be done either by lining of the wards with boards and nails
> to secure the planks from being boared through and taking out
> the bricks and whether a slight pallisade be not proper to be
> put on the top of the wall to prevent ropes being thrown over.[64]

The conditions of prison life allowed a constant assault to be mounted against the building, and over the next few years several groups of magistrates pondered ways of halting the decay of the New Gaol, still not yet ten years old. The committee that reported on the missing wainscotting in 1730 recommended that the walls be repaired "with ship plank or such like strong stuff," and the bench paid a carpenter in the following year to install six hundred and sixty feet of "old barge plank" in the women's wards and twelve hundred in the men's, the whole lined with elm boards and secured with nails "without heads and about three inches apart." At the same time, "iron hoop" was to be nailed around the edges of the chimneys and windows. The external walls were also by then in bad condition, the brickwork so decayed, it was reported that "the prisoners may get on top of it and assist one another to make their escape." The walls of the house of correction were also falling down and were inadequate anyway to keep the prisoners in: they needed to be raised all round, the keeper thought, and to have broken glass bottles set on top. The magistrates at the Easter quarter sessions in 1732 agreed to raise the walls three feet.[65]

One gets a sense from the repairs and improvements necessary in the ten years after the opening of the new institution in Southwark that there had been something of an onslaught on the building. It is possible that

---

[63] QS 2/6, Mich. 1730, 44.
[64] QS 2/1/12, p. 640 (1727).
[65] QS 2/6, Mids. 1731, 94a; Mich. 1730, 44; Ep. 1731, 17; Ea. 1732, 35.

it had not been adequately built in the first place, but the main point surely is that the response of the keeper and the justices had not been to improve their control over the prisoners by making rules or posting more guards, but to strengthen the fabric. The prisoners remained relatively uncontrolled within the building, and this inevitably made attempts at escape common. How commonly they were successful is another matter. Those who got away while awaiting trial would still be indicted and their case sent to the grand jury, but the indictment would then be inscribed "escaped" by the clerk. But of course more escaped than that. Those who got away while awaiting the death penalty or transportation or whipping or while serving a term of imprisonment would not necessarily be recorded, at least not in the court records. The number of escapes will thus remain a matter of impression. And my impression is that there were fewer than the expressed fears and the complaints of the jailers about the run-down condition of their prisons would lead one to believe.

Of course there were spectacular escapes and escape artists, Jack Sheppard being perhaps the most famous.[66] From time to time prisoners managed to get out of the Surrey prisons, disguised in their wives' clothing or simply slipping out in a crowd of visitors at night. And the walls of the jail were breached occasionally. Because the prison (as was so common) was simply another building along a main street in Southwark, backing on to alleys and courts and other buildings, escape routes could be more easily created than they might have been in a free-standing building with a perimeter that could be readily watched. A committee of magistrates inspected the jail in 1738 and discovered that since the men's ward adjoined several tenements in Angel Alley, which ran along one side of the prison, the inmates had been able to escape by taking bricks out of the wall and by getting friends on the outside to drop ladders and ropes from the tenements. They recommended that the men's ward be rebuilt so as to separate it from the wall that enclosed the yard.[67]

Outside support for an escape attempt could come in several forms. The most easily accomplished, since visitors could come and go at will without being searched closely, was the smuggling in of tools: files and crowbars and the like. Several such attempts were discovered in the Surrey county jail; and toward the end of the century, at a time when crime was thought to be especially serious and at an especially high level, jailers in London were being urged to take steps to prevent visitors to prisons from taking in saws and other tools.[68] But we should not exaggerate the laxness of the keepers and the guards (at least until the subject is studied), nor

---

[66] Howson, *Thief-Taker General*, chap. 19.

[67] QS 2/6, Ea. 1738, 42.

[68] QS 2/6, Ep. 1741, 48 (a crowbar smuggled in by a man seen to be limping); HO 42/1, ff. 344–45.

the ease of escape. The jailers were held responsible for prisoners escaping, and at the very least that could mean a troublesome search conducted at their expense. When a prisoner got away from the house of correction in Southwark in 1719 the keeper paid for advertisements in an effort to find him; and in general, as he told the clerk of the peace whose support he sought in case there were any complaints about him at the forthcoming sessions, he had been forced to be "very industrious" to try to get him back.[69] The keeper of the Kingston house of correction was ordered by the magistrates in quarter sessions in similar circumstances in 1778 to "advertize [the prisoner] with a full description of his person three times in the Morning Post and also in a paper commonly or known by the name of Sir John Fielding's Hue and Cry" and to pay a reward of two guineas for his apprehension.[70] If they did not commonly watch the prisoners' "behaviour and motions," as one keeper complained bitterly he had to do on one occasion when the walls had actually crumbled in several places,[71] that was not because they were indifferent but because they did not rely on internal controls or even on bricks and mortar to keep the prisoners inside. They depended mainly on other physical restraints, principally irons and chains.

There was some belief in the eighteenth century that jailers had no warrant in law to put fetters on their prisoners or to load them in other ways with irons, and certainly not before their trial, unless the prisoner was unruly or had made an attempt to escape. Jailers were forbidden in this view from putting their prisoners through "pain and torment."[72] But leg irons were used as a matter of course. Howard's evidence makes that very clear.[73] The keeper of the Surrey jail who complained in 1730 about having to watch his prisoners' behavior closely was forced to take that unusual step not only by the weakness of the walls but perhaps mainly because he had also discovered that many of the prisoners had managed to obtain tools and were cutting through their irons.[74]

Mere leg irons were relatively light restraints compared to what was possible: much harsher treatment was visited on those who tried to escape, especially condemned men whose "desperation" was feared. Three who killed a turnkey in trying to escape from Reading jail in the middle of the century were "put into the Collar, Handcuff'd, well loaded with Irons,

[69] QS 2/6, Mich. 1719, 64.
[70] QS 2/1/24, p. 544.
[71] QS 2/6, Mich. 1730, 44.
[72] See Sollom Emlyn, ed., *State Trials*, 6 vols. (1730), vol. 1, p. xiii; Howard, *State of the Prisons*, 4th ed., pp. 13–14.
[73] Quoted by Ignatieff, *A Just Measure of Pain*, p. 42.
[74] QS 2/6, Mich. 1730, 44.

and Stapled down in the Floor of the Condemn'd Room."[75] Chaining such men in dungeons was commonplace and many prisons (though not, apparently, the Surrey jail) had a dark hole underground used for such purposes.[76] Attempts to escape by main force were perhaps encouraged by the apparent weakness of the internal security in most jails, as well as by the ease of contact with the outside world that facilitated planning and supplying weapons and tools. But force could be matched on the other side too, as an attempted break-out by four condemned men at the Surrey county jail in 1735 makes clear. A highwayman called Macray and three other men had smuggled pistols into the jail, and two nights before their execution was to take place they were discovered "filing off their irons." The keeper, the *Gentleman's Magazine* reported,

> got his Assistants arm'd with Blunderbusses, Pistols, and Cutlasses, went to the Door, and desir'd Macray to make no desperate Attempt, for there was no possibility of his Escape. Macray replied, in their present desperate Circumstances they knew no body, and desir'd him to retire, for the first that enter'd was a dead man. Upon this Mr. Taylor [the keeper] order'd the Door to be unbolted and open'd a little way; which they sooner heard but they discharg'd eight Pistols, and one of the keepers a Blunderbuss, but without Execution, the Door between them being very strong. Then Mr. Taylor and his Guard rush'd in, attack'd them with their Cutlasses, and overpower'd them immediately. Macray was wounded in his Head, and his Arm disabled. Sellon desperately cut in several Places; Emerson had one Side of his Face cut away: James was but slightly hurt. On Mr. Taylor's Part very little Damage was done. The Pistols were brought to the Prisoners in two Smoking hot Pyes. . . .[77]

The weakness of internal controls encourged plans and attempts at escape. But the balance still lay with the jailer, who could keep them within acceptable limits because he had in practice the unsupervised power to load prisoners with irons and to treat some very harshly indeed.

THE COUNTY JAIL: HEALTH AND "IMPROVEMENT"

The weakness of control over the daily lives of prisoners was one aspect of the old regime that came in for serious criticism in the last third of

---

[75] *London Evening Post*, 11 Apr. 1748.
[76] On dungeons see Evans, *Fabrication of Virtue*, pp. 75–91.
[77] *G. M.* 5 (1735), p. 498.

the century, when reformers urged that jails be constructed and organized in such a way as to make full internal supervision possible. In the nineteenth century the proponents of penitentiaries strove to create such "total institutions" in which the inmates' every movement, every aspect of their lives, virtually every gesture, would be controlled by the prison authorities.[78] When that was achieved, leg irons could be abandoned. That exchange might not have been an entirely unmixed blessing for the prisoners. But one side of prison life that did change in the course of the eighteenth century and that changed unequivocally for the better was in the arrangements to protect the health of inmates.

Jails were unhealthy places. There were times when they were relatively clean and free from lice and not so pungently noisome that men could enter from the outside without gagging. But very often visitors found it impossible to stay in them for long because of the stench. On his tours of the prisons in the 1770s and 1780s, John Howard found dirt wherever he went, an absence of running water, and inadequate toilet facilities. Prisons were also perishingly cold in the winter. In the house of correction in Southwark, Howard found a dozen small rooms, with shutters and iron bars on the windows but no glass. There was no infirmary, and the several inmates who were ill when he visited simply lay on the plank floors among all the others. The county allowed no bedding or straw: only those who could pay 2s. 6d. a week had a bed. The rooms were all dirty and "in two or three of them were fowls."[79]

The stench arising from the jails in the eighteenth century was no doubt mainly a consequence of their primitive sanitary arrangements and the fact that the "vaults" of the "necessary houses" so often seem to have overflowed. When a new keeper was appointed at the Surrey jail in 1728, he discovered that "the vaults and drains thereto belonging were full and the passages stopped so as to overflow." But it was to be some months before the magistrates got the jails inspected and agreed to pay to have the system "emptied, scoured and cleansed" at the county's expense.[80] This was obviously a common problem, as was the delay before a complaint would be acted on. Later in the century, to take just one occasion as an example, when it was reported to the bench at the beginning of November 1769 that the "common vaults" of the jail were "so full that diverse unwholesome smells arise therefrom" and the court ordered two justices to get them emptied, it was to be seven weeks before they contracted with a "nightman" actually to do the work.[81]

[78] Ignatieff, *A Just Measure of Pain*, chap. 1.
[79] Howard, *State of the Prisons*, 4th ed., p. 276.
[80] QS 2/6, Mids. 1728, bundle 2, 20.
[81] QS 2/6, Ep. 1769, 33. People living near the prisons suffered almost as much as the inmates.

The jails and houses of correction were not always, however, at a maximum level of horror: much depended on how crowded they were. It must be remembered that before the 1770s the prisons were not meant to be places of long-term incarceration, at least not of felons.[82] In the late seventeenth century there would have been a regular rhythm and fluctuation in the size of the prison population—at its greatest just before the assizes, but almost immediately afterwards at its lowest, for there would have remained then (and for a few weeks at the most) only those condemned to death; while the rest, even if convicted, would have been discharged with a whipping or branding. This pattern was changed by the increasing use of transportation after 1718, for then some convicted prisoners were returned to jail to await a ship for America. After 1770 the jails began to be used actually as places of punishment. But even before the emergence of imprisonment, the large numbers of convicts sentenced to transportation meant that the courts were not clearing the jails as they had earlier. Transportation helped to make the prisons seem inadequate before the invention of imprisonment confirmed it. Very often in the eighteenth century suspects committed for trial must have found the jail already crowded. Often, though not always—for there is another rhythm of occupation that was obviously of great importance: the fluctuation of prosecutions. This may indeed have been the single most important factor affecting jail conditions in the eighteenth century, at least in Surrey (and other counties near London), where, as we have seen, there were substantial fluctuations in the levels of charges being laid.

By the standards of the nineteenth century and after, the level of prosecutions in the eighteenth century was not strikingly high. But it must be remembered that the jails were not large and that for the most part they had not been built to house stable populations of felons, so that what would be regarded as a modest intake in the later prisons might well have had a catastrophic effect in the eighteenth century. And it was the crowding that resulted from sudden increases in prosecutions that made the jails particularly noisome and dangerous.

In 1730 a widow who lived next to the Southwark house of correction complained to the magistrates that within a year of its being built

> the filth of the House of Office issued through the Walls of the House of Correction and the Walls of your Petitioner's Dwelling House in such great Quantities that it hath covered the Floor of her Kitchen. And the filth running in the new sink . . . and passing by your Petitioner's Door of her House is so great an Annoyance that your Petitioner hath lost all her Lodgers. And although [her landlord] hath abated your Petitioner £4 per annum your Petitioner is become utterly unable to pay her Rent or support herself as formerly. . . . (QS 2/6, Ep. 1730, 106)

[82] For the penal developments discussed in this paragraph, see chaps. 9–10.

Deaths in prison had of course been common before the eighteenth century.[83] Most were attributed to what was known as "gaol fever," a particularly virulent form of typhus carried by lice and spread by contact and thus at its worst in crowded conditions.[84] Typhus is a wasting disease that requires large intakes of protein if it is to be successfully resisted, so the prisoners' diets became an especially crucial matter when the jails were crowded. It is not easy to assess how well or badly fed prisoners were. If they depended entirely on the county allowance, they had to live for some weeks or months on a diet of bread and water and little else. The county did not of course expect them to be in jail for long, and the bread allowance was conceived as sufficient to keep men alive who had no other support and no means of earning money while in jail. In the early eighteenth century the Surrey allowance was one pennyworth of bread a day; by Howard's day it had been increased to three half-pence. At the prices prevailing in London in the 1740s and 1750s this would have likely brought three-quarters of a pound of bread.[85] This pitifully small ration might be supplemented by begging—the New Gaol provided a barred window through which the prisoners could appeal to passers-by for alms[86]—and those with friends on the outside or with money or credit had access to the shops and taverns of the neighborhood, for deliveries into the prison were allowed (for a fee), and some prisoners no doubt had frequent dinners, as had Macray and his three companions, of "smoking hot pyes." And, again for those with money, the prison tap provided nourishment in the form of beer.

How many prisoners typically languished merely on the county allowance I have no way of estimating. Some clearly did, and when the jails were crowded their undernourishment helped to make them particularly susceptible to jail fever. What appears to have been a fluctuating pattern of deaths in prison seems to be related in part to the number of prisoners being held (and beyond a simple proportionate increase). This certainly seems to explain the pattern of deaths in Surrey jails in the first half of the eighteenth century. There may well be more complete information about jail mortality than I have gathered. I regret, for example, that I have not been able fully to explore the possibility that coroners' inquests in the King's Bench records or the burial records of the parish in which the jail was located might have filled out the picture. But there is fragmentary evidence in the quarter sessions papers of the number of deaths

---

[83] Cockburn, *Assize Records: Introduction*, app. 2.

[84] Evans, *Fabrication of Virtue*, chap. 3; Linebaugh, "The Ordinary of Newgate," p. 253.

[85] Ashton, *Fluctuations*, p. 181. Full accounts of bread supplied to the jail by the man designated as the county baker are in QS 2/6 from 1701 on.

[86] QS 2/1/12, p. 504.

in the Surrey county jail at particular times.[87] These are claims for payment made by the jailer for burying prisoners. They are by no means complete, nor do they include everyone who died in jail, for presumably some were taken for burial by their friends and family. The jailer's claims provide a minimum figure. They do vary quite strikingly over time, though, and they raise some interesting questions (table 6.3). Between 1720 and 1739, for example, for which the figures on burials paid for by the keeper are available for a number of periods amounting to about ten years in all, deaths in the jail varied from about three a year to twelve. On average, the keeper claimed for the burial of eight prisoners a year. Twenty deaths, however, occurred in 1738, a year in which the county jail was particularly crowded and, it was said, "very sickly on account of the great number of prisoners there for selling spirituous liquors," that is, for contravening the Gin Act.[88] But worse was to come. In June 1740 five burials took place at the county jail, and the toll increased in the following winter. In December, nine men and women were buried at the county's expense (including five who had died in one day) and seven in January. In the next five months twenty-four prisoners were buried. From the summer of 1740 to the summer of 1741 the total had been fifty-two. Another thirty-four prisoners died in the first ten months of 1742. Over a period of about two years the annual mortality had been at the rate of forty deaths a year, eight times the average of the previous two decades.

The virulence of the jail fever in these years was such that when the Spring assizes came on in 1741, Lord Chief Justice Lee (with his own health no doubt very much in mind) ordered the prisoners to be examined

TABLE 6.3

Burials at the Surrey County Jail in Southwark

Period	Months	Deaths	Rate per Year
Jan. 1721–May 1723	29	23	9.5
June 1724–Dec. 1727	43	10	2.8
Apr. 1736–May 1740	50	50	12.0
June 1740–Sept. 1742	28	94	40.3
Jan. 1744–Jan. 1746	25	30	14.4

SOURCES: QS 2/6, Ep. 1723; Ea. 1724, 7; Ep. 1728, 132–33; Mids. 1740, 85; Ep. 1741, 56; Ea. 1741, 33, 63a; Ep. 1742, 9; Ep. 1744, 20; Ep. 1745, 40.

[87] Among the quarter sessions papers, QS 2/6, passim.
[88] S.A.P., Summer 1738, p. 8. One prisoner actually died in court at the Summer assizes (*London Evening Post*, 12 Aug. 1738).

and given medicine and for a doctor to attend at the court session and to fumigate the courtroom. Dr. Waterhouse of Kingston subsequently sent in his bill for attending during the four days of the session and for examining the prisoners, they "being ill and distempered and many of them dying before and some of them at the Assizes."[89] The magistrates themselves struck a committee at the following quarter sessions to look into "the cause of such sickness, whether by the closeness of the rooms or what other reasons may be assigned for the same and what method they think best to be taken to render the same more healthy and convenient." Rather than suggesting remedies, however, the four magistrates who reported four months later suggested only that two small rooms be set aside in the jail so that the "poor debtors" and "unhappy felons" who became ill could be separated from the rest.[90] It is possible that the jail fever in these years was complicated by smallpox, outbreaks of which were reported in Surrey in 1741.[91] As Howard was to point out, prisoners were readily subject to every epidemic that came along. But perhaps the most serious problem faced by prisoners in 1740 and 1741 was that for those who depended on the county allowance their usual scanty diet had been seriously reduced by harvest failures and a sharp rise in the price of grain. In the winter of 1740–41 the fixed allowance of one penny a day brought less and less bread: a quartern loaf that had averaged five pence in 1738 was seven and a quarter pence in 1740. So seriously undernourished did the county's prisoners become that in the spring of 1741 the magistrates raised the allowance first to three half-pence a day and then to a fixed two pounds weight because, as they said, they feared that many had died during the winter "for want of a better allowance of bread."[92] "Gaol fever" was perhaps the ultimate cause of most of the prison deaths in 1740–41, but it is also possible that some of the prisoners had simply died of starvation.[93]

That crisis passed with the falling away of prosecutions during the war and the recovery of the harvests. But similar outbreaks of fever were to reoccur whenever the prisons were crowded, as they were regularly in the second half of the century in the years immediately following the conclusion of wars. In the early 1750s, in 1763 and 1764, and again

[89] QS 2/6, Ea. 1741, 22a–b.

[90] QS 2/6, Mids. 1741.

[91] QS 2/6, Mids. 1741, 21c.

[92] QS 2/1/16, 16 July 1741. The bread allowance was increased at other times later in the century when prices rose sharply: in 1768–69, for example (QS 2/1/22, pp. 65, 94, 97, 225).

[93] At an inquest at the Wiltshire county jail in 1787 a prisoner was found to have died from the inclement weather and lack of sustenance. The coroner concluded that "the allowance of a twopenny loaf per day was and is a very short and scanty one, inadequate to and insufficient for the support and maintenance of the body of any man" (R. F. Hunnisett, ed., *Wiltshire Coroners' Bills, 1752–1796*, Wiltshire Record Society, vol. 36 [Devizes, 1981], p. 98).

twenty years later, there were to be complaints about the conditions in the jails and reports of high rates of mortality among the prisoners. For several years after 1749 the county jail was so crowded and so obviously unhealthy—even with the houses of correction at Southwark and Guildford pressed into service and even with the court of quarter sessions taking on for the first time a large number of simple felonies so that prisoners might be moved through as quickly as possible—that the magistrates considered building a new jail and another house of correction at Kingston. In the words of a grand jury presentment at the Summer assizes of 1751, the two buildings in Southwark were "greatly out of repair, too small, unwholesome and unsafe for the prisoners," several of whom, it was noted, had recently escaped while many others had died of "pestilential diseases."[94] Across the river, jail fever raged through Newgate. Indeed 1750 saw the most memorable outbreak of the century because it carried away not only dozens of prisoners but, following the April session at the Old Bailey, more than fifty people who had been in court, among them the lord mayor of London, two judges, an alderman, a lawyer, a number of court officials, and several members of the jury. Those who had been in court at this so-called Black Session, Sir Michael Foster reported, "were sensibly affected with a very noisome smell." Nonetheless he thought the outbreak of fever remarkable because it seemed to him "there was no sickness in the gaol more than is common in such places." In fact, sixty-two prisoners died in Newgate in 1750.[95]

Again, as ten years earlier, this crisis passed when the population of the jails diminished. Despite presentments of the jail and bridewells as inadequate, it began to appear to the magistrates of Surrey by 1752 and 1753 that they were large enough after all and that they would not have to engage in any expensive new building. A committee of justices examined the keeper of the jail in July 1752, and heard him say (or persuaded him, since it is curious to find a jailer declaring that he had everything he needed and that everything was fine in his prison) that he had "never complained there was any want of a new county gaol" and that the Surrey jail "was more wholesome" than those in Kent, Essex, and Sussex and decidedly better than Newgate. In fact he confessed himself astonished that several recent grand juries had seemed to think that there was room for improvement. This evidence provided decisive support to those magistrates who thought the jail "sufficiently large for all purposes," and the bench was able to congratulate itself on its having prevented an "unnecessary burthen and expense" being laid upon the county rate-payers.[96]

94 ASSI 35/191/12.
95 Linebaugh, "The Ordinary of Newgate," p. 252.
96 QS 2/6, Mids. 1752, 16; Ep. 1752, 21, 26; QS 1/18, pp. 192, 272, 295.

Despite this reprieve that came as the number of prosecutions declined, there was undoubtedly in the 1750s a growing concern about conditions in the jails, and particularly about jail fever—not the first evidence of such a concern, but more widespread and more sustained than ever before. Not everyone remained as complacent as Mr. Justice Foster or the keeper of the Surrey county jail. By the 1750s there is evidence of efforts being made to combat the effects of disease in prisons not merely by strewing the courts with herbs—"to prevent the smell of any stench that might arise from the prisoners," as was said on another occasion (in 1764) when the jails were again crowded at the conclusion of a war and jail fever was again taking its toll[97]—but now by tackling the fundamental causes. There was a broadening scientific interest in the nature of such institutional diseases as jail fever in the third quarter of the century, and that provided support and encouragement to laymen anxious to see the dirt and the stench of the jails removed. Better ventilation by machines was being advocated by the middle of the century, and there was quite clearly a growing anxiety to see the jails cleaned regularly and perhaps especially to open them up to fresh air, from a conviction that it was their close atmosphere that was mainly responsible for transmitting the fever so rapidly.[98]

There remained, it goes almost without saying, a reluctance to spend money. When the Surrey quarter sessions concluded that the "violent pestilential" that raged through the jail in 1764, when it was again very crowded, was due in part to a want of air and ordered that ventilators be installed, the magistrates were clearly delighted when the millwright they had engaged to give them advice reported that a few new windows would do as well.[99] Nonetheless, some improvements were to be made over the third quarter of the century in the conditions under which the county's prisoners were kept. There was certainly a deepening consciousness of the serious problems in the jails in Surrey. This may be seen in the presentment by the quarter sessions grand jury of the Southwark house of correction in 1759 because it was too small and inadequate, and in particular because "there was no room to keep the sick prisoners by themselves" to prevent the spreading of infections. They also found unacceptable the old practice of simply leaving the corpse of a dead prisoner among the other inmates until an order was made for its burial.[100] There were other piecemeal recognitions of the weaknesses of established practices: more regular provisions of medical services by a doctor who was given an annual salary to

---

[97] *The Public Advertiser*, 13 Jan. 1764.
[98] Evans, *Fabrication of Virtue*, pp. 99–115.
[99] QS 2/6, Ea. 1764, 19; Mich. 1765, 23, 34.
[100] QS 2/6, Ea. 1760, 8.

visit the jail and houses of correction; a growing awareness of the problems caused by dirt as well as of the value of fresh air; and a willingness to give sick prisoners a diet of "broth and other proper nourishment" when fever raged through the jail and to increase the bread allowance temporarily when the price of bread went up sharply.[101]

The emergence in Surrey of what appears to have been a heightened sensitivity and concern about the state of the prisons over the third quarter of the century seems to have been matched elsewhere. This is suggested by the acceptance by parliament in 1774 of a bill to encourage magistrates to take steps to eradicate jail fever, which, it announced, had been found to be caused by a "want of cleanliness and fresh air." Popham's Act, as it was known, authorized magistrates to order their jails to be scraped and whitewashed at least once a year, to be supplied with fresh air by some form of ventilator, and to be provided with baths and running water.[102] In addition they were encouraged to set rooms aside as infirmaries, and to appoint a surgeon or apothecary to make regular visits and to report to the quarter sessions on the health of the prisoners.

Anxiety about the jails in the 1750s and 1760s had no doubt been stimulated by a concern to protect those who had to come into contact with the prisoners, in the jail and especially in the courtroom, as much perhaps as the prisoners themselves. The "Black Session" at the Old Bailey cast a long shadow, and the protection of judges and magistrates and lawyers and jurors from "the putrescent tribe," as one man called the prisoners in 1800, was never far from the minds of those who put forward plans for combating jail fever, or from the legislation they inspired. Popham's Act, for example, also authorized justices to have courtrooms "properly ventilated" and to order inmates to change their own clothes for prison garb if the magistrates saw fit. The Surrey bench put all these provisions into effect immediately: they not only ordered that the jail and houses of correction be scraped and whitewashed but also that "commodious bathing tubs" be installed in each, in which the prisoners were to be washed before they came into court; and they provided each inmate with a coarse linen shirt, a flannel waistcoat, a pair of "strong flannel" drawers and woolen stockings, and a pair of "strong shoes."[103]

[101] QS 2/6, Ep. 1768, 24; Ep. 1771, 32.
[102] 14 Geo III, c. 59 (1774). This Act was amplified by 24 Geo III, c. 54, esp. s. 4 (1784).
[103] QS 2/1/23, pp. 523, 562. The bills for the purchase of the tubs and the clothes (including an additional four dozen "duck frocks") are at QS 2/6, Ep. 1775, 40–41, 43. The washing of prisoners was not apparently regularly instituted. It was reported at the end of the century as though it were new that jailers had been ordered to wash their prisoners' hands and faces with soap and their feet in salted water, and to comb and shave their heads before taking them to court (G. M. 70 [1800], p. 200).

The health of the prisoners and their proper management advanced together. The improvements in some aspects of jail conditions were nonetheless real enough. And they had been underway for two and more decades when John Howard first entered the jail at Bedford and was so appalled by what he saw that he devoted the rest of his life to prison reform.[104] Howard was to become immensely influential. But he did not initiate the complex and many-sided drive to change penal institutions and penal practices that was to have such fundamental influences in the late eighteenth century and into the nineteenth. He provided a great deal of information about all the jails in England and created a national context where none existed. His example and his recommendations inspired active "reformers." But he was influential in large part because the world was already moving in the direction he wanted it to go. There was by that time a constituency of men in the commissions of the peace and on the grand juries and beyond who were persuaded by successive crises of crime, and by the disasters that then ensued by the crush of bodies in jails that had not been designed as places of incarceration and punishment, that some other arrangements of internal management was necessary.

One should not exaggerate the changes that had occurred in the jails over the third quarter of the century, but Howard himself found much to persuade him in his tours of 1779 and 1782 that Popham's Act at least had had an immediate effect and that jail fever had been largely eradicated. He found very little of it in 1779 and three years later "not a single person labouring under that disorder throughout the whole kingdom."[105] In fact what he was recording was the old and well-established phase of wartime reduction of prosecutions, for when the jails became dangerously crowded again ("from the peace," Howard himself observed) reports of jail fever and of rising mortality in prisons again poured into the Home Office—and now not just from the London area, but from all over the country.[106]

Provincial as well as London jails were full in the mid-1780s, not only because of a steep rise in the number of prosecutions but in addition because those who before the American Revolution would have been transported could no longer be removed and were now being punished by a period of incarceration. This change in the pattern of punishment had been underway well before the American war, for there had been growing in the previous two decades a conviction that imprisonment, under the right conditions, would be a more effective punishment than transportation. The difficulties in the jails in the 1780s were thrown into sharper

[104] On Howard see Ignatieff, *A Just Measure of Pain*, pp. 47–59, and passim.
[105] Howard, *State of the Prisons*, 4th ed, p. 468.
[106] Ignatieff, *A Just Measure of Pain*, p. 109.

relief by the rapid development of these penal ideas during the war (under the considerable influence of Howard's *State of the Prisons*, first published in 1777), which resulted in a new penal program. The central statement of the new dogma came in the Penitentiary Act of 1779, which proposed the building of institutions that would be run on entirely new lines and in which prisoners would not merely be held for trial or incarcerated as a punishment, but would be transformed in their religious and social outlook and emerge as men capable and anxious to support themselves and their families by honest work. The prison as the preservative of social order emerged powerfully from the American war.[107]

Thus improvements in the conditions within prisons over the last two decades of the century were encapsulated within schemes that had broader social purposes than the mere security of the jails or the health of the prisoners, or even of the judges. What became in some quarters a passionate crusade swept up the hesitating and piecemeal improvements begun in the 1740s and 1750s and made them part of a more complex set of imperatives. In this crusade, narrowly "humanitarian" motives in the sense of a disinterested concern to relieve human suffering are difficult to disentangle from developing medical ideologies, and especially from the powerful vision of the prison as the key to social harmony. "Humanitarianism" provides an unsatisfactory explanation of the changes, including the "improvements," in the English prisons after 1780, and explanations that emphasize the role of the prison in a wide social and political context are surely moving along more satisfactory lines. But it is worth remembering that there were some very real changes distinctly for the better in the conditions under which prisoners were kept in the jails. These had begun in the second quarter of the century, as new penal practices and a particular rhythm of occupation produced some moments of heavy mortality that focused and concentrated sentiments developing independently that such suffering was wrong and unnecessary as well as dangerous for the community. And these sentiments broadened in the new context after the American Revolution in a concern for better sanitary arrangements in the jails, in the provision of clean water and fresh air, and in the establishment of medical services and better food for sick prisoners. It is true that the county authorities in Surrey continued to the end of the century to find it necessary to buy large quantities of vinegar and rue so that the courthouses could be made habitable for the judges, jurors, and spectators. But they also bought blankets and pillows and flock beds, and provided the prisoners with running water and fuel. It is necessary to remember the inmates who were ripping out the wainscotting in the New

[107] See chap. 10.

Gaol in the 1720s in order to make a fire, and their sleeping on the floor, the ill and dying (and dead) amongst the rest, to get some sense of the change that had occurred. When Surrey built a new jail in the 1790s it included individual sleeping cells with beds and bedding and with ventilators and glazed windows; it also had baths, and two surgeons were given salaries to examine the prisoners regularly and to make an annual medical report to the quarter sessions. Cleanliness advanced hand in hand with discipline and humiliation. But there were some improvements worth acknowledging in the conditions in which prisoners had been held for trial over much of the period we have been studying, in which there were times when they might have counted themselves lucky to have survived the jail experience at all and to have managed to get before the judge and jury.

THE TIMING AND PLACE OF COURT SESSIONS

The condition of the jails made the question of which court a prisoner was to be tried in a matter of crucial importance: those who went to the assizes were likely to have a much longer wait than those who came before the quarter sessions. Outside London and Middlesex, where the Old Bailey sat eight times a year, the assize courts met twice a year, the quarter sessions four times. The assizes met in the spring and summer, and there was commonly a gap of seven months or more from the end of a session in July or August to the Lent assizes, generally held in March in Surrey. If the dates fell in a particular way a prisoner could be in jail for as long as eight and a half months. The jail calendars in the assize files provide examples every year of men and women committed within a few days or weeks of the conclusion of the Summer assizes who had to wait in jail through the winter before their trials came on.

The engagement in the middle of the century of the Surrey quarter sessions in the trial of felonies was thus of the greatest significance, for that court met four times a year (generally in January, April, July, and October) and could meet for additional sessions by the device of adjournment. Adjournments were very common for administrative purposes, usually to enable a group of local justices to meet to deal with a bridge repair or some other particular problem. Occasionally criminal business had been dealt with at more general adjourned sessions,[108] but they took on a new character when the court began to deal for the first time with a significant

---

[108] There are references to adjournments at which indictments for assault and petty larceny were tried at QS 2/6, Mids. 1719, 67; Ep. 1727, 63; Mids. 1730, 41; Mich. 1738, 2, 13; and no doubt other sessions were adjourned to deal with similar business.

proportion of the property crimes tried in the county. Adjourned sessions were held after every regular meeting of the court in 1752 to 1754, always at Southwark because they were intended to deal specifically with felons. Southwark was the most convenient venue for that purpose since the prisoners were in jail there and, the offenses having been committed mainly in the urban parishes in the northeastern corner of the county, most of the prosecutors and witnesses lived there too. In 1752 it obviously seemed to the magistrates that an adjournment to Southwark was likely to be called at the conclusion of every session, and they made arrangements to mobilize the additional jurors who would be required.[109] But once the rush of postwar business abated by the mid-1750s it became clear that eight annual sessions of the court would not be necessary. Thereafter the January quarter sessions, held invariably at St. Margaret's Hill in Southwark (until the New Sessions House and county jail were built in Newington in the 1790s), was commonly adjourned to meet again at the same place in February to deal with more of the criminal business that was always at its heaviest at that time of year. Adjournments for criminal business of the other three annual sessions then became less regular.

The quarter sessions were not only flexible in being able to meet as often as seemed necessary, but the sessions themselves could last as many days as were needed to deal with the business at hand. The assizes had none of this flexibility. They were held by the judges of the central courts at Westminster and took place between the terms of these courts when the judges were free to go on circuit. The judges set out a schedule for a forthcoming circuit, establishing when they would be at various towns. It would not have been possible to calculate ahead how many days would be required to clear each jail, nor could the schedule be much altered once it had been set out.[110] This no doubt helps to explain why the Surrey quarter sessions were pressed into service when the jails became so crowded in 1749, and why they continued to deal with the bulk of simple larcenies thereafter.

The increasing engagement of the quarter sessions in the trials of

---

[109] Guildford Muniment Room, LM 1067/2.
[110] Even the duke of Newcastle as secretary of state found it difficult to get the date changed once it had been published. Mr. Justice Comyns told him in 1733:

> I have been very much troubled that the time of the assizes in Sussex was not agreeable to your Grace, and have used my best endeavors to get it altered, but find it will be difficult to do so without inconvenience. For the attorneys who saw the times published in Westminster Hall many of them made up their records accordingly and subpoena'd their witnesses which must all be brought back and signed over again. Besides the alteration in one county will require an alteration in the other counties of the circuit to which many are averse. (SP 36/29, f. 259)

felons in the second half of the century had a number of consequences—none of more immediate importance to those coming to trial than the effect it had on the time they would wait in jail. For some, the difference was considerable. Let us take the first year in which it had an effect. In the two weeks following the Lent assizes in March 1749, eleven men and women were committed to jail for offenses that would normally have brought them before the next sessions of that court, five months hence, in August. But with the quarter sessions now dealing with minor felonies—or pretending that felonies were minor in order to take them up—six of the eleven were in fact taken before the Easter sessions on April 4, and although they were all convicted and whipped, they were at least spared a long wait in jail, as well as the distinct possibility of being transported (though that is a different story).[111] By the end of 1750 the new criminal work of the quarter sessions was now so routine and the division between the prisoners so clear that two separate jail lists were prepared, one showing the offenders to be left for the assizes, the other the prisoners for the quarter sessions. The quarter sessions list for the Epiphany meeting in January 1751 contained the names of twenty-four men and women committed to jail since the previous October who would earlier have had to wait in jail for another two or three months. They might not all have been pleased to be pushed forward into the quarter sessions instead; but one, William Stoneman, must surely have been, for he was committed to jail on the very day the quarter sessions met, indicted for assault with an intent to rob, and acquitted and released a few days later.[112]

One other minor advantage of being tried at the quarter sessions in Surrey was that most of the prisoners were tried in Southwark, either at the January session of the court or at one of the adjournments, and they were mainly held in jail there. The other meetings of the quarter sessions were held regularly at Reigate, Guildford, and Kingston, and apart from the few felons held for trial in the houses of correction at Guildford and later at Kingston, those who were tried in these sessions had to be moved there from Southwark. But that was distinctly a minority of the accused felons at the quarter sessions: for the most part they were tried at the court on St. Margaret's Hill where they were jailed. On the other hand, the assizes met at Kingston, Guildford, Croydon, and occasionally Reigate—never after 1700 at Southwark. In the eighteenth century prisoners had to be brought in some cases substantial distances from the jail to the town in which the court was to sit: it was something on the order of twenty-six miles, for example, from Southwark to Guildford. For a good part of

[111] QS 2/6, Ea. 1749, 68.
[112] QS 2/6, Ep. 1750 (i.e., Jan. 1751), 1.

the period we are dealing with they are likely to have walked, and with their leg irons in place. It was John Howard's impression that prisoners continued to walk between the county jail and the assize town in his day. But in Surrey, from the 1730s if not earlier, they were taken in carts—or at least Surrey jailers were successfully claiming in their accounts expenses for carts and wagons for "carrying prisoners" to the sessions and assizes away from Southwark.[113]

Whether they walked or were bumped down in carts, one thing is clear: most of the time the prisoners went from bad conditions to worse. Few of the towns in which the quarter sessions and assizes were held had a jail, and a variety of makeshift arrangements were made for the week of the court, under which the prisoners suffered badly. In the summer of 1776 a memorial was received at the quarter sessions from "the principal inhabitants of Reigate," where the court met regularly at Easter, pointing out to the magistrates how inadequate their facilities were for holding prisoners while the court was in session. In fact the room always set aside for the prisoners brought down from Southwark, known as the "cage," was no larger than nine by twelve feet. In here for several days and nights as many as twenty and more prisoners, men and women, were "obliged promiscuously to lye like swine together and ease the calls of nature in a tub provided for that purpose." Such an arrangement they thought could only promote "wickedness and vice"; and what was perhaps as much on their minds since the cage was in the middle of the town "amidst the abodes of divers principal traders," they were fearful that it might be the source of "some dangerous and epidemic distemper."

The grand jury presented the Reigate "cage" as a common nuisance. But there was little the county magistrates could do, or wished to do, about such a local question that would clearly require some expenditure of money. The county did pay the next year for tubs in which the prisoners could wash at the Reigate sessions (with magisterial health no doubt partly in mind), and they paid for accommodation that would enable the women to be separated from the men. At the very end of the century they were paying for "beer and other liquors and meat and broth etc." for the prisoners at the Reigate sessions when the weather was bad. But the "cage" apparently remained as it had been. Howard, who knew about this memorial or perhaps had stimulated it by his visit and enquiry, mentions it. Ten years later "more commodious lodgings" were being promised for the prisoners at Reigate, but in 1801 they were still at the planning stage,

[113] Claims for carrying prisoners to and from the assizes are included among the sheriffs' cravings for 1733 and 1738 (T 90/146 and 147). For later bills for the carriage of prisoners see QS 2/6, Ep. 1741, 17; Ep. 1742, 43; Ep. 1744, 5.

for the clerk of the peace was assured that the inhabitants had raised money by subscription "to enlarge the prison or cage." Perhaps the fact that it was only in use once a year, and that only occasionally were there very large numbers of prisoners being held for the Easter sessions, had been sufficient to discourage and delay local initiative for so long.[114]

When the courts met at Guildford the house of correction was used for the prisoners, and at Kingston there was a town jail, the stockhouse.[115] At Croydon, Howard reported that the prisoners were kept chained together in stables at an inn, and indeed at the end of the century the jailer was still claiming repayment of his expenditure "for the use of three stables to put the prisoners in and also straw for them during the assizes."[116] From these jails and cages and stables the prisoners would be taken directly into the court to hear the charges against them, to plead guilty or not guilty and take their trial. There they had waited during the early stages of the session while the formal preliminaries were conducted and the grand jury was sworn and charged. But events now began to move quickly. When their names were called and they found themselves being arraigned before the trial jury, their fate was going to be decided in a matter of a few minutes.

[114] QS 2/6, Mich. 1776, 41–42; Mich. 1777, 17; Ep. 1785, 55; Ea. 1800, 21; Mids. 1800, 35; Ep. 1801, 63; Howard, *State of the Prisons*, 1st ed., p. 238.

[115] Howard, *State of the Prisons*, 1st ed., pp. 239–40; S.A.P., Lent 1739, p. 21.

[116] Howard, *State of the Prisons*, 3rd ed. (Warrington, 1784), p. 275; QS 2/6, Mich. 1795, 80.

CHAPTER 7

THE CRIMINAL TRIAL

That Englishmen enjoyed fundamental liberties beyond the reach of government was a commonplace in the eighteenth century. It was a notion shared across society and across the political spectrum, celebrated alike by Whigs and Tories, by Hanoverian oligarchs and their country and radical opponents. There might be disagreements about whether those rights were being threatened and by whom, but no one questioned that Englishmen had inherited liberties won by their forefathers in the struggle against despotic governments. Among the most cherished were those rights that guaranteed the rule of law and shielded the individual from arbitrary arrest and punishment, particularly trial by jury. The right of an Englishman to be tried by his peers, by a jury, as Blackstone said, of "twelve of his equals and neighbours, indifferently chosen, and superior to all suspicion," had been invested with near mystical powers, for the jury was celebrated as the institution that had preserved both the constitutional monarchy and the Church of England in the struggles of the seventeenth century.

It was accepted on all sides after 1689 that the jury elevated the English constitution above all others and preserved for Englishmen those rights that made them the happiest of men. "Of all the boasted privileges of our constitution," a contributor to the *Gentleman's Magazine* said in 1777, "there is none which shines more eminently conspicuous than trial by jury. This invaluable prerogative is the birthright of every Englishman, and distinguishes the laws of this happy country from the arbitrary decisions of other states."[1] It was, in Blackstone's phrase, the "grand bulwark" of English liberties which "cannot but subsist so long as this palladium remains sacred and inviolate."[2] It is the character of the encounter between an accused Englishman and the jury of his peers that this chapter seeks to investigate.

One of the striking characteristics of the administration of justice in the seventeenth and eighteenth centuries—and one reason no doubt why

[1] *G. M.* 47 (1777), p. 214.
[2] Blackstone, *Commentaries*, vol. 4, pp. 342–43.

the jury continued to be thought to occupy a crucial place between the citizen and the government—was that a high proportion of criminal cases were in fact dealt with by juries. In the nineteenth century numerous minor property offenses and assaults were transferred to the jurisdiction of magistrates acting summarily. This had begun in the eighteenth century and had gone far enough to worry libertarians like Blackstone who deplored the growth of practices that threatened "the disuse of juries."[3] But, significant as it was, the growth of magistrates' summary powers did not tilt the balance away from the jury in the eighteenth century. All felonies and many misdemeanors, including assault, continued in 1800 to be tried before juries at both the quarter sessions and the assizes. This remained possible because there were significantly fewer offenders to be tried than there were to be a generation or two later. But it was also possible because of the way jury trials were typically conducted in the eighteenth century, particularly the trial of the ordinary mainstream offenses against property and the person that occupied most of the time of the criminal courts. That is our subject.

The material available makes it inevitable that we will concentrate in fact on the assizes, but procedure at the quarter sessions followed substantially the same lines. As we will see, jury trials in both courts over this period differed in some fundamental ways from their modern equivalent, and not merely in their forms but to some extent in their purposes and intentions. My aim is to uncover something of those purposes and intentions in the course of exploring in this chapter what one might call as a shorthand the "old" form of trial, and in the following and subsequent chapters on the verdicts the juries came to and the punishments that flowed from them.[4]

[3] Ibid., p. 276.

[4] This chapter owes a good deal to the work of several recent writers, particularly John Baker, "Criminal Courts and Procedure at Common Law, 1550–1800," in Cockburn, ed., *Crime in England*, pp. 15–48; Cockburn, *History of English Assizes*, esp. chap. 6; and the two very important and pioneering articles by John Langbein, "Criminal Trial before the Lawyers," and "Shaping the Eighteenth-Century Criminal Trial." The chapter depends fundamentally on the printed accounts of the trials at the Surrey assizes (S.A.P.). These pamphlets fall within the century 1678–1774 but with a heavy concentration in two decades from the late 1730s. Much of my evidence thus inevitably comes from the mid-eighteenth century, a period in which some important elements in the trial were beginning to change, and my account is to some extent colored by that. The biggest problem, however, is that the absence of accounts from the last quarter of the century prevents as full an investigation of changing practice on the Home Circuit as I would have liked to make. To fill the gap a little I have dipped into the rich evidence from the Old Bailey for the 1780s and 1790s, but merely to suggest the character of changes that might have been going forward in Surrey, not to assert a major argument about it.

OPENING CEREMONIES

The courts strove, not always successfully, to create an atmosphere of dignity and solemnity in which the trials would take place. Part of the ceremonial that surrounded the holding of the quarter sessions and the assizes—the reading of the commissions under which the judges acted at the assizes, for example—ensured the legality of the proceedings. But there was also plainly an effort to heighten the natural drama of the courtroom by symbolic and pointed gestures and phrases. The deliberate theatricality of criminal courts has been frequently commented on.[5] It might have been at its height at the English assizes in the eighteenth century. For then the criminal law ensured that large numbers of prisoners would be condemned to death, and few sessions of the court, certainly in Surrey, ended without the judge putting the square of black cloth on his full-bottomed wig and pronouncing the terrible words of the death sentence. In the rare instances in which no one was condemned to death, the conclusion of such a "maiden-session" was marked by another piece of theater, the gift of a pair of white gloves to the judge.

The ceremony surrounding the holding of the assizes had begun as the judges reached the borders of the county, for they were met there and escorted to the assize town. There they made their entrance led by the sheriff, who, it was said in 1682, "attended with his Under-Sheriff, and Bailiffs, with their white Staves and his Livery-men with their Holberds in their hands, and accompanied with the chief of the Gentry of the County, do wait upon the Judges at the usual place, and conduct them from thence to their Lodgings. . . ."[6] In the heady days of Tory triumph in the last years of Charles II's reign, some of Judge Jeffreys' circuits resembled royal progresses. Everywhere he went he was met at his entrance to the assize towns by large crowds and often by fifteen-gun salutes.[7] Cannonades were not common in the eighteenth century, but the crowds were possibly larger, especially by the middle of the century, when political divisions

[5] Hay, "Property, Authority and the Criminal Law," in Hay, Linebaugh, and Thompson, eds., *Albion's Fatal Tree*, pp. 26–31; J. D. Morton, *The Function of Criminal Law* (Toronto, 1962), pp. 30–33.

[6] *Clerk of Assize*, p. 23. There is a great deal of information about the life of a judge on circuit in the 1690s in *The Diary of Mr. Justice Rokeby* (privately printed, 1887). Rokeby discusses his travel arrangements, his expenses, and the entertainments provided by sheriffs. Occasionally, he discloses details of procedural interest, but only rarely does he discuss the details of criminal cases tried before him. There is also a great deal of information about the entertainment of the judges and their role in the social side of the assizes in Ryder's Assize Diary.

[7] G. W. Keeton, *Lord Chancellor Jeffreys and the Stuart Cause* (1963), pp. 242–43.

were milder than they had been in the generations immediately before and after the Revolution and attendance at or absence from the assizes was no longer a significant gesture. When the leading families of the county were able to unite in support of the broader social and political functions of the courts and to detach that from a narrow partisan view of politics, as had certainly happened by the 1750s, the crowds that greeted the assize judges were larger and the ceremonial more elaborate. Triumphal entries continued well into the nineteenth century. The French visitor Cottu reported in 1820 that at their approach to the assize town the judges

> are received by the sheriff, and often by a great part of the wealthiest inhabitants of the country; the latter come in person to greet him, or send their carriages, with their richest liveries, to serve as an escort, and increase the splendour of the occasion.
> They enter the town with bells ringing and trumpets playing, preceded by the sheriff's men, to the number of twelve or twenty, in full dress, armed with javelins. . . .[8]

The court session itself began with further rituals. The judges in their scarlet robes went off to the local parish church where the sheriff's chaplain preached what was one of the Church's set-pieces, the assize sermon. When political divisions ran high, and especially when Church interests were engaged, as in Anne's reign, this might well be fiercely partisan.[9] More often the assize sermon turned on a theme more immediately suitable for the occasion, some variant on the theme of the Great Assizes before which in time every man would be called, or a homily on the wisdom of the laws and the rightfulness of the punishments that would be imposed in the coming session.[10]

Thus reassured, the company moved to the courtroom where the first business was immediately enacted: the opening and reading of the judges' commissions. Two of these, the commissions of assize and of *nisi prius*, gave them jurisdiction in civil cases, but it was the commissions of oyer and terminer and general jail delivery that were of particular relevance, for together they conferred upon the assize judges the unlimited jurisdiction that enabled them to deal with all the criminal cases pending.[11] In

[8] M. Cottu, *On the Administration of Criminal Justice in England* (1822), p. 43.

[9] Geoffrey Holmes, *The Trial of Dr. Sacheverell* (1973), pp. 237–38.

[10] Assize sermons were commonly published. Among those delivered in Surrey and published were a series in the 1730s by George Osborne, vicar of Battersea. He discoursed on such themes as *The Civil Magistrate's Right of Inflicting Punishment: The End of the Laws and the Necessity of a Due Execution of Them* (1733), and *Subjection to Principalities, Powers and Magistrates* (1735). For published assize sermons see J. N. Adams and G. Averley, *A Bibliography of Eighteenth-Century Legal Literature* (1982), pp. 249–52.

[11] Blackstone, *Commentaries*, vol. 4, p. 269; Baker, "Criminal Courts and Procedure," p. 28.

the spacious days of the mid-eighteenth century, when it is first possible to learn from the assize Agenda Book the order and timing of business on the Home Circuit,[12] the judges at the Surrey assizes commonly found the reading of the commissions to be sufficient business for one day, and they normally adjourned at that point until the next morning. They retired to their lodgings or perhaps to the house of a local worthy for some of the entertainment that made the assizes a social occasion for those on the right side of the law.

The next morning was taken up by several other preliminaries. One of the two judges who went on circuit together presided in the Crown court where the criminal cases were to be heard while the other took the civil pleas. On the criminal side several pieces of essential business had to be completed before the trials could begin. The clerk had to call over the names of the members of the commission of the peace for the county, noting those present, and also the mayors, coroners, stewards, bailiffs, and constables. This was followed by the calling of the grand jury and the judge's charge to them. It had been the sheriff's duty to summon men to serve on the grand and trial juries; when the preliminaries were completed the panel of grand jurors was called over and those present came forward to be sworn. It was their principal task to hear the charges that were to be brought against each prisoner and to decide whether he would go on to trial or not. Soon after their swearing-in they would retire to a separate room to receive the bills of accusation and listen to the evidence against each prisoner presented verbally by the prosecutor and his witnesses. On the basis simply of the prosecution evidence, the jury decided whether there was a case to be answered. They recorded their verdict on the back of the bill, finding either a "true bill" (*billa vera* before 1733), which sent the accused on to trial on the charge alleged, or "no true bill" (ignoramus—"we do not know"), in which case the prisoner would be discharged "by proclamation" at the conclusion of the sitting.

The grand jury verdict was thus a matter of crucial significance. And it was no mere formality, for grand juries continued to the end of the eighteenth century and beyond to take their work seriously. It is of some importance, before we go back to the court, to enquire a little more fully into the composition of this body and the character of its verdicts.

THE GRAND JURY

Over the long term, the role of the grand jury as the body making the decision whether or not a person accused of an offense would be sent to

---

[12] ASSI 31.

trial was undermined by the growing judicial character of the magistrate's enquiry. As magistrates extended their investigation by taking the defendant's evidence into account and by allowing the accused to cross-examine the prosecution witnesses and to be advised by counsel, and particularly when magistrates began to discharge those against whom the evidence was weak, it is clear that the brief and more partial enquiry that the grand jury could mount as the court session was beginning was bound to appear flimsy by comparison and then irrelevant. And when in the nineteenth century there were police forces to investigate the facts alleged, it became increasingly difficult for the grand jury not to relent when the magistrate committed someone to trial. As the judicial character of preliminary investigation took firmer shape over the first half of the nineteenth century the grand jury withered, and its abolition would be suggested in the interests of more efficient administration.[13]

At the end of the eighteenth century the role of the grand jury remained unquestioned. That the jurors heard only the evidence for the prosecution had been justified by Blackstone on the grounds that their finding of an indictment was merely an accusation, not a determination of guilt. He did go on to say that the grand jury "ought to be thoroughly persuaded of the truth of an indictment, so far as the evidence goes; and not to rest satisfied merely with remote probabilities."[14] There was undoubtedly an increasing desire at every stage of the investigation and trial of criminal offenses in the eighteenth century to be "thoroughly persuaded" of the truth of the charge being made, and that helped to enlarge the role of the magistrate's preliminary hearing and diminished that of the grand jury. But that had not gone so far by 1800 that the grand jury had ceased to take its duties seriously. At least it appeared to be working as it had over the century, for, as we will see, jurors continued in the 1790s to refuse to indict a significant number of accused offenders.

Besides making the crucial decision whether or not a case should go forward to trial, grand jurors were occasionally engaged in other aspects of criminal administration. Judges occasionally solicited their advice on the appropriateness of punishments in particular cases and received their recommendations about pardons.[15] But their second main duty was to act as the voice of the county about matters of broad interest or matters that

---

[13] Radzinowicz, *History*, vol. 3, pp. 463–64; Baker, "Criminal Courts and Procedure," pp. 19–20. The grand jury survived until 1933, but it is clear that it had lost its real purpose by the middle of the nineteenth century.

[14] Blackstone, *Commentaries*, vol. 4, p. 302. For changing conceptions of proof in the seventeenth century and in particular the standard of proof sought by grand jurors, see Barbara J. Shapiro, *Probability and Certainty in Seventeenth-Century England; A Study of the Relationships between Natural Science, Religion, History, Law, and Literature* (Princeton, 1983), p. 188.

[15] SP 36/64, f. 366.

required administrative attention. When the grand jury had completed its scrutiny of the bills, it turned to a consideration of presentments made by the various juries that were required to report to the court (the hundred and liberty juries, and so on) if there were problems that required action: a road or a bridge in need of repair, for example. And the grand jurors then came back into the court to make a presentment of their own, acting as "the grand inquest of the county" and putting forward for correction any fault that should be righted.[16] Most often they reported "all well." But their right to present the inhabitants of the county for failing to provide some necessary service or institution was very important, as indeed, in broader terms, was their status as the one authentic and legitimate voice of county opinion. It was the weight and authority that that status gave the grand jury that mainly explains why its membership changed so strikingly in the generation after the Restoration, when it became, much more than it had been before, the preserve of the county's social and political leaders.

The qualifications for service on the grand jury were inexact. The authorities spoke merely of the requirement that they be "honest and legal" men. It was said at the Restoration that they should be chosen from "the most sufficient freeholders in the county," and such a description seems to fit most of the men called to serve on the grand juries at both the quarter sessions and the assizes.[17] The practice at the quarter sessions of several counties was to make up a grand jury of the high constables of the hundreds who would have been called to attend the court in that capacity in any case. These were men of the right social bearing, of middling status—yeomen, craftsmen, tradesmen—and of some consequence in their own parishes. In Surrey and Sussex, the quarter sessions grand jury was so commonly composed of these officials that it was known indeed as the jury of constables.[18]

The grand jurymen called to the assizes at the Restoration were of broadly the same social status, not men of the meanest estates but yet not men who would have moved easily within the ranks of the gentry of the county. Morrill's conclusion that the grand jury of Cheshire in the first half of the seventeenth century was drawn from "a broad spectrum of middling freeholders with incomes and status well below that of the magisterial class" would certainly fit the Surrey grand juries of the 1660s. And, as in Cheshire, the men who served on the Surrey grand jury in this period were likely to find their social standing temporarily enhanced by

---

[16] Webb and Webb, *The Parish and the County*, pp. 446–56.

[17] Blackstone, *Commentaries*, vol. 4, p. 299; *Clerk of Assize*, pp. 16–17, 29–30.

[18] Webb and Webb, *The Parish and the County*, p. 447, n. 4. For Sussex, QR/W/96 (17) and (18); QR/E/129 (12) and (13). And see J. S. Morrill, *The Cheshire Grand Jury, 1625–1659: A Social and Administrative Study* (Leicester, 1976), pp. 17–18, 43.

their service.[19] A list of "persons as are to be retorned for Jury men" made up parish by parish in 1665 by constables (in accordance with an Act of parliament passed that year) provides evidence of the social status of eighty-five of the men who served on Surrey grand juries in the 1660s. Twenty-one of them were recognized in these parish lists as "esquires" or "gentlemen," men of high local status. The remaining sixty-four (three out of four of the grand jurors identified on this list) were yeomen or craftsmen or tradesmen.[20] On the grand jury lists they appear as "gentlemen," but it seems likely that this was not an honor they would continue to enjoy once the court session was concluded.

Within a generation of the Restoration men of such middling status were being excluded, for the Surrey grand jury was invaded by the gentry of the county and became their preserve. This was beginning in 1675, when two baronets, a knight, and at least eight justices of the peace sat on the jury at the Summer assizes.[21] But the transformation of the grand jury appears to have been particularly encouraged by the sharp divisions of the Exclusion controversy at the end of that decade. By 1680 and 1681 large numbers of magistrates and members of the gentry were serving on the grand jury in order to use the jury's right to issue addresses in the midst of the Exclusion crisis and the political struggle in the county between Whig and Tory factions. In 1681, as in several other counties, the Surrey grand jury published an address to thank the king for dissolving the Oxford parliament and preserving the hereditary monarchy.[22]

The meetings of the quarter sessions and assizes had always been in

[19] Morrill, *Cheshire Grand Jury*, pp. 17–18. Cockburn believes that on the Home Circuit the addition "gentleman" was being "indiscriminately" attributed to grand jurors in the early seventeenth century (*Assize Records: Introduction*). On the other hand, Cynthia Herrup has made a thorough study of a sample of grand jurors called to the Sussex assizes in the late sixteenth and early seventeenth centuries, and concludes that many may be characterized as minor gentry ("The Common Peace: Legal Structure and Legal Substance in East Sussex, 1594–1640" [Ph.D. thesis, Northwestern University, 1982], p. 145, and app. 6, pp. 431–57). Peter Lawson finds similarly that the grand jurors at the Hertfordshire assizes in the same period were drawn from the "lesser, parish gentry" ("Lawless Juries: The Composition and Behaviour of Hertfordshire Juries, 1573–1624" [forthcoming]).

[20] *Surrey Quarter Sessions Records*, 1663–65, pp. 58–64. The status or occupation of everyone listed is given in only twelve parishes; in the remainder only those who could be assigned at least the status of gentleman have an addition after their names. It is clear from the returns for the twelve complete parishes, however, that those not given a status in the list were craftsmen, tradesmen, and yeomen.

[21] ASSI 35/116/6.

[22] *To the King's Majesty: The Address of the Grand Jury at the Surrey Assizes, Kingston, July 20, 1681* (1681). For the political character of grand juries in the 1680s see Norma Landau, *The Justices of the Peace, 1679–1760* (Berkeley, 1984), pp. 50–54, 60–61; Keeton, *Lord Chancellor Jeffreys*, pp. 165–84. And for the influence of politics on the grand jury at the Southwark Borough sessions in this period see Johnson, *Southwark and the City*, pp. 254–55.

some senses political occasions. But they inevitably became more intensely and immediately political in the years that saw the fundamental struggle for supremacy in every county between the Whig and Tory parties from the late 1670s at least into the third and fourth decades of the eighteenth century. The composition of the commission of the peace itself changed regularly over several decades with the changing fortunes of the parties at Westminster,[23] and inevitably all the other institutions of the county that could contribute in any way to political advantage similarly reflected the political struggle. The grand jury was no exception. Not only might its powers to indict have immediate political relevance, but its right to speak for the community on matters of common interest was too powerful a weapon to allow it to fall into the wrong hands. Grand jurors were the authentic voice of the county, the spokesmen of that broad political nation that the parties fought to influence and that all governments had to appease and appeal to. Even after the party and electoral battles of the reigns of William and Anne gave way before the oligarchical security of the Whig administrations of Walpole and Pelham, grand jury addresses on important national issues retained sufficient significance that governments were frequently anxious about their influence.[24]

Even after the bitterness of the party struggle had waned in the second quarter of the century, the assizes were occasionally caught up in political questions. But attendance at the grand jury had in any case by then become one of the signs of a man's importance in the county, and its membership remained dominated in the eighteenth century by a much more elevated social group than had typically attended in the twenty years following the Restoration. Blackstone's description of assize grand juries as consisting of "gentlemen of the best figure in the county"[25] certainly fits the Surrey experience in the eighteenth century: the jury was usually headed by a baronet or knight as the foreman, and most often a majority of its members were esquires and the remainder "gentlemen," acknowledged as such in their own right and not simply by virtue of their service.

[23] Landau, *Justices of the Peace*, chaps. 3–4. Lionel K. J. Glassey, *Politics and the Appointment of Justices of the Peace, 1675–1720* (Oxford, 1979), passim.

[24] Following the loss of Minorca, to take one example, many of the dozens of addresses from around the country demanding an enquiry were from grand juries, and the Newcastle administration worked to limit their number. See Nicholas Rogers, "London Politics from Walpole to Pitt: Patriotism and Independency in an Era of Commercial Imperialism, 1738–63" (Ph.D. thesis, University of Toronto, 1974), pp. 190–93. At other points throughout the eighteenth century when issues of broad importance and interest were before the public, grand juries very commonly made some comment, either in the form of an address or by formally commending or condemning the ministry or other political figures. In the discussion over general warrants in 1764 the grand jury at the York assizes thanked the county members of parliament for the stand they had taken in favor of the Wilkite position (*G. M.* 34 [1764], p. 196).

[25] Blackstone, *Commentaries*, vol. 4, p. 299.

Between 1750 and 1769, to take two decades by way of example, the Surrey grand jury was led as foreman by Sir More Molyneux, Bart., of Loseley, Sir William Richardson, Sir Peter Thompson, Sir Francis Vincent, and such men of countywide reputation as George Onslow and John Evelyn. Other baronets and knights attended occasionally. Three-quarters of the jurors were recognized by the clerk who made up the grand jury list in the Agenda Book (in which the circuit business was recorded) as "esquires" and a fifth as "gentlemen."

There was a sharp distinction by the eighteenth century between the men called to the grand juries at the Surrey assizes and quarter sessions. The high constables of the hundreds continued to serve as the sessions grand jurors through the first half of the century, but there were frequent complaints about the social character of the jury that resulted, not least because it was said that the high constables occasionally appointed deputies who were "poor and illiterate."[26] A committee of magistrates was asked in 1743, to look into the qualifications of quarter sessions grand jurors, and they recommended that the constables should no longer form the grand jury and that the sheriff should make sure that every juror was a forty-shilling freeholder.[27] Nothing came of this until 1768, when the reforming Surrey justice William Man Godschall instigated another enquiry into "the present method of constituting a grand jury." That merged with a concern about the way trial juries were called to the sessions, as we will see, and resulted in a new method of summoning both juries.[28] Grand jurors were henceforth chosen as individuals. But the assizes and quarter sessions grand juries remained socially distinct. Indeed, if anything the grand jurors at the assizes became even more socially distinguished by the end of the century. In the 1790s the Surrey jury normally included a peer or the son of a peer and an even higher proportion of knights and baronets than it had earlier. Altogether, a fifth of its members were men in such elevated social categories. The remainder were all recognized as esquires (table 7.1).

The changes in the social character of the grand jury after 1680 clearly held significant implications for the administration of the criminal law. One consequence was particularly important: it made it possible (socially) for justices of the peace to sit on the grand jury at the assizes, and they began to do so regularly after 1680. Professor Cockburn has found magistrates as members of the Home Circuit grand juries on only one occasion in the reigns of Elizabeth and James I, in the summer of 1607. Complaints were made at that time that men who had committed the accused to trial

---

[26] QS 2/1/18, 2 Oct. 1750.
[27] QS 2/6, Mids. 1743, 42; QS 2/1/16, 4 Oct. 1743.
[28] QS 2/1/22, July 1768.

TABLE 7.1

Grand Jurors at the Surrey Assizes

Status	1750–1769 (39 Sessions)		1792–1801 (16 Sessions)	
	No.	%	No.	%
Peer, son of peer, baronet, or knight	34	3.6	73	20.2
Esquire	734	76.5	288	79.8
Gentlemen	191	19.9	0	0
Total	959	100.0	361	100.0

SOURCE: ASSI 31/2–19.

should not also have the power to decide whether they should be indicted, and magistrates were not returned to the grand juries thereafter.[29] Such concerns did not prevent justices of the peace from sitting as grand jurors in the late seventeenth century, once the social character of the jury changed. By the middle of the eighteenth century magistrates dominated the grand jury at the assizes. Between 1750 and 1769, for example, an average of just over fifteen magistrates sat on every grand jury in Surrey and accounted for sixty per cent of their membership.[30]

The transformation of the grand jury after the Restoration into a body that included some of the most influential men in the county made for a clear separation between grand and petty jurors. On the Home Circuit in Elizabeth's reign, men were likely to serve on both.[31] That was no longer the case in Surrey by the 1660s, but the emergence of separate classes of grand and trial jurors was particularly confirmed by the change in the social character of the grand jury after 1680.

How many men sat on the grand jury varied from session to session. The jury had to have at least twelve members to return an indictment; and an odd number was commonly recommended, to prevent a tied vote, though that was by no means slavishly adhered to.[32] The sheriff was instructed to summon forty-eight or more, some from each hundred, in order to ensure a reasonable attendance. The *Clerk of Assize* (1682) rec-

[29] Cockburn, *Assize Records: Introduction*, chap. 5.
[30] ASSI 31/2–9.
[31] For the pattern of jury service in Elizabeth's reign see Cockburn, *Assize Records: Introduction*.
[32] Zachary Babington, *Advice to Grand Jurors in Cases of Blood* (1677; 2nd ed., 1692), pp. 4–5.

ommended a grand jury of between thirteen and twenty-three, and in the
1660s and 1670s the juries at the Surrey assizes fell within those limits,
as they had indeed in the period 1559 to 1625: the average attendance of
17.6 in the two decades after the Restoration exactly duplicated that of
Elizabethan and Jacobean assize juries in Surrey (table 7.2).[33] The Surrey
jury began to increase slightly in size over the last two decades of the

TABLE 7.2

Size of the Grand Jury at the Surrey and Sussex Assizes

Number of Jurors	Surrey					Sussex
	1660–1679 (35 Sess.)	1680–1701 (41 Sess.)	1750–1773 (46 Sess.)	1780–1784 (9 Sess.)	1792–1801 (16 Sess.)	1748–1802 (77 Sess.)
13	4					3
14	3					3
15	3	4	1			10
16	2	2				4
17	6	5				7
18	5	7	2			2
19	1	10	1			2
20	4	4	2	1	1	4
21	1	5	6			3
22	5	1	4		1	6
23	1		11	8	14	31
24		1				
25		2	2			
26			5			
27			3			
28			2			
29			1			
32			1			
34			1			
37			1			
40			1			
51			1			
52			1			
Average	17.6	18.4	25.4	22.7	22.8	19.7

SOURCES: ASSI 31/2–19; ASSI 35

[33] *Clerk of Assize*, p. 30. For the size of grand juries on the Home Circuit, 1559–1625, see
Cockburn, *Assize Records: Introduction*, table 5, from which the average size of the Surrey grand
juries in that period has been calculated.

seventeenth century, when it averaged more than eighteen members. This is presumably to be explained by its changing social character and enlarging prestige. That is surely why the average size of the grand jury continued to increase in the first half of the eighteenth century, and why it was sometimes very large indeed. It is unlikely that a sheriff would have insulted the important men he had summoned by refusing to impanel anyone who attended, and it looks as though the practice until the last quarter of the eighteenth century was that all who came took part. The number of grand jurors thus varied considerably. Twenty-three came to seem an ideal number: in the third quarter of the eighteenth century almost a quarter of the sittings of the Surrey assizes had grand juries of that size and fully half ranged within two on either side of it. But the attendance fell in some years to as low as fifteen, and on two occasions rose to the astonishing heights of fifty-one and fifty-two. Between 1750 and 1773 the Surrey grand jury averaged just over twenty-five members.[34] The numbers fell over the remainder of the century, encouraged perhaps by a ruling of King's Bench in 1761 that came down firmly in favor of a jury of twenty-three.[35] In the 1780s and 1790s Surrey grand juries were being limited to that number. Presumably more of those summoned came to court than were impaneled, and thus service on the assize grand jury became an even greater mark of distinction. That no doubt helps to explain why its membership was even more socially elevated by 1800 than it had been earlier in the century.[36]

[34] One result of the increased size of the grand jury in the eighteenth century and of the change in the character of its membership was that it must have been more difficult to pack on those occasions in which a matter of national significance might be expected to be discussed and an address proposed. It was clearly much more difficult for one party to exclude another. Even as powerful a political manager as the duke of Newcastle could not ensure that the grand jury of Sussex, the county in which his influence ran most securely, would not issue an address at the height of the Minorca crisis that would add to his embarrassment as head of the administration. He told one of his followers that he hoped that he and "all our Friends will attend to prevent any such step as that" (Add Mss. 32866, f. 432, quoted by Rogers, "London Politics from Walpole to Pitt," p. 192).

[35] "It was intended by the sheriff, and pressed by the two knights of the shire for Middlesex, that all the principal gentlemen of the county (not fewer than fourscore in number) should be sworn of this grand jury, in order to their being included in an address to His Majesty, from and in the name of the grand jury of Middlesex, upon his accession to the Crown. But . . . it seemed [to Burrow] to be irregular and improper to swear more than twenty-three." His reasoning was that if a grand jury found a true bill, it would be "inconvenient as well as contradictory" for twelve or more men—that is, a complete jury—to have voted to reject it. Burrow adds that "Lord Mansfield concurred" with this view. See *Reports of Cases Argued and Adjudged in the Court of King's Bench . . . By Sir James Burrow*, 5 vols. (1812), vol. 2, p. 1088; *Eng. Rep.*, vol. 97, p. 724.

[36] The clerk at the Surrey Lent assizes in 1796 noted that twenty-three grand jurors had been sworn before William Man Godschall arrived. Godschall had been one of the most active Surrey magistrates for well over thirty years, and out of deference to him one of the grand jurymen

In Sussex the grand jury was no less socially distinguished in the eighteenth century, but it was always smaller than in Surrey. It was never over twenty-three in the seventy-seven sessions examined between 1748 and 1802, and it was more often than in Surrey just over the minimum possible size (table 7.2). Attendance in Sussex must have been limited to some extent by the inconveniences of distance and the difficulties of travel, particularly in the winter months. This is suggested by the sharp contrast between the size of the grand jury at Summer and Lent assizes: an average of 21.4 in the summer and only 17.8 in the spring. The difference in Surrey, 26.6 as against 24.3, was less marked.[37]

The change in the membership of the grand jury after 1680 did not alter one other characteristic of the Surrey jury that had been well established by then: many of those who served did so repeatedly.[38] Roughly half the men who sat on the grand jury between 1660 and 1700, and rather more than that by the middle of the eighteenth century, had served at least once before; indeed so common was the pattern of repeated appearances that on any twenty-three-man jury of the late seventeenth century nearly fourteen of those men would have had previous experience, and fifty years later an even higher proportion would have served before (table 7.3). Not many men matched the performance of John Middlemarsh, a Lambeth magistrate who attended the grand jury twenty-five times between 1751 and 1768, including a ten-year stretch in which he missed only once. But the habit of regular attendance was common, and even more common than the figures in table 7.3 suggest, for a number of men went regularly to either the Lent or the Summer assizes for several years together, and others served on the grand jury whenever the court was sitting in their neighborhood. Between 1758 and 1769, for example, Samuel Atkinson sat on the grand jury at all the sessions held in Croydon, that is, at the Summer assizes every other year.

The fact that most grand jurors were men of considerable property, that many of them were magistrates, and that many had considerable previous experience of jury service had implications for the verdicts they arrived at. We will take that up in the next chapter, in which the verdicts of both the grand and trial juries will be considered in detail. On the social side, the attendance of such large numbers of men of countywide reputation ensured that the meetings of the assizes (and to a lesser extent

---

withdrew so that Godschall might be sworn. Twenty-three was plainly the limit by then (ASSI 31/17, p. 228).

[37] ASSI 31/2–19.

[38] For repeated service on the grand juries of the Home Circuit in the reigns of Elizabeth and James I, see Cockburn, *Assize Records: Introduction*; for Sussex, Herrup, "The Common Peace," p. 145; for Herts, Lawson, "Lawless Juries," p. 12; for Cheshire, Morrill, *Cheshire Grand Jury*, pp. 9–10.

TABLE 7.3
Grand Jury Service at the Surrey Assizes

Times jurors served	1660–1679			1680–1701			1750–1769		
	No. of Jurors	No. of Appearances	% of Total	No. of Jurors	No. of Appearances	% of Total	No. of Jurors	No. of Appearances	% of Total
1	95	95	48.5	128	128	50.8	153	153	43.7
2	40	80	20.4	36	72	14.3	71	142	20.3
3	19	57	9.7	35	105	13.9	42	126	12.0
4	6	24	3.1	18	72	7.1	23	92	6.6
5	12	60	6.1	13	65	5.2	12	60	3.4
6	8	48	4.1	7	42	2.8	15	90	4.3
7	7	49	3.6	6	42	2.4	9	63	2.6
8	2	16	1.0	4	32	1.6	4	32	1.1
9	4	36	2.0	1	9	.4	5	45	1.4
10	2	20	1.0	2	20	.8	2	20	.6
11	1	11	.5				5	55	1.4
12				1	12	.4	2	24	.6
13				1	13	.4	3	39	.9
14							1	14	.3
16							1	16	.3
23							1	23	.3
25							1	25	.3
Total	196	496		252	612		350	1,019	

	1660–1679			1680–1701			1750–1769		
	No. of Jurors	No. of Appearances	% of Total	No. of Jurors	No. of Appearances	% of Total	No. of Jurors	No. of Appearances	% of Total
First-time attendees		196			252			350	
Jurors with previous experience		300			360			669	
Ratio of experienced jurors		.60			.59			.66	
Average number of experienced jurors on 23-man jury		13.9			13.5			15.2	

SOURCES: ASSI 31/2–19; ASSI 35.

the quarter sessions) were significant events in the life of the county and that they would take on a festive character. The magistrates and gentlemen in attendance often brought their wives and families to what became a fixed entry in the social calendar of provincial society, one of the "public occasions," and of course this in itself attracted many others. Newcastle's sister wrote to him in 1735 in response to his summoning his political allies and dependants to meet him at the forthcoming assizes:

> Sir John Shelley [Newcastle's brother-in-law] desires his humble service, and will be sure to meet you at the Assizes, and will go over the Finden to day to speak to Mr. Cheale. We neither of us intended going to Lewis [Lewes, where the assizes were to meet], but as you desire it, we will not fail being there if please God we are all well, and I will do the honours to the Ladys as well as I can. I did hear before I had your letter that all the Company from Horsham were to be there. Mr. Cheale did not intend being at the Races or Assizes as he does not love those Public things, but I believe now Sir John will persuade Him to come.[39]

Assizes week was thus marked by dinner and balls and other entertainment, and the holiday atmosphere extended well beyond the ranks of the gentry. It was often thought that the normal work week was disrupted when the assizes were on in the neighborhood. All of this meant that the assizes were an immensely valuable source of custom to the local inns and taverns and to the retailers of the small county towns where they were typically held, a sizeable enough consideration that the right to hold the assizes was jealously guarded. Influence over the choice of assize towns was political patronage of the first order. It was presumably superior influence that explains why the assizes had ceased to meet in Southwark by 1700. A struggle had clearly been going on for some time. Inhabitants of Southwark had complained in 1681 and 1683 when the Lent assizes were shifted to other towns, and in 1683 had even managed to get a recommendation from the king to the lord chief justice that "if any favour be shown [to any town], it may be to the borough of Southwark as having chosen very worthy men to the latter parliaments."[40] Some years later, it was clearly a measure of Speaker Onslow's decisive political influence that he was able to get the Surrey Summer assize session held in Guildford in alternate years, despite the view of the lord chief justice that Guildford was "inconvenient and will be complained of."[41]

[39] SP 36/35, f. 158.

[40] *Cal. S. P. Dom.*, 1680–81, p. 179; 1683 (1), p. 52.

[41] Ryder Assize Diary, p. 14. It was alleged that Lord Chief Justice Willes got the 1747 Buckinghamshire Summer assizes moved from Buckingham to Aylesbury, where his son was a

The meetings of the assizes and quarter sessions did not make a festive season for the men and women who waited in their chains for the moment when the grand jury adjourned to their room to begin considering the bills and to hear the evidence brought forward by the prosecutors. For them, the serious business of the session was about to begin.

THE CHARGE TO THE GRAND JURY

The grand jury was sent off to its task by a judge in the assize court or the chairman of the quarter sessions who delivered a charge to remind them of their duty after they had been sworn (three at a time) and as they were standing before him in the body of the court. Such charges could vary considerably, but most seem to have consisted of a general preamble in which the virtues of the constitution and the common law, the benefits of living under the present monarch, and the mutual dependence of liberty and property were the chief themes, followed by an outline of the laws that the grand jury were particularly charged to uphold. At the quarter sessions the chairman commonly concentrated on the preservation of the peace and especially on the laws relating to breaches of morality, emphasizing one of the fundamental points of belief about crime in the seventeenth and eighteenth centuries: that the major offenses like robbery and murder were committed by individuals who began their slide into crime by drunkenness and sabbath-breaking.[42] This notion had also been reinforced by the reading, as part of the preliminaries, of the royal proclamation against vice and immorality that was frequently renewed from the Revolution onwards.

The charge was another set-piece, especially at the quarter sessions, where the concentration on misdemeanors and minor offenses provided scope for reflections on the connection between crime and immorality and on the duty of the poor. Like the other sermon preached by the sheriff's chaplain at the assizes, charges were often published.[43] But even when they did not intend that, chairmen at the quarter sessions clearly took some pains over their restatement of and reflections on the laws the court would enforce. This is very strongly the impression given by the quarter

---

candidate in the parliamentary election, and that the diversion of custom to the borough was sufficiently appreciated to get him elected. The Grenville family, the political patrons of Buckingham, managed to get the assizes returned there the following year (R. R. Sedgwick, ed., *The History of Parliament, 1715–1754*, 2 vols. [New York, 1970], vol. 1, p. 197).

[42] A "Form of the Charge" at the quarter sessions was included in *The Office of Clerk of the Peace* (published with *Clerk of Assize*), pp. 118–39.

[43] A large number of published charges are listed in Adams and Averley, *Bibliography of Eighteenth-Century Legal Literature*, pp. 403–6.

sessions charges delivered annually over a twenty-year period from the mid-1730s by Sir More Molyneux, of Loseley, near Guildford, a leading landowner who was invariably named chairman at the Midsummer meeting that was always held in Guildford. Molyneux took this duty seriously. He used his good charges several times, and occasionally he borrowed a bit from one of the published charges. But in most years he sat down to compose a talk that must often have lasted half an hour or more on the tasks the grand jurymen would be performing and to point out to everyone in court the blessings under which, as it seemed to him from his great house at Loseley, they all lived. The theme he returned to over and over again was the relationship between law, liberty, and property, and the wisdom of the British constitution in providing for their mutual support. Thus in 1748 he told the grand jurors

> that Flow of Liberty, which both distinguishes and renders this Country so remarkably Free and Happy beyond all others, that we either know or read about in History is owing to the wise and admirable Constitution of its Laws. These Laws, whilst they are preserv'd and executed with their due Force and Vigour, must stand like so many Rocks of Defence, no ways to be impress'd upon by the High Hand of Tyranny or Arbitrary Power, nor in the least to be shaken and overborn by any Torrent of Popular Commotion or Confusion.

It was their duty, he said on another occasion, to punish all wrongdoers so that

> one Man's Person and property may not be exposed to the Violence of Another, and the Common Bonds of Society by that means be broken and dissolv'd; but that all things may rest in a peace inviolate under the Protection of the Laws and that the weakest among the People may find a sure Refuge in the Public Authority.[44]

Charges at the assizes also frequently developed such themes, as well as the other matter that particularly preoccupied chairmen at the quarter sessions—immorality as the fruitful parent of crime. But the assize judges had to concentrate on the more serious offenses against property and the person that their grand juries would in fact be mainly concerned with. At some point in the past this may well have been a genuine if brief introduction to the criminal law for men who knew little about it. By the eighteenth century this was clearly much less necessary, since not only were many grand jurymen experienced, but several were magistrates. The

---

[44] Guildford Muniment Room, Loseley Ms. 1066/10; 1066/3.

assize charge was thus also addressed to the court and to the society beyond, and served to restate and reinforce the general principles upon which the law and its legitimate administration rested. The gentlemen who stood before the assize judge might require some instruction on recent changes introduced by statute, but apart from the few occasions on which that might have been relevant they knew their duty well, and many were perhaps secretly glad when his lordship's rolling periods came to an end and they were instructed to go to their room with the first of the bills and begin their deliberations.

ARRAIGNMENT AND PLEA

The bills of accusation sent to the grand jury had been drawn up mainly by a clerk from the calendars of prisoners in the jail and the recognizances and informations taken by the magistrates. The prosecutor might also be consulted at this stage and might in fact exert considerable influence over the way the indictment was framed, particularly in the case of property offenses that could be brought within benefit of clergy or excluded from it by the way the alleged crime was described and the value placed upon the stolen goods. It was widely believed in the late eighteenth century that victims of minor property offenses commonly took advantage of these powers to circumvent capital punishment—as in the case reported in the press in 1783 of a woman who insisted at the indictment stage that the property she had lost from her house was worth thirty-nine shillings and "very humanely refused to say it was worth more."[45] It seems clear that such "downcharging" went on quietly throughout the century, not on a massive scale but commonly enough in the case of the more minor property offenses brought within capital punishment after the Revolution of 1689. One can get some sense of this by comparing the reasons given in the jail calendar for the commitment of the accused to trial and the offense stated in the indictment. In the six years 1738–43 in Surrey, which I take by way of example, only nine cases can be identified in which an original capital charge was reduced to a noncapital offense in the indictment. Four were for shoplifting, four for theft from a house, and one for picking pockets. Six of the nine accused were women.[46]

For the most part the bills drawn up by the clerk of indictments as the session began duplicated the evidence in the jail calendar, or at least did not significantly alter the category of the charge. Some of the longer

[45] *Whitehall Evening Post*, 16–18 Jan. 1783.
[46] Based on the jail calendars and the indictments in the Surrey felony files in ASSI 35/178–83.

and more complicated bills might have been prepared in advance of the session, those, for example, that listed dozens of items of clothing stolen or those relating to forgery charges that had to specify in detail the forgery alleged and were sometimes two and three feet long as a result. Some bills were written by the prosecutor's solicitor. But most of the indictments tried at the quarter sessions and assizes were relatively simple documents, and so long as the clerk who prepared them paid attention to getting the form correct they could be written as the preliminaries were going on. The process was simplified by the development of blank indictment forms in the second half of the eighteenth century with the right language for a specific offense and spaces left for the name and residence and occupation of the accused, the goods stolen, their value, and so on.

When the charge was concluded and the grand jury withdrew, the clerk of the court called forward the prosecutor and the witnesses in the first case (he having determined, no doubt in consultation with the judge, the order in which the cases would be heard).[47] The witnesses for the Crown had been listed on the back of the bill, and those present were now sworn and were sent off, each group with the appropriate bill and in the charge of a bailiff (who along with all the other clerks and officials needed his fee), to the grand jury room to give the evidence upon which the bill would be found or not. In the middle decades of the eighteenth century in Surrey it was still common for there to be another adjournment after the grand jury withdrew. By then it was mid-afternoon on the second day and time for dinner. Indeed the court might not reconvene until the next morning, although very commonly there was a brief session following a generous break for dinner at which no doubt the judges and the grand

[47] This gave the clerk a great deal of influence over matters of crucial interest to a large number of prosecutors and defendants, and he was besieged by interested parties before the session came on. This was particularly true at the quarter sessions, where the clerk had considerable leeway before the magistrates imposed tighter control over the order of business at the Surrey quarter sessions in the 1760s. The clerk was frequently urged by prosecutors to ensure that their cases came on quickly—an important matter for those waiting around with their witnesses, not only losing time at work but also paying for board and lodgings. Given sufficient interest with the clerk a man might well be able to stay at home until the precisely correct moment to arrive with his witnesses. For examples see the correspondence between the clerk of the peace of Surrey and Lord Baltimore's agent about the timing of the trial in which Baltimore was prosecuting a sheep-stealer. The agent wanted to be sent word when he should set off with the witnesses so as not to waste their time sitting around in court, and to avoid the expense of lodging them overnight (QS 2/6, Ep. 1737, 75). The clerk received numerous requests to get men excused from jury service, to get business delayed, and to arrange business at a convenient time for a prosecutor. For examples see QS 2/6, Ep. 1721, 10 (arranging order of business); QS 2/6, Mich. 1721 (arranging business); QS 2/6, Ep. 1739, 35 (to be excused from jury service); QS 2/6, 1701, 6 (the same); QS 2/6, Mich. 1729, 100 (to arrange a trial at a convenient time).

jury and the attorneys in attendance rewarded themselves amply for their morning's work.

What sort of dinner the prisoners had is unclear, but the time of decision was now fast approaching. With the grand jury at work it was not long after the resumption that a number of indictments would be returned. In the meantime, the jailer had brought the prisoners into the courtroom, and those whose names were called by the clerk from the first batch of indictments were now made to step forward until a sufficient number were assembled "as will serve for a petty jury to pass upon at once," perhaps as many as ten or a dozen.[48] They were brought forward to be arraigned.

Those whose bills had not been found by the grand jury and who had thus not been indicted were set aside at this point. They would be returned to the court at the conclusion of the session to be discharged. Others were also discharged if the prosecutor did not appear to give evidence. Occasionally a case was merely postponed by the nonappearance of the prosecutor or a witness when it was proved by affidavit that there was a legitimate reason for their absence. In that case the judge might allow a postponement, and the unfortunate prisoner would be returned to jail to wait through another six or eight months.[49] Other trials were delayed by the illness of the prisoner. Still others did not take place because the prisoner had in fact died or had escaped from jail or, having been bailed, had chosen not to appear.[50] Some cases of misdemeanor, mainly assaults and charges of riot, were not tried because the defendant had been granted a writ of certiorari that removed the case to King's Bench, the point of that being almost certainly to put pressure on the prosecutor to come to a settlement because the costs of the trial promised to be considerable.[51]

There were a number of reasons why a trial might not go forward, but the vast majority of accused offenders were in court and were arraigned when their names were called. They were made to step forward with as many as a dozen others, to acknowledge their identity by holding up a hand when they heard their name, and to plead to the indictment, guilty

---

[48] *Clerk of Assize*, p. 39.

[49] At the Lent assizes in 1744, for example, a man on trial for a simple larceny was sent back to the county jail when the prosecutor, a widow of Carshalton, proved that an important witness had not appeared "notwithstanding he was bound over by Recognizance to appear and give evidence"; the prisoner was convicted at the following session and transported to America for seven years (ASSI 35/184/7 [Massingham]). Delays for similar reasons or because the prosecutor was ill are noted as ASSI 35/191/12, jail calendar (Kelly); ASSI 35/191/8, jail calendar (Cosins), ASSI 31/5, p. 24; and ASSI 31/7, p. 74.

[50] For bills not found and for the variety of reasons why the accused might not be brought to trial, see chap. 8.

[51] For certiorari see Chitty, *Criminal Law*, vol. 1, pp. 371–402.

or not guilty, when the substance of the charge was read to them. (It was read in English, even when, before 1733, the indictment itself was in Latin.) If a prisoner confessed, he was set aside to be sentenced at the conclusion of the session. But that was rare, and at least in capital cases such a plea was actively discouraged: when a man charged with burglary at the Old Bailey in 1680 pleaded guilty the reporter noted that he could not "be persuaded to do otherwise." As we will see, judges in the eighteenth century were reluctant to accept a guilty plea in capital cases because it meant they had to sentence the prisoner to death without having the information a trial might provide upon which they might base a reprieve and a recommendation of mercy. There was less anxiety about confessions of guilt when the offense was within clergy, though in fact such confessions were not common in the late seventeenth century and became even less common in the eighteenth. So long as the consequences of conviction for simple grand larceny were certain to be the branding and discharge of clergy a few defendants were willing to plead guilty and accept that penalty; in Surrey six per cent did so between 1663 and 1715. And in the same period more than seventeen per cent of those charged with petty larceny also pleaded guilty and were whipped and discharged. But when after 1718, as we will see, conviction for grand larceny invariably meant transportation to America and when petty larceny could bring that same punishment, defendants became almost as reluctant to confess as those charged with capital offenses. Less than one per cent of the men and women charged with grand larceny and only four per cent of those indicted for petty larceny pleaded guilty in the Surrey courts between 1722 and 1802.[52] Virtually every prisoner charged with a felony insisted on taking his trial,

[52] These figures are based on the cases in which the defendant faced one indictment only and thus entered only one plea (drawn from the Surrey Sample, 1663–1802):

Offense	Pleaded Guilty	Pleaded Not Guilty	Total	Percentage Pleaded Guilty
Highway robbery	3	276	279	1.1
Burglary	1	414	415	0.2
Horse-theft	0	123	123	0
Capital larceny	0	444	444	0
Simple grand larceny				
1660–1715	33	484	517	6.4
1722–1802	16	1,949	1,965	0.8
Petty larceny				
1660–1715	12	56	68	17.7
1722–1802	20	451	471	4.3
Total	85	4,197	4,282	2.0

with the obvious support and encouragement of the court. There was no plea bargaining in felony cases in the eighteenth century.

If a prisoner declared himself not guilty the clerk asked him how he would be tried, to which the only acceptable answer was "by God and my Country," that is to say by the jury. Prisoners were presumably instructed in the correct forms by the clerk of the court, or possibly by the judge, who took an active role in pushing trials in the right direction and in getting prisoners and witnesses and prosecutors to do what was required of them. Some prisoners, instructed or not, actually refused to plead and brought matters to a halt. The point of thus "standing mute" was to prevent the forfeiture of lands and goods that in law at least was supposed to follow upon conviction for felony or petty treason. In high treason and misdemeanor, refusal to plead was simply taken as acknowledgment of guilt, and after sufficient warning the prisoner in such cases was punished as though he had pleaded guilty. This was also to be the case in felony and petty treason after 1772 (by 12 Geo III, c. 20). Before then, however, the courts refused to accept a nonplea, and a few men chose into the eighteenth century to undergo the unpleasant consequences. The first question the court asked was whether such a prisoner was incapable of pleading because of some disability (being deaf and dumb being the obvious possibilities) or whether he was deliberately refusing. This question was given to a jury, usually simply the trial jury, to enquire into immediately.[53]

If their verdict was that he stood mute deliberately and he continued to do so, the prisoner was subjected to the so-called *peine forte et dure*, which meant that he was taken to a dungeon, chained spread-eagled to the floor, and loaded with a gradually increasing weight of iron until either he agreed to plead or he died. This was still being practiced in the late seventeenth century and indeed well into the third quarter of the eighteenth.[54] Saussure reported in the reign of George I hearing of men "preferring to die in this fashion, after two or three days of atrocious suffering, rather than by the hands of the executioner," and he was told that they

---

[53] They gathered evidence from those in court who had had any dealings with the prisoner—magistrates, jailers, and if there happened to be a doctor in the court he might be asked to examine the prisoner—and the jury then declared whether the refusal to plead was willful or "by the providence and act of God." See, for example, ASSI 31/4, p. 118; R vs. Mercier: Leach, *Reports*, vol. 1, pp. 183–85; *Eng. Rep.*, vol. 168, pp. 194–95 (1777); R vs. Steel: Leach, *Reports*, vol. 1, pp. 451–53; *Eng. Rep.*, vol. 168, p. 328 (1787).

[54] Prisoners were pressed to death in Surrey in the 1660s and the 1720s (ASSI 35/105/7, calendar; S.A.P., Lent 1726, p. 2). In the latter case the man repented after "suffering great agony" and returned to court to plead not guilty. In Sussex in 1735 a man accused of murder was "gradually pressed to death, continuing obstinately dumb to the last moment" (G. M. 5 [1735], p. 497). For *peine forte et dure* generally, see John H. Langbein, *Torture and the Law of Proof: Europe and England in the Ancien Regime* (Chicago, 1977), pp. 74–77.

did so "in order not to leave a mark of infamy on their families and to save their possessions from going to the Crown according to the law."[55] But it was clear by then that the king in fact never insisted on the forfeiture of the lands or goods of convicted felons. In any case, juries returned as a matter of course the report that convicted men had "no goods," and the matter rested there. Why some men nonetheless insisted on this appalling death is unclear.

It was thought in the late seventeenth century that jailers were inclined to try other ways to persuade prisoners to plead, short of actually pressing them.[56] Blackstone was certain that in his day the full stretching out and crushing was not being put into practice: he was undoubtedly right that *peine forte et dure* was falling into disfavor after mid-century, for it was abolished by statute in 1772.[57] For half a century a refusal to plead was then treated as a confession, and the defendant was subjected to the established punishments, including hanging if the crime was capital. But this was changed further in 1827, when a nonplea was taken rather as a plea of not guilty and trial followed immediately.[58] In the case of deaf and dumb prisoners there was as yet perhaps no consistent treatment, but the courts were taking a strong line by the end of the century and insisting on a trial where that proved to be possible.[59]

[55] *A Foreign View of England in the Reigns of George I and George II: The Letters of Monsieur César de Saussure to his Family*, ed. Madame van Muyden (1902), p. 119.

[56] Babington, *Advice to Grand Jurors*, pp. 189–93. According to Kelyng, it was the "constant practice" at Newgate in the 1660s for jailers to encourage recalcitrant prisoners to plead by tying their thumbs together with whipcord rather than pressing them (R vs. Thorley: Kelyng, *Reports*, pp. 27–28; *Eng. Rep.*, vol. 84, p. 1066, quoted by Langbein, *Torture and the Law of Proof*, p. 183, n. 18).

[57] Blackstone, *Commentaries*, vol. 4, pp. 319–24. On the eve of the passing of the Act, which authorized the courts to take a refusal to plead to a felony as an acknowledgment of guilt, a man who stood mute at the sessions in Bristol was told that if he persisted and if the new law had not yet been proclaimed the consequences would be "fatal to him"; but in fact to avoid this the judge ordered that his refusal not be recorded and that an express be sent to London for the new Act (SP 37/9, f. 132).

[58] 7 and 8 Geo IV, c. 28, s. 2 (1827). For the significance of these statutes see Langbein, *Torture and the Law of Proof*, p. 184, n. 20. Hale had had some doubts about the legality of executing men who stood mute in cases of treason, but men had been hanged in the late eighteenth century after refusing to plead in capital cases (*G. M.* 47 [1777], p. 608; R vs. Mercier: Leach, *Reports*, vol. 1, pp. 183–85; *Eng. Rep.*, vol. 168, pp. 194–95 [1777]). At the Surrey quarter sessions in 1773 a man who refused to plead to a charge of petty larceny was whipped as he would have been had he been tried and convicted (QS 3/5/9, p. 140).

[59] A man indicted for burglary at the Surrey assizes in 1771 and found to be unable to hear the proceedings or to speak was not tried but ordered by the court "to be taken care of and conveyed to his last legal settlement" (ASSI 31/10, p. 68). On the other hand, a man similarly afflicted was put on trial at the Old Bailey two years later when it was discovered that he could communicate by sign language through a woman who was sworn "well and truly to interpret" for him. He was convicted of simple larceny and sentenced to be transported to America. And

Most prisoners responded when the clerk asked whether they were guilty or not guilty. It was possible to enter a plea that was not a direct answer to this question: several pleas in abatement were allowed—for example, that they had already been tried for this offense. But in fact such responses were extremely rare in ordinary criminal trials.[60] In virtually every case of felony in the eighteenth century, the prisoner declared that he was not guilty and announced that he would be tried by God and his country. After pleading, he was entitled to have his fetters struck off,[61] and when a sufficiently large group had thus been arraigned—as determined by the judge, who had had the calendar and knew the general outlines of the charges—their "country" was assembled in the form of twelve petty jurymen.

If the offense was a felony, trial followed immediately upon arraignment on the grounds that because the accused felon had been in jail he knew from his commitment what charge he faced and he could not mistake the day of the trial. The issues in felony were also thought to be simple matters of fact. In misdemeanors, on the other hand, issues were often complex and, as was said in the early nineteenth century about the case of a man refusing to do his stint of work on the parish roads, often turned on "intricate questions of civil rights and ancient liability." In such circumstances the defendant needed time to prepare an adequate defense after hearing the specific charge that had to be answered, and he was allowed to enter a "traverse" after pleading not guilty, which put the trial off until the next session of the court.[62] But for felons and for those pleading to traverses entered in a previous session, the trial went on immediately.

a deaf woman was put on trial in 1787 (and also transported) when the judges decided in conference that a jury verdict finding a prisoner "mute by the visitation of God" was not an absolute barrier to trial. See R vs. Jones: Leach, *Reports*, vol. 1, p. 102; *Eng. Rep.*, vol. 168, p. 153 (1773); R vs. Steel: Leach, *Reports*, vol. 1, pp. 451–53; *Eng. Rep.*, vol. 168, p. 328 (1787).

[60] Baker, "Criminal Courts and Procedure," pp. 34–35.

[61] Blackstone, *Commentaries*, vol. 4, p. 317, suggests that after Layer's case (1722) the court might insist that the prisoner remain chained during his arraignment and only have his irons removed when he came to trial. It was widely agreed that a man ought not to be in fetters during his trial, and presumably those who were chained throughout the proceedings (and examples can be found) were thought to be dangerous or likely to attempt an escape. At the trial of Quirk and Balse at the Old Bailey in 1769 on a charge of murder arising out of the disturbances at the Middlesex election, the prisoners, it was reported, stood at the bar throughout the long trial until at five in the afternoon the lord mayor "asked whether they had irons on, and being answered in the affirmative, he immediately ordered them chairs" (*Annual Register*, 1769, chronicle, p. 68).

[62] Chitty, *Criminal Law*, vol. 1, 484–87. Traverses were especially common in the quarter sessions, where the bulk of assaults and other misdemeanors were tried. The distinction between felony and misdemeanor is an eloquent comment on what was expected in the way of defense from men on trial for their lives. And the distinction was no doubt encouraged and sustained

As the trial jurors were sworn, the prisoners at the bar on trial for felony had the right to challenge up to twenty of them peremptorily and others for cause as they came forward to take their oaths. Elaborate rules governed the right of challenge, and the extensive discussion of the subject in the law books testifies to the importance attached to it. But few prisoners in fact exercised these rights. Occasionally a challenge was mounted at the Surrey assizes in the eighteenth century, but the system of jury trials could not have worked as it did if challenges had been frequently asserted since it depended, as we will see, on the high-speed processing of cases.[63] Most often the first twelve men called to the jury were sworn, and the first case began immediately. The trials would go on then at a cracking pace, and the prisoners needed to have their wits about them when they were called forward for a second time to hear the clerk once more read the charge for the benefit of the jury and they were again asked to raise their hand to acknowledge that they were the defendant named in the indictment.

TRIAL PROCEDURE

The dogma that a prisoner is to be regarded as innocent until he is proven guilty so pervades modern Anglo-American law that it is reasonable to

by the fact that respectable men on trial before the criminal courts would almost certainly be charged with a misdemeanor, while men in jail on suspicion of felony were not likely to be men with reputations and character. This suspicion is further suggested by the fact that as opinion moved against traverses in the eighteenth century those misdemeanors that were in effect offenses against property—obtaining goods by false pretenses, extorting by means of a threatening letter, and receiving stolen goods—were the first to be restricted (30 Geo II, c. 24; 39 and 40 Geo III, c. 87, s. 22). By the end of the century a more general objection was being put forward against traverses (perhaps as the courts felt the increasing burden of work and the need for more efficient administration), and in the 1820s the right to enter a traverse was so limited that in the future any defendant who had been admitted to bail or had been committed to jail at least twenty days before the court session was to take his trial immediately upon arraignment (1 Geo IV, c. 4, s. 3).

[63] For challenges see Hale, *Pleas of the Crown*, vol. 2, pp. 267–76; Hawkins, *Pleas of the Crown*, vol. 2, pp. 412–20; Chitty, *Criminal Law*, vol. 1, pp. 533–51. For examples at the Surrey assizes see ASSI 31/12, pp. 20, 24. An alien who could not speak English had the right to be tried by a jury "de medietate linguae," a jury composed of half denizens and half aliens. Such requests were not of course very frequent. It appears that on some of the occasions on which such a jury was requested, the sheriff had been forewarned and the jury was assembled immediately and the trial continued (ASSI 31/8, p. 147 [Derien]). But if no preparations had been made a request for such a jury would likely result in the prisoner's being returned to jail to await the next assizes. Antonio Welpes, who was indicted for murder in 1771, requested an interpreter and a jury "de medietate linguae" when he came to trial; he was held until the court met for the Summer assizes some months later when he was provided with both. He was convicted, hanged, and dissected (ASSI 31/10, pp. 117, 158).

assume that such a presumption of innocence has always been the rule at common law. In fact, the notion in its modern form arose as an active principle only toward the end of the period we are concerned with as one aspect of a complex change in the character of criminal trials. The idea that men ought actively to be regarded as innocent before being tried was being expressed in the 1780s, and by 1820 it could be confidently asserted that "every man is presumed to be innocent till he has been clearly proved to be guilty: the onus of the proof of guilt lies therefore on the accuser; and no man is bound, required or expected to prove his own innocency."[64] But it was only then that the characteristics of the modern jury trial were beginning to emerge, and only in the nineteenth century that they took firm shape: it was then that juries came to be selected specifically for each case, that the prosecution and defense were normally managed by lawyers, that the judge invariably summed up and instructed the jury to retire and deliberate over the evidence in a frame of mind that required that they be persuaded of the prisoner's guilt beyond a reasonable doubt before convicting him.

Little of that practice and few of the assumptions that underlie it are to be found in English jury trials before the nineteenth century. Certainly at the Restoration and well into the eighteenth century the attitudes toward the accused that characterized the Marian bail and examination legislation seem to have been carried over into the court. The prosecution was required to provide evidence that the prisoner was guilty of the charge laid. But if any assumption was made in court about the prisoner himself, it was not that he was innocent until the case against him was proved beyond a reasonable doubt, but that if he *were* innocent he ought to be able to demonstrate it for the jury by the quality and character of his reply to the prosecutor's evidence. That put emphasis on the prisoner's active role. He was very much in the position of having to prove that the prosecutor was mistaken. And for the most part he had to prove it on his own and by his immediate replies to the charges, rather than through a lawyer. In this fundamental way the "old" form of trial (if I may so describe it without implying that it had been unchanging since the dawn of time) was very different from its "modern" successor. Partly as a consequence

---

[64] Advocates of separation of prisoners in the 1770s included those who sought to keep the convicted apart from the accused, the guilty, as was said by a House of Commons committee, apart from "those who are presumed Innocent" (*J.H.C.* 37 [1778–80], p. 313). Some of the opposition to the spread of societies for the prosecution of felons and to the development of a professional police was founded in the belief that they would ignore the principle (as was said in the *Northampton Mercury* on 23 Feb. 1784) that "the Laws deem every Man innocent till he is proved guilty" (I owe this reference to Douglas Hay). See also Radzinowicz, *History*, vol. 3, p. 130. For the 1820 quotation see Sir Richard Phillips, *Golden Rules for Jurymen* (1820), rule no. 6. And see generally C. K. Allen, "The Presumption of Innocence," in *Legal Duties and Other Essays in Jurisprudence* (Oxford, 1931), pp. 253–94.

of that, trials differed in other important ways too: in the judge's role, for example; in the way that evidence was introduced and assessed; and in jury practice. It is this "old" form of trial that we are mainly concerned with in this chapter. It remained in many ways intact in 1800, although some of its elements were beginning to change over the second half of the eighteenth century, and we will have to attempt to identify these changes and assess their impact.

Virtually every jury trial in the eighteenth century began with the prosecutor, who was usually the victim of the offense, telling his story to the jury. He was followed by the witnesses for the Crown, often including a constable who might testify about the circumstances of the prisoner's apprehension—what he said, what was found, and so on—when this provided strong evidence for the prosecution. These witnesses gave their evidence under oath, and risked in doing so a prosecution for perjury if they were found to have lied.[65] Some prosecutors and witnesses perhaps simply made a statement about the matters at issue, but the common practice clearly was for the judge to take them through their testimony line by line, acting as both examiner and cross-examiner, until he was satisfied that the fullest possible case had been presented.

The role of the judge has to be emphasized. He might be joined on the bench by some of the county magistrates or by a local aristocrat of importance.[66] But the judge was very much in charge, and in the eighteenth century he was very active. In modern jury trials judges have been

[65] It was frequently alleged that perjured evidence was common in the criminal courts and especially in cases in which substantial monetary rewards depended on securing a conviction. (Men on trial were among the leading proponents of the view.) Some argued that in capital cases, at least, perjury ought to be capitally punished instead of being merely subject to six months' imprisonment, a fine, and a period on the pillory, as it had been laid down by a statute of 1563 (5 Eliz, c. 9), or, after 1729, transportation for seven years (2 Geo II, c. 25). The oath retained its religious basis in the eighteenth century in that the question of who was able to be sworn to give evidence in court was resolved by a general religious test. In the case of a black servant who was to testify at the Surrey assizes in 1738 the judge asked if he had been baptized and allowed him to take the oath and to give his evidence when he was satisfied on that score (S.A.P., Lent 1738, p. 4). A muslim was sworn on the Koran in 1764 (R vs. Morgan: Leach, Reports, vol. 1, p. 54; Eng. Rep., vol. 168, p. 129 [1764]). The rule applied later in the century was that witnesses might be sworn who had "a notion of eternity," some form of belief that would persuade them that perjury would be visited by eternal punishment (R vs. White: Leach, Reports, vol. 1, p. 430; Eng. Rep., vol. 168, p. 137 [1786]). This test was applied to children as well as to non-Christians. An eleven-year-old girl asked in 1799 "What becomes of persons who do not tell the truth, after they depart this life?" was allowed to be sworn and to give evidence at the Old Bailey when she replied they go "to the wicked man," by which she further said she meant "the devil" (OBSP, 1799–1800, p. 108).

[66] John Baker noted, for example, that at the Sussex assizes in 1772 the "Duke of Richmond sat all the time by Lord Mansfield," who was presiding in the Crown court (Philip C. Yorke, ed., The Diary of John Baker [1931], p. 242).

removed from detailed involvement in the management of the evidence and the examination of witnesses by the intrusion of lawyers on both the prosecution and the defense sides. (The prisoner has been largely removed from his own trial for the same reason.) The judge presides as the case is unfolded by others. He takes notes for the summing up of the evidence he will make for the jury, and he controls the flow of the evidence. But he is not actively engaged in its production. In the eighteenth century judges could not sit back in this way, because in most cases no counsel were acting for the prosecution or the defense. We will qualify that to some extent in a moment, for there were significant changes in this area in the course of the eighteenth century. For most of the period we are concerned with (and in the vast majority of cases), however, the ordinary felony trial was conducted without the involvement of lawyers, and the judge was fully engaged in getting the prosecutor to tell what he had lost or how he had been harmed, why he suspected the prisoner, how the prisoner had been apprehended, what he had said when examined by the magistrate, and so on, and then in taking each witness through his story in the same way.

We might presume a wide variety in the way this evidence was presented, but the printed accounts of trials that appear to be more a verbatim record than a mere summary of the evidence give the strong impression of the judge as examiner. Here, for example, is the beginning of the report of a case at the Surrey assizes in 1774 in which three men were accused of robbing Mrs. Elizabeth Appletree on the highway at Lambeth:

> *Elizabeth Appletree*: I am the wife of Robert Appletree; on the
> 2d of September I was coming home on foot from Kennington
> Turnpike to Newington Butts at about ten o'clock at night;
> as I came along the road, four men came up to me.

> *Question* [from the judge, Lord Chief Justice Edward Willes]:
> Was you alone?

> *Appletree*: No, Mrs. Corothers was with me; one of them patted
> me on my left arm, and putting a pistol to my left breast
> said, *Stop, Madam, your money.*

> *Q*: Can you tell who put the pistol to your breast?

> *Appletree*: John Brind.

> *Q*: Was it the same that put the pistol to your breast that patted
> your arm?

> *Appletree*: Yes. I stood quite still, and said if they would do me
> no harm I would give them my money directly; I took out
> of my pocket a guinea and a half and some halfpence; I held
> it in my hand and the halfpence; they left the half guinea,
> and I slipt that down into my bosom.
>
> *Q*: Was it light or dark?
>
> *Appletree*: It was quite light, moon shine.

And so on. Margaret Corothers came on next, and the judge took her
through her evidence too. One of the robbers had turned king's evidence,
and he responded in a similar way to the judge's questions.[67]

Mrs. Appletree's evidence came at the beginning of the trial. There
being no prosecuting counsel, there was no opening statement, no assertion
of what was going to be proved against the prisoner. Without preliminaries, the prosecution evidence was presented directly and briefly. The
trial got on rapidly, in part because the judge as examiner kept the
witnesses to the narrow track of evidence that related to the issue at hand,
aiming to produce the most serious matters that the prisoner would have
to confront if he was going to make a defense.

Occasionally one gets the impression that trials not only got rapidly
to the point but that the procedure at this stage was less tightly controlled
than it would be in a modern courtroom, that there was a certain hectic
quality produced by interventions from other quarters besides the bench
while the prosecution evidence was being given. The prisoner was allowed
to ask questions of the witnesses as they gave their evidence—while the
point at issue was in his mind and the opportunity at hand, as Nelson
said.[68] But his observations on this evidence and his responses to it were
meant to come when the prosecution case had been completed. Jurors
occasionally intervened too, asking questions or making comments, sometimes directed to the judge but often apparently simply fired at the witness
during his testimony. It is difficult to tell from reports that are far from
complete and that did not aim to reproduce these niceties of procedure
how commonly others besides the judges took part in clarifying the evidence being presented against the prisoner. But the scattered examples do
suggest that it was acceptable to the bench that such interventions take
place, even though they led to a certain amount of chaos in the court.[69]

---

[67] S.A.P., Lent 1774, pp. 3–5. On the engagement of the judge in the production of evidence
see Langbein, "Criminal Trial before the Lawyers," pp. 277–84.

[68] William Nelson, *The Office and Authority of a Justice of the Peace* (1711), p. 234.

[69] For jurors asking questions and making other interventions, see S.A.P., Lent 1738, p. 4
(Simms); Summer 1739, pp. 2–3 (Hitchcock); Summer 1739, pp. 14–15 (Willington et al.);
Summer 1739, p. 17 (Dunkley et al.); Summer 1741, p. 9 (Moore); Summer 1741, p. 10
(Rummels); and see Langbein, "Criminal Trial before the Lawyers," p. 288.

How the evidence was presented is not always clear. But what is abundantly clear at the assizes is the judge's immense influence on the way the jury received the evidence and the impression it made on them. He had ample opportunity to comment on the testimony as it was being given and to shape it as he thought it deserved to be presented, to emphasize and underline its strengths and weaknesses. Of course he had to take the evidence as he found it: he dealt with those bound over by the examining magistrate to prosecute and give evidence. But the scope for his influence on the way the case unfolded was obviously enormous. Nor need he be concerned that he might be criticized on appeal for browbeating prisoners or witnesses, for "making sport" of them, since there were no appeals. Even when prosecuting counsel became more common, the judge often remained the dominant figure and might still ask most of the questions.[70] Without counsel present it was his duty to get the evidence out and to keep the trial moving.

Because prisoners did not have the help of lawyers, at least until the middle decades of the century (a subject we will take up presently), the judge was thought to have a special responsibility to see that they were given every opportunity to prove their innocence. This was one of the aspects of criminal procedure that gave rise to the frequently repeated view that English law and the English courts were exceptionally humane and tender with regard to the prisoner's rights. The judge was thought to be counsel for the prisoner as well as for the king, and it was commonly claimed that this role led English judges to treat even the worst prisoners gently. Sir Thomas de Veil recommended to his fellow magistrates in their examination of prisoners "the examples of the judges" who, he said,

> behave always not only with the utmost impartiality, but with the utmost mildness and decency[;] their zeal appears in the execution of the laws, but without any diminution of that tenderness which humanity requires for those that, however bad they may be, are still our fellow creatures, and our fellow subjects.[71]

This had long been a common theme in the press, among law writers, and indeed in most comments on the legal system, and it was frequently repeated in the eighteenth century. "The learned judge showed the greatest humanity," a newspaper said in an account of a murder trial in 1783, "and was, what every judge should be, the advocate for the prisoner in every way where justice would permit it."[72]

[70] S.A.P., Lent 1739, pp. 18–19 (Cooke).
[71] *Memoirs of the Life and Times of Sir Thomas Deveil, Knight* (1748), p. 81.
[72] *Whitehall Evening Post*, 16 Jan. 1783. And see Foster, *Reports*, p. 31; *Eng. Rep.*, vol. 168, p. 16; and Cottu, *Administration of Criminal Justice in England*, pp. 90–91.

There is no doubt that a judge could do a great deal for the prisoner if he was so moved. Judges must have differed considerably in this respect one from the other—much obviously depended on their own character and views—but they all tended to support prisoners in certain circumstances, or at least to take a hard line with certain prosecutors, especially those they suspected of acting out of malice or of being suspicious themselves, or those they thought had brought their misfortune on themselves by acting foolishly. A good example of the latter were men who charged prostitutes with theft. Judges' questioning of them as they gave their evidence was often hostile: "Was it your money that drop't from the prisoner?" a judge asked one such prosecutor. "Had it any particular mark whereby you could know it. . . . How many thousands are there more than yours do you think?" And having cast doubt on the prosecutor's ability to prove that the woman had taken his money, the judge also managed to emphasize that the prosecutor had been with the woman for three hours and that he had fallen asleep in her room. It was hardly surprising that she was acquitted.[73] At the same session of the Surrey assizes the judge went after another prosecutor, a man who had advertised his loss after a theft, paid a reward for its return, and then prosecuted the thief. The judge heaped scorn on him. He pointed out to the jury a technical error in the indictment because the goods listed did not exactly agree with their description in the prosecutor's advertisement. But mainly he treated the prosecutor with contempt for bringing the case at all: "So you offer a Reward to tempt a Man to bring you your Goods, and then you would be so kind as to hang him for it." There were other encouragements to the jury to find an acquittal, and they did so.[74]

There are instances, too, of judges rounding on men who had induced a thief, often a servant, to confess by promising forgiveness and then using the confession against him in court. As we will see, confessions obtained by threats or favor were being regularly found unacceptable as evidence by the end of the century. In 1738 Lord Chief Justice Willes did not make that ruling, but he roasted a prosecutor for using a confession "extorted" from a servant. "No regard is to be had to what you say," he told the man as he gave evidence against his servant:

> It is the greatest Cruelty that can be practis'd, first to make her
> a fallacious Promise of Pardon, and then to bring her Confession
> in Evidence against her. I hope what you have said will have

---

[73] S.A.P., Lent 1738, pp. 16–17 (Sarnel and Falkener). For another prostitute acquitted after the judge intervened on her behalf, S.A.P., Summer 1739, pp. 9–10 (Williams).

[74] S.A.P., Lent 1738, p. 22 (Jennison and Payton).

no Weight with the Jury; for such a Man as you ought not to be trusted on any Account whatsoever.

The servant was acquitted.[75]

Apart from these what might be thought to be special cases, judges can certainly also be found clearly bringing their influence to bear in the middle of a trial in favour of a prisoner they had decided ought not to be convicted.[76] But the greater reality of the trial was that the prisoner (at least in offenses against property and other felonies) was mainly in a weak and disadvantageous position that was not fundamentally altered by these occasional examples of judicial benevolence and humanity. Indeed examples of judges' hostility to prisoners would not be hard to find, and for every prostitute protected by a judge who thought her victim a silly man or for every servant protected from a bullying employer there were prisoners whose feeble attempts to defend themselves were entirely undermined by the scorn and sarcasm of the bench. A woman who had excused her theft of meat on the grounds that she had been pregnant and "longed" for it was asked by the judge if she had also longed for the brass mortar she was accused of stealing in another indictment. That was not perhaps a damaging retort after she had already been convicted of one offense, but other sallies and judicial witticisms were more clearly calculated to weaken a prisoner's defense and to influence the jury. When a character witness said that he had known a defendant three months and knew "no Ill of him," Mr. Justice Carter scoffed, "That's a great Proof of his Righteousness. I have known him half a Day, that's almost as long as you." At the same session, after several exchanges with a prisoner who claimed to have been indicted under the wrong name, he said in conclusion that he would leave his name to the jury but for himself he fancied that "it is so long since you was christen'd, you have forgot your Name," which perhaps raised a laugh as the case concluded. The jury was clearly not troubled by the possibility that the indictment was faulty, for they convicted him of breaking and entering, and Carter sentenced him to death.[77]

This is no doubt not on the same level of bullying as Charles II's judges had been reputed to indulge in in court. Of course Scroggs and Jeffreys acquired their reputations for being full of jokes and "very witty with the prisoners" particularly in trials for treason in which they were

---

[75] S.A.P., Summer 1738, p. 6 (Wilcox).

[76] When an old man was charged with stealing ten sheep a few months after that offense had been made capital in 1741, the judge at his trial observed to the jury that he seemed "very ancient and sick" and wondered aloud whether he was "capable of driving so many sheep" (S.A.P., Lent 1742, p. 5 [Matthews]).

[77] S.A.P., Lent 1726, p. 2 (Hayward); Lent 1738, p. 18 (Heaford), pp. 19–20 (Lindon).

deeply engaged in the advocacy of the Crown's interests. It would be dangerous to assume that the taunting and insulting of prisoners from the bench in the trials that grew out of the Popish and Rye House Plots and in the trials following Monmouth's Rebellion could also be found in ordinary trials at the assizes. There is not a great deal of evidence to go by, certainly not for Surrey. But it seems reasonable to suppose that the attitudes and the behavior of judges in the state trials reflects (though perhaps it also exaggerates) the attitudes they are likely to have adopted toward ordinary prisoners, and that the freeing of the judges in the Act of Settlement from their immediate ties to the king encouraged a more detached and less hostile attitude toward all prisoners.[78]

But focusing on the judge's attitudes and his behavior toward the prisoners is, in any case, too narrow a perspective and makes a complex subject too simple. In most cases the judge displayed no particular attitude toward the accused or the prosecutor, and the character of the trial was much more fundamentally determined by the way the evidence was presented and the way the prisoner was expected to respond to it. In the "old" form of trial the prisoner was placed at what must seem from a modern point of view a serious disadvantage. The prosecution was organized by the State, at least to the important extent that the presence of the witnesses against the prisoner was ensured by their being bound in recognizances. As each completed his testimony, the prisoner had the right to ask him questions and to attempt by means of this cross-examination to throw doubt on his evidence. It was expected, however, that the prisoner would make his main defense when the prosecution case was completed. It was then that he was asked to provide an explanation of the evidence adduced against him. Of course if this evidence had not been especially strong, if it had not directly identified him or revealed circumstances that pointed strongly to his guilt, there might not have been much of a case to answer. But if it implicated him he was very much in a position of having to explain it. There was no thought that the prisoner had a right to remain silent on the grounds that he would otherwise be liable to incriminate himself. He was not to be put on oath, and he did not have to answer questions; and there was a developing notion by the middle of the eighteenth century that his examination before the magistrate ought not to have been taken on oath, since that did in fact lead to self-incrimination. But if he was without counsel, the prisoner had to cross-examine prosecution witnesses himself and to speak in his own defense. If *he* did not, no one would. And the assumption was clear that if the case against

---

[78] For the judges in the late seventeenth century see Cockburn, *History of English Assizes*, chap. 6; Keeton, *Lord Chancellor Jeffreys*, pp. 94–114; Alfred Havighurst, "The Judiciary and Politics in the Reign of Charles II," *Law Quarterly Review* 66 (1950), pp. 62–78, 221–52; idem, "James II and the Twelve Men in Scarlet," *Law Quarterly Review* 69 (1953), pp. 522–46.

him was false the prisoner ought to say so and suggest why, and that if he did not speak that could only be because he was unable to deny the truth of the evidence. When prisoners did speak, their own testimony was given great weight, especially the way they asserted their innocence—or at least that was always said on behalf of the rule prohibiting defense counsel.[79]

Because in the "old" form of trial the prisoner was required to provide his own defense, the advantages that derive from the presumption of innocence were largely absent in practice. It was only when the trial could be conceived as a contest not between two men but between a "case" put forward by the prosecution and a "case" put in answer by the defense that the prisoner could remain silent and the trial could be organized around his presumed innocence. That awaited "the coming of the lawyers," in Langbein's phrase.[80] When Lord Sankey declared in the House of Lords in 1935 in the case of Woolmington that the duty of the prosecution to prove the prisoner's guilt was a "golden thread" running through the history of the English criminal law, he could only assume that eighteenth-century judges and commentators who failed to emphasize this point had misread their sources. Thus, Sir Michael Foster's comment that in a homicide case in the eighteenth century the law presumed malice on the part of the prisoner and left it to him to persuade the jury otherwise led Sankey to conclude that if Foster meant that the burden of proof had shifted to the prisoner he did not understand the common law and had no authority for such views.[81] But Foster was not only right about the way the courts dealt with homicide (and since he was a judge that is not unexpected). He was also stating a general position that applied in all cases: the court's assumptions were simply a little clearer in homicide because of the variety of verdicts that were possible. The point applied to all felonies. When the evidence had been given for the prosecution, the judge turned to the prisoner and said in effect: "You have heard the evidence; what do you have to say for yourself?" The implications of the judge's question were perfectly clear. When one man responded simply "I am no thief" and the judge told him "You must prove that," he was stating plainly the situation that every prisoner found himself in.[82]

[79] The jury also made its judgment about the character of the prosecutor in the same way. In explaining on one occasion why the magistrates at the Surrey quarter sessions had given weight to a particular prosecutor's evidence, Sir Joseph Mawby, the chairman, told a secretary of state that "the manner in which she told a tale, seeming artless . . . stamped her narrative with credit" (HO 42/2, f. 193). The same "artless" quality would similarly stamp an innocent prisoner's explanations with credit, or so went the theory.

[80] Langbein, "Criminal Trial before the Lawyers," p. 307.

[81] Woolmington vs. D.P.P. (1935) A.C. 462, quoted in M. L. Friedland, *Cases and Materials in Criminal Law and Procedure*, 5th ed. (Toronto, 1978), pp. 380–85.

[82] S.A.P., Lent 1739, p. 20 (Durham).

How far prisoners were able to respond to the judge's invitation to address the jury and to cross-examine the prosecution witnesses must have depended on whether they had in fact objections of substance to offer, whether they had been able to prepare for the trial and whether, when it came to it, they were able to talk effectively in this public setting. Some "old offenders" no doubt knew the ropes, and others of the accused perhaps learned something about what to expect in the courtroom while they were in jail. Those who had friends on the outside would have been able to arrange to have their own witnesses present, and the prisoner was allowed to bring them on to support his own case, witnesses both to fact and to his character and reputation. Until Anne's reign the prisoner's witnesses were not allowed to give their evidence under oath. An Act of 1702 (1 Anne, st. 2, c. 9) put their testimony on the same footing as the prosecution witnesses', but there were still considerable difficulties preventing most men in prison from arranging counter-evidence, not least the likelihood that they did not know the precise evidence that would be introduced against them. Even if they could organize witnesses for the defense, their preparation for trial might well remain seriously limited. But such difficulties would not have seemed especially damaging to a man's chances of proving his innocence so long as the view persisted that the prisoner's best defense was his own natural and unprepared response to the charges as they were asserted by the prosecution in court. Associated with that central belief was the further conviction that witnesses to the prisoner's character were immensely important, since they encouraged the judge and jury to believe in his trustworthiness.

The prisoner had thus essentially to make his own defense. The strong impression formed by the printed accounts of trials at the Surrey assizes is that few did so very successfully. Their difficulties were compounded if they had confessed at their examination and the confession was introduced during the trial and certified as authentic by the magistrate or his clerk, or even if his acknowledgment of guilt was simply asserted by a witness. The evidence of an accomplice turned king's evidence might be equally damaging and as difficult to contend with. We will be concerned later to assess the weight that judges and juries commonly gave to confessions and accomplices' evidence, but whatever value was placed on such testimony it surely complicated the prisoner's task in court. Even without that to contend with, most men and women on trial found it difficult to mount a defense against the evidence. It is hardly surprising that men not used to speaking in public who suddenly found themselves thrust into the limelight before an audience in an unfamiliar setting—and who were for the most part dirty, underfed, and surely often ill—did not usually cross-examine vigorously or challenge the evidence presented against them. Not all prisoners were unprepared or tongue-tied in court. But the evidence of the printed reports of assize trials in Surrey suggests that it was the exceptional prisoner who asked probing questions or who spoke effectively to the jury on his own behalf.[83]

It was Henry Fielding's view that at the Old Bailey members of gangs and others with connections and money managed as a matter of course to find witnesses willing to provide them with an alibi, and that perjured evidence saved many such men from justice: "The usual defence of a Thief . . . is an *alibi*: To prove this by Perjury is a common Act of Newgate Friendship; and there seldom is any Difficulty in procuring such Witnesses."[84] This might have been true at the Old Bailey, where there were always more men in the jail, many of them experienced and with connections on the outside; it was plainly rare, however, at the Surrey assizes.[85] Occasional charges of perjury were laid against witnesses there, but a coherent defense based upon such evidence required even more coordination and preparation than the printed accounts of trials suggest the vast majority of prisoners could manage. And of course even when defense witnesses were brought in, their evidence was subject to scrutiny and might not hold up.[86]

[83] Some did both reasonably well. Stephen Sutton, indicted for highway robbery, was very active in his own defense compared with most prisoners. When the prosecutor concluded his account of how he had been robbed, Sutton requested the judge "to ask the gentleman if he did not say at Belsize that he was not sure that I was the man, only said that I looked much like him; and whether I did not go quietly with him before the justice." The prosecutor admitted as much. He later challenged another witness who claimed to recognize him as the robber; and when called upon by the judge to speak for himself ("If you can say anything in your defence, now is the time to offer it, and the court will hear you") he said that he was well known as a jockey in Surrey, that he "rode races for several lords and dukes, and the best of people," and that it was "a likely thing I should rob people at noonday on Banstead Down, when I was so well known all about the country." It did him in fact no good. "Take care you don't ride on the wrong side of the post," the judge said at the conclusion of his statement, and the jury convicted him. But Sutton had made as good an unaided attempt to defend himself as any prisoner whose trial was reported in the pamphlet accounts (S.A.P., Summer 1738, pp. 5–6; for two other effective defenses see Summer 1711, pp. 2–3 [Robinson], and Summer 1718, p. 4 [Hawsley and Rigby]).

[84] Fielding, *Increase of Robbers*, p. 116.

[85] The relative ease of finding supportive witnesses in a larger prison may be (if anything) what one man had in mind when he said at his trial in Surrey, "I have never a soul on this side of the world I can call to speak in my behalf. God send me to the Old Bailey again, where Christians are tried, for there is no more justice here, than there is in a common field. Now I see I will be hanged" (S.A.P., Summer 1751, p. 30 [Brian]). He was right on this last point.

[86] One man produced five witnesses "to prove that he was in the White Bear Pickadilly the time the robbery was committed," but their stories were slightly different and the judge "gave no credit to their evidence; nor did the jury (S.A.P., Summer 1751, p. 32). One effective defense by means of an alibi was put up by a prisoner in 1740 who brought witnesses who, as the *Gentleman's Magazine* said, "proved that he was in a different place at the time of the robbery, giving a distinct detail how he passed the day til 11 at night that he went to bed." He was acquitted largely on the strength of this evidence (G. M. 10 [1740]; for the case see S.A.P.,

For the most part, if prisoners said anything at all it was simply to deny that they had anything to do with whatever was alleged against them, or to make some ineffective comment that often only got them into deeper trouble. "Do you know me?" one prisoner asked a witness who claimed to have been his accomplice in a burglary. "Know you!" was the reply. "Why have not we been thieves together?" The prisoner said no more after this poor thrust and offered no other defense; he was convicted and sentenced to death. Many simply said that they had found the stolen goods, that they had been asked to hold them or, in the case of sheep, to drive them for an unknown third party ("a common excuse," one judge commented), or that they had just mysteriously appeared. A woman caught with stolen goods could say at her trial only that someone had "put all these things on my back."[87] A large number of prisoners apparently said very little, either in cross-examining or directly to the jury. It is true that this impression derives from brief printed reports of trials that were not likely to emphasize attempts at a defense, especially when the prisoner had been convicted. But there is also some slightly more positive evidence in these trial accounts of the ineffectiveness of prisoners' attempts to defend themselves in that the reporters from time to time record "no defence," "little to say in defence," "frivolous defence," or "trifling defence."

Prisoners who could not respond immediately and speak off the cuff were not necessarily convicted. That is a different question, as we will see when we enquire into the grounds on which juries based their verdicts. Nonetheless, those who could put the prosecution on the defensive and shift the burden of proof to some extent to that side were obviously at an advantage. It was of immense significance that there was to be an increasing emphasis in that direction as a result of the intrusion into felony trials of lawyers acting for the defense: this was a departure that was to bring momentous changes in the forms of trial we have been describing.

THE INTRODUCTION OF LAWYERS

The rule prohibiting defendants from employing counsel in trials of felonies remained fully in force at the Restoration and indeed well into the eighteenth century. A prisoner might have the assistance of a lawyer to raise points of law on his behalf, but few defendants could have anticipated such a need, and in practice counsel never appeared on the defense side.

Summer 1740, pp. 4–8). But this was unusual in so many ways—not the least because both the prosecutor and the defendant were gentlemen and had been acquainted before the alleged robbery—that it provides little evidence about the common run of trials.

[87] S.A.P., Lent 1752, p. 16 (Morgan); SP 36/44, f. 153.

Such a situation was justified, as we have seen, not merely as an aid to the court's discovery of the truth but as the means whereby the innocent prisoner might most readily exculpate himself. No such rule prevented the engagement of lawyers for the prosecution, however. In important state trials the case for the Crown was commonly put by the attorney general assisted by other counsel, and it was as open to a private prosecutor to hire counsel in a felony case as in the trial of a misdemeanor or a civil action. It is clear that until the early eighteenth century few did so, no doubt largely because it was thought unnecessary to go to such expense when an ordinary case of theft or burglary needed no special presentation since the accused had to answer on his own behalf. Virtually every felony trial was conducted as we have seen by the prosecutor himself.

Why lawyers came to be more commonly employed in prosecuting felonies is far from clear. The evidence from the Surrey assizes is not full or reliable enough to enable even the timing of their introduction to be established with certainty, but it would seem that few prosecuting counsel were engaged in ordinary cases before 1714 and that they began to appear in modest numbers during the reign of George I, when Langbein has found something on the order of one a year reported at the Old Bailey.[88] It is possible that some of this interest in more effective prosecution came from the encouragement of the government. In the face of popular disaffection, Jacobite plots, and a variety of disturbances,[89] the Whig governments after 1714 and especially in the 1720s vigorously pursued a wide range of presumed enemies by bringing them before the secretaries and privy council for examination and by carrying on prosecutions in the courts. The engagement of the administration in the prosecution of the so-called Blacks, whose protests over the erosion of customary rights was met with savage legislation and government-sponsored repression, has been fully documented.[90]

The Walpole administration also clamped down on the press, harried printers and sellers of "seditious" pamphlets and ballads, and encouraged the prosecution of men and women overheard uttering "treasonable" sentiments. In the 1720s Secretary Townshend, his undersecretary Charles Delafaye, and the Solicitor to the Treasury, Anthony Cracherode, encouraged and paid for numerous such prosecutions throughout the country. Some of these cases were carried on by counsel. The costs of prosecuting a clergyman in Westmoreland for treasonable words included a two-guinea fee for an attorney to manage the case at the assizes and money to get the

---

[88] Langbein, "Criminal Trial before the Lawyers," p. 311.

[89] Nicholas Rogers, "Popular Protest in Early Hanoverian London," *Past and Present* 79 (1978), pp. 70–100.

[90] Thompson, *Whigs and Hunters*.

indictment drawn to his specifications. A man charged at the Middlesex sessions in the same year, 1723, for saying in public "God damn your King George, he is no king" was prosecuted by a lawyer paid for by the government—or at least the soldier who had informed on him was encouraged to think he would be.[91] I am not sure that it was a strikingly new departure for the government to pay for such prosecutions. But it is clear that there were a large number of them in the 1720s, so many that Cracherode was referred to occasionally as the "Solicitor for Criminal Prosecutions" and three hundred pounds was transferred annually to him from the Treasury as the funds "for carrying on public prosecutions."[92]

It is not perhaps surprising that many of these prosecutions for sedition were carried on by counsel: the government was anxious that they should succeed, and there was no obvious victim to take the lead in court. It was a little more novel that this interest in effective prosecution of offenses extended to a number of more ordinary felonies. The government also paid, for example, for the prosecution of a man who had attempted to murder his brother-in-law "in a barbarous manner," and included in the charge were the fees of "an able Council and a proper Solicitor." Nicholas Paxton, Cracherode's assistant at the Treasury, was also sent to manage the indictment at the assizes at Bury St. Edmunds, and in the end the Treasury paid a bill of more than eighty-five pounds.[93] In 1723 and over the next few years the government paid the costs of at least two other murder trials, of another trial that involved rape and murder, and of a prosecution for robbery; they also paid some fees, for drawing indictments at the Old Bailey for example, in a number of other cases.[94] The government did not move into ordinary prosecutions in a large way in this period, but it does seem that their anxiety about the stability of the Hanoverian regime led them to take a close interest in the adminis-

[91] SP 35/49, f. 35; SP 35/45, f. 38. The mayor of Harwich wrote in this period to the secretary's office for advice on how to proceed in a case in which two men were to be prosecuted at the next assizes for riot, particularly to know whether "there should be council for the King" (SP 35/52, f. 83).

[92] SP 44/81, pp. 113, 438. For Cracherode's declared accounts for 1722–23 and 1723–27, showing fees paid to the attorney general and solicitor general and other counsel in prosecutions for treason, seditious words, and other offenses, see Public Record Office, AO 1/2321/49–50. For his charges incurred in one term in 1725 see T 1/253, ff. 305–9. And for Cracherode and his assistant, Nicholas Paxton, and the prosecution of the Blacks, see Thompson, *Whigs and Hunters*, pp. 212–13.

[93] SP 44/81, pp. 24, 69; *Weekly Journal*, 24 Mar. 1722.

[94] SP 44/51, p. 431; SP 44/81, pp. 176, 189, 372; SP 35/63, f. 258. In several cases in this period the attorney general and the solicitor general had a hand in organizing the prosecution, and in some (the prosecution of Arnold, who shot at Lord Onslow in Surrey in 1723, for example) the case was conducted in court by the attorney general (SP 44/81, pp. 189, 336, 391; SP 35/48, f. 210).

tration of the criminal law and to encourage the engagement of lawyers as prosecuting counsel.

I do not know that it was this interest and this stimulus that in fact initiated the more common appearance of prosecuting counsel in the criminal courts, but it is from the 1720s and 1730s that that is to be dated. Langbein found lawyers acting for the prosecution in a handful of cases at the Old Bailey in the 1720s and then in more substantial numbers in the following decade: in 1732–34 he notes prosecuting counsel in eight murder cases, four theft cases, one highway robbery, and a few others.[95] A similar pattern can be discerned in the scraps of evidence from the Surrey assizes in the same period. At the Summer assizes in 1718 a prosecution for seditious words was opened by counsel, and in 1726, when the next pamphlet account is available, a complex case against several members of a gang charged with murder was carried on also by prosecuting counsel; the latter, if not the former, was at the government's expense.[96] Murder trials were prosecuted by lawyers in 1729 and 1732, and in the five years from 1738 to 1742, for which printed accounts are complete, prosecuting counsel are mentioned on ten occasions (three in murder, four in theft or robbery, one each in rape, smuggling, and arson). It is of course possible that lawyers appeared in other trials but were simply not noted by the reporters.[97] At least one of these cases in 1738–42 was undertaken at the order of the secretary of state, and in addition a lawyer acted for the Post Office in two cases in which highwaymen were tried for robbing the mails. The East India Company engaged the lawyer in one of the larceny prosecutions.

This was not a massive invasion of lawyers. The fact that some (at least) of these prosecutions had been paid for by the government or by large institutions supports the view that the fashion for prosecuting counsel arose from the government's anxiety about cases that seemed particularly sensitive and serious. Why private prosecutors took up this option is more puzzling. It meant adding considerably to the expense, though of course for those who could afford it the advantages of a more coherent presentation of their case (and of having the burden lifted to some extent from their shoulders) must have been obvious. Lawyers themselves must have come

---

[95] Langbein, "Criminal Trial before the Lawyers," pp. 311–12.

[96] S.A.P., Summer 1718, p. 4 (Bedow); Lent 1726, p. 1 (Blewet et al.). In 1728 it could still be said that it was "not very usual in private criminal causes in the Country" to engage counsel "to manage the tryall" (SP 36/5, f. 81v).

[97] By comparing the OBSP with the trial notes of Chief Justice Ryder, Langbein has discovered that the printed reports of the Old Bailey trials do not always reveal the presence of defense and prosecuting counsel. Between 1752 and 1754 Ryder notes the engagement of counsel in seven cases in which that information is not included in the pamphlet account of the trials (Langbein, "Shaping the Eighteenth-Century Criminal Trial," p. 23).

to think of the trial of felonies as an area of regular employment, and so made themselves available. It seems, in any event, quickly to have become an option that men considered: when Lord Baltimore's agent was preparing to prosecute a man for stealing his lordship's sheep in 1737, he thought it necessary to ask the clerk of the peace in Surrey if it was "proper to have Counsel against the prisoner."[98]

The appearance of lawyers for the prosecution in the 1730s had a significance well beyond that suggested by their numbers, if only because their activities seem mainly to explain why judges began to allow defendants to engage counsel in these same years. And that was to be especially significant, for while prosecuting counsel made a difference to the way trials were conducted, they mainly did what the judge had always done, though perhaps more effectively. Defense counsel, on the other hand, were likely to want to do things that had not been done before, and their appearance at the assizes undoubtedly led to some fundamental changes in the conduct of trials.

DEFENSE COUNSEL

Prisoners charged with felonies had been prohibited from engaging counsel on the familiar grounds stated by Hawkins that "it requires no manner of skill to make a plain and honest defence, which in cases of this kind is always the best."[99] By the 1730s, however, counsel were being allowed to act for defendants. The Surrey evidence is too fragmentary to enable their appearance to be dated precisely, but defense counsel at the Surrey assizes seem to have followed by some years the more frequent engagement of lawyers for the prosecution. No accused felons were recorded as having lawyers in the two printed reports of the 1720s, nor any before that. The first example is in the account of the Lent assizes of 1732, when a woman charged with murder was defended by counsel.[100] When next there are printed reports of the Surrey assizes, the complete run for 1738–42, nine

[98] QS 2/6, Ep. 1737, 63. It is striking that the increasing employment of prosecuting counsel followed the establishment of statutory rewards for the conviction of certain kinds of offenders, particularly burglars and robbers, which suggests a plausible explanation of why a private prosecutor might want to employ a lawyer. The problem is that it was not typically in burglary and robbery cases that counsel were engaged, but in murder; and when they were brought into the major property cases, at least in Surrey in the 1720s and 1730s, counsel were as likely to be hired by the government as by a private prosecutor. But I would want to leave that an open question since my evidence is so flimsy.

[99] Hawkins, *Pleas of the Crown*, vol. 2, p. 400.

[100] S.A.P., Lent 1732, pp. 2–8 (Longley). In the preface to his edition of the *State Trials* published in 1730 (p. viii), Sollom Emlyn had complained about, among other things, the continued prohibition against defense counsel.

defendants over that five-year period were said to have had counsel, one accused of murder and eight in other felonies, mainly robbery and burglary. There may have been others unreported.

The impression formed by this piecemeal evidence is that while the engagement of prosecution counsel developed gradually, the rule prohibiting the defendant to have counsel gave way suddenly. This impression is confirmed by the fuller evidence from the Old Bailey, where, having noted none in previous years, Langbein found "unmistakable instances of lawyers examining and cross-examining for the defense" in 1734–35. In 1736 there were nine cases at the Old Bailey.[101] They were common if not numerous from then on. Similarly, at the Surrey assizes, where in the surviving printed reports after 1742 (eleven sessions up to 1774) there is evidence of prisoners with defense lawyers in six murder trials, two infanticides, and eight other felonies. There is no reason to think that the reporters felt obliged to note the presence of counsel, so these must be taken as minimum figures that suggest no more than that defense counsel had become accepted.

Why they were accepted by judges remains uncertain. There was undoubtedly some strong resistance against them, not so much out of hostility to prisoners as out of regard for a form of trial that put great stock in the defendant speaking for himself. On the other side, arguments had been advanced for some years in favor of prisoners being allowed the help of counsel, and in the case of treason they had actually won that right. That sentiment had emerged during the 1680s, as an aspect of a broader conviction that the highly political use of charges of treason during that decade had brought the judges and the courts into disrepute and that criminal trial procedure required reform.[102] There was widespread agreement that Russell, Sidney, and others had been unfairly treated by the courts, and in particular had been unjustly prevented from defending themselves by the established trial procedures. The Revolution itself—or at least "the growing disaffection of the nation to the late government"— was thought by some after 1689 to have stemmed largely from these "undue prosecutions," and those who pressed for reform in trial procedure in William's reign argued that there was some general obligation to do so.[103]

Several aspects of the treason trials in the 1680s had caused disquiet, particularly the fundamental unfairness that arose from the accused having to defend himself against charges that he had had no certain knowledge of beforehand, that were supported by what might be hours of oral tes-

[101] Langbein, "Criminal Trial before the Lawyers," p. 312.

[102] Stephen, *History of the Criminal Law*, vol. 1, pp. 383–416.

[103] Sir John Hawles, *Remarks upon the Trials of Edward Fitzharris, Stephen Colledge, Count Coningsmark, Lord Russel, Collonel Sidney, Henry Cornish, and Charles Bateman. . . .* (1689), p. 1.

timony in court and to which he was expected to respond immediately. What seemed to many especially unfair was the rule that deprived the prisoner of help in preparing for trial or in actually conducting his defense in the courtroom. Some aspects of these prohibitions were crumbling in practice even in the 1680s, but not the central rule against defense counsel, and this became the focus of the efforts made after the Revolution to reform trial procedure.

The most advanced opinion would undoubtedly have allowed all prisoners to be assisted by counsel, accused felons as well as those charged with treason. Sir Robert Atkyns, who had been a judge in Charles II's reign and was to be appointed chief baron in 1689, wrote after the Revolution that he had "ever thought it a severity in our Law, that a Prisoner for his Life is not allowed the assistance of a grave and prudent Lawyer, or some other friend, to make his defence for him, even as to matter of fact, as well as to Law."[104] He went on to ridicule the argument that the prisoner had no need of counsel because the court acted for him, a point taken up particularly by Sir John Hawles in his commentaries on some of the notorious trials of the recent past. In treason trials, Hawles thought, the judges inevitably supported the interests of "their better client, the king." But he also extended the argument to felonies and declared "foolish" the notion that a man needed no defense other than his own simple declaration of the truth. Hawles cited a case involving robbery and horse-theft in which a defense witness had provided the crucial evidence of the defendant's innocence to illustrate what he called the "folly" of the argument that sustained the opposition to defense counsel. Very often, he argued, the truth was not immediately apparent and required demonstration; keeping a man in prison before trial and then denying him the help of a lawyer in court, he concluded, was "downright tying a man's hands behind him, and baiting him to death."[105]

These were advanced opinions, but the sentiment was widely shared in 1689.[106] There was support for several attempts made early in William's reign (against the king's resistance and that of his largely Whig advisers) to eliminate what these critics thought was the unfairness of trial procedure, the result of which after a number of pushes in parliament was the compromise worked out in what came to be known as the Treason Act of

---

[104] Sir Robert Atkyns, *A Defence of the late Lord Russel's Innocency.* . . . (1689), p. 8.

[105] Hawles, *Remarks upon the Trials*, pp. 22–23.

[106] Even Jeffreys had confessed it his "own particular opinion" that it was "a hard case, that a man should have counsel to defend himself for a two-penny trespass, and his witness examined on oath, but if he steal, commit murder . . . nay, high treason, where life, estate, honor, and all are concerned, he shall neither have counsel nor his witnesses examined on oath" (*State Trials*, vol. 10, p. 267, quoted by Samuel Rezneck, "The Statute of 1696: A Pioneer Measure in the Reform of Judicial Procedure in England," *Journal of Modern History* 2 [1930], p. 14).

1696. This introduced some important changes in trial procedure, including the right to defense counsel, but confined them to high treason.[107]

There do not appear to have been any strong lines of argument between the 1690s and the breakdown in practice of the rules prohibiting defense counsel in trials of felony forty years later. The example of the Treason Act was no doubt crucial, but it would appear that the right to counsel was granted not so much as a result of shifting attitudes outside the court as much as from pressure within the courts themselves, pressure it seems reasonable to think that was derived from the increasingly common practice by the 1730s of the prosecution case being presented and argued by lawyers. This is likely to have produced exactly the kind of disproportion and unfairness that brought support for the reform of procedure in the Treason Act, for an unprepared prisoner trying to defend himself without help against a case being put by a lawyer was in an entirely different position from the man answering the charges put haphazardly by his accuser. It is unclear whether the first defense counsel were allowed as a result of an agreement among the judges; nor is it certain, though it seems likely, that the practice began in London at the Old Bailey, where the largest number of serious cases were tried and where lawyers were more readily available, and that it spread from there to the provincial assizes. It is clear, however, that prisoners were employing lawyers to help them in court by the 1730s, almost exactly a hundred years before their right to do so was acknowledged in statute.[108]

Defense counsel were admitted to court on the sufferance of the judges, and certainly more as a favor than a right. This meant inevitably that the help they were able to give their clients depended for some time on the leeway allowed them by the bench and that the role of the defense counsel developed unevenly. A barrister observed in 1741 that

> the judges, I apprehend, act as they see fit on these occasions, and few of them (as far as I have observed) walk by one and the same rule in this particular: some have gone so far, as to give leave for counsel to examine and cross-examine witnesses; others have bid the counsel propose their questions to the Court; and others again have directed that the prisoner should put his own questions: the method of practice in this point, is very variable and uncertain.[109]

[107] 7 and 8 Wm III, c. 3 (1695). For the legal and political argument surrounding the statute and its passage, see Rezneck, "The Statute of 1696."

[108] 6 and 7 Wm IV, c. 114 (1836).

[109] *State Trials*, vol. 17, p. 1022, quoted by Langbein, "Criminal Trial before the Lawyers," p. 313.

This was plainly the case in Surrey in the early years. A lawyer defending two men for burglary in 1738, for example, called six witnesses to establish their alibi and four to their character, but he did not ask them questions—the judge did. According to the printed report, he squeezed in one question, but the witnesses mainly gave their evidence in the traditional way, under the judge's guidance.[110] In some aspects of the defense all judges restricted the role of the lawyer. Certainly for a long time defense counsel were prevented from addressing the jury on their clients' behalf, making a general statement, for example, and putting forward a defense. At the trial of a man accused of robbing a postboy at mid-century, the prosecution evidence was supported by the testimony of no fewer than thirty-three witnesses, and it was marshalled by a lawyer engaged by the Post Office. At its conclusion, when the judge asked the prisoner what he had to say in reply, he said that he would like to leave his defense to Mr. Knowler, his counsel. But, the reporter notes, "Mr. Knowler declined it" and the judge commented: "Your counsel knows his duty very well, they may indeed speak for you in any matter of law that may arise on your trial, but cannot as to matter of fact, for you must manage your defence in the best manner you can yourself." The accused said nothing further and was convicted.[111]

How many prisoners had defense counsel at the Surrey assizes by the end of the eighteenth century and what precisely those counsel were permitted to do by the court is unclear. No printed accounts seem to have survived for years after 1774. But there is rich evidence from the Old Bailey that is likely to indicate the broad pattern that Surrey was following, if it did not duplicate it exactly.[112] In 1788, as an example, seventy-two defendants in property cases at the Old Bailey were reported to have been defended by counsel out of a total of 580 on trial. Again, these are minimum figures since it is likely that counsel were engaged by some prisoners whose trials were too briefly reported to have included this fact. But assuming that is reasonably accurate, one in eight prisoners charged with property offenses had the help of an attorney in court.[113] In 1800 the reported level was higher: between a quarter and a third of defendants in property cases had counsel.[114] Whether a similar proportion would have

---

[110] S.A.P., Summer 1738, pp. 7–9 (Ticknell).

[111] S.A.P., Lent 1752, pp. 2–11 (Derby).

[112] In the OBSP, for which see Langbein, "Criminal Trial before the Lawyers," pp. 267–72, and "Shaping the Eighteenth-Century Criminal Trial," pp. 3–5; Michael Harris, "Trials and Criminal Biographies: A Case Study in Distribution," in Robin Myers and Michael Harris, eds., *Sale and Distribution of Books from 1700* (1982), pp. 6–15.

[113] Based on OBSP, Dec. 1787–Sept. 1788.

[114] Based on OBSP, Dec. 1799–April 1800: defense counsel were reported in ninety-six of the trials of 335 defendants accused of property offenses (28.6 per cent).

been found in Surrey and on the provincial assizes generally I am not able to say, though Cottu thought in 1820 that it was "the general case in the country" for prisoners to have counsel.[115]

The precise numbers are not important. What is plain is that counsel were commonly engaged in the defense of accused felons by the late eighteenth century and that they made a great difference to the way trials were conducted. Despite the constraints they remained under, defense counsel were able to do a great deal for their clients. Even the rule that prohibited them from addressing the court and the jury on behalf of the prisoner must have been frequently ignored in practice. The printed reports of cases at the Surrey assizes include examples of counsel making statements to the court about the evidence submitted by the prosecution or outlining the defense the accused man would offer. After the witnesses for the prosecution had been examined at a trial in 1759, for example, defense counsel submitted that since there was only "presumptive proof against the prisoner, and that so very slender . . . , no credit ought to be given to it." The jury agreed.[116] Other such interventions were reported in the Surrey Proceedings. In addition, a lawyer was much more likely than the prisoner to spot errors in indictments (and invariably more likely than the judge to point them out) and obviously more able to move the court for dismissal of charges on technical grounds or to exploit other avenues of defense.

The area in which defense counsel had the greatest influence and the greatest freedom, however, was in the cross-examination of prosecution witnesses. At a murder trial in 1740 the reporter noted that "the prisoner was allowed Council by the court, who cross-examined the evidence. . . ."[117] That aspect of the defense, the area in which a prisoner on his own was likely to be at his weakest, developed fully thereafter. If counsel were not free to address the jury directly, they could at least cast doubt on a prosecutor's or witness's evidence as to the identity of the prisoner

[115] Cottu, *Administration of Justice in England*, p. 88.

[116] S.A.P., Summer 1759, p. 3 (Angel). At an earlier session of the Surrey assizes (in 1740) one defense counsel was allowed to make a long statement to the court—beginning, "May it please your lordship and you gentlemen of the jury"—in which he outlined the defense his client would offer. He may have been allowed this latitude by the judge because his client (most unusually in a robbery case) was a gentleman. The case is included in the printed account of the assizes in S.A.P., Summer 1740, pp. 4–8 (Greenwood), but that report does not disclose the full scope of defense counsel's work. That can be seen in the full account of the trial published as a separate thirty-two page pamphlet, *The Trial of Bartholomew Greenwood, Gent . . .* (1740). In a case at the quarter sessions, defense counsel managed to talk effectively about the prosecution's evidence under the guise of discussing a point of law. He was interrupted by the prosecuting counsel in the course of the speech with the complaint that he was in fact "observing on the evidence" (*The Trial of Humphrey Finnamore, Esq.* [1779], pp. 9–11).

[117] S.A.P., Lent 1740, p. 8 (Miller).

or the goods stolen; they could soften the effect of a prior confession by questioning the circumstances under which it had been obtained; they could question the prosecutor's motives when he stood to benefit from a large reward. In general, counsel could force the prosecution onto the defensive—and with particular effectiveness in cases in which blood money would be paid for the conviction of men who were on trial for their lives. Every witness in such cases was open to a searching examination of his motives in giving evidence, an examination of a kind that few prisoners could have mounted on their own and that went beyond the kind of questioning a judge would likely have thought appropriate. Judges had attacked certain kinds of prosecutors freely, as we have seen. Defense counsel made even greater sport with men who had been robbed by prostitutes,[118] and others who had got themselves into trouble by their own foolishness. But they not only questioned such men more vigorously and harshly than the bench might have done, they went after the blood-money prosecutors and witnesses (and there were numerous such cases in London) in a way and at a length that it is most unlikely a judge would have found possible. Private "thief-takers" and constables attached to the police offices were particularly vulnerable to the suggestion that the prosecution was being pressed for financial reasons, and they and other witnesses in such cases were often raked over by defense counsel in a way that seems to have been entirely different from the kind of questioning common before lawyers were allowed to cross-examine for the defense. We will return to the broader consequences of this developing "art of interrogation" (in Wigmore's phrase) that was increasingly brought to bear on the side of the defense as a consequence of the engagement of lawyers in the courtroom.[119]

RULES OF EVIDENCE

The increased vigor from the defense side was to have profound effects on the character of the criminal trial. Perhaps the most immediate influence

[118] See, for example, OBSP, 1787, pp. 616–22.

[119] John H. Wigmore, "The History of the Hearsay Rule," *Harvard Law Review* 17 (1904), p. 457. For this theme see Langbein, "Shaping the Eighteenth-Century Criminal Trial," pp. 123–34. It seems reasonable to suppose that one further consequence of the engagement of defense counsel was that some accused also engaged solicitors to prepare their cases, in particular to organize witnesses and make sure they were in court when the trial came on. In several trials reported in S.A.P. in which the defense was conducted by a lawyer there are signs of the case's having been prepared ahead of time, at least to the extent that witnesses were brought in to give the prisoners an alibi as well as to testify to character. See, for example, Summer 1738, pp. 7–10 (Ticknell and Downing). In the middle of the century a man convicted at the Old Bailey claimed in his petition for a pardon that he had been deprived of helpful character witnesses "by

was felt in the rules governing evidence, the kinds of evidence that might or might not be put before the jury and the weight it ought to be given. Such rules clearly did not owe their elaboration simply to the activities of defense counsel, but it does seem likely that it was their insistent objections against particular kinds of testimony that raised the issues that were then extended in other decisions and precedents and gave rise to what amounted to a law of evidence in criminal trials. In the seventeenth century there were few controls over the evidence that a criminal jury could hear, and no treatises dealing with the subject. Modern juries, on the other hand, hear only evidence that has been filtered by a system of exclusionary rules, the assumption being that they have to be protected from evidence that might be in some way prejudicial. The construction of these filters began mainly in the eighteenth century, and it was then and in the early decades of the nineteenth that a literature appeared dealing with the subject of evidence in criminal trials, a market having formed among lawyers practicing at the criminal bar.[120]

The printed accounts of the Surrey assizes are neither full enough nor numerous enough to permit a thorough study of the rules governing evidence at provincial assizes in the eighteenth century. But there are sufficient reports to make clear a growing concern by the middle decades

---

a mistake of his sollicitor" (SP 36/144, f. 148). For the possible attendance of lawyers at preliminary hearings in the eighteenth century, see chap. 6.

[120] William Nelson, *The Law of Evidence* (1717; 3rd ed., 1744), includes a brief, unsystematic chapter on evidence in criminal trials. The most widely cited text in the second half of the century was Sir Geoffrey Gilbert, *The Law of Evidence*, first published in Dublin in 1754 (London, 1756) but written earlier in the century; Gilbert died in 1726. Further editions appeared in 1760, 1769, 1777, and, enlarged by Capel Lofft, in four volumes in 1791–96. According to Holdsworth, it retained its importance throughout this period (*History of English Law*, vol. 12, p. 366). John Morgan published an *Essay on Evidence* in 1789, based on the 1777 edition of Gilbert. It is vol. 1 of his *Essays upon the Law of Evidence, New Trials, Special Verdicts, Trials at Bar and Repleaders*, 3 vols. (1789). The literature on evidence was particularly developed in the early nineteenth century. The first treatise specifically devoted to the subject of evidence in criminal cases and addressed to practitioners at the assizes was published in 1802 by Leonard MacNally, *The Rules of Evidence on Pleas of the Crown* (London and Dublin). In the preceding year Thomas Peake had published *A Compendium of the Law of Evidence*, which went into five editions over the next two decades but was overtaken by more substantial works by S. M. Phillipps, *A Treatise on the Law of Evidence* (1814; 10th ed., 1852), and especially by J. F. Archbold, *A Summary of the Law Relating to Pleading and Evidence in Criminal Cases* (1822; numerous editions). For the historical development of the law of evidence see J. B. Thayer, *A Preliminary Treatise on Evidence at Common Law* (Boston, 1898); Langbein, "Criminal Trial before the Lawyers," pp. 301–6; and idem, "Shaping the Eighteenth-Century Criminal Trial," pp. 96–105. And for a broad view of the intellectual climate within which the law of evidence developed see Shapiro, *Probability and Certainty in Seventeenth-Century England*, chap. 5. Shapiro makes the important case that the fundamental developments behind the emergence of the law of evidence as they were first embodied in Gilbert's work are an aspect of changes in thinking about the nature of evidence and the character of proof in science, religion, and philosophy in the seventeenth century.

of the century about evidence that might be thought to be in some way tainted. Hearsay evidence, for example, had come increasingly under suspicion after 1660, when doubts about the reliability and validity of the testimony of someone who could not be cross-examined were expressed in several state trials in Charles II's reign.[121] By the second quarter of the eighteenth century there had emerged the outlines of a "hearsay rule" that did not necessarily prevent such evidence from being given in court, but that did at least increase the sensitivity of judges and jurors to its dangers. Hearsay evidence continued to be received in the eighteenth century, and sometimes (if the reports from Surrey assizes can be relied on) without the judges apparently cautioning the jury about its character.[122] But by the middle of the century judges more commonly prevented its being given at all. "It don't belong to you to speak to that part," an excise officer was told from the bench as he was about to describe an arrest at which he was not present. "That is not evidence," a judge declared on another occasion when a witness offered to repeat what somebody had told him.[123] By the middle decades of the century there was also a growing reluctance to accept depositions as evidence if the deponent was not in court to be cross-examined. Hearsay remained acceptable on occasion when it illustrated and amplified other testimony, but the statements of those who were not in court to take an oath and be cross-examined were being regarded by the late eighteenth century as evidence that "cannot be admitted to prove any circumstance on the trial."[124]

There developed similarly in the first half of the century some sensitivity with regard to confessions made by prisoners before trial and entered as evidence. The confession of the prisoner in the presence of reliable witnesses was of course powerful prosecution evidence, whether it was simply introduced verbally during the trial by the prosecutor, or a constable, or some other prosecution witness, or brought in formally, having been made before a magistrate and taken down in writing. Such confessions

[121] Wigmore, "History of the Hearsay Rule," pp. 444–45.

[122] In a rape case involving a child under ten, in which the victim herself was unable or unwilling to tell the court what the prisoner had done to her in sufficient detail to prove the rape, the only evidence against the prisoner was given by a woman who said that "the girl had often declared to her, that the prisoner had abused her." I do not know whether the judge's comment on the weight of that evidence was responsible for the prisoner's being acquitted. But it is possible that he had allowed it to be given because it prepared the way for the prisoner's trial on another indictment that alleged attempted rape, a charge on which he had much more chance of being convicted on the evidence the girl was willing to give, along with this confirmation from the woman who alleged she had spoken to her about it. He was in fact convicted on this charge (S.A.P., Lent 1739, p. 22 [Bromley]).

[123] S.A.P., Summer 1739, p. 19 (Cobbing); Lent 1759, p. 7 (Edmundson).

[124] Chitty, *Criminal Law*, vol. 1, pp. 568–70.

were particularly influential when the examining magistrate or his clerk were in court to confirm the authenticity of the document, which happened occasionally but by no means invariably when a confession was introduced. [125] I have not found (in the admittedly skimpy Surrey assize reports) much concern being expressed in court before the 1730s about the way that confessions had been obtained. No doubt confessions were valued by the courts, if only because, as Langbein has pointed out, they made for speedier trials, and that was a matter of some importance when the calendar was long and the circuit schedule tight. [126] But by 1740 confessions were often scrutinized by the bench and were from time to time disallowed as evidence because they had not been made voluntarily. Inducements (in the form of promises of favor or forgiveness) or threats were frequently now held to be fatal. At the Surrey Lent assizes in 1738, the judge made a point of enquiring into the circumstances in which a confession had been given before a magistrate to ensure that it had been "voluntary, without threats or promises"; [127] and at the following Summer session a judge made such hostile comments about a confession extracted by promises in favor that he seems plainly to have induced the jury to acquit the prisoner. [128] As in this case, the consequence of confessions having been obtained by such methods depended to some extent on the judge's view of the prisoner. When he inclined toward an acquittal he could almost certainly get it by emphasizing to the jury the weaknesses of evidence so obtained.

Most often the judges appear to have left it to the jury to assign what weight they would to confessions. Even by 1740, however, they were likely in capital cases at least to prevent the reading of confessions that had been taken by a magistrate when the accused man was under oath, following the principle that a suspect should not be examined under oath since that compelled him to testify against himself. When it came to light that confessions had been obtained under those circumstances judges looked for evidence of the admission having been made before the magistrate's examination. Failing that, such confessions were not likely to be read in court, though since the discussion of that evidence went on in the presence of the jury and the fact that the prisoner had confessed was disclosed to them, it must frequently not have mattered a great deal whether the confession was actually read or not. [129]

[125] See, for example, S.A.P., Lent 1738, p. 17 (Smith); Lent 1740, p. 7 (Kerr); Lent 1745, p. 8 (Cavenaugh et al.); Summer 1756, p. 17 (Evans).

[126] Langbein, "Shaping the Eighteenth-Century Criminal Trial," p. 83.

[127] S.A.P., Lent 1738, p. 18 (Dixon and Washford).

[128] S.A.P., Summer 1738, p. 6 (Wilcox).

[129] S.A.P., Lent 1742, p. 5 (Johnson); Summer 1743, p. 13 (Scate). It was reported in the latter case that "the confession was produced; but it being taken on oath, it could not be read.

Objections against confessions obtained by force or promises of favor may not have been raised first by lawyers acting for the defense, but it is clear that counsel were ready with such objections whenever a confession was brought forward by the prosecution, since the prisoner's voluntary acknowledgment of his guilt when he was apprehended was powerful evidence in court. Such confessions convicted large numbers of defendants in this period.[130] Some "confessions" no doubt had been extorted or obtained in ways that made them less than trustworthy, especially when the prisoner was a servant and the prosecutor his master. It was a likely line of defense to question the voluntary character of a confession in these cases, and counsel took it whenever the chance arose. "The counsel for the prisoner," it was reported of a trial in 1756 in Surrey, "endeavoured to prove that she [the prisoner] was persuaded by the prosecutor to sign the confession on a promise that no harm should come on her. . . ." Had he succeeded, the report continued, it "must have acquitted the prisoner," but in fact he was not able "to prove the allegation" and she was convicted.[131]

Another evidentiary issue raised insistently by defense counsel in the eighteenth century concerned the weight that was to be attached to the testimony of accomplices who had turned king's evidence to save their own skins. Such evidence was very common in trials at the Surrey assizes from the late seventeenth century. It was then that pardons were first offered to accomplices by statute, the pardon (and commonly a reward) being granted in exchange for the evidence that would convict those who committed one of a number of specified offenses.[132] In addition, pardons were regularly offered in royal proclamations and even in private advertisements, if the victim got permission from the Crown.[133]

Both the authorities and private prosecutors actively sought the cooperation of accomplices as the most likely means of apprehending and

If it had been taken voluntarily it would have been admitted as good evidence; but the law supposes that an oath is a compulsion; and consequently that no man is obliged to swear against himself in cases where it affects his life."

[130] We will see in the following chapter that confession before a justice did not necessarily lead to conviction even when the confession appeared to be freely given; but the trials reported in the Surrey Assize Proceedings make it clear that, as one would expect, such a confession was very likely to lead to conviction by the trial jury.

[131] S.A.P., Summer 1756, p. 17 (Evans).

[132] For the statutes and offenses involved see Radzinowicz, *History*, vol. 2, pp. 40–42.

[133] Anne Markham, who owned a "toy-shop" in Fleet Street, petitioned the king when her shop was burgled and she lost two hundred pounds' worth of goods for permission to advertise the royal promise of a pardon "to any concerned in the said robbery that shall discover his accomplices, Your Petitioner having found all other means ineffectual, and being unable to sustain so great a loss" (SP 36/158, f. 108).

convicting offenders. What was offered was usually described as a pardon. But in fact, as Langbein has recently pointed out, accomplices were most often in practice granted immunity from prosecution.[134] The process by which one of a group of offenders was persuaded to become a witness for the Crown, or by which he persuaded the authorities to allow him to assume that role, frequently began as soon as one or two members of a gang of suspected offenders were apprehended. The negotiations commonly involved the victim of the offense and constables and others with an interest in seeing a successful prosecution, and must have often been conducted by means of a combination of threats and inducements. But the arrangement depended mainly on the examining magistrate, for it was his willingness to admit a suspect as "an evidence" that induced such men to confess and to act as witnesses for the Crown. The normal understanding was that in return they would not be indicted. Some men settled for less. A Surrey justice wrote to a secretary of state (about 1725) asking that

> William Luff now under sentence [of death] at Guildford, may be reprieved for transportation, upon his confession to me [when apprehended] and his discovering his two accomplices who are also under sentence at the same place. I promised to do all in my power to save him for transportation. I think it is of service to the public to encourage discoveries and is the chief inducement for this application. . . .[135]

Others who confessed also accepted transportation.[136] The usual bargain, however, was more simply immunity from prosecution and immediate freedom once the trials were over. The system depended entirely on the accused's willingness to trust the word of the magistrate, for no absolute right to nonprosecution (or to a pardon) was established in exchange for the accomplice's confession and evidence. The Crown witness, Henry Fielding said, had "no positive Title" to a discharge.[137] That point was clarified

---

[134] Langbein, "Shaping the Eighteenth-Century Criminal Trial," pp. 91–96.

[135] SP 35/64, f. 251.

[136] "John Willoughby was admitted as evidence against Solomon Harvey and James Higgs alias Hicks but he is by his own consent to be transported for [blank] years" (ASSI 35/172/5, jail calendar).

[137] Fielding, *Increase of Robbers*, p. 115. For the importance of trust in the Crown witness system see Langbein, "Shaping the Eighteenth-Century Criminal Trial," pp. 95–96. There remains something of a puzzle in the way the system worked. Langbein is clearly right that accomplices who confessed and impeached their colleagues were not pardoned but were simply not prosecuted. Yet, as he has pointed out, judges and magistrates like Mansfield and Sir John Fielding described the process as one in which the cooperative offender would earn a pardon— or "an equitable title" to a pardon, in Mansfield's phrase. It was distinctly unusual for a Crown witness to be indicted and thus to require a pardon. Was it that nonprosecution could not be

in 1775 in a King's Bench case that turned on this question. In the course of his judgment in the case of Mrs. Rudd, whose immunity from prosecution had been withdrawn when it was revealed that she had not disclosed as a Crown witness all she knew about the offenses at issue, Lord Chief Justice Mansfield said that the courts were not obliged to keep the implicit bargain that was entered into with a confessed accomplice. Indeed, he went on to commend the uncertainty the prisoner was under as a useful means of ensuring that he gave his evidence effectively. What was involved, he said,

> is a kind of hope, that accomplices who behave fairly and disclose the whole truth, and bring others to justice, should themselves escape punishment and be pardoned. This is in the nature of a recommendation to mercy. But no authority is given to a Justice of the Peace to pardon an offender, and to tell him that he shall be a witness against others. The accomplice is not assured of his pardon; but gives his evidence *in vinculis*, in custody: and it depends on the title he has from his behaviour, whether he shall be pardoned or executed.[138]

Things did indeed go wrong for some men who thought that their confession before a magistrate would ensure their freedom. Several men convicted at the Surrey assizes claimed that they had been promised they would be admitted as Crown witnesses only to find themselves indicted and their confession being used against them.[139] Others had simply been beaten to it by one of their colleagues who had confessed first (or more fully) and reserved the role of prosecution witness for himself.[140] But things also went wrong from time to time because people objected to the system, particularly when a committed and experienced offender bought himself immunity by bringing a young man to justice whom he had perhaps encouraged in the first place. Occasionally, grand juries insisted on indicting someone who expected not to be prosecuted, or trial juries balked at arrangements they found distasteful. At the trial of a woman for burglary

offered officially, and that the bargain between a magistrate and an accomplice could only be conceived as a process in which a confessed felon was in effect if not in law pardoned before trial? For Mansfield's views see Langbein, "Shaping the Eighteenth-Century Criminal Trial," pp. 91–96.

[138] R vs. Rudd: Leach, *Reports*, vol. 1, pp. 120–21; *Eng. Rep.*, vol. 168, pp. 162–63 (1775). For the significance of the Rudd case see Langbein, "Shaping the Eighteenth-Century Criminal Trial," pp. 91–96. The procedure before the judges at the Old Bailey to decide whether Mrs. Rudd should stand trial for offenses not confessed to but subsequently disclosed is reported in OBSP, Sept. 1775, pp. 493–98 (I owe this reference to John Langbein).

[139] S.A.P., Summer 1711, p. 3 (Wilson); Lent 1740, p. 5 (Flack); Lent 1742, p. 6 (Lancaster).

[140] S.A.P., Summer 1743, p. 9 (Whiting). And see Langbein, "Shaping the Eighteenth-Century Criminal Trial," pp. 87–88, on this competition.

in 1738, for example, at which her accomplice gave the crucial evidence against her, the prisoner claimed that she had been duped into taking part. The jury asked the judge to enquire into this allegation, but he declined to do so. The Crown witness system did not concern itself with questions of that sort. "That's not material," he told the jury. "Johnson is evidence and so secures herself."[141] Other opponents of the Crown witness system objected because the confessed accomplice was granted his absolute freedom and would, of necessity perhaps, return immediately to crime. It was for this reason that Sir John Fielding urged that such men be transported and not simply discharged.[142]

Despite the fears that offenders may have had about confessing, and despite the objections that were raised from time to time, the practice continued, and probably became even more common over the century. The fundamental fact was that in the absence of regular police and detective forces, immunity from prosecution (along with the offer of rewards) gave the authorities their only means of securing evidence, especially against members of gangs.[143] At the Surrey assizes convictions were regularly obtained by such means. In the second half of the eighteenth century more than three men and women a year on average were discharged "by proclamation" at the conclusion of the Surrey assizes after giving evidence, and it is likely that numbers of others acted as Crown witnesses without requiring to be formally discharged. As a judge said in 1775, the discretionary power of magistrates to select Crown witnesses who would escape indictment and punishment was "part of the criminal justice of the nation."[144]

The central question with regard to such evidence was not so much

---

[141] S.A.P., Lent 1743, pp. 3–4 (Sims).

[142] Sir John Fielding, *A Plan for Preventing Robberies within Twenty Miles of London* (1755), p. 11.

[143] As Hawkins said, "If no accomplices were to be admitted as witnesses, it would be generally impossible to find evidence to convict the greatest offenders" (*Pleas of the Crown*, vol. 2, p. 432). In his judgment in the case of Mrs. Rudd, Mansfield observed that "there is no doubt, if it were not absolutely necessary for the execution of the law against notorious offenders that accomplices should be received as witnesses the practice is liable to many objections" (Leach, *Reports*, vol. 1, p. 120; *Eng. Rep.*, vol. 168, p. 163 [1778]).

[144] OBSP, Sept. 1775, p. 497. The figures for the "discharge by proclamation" of Crown witnesses in Surrey were obtained from the Circuit Agenda Books (ASSI 31), in which in some periods the reasons for such discharges are specified. The pattern of appearances of such witnesses was very uneven: in some sessions there were none, in others as many as four or five. Altogether, in a total of twenty-nine sessions in the years 1771–75, 1782–84, 1786–87 and 1796–1800, in which the reasons for discharge are given, forty-seven men and women were labeled as "evidences." This merely suggests a minimum number of Crown witnesses acting at the Surrey assizes in these years, for the printed Proceedings make it clear that some men who do not appear among those discharged by proclamation at the conclusion of the session had given evidence as accomplices against their former associates.

whether it should be received but whether it required corroboration. It is difficult to tell from the entirely unofficial reports of the trials at the Surrey assizes how commonly the single evidence of an accomplice was sufficient to convict a prisoner. Clearly much depended on the offense. In coining trials there was no circumstantial evidence arising from a victim's testimony against which the inherent plausibility of the single evidence of an accomplice could be assessed by the jury, and such uncorroborated evidence was not likely to succeed in court. [145] In property cases at the Surrey assizes, juries can also be found refusing to convict on the word of an accomplice, apparently at the judge's order or on his advice. At the Summer assizes in 1738, the brief report of the trial of Abraham Coldcock for grand larceny says simply that "there being no other Evidence to affect the Prisoner, but that of Duffel Wood, an Accomplice, the Jury gave no Credit to what he said, and acquitted the Prisoner." Having reached that verdict in one case, the jury found four other prisoners not guilty at that session for similar reasons. [146] But the system relied too heavily on such testimony and strove too mightily to acquire it for uncorroborated evidence to be banned entirely. At the Surrey assizes, at least, it seems to have been generally left to the jury to decide how far such evidence should be trusted. This had been Hale's position, although he thought the courts should be cautious about such evidence, and especially in capital cases. It was his view that

> though [a *particeps criminis*] be admissible as a witness in law, yet the credibility of his testimony is to be left to the jury; and truly it would be hard to take away the life of any person upon such a witness that swears to save his own, and yet confesseth himself guilty of so great a crime, unless there be also very considerable circumstances, which may give the greater credit to what he swears. [147]

In the absence of fuller trial evidence than can be drawn from the printed reports from Surrey, it would be dangerous to assert that such "considerable circumstances" were not established in any particular trial in which an accomplice provided the main evidence leading to conviction (for the reporter may simply have left it out). But it is not difficult to find cases in which the corroboration *appears* to have been weak at best, as, for example, in the case of a woman who prosecuted six Irishmen for robbery but could identify only one in court; five of them were convicted

[145] John Styles, " 'Our Traitorous Money Makers,' " in Brewer and Styles, eds., *An Ungovernable People*, p. 228.

[146] S.A.P., Summer 1738, p. 6 (Coldcock), p. 10 (Proctor), p. 19 (Fossett et al.).

[147] Hale, *Pleas of the Crown*, vol. 1, p. 305.

when the sixth described the robbery very briefly and implicated them all. There was apparently no other evidence. Perhaps the fact that there were three other indictments pending against them was sufficient corroboration.[148]

It is not possible to draw firm conclusions from what are generally very brief reports about the way the Surrey assizes were dealing with accomplice evidence in the middle of the eighteenth century. Langbein has found evidence that a "mandatory corroboration rule" was being observed at the Old Bailey by the 1750s under which judges were directing juries to find not guilty verdicts when accomplices' testimony was not corroborated by some independent evidence.[149] Certainly, Henry Fielding's complaints about the timidity of the courts in this matter suggest that such a rule was being followed. It was not only troublesome and dangerous to apprehend gangs of robbers, Fielding told the readers of his *Enquiry* into the recent increases of crime in London (1751), it was also difficult to get them convicted after they were brought before the courts because their victims could rarely swear positively to their identity and the judges would not accept the uncorroborated evidence of confessed accomplices: "Though the Evidence of the Accomplice be ever so positive and explicit, nay ever so connected and probable, still, unless it be corroborated by some other Evidence, it is not sufficient."[150]

Whether the judges at the Surrey assizes were similarly insisting on mandatory corroboration in the 1750s and directing juries to acquit when it was not forthcoming is not at all clear from the scraps of evidence in the Surrey Proceedings. In the 1738 case quoted earlier the jury was said to have given "no credit" to the accomplice's evidence, as though they had made up their own minds about it—or at least as though they had not been directed to take this view by the judge. Other acquittals were worded in a similar way at that session: "There being no other evidence to prove the fact upon the prisoner but Richard Nicholas an accomplice, the jury acquitted him."[151] And in two cases in 1751, the year in which Fielding's *Enquiry* was published, accomplices gave what appears (from brief reports) to have been the only evidence against the accused on trial. The trial of two men for burglary was summed up in a few lines as follows:

Thomas Percival, who called himself an accomplice, gave the court and jury no room to doubt but that he had a hand in the fact: but the prisoners each had a good character given them;

[148] S.A.P., Lent 1738, pp. 6–8 (Moylon et al.).
[149] Langbein, "Shaping the Eighteenth-Century Criminal Trial," pp. 96–100.
[150] Fielding, *Increase of Robbers*, p. 111.
[151] S.A.P., Summer 1738, p. 10 (Proctor), p. 19 (Fossett et al.).

his account against them gained no credit with the jury, they were acquitted.[152]

It is possible, of course, that this accomplice's evidence was in fact corroborated and that that is why the judge allowed defense evidence to be given and why he left it to the jury. Some doubt is thrown on that, however, by the fact that the accused in this case had been committed to trial solely on the evidence of the accomplice.[153] In another case at that same session the accused man also defended himself against what appears to have been mainly the testimony of an accomplice.[154]

It remains an open question whether judges at the Surrey assizes in the middle decades of the century were instructing juries to acquit in the face of uncorroborated accomplice evidence. All one can say about the brief reports in the Surrey Assize Proceedings is that they do not reveal such a rule in operation, and that the scraps of evidence they do provide seem to point to the court continuing to follow Hale's advice, that is, that the testimony of accomplices should be treated with caution but left to the jury to decide how much credibility it should be given. That was certainly the practice endorsed by the judges when they were asked to pronounce on this question in 1788. The issue was brought to a conference at Serjeants' Inn by Mr. Justice Buller, following the conviction of two highwaymen at the Somerset assizes solely on the evidence of a third man who had confessed and had been admitted as a Crown witness. The judges agreed unanimously that

> an accomplice alone is a competent witness; and that, if the Jury, weighing the probability of his testimony, think him worthy of belief, a conviction supported by such testimony alone is perfectly legal. The distinction between the competency and the credit of a witness has been long settled. If a question be made respecting his competency, the decision of that question is the exclusive province of the Judge; but if the ground of the objection go to his credit only, his testimony must be received and left with the Jury, under such directions and observations from the Court as the circumstances of the case may require, to

[152] S.A.P., Summer 1751, p. 30 (Young and Brown).
[153] QS 2/6, Mids. 1751, 156, jail calendar.
[154] This was the case of James Turpin, indicted for stealing a load of logwood valued at over sixteen pounds from a ship in the Thames more than two years before the trial took place. The only evidence reported in the brief printed account was presented by a man acting as Crown witness. Again, the accused brought evidence to prove that he had in fact bought the wood, and he was acquitted (S.A.P., Summer 1751, p. 33).

say whether they think it sufficiently credible to guide their decision on the case.[155]

If the force of an accomplice's evidence turned on his credit as a witness (as well as on the general corroboration of what he said by other circumstances surrounding the offense), the prisoner with defense counsel was plainly in a better position than the man defending himself alone. Counsel might not have been able to prevent such evidence from being given, but they might throw some doubt on it if the accomplice's character could be blackened and his motives emphasized. At the Old Bailey in 1788, to take one example, an accomplice was asked the following questions by the counsel for one of two men on trial after he had implicated the two prisoners in a burglary:

How long have you been a thief?   *About a twelvemonth.*

How long is it since you were tried at Chelmsford?   *In July last.*

That was for striking a man?   *No, I was taken up for a robbery; I was six months in gaol in Chelmsford.*

You improved there, I suppose, very much; how many robberies did you plan in that gaol?   *None, I never planned robberies in gaol.*

How many have been executed for robberies you planned in Chelmsford gaol?   *I never plan robberies in gaol. . . .*

These two rewards will be better than the robberies?   *I do not expect to get nothing.*

Upon your oath did not you think you should forfeit your life for this robbery which you committed singly, if you had not hooked in some other person as a companion?   *I never did a robbery alone.*

You turned evidence to save yourself from being hanged?   *Yes.*

There was in fact a good deal of other evidence against one of the prisoners, and none against the other. Despite his counsel's efforts the first was convicted, though of a lesser charge than burglary, while the second was acquitted.[156]

[155] R v. Atwood and Robbins: Leach, *Reports*, vol. 1, pp. 464–66; *Eng. Rep.*, vol. 168, pp. 334–35.

[156] OBSP, 1788, pp. 261–62.

The credit of prosecutors and of their witnesses was frequently attacked by defense counsel whenever a reward was to be paid upon the conviction of the accused. The possibilities of collusion were too obvious to be left unexplored in court, especially perhaps when the evidence against the prisoner was particularly strong. "Have you never heard that there is a reward, if these men are convicted," counsel asked one witness who had identified his clients as the men who had robbed her father and mother. "I did not come upon that," she replied. Twice more, each time a little more insistently, he asked the same question with the same result. And then more vigorously: "But you must come upon it before I have done with you. . . . You must give me an answer, or my lord will be obliged to commit you to Newgate. . . . Have you not heard Mr. Hetherington [a thief-taker] and your father talking about the reward?" until at last she confessed that she had in fact come upon it.[157]

The disadvantages of the system of rewards became particularly apparent toward the end of the century, when it is likely that a significant number of accused charged with serious offenses had defense counsel. Patrick Colquhoun made this point in 1796. The payment of large rewards upon conviction tends to weaken the prosecution's evidence, he said,

> since it is obvious that the Counsel for all prisoners, whose offences entitle the prosecutor and officers to a reward, generally endeavour to impress upon the minds of the jury an idea that witnesses who have a pecuniary interest in the conviction of any offender standing upon trial, are not, on all occasions, deserving of full credit, unless strongly corroborated by other evidences; and thus it is that many notorious offenders often escape justice.[158]

Other and broader questions touching the competence rather than the credit of witnesses were raised in the eighteenth century in the course of the more active defenses being mounted by counsel. Not all were raised for the first time, but such questions as the circumstances under which a woman might give evidence against her husband or whether a child might testify in court and under oath or questions surrounding evidence given by the deaf and dumb and by non-Christians were actively discussed and considerably clarified in the course of the century.[159]

It is thus my impression that apart from the more skillful cross-examination that defense counsel might conduct, the engagement of law-

[157] OBSP, 1788, p. 477.
[158] Colquhoun, *Police of the Metropolis*, p. 222.
[159] For these subjects see the discussion in Chitty, *Criminal Law*, vol. 1, pp. 588–608.

yers on behalf of some prisoners over the second two-thirds of the eighteenth century began to shift the focus of the defense in a fundamental way by casting doubt on the validity of the factual case being presented against the defendant, so that the prosecution came increasingly under the necessity of proving its assertions. The notion was strengthened that the matters put in issue by the prosecution would have to be fully demonstrated before there could be a case to answer.[160] The involvement of counsel brought an elaboration of the rules under which trials were conducted and tended to shift the burden of proof from the prisoner to the prosecutor—to encourage the mental shift that is embodied in Sir Richard Phillips' *Golden Rules for Jurymen* (1820) in which he exhorts jurors to be careful in their judgments, to give the benefit of the doubt to the accused, to weigh all the evidence carefully, to guard against overbearing judges, and to regard the prisoner as innocent until he has clearly been proved guilty, that onus being squarely on his accuser.

One consequence of the increased vigor of defenses in the second half of the eighteenth century was that the balance in the courtroom tilted a little in the prisoner's favor. Not everyone, predictably, thought this a good thing. Sir John Hawkins, the Middlesex magistrate, said in 1787 that one of the reasons men were reluctant to report crimes and to go to court was the likelihood that when they got to trial their witnesses "may be entangled or made to contradict themselves, or each other, in a cross examination, by the prisoner's council."[161] And the numbers of defense counsel at work in the courts and the scope allowed them encouraged Patrick Colquhoun to favor a system of public prosecution. The balance between the two sides in court, he thought, had swung too far in favor of the prisoner.[162] Whether, of course, the engagement of counsel on the defense side had had any effect on the verdicts that juries were likely to reach is another matter. But that they had changed the dynamics in the courtroom and were by 1800 transforming the "old" mode of trial is beyond doubt.

We have run some risk in this lengthy discussion of the introduction of lawyers into criminal trials in the eighteenth century of overemphasizing and exaggerating changes going on in the courtroom. Even in 1800 at the Old Bailey something like seven out of every ten defendants, including many on trial for their lives, apparently had no counsel to assist them. Over the long period we have been dealing with, the vast majority of men and women tried at the Surrey assizes had made their own defenses. And

---

[160] For an elaboration of this theme see Langbein, "Shaping the Eighteenth-Century Criminal Trial," pp. 123–34.

[161] Sir John Hawkins, *The Life of Samuel Johnson* (1787), p. 521.

[162] Colquhoun, *Police of the Metropolis*, pp. 24, 245–46.

if few of them had managed to put forward a strong argument against the charges and if fewer still had addressed the jury to effect, they had not been left without defense of any kind, for many had brought on character witnesses whose testimony, as we will see, was taken seriously by both juries and judges. Their testimonials were given after the other witnesses had been heard, and when their brief evidence was taken the trial came to an end. The judge then customarily turned to the jury and charged them to find their verdict.

THE PACE OF TRIAL[163]

Only rarely did judges find it necessary to sum up for the jury. That became more common when lawyers began to play a larger role in trials, for their examinations and cross-examinations tended to produce more evidence and to make its implications less clear-cut. Cottu reported the judge at the provincial assizes in 1820 remaining "almost a stranger to what is going on" during the trial but taking notes so that he could provide the jury with a summary of what they had heard.[164] The chairman of the Surrey quarter sessions was also taking notes by the end of the century.[165] At both quarter sessions and assizes the chairman and the judge might well have found it increasingly necessary to sum up, but over most of the period we have been concerned with such summations had not been common except after the very occasional long and complicated trial.[166]

The dependence on the memory of the jury was more reasonable in the eighteenth century than it might appear to a modern observer because most trials were brief. Many could only have lasted a few minutes, for the point at issue was usually reached quickly, not a great deal of evidence was produced, and there was little dispute about it. Some trials, especially of murder charges and some robberies and burglaries, obviously took much longer, but a trial that lasted several hours was a matter for comment. Ordinary trials at the assizes never went beyond an adjournment. The expeditious dispatch of business at a typical session can be best illustrated by considering a meeting of the Surrey assizes for which we have both the

[163] For "the pace of trial" at the Old Bailey in the late seventeenth and early eighteenth centuries, see Langbein, "The Criminal Trial before the Lawyers," pp. 277–78, from whom I have borrowed this phrase.

[164] Cottu, *Administration of Criminal Justice in England*, p. 90.

[165] QS 2/6, Ep. 1795, 25–26: a solicitor's bill, including a fee for waiting on the chairman of the quarter sessions "for his minutes" taken on a trial.

[166] For example at the assizes, S.A.P., Lent 1738, p. 15 (Smith); Lent 1742, p. 7 (Topp). At the quarter sessions, *The Trial of Humphrey Finnimore, Esq.* (1779), p. 15.

account in the circuit "Agenda Book," which sets out the day-to-day work clearly, and the printed Proceedings, which provide some indication (without reporting the cases in any sense fully) if any of the trials were particularly complex and time-consuming. These sources overlap for seven sessions of the Surrey assizes, and I take the first of these, Summer 1751, by way of example.

The session began on Thursday afternoon, 16 August, with the opening of the commissions. The court then adjourned until Friday morning at 11:00, when the other preliminaries were completed, the grand jury was sworn, the charge given, and several orders were issued from the bench concerning accomplices who were to be taken to testify before the grand jury. The court then adjourned for dinner and reassembled afterwards (probably at 5:00 p.m.) for a brief session in which two cases were heard. One of these trials, in which the charge was receiving stolen goods, appears from the report in the Proceedings to have involved numerous witnesses and to have taken a good deal of time. The main work began on Saturday morning, when the court met at 7:00. They began immediately with an infanticide case in which ten witnesses were heard, and then went on to a series of other felonies, all of them property crimes, in most of which the accused faced capital charges. By the dinner adjournment, at about 2:00 in the afternoon, the court had tried ten cases altogether and the jury had found their verdicts: they had acquitted the woman charged with infanticide and an accused shoplifter, found convictions on reduced charges against five felons, and convicted three others of the offense charged, two of whom would later be sentenced to death. The impression given by the reports in the Proceedings is that all but two of these trials—the infanticide and a highway robbery—were over very quickly.

The court resumed after the dinner adjournment (again about 5:00 p.m.) and dealt with four more accused felons and two misdemeanor cases, including a charge against the inhabitants of Wimbledon for not repairing parish roads, before adjourning for the day. There was of course no meeting on Sunday, but the court put in full days on Monday, Tuesday, and Wednesday of the following week (including an evening session on Monday) and dealt with a total of thirty-seven men and women charged with felonies and six with misdemeanors—in the early 1750s even the Summer calendars were long. The sessions came to an end on the Thursday when sentences were pronounced and orders were issued from the bench for the discharge of prisoners whose bills had not been found or who had not been prosecuted, and for the transference of others to face charges in other courts.

This had been a slightly longer session than most in Surrey in the eighteenth century, but the level of work seems to have been entirely typical. Altogether, fifty-four accused felons had been put on trial over four days, a level that matches the average of close to fifteen cases a day maintained at the Surrey assizes in the second half of the century. Since on most days the court met at 7:00 a.m. (occasionally earlier), adjourned for dinner at about 2:00 in the afternoon, and then sometimes resumed for an hour or two afterwards, eight or nine hours seems a likely estimate for a typical day. The trials must thus have averaged somewhere near half an hour, including the arraignment, the plea, and the jury's deliberation.[167]

ASSIZE TRIAL JURIES

Given the brevity of most trials, the jury did not often need to be reminded about the evidence it had just heard. The rapid dispatch of business was further aided by the character of the jury itself and by the way it reached its verdict. Eligibility for jury service and the process of selection were set out by statute, but there appear to have been problems getting men to attend, for parliament was called upon several times in the late seventeenth century and in the early decades of the eighteenth to find ways of compelling acceptable men to take their turns on juries. A statute of 1665 that aimed to prevent the rich and powerful from avoiding jury service and leaving it to "poorer and simpler freeholders" laid it down that jurors were to have a freehold of twenty pounds a year value and that the sheriff was to deliver to the quarter sessions every Easter the names of those deemed eligible for next year's service. That proved to be too restrictive. The qualifications were broadened in William III's reign, in a statute of 1692 by which jurors were to have ten pounds a year in freehold

---

[167] Evidence on the structure of the assize sessions is derived from the Home Circuit Agenda Book (ASSI/31), which the clerk of assize began to keep in 1748. The figure of fifteen accused dealt with per day is derived from an analysis of forty-nine sessions of the court in the years 1750–58, 1766–72, and 1792–1802. There was of course great variety. On some apparently full court days the assize jury dealt with only half a dozen prisoners, on others as many as twenty-five or thirty. On one day at the Lent assizes in 1770 thirty-five accused were tried. The average of "about fifteen" must remain an approximation because it is occasionally difficult to tell from the Agenda Book whether the court had devoted a full day to trials or only part of a day. In computing the average, I have taken account of those days that were clearly only partially given over to trials—the day on which the grand jury was sworn in and charged, for example. But there may well have been other days on which the court's time was largely taken up with other business without that being revealed by the entries in the Agenda Book.

By the end of the century the assizes in Surrey tended to begin a little later in the day than they had at mid-century. The court still occasionally opened at 7:00 a.m. in the 1790s, but 8:00 a.m. was more common and they sometimes began at 9:00. The evening session after the dinner adjournment was still beginning at 5:00 p.m. in the 1780s but moved to 6:00 in the last decade of the century.

or copyhold land or tenements or in rents, a requirement that aimed to
ensure that jurors would be drawn largely from the middling groups
between the gentry and the laboring poor, that is, from among farmers,
tradesmen, craftsmen, and other established housekeepers. To prevent
some men from escaping service it was also laid down in William's reign
that constables were to make annual lists of eligible men in their parishes
between the ages of twenty-one and seventy, and that these lists were to
form the "Freeholders' Book" from which the sheriff was to make his
selection of jurors.[168]

The problems that these statutes had addressed were clearly not easily
solved, for an Act of 1706 placed responsibility on the high constables to
ensure that the constables in their hundreds actually did what was expected
of them, and laid it down that all officials were to be reminded of their
duty by the public reading of the statutes of William's reign at the
appropriate quarter sessions every year.[169] This had to be followed by other
efforts to prevent the familiar "evil practices" of unqualified men being
listed and the qualified avoiding service. A bill of 1720 failed to become
law, but an important statute that attempted to plug several loopholes
was carried ten years later.[170] In the first place, it enlarged the group of
eligible jurors by including men with long leases of twenty pounds a year
or more. The statute also established fines for nonattendance after being
summoned as a juror (of two to five pounds at the judge's discretion), and
attempted to ensure that the same men were not called too frequently ("to
prevent persons making a Trade of attending and serving on Juries," it
was said by a contemporary)[171] by forbidding men in most counties to
serve more frequently than once every two years. The sheriff was instructed
to keep a book in which each man's service would be recorded, and the
lists of eligible men were to be posted publicly within each parish. The
system by which the sheriff was to assemble jurors was changed to bring
it more in line with practice, for instead of summoning a series of juries
for specific cases known to be coming on at the next court session (panels
that generally repeated the same names), the sheriff was now to summon
one general panel of between forty-eight and seventy-two men from whom
the trial juries would be selected. To ensure fairness among those who did
appear, the statute created a system of balloting at the assizes by which

[168] 16 and 17 Chas II, c. 3 (1664); 4 Wm and M, c. 24, s. 15 (1692); 7 and 8 Wm III, c.
32 (1695–96). On jury qualification see Burn, *Justice of the Peace*, vol. 3, pp. 96–99; *The Complete
Juryman: or, a Compendium of the Laws relating to Jurors* (1752), pp. 21–33. Freeholders' Books
survive in Surrey for 1696–1703 and from 1762 on (QS 7/5/1–6).

[169] 3 and 4 Anne, c. 16, s. 5 (1704).

[170] *J.H.C.* 19 (1718–21), p. 288; 3 Geo II, c. 25 (1730).

[171] Add Mss. 33052, f. 69v.

the names of the jurors who actually would serve would be drawn from a box.

The system seems henceforth to have worked reasonably well at the assizes. The sheriff in Surrey got his "balloting box to draw jurys" and a book in which he was to keep a record of those summoned;[172] and both the grand juries and magistrates appear to have become more actively engaged in ensuring that constables made up their lists and that high constables sent them forward to the clerk of the peace.[173] Jurors were regularly fined for nonattendance unless they were excused. No further major statutes dealing with juries were found necessary in the eighteenth century. Whether it began to work simply because the law had been clarified and was being better enforced is less certain, however. Changing patterns of jury service over the period suggest that there was perhaps more to it than that.

Broadly speaking, in the late seventeenth century felonies were tried at the assizes by a series of juries that each dealt with one or more batches of arraigned prisoners. Thus one trial jury of twelve men would be chosen from those impaneled. They heard the cases of a group of prisoners, a number that could vary from one or two to a dozen or more, depending on the offenses involved and perhaps on the timing of cases coming from the grand jury. They heard those cases one after the other with hardly a pause between. When that group of trials had been completed and the verdicts given, that same jury might be sworn again to take on the next batch of arraigned prisoners; or it might give way to an entirely new jury. Occasionally, the first jury might change one or two of its members before going on to new cases, though that was less common in the late seventeenth century than it was to become in the eighteenth. Thus twenty-four or thirty-six jurors altogether were normally sworn at each sitting of the assize court; in the 1660s and 1670s the average in Surrey was just over thirty-one (table 7.4).

This pattern of jury service was beginning to change by the end of the century. There were distinctly more occasions in the 1690s when only one jury dealt with the entire calendar: that occurred at seven of the twenty sessions in that decade, as against only one in the fifteen sampled in the twenty years after the Restoration. The average number of men sworn for

[172] T 90/147, p. 56 (sheriff's cravings). If sheriffs in Surrey kept records of jury service, they seem not to have been preserved. For such records in Gloucestershire see Esther Moir, *Local Government in Gloucestershire, 1775–1800* (1969), p. 92.

[173] For constables and high constables presented and prosecuted for failing to do their duty see QS 2/6, Mich. 1751, 25; Ea. 1768, 22. For lists of freeholders submitted by constables (men qualified, they generally said, "to the best of my knowledge and belief") see QS 2/6, Mich. 1751, 9 (Town of Farnham); Ea. 1779, 2 (the Clink Liberty), and 95 (St. Mary, Rotherhithe).

TABLE 7.4

Trial Juries at the Surrey Assizes

Period	Sessions examined	Jurors Sworn	Average No. Jurors per Court Session
1660–69	7	202	28.9
1670–79	8	267	33.4
1690–99	20	450	22.5
1700–09	6	171	28.5
1710–19	12	289	24.1
1720–29	12	187	15.6
1730–39	8	131	16.4
1750–59	12	165	13.8
1760–69	20	283	14.2
1770–79	10	196	19.6
1780–89	6	148	24.7
1790–99	13	272	20.9
1800–01	4	88	22.0
SUMMARY			
1660–1719	53	1,379	26.0
1720–1769	52	766	14.7
1770–1801	33	704	21.3

SOURCES: ASSI 31/2–19; ASSI 35.

jury duty in the 1690s fell to just over twenty-two. By the 1720s this pattern had been firmly established, and through the middle decades of the century it was more common than not that the jury at the assizes would change by only one or two members (if any at all) when each batch of arraigned prisoners had been dealt with. Only very occasionally now was a new jury sworn, and then often because the judge in the *Nisi Prius* court finished his business and helped his brother judge in the Crown court by swearing a separate jury and taking some of the cases if time was pressing.[174] At the vast majority of assize sessions over the middle decades

---

[174] At the Lent 1784 Surrey assizes, for example, the trials began on a Wednesday afternoon, and between then and Saturday afternoon thirty-two indictments were dealt with by four juries before Mr. Justice Gould. At the same time, the other judge, Sir William Henry Ashurst, was hearing the *nisi prius* cases. By Friday the civil causes had all been dealt with, but the judges clearly thought that the criminal cases were taking so much time that a holdover until Monday was a distinct possibility. To speed up the trial of the indictments, Ashurst swore a jury in the *Nisi Prius* court and dealt with eleven cases. It is clear from the Agenda Book that the two judges were dealing with criminal cases simultaneously. The third jury before Gould was sworn on both

of the century the entire calendar of felons was tried by a jury that changed
by only two or three members during the course of a three- or four-day
sitting, a pattern of service that accounts for the fact that the average
number of jurors sworn rarely exceeded fifteen or sixteen.[175] This was
beginning to change again, perhaps under the pressure of the numbers of
cases, toward the end of the century. In the 1770s the average had crept
up to over nineteen. It was higher than that after 1780, and juries were
by then tending again to change as units (table 7.4).

Perhaps we might leave possible explanations of this changing pattern
of jury service for the moment, for it is worth noting first another consideration that played some part in determining who would be called to
serve on juries and who would attend: that is geography. Jurors were
summoned in disproportionate numbers from the towns and the hundreds
in which the court was sitting, presumably to ensure a good attendance.
I am not sure how the decisions were made that resulted in the imbalance
of service that is shown in table 7.5. There was no doubt a certain ran-
domness in the summoning and attendance of jurors. But it looks as though
the sheriff, or perhaps his bailiffs, not unreasonably concentrated on calling
jurors from the neighborhoods of the town in which the court was to
meet. The result was that over much of this period when the court met
in Kingston, for example, the eligible men of the town and hundred of
Kingston commonly supplied half of the jurors sworn, and many of the
remainder came from neighboring hundreds. Juries were never drawn
exclusively from Kingston or, when the court met elsewhere, from any
other part of the county. Broadly speaking, however, there was a tendency
over the period we are dealing with for a strong proportion of the assize
trial jury to be drawn from the area adjacent to the meeting place of the
court, or at least from the quadrant of the county in which it was located:
from Guildford and its immediate neighborhood when the court met there,
or at least from the western and southern parishes of the county; from
Southwark and its environs when the assizes were held there; and similarly
in other places.

Friday morning and Friday afternoon, and the fourth on Saturday morning and Saturday afternoon.
It was on the Friday afternoon and Saturday morning that Ashurst took on the criminal work,
the trial of eleven accused against which the clerk noted "the following prisoners were tried
before Mr Justice Ashurst in the *Nisi Prius* Court" (ASSI 31/13, p. 352). For other occasions on
which the two judges at the assizes tried criminal cases simultaneously, see ASSI 31/13, p. 31;
ASSI 31/14, p. 215.

[175] The juries at the Surrey Summer assizes of 1751, described earlier, were entirely typical.
Eight men sat on all the juries sworn and heard all the cases tried between Friday afternoon and
the following Thursday. Two other men began on Saturday and heard all but two. Altogether,
a total of only sixteen men served in the course of the week-long session (ASSI 31/3, pp.
53–63).

TABLE 7.5
Residences of Trial Jurors at the Surrey Assizes

A. SESSIONS HELD AT KINGSTON UPON THAMES

		Jurors' Residences								
		Town and Hundred of Kingston		Neighboring Hundreds		Southwark and Environs		Others		
Period	*Sessions Examined*	*No.*	*%*	*No.*	*%*	*No.*	*%*	*No.*	*%*	*Total*
1663–1665	3	70	78.7	7	7.9	12	13.5	0	0	89
1674–1676	3	46	47.4	4	4.1	45	46.4	2	2.1	97
1690–1701	13	142	47.2	61	20.3	66	21.9	32	10.6	301
1736–1740	9	59	46.5	44	34.7	7	5.5	17	13.4	127
1797–1800	4	4	4.4	37	40.2	10	10.9	37	40.2	88

B. SESSIONS HELD AT REIGATE

		Jurors' Residences								
		Reigate Hundred		Other East and South Surrey		Southwark and Environs		Other		
Period	*Sessions Examined*	*No.*	*%*	*No.*	*%*	*No.*	*%*	*No.*	*%*	*Total*
1677–1700	3	39	36.1	14	13.0	22	20.4	33	30.6	108

C. SESSIONS HELD AT SOUTHWARK

		Jurors' Residences						
				Environs of				
		Southwark		Southwark		Other		
Period	*Sessions Examined*	*No.*	*%*	*No.*	*%*	*No.*	*%*	*Total*
1663–1665	3	67	67.0	33	33.0	0	0	100
1674–1677	4	54	44.6	38	31.4	29	24.0	121
1690–1696	4	30	38.0	21	26.6	28	35.4	79

TABLE 7.5 *(cont.)*

D. SESSIONS HELD AT CROYDON

		Jurors' Residences							
Period	Sessions Examined	Croydon and Wallington Hundreds		Other East Surrey		Southwark and Environs		Other		Total
		No.	%	No.	%	No.	%	No.	%	
1691–1697	3	29	43.9	1	1.5	8	12.1	28	42.4	66
1797–1799	2	25	61.0	14	34.2	2	4.9	0	0	41

E. SESSIONS HELD AT GUILDFORD

		Jurors' Residences							
Period	Sessions Examined	Guildford and Neighboring Parishes		Other West and South Surrey		Southwark and Environs		Other		Total
		No.	%	No.	%	No.	%	No.	%	
1661	1	12	100.0	0	0	0	0	0	0	12
1700–1701	2	13	24.5	20	37.7	13	24.5	7	13.2	53
1738	1	3	23.1	10	76.9	0	0	0	0	13
1798–1800	2	0	0	37	100.0	0	0	0	0	37

SOURCE: ASSI 35.

The burden that this placed on a limited pool of eligible jurors might have been spread if the court had visited all centers of population equally. In fact this was not the case. In the late seventeenth century fully half of the sessions of the assize court were held in Kingston upon Thames (particularly the Summer sittings) and a quarter at Southwark. The remainder took place in Guildford and Croydon, though the court also met occasionally at Reigate and Dorking (table 7.6). In the eighteenth century the sessions were even more concentrated, for the regular meetings at Southwark were for some reason discontinued in 1700 (oddly, because that is where the county jail was). The burden was shifted mainly to Kingston, where over the first half of the century the court met for at least one of the two annual sessions and sometimes for both, with the others shared largely between Guildford and Croydon. After 1757 what had been a more random arrangement settled into an unvarying pattern, for the Lent assizes

TABLE 7.6
Place of Meeting of the Surrey Assizes

Period	Sessions Examined	Place of Meeting					
		Southwark %	Kingston upon Thames %	Guildford %	Croydon %	Reigate %	Dorking %
1660–1697	Lent: 28	54	36	4	4	4	
	Summer: 31		71	13	13		3
	Total: 59	25	54	9	9	2	2
1700–1756	Lent: 43		65	21	12	2	
	Summer: 45		76	16	9		
	Total: 88		71	18	10	1	
1757–1799	Lent: 30		100				
	Summer: 29			52	48		
	Total: 59		51	26	24		

SOURCE: ASSI 35.

were held exclusively thereafter at Kingston, and the Summer sessions alternated regularly between the other two Surrey assize towns.

These patterns of meetings and of juror recruitment not surprisingly encouraged and reinforced the practice of repeated jury service that, as Cockburn has revealed, had been common for some time. Cockburn has found that, depending on the county, between a third and a half of the men sworn for jury service at the Home Circuit assizes in the reign of Elizabeth served on more than one panel.[176] The same phenomenon can be found in the late seventeenth and eighteenth centuries, though my data on this point are not strictly comparable to Cockburn's, because I have counted as repeated service attendance at more than one session of the court whereas his figures are based on the number of times a juror was sworn on a separate panel. In the eighteenth century a man could easily appear on two or three panels at one session, but unless he returned to the jury at a subsequent meeting of the court I have not reckoned this as repeated service. By this more restricted view, the vast majority of jurors at the assizes—three-quarters over most of the period, rather more toward the end—were sworn for jury service once only. But a significant number were called frequently enough that some members of every trial jury in the eighteenth century had served before. Some were very experienced indeed. On average, more than a third of the members of every trial jury

[176] Cockburn, *Assize Records: Introduction*, table 7.

had seen previous service, at least until the last decade of the century, when the average appears to have fallen sharply (table 7.7). The Jury Act of 1730, which had attempted among other things to reduce the incidence of repeated service, did not have any noticeable effect on the average number of experienced men on each jury. Nor was it enforced absolutely stringently: at least eight men in the 1750s and 1760s, for example, served on more than one jury within the two-year limit the Act laid down. (Other men who served frequently fell into a pattern of attending every third year or so through this period, and that may have been encouraged by the statute. Joseph Davis, a Kingston shopkeeper, served on the assize trial jury in 1756, 1758, 1761, 1765, 1768, and 1771, always when the court met in Kingston; and several other men followed similar patterns.)[177]

That a third or more of every trial jury consisted of experienced men is not perhaps particularly striking on the face of it. But its significance has to be judged in the light of the way juries normally deliberated and reached a verdict, a process that as we will see was likely to exaggerate the importance of a few leaders on the jury and perhaps diminish that of

TABLE 7.7
Patterns of Trial Jury Service at the Surrey Assizes

	1690–1701		1750–1773		1792–1801	
Sessions examined	24		47		20	
Men sworn as jurrors at						
One session	298	74.3%	394	76.5%	266	85.5%
Two sessions	66	16.5	86	16.7	44	14.2
Three sessions	24	6.0	19	3.7	1	.3
Four sessions	7	1.8	7	1.4		
Five sessions	4	1.0	6	1.2		
Six sessions	1	.3	3	.6		
More than seven	1	.3				
Total individuals sworn	401		515		311	
Total juror "appearances" (T)	567		699		357	
First-time appearances	401		515		311	
Repeaters (R)	166		184		46	
Average number of repeaters per jury ($\frac{12R}{T}$)	3.5		3.2		1.6	

SOURCES: ASSI 31/2–19; ASSI 35.

[177] Based on the jury panels in ASSI 35/190–209.

the majority. The significance of previous service should also perhaps be judged in the light of the more general experience that jurors typically brought to the court.

The burden of jury service at the Surrey assizes was carried apparently by fewer and fewer men after the Revolution and into the eighteenth century. Does this mean that parliament had failed to remedy the evils identified at the Restoration of too many rich men escaping service by paying off the bailiffs, and of juries thus composed of their poorer neighbors and indeed of men not fully eligible? If that had been the case, it is odd that no further remedies were sought by statute after 1730. In fact it seems to me likely that the larger aims behind the parliamentary effort had been achieved by the early eighteenth century, and that concentration of service is a measure not that poorer and weaker jurors were being exploited but that sufficient men of the solid middling groups that parliament and the judges wanted to see on the juries were coming regularly. That is certainly the impression given by the lists of eligible jurors drawn up by the parish constables, which were headed by the gentry but made up mainly, as one would expect, of tradesmen and craftsmen and farmers. The jurors actually impaneled were broadly men of this latter type.[178] That mere description, of course, tells one nothing of their wealth and status, but an investigation of one small sample of assize trial jurors in the 1690s and in the second quarter of the eighteenth century suggests that for the most part they were in fact men of some significance in their communities, members of the broad middling ranks of respectable masters and employers.

In the 1690s, thirty-seven men from the Borough of Kingston upon Thames served on at least one trial jury. Of these, twenty-nine can be identified in the town records.[179] They were mainly tradesmen and craftsmen: a glazier, a cooper, a blacksmith, a mealman, a tanner. Most significant, they were also men who occupied other positions of authority and influence in the government of the town and the hundred, the manor, and the parish. During the years in which they sat as jurors (some several times), virtually all twenty-nine of these Kingston men filled such im-

[178] Those eligible for jury service can be found in the Freeholders' Books (QS 7/5/1–6); those impaneled are on jury lists included among the records kept by the clerk of assize in the "felony" and "general" files in ASSI 35.

[179] The following paragraphs are based on the rich records of the Borough of Kingston upon Thames that I was able to consult in the Surrey County Record Office through the kindness of the Borough archivist. The following classes were the most useful: KB1 (minutes of the Court of Assembly); KB12 (elections and appointments of Borough officials); KE (records of the Borough justices, sessions of the peace, coroner and market sessions); KF (manor court); KG (parish records). An excellent guide to these records is provided by the *Guide to the Borough Archives* (Kingston Borough Council, 1971), prepared by Anne McCormack.

portant local positions as high constable and headborough, overseer of the poor, surveyor of the highways, and churchwarden. In addition, some took their turns as searcher of the market or aleconner, as bridge warden and paving warden; they served on the vestry, on the coroner's jury, on the manor court jury; they were officials of the three trading companies in the town; they served on the Borough quarter sessions' grand and trial juries and on the hundred jury. Some of them held such posts several times over and moved from one to the other through many years of engagement in local affairs.

It is notable that few of these men attained the highest positions in the government of the town. Only one became a bailiff, the head of the corporation, and only three were ever members of the highest governing body, the court of assembly. That sense of their being solidly among the middling men of the town but not members of the elite who could aspire to the highest posts is confirmed by the (very approximate) indication of their wealth that is provided by assessments for the payment of local rates. In an assessment in 1697, for example, twenty-five of the assize jurors were included among the 345 citizens rated, and they fell largely in the middle ranks of the Kingston population as a whole. If one divides the population into five assessment ranks, few of the jurors are to be found in either the lowest or the highest categories. For the most part they are in the middle and lower middle groups.[180]

Fifty years later the same kinds of men, many of them clearly the descendants of the men in our sample from the 1690s, were sitting on the assize trial juries at the Surrey assizes. They continued to be tradesmen and craftsmen of the town and small property owners. They also continued to bring to their service at the assizes experience of the workings of local government and of a wide range of decision-making on juries at the manor court, at coroners' inquests, at the local Borough sessions.[181] They remained thus men in the middling ranks of local society, men of moderate wealth and secure social standing who manned the principal organs of local administration and for whom service on the trial jury was one aspect of the broader exercise of local governance.

If these small samples from one part of the country turn out to be typical of the trial jurors who served at the assizes through the century (and only a thorough study of a larger group of jurors could confirm that),[182]

---

[180] Surrey Record Office, KD9/4.

[181] Thirty-four men from Kingston sat on the trial juries at the Surrey assizes between 1736 and 1751. Of them at least twenty also held some kind of local office.

[182] It is possible that the corporate life of a borough provided a wider range of offices and placed more demands on its inhabitants than a rural parish might have done, and thus it is possible that these small samples of Kingston jurors exaggerate the extent to which assize jurors

it is clear that the twelve men who dealt so rapidly with large numbers of cases were not entirely unprepared for the task. What effect their experience on previous juries and in office-holding might have had on their verdicts is obviously a difficult question, but it is not unimportant that once the trials began and ten or more accused were arraigned together, the jurors were not likely to have been as confused in the rush of business as many of the prisoners surely were.

QUARTER SESSIONS TRIAL JURIES

If there was little difficulty in getting jurymen to attend the assizes in the eighteenth century, which seems to have been the case, it must have been because such service enhanced a man's standing as a respectable local citizen. It is possible that the prestige of the assize jury was enlarging in the decades after the Restoration because of the changes that made the grand jury, as we have seen, the preserve of the gentry and of those among the merchants and manufacturers and clergymen who could aspire to membership in the commission of the peace. Tradesmen, skilled craftsmen, small masters, and working farmers were no longer called to the grand jury in the 1680s and after as they might have been earlier. They were shut out by an aspect of the oligarchical narrowing of power that, it has been argued, went on apace in political and social life in the late seventeenth and early eighteenth centuries.[183] If their exclusion from the grand jury and their restriction to service on the trial jury raised the prestige of the latter body, that would explain why some men were willing to serve on the jury through entire sessions of the court and to serve often. If some men were "making a trade" of jury service, as Hawles complained in 1680 and as was said in explanation of the clause in the Act of 1730 that limited frequency of service,[184] the attractions were more likely to have been the confirmation of local prestige and standing that came with participation at the assizes than monetary rewards. The fact that fewer and fewer jurors were required for entire sessions of the court seems to confirm that.

That is a possible view of the jury at the assizes. It would fit the

---

in general were drawn from the group of local notables who largely ran their communities. That this is not the case is suggested by the work of Cynthia Herrup and Peter Lawson, both of whom find men of a similar character and similar experience on assize juries in the late sixteeth and early seventeenth centuries (Herrup, "The Common Peace," pp. 206–10; Lawson, "Lawless Juries" [forthcoming]).

[183] J. H. Plumb, *The Growth of Political Stability in England, 1675–1725* (1967), pp. 66–97.

[184] Sir John Hawles, *The Englishman's Right* (first ed., 1680; reprint of 1771 ed. in 1844), p. 72; Add Mss. 33052, f. 69v.

quarter sessions juries in Surrey less well over much of the eighteenth century. There was no sharp distinction between the kinds of men who served on the trial juries at the assizes and quarter sessions—as there was clearly between the trial jurors and grand jurors at the assizes. In some counties in the early seventeenth century, men apparently served indifferently on the trial juries in each court.[185] That was not unknown in Surrey at the end of the seventeenth century and in the eighteenth, but something of a distinction in status was apparent by then, and (though I have not done the full-scale study that would confirm this) it seems clear that jury service at the assizes was reserved for older and more experienced men. The nine men from the town of Kingston who can be identified as having served at both the assizes and the quarter sessions in the 1690s generally had been called first to the quarter sessions; another half dozen men saw service on the trial jury at the Borough sessions before being called to sit on the jury at the assizes. There was no invariable rule of succession, however. Many men served at the quarter sessions who would not be called to the assizes, and distinctions between the juries had clearly emerged by the eighteenth century, when complaints continued to be made with some frequency about the poverty and low status of jurors at the quarter sessions in Surrey but not about those at the assizes.[186]

That unqualified men were called to the Surrey quarter sessions is hardly surprising considering the way trial juries were assembled in that court. An extraordinarily cumbrous and complex system survived well past the middle of the eighteenth century and virtually ensured that the objectives of the statutes passed from 1665 to 1730 would be defeated. That system depended essentially on the calling to each session of the court of

---

[185] For the degree of overlapping service on the Home Circuit see Cockburn, *Assize Records; Introduction*, chap. 6. Cockburn shows that the degree of overlap varied a good deal from county to county. Lawson confirms that it was very low indeed in Hertfordshire ("Lawless Juries"). For Cheshire, where it was very common in the first half of the seventeenth century, see Morrill, *Cheshire Grand Jury*, pp. 19–20.

[186] For the complaint of a Richmond magistrate that two men had been called for jury service at the quarter sessions in 1731 whom he knew to be unqualified, see QS 2/6, Ea. 1731, 31. For a similar complaint, QS 2/6, Ep. 1737, 19. From time to time men who had been summoned petitioned the quarter sessions to be excused from jury service because they were not "housekeepers" or were too poor to attend (QS 2/6, Mich. 1724, 74; Ep. 1726, 22; Ep. 1737, 19). And employers similarly may be found writing to the clerk to get their servants excused; one farmer wrote to the clerk on behalf of a man who "works in my barn" and who "is a very poor fellow and has a great family and not able to bear the charge of attending" (QS 2/6, Ep. 1739, 35). There were complaints in the middle of the eighteenth century about the grand jury at the quarter sessions, too, because it was said that some of the high constables (who made up the grand jury) hired deputies who were often "poor, illiterate men" and "unfit to serve." The court ruled in 1750 that only those who were high constables in their own right could be allowed to serve on the grand jury (QS 2/1/18, p. 104).

a jury of presentment of twenty-four men from each of the hundreds of the county and from three towns, three liberties, and two manors. In addition, the high constables were called, as we have seen, to form the grand jury, and the constables of Southwark were also always called to form another jury if need be.[187] Altogether this could have resulted in the attendance of seventeen juries of presentment and a total of over four-hundred men, plus the constables. In the 1660s the juries more or less took it in turn, so that the hundreds and towns close to the place of the session would send juries and those more distant might not, though this was not apparently carefully controlled or consistent. The pattern in the years immediately after the Restoration was for seven or eight juries to appear, generally made up of about twenty men, so that a group of about 150 jurors assembled in the courtroom when the panels were called over. Unless they actually had a presentment to make, and few did, this was mainly a charade, for all, that is, except what came to be known as the "home jury," the jury of the town or the hundred in which the court was meeting, for those men formed the pool from which the trial juries would be chosen. Several juries were called, dozens of men were forced to attend on pain of being fined, and then all but two dozen were dismissed within a few hours of the beginning of the session. Perhaps the juries of presentment had once played a more active role, but there are few signs of that in 1660.

That means of finding a trial jury was still functioning in its essentials in the middle of the eighteenth century. Let us take as a random example the Michaelmas session in 1751 at Kingston.[188] On the opening day of the session the following juries were present: Brixton (twenty-four men); Lambeth (nineteen); Woking (twenty-one); Copthorne and Effingham (eighteen); Wallington and Croydon (eighteen); Godly (twenty-three); Kingston and Elmbridge (nineteen); and Manor of Southwark (twenty-two). A total of 186 jurors assembled. They were called over, and after them the high constables (who would form the grand jury); the customary Acts were read, and the chairman gave his charge. There was then an adjournment until 5:00. When the court reassembled, all the jurors were discharged except the nineteen men from Kingston and Elmbridge, who were ordered to return two days later at 10:00 in the morning to act as the trial jury for the prisoners at the bar and those who had entered traverses at previous sessions.

A system that required so many jurors to be assembled in court

---

[187] For the precepts summoning the juries and the returns made to the writs see the *Surrey Quarter Sessions Records*: for example, the Michaelmas session in Oct. 1661, *Surrey Quarter Sessions Records*, 1661–63, pp. 82–87.

[188] QS 2/6/7, Oct. 1751.

undoubtedly forced the sheriff's officers to call at least a few men who were not strictly qualified for jury service; hence the complaints in the first half of the century about the low status of some quarter sessions jurors. This seems not to have been recognized in the court as a particularly serious problem until after 1748, when the quarter sessions took on a much increased load of criminal cases. That new burden, which both sharply increased the seriousness of the court's criminal work and required that additional adjourned sessions be held at Southwark, clearly revealed weaknesses in the court's procedures, including the way trial juries were assembled. The magistrates patched up a means of finding juries for the four adjourned sessions they found it necessary to hold in the early 1750s,[189] and they made efforts then and some years later to insist that only qualified men be called for jury duty.[190] But the new burdens on the court led in the late 1760s to a much more fundamental rationalization of the order of business and of the way that juries were summoned.

Before this reorganization of their work, the quarter sessions in Surrey had not made a strict separation between the kinds of business they transacted. It is true that the first day had customarily been devoted to calling over the juries and reading the charge, the second to a variety of administrative business, including appeals, and that on the third the trials had generally begun. But the court might continue to deal with administrative matters to the end of the session interspersed among the jury trials. Thus at the Michaelmas session in 1751 after one case had been heard by the jury the court discussed a rating problem, went back to a series of assaults and petty larcenies, and then made an order concerning the inhabitants of Richmond.[191] This muddling of business was altered a little by a decision of the court in 1754 that appeals would be dealt with only if they were entered with the clerk before noon on the first day, to prevent them from being pressed forward chaotically throughout the session.[192] But the clearest reorganization came in 1767 when at the Midsummer sessions the magistrates decided that for the future they would deal with business in sequence: they would listen to appeals on the first afternoon and follow

[189] The four adjourned sessions being held in Southwark in the early 1750s clearly placed a great burden on the constables and eligible jurors of the Borough. The problem of assembling a grand jury for the adjourned session was solved by drafting the petty constables of Southwark, an arrangement that paralleled the well-established convention that the high constables of the county formed the grand jury at the quarter sessions. The trial jury was to be formed from "one of the Juries [of presentment] near the Borough," and those jurors and the Southwark constables were excused from their regular attendance at the ordinary sessions of the court (Loseley Mss. 1067/2 ["Case of the Southwark Juries"], and see QS 2/1/18, pp. 294, 331).

[190] QS 2/1/18, p. 368; QS 2/1/21, p. 236.

[191] QS 2/2/7, Oct. 1751.

[192] QS 2/1/18, p. 466.

with the trial of traverses, the trial of prisoners at the bar, and only then with the county business.[193]

This reorganization was followed by an effort to improve the quality of the juries by changing the ways they were assembled. A committee of justices meeting in Guildford in July 1769 declared that the practice of calling half a dozen or more juries to the quarter sessions was "unnecessary and an oppression upon the county" and "that two jurys only were requisite for the purposes of the said session." The magistrates went on to recommend that in the future the sheriff be asked to return two juries, "having regard to the quality and condition of the said jurys the one being to be considered as the grand jury, the other as the traverse [i.e., the trial] jury."[194] This was adopted by the court. A copy of the precept used by the Berkshire magistrates was obtained so that the Surrey sheriff could be properly instructed to institute this new system.[195] Twenty-four men were then called to sit on the grand jury and twenty-four to provide the trial jury for the traverses and the prisoners at the bar. Both were increased to thirty-six in 1771, when it was discovered that twenty-four did not provide sufficient margin, "what with allowing the excuses that are made for some, the real illness of others and the non-attendance of many returned on the panel,"[196] but in fact so far as the trial jury was concerned the quarter sessions aimed in essence to form a jury of twelve that would deal with most of the cases. The other administrative reorganization of the session went forward, too. It was ordered in 1770 that all recognizances be returned to the court on the first morning of business as against the customary second day so that the prisoners could all be tried together and early in the session.[197]

One of the aims of this reorganization of the quarter sessions had been to get jurors who were securely in the property-owning class. Under the new system the sheriff was ordered to have "regard to the quality and condition" of the jurors he called, and it would appear from the pattern of service by the end of the century that this aim had been largely fulfilled. In the last decade of the century the Surrey quarter sessions still met in four different towns throughout the year: the Epiphany session in January was invariably held in Southwark, commonly with an adjourned session

---

[193] QS 2/1/21, p. 451. It is perhaps significant that such a sense of separateness had developed in each of the sessions of the court (magistrates tending to go to the session closest to their residence) that the order was made simply for the Midsummer sessions. It was not until 1770 and 1771 that the other three sessions followed suit (QS 2/1/22, pp. 492–93, 532, 556).

[194] QS 2/6, Mids. 1769, 38; QS 2/1/22, pp. 304–5.

[195] QS 2/6, Mich. 1769, 22.

[196] QS 2/1/23, p. 33.

[197] QS 2/1/22, p. 456.

in February because of the press of criminal business at that time of year; the Easter session was held at Reigate; the Midsummer session at Guildford, generally in July; and the Michaelmas session at Kingston upon Thames in October. Each meeting of the court drew on a separate pool of jurors in the familiar pattern but with a distinct difference in this period between Southwark on the one hand and the other quarter sessions towns on the other. In the years 1792–99, 144 men were summoned from Southwark and neighboring parishes in the hundred of Brixton. Only ten of them served at more than one session, none at more than two in those eight years. They did tend to remain on duty through the whole session—four or five days or more—and commonly returned to serve at the adjournment in the following month. This was heavy duty and perhaps explains why, having once served, men were not likely to be called back in the immediate future. And of course there was a large population of qualified men in this corner of Surrey by the 1790s.

In the other three quarter sessions towns trial jury service conformed to a different and older pattern. Either because there were fewer eligible men available or because in a smaller town jury service was regarded by some men as a confirmation of their local standing and was deliberately sought, many fewer individuals were called to the quarter sessions in Reigate, Guildford, and Kingston in the 1790s (fifty-five, sixty-two, and fifty-nine respectively), and they served much more frequently than men in Southwark. In each town roughly half the jurors sworn between 1792 and 1799 served at more than one session. One man in Guildford was on the quarter sessions trial jury five years out of the eight, and four others served four times; in Reigate and Kingston several men served on four occasions. Altogether, an average of more than nine of the twelve men on every quarter sessions trial jury in these towns between 1792 and 1799 had had previous experience of jury service.

By the 1790s the jury lists and the Freeholders' Books reveal these jurors' occupations and status, at least in the case of the Reigate, Guildford, and Kingston men (the Southwark jurors are merely given their street address). A fifth of those who served in the 1790s were described as farmers, a quarter were skilled craftsmen, and forty per cent were shopkeepers and men in retail trades—from all appearances men of some property. Yet it is striking that no more than half a dozen of the 320 men who served on the quarter sessions trial juries also served in these same years on the juries at the assizes. There remained something of a gulf between those called to each court, a gulf that I can only presume, without undertaking a thorough and finely grained study of jurors over a long period, derived from differences in wealth and local standing. If that was indeed the case, it suggests that assize jurors were more firmly than ever from within the

property-owning classes at the end of the century. Whether changes in
the social character of both quarter sessions and assizes jurors over the
course of a century and more had had any effect on their verdicts, on their
willingness to convict or acquit the accused thieves who filled out the trial
calendars in both courts, is another matter, and a question that we will
leave to the following chapter, which is concerned with verdicts more
broadly.

JURY DELIBERATION

At the quarter sessions as at the assizes, it was still the case into the late
eighteenth century that a small group of men, often no more than a dozen
or fifteen, heard all the cases over the several days the court was in session.
That helps to explain why the trials could be conducted so quickly. But
that was also made possible by the way the juries reached and reported
their verdicts.

The established practice at the Restoration was for the jury to hear
the trials of all the prisoners who had been arraigned together before
deliberating on their verdicts. The jury might thus hear as many as a
dozen cases one after the other. As an aid to their memory (since the first
case might be a little hazy by the time they reached the last) it was
recommended that the clerk provide them with a list of the prisoners'
names and the offenses charged against them.[198] Sir John Hawles, the
most influential advocate of the rights of the jury, advised jurors in the
late seventeenth century to pay strict attention to the evidence presented
in court, and even to take notes, which jurors were said to be doing at
the Old Bailey in the 1730s. Whether they did so regularly at provincial
assizes in the seventeenth century and before is another matter.[199] Under
a system in which they might hear up to a dozen cases with hardly a pause
between them, the jurors must normally have left the courtroom to deliberate. A manual addressed to clerks of assize in 1660 assumed that the
jury would retire to reach its verdicts, for it laid it down that when the
last case was completed a bailiff was to be sworn "to attend them to some
convenient place" and to keep them together "without meat, drink, fire,
candle or lodging" until they were ready to return to the court.[200]

I am uncertain whether this was indeed the practice at the Surrey
assizes in 1660, but by then or soon thereafter that system was in the

[198] *Clerk of Assize*, p. 48.
[199] Hawles, *The Englishman's Right* (1844 reprint), p. 74.
[200] *Clerk of Assize*, pp. 48–49.

process of being abandoned, and at some point in the late seventeenth century or in the early decades of the eighteenth both on the Home Circuit and on other provincial assize circuits the jury began to reach its verdict at the conclusion of each case. The new system was not adopted at the Old Bailey until 1738, when what was described as "the practice in all other courts" was accepted there too. It was announced in the press that

> yesterday at the sessions at the Old Bailey, the right Hon. the Lord Mayor, as soon as the juries for London and Middlesex were sworn, acquainted them, that the court had taken notice of the inconvenience arising from the usual method of trying prisoners there; and that it had been thought improper for the juries to sit so long, and give their verdicts on so many trials (which have commonly been twelve or more together) depending on the strength of their memories or the assistance of their notes; it was therefore thought more consistent with the justice of the court to alter the method of proceedings, and their seats were accordingly now so placed, that they might consult one another, and give in their verdict on each trial immediately. . . . The Right Hon. the Lord Chief Justice Willes and Mr. Justice Probyn, coming into court soon after, his lordship was pleased to express his approbation of the regulation made by the Lord Mayor, which he observed was agreeable to the constant practice in all other courts.[201]

The change had been delayed at the Old Bailey because it was feared that this new system "would have considerably lengthened out the session."[202] But this proved groundless. Indeed it was found that it actually speeded up the proceedings when the jury returned a verdict at the conclusion of each trial.[203]

If that was the case one reason for it is plain: juries did not often find it necessary to leave the courtroom when they had only one case to decide. When the evidence was complex or the case especially difficult they might do so. The reports of assize trials in Surrey note the jury withdrawing on several occasions: for seventeen minutes (robbery), thirteen minutes (murder), twenty minutes (murder), and six and fifteen minutes (robbery).[204] But that was distinctly unusual, and even after long trials in which a great deal of apparently contradictory evidence had been presented

    [201] *London Evening Post*, 5–7 Dec. 1738.
    [202] Ibid., 9–12 Dec. 1738.
    [203] *G. M.* 8 (1738), p. 659.
    [204] S.A.P., Summer 1740, p. 8; Summer 1742, p. 9; Summer 1743, p. 7; Lent 1756, p. 10; Lent 1759, p. 18.

juries did not invariably retire to deliberate on their verdict. In virtually every case the jury seems to have simply gone into a huddle. "Always, or nearly so," Cottu said of the practice as he found it in 1820, "they gather round their foreman, and in about two or three minutes, return their verdict. . . ."[205]

One effect of this change in the way the juries deliberated was to bring the members physically together in the courtroom. In the previous system in which they heard a number of trials and then left to discuss them, the jury appears not to have invariably sat together. The *Clerk of Assize* manual recommended simply that they "divide themselves at the Bar, some on one side, some on the other,"[206] and the juries at the Old Bailey before 1738 had clearly followed some such pattern, for the new system required that their seats be now "so placed that they might consult one another." By the second quarter of the eighteenth century at least, the jury at the Surrey assizes was sitting together. When the judge charged them to return a verdict on the case they had just heard, they must often have had a very good idea what his views were of the evidence and of the accused. They had heard his hints and his instructions. But the verdict was theirs reach and by the eighteenth century, as we will see, free of his coercion. They brought in the verdict most commonly after consulting only briefly together and without leaving the court.

How that discussion was normally conducted is unclear, but it is certain that in the two or three minutes that Cottu estimates was normal they could not review the evidence they had heard. There was neither time nor opportunity for one member of the jury to provide counter-arguments against what might appear immediately to be the majority view. How did they normally proceed, these twelve men huddled together in a crowded courtroom while the prisoner, whose life they were all too often deciding, looked on? How did they discover they were unanimous, since that was required? They took no ballots, no formal votes. There could have been little discussion. Most often the majority must simply have acquiesced in a verdict arrived at by one or two dominant figures on the jury. It is likely that the lead was normally taken by the man named as foreman and that the process of reaching a verdict involved a rapid survey to discover if his decision, and possibly that of those who sat near him, was acceptable.

---

[205] Cottu, *Administration of Criminal Justice in England*, p. 99. In some of the new courthouses built in such numbers in the second half of the eighteenth century, often within new county and shire halls, provision was made for a room in which the trial jury might retire to deliberate. The courts of justice built at York in 1774, for example, included a "jurymens verdict room" (George Richardson, *The New Vitruvius Britannicus* [1802–8], vol. 2, pls. 3–4, a reference I owe to Carl Lounsbury). How often such rooms were used is another matter.

[206] *Clerk of Assize*, p. 45.

It is here that previous experience on the jury was surely decisive, for some of those present, no doubt including the foreman, had tried dozens of prisoners in previous sessions and they would be familiar with the variety of verdicts possible under the law and that indeed had to be considered in most cases. For the jury in the eighteenth century exercised a wide discretion not only to convict or acquit the prisoner of the offense charged against him; the administration of capital statutes in particular required them to consider in each case whether the prisoner might not be convicted of a lesser, and noncapital, charge. They might get some help on this matter from the judge, but obviously some familiarity with the complications of the law was an asset that would further enlarge the influence of some jurors.

On occasion, foremen appear to have made decisions on behalf of the jury without apparently consulting the other members, in effect announcing a verdict before the trial had been completed.[207] That dominating leadership was doubtless exercised very commonly. Hawles thought that experienced men, especially the foremen, exercised a great deal of influence in the late seventeenth century, when juries were still leaving the courtroom to deliberate and vote in private. "Sometimes," he said of their discussion of these cases,

> without one serious thought, or consulted reason, offered *pro* or
> *con*, presently the foreman, or one, or two, that call themselves
> antient jurymen . . . rashly deliver their opinions; and all the
> rest, in respect to their supposed gravity, and experience, or
> because they have the biggest estates, or to avoid the trouble
> of disputing the point, or to prevent the spoiling of dinner by
> delay, or some such weighty reason, forthwith agree blindfold.
> . . .[208]

If the foreman or one or two experienced men could exercise influence in the jury-room, such leadership would be even more natural when the verdict was being reached not after deliberation in private but by twelve men in the open court.

It is worth remarking on one other aspect of the circumstances in which the juries reached their verdicts in the eighteenth-century courts: deliberation was ordinarily conducted in public and, in many courtrooms, in what must have been close proximity to the prisoner and to the spectators

[207] There are some instances in the S.A.P. similar, for example, to the report that in the trial of Tom Paine in 1792 following the publication of *The Rights of Man*, when the attorney general rose to reply to Erskine's defense submissions, the jury foreman told him that "a reply is not necessary" and the jury returned a guilty verdict (*State Trials*, vol. 22, p. 472).

[208] Hawles, *The Englishman's Right*, pp. 69–70.

and in an atmosphere not always of calm and quiet. Some of the rooms in which the Surrey assizes met appear to have been very small, and several were thought by the middle of the century to be seriously inadequate. We have perhaps been in some danger of exaggerating the dignity and order of the eighteenth-century courts and perhaps of overemphasizing their success as theater—taking the robes, full-bottom wigs, and black caps as guarantees, as it were, that the solemnity and hushed seriousness the judges would have wanted was in fact always achieved. There is on the contrary a good deal of evidence that the courts were often crowded and noisy. It was reported in the course of a murder trial in Surrey that when a statement made by the victim just before he died was to be read, the cryer "commanded a profound silence [and] the jury was desired to be very attentive," as though silence and close attention were not routinely to be expected. The jumble and confusion at the quarter sessions was such that a body of constables were regularly ordered to attend the court "with their long staves, to prevent all noise and disturbances."[209] They were also found to be occasionally necessary at the assizes, as for example in 1783 when the constables of Kingston were brought in because of the "many disorders committed during the sitting."[210] The precise nature of these "disorders" is unclear, but they had been directed principally against the jury who had been insulted "at their coming to and departure from the court."

We might discount a little the strictures of men like Martin Madan who complained about the way the "low rabble" filled the courts and about the "noise, crowd and confusion" at the provincial assizes after a dinner adjournment had allowed everyone—not excluding the jurors— ample opportunity for feasting and drinking. He was making an argument in favor of dignity and solemnity, since it did no good to condemn men to death if no one was paying attention.[211] Nor does one have to think that the jury deliberated always in a charged atmosphere to recognize that from time to time the presence of the thronging spectators and the local interest in particular cases must have weighed with the jurors as they gathered round their foreman to decide a prisoner's fate. When one re-members that the law being administered was notably harsh, that as many as a third of the defendants at the assizes were on trial for capital offenses, serious questions are raised about the verdicts that juries were reaching in this way.

---

[209] QS 2/1/18, pp. 14, 77, 148, 149; QS 2/1/22, p. 61.

[210] ASSI 31/13, p. 245. For other evidence of crowding and disorder at the assizes see Cockburn, *History of English Assizes*, p. 110.

[211] Martin Madan, *Thoughts on Executive Justice, with Respect to our Criminal Laws* (1785), pp. 85, 142–46.

CHAPTER 8

VERDICTS AND PARDONS:
DISCRETIONARY POWERS IN THE
ADMINISTRATION OF THE LAW

Not every suspect committed for trial by an examining magistrate would in
the end come before the grand and trial juries at the assizes and quarter
sessions. Some did not survive the experience of being held in jail; a few
escaped. Others were not put to their trial because the victim of the offense
or his agent did not appear in court and without their evidence there
would normally in property offenses be no case to answer. Unless the
prosecutor's absence was explained by affidavit and the trial postponed,
the judge had little choice in such circumstances but to discharge the
defendant "by proclamation" at the conclusion of the session. One or two
of the accused, on average, were discharged for such reasons at every
meeting of the Surrey assizes in the eighteenth century.[1] Others escaped
trial for reasons that are not always clear. But the vast majority of those
committed by magistrates to stand trial for felonies were charged and
brought to court, and it is with their fate that this chapter is concerned.
We will deal in turn with two subjects—the pattern of jury verdicts, and
the use of the royal prerogative of pardon to mitigate the harshness of the
law—both broad areas of decision-making that worked in complementary
ways to achieve the flexibility that characterized the administration of the
criminal law in the eighteenth century.

GRAND JURY VERDICTS

Fortunately, the court records in Surrey make it possible for us to study
the work of the grand jury as well as the trial jury. That would not be
possible in all counties, for on some assize circuits the clerks threw away
bills returned "ignoramus" and thus kept no record of the grand jury's

[1] Thirty-six men and women committed for trial in property cases were listed in the Agenda
Book as having been discharged for lack of prosecution in twenty-two sessions of the Surrey
assizes in the years 1771–75, 1783–87, and 1796–1800.

work. On the Home Circuit, however, the habit was established before 1660 of keeping rejected bills, and that remained the practice throughout the eighteenth century. At the quarter sessions, grand jury verdicts were recorded in the court's "process book."

Perhaps the most surprising point about the grand jury, considering that it heard only the evidence of the prosecutor, and that obviously in something of a rush, is that it threw out any bills at all. It did, and in significant numbers. As one might anticipate, the grand jury's willingness to find true bills varied with the offense. In some categories of crime there were so few prosecutions that little significance can be attached to the proportion found as true bills: it would not seem wise, for example, to read too much into the fact that almost ninety-two per cent of forgery accusations were found by the grand jury in Surrey, since there were only three dozen cases altogether in the sixty-one years examined (table 8.1). But in the larger crime groups that dominated the calendar session after session, particularly crimes against property and the person, the level of grand jury verdicts provides a more reliable guide to the juries' attitudes and values.

Considering the dread with which theft and robbery were regarded, it is hardly surprising that the grand juries were more anxious to send suspects in property cases to trial than those accused of offenses that were not thought to strike at a broader public interest (assault, for example). More than a quarter of the bills alleging such minor personal violence were marked "ignoramus" by the Surrey grand juries, compared with just over fifteen per cent in property offenses. Such broad categories lump numbers of offenses together that have little in common, and within each there were differences and distinctions in the levels of true bills. The Surrey juries were more ready to endorse bills in capital than in noncapital cases—though the difference was not enormous: eighty-nine per cent to eighty-three per cent (table 8.1). Among violent offenses against the person the grand juries were more encouraged to find bills in homicide than in infanticide or assault cases; and, though this is not shown in the data in Table 8.1, when faced with an allegation of assault they were naturally more inclined to indict when the complainant was a constable or another officer than a private citizen. There were even sharper differences in the grand juries' treatment of rape charges—hardly surprising, given the view of rape taken by the courts. Grand jurors did not perhaps think capital punishment too harsh a penalty for rape when the evidence was plain and unambiguous, but they clearly wanted the case to be overwhelmingly persuasive before a man was sent to trial. In Surrey they refused to indict in almost half of the (very few) cases they heard; on the other hand they were much more willing to see men go to trial for the less serious charge

TABLE 8.1

Grand Jury Verdicts in Surrey by Court of Trial, 1660–1800

Offense	Q.S. (No.) T.B.	Ig.	Total	Assizes (No.) T.B.	Ig.	Total	Q.S. % T.B.	Ig.	Assizes % T.B.	Ig.	Both Courts (No.) T.B.	Ig.	Total	Both Courts % T.B.	Ig.
Property offenses, capital				2,301	298	2,599			88.5	11.5	2,301	298	2,599	88.5	11.5
Property offenses, noncapital	2,161	440	2,601	2,147	463	2,610	83.1	16.9	82.3	17.7	4,308	903	5,211	82.7	17.3
Forgery				33	3	36			91.7	8.3	33	3	36	91.7	8.3
Fraud	142	15	157	64	11	75	90.5	9.5	85.3	14.7	206	26	232	88.8	11.2
Murder				251	44	295			85.1	14.9	251	44	295	85.1	14.9
Infanticide				45	17	62			72.6	27.4	45	17	62	72.6	27.4
Assault (and wounding)	2,730	943	3,673	602	218	820	74.3	25.7	73.4	26.6	3,332	1,161	4,493	74.2	25.8
Rape				25	20	45			55.6	44.4	25	20	45	55.6	44.4
Attempted rape	52	10	62	22	8	30	83.9	16.1	73.3	26.7	74	18	92	80.4	19.6

SOURCES: Sample and Homicide Count.

NOTE: These data represent all grand jury verdicts, including multiple indictments against an offender. The effect of including all indictments is slightly to inflate the number of individuals sent on to trial or discharged by proclamation. That seems most likely to give a fair reflection of the grand juries' work, though in fact reducing the multiple cases to one 'effective' verdict for each accused produces almost exactly the same proportion of true bills to ignoramus bills.

of attempted rape, a charge that women were obviously encouraged to make whatever had in fact happened to them.

Grand jurors were more likely to send one type of case than another to trial. They were also more prepared to indict a man than a woman accused of the same offense. In murder allegations a third of the women accused were discharged by the grand jury as against twelve per cent of the men (table 8.2). In other offenses the differences were narrower but not insignificant, since women were less likely to be prosecuted in the first place and the evidence against those who were charged—the evidence the grand jurors heard—must thus have been at least marginally more compelling than in the case of the typical accused man.

In finding true bills, the grand juries were no doubt mainly persuaded by the prosecutors' evidence. But they were clearly not unwilling to consider matters other than the narrow factual issues put to them. Neither the personal requirements of a particular prosecutor nor the broader needs of the society would have been seen as illegitimate influences on their verdicts. A Surrey magistrate did not think it improper, for example, to ask the clerk of the peace to "speak to the foreman of the grand jury in favour of the bill" when a case was to come up to quarter sessions in which he had a personal interest, and in which his own dignity and his local authority were very much engaged.[2] Prior knowledge on the part of jurymen was indeed more likely to be thought an advantage than a reason for their disqualification, for the jury was not engaged in administering the law in the interests of a narrow and abstract ideal of justice, but rather in pursuit of the more general aim of preserving order and harmony in society by a variable and personal application of the State's coercive powers.

The grand jury applied the law with discretion, and in deciding whether or not a prisoner should be sent to trial a range of concerns outside the narrow matters in issue would come into play. The nature of the charge was not unimportant; nor who the offender was. Another important influence appears clearly to have been the apparent state of crime and the need at that moment for examples to deter potential offenders. As we will see more fully when we look at the verdicts of the trial jury and the sentencing policies of the judges, the work of the grand jury fitted in this

---

[2] An inhabitant of Dorking, where Thomas Harris, the magistrate, lived, had gone around for some time saying "whatever he thinks . . . upon persons characters." Not only had he charged the keeper of the poorhouse with starving the inmates; he had gone so far as to call Thomas Harris himself "Turpin the highwayman," which it seemed to the magistrate was beyond a joke. Harris had thus charged him as a common disturber of the peace and made it plain to the clerk that his authority in his parish depended on getting this unruly man silenced. Hence his concern that the grand jury be informed privately of the circumstances surrounding the bill (QS 2/6, Ep. 1753, 53).

TABLE 8.2

Grand Jury Verdicts in Surrey Courts by Gender of Accused, 1660–1880

Offense	Men Accused (No.)			Women Accused (No.)			Men (%)		Women (%)	
	T.B.	Ig.	Total	T.B.	Ig.	Total	T.B.	Ig.	T.B.	Ig.
Property offenses, capital	1,923	240	2,163	378	58	436	88.9	11.1	86.7	13.3
Property offenses, noncapital	3,275	642	3,917	1,033	261	1,294	83.6	16.4	79.8	20.2
Forgery	32	3	35	1	0	1	91.4	8.6	100.0	0
Fraud	170	18	188	36	8	44	90.4	9.6	81.8	18.2
Murder	232	34	266	19	10	29	87.2	12.8	65.5	34.5
Infanticide	0	1	1	45	16	61	0	100.0	73.8	26.2
Assault	2,789	926	3,715	543	235	778	75.1	24.9	69.8	30.2
Rape	25	20	45				55.6	44.4		
Attempted rape	74	18	92				80.4	19.6		

SOURCES: Sample and Homicide Count (all verdicts, including multiple indictments).

way into a broader pattern of discretion in which the law was likely to be applied vigorously or leniently depending on what was thought to be the present level of crime. That was particularly true in Surrey, where an increase in prosecutions most often centered on the urban parishes in the metropolis, and many of the prisoners coming before the courts were likely to be suspected of being "old offenders" and to appear to be men who could not easily provide the court with good character witnesses. At times of rising prosecutions the grand jury in Surrey was more than likely to tighten the screws and to send more marginal cases to trial than they might have done in calmer times. In a very broad way, that is suggested by the differences in grand jury verdicts in years of war and peace. During wars, when prosecutions in Surrey were invariably at their lowest, an average of eighty-two per cent of bills before the grand jury for property offenses were returned as "true"; in peacetime, with prosecutions always at a higher level, the juries indicted close to eighty-seven per cent of those accused.[3]

This toughening of the attitude of the grand jury when crime seemed to increase—if that is indeed what it was—appears to have been encouraged as much by the fact that the increases in peacetime came generally in the urban parishes of Surrey as by the simple press of numbers. That is suggested at least by the grand juries' response to another moment of enlarging crime, on this occasion in the countryside, when in 1740–41 poor harvests and rising food prices brought distress to a considerable proportion of the rural population. In those years the grand jurors heard an increasing number of stories from prosecutors about barns being raided and sheep stolen. But many of them were landowners themselves, and they could hardly have failed to be aware of the difficulties being faced by their own tenants and their own laborers, of the struggles that so many of the rural poor must have been having to make ends meet.

It was presumably this understanding and sympathy that encouraged the grand jurors in 1740 and 1741 to discharge the cases against a much higher proportion of rural prisoners than they normally would have done. Over the whole period, rural property cases in Surrey were indicted at the rate of about eighty-three per cent by the grand jurors of both courts. Just before the harvest failure, true bills were running closer to ninety per cent of grand jury verdicts. But in 1740 and 1741, faced with increasing

---

[3] Based on the years in the Sample. In years of war the level of true-bill verdicts in the Surrey courts ranged between sixty-eight per cent and ninety per cent; in years of peace between seventy-four per cent and ninety-five per cent. In nine years of war and only three of peace true-bill verdicts fell below eighty per cent. Even more strikingly, in ten years of peace more than ninety per cent of bills were found by the grand jury in property offenses; they never reached that level during any war year.

numbers not of vagrants and ruffians from the city but with the rural poor in trouble, the Surrey grand juries found true bills in only seventy-three per cent of the cases of theft involving accused from rural parishes; that is, they threw out more than a quarter of the cases. When good harvests returned and the distress in the countryside eased, the grand juries again indicted a higher proportion of accused rural offenders. In years of distress they had been apparently willing to forgive some men and women who had acted out of necessity. They appear to have thought that at least some of the accused had been punished sufficiently by being held in jail and did not deserve to be sent on to trial, quite possibly to be transported.

I would want to make no more argument about this evidence than that it is suggestive of the influences that shaped grand jury verdicts and of the degree of discretion with which they assumed the law had to be applied. In this they were not running counter to the forces more broadly at work at the assizes and the quarter sessions. On the contrary, at every stage of the trial and in the administration of punishment, the system was shot through with discretionary powers. Indeed it could hardly have worked had it not been. In the courtroom itself the trial jurors and the judges and magistrates were also keenly aware of the character of the prisoner and of the prosecutor, and of the wider social needs to be served by their verdicts and by the penalties that would follow. The grand jury stage of trial procedure survived unchallenged to the end of the eighteenth century, despite the fact that the jury heard only the prosecutor's evidence, in part at least because judgments that took character and circumstance into account continued to be valued.

THE TRIAL JURY AND THE JUDGE

When the trial jury considered its verdict three alternatives were possible: it could find a general verdict of guilty or not guilty; or it could find the prisoner guilty of a reduced charge, what some contemporaries called a "partial" verdict, by which he was acquitted of the indicted offense but convicted of one of lesser seriousness contained within it.[4] Trial jurors thus had considerable discretionary power to tailor the application of the law as they thought necessary in particular cases. And since the law being enforced was increasingly shaped in the eighteenth century by the removal of clergy and the broadening scope of capital punishment, how they used those powers was of great consequence. Before examining the pattern of verdicts, however, we should first consider the relationship in the court-

---

[4] For the term "partial verdict" see Chitty, *Criminal Law*, vol. 1, p. 637.

room between the judge and the jury and the extent to which jurors were able to come to their own conclusions about the evidence they had heard. Given the trial procedures prevailing in the eighteenth century—the absence of counsel, the domination of the judge, the speed of the trial, and the brevity of deliberation—it is worth enquiring into the jurors' freedom to make up their own minds and the extent to which they may in fact have been led or driven to their verdicts.

The relationship of the judge and jury raises a complex set of issues, and we can merely skim the surface of this vast subject here.[5] The central question for us was the jury's right to find a verdict contrary to the judge's direction and free of his coercion. This issue had been raised sharply at the beginning of the period we are dealing with by complaints about judicial bullying, particularly by Chief Justice Kelyng on the Western Circuit in 1667, when he was alleged to have threatened and fined jurors for bringing in verdicts against his directions in a number of homicide cases and in others involving prosecutions of Quakers. Kelyng was brought to answer at the bar of the House of Commons. The issue came to a head not in parliament, however, but in the courts, when in 1670 Edward Bushel refused to pay a fine imposed on him as a juror for bringing in a verdict found unacceptable by a judge and took his case to the Court of Common Pleas. The argument against Bushel and his fellow jurors was that they had refused to find a verdict "according to the direction of the court in matter of law." The contention behind that was that there was a division of function between the jury as finders of fact and the judge as declarer of the law, and further that it was within the judge's province to deduce for the jury the legal implications of the facts they accepted as established. That contention and that view of the jury was decisively undermined by the judgment delivered in Bushel's favor by Mr. Justice Vaughan, or at least by the uses made of it by political and legal writers anxious to extend and establish the rights of an independent jury over the following decades. Vaughan's judgment was glossed and elaborated most influentially by Sir John Hawles, whose tract *The Englishman's Right: A Dialogue between a Barrister at Law and a Juryman* was published in 1680 and remained through the eighteenth century the foundation text of the ideology of jury independence and of the jury as the bulwark of English liberty.[6]

The question of the jury's right to convict or acquit the prisoner on

---

[5] For this subject see especially Thomas A. Green, *Verdict According to Conscience: Perspectives on the English Criminal Trial Jury, 1200–1800* (Chicago, 1985).

[6] For the significance of Bushel's case and Vaughan's judgment, and the uses made of it by the advocates of jury rights, especially Hawles, see the excellent account of these matters in Green, *Verdict According to Conscience*, chap. 6.

the whole matter charged against him remained an issue only in the case of seditious libel in the late seventeenth century and through the eighteenth—until that was also settled in the jury's favor by Fox's Libel Act of 1792.[7] In the ordinary trials that made up the day-to-day work of the criminal courts the jury's right to find a general verdict free of the judge's coercion was never in issue. To emphasize the legalities of the relationship between the judge and jury runs the risk, indeed, of missing both the essential harmony that existed between them most of the time and the natural authority and influence the judge exerted in the courtroom.[8] The judge's dominance was partly a result of the role he played in the absence of counsel and of the opportunities that gave him to comment on the evidence as it was being produced and to shape the testimony he was eliciting from the witnesses. Beyond that, juries were clearly willing for the most part to accept advice from the bench and indeed to accept the judge's directions when in his view the evidence was too weak to require an answer or the facts did not amount to a felony or when for some other reason he thought the matter should not be left to the ordinary verdict of the jury.[9]

Serious disagreements between the bench and the jury were perhaps most likely to occur in homicide cases, in which the jury had to decide whether a particular set of facts amounted to murder or manslaughter or to an excusable homicide, and in circumstances in which prejudice and local knowledge were deeply engaged. If in such cases or in other felonies the jury acquitted the defendant against the judge's view of the evidence, he might chide them and ask them to reconsider, he might express the

---

[7] In trials for seditious libel in the eighteenth century, in which an author, printer, or publisher was charged with composing and circulating matter that could be considered seditious, the bench continued sucessfully to insist that it was the jury's responsibility merely to decide whether the accused had published or printed the material in question while the judge ruled on its seditious character. The intent of the accused in writing or publishing and the possible seditious nature of the material were both excluded from the jury's purview, a circumstance that provoked a massive literature at a number of points over the course of the century (mainly, of course, when important seditious libel trials were staged) until the Act of 1792. On this eighteenth-century debate and the analogies drawn between seditious libel and ordinary criminal trials, see Green, *Verdict According to Conscience*, chap. 8.

[8] See on this subject generally Langbein, "Criminal Trial before the Lawyers," pp. 291, 295.

[9] Dudley Ryder records several instances in his notebooks of verdicts that had clearly been encouraged by his questioning or summing up or by his explicit direction. In one, he "directed the jury" to acquit the prisoner because the offense charged was not supported by the facts alleged. In another, in which a prostitute was charged with robbing a client, the evidence showed that the man had been very drunk and in no condition to know who had taken what from him. Ryder brought it quickly to an end and told the jury that "the case was so plain that . . . [he] supposed they would not have any doubt." The woman was acquitted (Ryder Notebook, pp. 6, 15).

hope that they would not be the accused's next victim—that they would not "hereafter complain if they received bad money," as a judge told a jury that had just acquitted a man charged with coining.[10] But in the end he would have to take their verdict if they insisted on it. Occasionally a judge dug in his heels and ordered an acquitted man to be sent to the house of correction as idle and disorderly or to be held until he could give securities for his future good behavior.[11] But such engagement on the part of the judge was rare. In homicide cases the next of kin could still institute an appeal of felony if the jury acquitted or if a convicted murderer was pardoned. The widow of a man killed with a sword in Surrey in 1757, perhaps in a duel, lodged such an appeal when his assailant was pardoned and the man charged with aiding and abetting him was acquitted by the jury. Both men were allowed bail but the case did not in fact go further because she failed to appear at the next session of the court to take it up. The appeal of felony was obsolete by the end of the century.[12]

If a jury convicted against the judge's advice and his view of the evidence, he again would have to accept their verdict if they insisted on it. In the case of a capital offense he would have no choice but to sentence the convicted offender to death, though he could overturn that sentence, if he chose to do so, by reprieving the condemned man and recommending that he be pardoned. Judges sought pardons in murder cases in the eighteenth century for men who they thought had been wrongly convicted by juries that had acted out of prejudice or that had been heavily influenced by local opinion or that had misunderstood the evidence and had insisted on convicting in the face of judicial advice that the facts could not sustain such a verdict in law. In other felonies judges can be found occasionally recommending a pardon for men convicted upon evidence that in their view was insufficient to sustain the charge.[13]

---

[10] Quoted by John Styles, " 'Our Traitorous Money Makers,' " in Brewer and Styles, eds., *An Ungovernable People*, p. 181.

[11] ASSI 35/104/7 (five men acquitted of felony but sent to the house of correction until the next jail delivery, 1663); ASSI 35/105/7 (three men acquitted of felony and sent to the house of correction until the next jail delivery, 1664); ASSI 35/135/7, jail calendar (a man acquitted of burglary declared to be a dangerous offender, to remain in jail); ASSI 35/177/7, jail calendar (Thompson and Bull acquitted of highway robbery, but "being of bad reputation must remain in gaol until they find sureties for their good behaviour").

[12] ASSI 31/5, pp. 70, 106 (Mitchell and Shuttleworth). For appeals of felony and their rarity in the eighteenth century see John Baker, "Criminal Courts and Procedure at Common Law, 1550–1800," in Cockburn, ed., *Crime in England*, pp. 17–18.

[13] Judges' recommendations for pardon in murder cases as a means of rectifying the verdict can be found at SP 36/5, ff. 76–83; SP 36/11, f. 98; SP 36/22, f. 206; SP 36/32, f. 32; SP 36/50, f. 321. And in cases involving robbery, rape, burglary, horse-theft, and sheep-stealing at SP 36/2, f. 111; SP 36/10, f. 89; SP 36/28, f. 203; SP 36/55, f. 260; SP 36/57, f. 92; SP 36/129, f. 231. For a case at the Surrey quarter sessions in which the jury insisted on convicting a

These are exceptional cases in the everyday work of the courts in the eighteenth century, however. There seems rather to have been broad agreement between the bench and jury about the purposes and procedures of the criminal law, an agreement that was surely essential if the courts were to get through as many as fifteen or twenty cases a day.

TRIAL JURY VERDICTS

The verdicts reached in the Surrey courts in the cases we have been mainly concerned with are recorded in table 8.3. Relatively few of the verdicts in assault cases have been recovered, but in any case those verdicts and the fines that so often followed conviction were commonly less significant than the private arrangement the parties had arrived at. In the case of several other offenses, so few defendants were brought to trial that it seems unwise, to say the least, to make too much of the pattern of verdicts. In property offenses, however, as in homicide and other cases of serious violence, our sources provide complete evidence of jury decisions, and our discussion of verdicts will be based largely on such cases, especially on the five thousand verdicts in property offenses.

Although one would not want to read too much into the patterns of verdicts in table 8.3, one tendency seems common in all these offenses and is perhaps unexpected: the Surrey juries acquitted a considerable proportion of the prisoners who came to trial. It has been suggested that a more "democratic" jury—a jury composed of men who did not have to satisfy a property qualification—might have convicted fewer still.[14] That is possible. But it is surely striking that juries composed for the most part of small masters, shopkeepers, farmers, and other minor property owners and employers should have acquitted so many offenders; and not simply for offenses that might be thought to pose no particular threat to their interests, such as assault or rape or infanticide, but for activities that most certainly did—forgery and fraud and malicious damage, for example. There might have been particular reasons why juries disliked convicting in certain kinds of offenses, even when they involved property in some way. Certainly it was well known by the end of the eighteenth century that jurors were reluctant to convict in forgery cases out of a dislike of the capital punish-

---

wealthy man for larceny in the face of the bench's insistence that the actions complained of did not amount to felony, see *The Trial of Humphrey Finnamore* (1779), pp. 17–33. In that case, too, the defendant received a pardon with the support of the magistrates.

[14] Douglas Hay, "Property, Authority and the Criminal Law," in Hay, Linebaugh, and Thompson, eds., *Albion's Fatal Tree*, p. 39.

TABLE 8.3

Trial Jury Verdicts in Surrey
(Quarter Sessions and Assizes Together), 1660–1800

	Number of Verdicts				Percentage of Verdicts		
Offense	*Not Guilty*	*Guilty*	*Partial Verdict*	*Total*[a]	*Not Guilty*	*Guilty*	*Partial Verdict*
Property offenses	1,782	2,571	817	5,170	34.5	49.7	15.8
Forgery	15	6	1	22	68.2	27.3	4.6
Fraud	38	40	2	80	47.5	50.0	2.5
Murder	114	57	81	252	45.2	22.6	32.1
Infanticide	34	9		41	79.1	20.9	
Assault	320	391		711	45.0	55.0	
Rape	15	3		18	83.3	14.7	
Attempted rape	10	21	2	33	30.3	63.6	6.1

SOURCES: Sample and Homicide Count.

[a] Known verdicts of *individual* accused. Verdicts in multiple indictments against one accused have been reduced to one composite verdict on the grounds that that would be the least misleading way of judging the effect of the juries' verdicts. If a man was convicted and hanged on one indictment it would not matter a great deal that he had been tried or had even been acquitted on several others. To add such acquittals to the not guilty column would be misleading. This reduction of the verdicts to one effective decision for each accused on trial helps to account for the discrepancy between the total number of verdicts in this table and the number of true bills found by the grand juries. That is further exaggerated by the fact that some of the accused pleaded guilty and by some verdicts simply being unknown.

ment that would follow,[15] and the few cases from Surrey suggest that that had been true over a long period. It was also difficult for the government to convict counterfeiters (at least those charged with treason), because the courts required not simply evidence of possession of false money but evidence that those so charged had actually possessed and used coining implements.[16]

Dislike of the law and the harsh penalties it imposed was also evident in the case of some property offenses, particularly toward the end of the eighteenth century. Such attitudes were largely confined to crimes made capital by parliament after 1689, however; and as we will see, juries were

[15] *Report on Criminal Laws* (1819), p. 54.

[16] SP 36/13, f. 19. On the difficulties of getting convictions in coining cases in the 1760s see Styles, " 'Our Traitorous Money Makers,' " p. 228.

most likely anyway not to acquit in such cases but rather, when they intended to be lenient, to find the offender guilty of a reduced charge. Dislike of the law does not appear to have been strong enough over the whole period to explain why one in three of those on charges of theft or robbery or burglary were found not guilty by the juries of propertied men. Such an acquittal rate is striking enough to raise a question about the grounds upon which the juries are likely to have acted, the standard of proof they were looking for in criminal trials.[17]

It is worth recognizing initially that not every not guilty verdict represents a judgment of the jury on the merits of the case. A number of these verdicts (exactly how many it is not, I think, possible to know) were in a sense technical acquittals. Some prisoners were acquitted, for example, because there was a problem in the way the indictment had been written or the way the offense had been charged, and the judge terminated the trial and directed the jury to acquit. The published account of the assize trials at the Lent 1715 session in Surrey notes simply that two men were indicted for stealing sheets "but the indictment being laid wrong, they were both acquitted." At another session two others were acquitted of shoplifting because there was "a fault in the indictment." And to take a third example from the published accounts of the Surrey assizes, even a man who had stolen things of great value from a ship, who had confessed before the magistrate, and whose guilt was confirmed by a good deal of other evidence was acquitted when it was revealed that the goods had been described as the property of William Blake whereas they really belonged to his brother Matthew.[18] In all these cases the indictment and the assize calendar are marked simply "not guilty": process was not quashed on a technicality; the jury accepted the judge's instruction to acquit, and the prisoner went free. It is thus possible that a larger proportion than I realize of the not guilty verdicts were arrived at by these means. Certainly there was room for objection on technical grounds against many indictments,

[17] For this subject in general see John H. Langbein, *Torture and the Law of Proof: England and Europe in the Ancien Regime* (Chicago, 1977), which, though it is largely concerned with the period before 1660, makes an important argument relevant to the eighteenth century about the relationship between the standard of proof demanded for conviction and the punishments that could follow upon it. And also Barbara J. Shapiro, *Probability and Certainty in Seventeenth-Century England: A Study of the Relationships between Natural Science, Religion, History, Law, and Literature* (Princeton, 1983), who argues (chap. 5) that important changes in the evaluation of evidence and in the standard of proof in criminal trials emerged in the seventeenth century as an aspect of wider changes in thinking about evidence and proof in science and religion and other areas of intellectual life.

[18] S.A.P., Lent 1715, p. 3 (Draper and Newman); Lent 1726, p. 3 (Goodbury and Lovel); Summer 1739, pp. 13–14 (Matthews). And on this see Radzinowicz, *History*, vol. 1, pp. 97–103.

for despite the insistence on accuracy in the drafting of bills, it is clear (in the seventeenth century at least) that technical flaws were common.[19] But the printed accounts of the eighteenth century suggest that in fact such objections were rare. On occasion judges simply swept them aside; in other cases they searched them out and brought them to the jury's attention. It is my impression that weaknesses in indictments were treated by the bench like any piece of evidence: to be exploited when it worked in the favor of a prisoner to whom they were sympathetic, and otherwise ignored.

The engagement of defense counsel undoubtedly had some effect on this aspect of trial (as it had on others). I do not have sufficient Surrey evidence to know what that effect was, but my guess is that it was of marginal importance only. For one thing, it is likely that indictments were in fact being drawn more accurately by the second half of the eighteenth century, partly because many were now being drawn by lawyers for the prosecution. This would also help to explain why so many of them became more elaborate, and in particular why offenses became commonly charged in multiple "counts"—an effort, it would seem, to ensure that if the evidence was not strong enough for the main offense the prisoner might be caught on another, and perhaps also to ensure that he not escape on a technicality. But in any case, small faults in the drafting could be changed so long as the grand jury was still in session. And even more crucially, a man who was acquitted because his indictment was faulty could in fact be indicted again (at the judge's discretion?) and so might simply be giving himself more trouble and a longer stay in jail if he objected too strenuously to a fault that was not too serious.[20]

A number of other verdicts registered as not guilty were similarly ordered by the bench. When a judge thought, for example, that a confession had been improperly obtained—the prisoner having been threatened or induced by a promise of favor to confess to the prosecutor and to a magistrate, or a prisoner having been put on oath by a magistrate and thus placed in a position of giving evidence against himself—he might disregard the impropriety if there was other strong evidence of the prisoner's guilt. But he might equally reject the confession entirely, particularly when it formed the core of the prosecution case. "The confession of the prisoner, taken before E. Baker, Esq. [a magistrate], was read," it was reported at a trial for housebreaking in 1740, "but the court not being satisfied that the said information was made voluntarily, and there being

[19] J. S. Cockburn, "Early-Modern Assize Records as Historical Evidence," *Journal of the Society of Archivists* 5 (1975), pp. 221–31, and "Trial by the Book? Fact and Theory in the Criminal Process, 1558–1625," in J. H. Baker, ed., *Legal Records and the Historian* (1978), pp. 61–66.
[20] For a case of a new trial being ordered see OBSP, Apr. 1788, p. 404.

nothing else to affect the prisoner but his own confession, the jury acquitted him." They acted in doing so almost certainly under directions from the bench.[21]

There were also cases of men turning king's evidence and yet being indicted, and some of them (though perhaps not all, for men can be found claiming that they had been duped) were acquitted by the juries under the judge's direction.[22] Similarly, some of the women tried for felonies with their husbands were acquitted because they were thought to have acted under their husbands' commands and not of their own free will. There was no absolute rule about this; each case was tried on its merits. But there was a broad assumption in a woman's favor that she might be expected to be acting by her husband's orders, so that if evidence was not produced to the contrary it is likely that judges would instruct the jury to find such a woman not guilty, especially if the offense amounted to no more than simple larceny. Women were regularly acquitted as "acting under the direction" of their husbands, as was said of one in 1745.[23] But if the evidence was plain that a woman had in fact instigated the offense or if her husband with whom she was charged was acquitted, a wife might be convicted and punished.[24] And if the offense was treason, murder, or robbery, a woman, married or not, would also be held fully responsible for her involvement. But the presumption was still very strong in the eighteenth century that a woman in company with her husband could not exercise independent judgment.

A number of prisoners were thus acquitted at the judge's direction rather than as a result of the jury's assessment of the evidence against them. How many there were it is not possible even to guess, for in the absence of full accounts of trials they are indistinguishable from prisoners acquitted in the ordinary way. There is no reason to think that the compiler of the published reports of the Surrey assizes would have paid a great deal of attention to the possible reasons for the juries' verdicts (particularly the cases that are given merely a line or two—a considerable proportion of the total especially before the 1730s), so these pamphlets do not provide a reliable guide in this area. What they do suggest, however, is that

[21] S.A.P., Summer 1740, p. 10 (Tigwell). "I cannot admit of a confession so obtained to be given in evidence," a judge said on another occasion when it was revealed that three boys had admitted to stealing only while they were being whipped as vagrants; the trial came immediately to an end at that point, and they were acquitted (S.A.P., Lent 1774, pp. 7–8 [Paterson, Hyde, and Whiffen]).

[22] S.A.P., Lent 1774, p. 14 (Stevens).

[23] S.A.P., Lent 1745, pp. 13–14 (John and Elizabeth Hood). See also Summer 1738, p. 6 (Taylor); SP 36/113, f. 39; QS 3/5/9, p. 140 (Elizabeth Jones).

[24] ASSI 35/216/7/12 (Hutton); ASSI 35/139/7/33 (Kent).

directed verdicts of not guilty were not numerous and that, even when judges had doubts about some aspects of a case, they were generally content to leave the jury to reach its verdict on broader grounds. My impression is that even if one could recover all the acquittals that might be explained by faults in the indictment or rulings by the bench, the broad picture of jury decision-making as shown in table 8.3 would not be much altered.

Juries in felony trials rarely took long to deliberate. What were they mainly looking for as they heard the evidence given on both sides? One important matter was their assessment of the character of the prisoner, and occasionally of the prosecutor. So far as the factual evidence was concerned, the juries looked in property cases for direct and positive proof of the prisoner's guilt from witnesses who seemed to be trustworthy, or strong circumstantial evidence that the prisoner would have to explain away. Direct identification on oath by the victim or an eye-witness was persuasive evidence, as was testimony that the prisoner had been apprehended with the stolen goods in his possession. In some cases juries may have had the benefit of the judge's advice on the bearing of the evidence they had heard; but even at the end of the eighteenth century, when counsel were acting more frequently for both the prosecution and the defense and were producing more extensive evidence on both sides, judges were still not routinely summing up or guiding juries through the evidence at the conclusion of the trial, though they no doubt commonly pointed the jury toward the verdict that seemed reasonable to them. After a long trial at the Old Bailey in 1784 in which Sir Thomas Davenport swore positively to the identity of a man he accused of robbing him but in which on the other side the prisoner had brought effective witnesses to provide him with an alibi, the *Gentleman's Magazine* reported that the judge merely observed

> that as the jury had been attentive to every thing that had been sworn, he should not take up their time with recapitulating the evidence. He would only remark on the great fallibility there was in swearing to the appearance of persons. Sir Thomas Davenport, who is a person of character and respectability, was no doubt convinced in his own mind that the prisoners were the persons who robbed him; yet it must be owned there had been sufficient evidence to the contrary.[25]

[25] G. M. 55 (1785), pp. 56–60. Of course, since judges had ample opportunity to comment on the evidence as it was being given, their observations and asides must occasionally have influenced the verdict. In a case in which a man accused a servant of stealing stockings from his house, Mr. Justice Thompson observed as soon as the prosecution evidence was concluded and before he asked the accused if she had anything to say that "it looks very improbable that the

Evidence that went to convict the prisoner was of course strengthened if it could be supported and amplified by the prisoner's own confession, given voluntarily before a magistrate, or the testimony of an accomplice. Confessions made at the time of arrest, taken down by the examining magistrate, and then certified by him or his clerk in court as authentic were difficult to explain away. But they were not always introduced as evidence in this formal way, and as far as one can tell from the printed accounts of Surrey trials, confessions were often simply treated as another piece of information that might or might not be decisive. Some prisoners who had confessed—according to the jail calendar, which recorded the grounds upon which they had been committed for trial—were acquitted by the jury, generally it would seem because the evidence of prosecution witnesses was sufficiently weak or inconsistent that the judge chose not to make much of the prisoner's prior confession.[26]

The evidence of accomplices was also clearly very powerful, especially when it was corroborated by the testimony of the prosecutor and his witnesses. Apart from that, the evidence that seems to have been partic- ularly persuasive to juries in the eighteenth century was the identification of the accused by the victim and by eye-witnesses under oath, especially of course when those taking the oaths were men and women of obvious good character and respectability. Beyond that, circumstantial evidence

---

prisoner should take the stockings out with her, and bring them back again, when she might have left them behind her." The servant denied the theft and brought two character witnesses, but the judge's skepticism about the charges no doubt encouraged the acquittal that concluded the case (S.A.P., Lent 1737, pp. 3–4 [Dolton]).

[26] In 1738–42, the years in which printed reports of the assize trials in Surrey are complete, seventy-five prisoners (fifty-eight men and seventeen women) were committed to trial "by their own confession," according to the jail calendars in the jail delivery files (ASSI 35). Of these, eleven men and two women were among those who eventually turned king's evidence, and they were discharged. Thirteen others either died or their fates are unknown. Of the thirty-five men whose cases went through to a verdict, more than eighty-five per cent were convicted, partly on the strength of their confession. But six were acquitted, and five of the fourteen women who had apparently confessed were also found not guilty. The reports of these trials are very brief for the most part; indeed two involving men are not even reported. But in some cases it seems that these confessions were not introduced during the trial. In the case of one of the acquitted women it is unclear why the jury reached that verdict. The other four were acquitted, it would seem, because the prosecution evidence was weak or because the jury simply wanted to find some reason to discharge this particular woman: in one case the prosecutor failed to provide identification; in another the accused's son had turned king's evidence and told a series of inconsistent stories; in another a witness thought the accused "crazy." It is less clear why the men were discharged, but in most cases it seems that the prosecution evidence did not amount in itself to a very serious charge and the jury (and presumably the judge) simply ignored the confession. Ten of these cases are included in S.A.P.: Lent 1738, p. 21 (Sission); Summer 1738, p. 20 (Digwood); Summer 1739, p. 17 (Lynch), pp. 16–17 (Fox and Keyt), pp. 13–14 (Matthews); Lent 1740, p. 7 (Huler); Lent 1741, p. 3 (Carter and Jones); Summer 1741, p. 10 (Rummells).

that pointed to the accused's guilt and that he was not able to explain and turn aside would commonly lead to conviction. It would appear from the printed assize reports in Surrey that it was the lack of direct identification of the accused or of persuasive circumstantial evidence that led to most acquittals. And of course so long as magistrates were required to send to trial any charge of felony, especially a charge made on oath, whatever the strength of the evidence, there were bound to be cases in which the evidence was fatally weak. This appears to have been particularly common in the late seventeenth century and the early decades of the eighteenth in which magistrates were still apparently narrowly constrained by the Marian bail and committal legislation. The impression given by the few printed reports from that period is that in a substantial number of trials of property offenses the prisoner was acquitted because there was in fact little case to answer beyond the merest suspicion and that that could not be brought home to the defendant in court. According to the reporter who prepared the account of the Lent assizes in 1688, for example, the dozen or more not guilty verdicts at that session followed from evidence that was "slight" or "slender" or "not positive" or "not charged fully upon the prisoner"; or that they came in cases in which the witnesses could not identify the prisoner or because "nothing appeared upon proof."[27] It was Roger North's view, in this same period, that "a criminal hath great odds to escape by trial, unless he hath very ill fortune in the circumstances of his taking," because the judges were "careful of the evidence" and required that "against life, it be almost demonstrative, which seldom happens."[28] He was exaggerating the acquittal rate (he also thought that the "law itself is mild and favourable"), but there seems no reason to doubt that juries were looking for what they could take to be positive proof before returning a guilty verdict. At the Surrey assizes in the early decades of the eighteenth century the reporters' brief explanations of why defendants were convicted were commonly that the evidence had been "full" or "plain," which most often seems to have meant that the prisoner had been identified on oath by the victim of a robbery or that he had been caught redhanded with goods near the scene of a theft and had been unable to explain how he had come by them.

Some defendants were acquitted when it became clear in court that they were victims of false charges that arose from malice or greed. Occasionally such a defendant was granted a copy of the indictment, the indispensable foundation of an action for malicious prosecution.[29] But the

---

[27] S.A.P., Lent 1688, pp. 1–3.

[28] Roger North, *A Discourse of the Poor* (written 1688; first pub. 1753), p. 27.

[29] S.A.P., Summer 1718, p. 5 (Howsley and Rigby); Lent 1745, pp. 2–3 (Badham and Curtis); Summer 1751, p. 33 (Duncomb); ASSI 31/15, p. 195.

criminal courts had long been reluctant to take a hard line in such cases, out of an anxiety not to discourage prosecutors generally. By the eighteenth century they did not grant copies of indictments freely, even when the charges were obviously malicious.[30] Such cases seem to have resulted most commonly simply in an acquittal, though on one or two occasions judges made a point by discharging the defendant as soon as the verdict was given to save him from having to wait until the end of the session, or by rescinding the fees that a discharged prisoner had to pay the jailer.[31]

The vast majority of acquittals no doubt resulted from weak evidence. Up to the 1730s in particular those who reported the trials at the Surrey assizes in the surviving Proceedings explained a considerable number of acquittals on such a basis. One cannot make too much of their view of the prosecution case as "slight" or "not positive," for such a formula, especially in what were mainly very brief reports, might well cover a myriad of circumstances and be simply a convenient shorthand. Beyond that, we are of course dealing with the reporters' *impressions* of why verdicts were given, not the juries' explanations. It thus may be in part because of a change in reporting styles, as well as the fact that the published accounts became longer in the 1730s, that one gets the impression from the Surrey pamphlets that there were fewer cases in the second quarter of the eighteenth century and after in which the prisoner was acquitted because of the obvious weakness of the prosecution case. There was surely no sudden or massive change in the evidence being presented or in the standard of proof demanded; but there seems to have been a gradual tightening up over a long period in the cases that came to trial, a gradual weeding out of weak charges as a result of the changes we have speculated were taking place in preliminary hearings by the second quarter of the century and that encouraged examining magistrates to discharge the accused when they judged the evidence to be inadequate. There is some support for the notion that the weakest cases were more likely to be eliminated at the magistrate's stage by the middle decades of the eighteenth century than a century earlier in the changing levels of not guilty verdicts in the Surrey courts over this period. In property cases acquittals were running at about forty per cent in the last four decades of the seventeenth

[30] Among the "Orders and directions to be observed by the justices of the peace, and others, at the sessions in the Old Baily" issued by a panel of judges in 1665 was included the following: "That no copy of any indictment for felony be given without special order upon motion made in open Court, at the general gaol delivery upon motion, for the late frequency of actions against prosecutors (which cannot be without copies of the indictment) deterreth people from prosecuting for the King upon just occasions" (Kelyng, *Reports*, p. 3; *Eng. Rep.*, vol. 84, p. 1056).

[31] On one occasion in Surrey the trial jury took up a collection in court on behalf of a discharged prisoner (S.A.P., Lent 1739, p. 19 [Dibley]).

century and at close to thirty-four per cent in the first forty years of the eighteenth. They held at that level, though with a good deal of annual variation over the remainder of the century.[32]

Such a change in the level of not guilty verdicts cannot, however, be attributed simply to the elimination of obviously weak cases. Too many other variables were at work for it to be as simple as that, particularly the shifting attitudes that juries were likely to take toward property offenses at different moments depending on their view of crime in general. There is the further complication that juries undoubtedly thought about their verdicts at least to some extent in light of the punishments that would follow, and since there was a sharp change in the secondary punishments available to the court in the very period in which the acquittal rate apparently fell most significantly (as we will see), that may well have encouraged trial juries to convict a larger proportion of the accused. Such an explanation is further suggested by the fact that it was partial verdicts rather than guilty verdicts that increased as acquittals diminished. On the other side, the change in the character and quality of defenses being offered in court because of the fuller engagement of lawyers in criminal trials may have had some effect on the level of acquittals over the long term. Only a minority of defendants employed counsel even at the assizes and at the end of the century, but there had occurred by then a shift in emphasis in the courtroom toward an obligation on the part of the prosecution to prove the case it was alleging (and less on the prisoner to prove his innocence), which may have been to the general advantage of all defendants. Whether the result was that some prisoners were acquitted who might have been convicted earlier is, however, impossible to say.

JURY DISCRETION: PARTIAL VERDICTS

A general verdict of guilty or not guilty of the charge in the indictment was not the only option available to the trial jury: they could also find

[32] Trial-jury verdicts in property cases at the Surrey assizes and quarter sessions (together) in four periods, male offenders only (from the Sample and the Count):

		Verdicts of the Trial Juries			
Period	Years included	Not Guilty %	Guilty %	Partial Verdict %	Number of Cases
1660–1699	18	40.5	42.7	16.8	745
1700–1739	16	33.7	41.4	24.9	884
1740–1779	40	33.0	54.1	12.7	2,384
1780–1802	23	32.7	59.8	7.5	2,891

the defendant guilty of a lesser offense. Further, the consequences of a jury conviction in capital cases could be profoundly altered by the judge's power to reprieve a condemned man and recommend that he be pardoned by the king. How juries and judges interpreted these discretionary powers and the grounds on which they acted tells one a great deal about their broader views of their duties and the function of the courts. Certainly no study of the judicial system in the seventeenth and eighteenth centuries could uncover its central devices and inner workings without paying full attention to the juries' right to find a verdict that in effect altered the charge the prosecutor had made or to the judges' right to grant a reprieve or the king's right to pardon.

One of the reasons why in the "old" trial there seems to have been little disposition to regard the defendant as innocent until proven guilty was that there was in general little apparent anxiety about guilt or innocence as abstract issues. Cottu was struck by the indifference of the English courts even in 1820 to the details of the offense and the outcome of the trial, in contrast to the French authorities, for whom, he said, "the conviction of the criminal and a knowledge of all the circumstances of the case appear like a devouring appetite."[33] The English attitude was strongly encouraged in the seventeenth and eighteenth centuries by the prevailing view of what crime was, what caused it, who committed it, and thus what its significance was, and of the related matter of the nature and purpose of the criminal law.

Hundreds of men and women in the eighteenth century faced a possible death sentence in the English courts every year because numerous offenses had been removed from benefit of clergy by Act of parliament. It is clear from the way the courts put these statutory changes into effect, however, that few men thought that all these laws needed to be rigidly enforced to serve their purpose. Even as parliament passed new statutes after 1689, the courts showed little inclination to execute men for the relatively trivial offenses they mainly dealt with.[34] The instruments of mitigation were at hand in the jury and in the royal prerogative of pardon, and together they made it possible for the law to be applied with rigor or leniency as conditions seemed to require. Jurors and judges were both agents in this manipulation; both possessed discretionary powers that

[33] M. Cottu, *On the Administration of Criminal Justice in England* (English trans., 1822), p. 97.

[34] Two men indicted of shoplifting to the value of £3.15 at the Surrey assizes in the summer of 1699 immediately following the passage of the Shoplifting Act were found by the jury guilty to the value of ten pence (on the significance of that amount see below) and ordered to be whipped; other examples were to follow in the next session (ASSI 35/140/8/10; ASSI 35/141/7/21). For an excellent discussion of jury mitigation in the eighteenth century see Green, *Verdict According to Conscience*, chap. 7.

enabled them to temper the application of the law so as to achieve a result that seemed appropriate. Cooperation and agreement between them was essential to the working of the system.

It is likely that parliament expected the law to be enforced with discretion, though that could hardly have been announced in the statutes themselves. The withdrawal of clergy from so many specific offenses provided the courts with a weapon, a tool, not a fixed set of rules, and it seems clear that in parliament as in the courts it was understood that a range of considerations beyond mere guilt or innocence would determine whether any particular offender would suffer as the statute directed or be spared by the discretionary powers exercised by the jury or the judge (and beyond the judge, the king). A personal and particularistic administration of the criminal law, especially of the capital laws, was upheld as an ideal. There was clearly no intention of hanging everyone who might have been guilty on the evidence. Equal treatment of prisoners was the ideology of the future, the cry of those inspired by the rationalism of the Enlightenment (and the evident failures of the existing system) who in the last third of the eighteenth century began to press for fundamental changes in the law and its administration. In arguing for certainty of punishment and a milder tariff of penalties applied uniformly, such "reformers" were striking, as they knew, at the fundamental premises of the "old" system, for the administration of the law in the seventeenth and eighteenth centuries relied on its selective application—some men punished one way, some another, others not at all—aiming to deter future offenders by the suffering of a few convicts selected as examples.

This view of the criminal law and of the courts and the function of punishment depended on a particular notion of crime and criminals. It depended especially on the view that men who committed the most serious offenses had been led to that by a gradual corruption of their morals, by a kind of apprenticeship in wickedness in which they proceeded from minor wrongs to the very greatest crimes and eventually reached a point at which they were beyond redemption. The slide into such a moral abyss began, it was widely believed, when men were tempted to stray from the narrow path of respectability by carousing and gaming at the alehouse, by neglecting their work, and in other ways falling into evil habits of life. Debauchery and seeking after pleasure bring men and their families into ruin, John Disney said in the early eighteenth century, and finally would bring men of all classes to the point at which they were ready "to venture upon capital crimes . . . either to relieve the poverty . . . or to open their way to new opportunities of Lust." There were many laws against excessive drinking and gambling and the rest of the corrosive temptations, "and therefore," Disney concluded, " 'tis to the Advantage of Society to have those crimes vigorously punished that these [capital offenses] might be prevented."[35]

It was indeed a constant refrain that if immorality grew apace the fault lay not with the laws but with the officials whose duty it was to put them into effect, in particular magistrates and parish constables. It was a fundamental belief over a long period of time (more emphasized at some points than others, but always at the center of thinking on such matters) that if only the laws against immorality were enforced, if alehouses could be controlled and drunkenness prevented, if fornication was punished and gambling suppressed, and if men could be properly instructed in the truths of religion, the foundations of a stable and prosperous society could be secured. Men would then be inclined to work hard and to sustain that natural obedience to their superiors that a healthy social order was assumed to rest on. One important consequence of that would be a falling away of all the serious forms of crime, for men who remained sensible of their duty and their own self-interest would be able to resist the temptations that led men into robbery and burglary and similar offenses. The magistrates in their parlors and at their sessions thus bore a special responsibility to deal with immoral and antisocial behavior. This need to pursue the petty offender was a theme of countless charges to grand juries at quarter sessions. Sir More Molyneux reminded the grand jury at the Surrey quarter sessions of this in 1740 (they had heard it many times before, even from him). "As no man is completely wicked at once," he said,

> but becomes so insensibly by a Gradation of Wickedness, which would continually gain Strength by Impunity, till the Offender loosing all sense of fear and remorse, grows hardened to the Commission of Crimes of the deepest Dye, and Capital Crimes must be attended with Capital Punishments. Therefore, Gentlemen, to prevent these Consequences, the Wisdom of the Government has provided this Court of Quarter Sessions . . . to nip Offences in the Bud and deter Offenders by gentle Chastisements into a due sense of what they owe their King, their Country and themselves, before their Offences grow too extream.[36]

This view of crime and of its relationship to morality and social order encouraged in turn particular views of the purpose of punishment, and indeed of the limits of punishment. The hope that men might be saved by chastisements, gentle or not, was largely confined to those still in the

[35] John Disney, *An Essay upon the Execution of the Laws against Immorality and Prophaneness* (1708), p. x.
[36] Loseley Mss. 1066/3, ff. 1–3.

early stages of crime, to minor offenders like vagrants, prostitutes, drunkards, petty thieves. For them and for the poor who refused to work, the houses of correction had been founded in the late sixteenth century in which they might be coerced into correcting their misbehavior. But there was as yet little conviction in the first half of the eighteenth century that more serious offenders might be "reformed." "Capital Crimes must be attended with Capital Punishments," said Molyneux; there was in the execution of the felon a recognition of the irreversible nature of his moral collapse and a confirmation of the doleful predictions of the moralists and social commentators. The execution of a thief or a robber sent a message to the broad ranks of the laboring poor as a terrible example of the consequences of falling into immoral habits and breaking the law. The gallows also got rid of the occasional individual who was permanently committed to a life of crime. But fundamentally the value of public hangings (and of course of other public punishments like whipping and the pillory) was the reminder of what eventually lay in store for those who strayed from the paths of duty and obedience. That required not hundreds of victims—for that could only have confused the message—but a few only, and a number that could be varied depending on the state of crime and the present danger to the social order. The regulation of that flow and the choice of those who would serve as examples was very much the business of the courts and the criminal trial.

There is no doubt that one consideration in the jurors' minds as they contemplated their verdict was the character of the charge being made in the indictment. We have seen that the withdrawal of benefit of clergy from property felonies took place broadly in two periods and produced what I have described somewhat artificially as two groups of "capital" crimes: the "old" offenses removed from clergy in the sixteenth century, which included the most feared and most widely regarded as serious (robbery, burglary, certain forms of housebreaking, horse-theft, and picking pockets); and the "new" offenses made capital after the Revolution of 1689 and through the eighteenth century that were mainly forms of larceny defined as serious by parliament because of the character of the offenders (servants, for example) or the place stolen from (shops, warehouses, ships, mines) or the object stolen (sheep, cattle). These two groups of offenses are not of course absolutely distinct: horses were protected by a stiffer penalty because of their value and the relative ease with which they could be stolen—the kind of argument that would lie behind many of the extensions of capital punishment in the eighteenth century—and picking pockets was not universally regarded after 1660 as deserving of hanging. The broad distinction between these two groups of offenses nonetheless holds, and it was a distinction that juries in the eighteenth century accepted.

There are two general reasons why some offenses were subject to jury mitigation more than others: juries did not think that all capital offenses deserved the death penalty; and some offenses were technically more open to manipulation than others. In the case of many of the larcenies removed from clergy, the circumstances that defined the offense were that the theft had to be from a particular place and of goods of a particular value: theft from a dwelling house of goods valued at forty shillings or more; shoplifting to the value of five shillings; and so on. The jury could thus restore clergy simply by finding the offender guilty of a theft of less than forty shillings from a house or of less than five shillings from a shop. Such mitigations had occurred before the late seventeenth century, particularly in the case of women accused of thefts of over ten shillings in value, for after 1622 women were admitted to clergy in larceny cases in which the goods stolen were under that value. Juries commonly brought women within the statutory limit by reducing the value of the theft in their verdicts. Thus a woman charged with larceny to the value of £1.8.0 at the Surrey Lent assizes in 1663 was convicted of theft of goods worth nine shillings. She was enabled to claim the benefit of the 1623 statute and was ordered to be burned on the thumb and discharged.[37] The opportunity to exercise such discretion on behalf of both men and women vastly expanded after 1689, when parliament removed many particular forms of larceny from the privilege of clergy.

Not every prisoner charged with such an offense was treated lightly by the jury, but many of those convicted of one of the more minor larcenies made capital above a certain value by the removal of clergy (the "new capital" offenses) were saved from the gallows by the jury's simply valuing the goods below the crucial line (table 8.4). Such "pious perjury" was a central element of criminal administration throughout the century, and the scale of undervaluation was frequently staggering. Law reformers gathered some of the more striking examples from the Old Bailey proceedings at the end of the eighteenth century and the first decades of the nineteenth to demonstrate the inappropriateness of the criminal law: a theft of twenty-three guineas from a house valued by the jury at thirty-nine shillings in order to bring the offense within clergy; lace valued at more than a hundred pounds in the indictment declared by the jury to be worth thirty-nine shillings; gold rings and jewelry stolen from a ship and valued by the owners at more than three hundred pounds but again found by the jury

[37] ASSI 35/104/7/21 (Draper).

TABLE 8.4

Trial Jury Verdicts in Property Cases
in Surrey, 1660–1800

Offense	Number of Verdicts	Percentage of Verdicts		
		Not Guilty	Guilty	Partial Verdict
"Old" capital offenses	1,197	36.4	46.9	16.7
"New" capital offenses	598	28.4	22.2	49.3
Noncapital offenses at assizes	1,637	35.7	45.7	18.6
Noncapital offenses at quarter sessions	1,734	34.1	64.9	1.0
All property offenses	5,166	34.5	49.7	15.8

SOURCE: Sample.

to be thirty-nine shillings' worth.[38] From Surrey they could have added watches stolen from a ship in 1776 and reduced by the jury from the fifty-six pounds in the indictment to the familiar thirty-nine shillings to bring the offense within clergy. The huge sums involved in these cases dramatize the point, but the principle underlying these verdicts could have been illustrated in any assize court in England in the eighteenth century: that the offenses removed from clergy since the Revolution were rarely so threatening in themselves that the purpose of the law could not be served by an occasional example, chosen either because the times demanded it or because the particular individual seemed to be a good candidate for the gallows.

In their manipulation of the charges, juries must normally have worked with the agreement and advice of the trial judge. Given the way verdicts were reached, with the jurors milling around their foreman for a few minutes at best, someone had to take the lead and make the suggestion that mitigation was reasonable or not in the case at hand. Of course the previous experience of several of the jurors was important here: they knew the options in all but the trickiest cases, and they would not need to be told the law. But the judge must often have reminded them briefly of the possible verdicts they might reach as the trial came to an end, and perhaps

[38] Radzinowicz, *History*, vol. 1, p. 95, n. 52.

nudged them toward a conclusion they could all agree on. Ryder reports a case from the Old Bailey of theft from a house in which the jury, he says, found the accused guilty to the value of thirty-nine shillings after he "told them that 40s was necessary to make him guilty of felony that was without benefit of clergy."[39] Other judges "recommended" verdicts, "intimated" to the jury the conclusion they themselves had reached, or merely hinted at the options the jury had before them. Richard Gough tells of a judge at the Shropshire assizes who told the jury in a case involving the theft of two dozen fowl that the evidence was such "that the matter of fact was soe fully proved that they must find the prisoner guilty, but they would doe well to consider of the value," whereupon the jury found the defendant "guilty of fellony to the value of eleven pence, at which the judge laught heartily and said he was glad to heare that cocks and henns were cheap in this country." There was no need for the judge, if this report is in fact complete, to tell this jury that a theft of under a shilling in value would make it possible for him to order the man to be whipped instead of being granted clergy, a bargain the convicted man might rather not have had.[40]

Things did not always work in the courtroom as smoothly as that. Some verdicts were redundant in that they involved the mitigation of a noncapital charge and made no difference to the punishment that would have to be ordered; others were muddled or deliberately obtuse in that, though the jury reduced the value of the goods stolen, the reduction was insufficient to restore the offense to clergy, and the judge was obliged to sentence the convicted prisoner to death.[41] Some muddled verdicts could

---

[39] Ryder Notebook, p. 11.

[40] Richard Gough, The History of Myddle, ed. David Hey (Harmondsworth, 1981), pp. 145–46. This "mitigation" may not in fact have been intended by the jury as merciful. As we will see, juries in Surrey reduced numerous grand larceny charges to petty larceny in the late seventeenth century and early decades of the eighteenth (especially before the establishment of transportation as a regular punishment) in order quite clearly to increase rather than to diminish the punishment the convicted offender would suffer. It is true that grand larceny remained technically a capital offense and that before 1706 offenders who failed the literacy test could be denied clergy. But in practice few were, and the reduction of the charge by the jury to petty larceny meant that the convicted felon would not simply be branded on the thumb and discharged but would be whipped, probably in public.

[41] Some verdicts make it seem that the jury had paid more attention to the evidence given during the trial than to the charge in the indictment. A man was indicted at the Surrey Lent assizes in 1737, for example, for grand larceny of goods worth almost seventeen pounds. This was a clergyable offense, and by that time conviction would have almost certainly brought him a sentence of transportation for seven years. The jail calendar makes it clear that the theft had taken place in a dwelling house that was also a shop, and this of course would have been revealed in the trial. This is presumably why the jury decided to reduce the value of the goods in their verdict to thirty-nine shillings, although he was not charged with a capital offense of stealing from a shop to the value of five shillings or from a dwelling house to the value of forty shillings.

be explained by the hurry of business. Given the speed of trial and of the jury's deliberation and the complexity of the law, occasional confusion would not be surprising. But some may have arisen from resistance in the jury to pressures from the bench, verdicts given in defiance of the judge's recommendations. What else could explain the verdict given in a burglary case at the Surrey assizes in 1772 in which three men were charged with breaking into a house at night and stealing sixty pounds in money? One of them was acquitted; the other two were found "not guilty of burglary, guilty of stealing in a dwelling house value £60." They were saved from hanging on the burglary charge in the entirely ordinary way, but the jury in fact seemed determined to hang them because stealing in a dwelling house more than two pounds was still nonclergyable, still capital. There is a clue perhaps to this distinctly unusual verdict in the second count, which lays the sixty pounds to be the property of thirty persons who held a club at the house in question. It was a friendly society of some sort. The jury perhaps had some local knowledge, possibly friends and relatives who had suffered. Perhaps, too, they were pressed by the judge to find a partial verdict and had stuck fast in what was an in-between land. The judge respited sentence and took it to a conference at Serjeants' Inn at which he asked the other eleven judges present whether they thought the verdict capital or not. They decided it was, and he returned at the next assizes to pass sentence accordingly.[42]

Such cases were, however, quite rare. In the main, judges and juries reached results that both found acceptable, and since those agreements meant the reduction of the charge from a capital to a noncapital offense, they were results that made a great deal of difference to the fate of numerous prisoners. The juries at the Surrey assizes reduced the charges in about a quarter of the nonclergyable property cases they dealt with over the period 1660 to 1800. Some offenses were much more likely to result in a partial

He was sentenced to transportation for seven years (ASSI 35/177/7 [King]). Another example of this kind of confusion (though it should be said they are not numerous) occurred at the Surrey Summer assizes in 1775. And other forms of muddle can be found. Occasionally, for example, the jury verdict did not quite achieve the result apparently intended, and one can find the verdict being repaired (apparently on the quiet) by the clerk. When the jury found men who had been charged with burglary or breaking and entering "guilty to the value of 39/-," they were presumably aiming to find a partial verdict that would restore benefit of clergy and save the prisoner from the gallows. But in fact their actual verdict did not do so, since it was the act of breaking that made it capital: stealing from a house above the value of forty shillings (without having broken in) was the capital offense they thought, incorrectly, they were mitigating. In at least one such case (and I think more could be found) the clerk of the court, or some other official, simply added to the indictment in a hand that makes it clear that it was after the verdict had been given, "not guilty break and enter," and judgment was given as in a noncapital larceny (ASSI 35/218/7/33 [Noy]).

[42] ASSI 35/212/8/17. R vs. Withal and Overend: Leach, *Reports*, vol. 1, p. 88; *Eng. Rep.*, vol. 168, p. 146 (1772).

verdict than others (table 8.5). This reflects differences in their seriousness; but it also derives, as we have said, from the technical ease with which mitigation could be accomplished in the case of some offenses and from its impossibility in others. It was a straightforward matter for jurors to reduce burglary and housebreaking to the clergyable offense of simple larceny if they wished to do so by finding that the offender had not broken into the premises in question, but had simply taken the goods. That lesser offense was contained within the original charge, and the ease with which the reduction could be managed helps to explain why a third of those on burglary charges and more than half of those accused of nonclergyable housebreaking were saved from a capital sentence by the jury's verdict. It is hardly surprising that they took a harder line with burglars than with those who broke into houses during the daytime. That same willingness to mitigate when the offense was relatively trivial surely explains why the Surrey juries found partial verdicts in the case of many of the property offenses made capital after the Revolution, at least when the offense was defined in such a way, by place of theft and value of goods, that reduction could be easily accomplished. There were not many prosecutions of any of these offenses, and that no doubt helps to explain why in dealing with shoplifting and thefts from houses, shops, and warehouses the juries found reduced charge verdicts in the trials of between half and two-thirds of the accused.

TABLE 8.5

Verdicts in Selected Capital Property Offenses
at the Surrey Assizes, 1660–1800

Offense	Number of Verdicts	Percentage of Verdicts		
		Not Guilty	Guilty	Partial Verdict
Robbery	444	37.2	57.7	5.2
Burglary	502	36.9	32.5	30.7
Housebreaking	177	23.7	22.0	54.2
Horse-theft	163	30.7	69.3	0
Theft from houses	201	32.3	17.4	50.3
Theft from shops or ships or warehouses	134	17.2	17.2	65.7
Theft from place of manufacture	31	32.3	45.2	22.6
Sheep-stealing	61	52.5	47.5	0

SOURCE: Sample.

Not all of the more minor capital offenses were as easily mitigated. When sheep-stealing was removed from clergy in 1741 there was some immediate willingness in Surrey juries to hang a few sheep-stealers to deter what were thought to be large numbers of offenders in the London area. But it was not because of the harshness of the jury that sheep-stealing was never reduced to a clergyable offense after 1741, but because there was no lesser offense the jury could retreat to: if the offender was found not to have stolen a sheep the whole indictment fell. In more than half the cases they dealt with, the Surrey juries entirely acquitted the prisoner— a much higher level of not guilty verdicts than can be found in other "new" capital offenses—in order presumably to save more minor sheep-stealers, or men whose guilt was not entirely clear, from the possibility of being hanged. Such difficulties also prevented the juries from restoring clergy to horse-theft; juries can be found recommending to the judge that a convicted horse-thief be reprieved and pardoned, but there was little they could do themselves short of acquitting him.[43] But perhaps the archetypically "serious" offense was robbery because it combined real danger to the victim with the loss of his valuables, and because in some of its forms it threatened free communication and therefore the commercial life-blood of the nation. Until the late eighteenth century it was widely believed that robbery could not be reduced to simple theft, and this helps to explain why such a small proportion of robbery charges resulted in mitigated verdicts of clergyable larceny (table 8.5). Even when that notion was overthrown in the 1780s,[44] the Surrey juries did not show the same willingness to save robbers from the gallows as they did lesser offenders.

In reaching their verdicts, and particularly in exercising their discretion to alter the charge laid in the indictment, trial jurors were undoubtedly influenced by a variety of considerations. The character of the defendant as well as of the offense were of prime importance. But there was also the question of the penal consequences of their verdicts: jurors could anticipate precisely the sentence that would follow particular decisions, and their willingness to mitigate capital charges must have been influenced to some extent by the punishments available to the courts as alternatives to the gallows, punishments that were to change strikingly over the century and a half after 1660. Juries thus determined not only the general issue of the accused's guilt or innocence but also, for many of those they did convict, the sentence that would follow.

For other prisoners, however, the important discretionary powers were

---

[43] For the mention of such petitions see SP 36/32, f. 66, and SP 36/53, ff. 48, 111.

[44] For men found not guilty of "violent taking" but guilty of "stealing only" see ASSI 35/223/7/13; ASSI 35/225/8/3; ASSI 35/229/7/3, 21.

not those wielded by the jury but those in the hands of the judge and the king, that is, the power to reprieve and pardon. So many offenses became punishable by hanging in the eighteenth century that, despite the juries' willingness to find partial verdicts, large numbers of men and women were sentenced to be executed. For them the possibility of a pardon was of course a crucial matter, and the post-sentencing decisions revolving around the granting of pardons became a regular and important part of the process by which the punishment of convicted offenders was determined.

REPRIEVES AND THE PARDON PROCESS

That the bench shared jurors' views of the capital laws of the eighteenth century and were willing to put some into effect and anxious to limit others can be seen in the judges' tendency to narrow the scope of the less serious offenses by strict interpretation of the statutes,[45] and in the way they exercised their own considerable discretionary power to reprieve a convicted offender and recommend him for a royal pardon. At the conclusion of the assize session the judges virtually always reprieved some of those they had condemned to death in court, a reprieve being, in Blackstone's words, "the withdrawal of the sentence for an interval of time."[46] The judge might do so if he was not satisfied with the verdict; and he would do so if a female prisoner was proved by a "jury of matrons" to be pregnant after "pleading her belly." In the latter case, the woman was to be held in jail and then hanged after the birth of her child. I am not

---

[45] In the course of the eighteenth century the courts, for example, construed the Shoplifting Act of 1699 in such a way as to exclude a number of thefts from its provisions: it was held that if the shopkeeper saw the thief taking the goods the accused could not be guilty of the non-clergyable offense of stealing "privately" in a shop to the value of five shillings; similarly there could be no stealing "privately" from a person, that is, pocket-picking, if the victim was drunk. In each of those cases the offense could only be simple larceny, which was clergyable. In the case of thefts from warehouses it was held that what was intended in the statute that removed such an offense from benefit of clergy was a theft from a place where merchants displayed goods for sale and where their customers went to view them—not a place where they were merely stored. It was also held that breaking into a house at night and stealing goods was no burglary if the owners or tenants had not yet actually moved in, for it was not then a "dwelling house." The Act that removed clergy from the offense of stealing from a ship in a navigable river was held to apply only when the theft was of goods, not money. Theft from a stable, another offense removed from clergy by the Act of 1699, was said to amount to the capital offense only when the goods stolen were usually kept in a stable and were "proper to it." For the cases involving these and other interpretations, in Foster's phrase, "in favour of life" see Radzinowicz, *History*, vol. 1, pp. 83–91, and esp. app. 1 (pp. 660–86, for offenses against property).

[46] Blackstone, *Commentaries*, vol. 4, p. 394. For the significance of pardon in general see Hay, "Property, Authority and the Criminal Law"; and Radzinowicz, *History*, vol. 1, chap. 4.

certain how many women were actually hanged after receiving such a reprieve: there is little reliable evidence to go on. It is possible that three women of eleven who successfully pleaded pregnancy in Surrey in the late seventeenth century were eventually put to death, but that is by no means clear. My sense is that few women were in fact executed after the termination of their pregnancy and that a reprieve on such grounds was likely to be tantamount to a pardon. In his thorough investigation into the functioning of the jury of matrons, James Oldham is inclined to be a little more cautious than that, but he concludes that while it was by no means automatic, a reprieve granted for pregnancy was likely to result in some form of pardon.[47]

Most reprieves were more directly for such a purpose: to allow the king to show mercy if he chose to. This was seen principally as a means of regulating the level of capital punishment so that an acceptable number of offenders would be sent to the gallows. At the same time, it was hoped that the sentence of death, the solemnity of its pronunciation, and the judge's condemnation would frighten the prisoner into obeying the law in the future. The reprieved prisoner would most often be held in jail and returned to court at a later session to plead to the pardon when it had been issued under the Great Seal.

By the late seventeenth century pardons had become a fundamental element in the administration of the criminal law. The judges submitted a "circuit pardon" or "circuit letter" at the conclusion of their assizes listing those they recommended, which when approved by the king began the process by which the pardon would be issued by the Chancery. The pardon might be absolute, in which case the prisoner would go free, as if he had been acquitted. Such pardons were often granted to those wrongfully convicted in the judge's view and occasionally to others who were thought incapable for reasons of age or infirmity of withstanding an alternative punishment. But an alternative was most commonly imposed after 1660 and was inserted into the pardon as a condition; and it was surely the development of a satisfactory sanction in the form of transportation (as well as the enlarging scope of capital punishment itself and the increasing numbers of convicts in danger of being hanged) that further encouraged the use of royal pardons and allowed it to become fully routinized by the third decade of the eighteenth century. Especially after transportation was firmly established in 1718, the judges were in effect allowed an almost free hand to choose among those convicted of capital

---

[47] James C. Oldham, "On Pleading the Belly: A Concise History of the Jury of Matrons" (forthcoming; I am grateful to Professor Oldham for allowing me to read this article in advance of its publication).

offenses who would be hanged and who sent to America for fourteen years, the condition that had become by then a virtually automatic consequence of a pardon.[48] In 1728 the judges were told to send in their lists of prisoners to be pardoned with those they wanted transported distinguished from those who deserved to be pardoned absolutely, an instruction that makes it clear that they were not required to justify these decisions, nor to send in explanations, and that their reprieve was almost certain to result in a pardon.[49]

That same letter to the judges also encouraged them not to "appoint an unusual distant time for the Execution" when they left a convict to be hanged. This was to discourage him or others on his behalf from appealing for a pardon directly to the king. But in fact such appeals could not be prevented, especially when the prisoner had family or friends to take up his case. Petitions on behalf of condemned prisoners were routed by way of the secretary of state to the trial judge, whose recommendation was invariably sought. For the most part judges explained in their replies why they had left the condemned prisoner to be hanged, but unless they felt strongly about the case or unless powerful local opinion had formed against the offender, they often went on to provide reasons that would justify the king's extending his mercy if he chose to do so. Judges kept notes on trials, partly at least to be able to respond to those requests.[50]

The vast majority of pardons, however, almost certainly originated in the judges' decisions at the conclusion of the session to reprieve some

---

[48] For the development of pardon in the seventeenth century and its relationship to the growth of transportation see Smith, *Colonists in Bondage*, pp. 96–97.

[49] The judges were told that in cases in which they thought a royal pardon was deserved they were at the end of their circuits "to send to one of the Secretarys of State, to be laid before His Majesty, a particular List distinguishing therein those whom you shall judge proper to be freely pardoned, and those who in your opinion should be transported to His Majesty's Plantations according to the Act of Parliament in that behalf" (SP 36/9, f. 149). The automatic character of the pardons recommended by the judges is further revealed by the instructions given by George II to the lords justices of the Regency when he went to Hanover. In 1743, for example, his instructions concerning their use of the pardoning power made a sharp distinction between pardons to be granted to condemned men recommended by the judges and those left to be hanged who petitioned for mercy. The lords justices were told that in an emergency they might delay the execution of men not reprieved by the judges in order to seek the king's instructions. But they were to use even those powers only "in Cases of Necessity." On the other hand, they were free to pardon convicts recommended by the judges at the conclusion of their assize circuits or at the Old Bailey, "which pardons," the king's instructions conclude, "We do leave you at Liberty to sign, without any Application to Us" (SP 36/60, f. 176).

[50] For evidence of the judges keeping notes see SP 36/43, f. 31; SP 36/58, f. 15; SP 37/15, f. 3. And see Langbein, "Shaping the Eighteenth-Century Criminal Trial," pp. 5–10, 18–21. Peter King has analyzed the factors most commonly mentioned by judges in their reports in supporting and opposing pardons ("Decision-Makers and Decision-Making in the English Criminal Law, 1750-1800," *Historical Journal* 27 [1984], pp. 42–51).

of those they had just sentenced to death.[51] In making those decisions they were undoubtedly moved by a variety of influences. The seriousness of the offense must have been a major consideration. Since eighty-five per cent of the prisoners condemned to death at the Surrey assizes between 1660 and 1800 had committed some form of property offense, the judges' dispositions in dealing with other offenses is not easy to measure (table 8.6). Only in homicide and coining cases were more than a handful of prisoners convicted by the Surrey juries; the judges also took a relatively hard line with both. In dealing with convicted murderers, judges mainly reserved reprieves for those they thought had been wrongfully convicted on the evidence, as a way of overcoming the persistence of juries who ignored their advice and direction. For the most part judges and jurors agreed on the justice of the execution of those who killed in cold blood

TABLE 8.6

Royal Pardons and Capital Punishment
in Surrey, 1660–1800

Offense	Sentenced to Death (No.)	Pardoned (No.)	Hanged (No.)	Pardoned (%)	Hanged (%)	Percentage of All Offenders Hanged
Property offenses	1,139	703	436	61.7	38.3	84.2
Forgery and fraud	8	3	5	37.5	62.5	1.0
Coining	31	18	13	58.1	41.9	2.5
Murder	55	13	42	23.6	76.4	8.1
Infanticide	9	5	4	55.6	44.4	.8
Rape	5	3	2	60.0	40.0	.4
Sodomy	4	0	4	0	100.0	.8
Offenses under the Black Act	5	1	4	20.0	80.0	.8
Offenses under the Riot Act	5	3	2	60.0	40.0	.4
Arson	1	0	1	0	100.0	.2
Returning from transportation	17	12	5	70.6	29.4	1.0
Total	1,279	761	518	59.5	40.5	100.2

SOURCE: Hanged Count.

[51] For the pardon process and the uncertainties of the evidence concerning the numbers pardoned see the appendix.

and with premeditation. And few were likely to be saved by the king if the judge passed them over. This was especially true when the so-called Murder Act of 1752 fixed the time between conviction and execution at three days in order indeed to prevent campaigns for a pardon and thereby to intensify the deterrent effects of the punishment.[52] The result was that condemned murderers were likely to be hanged: in Surrey, of the fifty-five men and women convicted in the ninety-five years sampled, close to three-quarters were executed.

Prisoners were not convicted in large numbers for other nonproperty capital offenses, indeed not even one a year on average in Surrey. Judges tended to take a harder line when the offense had involved violence toward the victim, as for example in the convictions under the Black Act that brought four men to the gallows for "shooting at" someone. The four men convicted of sodomy in our sample were shown no mercy by the bench, and four of the women found guilty under the Infanticide Act were also executed, though both convictions and executions for infanticide were less common after the first quarter of the eighteenth century than they had been before.

There are perhaps too few cases here to allow conclusions to be drawn about the judges' views of the law, and of course not every pardon was initiated by the bench anyway. But the tendency of both the judges (and those who advised the king) to take a hard line with crimes involving violence is more amply confirmed by their treatment of prisoners convicted of crimes against property, for three-quarters of those hanged for such offenses had been convicted of robbery or burglary (table 8.7). A number of forms of housebreaking (especially when someone was present in the house broken into who was "put in fear") also brought harsher treatment for similar reasons. Those who were pardoned after conviction for such offenses were likely to have treated their victims with some consideration, at least to have avoided threatening them. "Aggravating circumstances" in robbery and burglary in the form of actual violence, pointing weapons, or threatening behavior of any kind, made it unlikely that the judge would feel inclined to reprieve and to recommend a pardon to the king. As the duke of Newcastle told a judge whose opinion on a petition for pardon he was seeking in a case in which two men convicted of burglary were thought to have threatened to kill their victim, "if that should appear, by your Report, to have been proved against them by credible Witnesses at their tryal, it would then be highly improper to move his Majesty to extend His Mercy to them."[53] Petitions for pardon in such cases and the

[52] See chap. 10.
[53] SP 36/50, f. 288.

TABLE 8.7

Rate of Pardons in Property Offenses, 1660–1800

Offense	Sentenced to Death	Pardoned	Hanged	Percentage Pardoned
Robbery	463	250	213	54.0
Burglary	253	135	118	53.4
Housebreaking	55	32	23	58.2
Theft from house	63	54	9	85.7
Theft from shop	27	22	5	81.5
Theft from warehouse	4	1	3	25.0
Theft from ship	8	8	0	100.0
Theft from manufactory	2	0	2	0
Picking pockets	22	14	8	63.6
Sheep-stealing	40	34	6	85.0
Cattle-theft	4	4	0	100.0
Horse-theft	178	132	46	74.2
Simple larceny	18	15	3	83.3

SOURCE: Hanged Count.

judges' recommendations make it abundantly clear that the actual character of the offense was a crucial consideration in the choice of those to be saved from the gallows. Robbery, burglary, and housebreaking account for something like four out of five of those executed for property crimes in Surrey between 1660 and 1800, and for more than two-thirds of all men and women hanged in the county for any offense whatsoever.

In the case of property offenses that did not threaten violence as directly, the judges' decisions about reprieves (and the king's pardon) supplemented the juries' verdicts. In the case of horse-theft and sheep-stealing the judges to a considerable extent made up for the juries' inability to find a reduced-charge verdict by recommending close to three-quarters for a pardon, including no doubt many whom the jury would have treated more leniently had that been possible. The judges' decisions also complemented the juries' verdicts in cases under the statutes that had removed clergy from property offenses after 1689—theft from shops and houses and ships and the like. The juries were more than likely, as we have seen, to find such prisoners guilty of the reduced and noncapital charge of simple larceny, leaving only a few to be frightened by the sentence of capital punishment. But in fact, with the exception of the very few men who had stolen from a warehouse, those convicted capitally under the post-1689 statutes were mainly reprieved by the judges after sentence.

If the Surrey evidence is any guide, the eighteenth-century capital statutes that aimed to protect property from pilfering servants and shop-lifters and men who worked on the river did so more by threat and by the occasional example than by frequent demonstrations on the gallows. The choice of these examples, of the prisoners to be hanged and the effect to be made, was much more in the judge's province than the jury's. The jury had dealt with each case in turn, not knowing at the beginning of the session how many would in the end be convicted of a capital offense. The judge made his decisions about reprieves with the completed calendar before him, and his recommendations to the king could be made in the light of the numbers convicted and the need at that time and place to demonstrate the power of the law and the courts.

In making their calculations, judges and jurors were influenced not simply by the abstract character of various offenses. Crimes came forward for consideration as the deeds of actual men and women who obviously differed hugely: some of them young, some old; some apparent first-timers, some clearly experienced; some timid, some defiant. The jury and the judge regarded this as important information that ought to play a crucial role in their decisions. Who the prisoner was—his character and reputa-tion—was as critical a question as what he had done (and even in some cases whether he had done it), and it was centrally the business of the trial to find the answer. The discretionary options available to both the juries and the judges were exercised with that question and with those answers very much in mind.

VERDICTS AND PARDONS: THE MATTER OF GENDER

Offenses and offenders could not be neatly separated. A robbery would have been differently regarded when committed by a woman or a young boy or a man or a gang, for its significance would be read in the light of the threat that each posed to the security of the society. In addition, the effectiveness of hanging as an exemplary punishment depended on the offender who was providing the example. It was plainly more advisable to execute those whose death would confirm the wisdom and justice of the law rather than those whose suffering might excite pity, perhaps even hostility. Such considerations help to explain why women were treated more leniently than men by juries and if convicted were more likely to be reprieved and pardoned.

It is a reasonable assumption that women were less likely to have been prosecuted than men, that their crimes were overlooked more readily. The evidence against the women who *were* prosecuted is likely to have been at least marginally fuller and more positive than in similar cases against men. In addition, a larger proportion of women were discharged by the grand jury, so that it would seem that cases with any obvious weakness would have been thrown out at that stage. The least one can say is that weakness of evidence is not likely to explain why women were acquitted more readily than men and more frequently convicted of a lesser charge. But that was precisely their experience (table 8.8). The difference was most striking in property offenses. In the case of homicide, few women were charged with killing someone in a quarrel or by accident so they were less likely than men to be convicted of the reduced charge of man-slaughter. Women charged with homicide were generally accused of an offense that genuinely amounted to murder. The homicide cases of men and women are thus hardly comparable, and the treatment of the nineteen women indicted for murder cannot be measured against that of the 233 men whose bills were found in the same period.

Property offenses are more reliable as indicators of differential treat-ment because the numbers on trial were larger and the actual events behind

TABLE 8.8

Trial Jury Verdicts in Surrey, 1660–1800

	Men Accused				Women Accused			
Offense	Verdicts (No.)	N.G. (%)	G. (%)	Partial Verdicts (%)	Verdicts (No.)	N.G. (%)	G. (%)	Partial Verdicts (%)
"Old" capital property	1,032	34.7	50.8	14.5	165	47.3	22.4	30.3
"New" capital property	421	29.9	25.2	44.9	177	24.9	15.3	59.9
Noncapital property, assizes	1,180	33.9	24.7	41.5	457	40.5	34.6	25.0
Noncapital property, quarter sessions	1,305	33.0	65.9	1.2	429	37.5	61.8	.7
All property offenses	3,938	33.4	52.8	13.8	1228	38.1	39.7	22.2
Murder	233	43.8	22.3	33.9	19	63.2	26.3	10.5

SOURCE: Sample.

the charges were roughly similar. The difference in the juries' treatment of men and women is very plain. If one looks at the harshest judgment the jury could make, guilty as charged, and at the most serious offenses, those made nonclergyable before 1660, there is a striking contrast between the conviction of half the men on trial as against less than a quarter of the women (table 8.8). The jury also convicted fewer women than men charged with what I have called the "new" capital crimes and more frequently reduced the charge against them to noncapital larceny. In simple larceny, too, a higher proportion of women were acquitted, and fewer were found guilty as charged. Taking all property crimes together, the treatment of women was substantially different from that of men, for women were more likely to be acquitted and, if convicted, to be found guilty of a lesser charge than that stated in the indictment.

That was not the end of the courts' reluctance to subject women to the full rigor of the law. Notwithstanding the finer screens that had removed many at the grand jury stage and at the trial, the judges were much more favorably disposed toward women when they considered whom to reprieve, as was the king in granting pardons (table 8.9). The result was that, with the exception of murder (and by the end of the process only five women were executed for murder in Surrey in the ninety-six years examined between 1660 and 1800), women convicted of capital crimes had a good chance of escaping the gallows. In property crimes almost eighty per cent were reprieved (and I assume pardoned), as against forty per cent of the men. The qualification is necessary because I count as pardoned the women who were reprieved as pregnant. That might understate by a few the numbers who were actually hanged, but I do not think that it affects the broad truth that at every point in the administration of justice the courts were more likely to take a harder line with a man than with a woman. Women made up almost eighteen per cent of the prisoners charged with capital property offenses before the grand jury, but only seven per cent of those hanged. Altogether, over the 140 years after

TABLE 8.9

Pardons and Capital Punishment in Surrey

	Convicted of Capital Offense	Number Pardoned	Number Executed	Percentage Pardoned	Percentage Executed
Men	1,130	649	481	57.4	42.6
Women	149	112	37	75.2	24.8

SOURCE: Hanged Count.

1660 about fifty men were hanged every decade in Surrey on average; at the same time, an average of about four women were executed every ten years.

This might be explained in part by what has been called "an often instinctive chivalry, or if you like embarrassment, which was a common reaction of that day when confronted with women who broke the rules."[54] Undoubtedly men were reluctant, and perhaps embarrassed, to see women suffering in public. But how far a sense of chivalry extended to women of the laboring poor has yet to be established, and any embarrassment they might have felt did not prevent men in the eighteenth century from burning women at the stake for treason (including the murder of their husbands), nor from stripping them to the waist and whipping them through the streets at a cart's tail. Chivalrous instincts do not sufficiently explain a persistent tendency to let women off more lightly than men for the same offenses—not necessarily to let them go scot free, but to let them off more lightly. That is mainly explained by the general purposes that were thought to be served by punishment, and by the absence of a conviction that what is meted out to one ought in justice be done to all. Punishment was thought of less as a means to reform and rehabilitate offenders than as a much blunter weapon that would either rid the community of someone who had proved himself incorrigible or, by public and violent chastisement, to deter him and others in the future. Any chivalrous feelings in the jury box and on the bench were encouraged and allowed expression by the fact that women were less frequently charged with serious offenses, that they posed a less serious threat to lives, property, and order. It was not necessary that large numbers of women be punished in public. The broader purposes of the law and of the administration of justice could be served by the very occasional example of a woman harshly dealt with.

VERDICTS AND PARDONS: THE IMPORTANCE OF CHARACTER

The treatment of women suggests that the courts were engaged to some extent in a form of selection of prisoners to suffer in particular ways, that the crime and the criminal were to fit the punishment. That ambition and intention should not be overemphasized. But there is no doubt that the character of the capital laws encouraged the courts to pay attention to the identity of the prisoner, and surrounded the issue of guilt and innocence with concern for who the prisoner was who might suffer in a particular

[54] G. R. Elton, "Introduction: Crime and the Historian," in Cockburn, ed., *Crime in England*, p. 13.

way. Not only were women thus distinguished from men, some men were distinguished from others. To some extent, for example, age had a bearing on the way a prisoner would be treated by the jury and by the judge when he considered reprieves, and it is clear that age was an influential factor in the granting of pardons. But of course it is difficult to abstract age from other characteristics of the prisoners, some of which were almost certain to have been more influential in themselves. Indeed the prisoner's age may well have been important mainly as an indicator of other things that the courts were more deeply sensitive toward, in particular the prisoner's character and reputation, whether he was a habitual offender or a beginner, and thus how he might be most effectively and usefully punished.

When the jurors, judges, and magistrates listened to the brief interchange between the prosecutor and the defendant that was the essence of so many criminal trials in the eighteenth century, it is clear they paid attention not just to the facts alleged and the defense offered. They were in addition anxious to discover something about the men and women on each side. The character of the prisoner (in the sense of both his disposition and his reputation) was especially important information and was often crucial to the outcome of the trial. That consideration encouraged prisoners to bring character witnesses to speak on their behalf. One can see from the questions often put to such witnesses that what was important was their evidence about the prisoner's habits of life: did he work regularly; did he support his family; was he sober and honest in his dealings with others; did he, in other words, have an established place in a community, and was he known to his respectable neighbors as a man who could be trusted? Or, on the other hand, was he a troublemaker and an idler, a man without visible means of support who might be presumed to live dishonestly? A man who could produce no witnesses was likely to have a difficult time in court.

Men were not all equal before the law; nor was that sought as an ideal. According to Zachary Babington in the late seventeenth century, trial jurors were supposed to be drawn from the neighborhood of the offense because they might then be expected to know something not only of "the truth and nature of the offense" but also of "the quality of the [prisoner] . . . and happily the credit of the accuser and his witnesses."[55] Much of this was fanciful, for trial jurors had by then long ceased to be self-informing. The "quality" of the defendant and the "credit" of the prosecutor remained highly relevant considerations, but they had to be discovered in the same way that the facts of the case were revealed, by

[55] Zachary Babington, *Advice to Grand Jurors in Cases of Blood* (1677; 2nd ed., 1692), pp. 3–4.

the examination of witnesses. And as the Swiss visitor Saussure observed in the early eighteenth century, if the witnesses who appeared for the prisoner testified that he had "always been an honest man, his case will be considered in quite a different light to what it would have been had he been suspected of other cases of villainy."[56] Indeed, there is evidence that where the proof of guilt was not persuasive or the character of the prosecutor himself was not entirely certain, strong witnesses to the good reputation of the accused could well bring an acquittal, as for example in the case of a man indicted for theft at the Old Bailey in 1687 who was acquitted by the jury (according to the reporter, at least) because several witnesses testified "to his long inhabiting" his parish in good repute.[57]

The reporters who made up the brief accounts of trials at the Surrey assizes in the late seventeenth century and the early decades of the eighteenth did not often speculate why juries found as they did, but there are suggestions from time to time that in that court too character witnesses provided decisive evidence leading to acquittals. In the trial of a man and a woman for breaking into and stealing from a house in 1726, the jury was undoubtedly led to convict the woman and acquit the man by the fact that she was caught carrying the stolen goods. But character evidence seems also to have been strongly influential in the man's favor, despite the prosecutor's testimony that he had seen both of them "loitering" near the house. The man "proved that he had lived in the parish many years and always bore a good character." As for the woman, she could give no account at all of herself, "whereupon," the report concludes, "the jury acquitted the man and found the woman guilty." She was sentenced to death.[58] A number of cases in the printed report of the Summer assizes in 1718 also concluded in ways that suggest that the reporter thought character evidence had played an important part in the prisoner's acquittal.[59] Such testimony could certainly overturn the evidence of an ac-

[56] *A Foreign View of England in the Reigns of George I and George II. The Letters of Monsieur César de Saussure to his Family*, ed. Madame van Muyden (1902), p. 121.

[57] At the same session, a man accused of stealing a silver tankard from a public house also brought witnesses to testify to his "honest reputation," and the reporter again thought that that had been sufficient to persuade the jury—"supposing the prosecutor might have been mistaken in the man"—to acquit him. Several other acquittals at that session of the Old Bailey were apparently encouraged by favorable character evidence (OBSP, Apr. 1687).

[58] S.A.P., Lent 1726, p. 4.

[59] In one case it was said that "the prisoner called several people of credit to her reputation, who said she worked honestly for her living, and that they had never heard any ill of her: the jury considering the matter acquitted her." In another, "the prisoner denied the fact, and called persons to his reputation, who said they had never heard any ill of him, nor did they believe he would be guilty of such a crime. The jury acquitted him" (S.A.P., Summer 1718, pp. 1–2).

complice.[60] And indeed the enquiry into character could as easily turn into an investigation of the prosecutor and his witnesses, particularly when there was some suspicion that the prosecution was malicious or was being carried on entirely for the sake of a reward.

Some trials give the appearance of having involved as much a weighing up and balancing of the reputations and social worth of the principals on each side as of the evidence. When a woman who sold shrimp around the county brought a charge of robbery against two men with whom she was acquainted, the story she told was not very plausible and was contradicted even by some of her own witnesses. But what seems to have been particularly decisive in explaining the acquittal of these men was the testimony of defense witnesses that she was a woman of "very ill character" who "would swear anything." Other witnesses said that the prisoners were honest men, "true and trusty." It is interesting that one of these men was immediately indicted again for another robbery, but this time for stealing not from a woman of doubtful character but from a man of some substance who identified him as the robber who had stopped him on a highway between Kingston and London and had taken his silver watch and spurs, a gold ring, and money. This prosecutor's character could not be blackened by the prisoner's neighbors, and they turned out now not to be as effective against this more formidable man. Five character witnesses appeared for the prisoner, all from Wandsworth, several of whom spoke of having done business with him over many years; they agreed that he had always "behaved very well and worked hard." The central issue turned out to be the direct conflict between the prosecutor's identification of the prisoner and the prisoner's denial. There was no other evidence, for other witnesses brought by the prosecution failed to add anything substantial, and three witnesses who gave the prisoner an alibi for the time of the robbery appear to have had little influence. What it came down to was the conflict not of evidence but of character and reputation. After his eight witnesses had spoken for him, the judge asked the prisoner not for a better factual defense but for better character witnesses: "Have you any of the substantial inhabitants of Wandsworth to your character?" he wanted to know. The implication was clear that while his witnesses were effective against the flimsy evidence of a shrimp-seller, they could not deflect the sworn testimony of a man whose own character could not be impugned. In the end the prisoner could only repeat that he was "innocent of this fact. I never robbed any one in my life." He was, however, convicted and hanged.[61]

    [60] S.A.P., Lent 1732, p. 2 (Chick); Summer 1751, p. 30 (Young).
    [61] S.A.P., Summer 1738, pp. 13–15 (Hoare and Oliver). For another case in which the character of the prosecutor was attacked by the defense see S.A.P., Summer 1739, p. 17 (Dunkley et al.).

Character evidence occasionally won an acquittal, but it was perhaps especially effective in persuading juries to find partial verdicts. This was particularly true when the charge was one of the more trivial capital offenses. But even in robbery, burglary, and horse-theft good character evidence could well influence the jury's decision. Who was being charged and by whom were critical issues in all criminal trials, and the evidence drawn out to elucidate them could clearly influence a jury's verdict. But perhaps the crucial influence of character evidence in capital cases was its effect on the judge when he decided who to recommend to the king for a pardon and who to leave to be hanged. The factual evidence he had heard made a great deal of difference. He also, however, had clearly in mind who the prisoners were, as far as he could discover, and his selection of men and women to be hanged was decidedly influenced by his view of their character and disposition and reputation. He must have formed his impression of them partly directly—from the way they were dressed, the way they spoke and acted in court—and from what was said about them by their accusers and their own witnesses.

The principal question in the judge's mind was likely to be whether the prisoner was an "old offender" or a first-timer who had been led to commit this offense by some momentary difficulty. Character evidence that stressed the prisoner's youth and inexperience and the ease with which he had been tempted by bad companions or by lust or poverty into this one aberration would almost certainly incline the judge toward a reprieve. It was to the prisoner's benefit if he could be shown to have been brought up in a respectable household, and given religious training and a good education by parents long established in a community. Good character evidence also stressed that the prisoner had worked hard, that he was not a man to stay out late carousing, spending his money at an alehouse. The more visible his means of support and the more regular his life, the more plausible would be the argument to which all this related—that if his life were spared he would not go back to crime. The Irishman of whom it was said in court that he left home every morning carrying his spade and the man who said in court that he had always striven to get his living were attempting to give the right impression and endeavoring to get a favorable answer when the judge asked himself, in the duke of Portland's words in 1717, whether the convict "be an old offender or not, and whether he deserves mercy."[62]

The trial judge must have heard a good deal about certain prisoners outside the court. Magistrates and local gentlemen were not likely to leave it to chance that the judge would get the right impression of prisoners

[62] S.A.P., Lent 1738, p. 7 (Moylon et al.); SP 35/9, f. 231.

who in their view deserved mercy or (and this was more certain to stir them to action) to be dealt with severely. There is nothing to suggest that judges did not welcome such information from local worthies about the troublemakers and dangerous characters on the upcoming calendar. Judges frequently acknowledged in their reports on capital cases that they had relied on such local information in deciding for and against reprieves. Mr. Justice Eyre reported in 1714, for example, that when two men were convicted of horse-theft, he reprieved one "in compassion to his wife and nine small children." But the other man was "represented to me by several gentlemen and Justices of the Peace, to be a man of ill fame and dangerous to the country [and] was left to be executed."[63] A judge said of another man that "I should have been inclined to have saved his life, as far as it lay in my power to do it, had not the Gentlemen present assured me that he was so incorrigeable a Villain as to be past all hopes of amendment . . . [which] induced me to leave him to the Severity of the Law."[64] A prisoner given "a very ill character from the Gentlemen of the Country" was left to suffer; another was reprieved when "Gentlemen of distinction in the Country [represented] the witnesses against him to be persons of no credit."[65]

   Judges were bound to pay attention to the recommendations of the men upon whom the administration of justice and the government of the county largely rested, and it is plain that on occasion they went against their own personal view of the merits of a case in bowing to the pressures from local interests whose goodwill it would be unwise to lose. Opposition to a pardon from groups of local gentlemen was taken seriously in London.[66] On the other side, the king was clearly open to persuasion by men with influence and interest at court when they were drawn in to support a petition.[67] But it would be a mistake to concentrate too narrowly on the

---

[63] SP 35/1, f. 32.

[64] SP 36/8, ff. 130–31.

[65] SP 36/28, ff. 64, 111. A magistrate who was not going to attend the quarter sessions wrote to the clerk of the peace in 1727 about a man from his parish who was to be tried for a petty theft. He has a very bad character, he told the clerk, and is thought to have committed much worse crimes than the one charged, and "therefore" he wanted him to "receive the full punishment the law directs" (QS 2/6, Ep. 1727, 31).

[66] For petitions from groups of local gentlemen or prosecutors opposing pardons see, for example, SP 35/61, f. 200; SP 36/28, f. 8; SP 36/63, f. 462; SP 36/62, f. 277. For the withdrawal of support for a pardon when it was revealed that it "raised a very great Clamour" among "the Gentlemen of the County" of Nottingham, SP 35/42, f. 439.

[67] Pardons were occasionally sought as a favor not to the prisoner but to a peer or a man with political clout, as a means of demonstrating interest to a constituency's electors. For petitions advanced for narrowly political reasons see SP 35/57, f. 181; SP 36/11, f. 120; SP 36/14, f. 98; SP 36/15, f. 13; SP 36/117, ff. 181–82; SP 36/118, ff. 127–28. In such cases, as Douglas Hay has said, "mercy was part of the currency of patronage" ("Property, Authority and the Criminal Law," p. 45).

influence of the political and social elite and to stress too sharply the claims of class, not because when brought to bear they were unimportant, but because that tends to divert attention from the ordinariness and the centrality of pardoning in the administration of justice. The vast majority of pardons were granted without the direct intervention of a member of the gentry or nobility, since they arose as part of the system of mitigation in the hands of the courts. Only when a judge failed to reprieve a condemned man was a petitioning campaign necessary. Even then a petition did not require a great man's support to bring success. Undoubtedly that helped, for it strengthened the substance of the case being made and ensured that the petition got a hearing. But large numbers of petitions supported merely by the signatures of the inhabitants of the prisoner's parish also came before the king. Such local petitions often, though by no means always, included the names of local gentry. Much more commonly they were headed by the signatures of the parish worthies—the clergyman, churchwardens, overseers, the constable—and included a large number of the names or marks of the inhabitants, occasionally as many as fifty or a hundred.[68]

The local officials were pre-eminently the respectable men of the parish. Their word and their guarantee counted for a great deal because what the judge and the government were particularly interested in, in the day-to-day administration of the law, was separating the "old offenders" from the rest, and ensuring that the former did not escape. What happened to the others was less important. The guarantee provided by local men was that the prisoner was a man of previously good character, that he came from a respectable family, that he was known and had a place in the community.[69] There was undoubtedly some truth in Mr. Justice Foster's view that parish notables frequently supported petitions on behalf of a local man out of a concern for the financial burdens they would have to assume if he were executed and left a wife and children to be cared for by the parish. Foster thought that such considerations were "too often an

---

[68] Peter King has analyzed the petitions submitted on behalf of condemned men in the years 1787 and 1790 and concludes that of those whose social background can be identified "the largest petitioning group were middling men—traders, petty jurors, town inhabitants and poor law officials" ("Decision-Makers and Decision-Making," p. 49).

[69] In his analysis of the petitions submitted in 1787 and 1790, King adopted a "factor-mentions system" to provide as systematic an account as could be devised of the reasons given by petitioners in favor of condemned men. This reveals that such petitioners commonly stressed the prisoner's character and his previous good conduct as mitigating factors (ibid., pp. 42–51). A condemned man who had no settled community, no respectable witnesses, to appeal to would have difficulty raising a petition that would be considered. One man in Sussex thought it absurd that he should be asked to support a campaign on behalf of a condemned prisoner who was "an Irishman and quite a stranger to these parts." He thought the local community should not interpose "without grounds or reason in the execution of the public justice of the kingdom for a man we know nothing about" (Philip C. Yorke, ed., *The Diary of John Baker* [1931], p. 264).

Inducement to the Parishioners to interpose. They frequently choose rather to continue a pilfering Fellow among them than take the Burden of Wife and Children."[70] That could not have applied to more than a fraction of the cases, however, for most petitioners were attempting to save men from the gallows not in order that they might go free but that they might be transported or, in the last decades of the century, imprisoned, neither of which would have saved the parish from having to look after the abandoned family.[71]

In making decisions about reprieves, judges were by no means limited to the evidence presented in court, but the trial was their fundamental source of information about most of the offenders who came before them. That helps to explain why judges resisted guilty pleas from accused felons in the eighteenth century. It is odd on the face of it (particularly in view of the modern courts' anxiety to bargain toward a guilty plea) that eighteenth-century judges were so insistent that a trial take place and evidence be produced, especially in capital cases. There was undoubtedly some feeling that every man accused of a felony ought to have the benefit of a trial by a jury. But the anxiety of the judges that a trial take place derives from their need to form an impression of the prisoner in order to decide how he should be punished, and particularly whether he should be reprieved or not. A man who pleaded guilty at the Old Bailey in 1743 and expressed the hope that the jury and the judge would recommend him to his majesty's mercy was told that "if there were any favourable Circumstances in his Case, if he pleaded guilty, the Court could not take any Notice of them [that is, would not learn about them]; and that the Jury cannot report any favourable Circumstances, because the Circumstances do not appear to them: Upon which he agreed to take his Trial."[72] On another occasion a judge explained that he had left a man to be hanged because he had pleaded guilty and he thus had no alternative. He explained to the secretary of state that he had been "shut out from all Evidence and Circumstances favourable and disfavourable which might have Appeared in his Case and Trial if he had pleaded not Guilty and having no Rule to direct me in my Duty but the Charge in the Indictment, which was

---

[70] SP 36/145, f. 105.

[71] In one case in Surrey the minister and churchwardens and half a dozen inhabitants of the parish of St. John in Southwark supported the petition of a woman whom they knew "to be a very poor Industrious woman of honest repute having lived in the said Parish upwards of 20 years" who in 1758 wanted to get her son pardoned from transportation and sent to the army instead, on the grounds that she could not afford to support him in prison while he waited for shipping (delayed no doubt by the war). There may have been some indirect financial benefit to the parish in this, but it is not likely to explain the support given by these officials (SP 36/140, f. 238).

[72] Quoted by Langbein, "Criminal Trial before the Lawyers," p. 278.

confessed, I left him for Execution."[73] Chief Justice Willes said the same
thing about another confession in a capital case. It meant, he said, that
he "had no opportunity of knowing what his Character was, or with what
Circumstances the Crime was committed."[74] In such cases the judges
commonly went on to say that they would have been ready to grant a
reprieve if, in the words of one of them, "persons of worth and reputation"
had given him "a favourable account of [the prisoner's] character and former
manner of life."[75] But it was likely that local interests were not engaged
one way or the other in the case of most offenders, particularly in the
courts in and around London, where information produced at the trial
(supplemented perhaps by the opinion of the keeper of the jail or the
chaplain) might be all that could be learned about many prisoners.[76]

Prisoners obviously understood the importance of character evidence,
and, to judge by even the brief and incomplete printed reports of the trials
at the Surrey assizes, large numbers managed to arrange from jail to get
one or two witnesses to come to court to speak on their behalf. Those who
could not frequently offered the excuse, no doubt genuine enough, that
they were too poor and too far from those who knew them to be able to
bring witnesses. A boy of fourteen, charged with street robbery at the
Surrey assizes at Guildford told the court that he "should have several
People here to speak for me, but they are so poor, and it is such a long
way from London, that they could not spare Time to come down." He
knew what their helpful message would have been had they come, for he
added, "I hope you will consider my Youth. I never was before the Face
of a Justice in my whole Life." He was reprieved, pardoned, and transported, no doubt largely on account of his age. Another man at the same
session of the Surrey assizes said simply "I have No Body to speak to my
Character. I am from my Friends."[77] Undoubtedly the more respectable
the witnesses, the more effectively the prisoner's character could be es-

[73] SP 36/116, ff. 105–6.

[74] SP 36/63, f. 356.

[75] SP 36/116, ff. 105–6. Even if the prisoner pleaded not guilty and a trial took place, the
crucial evidence would not emerge if the prisoner did not call witnesses to his character. Asked
to respond to a petition for pardon in 1724 in which the prisoner alleged his previous good
behavior as grounds for mercy, Mr. Justice Eyre told the secretary of state that he had learned
nothing about that at the trial, "for the Petitioner call'd no witnesses to his reputation or good
behaviour, to show that he was settled in any industrious course of life, or that he was seduced
and drawn in by others to commit the offence" (SP 35/52, f. 57).

[76] When the Recorder of London was told in 1784 to choose a hundred prisoners from Newgate
to be transported to Africa, he reported that he got the best information he could "from the
evidence given on their respective Trials as from their general Character and other Demeanor
since their confinement in Newgate" (HO 7/1).

[77] S.A.P., Lent 1742, pp. 4–5 (Burroughs), p. 9 (Prew).

tablished. But to have no witnesses at all was almost certain to be disastrous, especially if the crime charged was particularly serious. Being "from" your friends encouraged condemnation not pity in the court, and the odds were heavily against a stranger who brought no support of any kind.

The strong impression given by the printed accounts of Surrey assize trials is that the prisoner who had been convicted of a burglary or a robbery or who had stolen a horse, and who was clearly not a youth and could not bring anyone with standing in the community to vouch for him and remove the impression of his being a habitual offender, was likely to be hanged. Many of those who were executed for crimes against property shared two characteristics: they had been convicted of one of the "serious" offenses; and they were men who appeared to be "old offenders," or at least vagrants, and wanderers, men who lived anonymously in the larger urban parishes, strangers, Irishmen, men with no fixed place who could not bring an employer or a group of neighbors to speak for them to remove the impression that they were detached and dangerous. The only men in a weaker position were those who were in fact *known* to be old offenders and who had made enemies who seized the opportunity to speak against them. It was such men whose pardons were opposed. One man was certain that his local reputation had condemned him when he was charged with murder along with two prostitutes who had thrown a client out of a window to prevent him from calling for help as he was being robbed. He was hanged. In his *Life and Dying Words*, sold at the gallows on the day of his execution, he said that he had had no hope of a pardon because the parish officers and others were out to get him as the keeper of a brothel. When he was convicted "the mouths of both the rich and poor were open against me and many things were said to my prejudice. . . ."[78]

A swirl of rumor and prejudice no doubt surrounded many of those on trial. It was the kind of testimony the courts were anxious to hear, since the fierceness of the law required the courts to deal with the factual aspects of the cases before them in the light of the prisoners' reputations and characters so that capital punishment might be kept to acceptable levels. "The prisoners selected for capital punishment as an example to others," Sir John Fielding said, "should be chosen from the dangerous and incorrigible offenders." He went on to advocate that their selection should be based on their "record," which he proposed to keep at public office in Bow Street to provide "reliable information as to the criminal antecedents of every offender."[79] In this way, as in others, Fielding an-

[78] *Lives of the Malefactors* (1743), p. 10.
[79] *Cal. H. O. Papers*, vol. 4, pp. 10–11.

ticipated the future. For the most part such information continued to be gathered in the eighteenth century at the trial, which was in part at least a form of pre-sentencing hearing and where witnesses to character were of fundamental importance. "What character do the Neighbours give of him?" judges wanted to know of such witnesses. "Is it that of a sober industrious one, or an indifferent Character?" Or, in another case, has the prisoner "worked at his Trade lately? How has he supported himself? Has he worked for a Twelvemonth last past?" Or, of another prisoner, "You have been saying that the prisoner was a very hard working woman, but what was her moral character?"[80]

The offense contained in the indictment, the factual evidence brought to support it, the prisoner's defense, and the witnesses he brought to speak for him all had some bearing on the way the prisoner would be regarded by the jury and the judge, and particularly in their exercise of discretionary powers. That made a great difference to the way a convicted prisoner would be punished. And it is likely that that was very much in the jury's mind when they considered their verdict, and in the judge's when he thought about reprieves. It is also likely that the need for examples would have some influence. But none of those calculations went on in a vacuum. There was also the crucial matter of the punishment that particular decisions would lead to. How ready the juries were to convict, and how amenable the judge to reprieve and the king to pardon, would turn in part on their views of the punishments available to the courts and how they saw these punishments serving the broader purposes of the law. The changing character of punishment over the century and a half we are concerned with was thus another crucial and fundamental aspect of the administration of justice. We will turn to that next to follow further the fate of those brought before the courts.

[80] S.A.P., Summer 1738, pp. 8, 17; Lent 1759, p. 14.

CHAPTER 9

PUNISHMENT, 1660–1750: THE IMPACT OF TRANSPORTATION

When the last trial had been completed and the jury had given its final verdict, the prisoners were once again returned to the court in a body to be sentenced. It is unlikely that many were surprised by what they heard, for even the youngest and least experienced of them must have known that the range of possible punishments was very narrow indeed. It was certainly the case at the Restoration that in the most serious offenses, in treason and felony, what the judge could do had been in large part determined by the jury's verdict. He had merely to pronounce the judgments prescribed by law. With few exceptions, prisoners convicted of treason or of a felony—and that meant the vast majority of those tried at the assizes—could only be sentenced to death.[1]

It is necessary to emphasize these constraints because they were to be significantly broken over the next century. The poverty of choice available to the bench at the Restoration was by no means new.[2] But it was clearly being felt then as a serious problem, and a central theme in the administration of the criminal law in the last decades of the seventeenth century and into the eighteenth is the variety of attempts made to broaden the penal options open to the courts. Indeed, the history of punishment over the century and a half after 1660 that we will follow in the next two chapters is most notably the story not of the enlargement of the capital code that is so frequently emphasized (important as that is) but of the remarkable broadening of secondary punishments, particularly transpor-

---

[1] John Baker, "Criminal Courts and Procedure at Common Law, 1550–1800," in Cockburn, ed., *Crime in England*, pp. 42–44.

[2] This emerges clearly from the data collected by J. S. Cockburn from his calendar of Home Circuit assize files for the reigns of Elizabeth and James I and published in appendices in the introductory volume to his series. This reveals that between 1558 and 1625 convicted felons were either granted clergy or sentenced to be hanged. Cockburn, *Assize Records: Introduction*, apps. 5 and 6. Of all the accused convicted of crimes against property at the Surrey assizes in the 1650s (ninety-five between 1654 and 1659), almost half were granted a clergyable discharge and close to a quarter were sentenced to death (though several were subsequently pardoned and transported) (ASSI 35/95–100).

tation and imprisonment, which were to transform the punishment of convicted felons in England by the second half of the eighteenth century.

CAPITAL PUNISHMENT

Neither transportation nor imprisonment was available in the 1660s when judgment was passed on those convicted of treason or felony. In treason, the punishments prescribed sought to combine the maximum of pain and ignominy. The convict was to be "drawn to the place of execution upon a hurdle" and there hanged, cut down while still alive, disembowelled and castrated, beheaded and quartered. For the petty treason of killing his master, a man was to be drawn on a hurdle and hanged. Women were not subjected to disembowelling and other mutilation, but for both forms of treason—acts against the king, including counterfeiting the coinage, and the petty treason of killing husband or master or mistress—women were subjected to the equally terrifying sentence of burning at the stake. It was widely believed in the eighteenth century that executioners generally allowed men to die on the gallows before cutting them down to be dismembered and that they commonly strangled women with a cord before lighting the fire that would consume them.[3] But clearly these were limited benefits, and not all such merciful deliverances were in any case successfully managed.

The principal offenses dealt with at the assizes were felonies. With the exception of petty larceny, which was occasionally described as a "noncapital felony" and which in the seventeenth century was commonly punished by whipping, felonies were capital offenses. Not every convicted felon was sentenced to death, however, because, as we have seen, many were able to plead benefit of clergy before judgment was passed. Despite the withdrawal of clergy from the most serious crimes in the previous century, a large number of convicted men (though a smaller proportion of women) continued in 1660 to be eligible to plead its benefits and thus to escape with a mere branding on the thumb. Simple larceny remained a clergyable offense at the Restoration, and that always accounted for the largest number of accused felons at any session of the assize courts.

At the conclusion of the trials, when the prisoners were brought forward to be sentenced, they were asked (at the stage known as the *allocutus*) if they could offer any reason why judgment should not be pronounced against them.[4] About sixty per cent of those convicted of

[3] Blackstone, *Commentaries*, vol. 4, pp. 376–77.
[4] Baker, "Criminal Courts and Procedure," p. 41.

simple grand larceny at the Surrey assizes in the half century after 1660 successfully pleaded clergy at that point. The women among them had merely "prayed the benefit of the statute," the benefit, that is, of the statutes of 1623 and 1692 that together fully extended the privilege of clergy to women. Until 1706, men who pleaded clergy were put immediately to a literacy test in court. They "prayed for the book" and were meant to demonstrate that they could read it before clergy was allowed. Most did so, or at least were said to have done so by the clergyman who was in court to administer the test. The judges occasionally insisted on a strict interpretation of the rules and a clear demonstration of a prisoner's literacy, in order to punish particular offenders more severely than merely branding them on the thumb and discharging them immediately from the court. By the late seventeenth century, when it had been extended to both men and women, clergy was being granted more or less automatically to most who applied. Nonetheless the judges retained a discretionary power that was virtually uncontrollable to decide whether a man had read well enough to save his life. And it was thus profoundly important that the literacy test was abolished in 1706. This is insufficiently emphasized in discussions of the English criminal law in the eighteenth century. It is true that the law became increasingly harsh as parliament excluded numerous offenses from the privilege of clergy or created others to which clergy would not apply. But it is worth remembering that for illiterate men all felonies were potentially capital before 1706. The fact that the literacy test had not been administered strictly (nor the rule that denied clergy to those convicted of felony a second time) does not make those laws less harsh, any more than the mitigation by "pious perjury" was to make the law in the eighteenth century any less brutal. A witness before the House of Commons committee on the criminal law in 1819 reminded the members of this crucial point when he was asked to confirm their belief that "the laws of England at this time are much more severe than they were at earlier periods." "Yes," he said, "on those who can read certainly, but not on non-readers."[5] After 1706 the scope of benefit of clergy was increasingly restricted, and it was technically available only for a first offense. But where it applied, it applied to all men and women equally.

Before 1706 the threat of capital punishment hung over many more men and women, though in practice those actually executed had mainly been convicted of offenses removed from clergy, not because they failed as individuals to qualify or because they had had the privilege before. In twelve years sampled between 1663 and 1694 a total of ninety-seven men

[5] *Report on Criminal Laws* (1819), p. 37.

and thirty women were sentenced to death at the Surrey assizes (table 9.1).[6] Half the men and twenty-two women were subsequently pardoned. The remainder were executed, mainly on the gallows. Forty of the men put to death, over eighty per cent, had committed one of the offenses against property made nonclergyable in the sixteenth century (robbery, burglary, housebreaking, and horse-theft), as had five of the eight women executed. The others had been convicted of homicide and clipping or counterfeiting the coinage. Fewer women were found guilty than men, and they were also more likely to escape execution. Of the thirty convicted of capital offenses, eleven pleaded pregnancy and were reprieved, of whom it appears three were subsequently hanged and the remainder pardoned. Fourteen others were also eventually pardoned, so that a total of eight were apparently executed, about a quarter of those condemned.

Two convicts, a man and a woman, were apparently executed in these years for simple larceny.[7] On the whole, however, those hanged in Surrey had been convicted of offenses removed from clergy in the sixteenth century, principally murder, robbery, and burglary, offenses for which capital punishment continued to be accepted as a justifiable sanction. The large crowds that gathered at Kennington Common and at other places of execution in the county might in the end come to pity the man or woman being hanged; and there were conflicts around the gallows from time to time over the disposal of the prisoner's body.[8] But there is little evidence of a serious disagreement in society about capital punishment itself. It was justified on grounds of both social utility and religious authority: on the one hand, the right of society to protect itself against dangerous offenders; and on the other, the biblical commands that authorized capital punishment for offenses against the law of nature that were universally condemned, such as murder.[9]

---

[6] I have not reported the level of executions in Sussex before 1749 because I have not conducted a full search for pardons. After 1749 I have relied on the Agenda Book to identify pardons (as in the case of Surrey) and have included data on hangings in Sussex in chapter 10.

[7] Women were in theory more liable than men to be executed for such offenses since until 1692 they were denied clergy for any simple theft over ten shillings in value. In the twelve years we have examined, close to half the women convicted had been charged with such a nonclergyable offense; all but one were reprieved. In the case of men, all simple larcenies were clergyable, but as we will see judges occasionally insisted on a strict literacy test, and in this way a number of men were threatened with a death sentence. For the most part that threat was removed by the judge's reprieving them before sentencing in order to recommend their pardon and subsequent transportation. But five were sentenced to death, of whom one appears in fact to have been hanged.

[8] Peter Linebaugh, "The Tyburn Riot against the Surgeons," in Hay, Linebaugh, and Thompson, eds., *Albion's Fatal Tree*, pp. 79–88.

[9] Even an early advocate of proportionality in punishment like Sollom Emlyn, the editor of the *State Trials*, believed that the law given by God to Noah—"Whoso sheddeth man's blood,

TABLE 9.1

Capital Punishment in Surrey, 1663–1694 (12 Sample Years)

Offense	Men			Women			Total Number Hanged	Percentage of Total Executed
	Sentenced to Death	Pardoned	Executed	Sentenced to Death	Pardoned	Executed		
Property offenses								
Robbery	24	15	9	1	0	1	10	17.9
Burglary	17	6	11	7	3	4	15	26.8
Housebreaking	9	2	7	2	2	0	7	12.5
Horse-theft	28	15	13	0	0	0	13	23.2
Picking pockets	0	0	0	2	2	0	0	0
Simple larceny	2	1	1	13	12	1	2	3.6
Total	80	39	41	25	19	6	47	84.0
Murder	11	6	5	1	0	1	6	10.7
Infanticide	0	0	0	3	2	1	1	1.8
Coining	6	4	2	1	1	0	2	3.6
Total	97	49	48	30	22	8	56	100.1

SOURCE: Hanged Count (1663–65, 1674–77, 1690–94).

Execution was further legitimized by being encased within a religious context. A clergyman was appointed to minister to the condemned prisoner, to preach on the eve of the hanging, and to accompany him to the gallows.[10] He would also strive to persuade the prisoner to make a full public confession and to accept the justice of his treatment by the courts, a declaration that would have the double significance of acting as a means to his own salvation and providing justification of the law and of the sentence passed upon him. Capital punishment did not, however, bring atonement for the crime: that, as Blackstone was to say, "must be left to the just determination of the supreme being."[11] Its purpose, and the purpose of all punishment, was more directly secular: to prevent crime in the future by disabling particular offenders and terrifying others into obeying the law. Punishments that were directed toward society provided examples, and this was especially important in capital punishment since it was the only penalty regularly available to the courts in felonies. Public execution thus served two immediate purposes: it rid society of particularly wicked individuals, those who had proved themselves dangerous and incorrigible or who had committed an offense that could not be forgiven; beyond that, it demonstrated to the broad ranks of the laboring poor the ultimate consequences of disobedience and immoral habits and law breaking. But of course the number of examples needed to convey that message was a matter of judgment, a judgment that was exercised, as we have seen, by juries and judges and the king. The power of juries to find mitigating verdicts and of the king to pardon meant that the actual level of hanging could fluctuate sharply over time without capital punishment itself coming seriously into question. And while there was no reluctance to hang certain kinds of offenders or, if circumstances required it, a large number of condemned men together, there does seem to have been a tendency by the seventeenth century for the courts to use their discretionary powers in such a way as to limit the number of prisoners sent to the gallows.[12] One result of this may have been to emphasize the lack of

---

by man shall his blood be shed" (Genesis 9:6)—remained binding; in cases of murder no other punishment would serve (*State Trials* [1730], vol. 1, p. ix).

[10] For the role of the ordinary and the significance of the prisoner's dying speech and confession see Peter Linebaugh, "The Ordinary of Newgate and His 'Account' " in Cockburn, ed., *Crime in England*, pp. 246–69. Pamphlet accounts of the lives, crimes, and confessions of condemned prisoners were not published in Surrey with the regularity with which they appeared from the ordinaries of Newgate. For one example, written by the Reverend Mr. Wilson, curate of St. George the Martyr, Southwark, see *A Genuine Account of the Lives, Characters, Behaviours, Confessions and Dying Words of the Six Malefactors that were Executed at Kennington Common on Friday the 14th of September 1739* (Southwark, 1739). Similar pamphlets were published in 1742 and 1743.

[11] Blackstone, *Commentaries*, vol. 1, p. 11; Hale, *Pleas of the Crown*, vol. 1, p. 13.

[12] J. A. Sharpe, *Crime in Seventeenth-Century England: A County Study* (Cambridge, 1983), pp. 142–44.

alternatives to execution as a punishment for convicted felons. At least it is clear that that was being recognized as a problem by the 1660s, and the dissatisfaction it gave rise to encouraged a great deal of penal experimentation in the decades that followed.

LESSER SANCTIONS

If the judges had few choices when they passed sentence on convicted felons, they were much less constrained in the case of other common law offenses not regulated by statutes, including misdemeanors. Within certain limits, they were freer to choose among a range of punishments that in 1660 included imprisonment, fines, whipping, and public exposure in the stocks or pillory, or some variant of this, such as the ducking stool. A number of prominent political cases in King's Bench in the reigns of Charles II and James II reminded those who might have forgotten the activities of Star Chamber before the Civil War just how crushing such punishments could be: the thirty thousand pound fine assessed, for example, against the Duke of Devonshire in 1687 for striking someone within the verge of the king's palace, which fine was adjudged by the House of Lords to be oppressive and illegal; or the punishment of Titus Oates, who upon his conviction for perjury was sentenced to be fined a thousand marks, whipped severely in public, imprisoned at the pleasure of the Crown, and placed upon the pillory five times a year.[13] It was such penalties that explain the limits imposed by the Bill of Rights, specifically making excessive fines illegal and prohibiting cruel and unusual punishments.[14] Of course in ordinary, nonpolitical trials at the assizes and quarter sessions, judges and justices were more restrained in their use of discretionary punishments even before these limits were drawn.

Fines

Minor game offenses, petty fraud, and cheating, a number of crimes that would fall into the category of offenses against justice (contempt of officials, for example, or obstructing justice, refusing to aid an officer when called upon, or aiding an escape), seditious or insulting words spoken against the monarch, and a variety of other charges could all be punished by fines.

[13] F. Hargrave, W. Cobbett, T. B. Howell, and T. J. Howell, eds., *State Trials* (1809–20), vol. 11, col. 1353; vol. 10, col. 1325. And see Baker, "Criminal Courts and Procedure," p. 44.

[14] A. F. Granucci, "Nor Cruel and Unusual Punishments Inflicted': The Original Meaning," *California Law Review* 57 (1969), pp. 839–65.

Where the public interest was engaged the fines could be large and damaging.[15] But the majority of offenders fined in Surrey had been convicted
of assault, and for the most part the courts' assessments in such cases were
modest. At the quarter sessions, where assault cases were generally tried,
the range of fines in the late seventeenth century was from six pence to
ten pounds, but the latter was unusually heavy and since the prisoner in
this case was a laborer it seems likely that it was intended as a way of
putting him in the county jail for a long period. The median of ninety-
three fines for common assault was two shillings and six pence, and if one
excludes eight that were at the highest end and that were plainly unusual,
the average was about 3*s*. 6*d*. More than a third of the fines assessed in
assault cases at the quarter sessions were six pence or a shilling, an amount
that seems not so much an assessment made on behalf of the Crown to
discourage similar behavior in the future as a token that the two parties
in conflict had reached an agreement. A larger fine might well result when
such agreement was not forthcoming, and its threat, along with the further
threat that the nonpayment of a large fine could result in a period in jail,
was clearly used by the courts as a way of persuading a recalcitrant prisoner
to come to terms with the complainant.

Two cases in the eighteenth century illustrate the role the courts
played in these quasi-civil settlements. The chairman of the Middlesex
quarter sessions, asked to report on the case of one Hutchinson Little who
had been held in jail for eleven months, told the secretary of state that
Little had recently "agreed to make and has since accordingly made Satisfaction to the Prosecutor." He went on to explain that "it was Inducement
to the Court to set the Fine they did on the said Hutchinson Little that
he might talk with the said Prosecutor, he having done so, and the
Prosecutor being satisfied" he could now be released.[16] The connection
between the private satisfaction and the public fine was made even more
explicit by the Recorder of London in 1729. In discussing an assault and
battery, he said that it was "usual in these cases for the Defendant to make
satisfaction to the Prosecutor for his wounds, and costs and charges—
before the Court sets the fine . . . which is usually greater if a Defendant
won't make a Prosecutor easy as the Court directs." That being the case,
he went on to say, it was better for the defendant or his friends to speak
with the prosecutor before the trial "and then if he forbears to appear and
prosecute [the defendant] will be discharged, and all charges of a Tryal

---

[15] It should be emphasized that the evidence for the fines imposed is incomplete. Even when
it is clear that a case reached a conclusion and the defendant was convicted, the fine assessed is
not always revealed in the court record. It is possible, too, that some of the fines imposed were
in the end remitted.

[16] SP 36/54, f. 94.

saved, which would be a greate expence."[17] Blackstone disapproved of this engagement of the criminal courts, particularly the quarter sessions, in thus encouraging private settlements in assault cases.[18] But it was surely simply an extension of the attitude toward such conflicts that magistrates were encouraged to take when the parties first came before them, and it was plainly very common indeed.

A heavier fine might thus have resulted from a failure of the parties to agree. But some were exacted as punishments and registered the court's disapproval of the offense itself. One of a number of circumstances often seems present when a hefty fine was demanded: the high status of the victim; the possibility that an attack on a woman had been with the intention of raping her; or the disturbance's engaging public concern in some way. In one offense in which the offender was fined a pound the victim alleged that her attacker had intended to rape her; and it is entirely possible (though I have no evidence) that in four other cases in which a man was fined the relatively large amount of ten shillings or more for assaulting a woman, the judge or the magistrates were persuaded that rape had been the motive on those occasions too. Certainly it was not the mere fact that a man had assaulted a woman, for many such cases ended in the nominal fine of six pence or a shilling.

The status of the victim seems also to have influenced the size of the fine in assault cases. The ten-pound penalty noticed earlier was for an assault on a gentleman, and several of the heavy fines had similarly been imposed on workmen for attacking their social superiors: a carpenter who assaulted a gentleman had to pay one pound; a tanner was assessed £3.6.8 by an assize judge for attacking an esquire. But there was no simple tariff of fines linked to status. Private agreements were also possible in cases in which a gentleman was attacked by his social inferior, and that may explain why a waterman who assaulted a gentleman was fined a mere 3s. 4d. and why a victualler who got into a quarrel with Sir William Russell, Bart., had to pay only a shilling when he was convicted of assault.

It would be reasonable to expect that attacks on constables and other officers, overseers of the poor and the like, would bring a heavier fine than would a mere private squabble. Of the six such cases in Surrey in the late seventeenth century for which the evidence of the fine assessed survives, one was for a pound, and another involving an attack on a constable by a gentleman and tried at the assizes was for two pounds. Again there was no invariable reflex in the courts to defend officialdom by heavy fines, however, for the others were a shilling.

[17] SP 36/15, ff. 183–84.
[18] Blackstone, *Commentaries*, vol. 4, pp. 356–57.

It does not appear that the damage done to a victim of an assault had a direct bearing on the court's assessment: that would be mainly taken into consideration in a private settlement. The courts were perhaps more sensitive to offenses that had caused a public disturbance or had threatened to do so. There were some stiff fines in cases in which the offenders were indicted for unlawful assembly and riot and trespass as well as for mere assault: £10 on one occasion at the Surrey assizes and £6.19.8 on another, £4 at the quarter sessions. But for the most part such fines were also concentrated at the lower end of the scale, mainly a shilling or 2s. 6d., sealing a settlement as much as being the settlement itself.

The amount of the fine was in the court's hands to set. The bench had considerable leeway, and without doubt it imposed crushing burdens on some men. Fines of five pounds or more, along with the order that he remain in jail until it was paid, could threaten a poor man with life imprisonment. Peter Black, fined £6.13.4 in 1690 for speaking seditious words against William III, was described by the trial judge when he recommended his pardon in the following year as "a poor indigent person, not able to pay the said fine."[19] Fines of fifty or a hundred pounds were extracted for particularly heinous offenses. Attempted buggery by a clergyman in 1699, for example, and seditious words spoken by a gentleman, also in William III's reign, both led to fines of a hundred pounds. The assize courts dealt with many fewer cases of assault than did the quarter sessions, but no doubt some of the more serious incidents were reserved for the judges on their circuits, and some of those cases led to heavy fines: a man convicted of assault in 1702 was fined forty pounds at the Surrey assizes, for example; four years later another was assessed fifty pounds for a similar offense. The sentence commonly specified that the defendant was to be held in jail until the fine was paid, and fines of this magnitude must often have meant that the convicted man was held in the county jail for a number of years at the pleasure of the bench. That was certainly the fate of the man fined fifty pounds in 1706 who was still in jail three years later, and it may have been some time after that before his fine was remitted and he was allowed his freedom.[20]

Such large fines were not common, particularly at the quarter sessions. But of course a fine of a pound or two, or even of five or ten shillings

---

[19] C 82/2674, warrant dated July 1691. Not all seditious words were so expensive. The man who said in public that "the Queen Dowager is a whore and a bitch and I will prove her a whore" was fined merely five shillings in the same period (ASSI 35/131/12/3).

[20] ASSI 35/140/7, calendar. I have not investigated the payment and nonpayment of fines systematically, but my impression is that well before imprisonment became instituted as a regular punishment it would not have been uncommon to find men being held in jail for long periods because they could not pay a fine.

(and about a fifth of the fines over the late seventeenth century in Surrey were more than five shillings), would have been serious for many a working man, especially when the other expenses of the trial were added in. And in addition to occasional petitions to get men released from jail who had no prospect of paying a huge sum,[21] attempts can be found being made by men who had some influence on the bench to get the magistrates to set modest fines for their friends or dependents. One magistrate, for example, was asked by a man who may have been the prisoner's employer to advise the offender in an assault case whether he should plead guilty or not and then to "assist to get the fine if any as low as possible [since] he is very poor and expedition in bringing it on may ease expenses one way as your influence in the court will the other. . . ." He also tried to engage the interest of the clerk of the peace who, for earlier favors done, had promised "he would at any time be ready to render me service."[22] Other petitions came into the court to forestall heavy fines. On the whole, however, the courts in the late seventeenth century followed the rule ultimately derived from Magna Carta that, as Blackstone was to define it, they would not "assess a larger fine than a man is able to pay, without touching the implements of his livelihood."[23] If they wanted to impose a heavier punishment, he went on to say, they should take it out on his hide by way of imprisonment or whipping.

When Blackstone wrote that passage, imprisonment was perhaps becoming more widely accepted as a punishment at the quarter sessions and assizes. There had indeed been one period in the early eighteenth century when, for reasons we will discuss later, imprisonment at hard labor had been widely employed against convicted felons in some counties. Apart from that brief experiment with a particular form of imprisonment, however, neither the magistrates in quarter sessions nor the judges seem to have thought of incarceration as a useful punishment in the century after the Restoration. They did occasionally order that a prisoner be held in jail for a term of years, especially in cases that aroused public disapproval or in which the interests of the state were engaged. But often such imprisonment was in addition to a heavy fine or to more physical and public punishments such as whipping or the pillory. A man who in 1723 had attempted to rob the couple with whom he lodged, wounding them severely with a knife in the process, was ordered by the Middlesex magistrates to be imprisoned for four years and to be publicly whipped twice in the course of that term.[24] Sentences by which men were to be held in

[21] For example, SP 35/14, f. 144; SP 35/42, f. 456; SP 36/28, f. 131; SP 36/59, f. 30.
[22] QS 2/6, Mich. 1733, 39.
[23] Blackstone, *Commentaries*, vol. 4, p. 380.
[24] *British Journal*, 7 Sept. 1723.

jail so that they might be whipped or pilloried more than once, while not common, were also ordered in Surrey from time to time. But imprisonment on its own was not frequently imposed. The magistrates and judges were much more likely in noncapital cases to order sanctions that engaged the community in the punishment of the offender, sanctions that caused physical pain and also humiliated the prisoner and heaped ignominy upon him. The two such punishments principally employed were whipping and the pillory.

Whipping

The whipping of prisoners was carried out both in "private," within a jail or house of correction by the jailer or someone hired by him, and in public by the common hangman or a constable or a man hired for the occasion and paid out of county rates. Vagrants and others sent by the summary powers of magistrates to the house of correction were subjected to punishment by whipping, and occasionally men and women convicted of misdemeanors were similarly punished. The offense that most often resulted in corporal punishment was petty larceny, the theft of goods worth less than a shilling. By the middle of the eighteenth century some of those convicted of grand larceny were being sentenced to be whipped, but for the most part before 1750 whipping was reserved for those convicted of the lesser charge. There was also perhaps a tendency by the middle of the eighteenth century for whippings to be carried out more in private than might have been the case fifty or a hundred years earlier. Chief Justice Ryder was told by the clerk of assize when he first went on circuit that unless he specified otherwise a sentence of whipping would be administered privately.[25] Public whippings continued to be ordered, however, particularly at the quarter sessions, until the end of the eighteenth century.

Parishes were supposed to provide "whipping posts" at which the prisoner would be tied by the hands, and there is evidence of their being used in this period and of concern from time to time that they were falling into disrepair.[26] But the most common method of public flogging was "at the cart's tail": the prisoner was tied to the back of a cart, stripped to the

[25] Ryder Assize Diary, p. 5. Ryder was also told by Mr. Justice Foster that women were never sentenced to be whipped, but that was quite incorrect, as the clerk of assize later informed him (p. 15). The clerk also implied that women were invariably ordered to be whipped privately. That may have been the case at the Home Circuit assizes by the 1750s, but it was not the practice at every court, for women were still being whipped in public at the Surrey quarter sessions in this period (QS 2/1/18, p. 95).

[26] *Surrey Quarter Sessions Records*, 1663–66, p. 145; QS 2/6, Mids. 1716, 22; QS 2/6, 1715, 56.

waist, and whipped over a specific route or "until his back be bloody." Such whippings must have been common throughout the country over the whole period we are dealing with, at least until the very end of the eighteenth century. The course over which the punishment would take place was usually laid out by the magistrates in quarter sessions. A man convicted of petty larceny in 1731, for example, was ordered to be "stript from the middle upwards and whipped at the cart's tail tomorrow from the county gaol {in Southwark} to St. Thomas's Gate till blood come." Another, some years later, was "to be taken to Carshalton [where the offense had taken place] and delivered to the constable there and publicly whipped at the cart's tail there, and from the Church gate to the stocks."[27] Whipping at the cart's tail was included in a volume of illustrations of punishments published in 1681.[28] It was undoubtedly the form that most whipping sentences took then, and it continued to be for more than a century. It is likely indeed that the order concerning the course over which the prisoner would be whipped and the day and time at which the punishment would be administered became even more precise in the second half of the eighteenth century in the interests of attracting the largest possible crowd.

Wherever it was carried out, the actual punishment inflicted by a sentence of whipping must have differed considerably from one case to another. Carts could go quickly or slowly, over long or short distances; the man with the whip might be strong or weak, sympathetic or pitiless. Unlike military floggings (and unlike the practice in some counties) whipping sentences against criminals in Surrey and Sussex were apparently never specified by the number of stripes.[29] Sentences sometimes directed that the prisoner be whipped "severely." But such instructions, and the more common formula "until his back be bloody," did not make for precision,

[27] QS 2/6, Ep. 1731, 59; QS 2/6, Ea. 1735, 78.

[28] *A book of punishments of the common laws of England* (1681). I owe this reference to John Langbein.

[29] I owe to Joannes Innes the information that in the 1760s and 1770s the Cambridge quarter sessions specified the number of lashes to be administered to convicted prisoners ordered to be whipped: the number varied between two and twelve in the period 1763–74 (evidence drawn from the quarter sessions Order Book). She has also found instances of whipping sentences laid out in the number of stripes at the Norfolk quarter sessions in January 1755 and in the Minute Book of the Norwich Corporation of the Poor in October 1761. Sollom Emlyn remarked in 1730 on the unfairness of allowing a prisoner ordered to be whipped to be "at the mercy of a vile executioner" who had it in his power "to make that whipping as severe or as favourable as he pleases" (*State Trials*, vol. 1, p. xi). For military floggings, the number of stripes ordered by courts-martial, and the mitigation by the king of what were often very heavy sentences, see Arthur N. Gilbert, "Military and Civilian Justice in Eighteenth-Century England: An Assessment," *Journal of British Studies* (Spring 1978), pp. 50–55.

and certainly not for uniformity of treatment. One common element, deliberately aimed at, was humiliation. That was the point of the punishment's being carried out in public. The shame of being whipped before people who knew the prisoner and his family was calculated to increase the terror and the effectiveness of the punishment as a discouragement of minor crime beyond the pain it inflicted.

Corporal punishment of this kind was class based. Gentlemen (and, it goes without saying, gentlewomen) were not subjected to whippings in public because the loss of honor they would incur would be a greater punishment than the law intended. A man convicted before the King's Bench in 1719 for conspiring with another to extort money from Lord Sunderland by threatening to accuse him of sodomy was told that "nothing but his being a clergyman protected him from a corporal punishment." He was fined five hundred pounds, sentenced to a year's imprisonment, and ordered to find sureties for his good behavior for seven years beyond that.[30] Plebeians, being without honor in the same sense, were thought to have less to lose: "Marks of ignominy and disgrace which would be shocking and grievous to a person of liberal education," one man asserted confidently, "would be slighted and despised by one of the vulgar sort." But many men of the "vulgar sort" (according to this social vision) who were sentenced to be scourged in public did have a reputation and character that would be diminished by the indignity of being whipped like an animal before a crowd. If the crowd was hostile that would undoubtedly have added to the pain of the punishment; their hostility might also have encouraged the man with the whip to lay on with a will. The large crowd that watched the young man who had wounded his landlord and his wife being whipped through the streets of London in 1723 was said to have been "so far from pitying him that many of them called out for justice."[31] But the longer-term effect for those who underwent such punishment in their own communities, rendered infamous among those who knew them well, was much more serious. It was calculated to shame and to dishonor the offender, to diminish his moral worth. The loss of reputation and the blow to the respectability of his family must surely have been sharply felt by many. Few thought it possible, or worth their while, to petition against the sentence on those grounds. But it is likely that many looked upon such a punishment as did John Merry, a plasterer of Westminster, who was convicted of petty larceny (for taking what he regarded as scrap wood from a building site) and ordered to be whipped. He petitioned for a royal

[30] R vs. Kinnersley and Moore: Strange, *Reports*, vol. 1, p. 196; *Eng. Rep.*, vol. 93, p. 469 (1719).
[31] *British Journal*, 14 Sept. 1723.

pardon and for a remission of the sentence that, he said, was "to be put in execution in his own neighbourhood, on Friday the 11th of this instant December 1719, to the great reproach and utter ruin of himself and his two sisters, who have always lived in very good reputation in the Parish of St. James in the Liberty of Westminster."[32] Another man asked the Surrey magistrates to alter his sentence from a public to a private whipping so that he would be able to continue to find employment in Southwark and to continue to support his family.[33]

The Pillory

The sharp warning that whipping was intended to deliver was studiously enhanced by the participation and engagement of the public as audience in a consciously theatrical performance. Another punishment that sought even more directly to stigmatize and dishonor and to mark out an offender as unworthy of trust or respect was the pillory, in which the prisoner was made to undergo a form of public penance by being exhibited on a platform with his hands and head fixed in a wooden structure.[34] What actually happened while the prisoner was exposed (generally for an hour, though the offender might be pilloried several times) depended largely on the mood of the spectators. That in turn depended on the prisoner's offense, which was usually announced on a paper placed on his head.

The offenses that judges and magistrates were anxious to punish by the pillory were acts that aroused deep public anger and hostility, either because of the vulnerability of the victim (a child, for example) or because the offense was both damaging and difficult to prevent. The point of punishment by public exposure was in those cases not only to chastise the offender and to deter him and others from such behavior in the future, but also quite simply to make his identity known so as to forewarn potential victims—"to mark him out to the public," as was said in 1730, "as a person not fit to be trusted, but to be shunned and avoided by all creditable and honest men."[35] Men and women were thus pilloried for various forms

---

[32] SP 35/67, f. 57.

[33] QS 2/6, Ep. 1746, 35.

[34] Magistrates could order similar forms of exposure in the village stocks or simply in some other public place. A man who was convicted summarily of swearing a hundred oaths and who could not pay the fine nor had any goods to forfeit was ordered to sit in the stocks at Newington, for two hours, for example. And in the middle of the eighteenth century a woman who had stolen a sheet from the workhouse of St. Saviour's parish in Southwark was ordered to stand once a week for a month in the workhouse yard; another woman convicted of stealing a turnip was made to stand on a stool in Wandsworth for an hour. See QS 2/6, 1705, 26; QS 2/1/18, p. 177; QS 2/5, Ea. 1751, 24–26.

[35] Emlyn, ed., *State Trials*, vol. 1, p. xi.

of fraudulence and cheating: pretending to tell a fortune; cheating at cards and other games; taking a watch as a pledge for a loan and not giving the full sum promised; offering to bury the body of a dead infant for ten pence and then not doing so; pretending to be a servant collecting for his master. Perjury occasionally brought offenders to the pillory, as did conspiracies to extort money by threatening a false accusation, especially when the mere accusation would have been very damaging, as in the case of a woman who threatened to accuse a clergyman of fathering her bastard child or a man accusing another of attempted sodomy. Women were occasionally pilloried for keeping bawdy houses.[36]

Punishments in the pillory were not as common in Southwark as they were in the much more populous parts of the metropolis across the Thames. There were frequent reports of men and women standing on the pillory at Charing Cross throughout the eighteenth century. In Surrey, the courts ordered such a sentence on average over the whole period we are dealing with once every eighteen months or so. Two of the most common offenses punished in Surrey by such public exposure were also the two that tended to draw the greatest hostility from the crowd: "assault" with the intention of committing a homosexual act; and molesting children, sometimes described as rape or attempted rape of an infant. A man convicted at the Summer assizes in 1663 of "a fowle and great trespass in attempting an Act of uncleanness with a girl about eight years old" was set on the pillory in Southwark on a market day at eleven in the morning for two hours.[37] This was not the invariable punishment for attempted rape, but it was imposed on at least eight men in the sixty-two years sampled over the whole period, and the courts were especially likely to order the pillory when the victim was a child under ten. John Bromley, who was convicted of such offenses against two children in a workhouse, was jailed for a year and sentenced in addition to stand on the pillory for an hour.[38] Another Surrey man found guilty in the mid-eighteenth century of a sexual act with a four-year-old child was pilloried twice.[39] And similar punishments were ordered in other sexual cases. A man convicted of attempting to commit buggery with a mare was imprisoned in the house of correction for a year and ordered to be set on the pillory in three different market towns in Surrey in the course of that period, the third time just before he was released.[40]

[36] ASSI 35/163/6, calendar; ASSI 35/176/15/35; QS 2/5, Ea. 1754, 65; QS 2/5, Ea. 1752, 8; QS 2/5, Mids. 1750, 36; *Weekly Journal or British Gazeteer*, 3 Mar. 1722; S.A.P., Lent 1752, pp. 18–21 (Lingard); QS 2/1/18, p. 54.

[37] ASSI 35/104/8 (Fletcher).

[38] S.A.P., Lent 1739, pp. 22–23.

[39] S.A.P., Summer 1751, p. 40 (Bland).

[40] ASSI 35/218/7/35.

In these cases, as indeed in cases of fraud and cheating and most of the other offenses that led to punishment by exposure on the pillory, the authorities could be reasonably certain that their view of the community's standards and the justice of the sentence would be fully accepted by the crowd around the pillory and that the offender would be denounced. For some offenses the sympathies of the public must have been much less predictable, however. When they put a man in the pillory for speaking seditious words or for slandering a public figure like a magistrate or for refusing to pay an unpopular tax, the courts were clearly risking a demonstration of support for the prisoner that would turn his punishment into a triumph and undermine authority and the law. They nonetheless did so, and at moments when feelings were running high. In the years after the Revolution of 1689, for example, men were put in the pillory at Southwark for drinking toasts to the Jacobite cause and for saying that William III "was a rogue" or that James II "was King of England and they were all rogues and dogs who said the contrary" or that William was a villain and no king.[41] How these men fared is unclear. But at other times men in such circumstances were treated indulgently and as a victim of an oppressive regime. On at least one occasion in London following the Hanoverian succession a man convicted of speaking seditious words against George I was rescued by the crowd and released from the pillory at the Royal Exchange. The judge had simply provided the anti-Hanoverian crowd with an opportunity for an effective demonstration of its opposition to the new regime. A number of similar miscalculations of public sentiment occurred throughout the century.[42]

These were exceptional moments, however, around the London pillories. For the most part the pillory was a scene not of triumph, but of terror. With good reason prisoners spoke of their "dread and apprehension" of their hour before the public, or "begged for any chastisement rather than the pillory."[43] For some indeed it proved to be fatal. The expectation was that a large crowd would gather. Pillories were erected in open spaces and in Surrey for the most part in the densest areas of population, some-

[41] ASSI 35/131/7/22 (Powell); ASSI 35/132/7/33 (Edwards); ASSI 35/135/11/5 (Shotter). Even more curious perhaps was the decision in 1723 to place men in the pillory for deer-stealing in Waltham Forest in Essex and in Endfield Chase. See *The London Journal*, Aug. 1723; Derek Barlow, *Dick Turpin and the Gregory Gang* (1973), p. 4; and Thompson, *Whigs and Hunters*, p. 172.

[42] Nicholas Rogers, "London Politics from Walpole to Pitt: Patriotism and Independency in an Era of Commercial Imperialism, 1738–63" (Ph.D. thesis, University of Toronto, 1974), p. 533. A man pilloried in 1738 in Cheapside for not paying the duty on soap was treated indulgently. The crowd allowed him to stand quietly, a newspaper noted, and "on his coming on the pillory, and on his going off, he made several bows to them" (*London Evening Post*, 9, 19 Sept. 1738).

[43] SP 36/140, f. 376; *London Evening Post*, 6 Apr. 1738.

times near the place where the offense had occurred. They were arranged usually for mid-day,[44] and often on a market day. There was clearly a hope behind these arrangements that the crowd would make the offender very uncomfortable, that he would be taunted, perhaps pelted. But there was always the danger of more severe treatment, particularly of men whose offenses outraged the public. This was not in fact uncommon throughout the eighteenth century and within the larger metropolis of London. Vicious attacks occurred frequently on offenders pinioned in the wooden frame. Sometimes there was more than a suggestion that the constables and other officials on duty did less than they might have to protect them; more often, the crowds were so large and determined that, as a newspaper said of one occasion in the middle of the eighteenth century, they threatened "not only the lives of the persons in the pillory, but of the very officers who attend."[45] There were reports of men in the pillory in Southwark being "severely pelted" with dirt and stones and sticks until their heads were bloody, and of a woman who kept a bawdy house being "severely handled" by the populace as she stood in the pillory near the New Gaol in Southwark.[46] The treatment of a sixty-year-old man pilloried in Cheapside for a homosexual offense was all too typical: "the populace fell upon the wretch," it was reported,

> tore off his coat, waistcoat, shirt, hat, wig, and breeches, and then pelted and whipped him till he had scarcely any signs of life left; he was once pulled off the pillory, but hung by his arms till he was set up again and stood in that naked condition, covered with mud, till the hour was out, and then was carried back to Newgate.[47]

Some men were dealt with even more harshly in London. In 1723 one John Middleton was convicted of attempting to earn rewards by making false accusations of treasonable practices, at a time when the Walpole-Townshend administration was alarmed by the level of popular disaffection in London and was trying all ways to get evidence against printers and pamphleteers and ballad-singers. The government prosecuted him, and he was sentenced to stand on the pillory at Charing Cross for an hour. He

---

[44] The time that, according to Francis Place in the 1820s, was the "common dining hour for all sorts of persons who earn their livings by the labour of their hands and consequently the time when the streets were crowded by such people" (Add Mss. 27826, p. 172).

[45] *Evening Advertiser*, 20 Mar. 1756.

[46] *G. M.* 22 (1752), p. 190; *Whitehall Evening Post*, 10 May 1783.

[47] *G. M.* 32 (1762), p. 549. For the treatment of a man pilloried in the reign of James II for saying that "he hoped to see all the Protestants fry in their owne grease before Michaelmas next," see Richard Gough, *The History of Myddle*, ed. David Hey (Harmondsworth, 1981), p. 174.

did not survive it. Few figures were hated more in the eighteenth century than the informer, but a false, a perjured, informer was the most infamous and despised of men. As soon as Middleton was placed in the pillory he was attacked. "The Mob was so numerous and violent," an eyewitness said, "and pelted the said Middleton so barbarously that tho' this Deponent hath seen several persons before stand upon the pillory he never saw any so much abused." In the end he was choked by the mud and dirt heaped upon him and died before he was taken down.[48] A few years later one John Waller was killed in the pillory at the Seven Dials after being convicted of attempting to bring a false prosecution for the sake of the reward. Within a few minutes of his being exposed, the pillory was pulled down and he was trampled by the crowd. "As he lay on the ground," a contemporary account reported, the crowd "stamped so hard upon his body, that they broke his ribs." His skull was fractured, and he died before he could be returned to Newgate.[49] And in 1756 four members of an infamous gang of so-called thief-takers who had drawn unsuspecting young men into committing highway robberies so that they could then prosecute them for the substantial rewards offered by the government were similarly treated, and one, surrounded by an enormous crowd of butchers and drovers at Smithfield Market where the pillory was set up, was stoned to death.[50]

CHANGING PENAL OPTIONS

We have strayed a long way beyond the late seventeenth century (and across the river into the wider metropolis of London) in this brief discussion of the pillory, but it is unlikely that its character changed substantially over the century following the Restoration.[51] It is useful to get some sense of the nature of this punishment by public exposure because the pillory reveals in their clearest form the attitudes and assumptions that much of the broader penal practice of 1660 rested on. Public punishments on the gallows and at the whipping post or cart's tail, as well as on the pillory, were at least in the part moral-degradation ceremonies in which the crowd that watched played an important part. They were engaged in a renewal

---

[48] SP 35/44, f. 232.

[49] The Life and Infamous Actions of . . . John Waller who made his Exit in the Pillory at the Seven Dials Tuesday 13 June. . . . (1732), p. 29; and see G. M. 2 (1732), pp. 774, 823. For the implications of the charge against Waller see Langbein, "Shaping the Eighteenth-Century Criminal Trial," p. 108, n. 441.

[50] G. M. 26 (1756), pp. 90, 116, 166, 297–300; Radzinowicz, History, vol. 2, pp. 326–32.

[51] On the pillory in the second half of the eighteenth century see chap. 10.

of community values by their recognition and disapproval of the deviant act committed by the offender on display.[52] His exposure and punishment were intended to discourage him and others from committing other offenses. And beyond that, public punishment performed the wider function of reaffirming the moral boundaries of the society. The crowds that came to watch the "hanging matches" or a public whipping or a man on the pillory confirmed and reestablished the acceptable by participating in the condemning of the unacceptable. These measures could become confused if the crowd sympathized with the offender, or disapproved of his conviction and punishment. But such views were rarely demonstrated or expressed in the late seventeenth century. Little disapproval appears to have surfaced in the late seventeenth century concerning the punishment of the mainstream offenses against property and against the person dealt with at the assizes and quarter sessions.

On the other hand, there is evidence of a growing dissatisfaction after 1660 with the lack of options available to the courts for the punishment of convicted felons, and in particular with the lack of an effective secondary punishment short of death. There appears to have been a sense by 1660 that the courts were inadequately armed against serious offenders, and that some real noncapital punishment more damaging than the branding that followed a successful plea of clergy was required to deter them. It is significant that there was apparently no anxiety to discourage crime by increasing the numbers of offenders hanged. Indeed, the reverse seems to have been the case, at least in practice. It has been shown that over the seventeenth century there was a decided decline in several counties (and apparently nationally) in both the absolute number of felons hanged and the proportion of accused felons eventually brought to the gallows.[53] That decline may have been encouraged by a falling away in the level of property offenses. But it is obviously more complex than a mere response to the number of prosecutions. There is no evidence, for example, that crime and social disorder were thought to be less of a problem in the metropolis of London in the last decades of the seventeenth century. Indeed, there was if anything a growing anxiety about such problems in the capital and a determination to find ways of dealing with them. And yet, if evidence from Surrey is any guide, the level of capital punishment declined in the metropolis as well as in provincial centers in the seventeenth century.

[52] On this see Stephen Box, *Deviance, Reality and Society* (1971), pp. 36–42; Kai T. Erikson, *Wayward Puritans* (New York, 1966), pp. 3–29.
[53] J. A. Sharpe, *Crime in Seventeenth-Century England. A County Study* (1983), pp. 141–42; idem, "The Prosecution of Felony and Capital Punishment in Seventeenth-Century England: Towards a National Pattern?" (paper presented to the Conference on the History of Law, Labour and Crime, University of Warwick, Sept. 1983).

An apparent disinclination in the courts to send large numbers of offenders to the gallows in the second half of the seventeenth century thus suggests that there may have been some change in attitudes toward capital punishment itself. And both the smaller numbers of offenders hanged and changing sentiment about punishment may in turn have helped to exaggerate and to underline the narrow range of punishments the courts could call upon in dealing with convicted felons. The fact that, as a contemporary said, the numbers of offenders hanged were "very few in Comparison with the Escapers"[54] and that those who were not sent to the gallows were merely branded on the thumb and discharged was a matter of wide concern by the 1660s. That concern gave rise to a variety of efforts to enlarge the punishments that might be imposed on convicted felons.

THE ORIGINS OF TRANSPORTATION

Over the period from 1660 to 1720 a number of expedients were tried, some originating in the courts, others in parliament, to find alternatives to the simple discharge that followed the granting of clergy. The outcome was to be a striking departure in the patterns of punishment in England, when in 1718 parliament established transportation to the American colonies as a regular punishment for noncapital offenses. It was to transform the way the courts dealt with serious offenders.

The emergence of transportation was by no means straightforward; nor was it the only new departure in penal practice in this period. My intention here is to sketch some of the expedients out of which this substantially altered system emerged. Recovering the fragmented evidence of those efforts is difficult enough. Explaining them, or rather explaining why alternatives were sought (by whom and for what purpose) and the success of some over others, is much more difficult because changes in punishment are almost certain not to arise from a simple, one-dimensional effect. The forms of punishment employed by a society at any moment are shaped by a variety of interests and intentions. They arise in response to what must often be antagonistic considerations, including the framework of law, what is technologically possible, what seems desirable or necessary in light of the apparent problem of crime, what society is willing to accept and to pay for. Why one method of punishment loses favor over time and gives way to another is a complex question because penal methods evolve within a larger social and cultural context that in imperceptible ways alters the limits of what is acceptable in that society and what is not.

[54] Roger North, A *Discourse of the Poor* (written 1688; pub. 1753), p. 29.

Broad shifts in sentiment and large-scale social and economic changes thus form the fundamental levers of change in penal systems. But within those larger forces, as it were, the speed and character of change is shaped by more immediate decisions of men in the courts or in the government, men who contributed to the making of what one might loosely call "penal policy." Several possible agents of change in penal matters can be discerned in the period we are dealing with in England: the judges, whose discretionary powers gave them considerable influence over the way the law was administered; the king and the privy council (and in the eighteenth century the cabinet), who not only determined policy with regard to pardons from capital punishment but also exercised a broad supervision over the judges; and, over the longer term and with regard to the broad framework of the law, parliament, whose capacity to act in a policy-making role was significantly advanced when annual sessions became the norm after 1689. Important changes in the forms of punishment (as in the criminal law) were to be introduced by statute, particularly in the eighteenth century. For the most part the impulses behind these statutory changes have not yet been uncovered, but it seems clear that while some were likely to have been initiated by the government, much of the legislation had been introduced by private members in response to petitions from ad hoc interest groups of farmers or merchants or others, or as the result of addresses from grand juries or such influential bodies as the mayor and the corporation of the City of London.

It is difficult to discover where the main thrust for changes in penal practice was coming from in the late seventeenth century, but it seems clear that there was a considerable interest in seeing some such changes, and particularly in stiffening the consequences of conviction for clergyable felonies to prevent some men and women from merely being branded on the thumb and returned to society. There was an attempt soon after the Restoration, for example, to replace clergyable discharge with transportation. A bill introduced into the House of Commons in February 1663 would have authorized "the transporting of felons"; another submitted to the Lords some months later would have made it possible for the courts to transport "persons convicted of felony within clergy, or for petty larceny."[55] Neither passed, but the belief in the usefulness of such a penalty seems to have been widely shared. Some of the judges clearly held such a view, for there was a strong push from the bench in the 1660s (probably

[55] *J.H.C.* 8 (1660–67), pp. 437, 438, 443; *J.H.L.* 11 (1660–66), p. 529, and see pp. 330, 561, 587, 588, 591 (I owe these references to Joanna Innes). A Bill (eventually joined to the Felons Bill) was also introduced into the House of Commons at the same time to authorize the transportation of rogues and vagabonds; the power to suggest names of such rogues to the privy council with a view to their being transported was granted to the quarter sessions by the Act of Settlement, 14 Chas II, c. 12, s. 6 (1662).

with the support of the Privy Council) to introduce transportation by manipulating the rules governing the granting of benefit of clergy.

While it was not available to the courts as a regular punishment in 1660, transportation to the American colonies and to the West Indies had in fact been imposed on a number of convicts over the previous sixty years, principally as a condition of a royal pardon. Virtually as soon as the colonies had been established in the early seventeenth century the government had been persuaded of the mutual advantage of sending condemned criminals (who would otherwise have been hanged) to build up their populations. As Langbein has pointed out, transportation developed as the English equivalent to the galley service of France and Spain. Indeed he has traced a connection between the beginnings of transportation and a "stillborn attempt to introduce the galley sentence in England" in 1602. A commission issued in that year to a number of privy councillors and judges authorizing them to reprieve condemned felons for service in galleys was the model, in his view, for another issued by James I in 1615 that empowered a committee of the council to select from condemned prisoners those that it might be appropriate to pardon and send to the colonies, prisoners "whoe for strength of bodie or other abilities shall be thought fitt to be ymploied in forraine discoveries or other services beyond the Seas."[56] Under such authority, small groups of pardoned convicts were transported to the East and West Indies and to Virginia and other mainland colonies over the next quarter century.[57] The total probably did not exceed, however, a few hundred at best.

The next, and what was to be a middle, stage in the history of transportation to America began in 1654 when a group of convicts condemned to death at the Surrey assizes were pardoned by the Protector on the condition (a condition included in the pardon itself) that they be transported by the sheriff "to some English Plantation," and that if they returned within ten years the pardon was to be considered null and void.[58] This method of transporting prisoners by means of a conditional pardon was continued, after some hesitation, at the Restoration. A number of merchants with interests in Jamaica were given permission in 1661, for example, to take a number of pardoned convicts from the London jails (including the Surrey county jail) and to transport them to the island to help bolster its population.[59]

Transportation had obvious attractions. It provided a relatively simple

---

[56] Langbein, *Torture and the Law of Proof*, pp. 40–41; Smith, *Colonists in Bondage*, p. 93.

[57] Smith, *Colonists in Bondage*, pp. 93–95; and see his "The Transportation of Convicts to the American Colonies in the Seventeenth Century," *American Historical Review* 39 (1933–34).

[58] C 66/2912 (3).

[59] *Acts of the Privy Council (Colonial)*, vol. 1, pp. 310, 314–15.

way of ensuring that convicted men who were not entirely corrupted, but who had committed offenses that made them a danger to the community, could be disposed of without being hanged. It provided a way of regulating the level of capital punishment while providing proof of the king's care for his people and frequent demonstrations of his exercising his proper role by tempering justice with mercy. In addition, it provided the convict himself with an opportunity to make a new start, and there was present from the beginning the hope and expectation that men who had lost their characters in England might well become productive citizens in a new society, that the harsh discipline of the raw society across the Atlantic would reclaim men from the laziness and the bad habits that it was assumed had gradually led them into crime in the first place.[60] The rehabilitation of offenders was not a major consideration in the seventeenth century, but it was obviously recognized as a secondary advantage of transportation. Condemned offenders occasionally thought it valuable to strike this note in petitions to be pardoned from hanging, asking instead to be sent to the colonies, "where," as one man said in 1663, "there is hope and encouragement" for his being "advanced by industry, being a single man and aged but 23 years." Other men petitioned on the grounds that they were "unmarried and all able to do good service and steadfastly resolving through God's assistance to amend their lives for the future."[61]

The transportation to the colonies in the West Indies and North America of convicts who had committed capital but not particulary vicious offenses and who were at the same time "able and strong of body" was accepted at the Restoration, in the words of a royal warrant in 1663, as a policy "that might become our royal clemency and be likewise an advantage to the public." By then, conditional pardoning of convicted capital offenders was well established. In Surrey, at least nine men and women in 1663–65 and twenty-one in 1674–77 were pardoned from the death penalties passed upon them at the assizes on the condition that they be transported to the American mainland colonies or to the West Indies. Not every pardoned offender was sent to the plantations, but that condition was so commonly imposed that the judges were given instructions in 1665 on how to deal with "such prisoners as are reprieved with intent to be transported."[62]

[60] Even "the basest and worst men," the Rev. William Crashaw said in a sermon preached before the Virginia Company in London in 1610, "trained up in severe discipline, under sharpe lawes, a hard life, and much labor, do prove good members of a Commonwealth" (quoted in Darrett B. Rutman, "The Virginia Company and Its Military Regime," in Rutman, ed., *The Old Dominion* [1964], p 10).

[61] SP 29/78, f. 68; SP 29/89, f. 61.

[62] As was noted above, such a policy was introduced on a small scale in the 1650s. It appears

Most of the men transported in the 1660s and 1670s had been convicted of highway robbery or burglary or horse-theft; five of the nine women ordered to be banished had been sentenced to death for simple larceny above ten shillings, an offense that until 1692 was nonclergyable for women, though not for men. But there was a striking and apparently new departure at the Restoration. In addition to these men and women pardoned from a death sentence, a number of others were transported after being charged with offenses within clergy and for which they would have had every expectation if convicted of being allowed to mumble through the reading test and to be branded on the thumb and discharged. Bills that would have authorized the courts to transport such offenders directly had failed in 1663. That result was nonetheless being achieved by indirect means in the 1660s. At the Winchester assizes in 1666, for example, Kelyng refused to accept the clergyman's announcement that a particular prisoner who had pleaded his clergy had in fact demonstrated his ability to read. "I directed him," Kelyng reports

> to deal clearly with me, and not to say *legit* in case he could not read; and thereupon he delivered the book to him, and I perceived the prisoner never looked upon the book at all, and yet the bishop's clerk, upon the demand of *legit* or *non legit*, answered *legit*. . . . I bid the clerk of the Assizes not to record it, and I told the parson he was not the judge whether he read or no, but a ministerial officer to make a true report to the Court; and so I caused the prisoner to be brought near, and delivered him the book, and then the prisoner confessed he could not read.[63]

This was not an isolated incident but the result of a broader decision to prevent some offenders, selected at the judges' discretion, from simply slipping through the courts with what was clearly recognized in the 1660s as the slightest of chastisements. The literacy test was a crucial fiction in the administration of the law: if it had been taken seriously in all cases, hundreds of offenders would have gone to the gallows every year for the most minor offenses against property. It amounted in fact to a pre-sentence pardoning system in the broad range of offenses to which it still applied—most simple larcenies for men and those below ten shillings for women. It is almost certainly the case that most offenders could have been denied clergy on the grounds of their illiteracy had the courts insisted. "Were it

---

that two men were ordered to be transported at the Surrey assizes at the Lent session of 1654 (ASSI 35/95/7), three more in Lent 1655 (ASSI 35/96/7), and one in the Summer of 1656 (ASSI 35/97/8).

[63] Kelyng, *Reports*, p. 51; *Eng. Rep.*, vol. 84, p. 1078.

not for the favour of the Court," it was said in 1652, "not one in twenty could save their lives by reading."[64]

What the new policy of the 1660s amounted to was a decision to operate this pardoning system a little more strictly in order to prevent some prisoners from getting their clergied discharge automatically. This was done by the judges applying (no doubt roughly) the criteria that were most influential in the granting of pardons to those sentenced to death for non-clergiable offences: the crime they had committed and, most crucially, their character, particularly their previous criminal experience and previous convictions. On this last issue the branding of clergied convicts provided immediate information, and since it was being used informally (as it might have been used by the jury in reaching their verdict) there was no need to prove previous conviction by a court record. The judges selected some men and women on the basis of what they learned about them in their trial (and perhaps from local information), forced them to fail the reading test, and thus denied them their clergy. The central device of the new approach then came into play. Instead of sentencing them to death, as they might have done, the judges reprieved them *before* passing that judgment and ordered that they be held in jail without bail so that the king might pardon them. Their pardon would then be granted on the condition that they accept transportation. Men and women who might have left the court with a branded thumb, as most of the prisoners charged with similar offenses continued to do, found themselves returned to jail for what might turn out to be many months and then transported to America. It was a roundabout but effective way of creating a secondary punishment where none existed, a way of severely punishing some offenders without hanging them. It was clearly legal, but it also involved the manipulation of some long-standing rules and practices.[65]

It is likely that the devices employed in this new departure in penal policy emerged from agreements among the judges, since they better than anyone knew the fictional character of the literacy test and the ease with which it might be exploited. Nor was it a matter of individual judges deciding in isolated cases that particular individuals deserved to be punished harshly. It was so common in the 1660s that it is clear that the

---

[64] J. March, *Amicus Reipublicae*, 19 May 1652, quoted by Donald Veall, *The Popular Movement for Law Reform, 1640–1660* (1970), p. 4, n. 4.

[65] The main form of manipulation was that involving the literacy test, but a number of prisoners were also denied clergy because they had been allowed it once before, the evidence being an already branded thumb. A man convicted of stealing a sheep at the Sussex assizes in March 1663 pleaded his clergy "but being already burned in the hand" was denied it. He was reprieved by the court before judgment—as he might have been if he had failed the literacy test (ASSI 35/104/9/19).

policy either originated in the privy council or at least had support at the
highest levels of the court and administration, not least because the royal
pardon, granted simply at the judges' recommendations, was essential to
its working. In any event, the judges put it into effect with a will. In
1662 twelve prisoners convicted of clergyable offenses at the Old Bailey
"prayed their book" but were declared by the court to have "read not as
clerks" and were then reprieved before sentence of death was passed upon
them and ordered to be held without bail.[66] What happened to them is
clear from the pardons granted in subsequent years to prisoners treated in
a similar way. In 1664, for example, a pardon was issued

> to one and fifty poor prisoners in Newgate whereof some were
> attainted and after reprieved and the most were convicted of
> several felonies for which clergy is allowable but could not read.
> All which persons except Rose Gwynn are by his Majesty's order
> to be transported beyond the seas upon agreement made for
> serving there seven years. And this pardon is to be void to them
> that depart not within two months after the date thereof or
> return within seven years.[67]

In Surrey, at least seventeen felons were denied clergy in the years
1663–65 and ordered to be transported. Prisoners in other years in Surrey
and in other counties were treated similarly, including some at quarter
sessions that continued in this period to deal with clergyable larceny.[68]
By the mid-1660s transportation was being spoken of as though it had
been invented by the prisoners themselves as a way of their getting passage
to the colonies so that they might enjoy the benefits of land and work in
the new world. In 1665, for example, Kelyng said that in recent years it
had been the practice of the courts

> for felonies within clergy, if the prisoner desire it, not to give
> his book, but to procure a conditional pardon from the King,
> and send them beyond the sea to serve 5 years in some of the
> King's plantations, and then to have land there assigned them
> according to the use in those plantations, for servants after their
> time expired. . . .[69]

---

[66] *Cal. S. P. Dom.*, 1663–64, p. 1.

[67] C 231/7, p. 221.

[68] In 1666 two men convicted of stealing hens in Surrey pleaded their clergy but appear in
the jail calendar as having been ordered to be "safely kept in Gaole without baile untill they
shall be pardoned to be transported" (ASSI 35/107/5/8). Similar transportations following a denial
of clergy were recorded at the Wilts quarter sessions in January 1665 (QS Roll), and at the Sussex
quarter sessions in January 1663 (QS/E/137).

[69] Kelyng, *Reports*, p. 45; *Eng. Rep.*, vol. 84, p. 1075. Whether or not transported convicts

In the same year, a pardon warrant spoke of the ten men involved as having been convicted of clergyable offenses, but "in respect they could not read, they waved their clergy and put themselves upon your Majesty's Grace and Mercy."[70] Such language perhaps reflects in part the legal requirement that the prisoners had to agree to transportation. But the reality was that they had been maneuvered into accepting transportation as their option to death. They were the objects of a new policy, the intention of which was clearly to create a punishment that would work more effectively to prevent crime than the sanctions currently available to the courts. Such a punishment, it was said in a warrant in 1664, would "prevent the like crimes for the future" by getting committed offenders out of the country instead of allowing them simply to return to society.[71] A group of prisoners at the Old Bailey later in the century were "held to strict reading," the report of their trial announced, "in order to transportation, if their Majesties so please, to prevent the danger of further mischief to their Majesties' subjects, in case they should have been set at large."[72]

Transportation by means of the manipulation of clergy was so well established and so attractive by 1670 that it was actually incorporated into a statute passed in that year to remove from the protection of clergy the offense of cutting and stealing at night cloth stretched on racks in the process of manufacture. Henceforth a convicted offender would not be able to claim clergy and would thus be liable to be sentenced to death. But the judges were authorized to reprieve such convicted prisoners before sentencing, at their discretion, in the way that had become familiar over the previous decade, and to offer them transportation. If the offenders refused what was in effect a conditional pardon they would then be hanged.[73] The courts, and now perhaps parliament, were well on their way toward filling the broad unoccupied middle ground in the penal system

---

were in fact treated in the colonies like indentured servants at the expiry of their term of mandatory labor, there was clearly some intention on the English side in the early years that they should be, at least in the West Indies. A pardon was granted to twenty-five condemned prisoners on the Home Circuit in 1664, for example, who were "to be transported beyond the seas upon agreement made for serving five yeares after their landing and if at Jamaica at 5 yeares end to have 30 acres of land a piece and if at the Barbadoes the value of £10 sterling in Sugar and in the mean time to be maintayned" (C 82/2318, 24 Mar. 1663/4). Other pardons spoke of the prisoners being transported for seven years, "the last three for their own benefit" (C 82/2305, Apr. 1663). On the treatment of indentured servants at the expiry of their indentures see Smith, *Colonists in Bondage*, pp. 291–92; and on that subject generally, David W. Galenson, *White Servitude in Colonial America: An Economic Analysis* (Cambridge, 1981).

[70] C 82/2337, Aug. 1665.

[71] SP 29/92, f. 123.

[72] *An Account of the Malefactors that Received the Benefit of Their Majesties . . . Pardon at . . . the Old Bailey . . . 11 Dec. 1693* (1693).

[73] 22 Chas II, c. 5, s. 4 (1670).

with a punishment that they hoped would prevent crime without raising
the incidence of hanging to unacceptable levels. Transportation to America
came to seem such an attractive solution to the problem of incorrigible
minor offenders in general that the Middlesex magistrates were authorized
in the mid-1660s to transport "vagabonds, idle and disorderly persons,
[and] sturdy rogues and beggars," to be "disposed of in the usual way of
servants for the space of seven years."[74]

A number of men and women were thus transported across the Atlantic in the years after the Restoration, some of them pardoned following
conviction on charges that might be called genuinely capital, that is to
say offenses removed from clergy, others who had been jockeyed into a
position from which they needed to be rescued by the royal clemency.
Had transportation continued to develop strongly after 1670 the transformation of clergyable discharge may well have been broadened in further
statutes and in the practice of the courts. In fact, however, transportation
ran into a number of difficulties, and the big push toward its establishment
as an effective secondary punishment slackened considerably. Sentences of
transportation as a condition of a royal pardon from an actual death sentence
for a nonclergyable offense continued to be awarded to the end of the
century and beyond, and the banishment of English convicts to America
did not cease entirely.[75] But nor did it flourish. And it is probably for
this reason that the manipulation of the literacy test in order to get prisoners
into the position from which they could be legally transported seems to
have diminished in the 1670s and after. At least that is what the Surrey
experience suggests. In the years 1674–77 and 1687–88, which are the
only years of complete data in these decades, no prisoner at the Surrey
assizes seems to have been refused clergy on the grounds of his illiteracy
and then reprieved before sentence. The practice was revived in the case
of perhaps half a dozen felons in the years 1699–1701, and it had not in
the meantime entirely disappeared, for we have seen that at least in 1693
at the Old Bailey a group of prisoners were "held to strict reading in order
to transportation." But it seems quite clearly to have diminished sharply
after the initial enthusiasm in the 1660s.

There may have been objections to the manipulation of sentences that
I am not aware of, but the principal reason for its petering out was no
doubt the difficulties that beset transportation generally. These arose both

[74] *Acts of the Privy Council (Colonial)*, vol. 1, pp. 370–71, 389–90.

[75] Mr. Justice Rokeby clearly thought of transportation as the inevitable condition of a royal
pardon in the 1690s. At the Surrey Lent assizes in 1692, he notes in his diary, two men were
convicted before him for burglary and sentenced to death, but at the intercession of the jury he
went on to say, "I reprieved one for transportation" (*The Diary of Mr. Justice Rokeby* [1887],
p. 19).

from opposition in the colonies and from weakness in the way the system was organized in England.

From the beginning the actual machinery of transportation was in the hands of merchants trading to Virginia, Maryland, and the West Indies who looked upon the trade in convicts as they would any other commodity: their willingness to engage in it depended on the supply of convicts available, on the demand on the other side, and on the profit to be made. The business was managed in the 1660s and 1670s by the sheriffs who contracted with a merchant (at a price per head that included jail fees, the fees of the clerk of the appropriate court, fees for drawing up the pardon, and so on) to transport those in jail pardoned on that condition. The merchant made his profit by selling the convicts as indentured servants in the colonies.[76] This worked reasonably well from the English side if the merchants could pick and choose among the convicts. They naturally preferred to take only the young and able-bodied, and of course men with skills were particularly valuable. That merchants were selecting among the convicts in jail, taking some and leaving others, is suggested by a list drawn up in 1664 of men and women sentenced to be transported that included their ages and in the case of one man, his occupation.[77] Women were harder to dispose of than men, and it seems clear that under the arrangements made at the Restoration the merchants simply left some women in jail, along with men too old or ill to be easily disposed of.[78] This difficulty of getting certain classes of convicts sent abroad under the system of private enterprise may well have been one reason why it began to break down.

Another reason was the reluctance of the colonies to receive English convicts and the unwillingness or inability of the government to force them to do so. The mainland colonies that might have been expected to welcome labor in any form, Maryland and Virginia, both passed laws to prohibit them in the 1670s. In 1670 the General Court of Virginia argued that "the great numbers of felons and other desperate villains" presented a "danger to the colony" and ordered that no more English prisoners be landed. This order was not challenged in England; indeed the king was persuaded (by what means is unclear) to allow this prohibition to stand. The privy council ordered in 1670 that "no felon or other condemned persons shall be sent or transported from hence to his Majesty's said Colony of Virginia, but that they be sent to any other of his Majesty's plantations in America."[79] If an earlier privy council had supported the policy of

[76] Smith, *Colonists in Bondage*, pp. 97–106.
[77] SP 29/92, f. 125.
[78] Smith, *Colonists in Bondage*, pp. 99, 103.
[79] *Acts of the Privy Council (Colonial)*, vol. 1, p. 553.

broadening transportation as a secondary punishment, this political response in 1670 clearly diminished its chance of success, especially since other colonies were equally unwilling to accept convicts and took this as a cue to stiffen their own opposition. Maryland passed a similar prohibition in 1676. Massachusetts had always resisted and continued to do so.[80] There was still interest in accepting transportees on some of the islands in the West Indies—although only if the government was willing to help with the costs by paying their jail fees—but it seems clear that transportation to the mainland colonies was being seriously curtailed by the 1670s. A detailed investigation of the pardon evidence has revealed that no English prisoners were sent to Maryland or Virginia between 1670 and 1718.[81]

It appears, then, that the development of transportation was successfully resisted soon after the Restoration by the colonies themselves and that the English government could not or chose not to press the matter. Apart from the colonial reaction, it is also clear the transportation was not encouraged by the dominant thinking on economic questions in the late seventeenth century. The value of the productive power of labor as the source of the nation's wealth was a constant theme in the economic writings of the mercantilists after 1660, and this was in turn associated with arguments supporting schemes to enlarge the population, not to diminish it. There was thus little support in the late seventeenth century for schemes to encourage immigration in general, and it is unlikely that a system of transportation that allowed merchants to pick and choose among those sentenced and actually to send abroad only the able-bodied would have found much favor.[82]

The difficulties of transportation were felt perhaps most acutely in the 1690s, when they were compounded by the interruption of merchant shipping during the war,[83] and when the number and the character of

[80] Smith, *Colonists in Bondage*, p. 104.

[81] Ibid., p. 361, n. 37.

[82] Charles Davenant, Josiah Child, William Petyt, and others repeated in various ways and contexts the belief that people constituted a nation's chief source of strength, and that when large numbers were fully employed in productive work wages would be kept low, trade would be profitable, and the nation would flourish. These views underlay what Eli Hecksher called "an almost fanatical desire to increase population" in the second half of the seventeenth century (*Mercantilism*, 2nd ed., 2 vols. [1955], vol. 2, pp. 157–63). See also Edgar S. Furniss, *The Position of the Laborer in a System of Nationalism: A Study of the Labor Theories of the Later English Mercantalists* (repr. New York, 1965), pp. 12-28; E.A.J. Johnson, *Predecessors of Adam Smith: The Growth of British Economic Thought* (New York, 1938), pp. 243–47.

[83] During the war, trade was controlled by means of shifting embargoes issued in Orders in Council and was directly affected by other factors besides the dangers of losses to enemy ships and privateers. The Atlantic trade was seriously restricted by the demands of the navy for sailors. And, especially when the approaches to the channel were particularly dangerous, trade was crippled by the need to organize into convoys. There were generally only two convoys to America a year

prisoners to be transported presented particular problems. One source of such problems in London arose from the effort that was made at the time of the great recoinage to discourage clipping and counterfeiting. Twenty-one men and women were convicted at the Surrey assizes in the 1690s of clipping and coining, at least eleven of whom (including five women) were pardoned from the death penalty passed upon them and ordered to be transported. Across the river in the city proper and in Westminster and the London parishes of Middlesex even more were convicted, and as the jails filled up with prisoners pardoned from the traitor's gruesome death that might have befallen them, the limitations and the difficulties of transportation were plainly revealed. The reluctance or inability of merchants to transport women, so long as they had to depend on the price they could get for their services on the other side of the Atlantic, and the unwillingness of the colonies to receive them anyway became all too evident in 1696, for many women were among those arrested on coining and clipping charges, and the jails in London were filled with women pardoned from the death sentence on condition of transportation. Some of the West Indian islands were willing during the war to consider taking men who might bolster their defenses. But women were not wanted. An enquiry undertaken by the Board of Trade revealed that Barbados agreed to take prisoners who were fit for labor but not "women, children nor other infirm persons." Similarly in Jamaica: a group of merchants refused to take eighty prisoners in December 1696 "because most of them were women, and because persons of bad character were not wanted in Jamaica." Again in the following summer Jamaica objected to the transportation of women who "would only be a burden to us and would contribute nothing to our defence."[84]

These problems in transportation had been thrown into sharp relief by a combination of special circumstances: an unusually large number of women pardoned from execution during a war in which some of the colonies that might have received them were desperately concerned about their defenses. But what these circumstances revealed was a long-standing weakness in the arrangements for the transportation of convicts that derived from the fact that policy was being made in the colonies rather than in London. The lords justices who in William III's absence in 1697 had to deal with the problem of the nontransportable women expressed surprise

---

during the war in the 1690s. See John Ehrman, *The Navy in the War of William III, 1689–1697* (Cambridge, 1953), pp. 113–14; T. S. Ashton, *Economic Fluctuations in England, 1700–1800* (Oxford, 1959), p. 56, Ralph Davis, "English Foreign Trade, 1660–1700," *Economic History Review*, 2nd ser., 7 (1954–55), p. 161.

[84] *Cal. S. P. Colonial: America and the West Indies (1696–97)*, pp. 271, 341, 543.

when it became clear that the difficulties arose from colonial opposition.[85] But apart from calling for an investigation into these prohibitions, they were clearly not disposed to assert London's authority. Control had been imposed on colonial trade and on other aspects of the colonial economy over the previous fifty years, but immigration and settlement policy had been largely left to the colonies themselves.[86]

On the other hand, the king's ministers also resisted in 1697 the "solution" that was being adopted in practice in London and that appears to have had the support of the recorder and a number of magistrates: simply to release the women who could not be sent overseas. Some of them were indeed discharged from jail.[87] But the lords justices ordered that "no distinction" be made between men and women; they also concluded that it would be necessary for the government to pay to have these women transported, and that brought a solution to this particular crisis: fifty women awaiting transportation in the London jails were sent at the Treasury's expense to the Leeward Islands, the only colony that could be found to take them.[88]

A further difficulty of a more general kind was added in the last years of the decade, when the number of offenses prosecuted in the London area rose, if not massively, at least sufficiently to be felt in the populations of the jails. Whether stimulated by the demobilization of the forces at the conclusion of the war in 1697 or by the dearth and sharp rise in food prices in the middle years of the decade (particularly 1696 and 1697) or by a greater willingness of victims of property crimes to prosecute, there is no doubt that the jails were more crowded at the end of the decade than at the beginning. In the face of what appeared to be a sharp increase of offenses, the assizes judges in Surrey were clearly determined to deny the easy clergyable discharge to a number of the accused who might have expected it, in order to punish them more seriously.[89] The Surrey juries convicted sixty-seven prisoners of capital property offenses in the four years 1697–1700 as against twenty-seven in 1690–93. And where in the early

[85] Ibid., p. 666.
[86] Marcus Lee Hansen, *The Atlantic Migration, 1607–1860* (Cambridge, Mass., 1940), p. 35.
[87] *Cal. S. P. Dom.*, 1697, pp. 160, 167, 458.
[88] *Cal. S. P. Colonial: America and the West Indies (1696–97)*, p. 559.
[89] The case of Jane Perkin is typical of the way several of the accused were dealt with at the Surrey assizes in 1699–1700. She was indicted for stealing a gown worth ten shillings and was convicted. The indictment notes that she petitioned for transportation. Why she did that rather than petitioning for "the benefit of the statute" to which she was entitled is unclear. She was in fact sentenced to death and then reprieved and pardoned on condition of transportation (ASSI 35/140/8/34, and calendar). A man indicted for stealing a cow—a clergyable offense in 1699— was treated in a similar way: he too was said to have petitioned for transportation, was condemned to death, and was then pardoned on condition of transportation (ASSI 35/141/7/56).

years of the decade three offenders a year on average had been reprieved from the capital conviction and returned to jail to await transportation, by 1697–1700 more than ten prisoners every year were in that position. These are not large numbers. But when the jails were small and when transportation was not working effectively and regularly to clear them of the prisoners waiting to be shipped to America, even modest numbers building up over several years could make them seriously overcrowded. It is no doubt the difficulties of transportation in the 1690s, and the pressure of accommodation in the jail, that explains why ten of the forty-five men pardoned and at least four of the women were granted an absolute pardon, without conditions, so that they were able to leave jail as soon as it was granted and to go free. No such pardon had been granted in the years examined in the 1660s and 1670s.

The Surrey experience in the 1690s is perhaps most interesting as a pointer to what was undoubtedly happening on a much larger scale across the river, particularly in Newgate. The problems that arose from the difficulty of getting women convicts transported have already been noted. The situation in Newgate was eased by the government's agreeing to pay eight pounds per head to get fifty women taken to the West Indies in the summer of 1697. Before that, the authorities in London had been applying their own solutions and defying the orders of the central government in doing so. The cabinet objected to a proposal made by the Recorder of London in May 1697 that women be released from jail while awaiting transportation; it was this that had caused the lords justices to insist that no distinction be made between the sexes and that brought them to the decision that the government would have to pay to have the women taken abroad. In any event, they were adamant that the women should not simply be discharged from jail. Five days after that order was issued the recorder was at the council to explain why it had not been obeyed.[90] In November the recorder was again having to explain why twenty-five convicts had been released from Newgate "upon pretense only of transportation."[91] By then the situation in London was apparently so critical and the transportation arrangements so unable to cope that the cabinet council asked the Board of Trade to see whether there were places where transported prisoners might be "disposed of" or, failing that, "what punishment might be more proper for such prisoners in lieu of transportation."[92]

[90] *Cal. S. P. Dom.*, 1697, pp. 160, 167.
[91] Ibid., p. 458.
[92] *Cal. S. P. Colonial, America and the West Indies (1697–98)*, p. 36. The failure of transportation as an effective penal sanction, especially in the case of the more hardened and committed offenders, was most starkly revealed by the development of the practice of allowing those so sentenced in effect to transport themselves within a given period, and allowing them to be released from jail

OTHER PENAL EXPERIMENTS, 1660–1717

Transportation had been welcomed after the Restoration because it provided both a way to mitigate the rigors of the capital laws by offering a satisfactory alternative to hanging and a stiffer penalty for clergyable felonies. It failed to develop as a secondary punishment that the courts might use for noncapital offenses. And although prisoners who had been condemned to death continued to the end of the century and beyond to be pardoned on condition of transportation and continued to be sent abroad, the difficulties of finding suitable places to send them was clearly throttling this policy too, particulary in years of heavy prosecutions. It was significant that the courts did not seek a solution in capital punishment. The number of offenders hanged in Surrey in the last four years of the 1690s did increase to between six and seven on average each year as against just over three in 1690–93 and an average of about four per annum over the late seventeenth century generally. But that was directly a reflection of an increase in prosecutions. The rate of pardons did not decline, and there was no obvious attempt to compensate for the difficulties in transportation at the end of the century by leaving an unusually large proportion of prisoners to be disposed of on the gallows (table 9.2).

TABLE 9.2

Capital Punishment for Property Offenses
in Surrey, 1690–1700

Period	Convicted	Pardoned	Hanged	Number Hanged per Year	Percentage Hanged
1690–1693	27	14	13	3.25	48.2
1694–1696	36	21	15	5.0	41.7
1697–1700	67	41	26	6.5	38.8

SOURCE: Hanged Count.

if they gave adequate sureties that they would do so. See, for example, ASSI 35/143/7, Summer 1702, assize calendar. It was presumably this that Roger North was complaining about in 1688 when he said that many men were escaping transportation. A man pardoned from hanging on condition of transportation "sails to the next highway," he said, "from whence you may shortly hear of his prosperous voyages" (*Discourse of the Poor*, p. 28). The grand jury of London complained about this practice in 1704.

The other use to which transportation had been put in the 1660s, the punishment of clergyable felons by the manipulation of the reading test, had faded much earlier. By the 1690s other solutions were being tried to the problem of persistent minor offenders who were not discouraged by the branding of clergy and who, it was assumed, would go on if they were not dissuaded to more and more serious crimes and end inevitably on the gallows. One alternative that gradually emerged in the practice of the Surrey courts was the broader use of corporal punishment.

The Extension of Whipping

Whipping was reserved for the punishment of petty larceny and was thus much more frequently ordered at the quarter sessions than at the assizes. In the late seventeenth century, however, whipping became increasingly common at the assizes in Surrey. Indeed, more than a quarter of the men and women accused of even nonclergyable (and thus capital) felonies and forty per cent of those accused of clergyable grand larceny were whipped and discharged. They were subjected to this punishment because the trial juries had found them guilty not of the charge in their indictments but rather of petty larceny (table 9.3). For some, that must have represented a genuine and welcome mitigation of the charge against them. Women indicted for theft of more than ten shillings in value before 1692, for example, were not eligible to apply for "the benefit of the statute" and were thus in danger of being sentenced to death; a conviction for petty larceny could only have been regarded as a favorable verdict in those circumstances, even if it meant their being whipped. Similarly, men in-

TABLE 9.3

Noncapital Punishment for Property Offenses
in Surrey, 1660–1715 (16 Sample Years)

Offense Charged in Indictment	N	Clergy Allowed: Branded and Discharged (%)	Clergy Refused: Transported (%)	Whipped (%)
Nonclergyable felony[a]	99	71.7	1.0	27.3
Clergyable larceny	371	56.3	4.6	39.1
Petty larceny	27	—		100.0
Total	497	56.3	3.6	40.0

SOURCE: Sample (1663–65, 1674–77, 1690–94, 1708, 1710, 1714–15).

[a] I.e., nonclergyable felonies mitigated by juries' verdicts.

dicted for nonclergyable felonies who were given what amounted to a
double reduction by being convicted of simple theft of less than a shilling
must have thought themselves very fortunate indeed to be merely whipped
before being released.

Most of the reduced-charge verdicts in the late seventeenth century,
however, were in cases in which the accused would have been eligible to
apply for clergy had they been convicted of the offense in the indictment,
and the conviction for petty larceny in those cases seems less of a mitigation
and rather less straightforward. A woman charged in 1691 with stealing
six hens valued at nine shillings might not have been gratified to be
convicted, as she was, of theft to the value of ten pence, for instead of
being allowed her clergy, branded on the thumb, and discharged, she
found herself ordered to be whipped in public before being released.[93] In
the case of men charged with clergyable offenses, there is the slight complication that before 1706 they had to prove their literacy before being
allowed their clergy, and we have seen that that requirement could in fact
mean the denial of clergy and a more serious punishment than a mere
branding on the thumb. A petty larceny conviction before 1706 might
possibly have been a real mitigating verdict. But the vast majority of men
had not been punished seriously for clergyable larcenies and it seems clear
that the point of their being convicted of the reduced charge of petty
larceny was to substitute the sharp and humiliating sanction of a public
whipping for the less painful and discredited branding of clergy. This
surely explains why four out of ten of those convicted of theft at the Surrey
assizes over the late seventeenth century and in the early years of the
eighteenth who were originally charged with grand larceny were in fact
found guilty of stealing to the value of less than a shilling.

The whipping of so many offenders at the Surrey assizes resulted from
the conscious decision of the trial jurors to reduce the charges against them
to petty larceny. It is likely that the assize judges had encouraged jurors
to adopt this strategy, for both jurors and judges seem to have agreed that
a clergyable discharge was no longer an adequate penalty for many of the
offenses tried at the assizes. This sentiment strengthened as transportation
ran into difficulties. There were few such partial verdicts in larceny cases
in the 1660s. There were more in the 1670s, and they continued to increase
into the third and fourth decades of the eighteenth century, when they
fell off sharply. There was thus a steady rise in the proportion of convicted
offenders who were whipped and discharged in Surrey, from about a fifth
of those convicted either of clergyable larceny or of petty larceny by means
of a partial verdict in the 1660s and 1670s, to thirty-seven per cent in

[93] ASSI 35/132/7/5–6; ASSI 35/133/8/9, 26, 30.

1690–94, and to about half in the first two decades of the eighteenth century. By 1722–24 the proportion of whipping sentences had fallen back to half that level, and by 1736–39 it was about twelve per cent (table 9.4). It is not necessarily the case that the steady increase over the late seventeenth century and into the early eighteenth was encouraged by difficulties with transportation, but the rapid falling away by the 1720s was certainly connected with the firm establishment of transportation in 1718. The curve of partial verdicts in clergyable felonies rose and fell over the sixty years after the Restoration in such a way as to strongly reinforce the conclusion that the courts were anxious to find some punishment that would be more substantial than the branding and discharge of clergy.

Harsher Views Inside and Outside Parliament

Manipulations of verdicts and sentences suggest some fundamental dissatisfaction in the courts with the penal weapons available to them, and this dissatisfaction appears to have been particularly acute in the 1690s. That context perhaps helps to explain the engagement of parliament in the matter of the criminal law when the Revolution of 1689 and all that followed from it led to a continuity in the life of parliament—annual sessions following one after the other with established regularity—that enabled the members to translate into legislation their notions about how the problems of crime might be dealt with.[94] Some members of parliament

TABLE 9.4

Whipping as a Sanction for Felony, 1660–1739

Period	Number of Convictions for Grand or Petty Larceny	Sentenced To be Whipped	
		No.	%
1663–65	48	9	18.8
1674–77	131	25	19.1
1690–94	125	48	38.4
1708, 1710	42	20	47.6
1714–15	121	61	50.4
1722–24	102	25	24.5
1736–39	94	11	11.7

SOURCE: Sample

[94] Henry Horwitz has pointed out that the annual and prolonged sessions of parliament resulted in more legislation being passed. In William's reign parliament sat for just over fifty-three

were clearly as concerned as judges and jurors about the inadequacy of the laws protecting property, particularly when offenses appeared to be on the increase. Their responses also concentrated on the weaknesses of clergy. But those who ran the courts could only manipulate, not change, the law. Parliament attacked clergy directly by taking up again the approach accepted in the sixteenth century of restricting the offenses to which it applied. In 1691 clergy was removed from certain forms of housebreaking in which it had been available earlier; breaking into shops and warehouses and stealing goods to the value of five shillings or more also became a capital offense.[95] It is true that this statute also broadened clergy to include all women on the same terms as men, but it began a gradual restriction of the circumstances in which that benefit of the statute would apply. There were to be several other major Acts along these lines in Anne's reign.[96]

This toughness of mind was very much in tune with what appears to have been a broad public sentiment at the end of the seventeenth century. I take as examples of that two pamphlets published in 1700 and 1701 that advocated considerably increased harshness in the courts. In explaining why there had been an "increase of Highway-Men and Housebreakers" in recent years, the author of *Hanging Not Punishment Enough* (1701) acknowledged that there were thousands of disbanded soldiers and sailors "driven upon necessity" and unable to find work, and that "the Poor are exceedingly numerous." But he blamed the increase of crime especially in and around London at the end of the seventeenth century on the failure of capital punishment to restrain all these wretches. "Sanguinary Laws," he affirmed, "are not *chiefly* intended to punish the present Criminal, but to hinder others from being so; and on that account Punishments in the Learned Languages are called *Examples*, as being design'd to be such to all mankind." There were two problems, he thought, with the capital laws in England. One was that unequal offenses were all punished by death. The other was that convicts were often insufficiently frightened by the prospect of having to face that penalty. These were themes that would be widely discussed over the coming century, the second initially with more urgency, and on this issue especially the author of *Hanging* anticipated future arguments on several counts.

Like many after him, he was outraged that some men were defiant on the gallows and refused to show remorse or play their part in the

months, a dozen more than in Charles II's much longer reign, and 809 bills were enacted between 1689 and 1702, as against 533 between 1660 and 1685 (*Policy and Politics in the Reign of William III* [Manchester, 1977], p. 325).

[95] 3 and 4 Wm and M, c. 9 (1691).

[96] See above, chap. 4.

morality tale the state wished to mount on this public stage. Men even made light of the sentence as the judge pronounced it, joked and grinned in court, cracked nuts, waved to their friends, shrugged and winked, and made noises while the judge uttered the solemn words of the capital judgment and made his moralizing comment on the wickedness of the prisoner's life and deeds for the benefit of the assembled audience, Even worse was the man who lived his last days with riotous company in the jail and who went cheerfully to his death, dressed in his finery, pausing along the route to the gallows to drink the health of the crowd, making a brave end at the last, and earning admiration and sympathy.[97] For every such man it is certain that fifty went to their deaths terrified by the prospect and by the reality of the gallows, and probably already half-dead from starvation and disease. But the defiant men stood out, and they were sufficiently numerous to gall those who saw the failure of the deterrent power of the gallows as the cause of serious crime. They could easily get themselves to believe that the course of tenderness and humanity lay in ensuring that death was frightening.

The author of *Hanging Not Punishment Enough* anticipated proposals that would be made at various points over the eighteenth century, some of which were adopted, though not always in the form or the context he proposed. He thought, for example, that trial should follow immediately upon arrest; that the worst convicts should be put in solitary confinement and on bread and water, to humble them and to make jail more dreaded; that they should be hanged in a drab costume to prevent their going out in triumph. Mainly he thought it necessary to make the pain of their execution "much outbid the Pleasure" of the life of crime, "by inflicting somewhat [*sic*] they will tremble at *here*, since they fear nothing *hereafter*." If hanging did not frighten the most hardened criminals, then "Hanging them in Chains, and Starving them, or . . . breaking them on the Wheel, or Whipping them to Death, a *Roman* Punishment should." With those prospects in mind, few would want to commit offenses, and the criminals would either go to work or leave the country.[98]

This man was not alone in suggesting such courses. Timothy Nourse also thought that the solution to serious and violent crime lay in increasing the horror and the suffering of the gallows. He too thought that such afflictive punishments as breaking on the wheel—commonly employed on the Continent[99]—should be introduced. He acknowledged that

[97] On this theme see in particular Peter Linebaugh, "The Ordinary of Newgate and His 'Account,' " pp. 246–69.

[98] *Hanging, Not Punishment Enough, for Murtherers, High-way Men, and House-breakers. Offered to the Consideration of the two Houses of Parliament* (1701), pp. 9, 11, 18, 23–24.

[99] Langbein, *Torture and the Law of Proof*, pp. 27–28.

this sort of Punishment carried the face of Cruelty in respect of him who suffers, where a Man's Bones are broken to pieces, and his Nerves and Sinews beaten to a Pulp, which must needs be very dolorous; and to continue so for twenty four hours or more perhaps, must needs be very grievous to him who suffers, and fearful to the Spectators.[100]

It was nonetheless justifiable and necessary. The end of capital punishment was the prevention of like offenses in others: "It must be therefore *in terrorem.*" And if one method of punishment fails "Religion and Justice do advise the Magistrate . . . to have recourse to one which is more severe."[101]

Branding on the Cheek

Parliament did not in the event order wheels and racks to be erected in every county town. But some of the harshness and logic of these arguments was reflected in other solutions (apart from the mere extension of capital punishment) being proposed in the House of Commons in the 1690s and the early years of the eighteenth century. The dissatisfaction with benefit of clergy took the form, for example, not only of restricting its scope but of seriously stiffening the consequences that followed from it, indeed of transforming it. After the brief attempt in the 1660s to use the literacy requirement as a means of transporting noncapital offenders, clergy reverted to being simply a penalty that applied to certain offenses and offenders, widely regarded as singularly ineffective as a deterrent since, as Nourse said, it consisted merely of "frizzing [offenders] a little in the Fist . . . a Punishment of no great pain, and of short continuance."[102] Moreover, the mark of the brand was hidden and could hardly act as a deterrent to others. The kind of argument that informs Nourse's advocacy of violent physical punishments—let some suffer horribly in public so that many will be deterred from crime—led parliament to try again to repair the weaknesses of clergy. In the Act that made shoplifting a nonclergyable offense in 1699 it was also enacted that men and women granted clergy were to be burnt not on the thumb but "with the usual mark . . . on the most visible part of the left cheek nearest the nose."[103]

[100] Timothy Nourse, *Campania foelix. Or, a discourse of the benefits and improvements of husbandry. . . .* (1700), p. 230.
[101] Ibid., p. 231.
[102] Ibid., p. 229.
[103] 10 and 11 Wm III, c. 23, s. 6 (1699).

By May 1699 that Act was being enforced at the Old Bailey.[104] In Surrey several prisoners suffered the new penalty at the Summer assizes of that year. Counties provided themselves with an instrument with which convicts' heads could be held while the brand was applied—"an Engine to burne Felons in," as it was described in Sussex.[105] But it was clear immediately to the courts (as it was indeed in the case of many of the new ~~capital felonies being decreed by parliament~~) that the law was too harsh to be fully enforceable and that juries and judges would apply it with discretion, taking account, that is, of the character of the individual and of his offense. Even at the Summer assizes in 1699 in Surrey not all the prisoners allowed their clergy were burned in the face. Some were presumably thought by the judges to be unsuitable candidates for such treatment because of their age or physical condition.[106] In the Spring session of 1700 only one of several clergied offenders was in fact branded on the face, despite the insistence in the Act that the punishment be carried out "in open court, in the presence of the judge, who is hereby directed and required to see the same strictly and effectually executed."

Such mitigation continued until 1706, when that clause was repealed and the branding of clergy was returned to the thumb. The reason given in the new statute was that the permanent and visible stigmatization of prisoners had made them "unfit to be intrusted in any service or employment to get their livelihood in any honest and lawful way," and by thus making them "more desperate" had obliged many to follow a life of crime.[107] There is strong evidence that the real reason was that branding on the cheek had been in fact evaded by court officials, that even when the bench had insisted that the branding be visible prisoners were leaving court with brand marks so faint that the effect was worse than under the old system, for "old offenders" were now more difficult to recognize. That was the conclusion of the grand jury of London, who complained in a presentment in 1704 "how ineffectuall the several laws now in force against Felons . . . had proved for want of due Execution."[108] They were particularly concerned with the branding, or nonbranding, of clergy on the cheek, though they also complained about the ease with which women escaped justice by claiming pregnancy, and the ineffectiveness of self-administered transportation. Their observations on these subjects were to be

[104] OBSP, May 1699.

[105] QO/EW 11, Jan. 1700. In Surrey, some years later, it was called a "scull-cap . . . to keep their heads steddy" (S,A,P., Summer 1729, p. 2 [Acton]).

[106] ASSI 35/140/8/2, 9, 12, 21, 27, 30, 33.

[107] 5 Anne, c. 6, s. 1 (1706).

[108] Old Bailey, Sessions Papers, 1704 (Corporation of London Record Office). I owe my knowledge of this presentment to Joanna Innes and to Steven MacFarlane, who unearthed it.

of great significance, for this presentment appears to have provided the
starting point for a petition to the House of Commons from the City of
London that resulted in a clause in the Act of 1706 (the Act that returned
the branding of clergy to the thumb and at the same time abolished the
literacy test) that gave the judges the right to commit a clergied offender
to a house of correction or a workhouse for a period of hard labor. This
was not an entirely new power, for the Elizabethan statute that had severed
the connection between the lay and ecclesiastical courts in the administration of the privilege of clergy had authorized judges to imprison clergied
offenders for up to a year. That appears rarely to have been implemented,
however. The Act of 1706 was a new departure and a new intention. To
examine its significance we need to look briefly at the houses of correction
and notions surrounding the reform of offenders in this period.

Imprisonment at Hard Labor

Houses of correction had been first established in the reign of Elizabeth
specifically to punish and to attempt to reform the able-bodied poor who
refused to work.[109] They were to be institutions in which vagrants and
the idle and disorderly and all the "thriftless poor" could be punished and
disciplined and given those habits of life that the established and respectable men of the parish approved of as the foundation and guarantee of
social order. Those who shied away from regular work were to be committed there so that, as Michael Dalton said, "by labour and punishment
of their bodies, their froward natures may be bridled, their evil minds
bettered and others by their example terrified."[110]

Little is known in detail about the English houses of correction in
the seventeenth and eighteenth centuries. But several points are clear. One
is that they grew in number.[111] Another is that despite the Webbs' insistence that they had lost their purpose, they remained in intention and
to some extent at least in practice places of work and labor discipline well
into the eighteenth century. It is true that in the eighteenth century the
houses of correction also took on some of the functions of the jails as places

[109] Sidney and Beatrice Webb, *English Prisons under Local Government* (1922; repr. 1963), pp.
12–17. Workhouses and houses of correction were also established in Europe in the sixteenth
century. For the European institutions in the early modern period see Langbein, *Torture and the
Law of Proof*, pp. 33–39, and the works cited there; and Thorsten Sellin, *Pioneering in Penology:
The Amsterdam Houses of Correction in the Sixteenth and Seventeenth Centuries* (Philadelphia, 1944).

[110] Michael Dalton, *The Country Justice* (1661 ed.), p. 122.

[111] About twenty houses of correction were established between 1680 and 1720, by which
time there were approximately 120 altogether (Joanna Innes, "Imprisonment and Punishment
in Early Modern England," paper delivered at the conference of the International Association for
the History of Crime and Criminal Justice, Washington, D.C., 1980, n. 14).

of confinement for petty offenders awaiting trial. But the addition of such prisoners did not change their aims and purposes, for the Surrey magistrates ordered in 1724 that "all persons committed thither as lewd disorderly persons should be kept to labour as the comittal directs."[112] The majority of inmates continued to be the vagrant and disreputable poor, prostitutes, and street urchins, those who refused to work ("wanting more wages than the law allows"), servants and apprentices who disobeyed their masters, and unmarried mothers. Undoubtedly the threat of such incarceration was used to force compliance with the orders of magistrates and other local officials, as in the case of a man in Sussex who was told by the justices in 1691 "to marry widow Lewer in a month or leave her company or else to be sent to the house of correction."[113]

It is significant therefore that the Act of 1706 allowed judges to commit convicted felons who had been allowed benefit of clergy to a period of six months to two years in a house of correction or a workhouse in order to be "set at work and kept at hard labour" and to be given "such due correction as shall be fit and necessary in that behalf." A punishment previously reserved as a means of coercing the poor was specifically sanctioned for those convicted of felonies upon indictments.[114] This had been

---

[112] QS 2/6, Ep. 1724, 1. At the Southwark house of correction it was reported in the 1730s that a supply of "blocks and beetles" was kept in several rooms so that the prisoners could beat hemp; it was also said that the hempdressers in the Borough sent in raw materials to be prepared by the prisoners (QS 2/6, Mich. 1731, 30; Ea. 1738, 2b). An inspection by three magistrates revealed in 1739 that "the prisoners . . . are kept to labour and work as they ought" (QS 2/1/15, 15 Feb. 1739). A complaint that the inmates at the Guildford house of correction were not being kept at hard labor was investigated in 1741 (QS 2/1/16, 14 July). At the Tottlefields Bridewell, across the Thames, the Swiss visitor César de Saussure found thirty or forty inmates in a room, each sitting "in front of a large wooden block of wood, on which to beat the flax with a large and heavy wooden mallet." Men and women sat on opposite sides of the room, and "between these two lines walked the inspector, or Captain Whip'em. This man had a surly, repulsive countenance; he held a long cane in his hand about the thickness of my little finger, and whenever one of these ladies was fatigued and ceased working he would rap them on the arms, and in no gentle fashion" (*A Foreign View of England in the Reigns of George I and George II. The Letters of Monsieur César de Saussure to his Family*, ed. Madame van Muyden [1902], p. 300). That scene was recorded by Hogarth in plate 4 of "A Harlot's Progress" (1732). A statute of 1720 (6 Geo I, c. 19, s. 2) authorized magistrates to commit "vagrants and other criminals, offenders [and persons charged with minor offenses] . . . either to the common gaol or house of correction, as they in their judgement shall think proper; any law, custom, or usage to the contrary notwithstanding." The Surrey houses acquired sets of iron fetters to prevent prisoners sent there to await trial from escaping (QS 2/6, Mids. 1723, 81), and magistrates began sending a small number of felons to them.

[113] QM/FW/3 (Minute Book, Ea. 1691).

[114] Though not for the first time. As we have seen, the statute of 1576 that had broken the link between benefit of clergy and the church had also authorized judges to commit clergied offenders at their discretion for a period of up to a year, though to the county jail. Article 10

encouraged no doubt by the problems in transportation (exacerbated again by the interruptions in merchant shipping during the war of Spanish Succession then in progress) and by the obvious failure of burning on the cheek as an alternative to the established and unsatisfactory consequence of the allowance of clergy. But it was also encouraged by what appears to have been a positive argument in favor of applying to minor felons the punishments that had been designed as a means of reforming and correcting the disorderly poor.

It was not a new idea that magistrates ought to enforce the laws against immoral behavior in order to prevent men from falling into habits of crime; or that such prevention and the provision of employment for the poor and the proper education of their children would be more effective in reducing crime than a severe criminal law. Sir Matthew Hale had written in 1683, for example, that "the prevention of poverty, idleness and a loose and disorderly Education, even of poor Children, would do more good to this Kingdom, than all the Gibbets and Cauterizations, and Whipping Posts and Jayls in this Kingdom, and would render these kinds of Discipline less necessary and less frequent."[115] There was no clear division, but rather an overlap and continuity between those who might be thought to be acting immorally and in a disorderly way and those committing the most minor criminal offenses, an overlap that is cleary signaled in the commitment of men and women to the houses of correction in Surrey not only as "idle and disorderly" but also frequently as "pilfering persons."

If the reformative discipline of an institution in which habits of industry were taught by hard labor was thought to be the best means of correcting and punishing those who occupied the gray area between social indiscipline and crime, it is hardly surprising that in places and at times when immorality and petty crime seemed to be particularly acute corrective discipline was not only emphasized for the idle and disorderly but also extended to the lower ranks of those who had actually been convicted of minor thefts. The last decade of the seventeenth century and early decades of the eighteenth were such a time. The perceptions of clergymen and social commentators and moralists in London and other cities (Bristol, for example) in the 1690s were that at a time when labor was believed to be the foundation of the national strength, many thousands of men and women were withholding their labor out of laziness and corruption of mind. There was a widespread sense of moral crisis and social dislocation made visible

---

of the Book of Orders (1631) had urged magistrates to ensure that prisoners committed to jail should be reformed by being made to work in the house of correction, and to make this possible it was further suggested that the house of correction should be built next to the county jail (J. P. Kenyon, *The Stuart Constitution* [Cambridge, 1966], p. 501).

    [115] Matthew Hale, *A Discourse Touching Provision for the Poor* (1683), preface.

not only in the poor districts of London but in the crowds of beggars, vagrants, and street urchins noticed by every visitor to the capital.[116]

Soon after the Revolution small groups of men (stimulated perhaps by the example of the religious societies founded in the 1670s) were coming together in London to find ways of opposing what was widely regarded in the middling and upper ranks of society as a dangerously rising tide of immoral behavior. Their ambitions were to root out drunkenness, pro fanity, non-observance of the Sabbath, gambling, and other vices—to effect, in short, a "reformation of. manners." They were motivated fundamentally by religious sensibilities, by a deep concern that a society in which immorality was allowed to flourish unchecked was not fulfilling its duty to promote "the advancement of the honor and Service of almighty God," as one group announced when they formed in 1693.[117] The service of God and the interests of society were of course identical in this respect, for a healthy social order was assumed to rest on a religious and thus a moral foundation. Numerous laws prohibited immorality in various forms: blasphemy, drunkenness, trading or working on a Sunday, and similar evils. Their enforcement was from time to time enjoined upon magistrates and the judges of assize in royal proclamations addressed to the civil authorities to prosecute all who broke these laws, and to ensure the vigilance of constables and other local officials. Such proclamations had been issued soon after the Restoration, for example. But they were particularly numerous and particularly effective in the years after the Revolution of 1689. A letter on the subject of immorality from Queen Mary to the Middlesex magistrates in 1691 was especially influential in stimulating a wave of vigilante activity in the early 1690s; and a second wave was encouraged by further royal proclamations in 1698 and 1699 in response to an address by the House of Commons and particularly stimulated by the plea issued in April 1699 by Archbishop Tenison on irreligion that, in Bahlman's words, "mobilized the clergy . . . to make a special effort for the cause."[118] Queen Anne proclaimed her own endorsement of the prosecution of immorality and vice within weeks of coming to the throne in 1702.[119]

[116] Dudley W. R. Bahlman, *The Moral Revolution of 1688* (New Haven, 1957), chap. 1.

[117] Their "Agreement" is printed in Radzinowicz, *History*, vol. 2, p. 431. On this subject generally see Bahlman, *Moral Revolution*; G. V. Portus, *Caritas Anglicana, or an Historical Inquiry into those Religious and Philanthropical Societies that Flourished in England between 1678 and 1714* (1912); W. A. Speck and T. C. Curtis, "The Societies for the Reformation of Manners: A Case Study in the Theory and Practice of Moral Reform," *Literature and History* 3 (1976), pp. 43 64, A. G. Craig, "The Movement for the Reformation of Manners, 1688–1715" (Ph.D. thesis, University of Edinburgh, 1980).

[118] Bahlman, *Moral Revolution*, pp. 23–24.

[119] William's proclamation of 1699 is printed in *Cal. S. P. Dom.*, 1699–1700, p. 313, and

The cells of reformers that formed in the capital and elsewhere to advance this work were considerably encouraged by this umbrella of royal approval. The Societies for the Reformation of Manners, as they became called, saw their main task as prosecuting individuals for cursing or swearing or breaking other laws, but they also raised money to encourage informers and provided blank warrants and summonses and the like. Their influence, like that of the royal proclamations, was felt throughout the country.[120] But the greatest concentration of immorality and debauchery was in London and there is no doubt that the campaign for the reformation of manners was carried on in the metropolis with the greatest intensity.

Immorality was not restricted to the poor, and from time to time men pointed that out. But the Societies for the Reformation of Manners were concerned principally with the behavior and the habits of the working population. The repressive climate that their campaigns created at the end of the seventeenth century and in the early decades of the eighteenth was further extended by other schemes advanced in these same years to concentrate the dependent unemployed poor in workhouses (an idea born in Bristol in 1697 and taken up subsequently in London) and to create charity schools in which the children of the poor might be taught to read the scriptures and be trained for a life of work and service. That effort was coordinated from 1699 by the recently founded Society for the Propagation of Christian Knowledge.[121]

There is no doubt that this same repressive climate strongly influenced reactions in the 1690s and in the first quarter of the new century to the evident failure of the courts to create systems of punishment that would discourage crime and prevent the hordes of immoral and debauched individuals, whose lives were being attended to by the reformers of manners, from going on to even worse offenses. Concern for the moral health of society made the weakness of the punishments available to the courts especially dismaying to large numbers of men. That helps to explain the willingness of juries to convict in such a way that minor offenders could

---

see pp. 237 and 388 for instructions given to the judges before their Lent and Summer circuits in 1699 on the need to punish vice and immorality. Many county courts of quarter sessions responded to such royal proclamations by reminding constables of their duties under the statutes. Following Queen Anne's proclamation in 1702, for example, the Surrey quarter sessions ordered the high constables to summon their petty constables to hear the proclamation and the court's order read (QS 2/1/9, pp. 127–28).

[120] Bahlman, *Moral Revolution*, pp. 38–40.

[121] M. G. Jones, *The Charity School Movement* (1938), pp. 15–41; David Owen, *English Philanthropy* (Cambridge, Mass., 1964), pp. 20–21. For a broadly based account of the variety of schemes in the late seventeenth and early eighteenth centuries for employing and reforming the poor, see Donna T. Andrew, "London Charity in the Eighteenth Century" (Ph.D. thesis, University of Toronto, 1977), chap. 2.

be whipped instead of simply discharged with a branded thumb.[122] It helps to explain the experiment introduced in 1699 with branding on the cheek. And it undoubtedly encouraged the passage of the several major statutes in William's reign and in Anne's that altered the criminal code substantially. These were not, on the whole, statutes that responded to crises of particular crimes, as enactments removing clergy from specific offenses often were in the eighteenth century (in the case, for example, of sheep-stealing, thefts on the river, and the stealing of black lead from mines). In the 1690s there were no unusual outbreaks of thefts by servants, or shopliftings or even breaking and entering houses in the daytime. The Acts that removed these and similar offenses from the privilege of clergy were not aiming to diminish a crime wave of a specific kind, but rather of a generalized kind, crime that resulted largely from immorality and from social breakdown. This might help to explain why these new capital offenses were never in fact enforced with great strictness, even when they were first passed.

The conjunction on the one hand of widespread concern for the habits and behavior of the poor and the liveliness of the notion that what was required was their *reform*, and on the other of the failure of the penal alternatives to the simple branding of clergy, also helps to explain the emergence in Anne's reign of the notion that the institutions and the discipline previously reserved for the vagrant and disreputable poor might be usefully extended to reform and to rescue those who had been convicted of minor offenses. This is the significance of the clause of the 1706 statute that empowered judges to send prisoners convicted of clergyable felonies to hard labor in the house of correction for six months to two years. The idea was pressed upon the House of Commons in a petition drawn up in London, which was itself an amended version of the 1704 grand jury presentment noticed earlier that had urged more effective administration of the criminal law in the face of complaints made to them "by many eminent tradesmen" about the level of crime in the city.[123] The amendments were made by a committee of aldermen, which included the lord mayor and also Sir Robert Clayton, who as the governor of the London

---

[122] The apparent concentration of such immorality in urban parishes, particularly in the metropolis of London, also perhaps helps to explain why juries in Sussex reduced the charge of grand larceny to petty larceny much less frequently than those in Surrey. In the years 1662–63 and 1690–94, for example, only three offenders at the Sussex assizes were convicted of petty larceny and whipped after being indicted for a more serious offense.

[123] The petition submitted to the Commons in 1704 by "the Grand Jury, Citizens, and Shopkeepers, of the City of London" argued that "if instead of burning in the Cheek, such Criminals should be confined to some Work-house, there to be kept to hard Labour for a Year, for the First Offence, for the Second Offence, Two Years, and for the Third Offence, to suffer Death, it would more effectually prevent their wicked Practices" (*J.H.C.* 14 [1702–4], p. 463).

corporation of the poor was heavily engaged in the management of the poor of London. It appears likely that the clause that made it possible for felons to be imprisoned and punished at hard labor arose at the urging of a man who, it has been said, was especially interested in the reformative effects of poor law discipline.[124]

Others had indeed urged this before. Timothy Nourse thought, for example, that

> as for lesser criminals, as pick-pockets, petty-larceny, pimps, common-whores, sheep-stealers, coney-catchers, hedge-breakers, and other like offenders, whose crimes deserve not death, 'twere very good they were condemn'd to *bridewell* for a year or two, or more, as the nature and circumstances of their crimes do require. . . .

Nourse would have liked to see more of them transported, but he thought "the best way . . . would be to keep them to work in Houses of Correction."[125] Another argument in favor of the imprisonment at hard labor of convicted offenders was that such a punishment was already being tried as a condition of pardon. In 1705 eleven women who had been convicted of capital offenses at the Old Bailey were pardoned by the queen on condition that they be "removed to the Prison of Bridewell London to Labour as idle and disorderly persons for the space of one whole year and afterwards untill [her] Majesty's further Will and pleasure should be known for their delivery."[126] Further pardons on such conditions were issued later in Anne's reign. A man was pardoned and sent to a workhouse for three years in 1709; and five women and a man, again from the Old Bailey, were sent to various terms to the house of correction in 1710.[127] There may well have been others. This condition was largely reserved for women, for after 1705 men could be sent to the army, unless they were too old or physically incapable of service.[128] Women could not be so easily disposed of.

Imprisonment at hard labor was thus encouraged in Anne's reign by the arguments of those who thought it right to attempt to "reform" as

---

[124] Innes, "Imprisonment and Punishment," p. 8 and n. 21.

[125] Nourse, *Campania foelix*, p. 229.

[126] SP 34/9, f. 8.

[127] SP 34/11, f. 63; SP 34/13, f. 195.

[128] SP 34/11, f. 63. Authority to send men to the army as a condition of a pardon from capital punishment was provided by a clause in the Mutiny Act of 1705 (4 Anne, c. 10). Pardons had been granted earlier to men whose conditional transportation had been accomplished by their being enlisted in a regiment bound for the West Indies, but I believe that this Act marked the beginning of service in the army as a condition of pardon.

well as punish certain kinds of offenders, and by the difficulties and failures of alternative punishments, particularly transportation and branding on the cheek. The clause in the Act of 1706 that gave power to the judges to send offenders convicted of clergyable felonies directly to the house of correction was used over the next decade, extensively in some parts of the country. In Devon, for example, it has been calculated that almost a quarter of those accused of felony before the assizes were imprisoned in the years 1707–17.[129] In the same period, the judges at the Old Bailey took advantage of the 1706 Act to sentence a substantial number of men and women (particularly women, at least in the early years) to terms of hard labor in the house of correction after they had been burned in the hand for a clergyable felony.[130] How frequently such sentences were imposed on the Home Circuit is not easy to determine because the records are incomplete in this period. Some clergied felons at the Surrey assizes certainly were ordered to be imprisoned. At the Lent assizes in 1710 one man and seven women were convicted of simple larceny, burned in the hand, and sent to the Southwark house of correction for six months. In the following year three women and a man were similarly "put to hard labour" after being allowed their clergy.[131] It is entirely possible that at least some of the others burned in the hand in these years were in fact also committed to the house of correction, though it looks as though the judges did not for some reason find it necessary or advisable to order that as frequently as they were doing in other courts.[132]

Clearly, imprisonment at hard labor became acceptable in Anne's reign as a way of punishing more than mere immorality or of disciplining the disorderly poor. The imprisonment of felons did not in fact develop from this point in a major way: as we will see, transportation returned

---

[129] Innes, "Imprisonment and Punishment," p. 3.

[130] I owe this information to Joanna Innes.

[131] ASSI 35/150/6, calendar; S.A.P., Summer 1711, p. 4.

[132] About half the noncapital offenders convicted in Surrey in 1707–17 were whipped and the remainder burned in the hand. The latter were listed in the assize calendars that have survived as having been burned and discharged. It is possible, however, that they were subsequently ordered to be confined to a period of hard labor without that being recorded in the calendar, and since in any case six of the assize calendars for these years are missing and several others are very badly damaged the possibility clearly exists that many more Surrey offenders than I have estimated were imprisoned at hard labor, 1707–17. Even when such punishment was ordered it seems to have been used selectively: at the Summer assizes of 1716, for example, two convicts were sent to terms in the house of correction after being granted clergy, but twelve others were burned in the hand and discharged (ASSI 35/156/7, calendar). It looks distinctly as though the authorities in Surrey simply did not grasp the opportunities offered by the 1706 Act. A possible explanation of that may lie in the state of the county jail. As we have seen, the magistrates of Surrey were still without their own jail in this period, and that may well have played some part in the sentencing decisions of the assize judges.

powerfully in the reign of George I and established a greater stability in penal matters than had been in evidence at least since the Restoration. But the conviction that imprisonment was a legitimate penal alternative, and the persuasion (lying behind the use of the house of correction rather than the county jail) that the *reformation* of the prisoner might do more to prevent crime than would mere punishment, established a significant connection that was never wholly abandoned and that re-emerged powerfully in the third quarter of the century at the heart of a new dominant penal ideology.

THE TRANSPORTATION ACT, 1718

From the Restoration and into the second decade of the eighteenth century, the courts and parliament were engaged in a search for a usable secondary punishment that would deter crime by stiffening the penalties following upon a successful plea of benefit of clergy. None became firmly established. In 1714 the circumstances in which these shifting expedients had been tried began to change. Not least was the beginning of a long period of peace. Coupled with that were significant changes in the character of the administration, for the Hanoverian succession brought to power a king and a group of politicians anxious to establish an effective government that would safeguard the regime and the Revolution.

The succession also took place in the midst of a postwar crisis of crime and disorder, in and around the capital, that was reflected in a considerable increase in prosecutions for robbery and burglary and other violent offenses against property. The Surrey assizes dealt with a large number of such cases in the summer of 1713, the first year of peace, and even more in 1714 and 1715, when thirty-nine prisoners were convicted of capital offenses against property and twenty-one were hanged (table 9.5). There was a good deal of reluctance on the bench and at court to pardon many of these convicted offenders, especially men who had committed the most serious offenses. That toughness of mind reflects attitudes that had been evident for twenty years and more. But it may also owe something to the unsatisfactory character of the alternatives to hanging, to the lack of an effective punishment to impose as a condition of the royal clemency.

Certainly transportation of felons across the Atlantic was no more easily accomplished under Anne or in the early years of George I than it had been in the 1690s. The evidence of pardons granted under Anne is fragmentary for Surrey, but about a third of them appear to have been free and absolute, allowing the convict immediate discharge without any

TABLE 9.5

Capital Punishment for Property Offenses
at the Surrey Assizes, 1714–1715

Offense	Total Sentenced to Death	Pardoned	Hanged
MEN			
Robbery	5	2	3
Burglary	16	6	10
Housebreaking	3	1	2
Horse-theft	3	1	2
Picking pockets	1	1	0
Theft from house	2	1	1
Total	30	12	18
		= 40%	= 60%
WOMEN			
Burglary	1	0	1
Picking pockets	6	5	1
Theft from house	1	1	0
Theft from shop	1	0	1
Total	9	6	3
		= 67.7%	= 33.3%

SOURCE: Hanged Count.

condition at all (following a pattern established, as we have seen, in the 1690s). Roughly another third were granted to men on condition that they enlist in the army or navy. The remaining prisoners, perhaps unsuitable for the forces, continued to be pardoned on condition of transportation, but it is plain that such convicts were being released on the understanding that they would banish themselves within a certain period, having provided sureties that they would do so. The difficulties of transportation may be judged by several cases at the Old Bailey in 1711: one man convicted of burglary after breaking into the offices of the East India Company in London was pardoned from the death penalty on condition that he be transported by the Company to the East Indies for his life; two others pardoned with him were also banished for life, one to "any of the plantations in America," the other anywhere he chose, other than a country with which Britain was then at war.[133] The coming of peace did not make

[133] SP 34/16, ff. 143–45.

things much easier, for at least one man was pardoned in 1714 on condition that he transport himself to the Island of Minorca, recently acquired at the Treaty of Utrecht.[134]

The prisoners convicted of noncapital felonies in Surrey in Anne's reign and in the early years of George I's (as far as the records reveal) continued to be either burnt in the hand and discharged or, having been convicted of petty larceny by the trial jury, whipped and discharged. Some advantage had been taken of the clause in the Act of 1706 that allowed the judges to imprison clergied offenders for up to two years, but apparently not in Surrey as often as in some other counties. The difficulties in transportation and the large numbers of offenders hanged thus made even plainer than ever the weaknesses in the penal system that had encouraged the search for alternative punishments since the Restoration. The need for an effective noncapital punishment must have seemed particularly acute in view of the long criminal calendars to be dealt with.

Why imprisonment at hard labor failed to develop as that punishment is not entirely clear. Considerations of cost may have been decisively influential, especially in Surrey, given the inadequacy of the prison arrangements before the New Gaol was built in the 1720s. But the main point is that imprisonment was not conceived as stern enough for persistent serious offenders or for those pardoned from capital convictions, for whom in the early decades of the eighteenth century transportation appears to have been the preferred punishment. The problems that had prevented its firm establishment in the decades after the Restoration did not diminish the attractiveness of a punishment that would remove such prisoners entirely from the community and quite possibly terrify others by the prospects of a similar journey across the Atlantic. Support for such a penalty was rekindled in the midst of the massive increase in violent crime that appeared to overtake the capital at the end of the war of Spanish Succession and the early years of George I's reign, and in the new political arrangements that the accession of the Hanoverians created. There was then a return to the initiative begun in the 1660s, but now under different circumstances. Now the government seems to have been not only actively in favor of it but willing to create the circumstances in which it could succeed, willing to remove obstacles. The problem was also tackled head-on, and (possibly because the option of manipulating the literacy exam had been removed by the Act of 1706) the new plans did not depend on sleight of hand in the courtroom. The Whig governments after 1714 were clearly anxious to bolster the courts in the face of mounting crime and popular disaf-

---

[134] R vs. Bigg: Strange, *Reports*, vol. 1, pp. 18–20; *Eng. Rep.*, vol. 93, pp. 357–58 (1717).

fection—no doubt largely in the interests of the firm establishment of the regime—and they were strong enough, politically and financially, to ensure that any new powers they were granted could be put into effect. One result was the Transportation Act of 1718.[135]

It is not clear whose initiative lay behind this legislation, but it has the appearance of a piece of government business. It was introduced into the House of Commons in December 1717 by the Solicitor General, William Thomson, as a bill "for the further preventing Robberies, Burglaries, and other felonies; and for the more effectual Transportation of Felons." Thomson was Recorder of London as well as Solicitor General, and he had thus sat regularly as a judge at the Old Bailey. It is possible that he personally pressed for such a bill and that it was the interests of the busiest of the English courts that lay behind it. London had been particularly troubled by crime in the postwar years, and the special concern of the metropolis was recognized by the inclusion on the committee appointed to consider the bill of all the members for the counties of Surrey and Middlesex and for the City of London.[136] But this was no narrow piece of local business. It may have been pressed forward by members for London, but it took no special knowledge of the courts to recognize in 1715 and 1716 that despite the frequent hangings in and around the capital, robberies and burglaries were apparently at a very high level; and it could not have been news to men like Sunderland who had sat in the cabinet in Anne's reign that there was a problem in getting men transported to America and the West Indies. In addition, the bill was but one aspect of a broad policy that suggests that the administration was fully engaged in pressing a new policy forward and not merely acquiescing in others' initiatives.

There seems little reason to doubt that the main argument behind the Act was that stated in its preface: "The punishments inflicted by the laws now in force against the offences of robbery, larceny and other felonious taking and stealing of money and goods, have not proved effectual to deter wicked and evil-disposed persons from being guilty of the said crimes." It went on to make it possible for the courts to sentence a noncapital felon directly to a term of transportation to America for seven years, and to establish a term of fourteen years for those pardoned by the king from a capital sentence. The Act also laid it down that returning to England before the expiration of the full term of transportation was itself to be a capital offense.

[135] 4 Geo I, c. 11 (1718).
[136] *J.H.C.* 18 (1714–18), pp. 667, 671, 675.

This was one aspect of the new policy and program. The second was equally important and gave it teeth. The preamble to the Transportation Act noted that "whereas many of the offenders to whom royal mercy hath been extended, upon condition of transporting themselves to the West-Indies, have often neglected to perform the said condition, but returned to their former wickedness. . . ." It had indeed been frequently pointed out that transportation had failed in part because there had been no machinery to guarantee that the court's orders would be obeyed or the condition of a pardon fulfilled. A system that depended on the merchant's willingness to take convicts across the Atlantic had broken down because even if the colonies had not opposed the trade and the wars interrupted it, merchants simply could not dispose of everyone the courts wanted to send. That had given way to a more piecemeal system of individuals finding sureties to guarantee voluntary transportation, a system that was almost certain to fail.

It was the recognition that a proper transportation system would in fact cost money that made the new policy so successful—and that made it primarily a piece of government legislation. The government was perhaps in a much better position by 1718 than any previous administration to make a financial commitment of this kind, since it was the beneficiary of a "financial revolution" that over the previous twenty years had greatly expanded its capacities to tap the wealth of the nation,[137] and at the same time the country was in a period of peace that had all the appearances, unlike that of 1697, of taking root. In any event, the commitment of money to the new program was undoubtedly crucial to its success. The Treasury agreed to put the whole business of transportation from Newgate and the counties surrounding London by contract into the hands of a London merchant, Jonathan Forward, and to pay him a fee of three pounds for each convict he took across the Atlantic. The Treasury also paid for the transportation of felons from the Home Counties, but prisoners from the provincial assizes were to be subsidized by a county rate, and a contract was to be made between a merchant and the local magistrates.[138]

In London, Forward kept the contract for twenty years. He was succeeded by other merchants who kept it as long, which confirms what one might expect from the terms, that it was extremely lucrative.[139] The

[137] P.G.M. Dickson, *The Financial Revolution in England: A Study in the Development of Public Credit, 1688–1756* (1967).

[138] Authorized by 6 Geo I, c. 23. See *Calendar of Treasury Papers, 1714–1719*, p. 389; Smith, *Colonists in Bondage*, pp. 113–15.

[139] According to Smith, *Colonists in Bondage*, the contractors were Jonathan Forward, 1718–39; Andrew Reid, 1739–57; John Stewart, 1757–72; and Duncan Campbell, 1772 to 1775, when the trade came to an end.

contractor not only got the government's subsidy (which rose to five pounds in 1727); he was also free to sell the services of the prisoners to the highest bidder, and it is clear that that brought substantial returns.[140] This arrangement and the powers given to the courts under the Act together transformed the English penal system. Colonial objections to receiving convicts could not prevail against an English government determined to punish men by sending them to the New World, and especially a government as anxious about crime and social disorder as the new Whig administration was.

Perhaps the American mainland colonies were now sufficiently populous and developed to absorb more easily a few hundred convicts every year. Virginia still protested, not directly, but by passing an Act in 1723 that established such complex rules for the reception of convicts that merchants would have been discouraged from bringing them. The reaction in England was swift and decisive. Forward complained immediately to the Board of Trade that the Virginia regulations would "disable me from performing my contract with the government for transporting felons, and in a great measure destroy the intent of the Act of Parliament lately passed for that purpose." In less than two months the Board had obtained legal advice and reported to the cabinet, and the Act was disallowed.[141] Despite the struggles for power that had begun almost immediately within the administration, the Whigs were strongly in control of parliament; and as they demonstrated in the Riot Act of 1715 and would again in the Black Act of 1723, they were willing to strengthen the hands of the courts and to take strong measures in the face of threats to lives and property and to the stability of the Hanoverian regime. The establishment of transportation

[140] Campbell reported that in the last years of the trade he got an average of ten pounds each for male laborers and eight or nine for women. His great profit was made on craftsmen—carpenters and blacksmiths and the like—who brought from fifteen to twenty-five pounds, and that made up for the premium that had to be paid "to humane people" to take the old and infirm convicts off his hands. By the 1770s there was a great demand for English labor in the colonies, and the sums reported by Campbell may not have been enjoyed by all the contractors before him. Nonetheless, the profits were clearly handsome. For Campbell's evidence to a House of Commons committee see *J.H.C.* 37 (1778–80), p. 310. See also Smith, *Colonists in Bondage*, pp. 113–15, 362, nn. 6–10; and Wilfred Oldham, "The Administration of the System of Transportation of British Convicts, 1763–93" (Ph.D. thesis, University of London, 1933).

[141] *Cal. S. P. Colonial: America and the West Indies (1722–23)*, pp. 293–94, 301, 303; *Acts of the Privy Council (Colonial)*, vol. 3, pp. 54–55. The governor of Jamaica reported with some dismay that the first convicts sent there under the Act were "so farr from altering their evil courses and way of living and becoming an advantage to us, that the greatest part of them are gone and have induced others to go with them a pyrating, and have inveglied and encouraged several negroes to desert from their masters and go to the Spaniards in Cuba, the few that remains proves a wicked lazy and indolent people, so that I could heartily wish this country might be troubled with no more [of] them" (*Cal. S. P. Colonial: America and the West Indies* [1717–1718], p. 345).

as a regular punishment at the disposal of the courts was an act of a government strong enough to override objections. It was one of the fruits of the stability that the Whigs brought to English government after 1714, and it brought in turn stability to the penal system.[142]

NONCAPITAL PUNISHMENT, 1718–1750

How many of the judges had been consulted before the introduction of the Transportation Act is unclear, but once it had passed they gave it their enthusiastic endorsement by taking immediate advantage of its provisions. At a session of the Old Bailey in 1719, for example, twenty-five of twenty-seven prisoners convicted of clergyable offenses were sentenced to be transported.[143] In Surrey the first transportation sentences were handed down at the Lent session of 1719, when twelve men and women (of the fifteen who might have been) were ordered to be sent to America for seven years. The importance and influence of the Act can be seen in the sentences awarded in 1722–24, the first run of years for which complete evidence survives, in which more than half the prisoners convicted of noncapital felonies against property were ordered to be transported.

A significant aspect of the Act was the blurring of the distinction between petty and grand larceny that resulted from making both subject to transportation. They had previously been entirely different species of offense: the one, a felony for which a convicted prisoner might have been hanged; the other, a noncapital felony subject only to corporal punishment. The difference had immensely broadened the jury's discretionary power, for by finding a prisoner guilty of simple larceny of under a shilling in value they had ensured that he would be whipped—and only whipped— and discharged. The Transportation Act removed that discretion from the jury and gave it to the judge. A prisoner convicted of any noncapital offense could now be dealt with as the bench decided. Twelve of the men sent to America in 1722 and 1723 from Surrey had in fact been convicted of petty larceny by the jury, no doubt in the expectation that they would be whipped. It was the judge's decision that sent them to America for seven years. This transference of power from jury to judge was surely no accidental byproduct of the Act: it strongly suggests that the statute had

---

[142] For American opposition to the Transportation Act see Smith, *Colonists in Bondage*, pp. 119–22. There has been remarkably little work on the way transportation was organized in England, on the way the convicts were actually conveyed across the Atlantic and their fate once they arrived. These questions are all addressed, however, in a forthcoming study by Roger Ekirch, *Bound for America: The Transportation of British Convicts to the Colonies, 1718–1775*.

[143] OBSP, Dec. 1719.

TABLE 9.6
Noncapital Punishment for Property Offenses in Surrey before
and after the Transportation Act of 1718

Period	Years	Number of Punishments		Clergy allowed: Discharged		Transported		Whipped		Imprisoned	
		N	%	N	%	N	%	N	%	N	%
MEN											
1663–1715	16	334	100.0	193	57.8	15	4.5	126	37.7	0	0
1722–1749	14	332	100.0	29	8.7	198	59.6	103	31.0	2	.6
WOMEN											
1663–1715	16	163	99.9	87	53.3	3	1.8	73	44.8	0	0
1722–1749	14	130	100.0	18	13.9	60	46.2	51	39.2	1	.8

SOURCE: Sample.

been heavily influenced, and perhaps drafted, by a judge or by a man who had had a great deal of experience on the bench, a man who knew intimately the limitations on judicial discretion that particular jury verdicts produced and who wanted to broaden the discretionary sentencing powers of magistrates and judges.[144]

The extent to which the Act transformed the patterns of punishment may be seen by comparing noncapital sentences imposed on prisoners convicted in the Surrey courts in the thirty years following its passage with those of the previous half century (table 9.6). Whereas before transportation became available to the courts as a direct punishment sixty per cent of the men convicted of clergyable offenses or petty larceny were allowed their clergy and were branded on the thumb and discharged, in the generation after 1718 that same proportion was sent to the American colonies and fewer than one in ten were granted clergy. Transportation also reduced the number of men who were whipped and released. The change in the punishment of women was a little less dramatic in that a smaller proportion were sent to America, and rather more than in the case of men were whipped at the conclusion of the court session and discharged.

[144] It seems to me entirely likely that that man was William Thomson, the Recorder of London who was also the solicitor general, 1717–20, and who introduced the Bill into parliament. He was clearly a man who strongly valued both the stern punishments and the wider discretion the Act put into the hands of the bench.

The effect of the Act on the treatment of women was nonetheless significant, for it ensured that the largest proportion of the women convicted
of noncapital property offenses would be banished from the country. Both
men and women who previously would have had every expectation of
immediate discharge (though with the pain and humiliation of a whipping
or a branded thumb) were now more than likely to be returned to jail to
await the arrangements that would send them to Maryland or Virginia to
be sold into servitude for seven years. The Transportation Act had a similar
effect on sentencing in Sussex. In the decades that followed its passage
clergyable discharges all but disappeared in that county. The vast majority
of those convicted of noncapital felonies were transported (sixty-one per
cent), and the remainder largely whipped and discharged (thirty-six per
cent). Even in a county in which only modest numbers of accused were
being tried every year, transportation was welcomed as a substitute for
the branding and discharge of clergy.[145]

It is worth noting that at least in London and on the Home Circuit
the arrangements by which men were transported were placed in the hands
of one man who not only gave a bond to guarantee that the transportation
would take place as ordered but who developed a routine for carrying it
out, and no doubt in time captains and crews who became experienced in
the business. It remained possible for a prisoner ordered to be transported
to make his own arrangements. But after 1718 that was distinctly a favor,
and in the early years at least it was vigorously opposed—by William
Thomson, for example, who argued that the advantage of leaving all
transportation in the hands of the merchant who had the contract for
Newgate and the Home Circuit was that he provided some guarantee that
the convict would actually leave England. "This merchant," Thomson told
the secretary of state in 1736, "is esteemed an Officer with a publick trust,
and if he should wilfully misbehave does not only forfeite his bond but is
liable to public censure."[146]

---

[145] Based on the records of the Sussex quarter sessions and assizes for 1720–21, 1736–38, and
1750–52. A total of only twenty-eight men and three women were convicted of noncapital
offenses against property in those years: one man was granted clergy and discharged; seventeen
men and two women were transported; ten men and a woman were whipped and released.

[146] SP 36/38, f. 162. Some men continued to be allowed to transport themselves after 1718,
as a favor or in recognition of their superior social position and the added disgrace therefore of
being transported among the common criminals. For such a favor won by Lord Scarborough in
1732 for the brother of "a very good friend of mine," see SP 36/38, f. 147; and for a grocer in
Newington putting up a bond to ensure the transportation of his brother, QS 2/6, Ea. 1752,
60. Thomson was strongly opposed. "Such presidents," he said on one occasion, could lead to
a dangerous weakening of the system of transportation set up under the contractor in 1718; if
the favor were easily obtainable "it would almost change the terror of the punishment" (SP 36/
27, ff. 34, 43).

Not all who were convicted of noncapital felonies after 1718 were sentenced to be transported. The Act did not eliminate the branding of clergy, with or without a term in the house of correction. And those convicted of petty larceny could still be whipped and immediately discharged.[147] The introduction of transportation significantly widened the judges' discretionary sentencing powers. The patterns of punishment in Surrey over the following thirty years suggest strongly that their deployment of these powers was influenced (hardly surprisingly) by the same considerations that led them to reprieve some condemned prisoners and to leave others to be hanged. That is to say, they paid attention in sentencing in noncapital property cases to the seriousness of the offense and to the character of the prisoner, as far as they could learn about him in court or from his friends and enemies in the locality.

In general the tendency seems to have been for judges to impose the most stringent penalty—transportation—unless there were circumstances that might in mitigation induce them to sentence an offender (depending on the value of the goods stolen) to be whipped or branded and discharged. In explaining one such decision, Lord Chief Justice Raymond said in 1728, for example, that "the prisoner gave no Account of himself nor Examined any witnesses in his behalf"; when the jury convicted him of an offense "for which he was either to be burnt in the Hand or Transported, and no body appearing in his behalfe and no Account being given to him, I left him for Transportation."[148] Of another prisoner a judge reported, "I did not think him an Object of mercy and therefore I ordered him, instead of being burnt in the hand, to be Transported for Seven Years."[149] Those who were not objects of mercy, like those who in other circumstances were left to be hanged, were men and women without character witnesses to establish their place in a community, or who had offended so often that influential men wanted to expel them from the community. "The whole family of them have but Indifferent Characters," the mayor of Hastings told the Duke of Newcastle about a woman convicted at the Sussex assizes, "and it would be of Service to this Part of the Country if they were all Transported." He was in fact in this case petitioning to save her from being hanged, but his assessment of the value of transportation as a way of ridding a parish of a troublemaker, or a family of troublemakers,

---

[147] The fact that those convicted of petty larceny could now be either whipped or transported at the judge's discretion was one way in which the distinction between grand and petty larceny was diminished. As we will see, that distinction was all but eliminated in the middle decades of the century, when apparently without legal authority the courts began to order the whipping of some of those convicted of grand larceny.

[148] SP 36/6, ff. 194–95.

[149] SP 36/57, f. 56.

expresses a common sentiment.[150] If influential men in the community wanted a man transported it is unlikely that judges would have been unwilling to oblige them.

Offenders who might not be deterred by whipping or by the mere branding of clergy were strong candidates to be sent to America. The London courts in particular must have welcomed transportation as a way of dealing with petty but persistent offenders whose individual crimes would be unlikely ever to justify their being hanged but who were beyond the reach of other punishments. In objecting to the prospective pardoning of a man sentenced to transportation at the Old Bailey, Thomson, the recorder, told the secretary of state that he thought it necessary to transport persistent minor offenders because when "such persons are set at liberty, they very seldom if ever, leave off that ill habit, and persons of credit will not venture to employ 'em, and so they are generally observed to follow the same course of life." The value of transportation and "the intent of the Law," he went on to say was to "prevent their doing further misschiefe."[151]

There was a strong inclination in the Surrey courts to order transportation for men convicted of theft, unless there was some obvious reason why this was inappropriate—perhaps physical disability or great age. But not everyone who was sentenced actually went. For one thing, as the king could pardon from the death penalty, so he could pardon prisoners sentenced to transportation, and the monarchs did pardon some (after being petitioned by the prisoner or his friends or by parishioners who would have to look after his family while he was gone), generally on the condition of one of the lesser penalties, branding or whipping.

A system of such "pardoning" was actually operated by the court itself at the Old Bailey for some fifteen years after the passage of the Act: having ordered a number of prisoners to be transported at one session, the court then changed some of those sentences to whipping or burning in the hand at a subsequent session, as a result no doubt of having learned more about the prisoner in the meantime and having been importuned by interested parties on his behalf.[152] The Old Bailey was unique, however.

[150] SP 36/50, f. 233.

[151] SP 36/40, f. 229.

[152] At its height in the years 1721–35, the "pardoning" system of the Old Bailey changed the sentences of about fifteen per cent of those originally sentenced to transportation to burning in the hand or whipping. Thomson's interest in broadening the discretion of the bench and his influence in the creation of this "pardoning" system by which original sentences were subsequently diminished by the court itself may be judged by the observation of a clerk at Newgate in 1721 that

No other court had such continuity of membership on the bench from one session to the next (including the recorder himself). Even more important, no other court met as frequently. The Old Bailey sat eight times a year, whereas the provincial assize courts met twice. There was no possibility of the judges at the Surrey assizes reviewing in a regular way the sentences of transportation handed down at the previous session, some six or eight months earlier, for most of those prisoners would already be in America.[153] They had to make up their minds whether to order transportation or not on the basis largely of the evidence of the trial. If there was to be any reduction from that sentence it would normally have to come from the king in the form of a pardon, and it would have to be sought in the way that pardons from hanging were sought, by means of a petition addressed to the Crown that the secretary would route to the trial judge for his report and recommendation.

In the judge's original decision to transport or not, and in the deliberations around the king whether to grant a petition against banishment,

---

it was a Dispute some Sessions past whether a person convicted of felony, should be burnt or whipt (as the fact appeared). But last Sessions it was over ruled by Mr. Recorder who brought the Act into the house, that there remained a Discretionary power in the Court whether they wo'd transport, Burn or whip.

Accordingly several were burnt, who gave very good recommendations that they should be taken care of not to committ the like. (SP 35/26, f. 19)

When the system had been abandoned, Thomson himself said that "the court at the Old Bailey . . . have a power by Law to change the sentence of Transportation to corporal punishment and the discharge of the prisoners where they find them real objects of compassion." In 1729, replying to the duke of Newcastle about a prisoner's request to the king for a pardon from transportation, Thomson said that the prisoner ought to apply to the court "to order his being burnt in the hand instead of transportation, by which meanes there will be no occasion on any further trouble to the Crown in relation to his being pardoned or released from transportation" (SP 36/15, f. 89). The system was abandoned, Thomson said in 1735, because applications to the court became so numerous, particularly from parish officials, that the court "came to a Resolution that no Sentence of Transportation should be changed but at the same Sessions as the Tryal and when any real object of Mercy is observed that sentence is usually mitigated accordingly" (SP 36/35, f. 141). Thereafter prisoners at the Old Bailey were on the same footing as those at the provincial courts, that is, they had to apply to the Crown for a pardon if they were to escape a sentence of transportation. (I owe my knowledge of this practice at the Old Bailey to Joanna Innes, who has generously shared with me the results of her work on the subject in the records of the court.)

[153] It would be possible for a prisoner to wait in jail for a long period for transportation. The delays on the Northern Circuit were notorious, for example, and it is clear that in counties in which few were sentenced it was sometimes difficult to interest a merchant in taking the contract. But in Surrey such delays were, I think, unusual. The merchant who held the contract regularly entered into bonds for the transportation of offenders, and it is my impression that they were taken at least once or possibly twice a year. In 1725, for example, two batches of twelve and fifteen were taken on 15 April and 10 November, respectively, within weeks or certainly a few months of the previous assizes (QS 2/6, Mich. 1726, 50).

the main considerations tended to be those appealed to in capital cases: the prisoner's youth or inexperience, for example, and the likelihood of his being a danger to the community if he stayed at home.[154] Illness and old age were taken into account occasionally. And a good deal of pressure in favor of the lighter sentence arose from time to time from local officials when they saw that the transportation of the breadwinner of a family might leave them to look after his wife and children. Judges undoubtedly resisted such arguments when they thought that the offense or the offender deserved to be seriously punished.[155] Concerns about costs to the parish perhaps influenced the sentencing of some women, but the differences in the treatment of men and women by the Surrey courts in the second quarter of the century (table 9.6) are as likely to have arisen from the more general influences that shaped all verdicts and sentences. It is most likely that women were less frequently transported than men because their offenses were less serious and because they were thought to pose less of a threat to life and property.

An accurate count of pardons granted to prisoners ordered to be transported is probably not obtainable, but it is clear that they were not numerous enough to alter the fundamental fact that transportation to America became the dominant punishment for noncapital felonies after 1718 and, certainly for men, the normal consequence of conviction for a property crime (even petty larceny) for which they were not liable to be hanged.[156] Transportation had decisively broadened the options available

---

[154] Petitions for pardon from transportation, like those for pardon from hanging, are scattered among the State Papers, Domestic, because they too were sent to the judges for their opinion.

[155] Thomson said that the petitions of churchwardens and other parish officials against the transportation of one of their parishioners should always be resisted, for one reason in particular: whatever the man's character before, being convicted of theft placed him under such a stigma that "he cannot expect to be employed again as to maintain his family in an honest way and what necessity will prompt him to may be reasonably presumed." Once labeled, he would be unemployable among those he knew; without a character he would be unemployable elsewhere. He ought therefore to be transported to avoid "great inconvenience to the publick" (SP 36/35, f. 141).

[156] It is this eradication of the crucial distinction between grand and petty larceny that made it possible for the Surrey quarter sessions to take on so many of the grand larceny cases tried in the county in the years after 1748, even though they initially disguised their taking on new tasks by calling them all petty larceny and evaluating every object stolen in the county for several years at ten pence (see above, chap. 4). The practice of the courts since 1718 had made it clear that the value of the theft did not matter as much as the character of the offender and the impression he had made in court. Most of the men indicted at the quarter sessions around the middle of the century struck the magistrates as having characters that would benefit from seven years in America, so that despite the shift of the bulk of the larceny prosecutions from the assizes to the quarter sessions more than seventy per cent of the offenders convicted of noncapital property offenses in the years 1750–54 were nonetheless ordered to be transported.

to the courts and transformed the patterns of punishment in the second quarter of the eighteenth century. It removed the deep misgivings about benefit of clergy that had been so evident at least since the Restoration. Perhaps it also pleased some who thought the colonies needed labor. The Transportation Act itself had noted a "great want of servants" in America. But the judges, juries, and magistrates were not likely to have been thinking about that when they seized the opportunity to punish more effectively the largest group of offenders they dealt with at every court session. Transportation was immediately taken up because it bridged the wide gap between capital punishment and the branding of benefit of clergy that had typified the penal system at the Restoration. Since it could also be employed to punish vagrants,[157] it created a large middle ground in which the punishment of serious and petty offenders overlapped. Transportation created a penal system that could never again operate without a centrally dominant secondary punishment.

CAPITAL PUNISHMENT, 1720–1750

The firm establishment of transportation also had important consequences for the way the king dealt with that other large element in penal practice in this period, the question of pardons for prisoners condemned to death. The Transportation Act itself established the connection and authorized the judges to grant a pardon under the great seal on condition of transportation for fourteen years, when they were notified of the king's decision by a secretary of state. The availability of an acceptable alternative punishment had an important influence on the administration of the ever-enlarging capital code.

The level of capital punishment was, however, determined by the combined decisions of the trial juries, the judges, and the king, and there was clearly much more behind these decisions than mere sentiment and mere concern about the punishment that the "saved" offender would be subjected to instead of being executed. The selection of those to be hanged depended upon several considerations, particularly the character of the offenders on trial, their offenses, and the state of crime in general. This made for frequent and sometimes substantial fluctuations from one period to another. Such fluctuations were especially striking in the second quarter of the eighteenth century.

We have seen that there was an overwhelming disposition in the courts to reserve capital punishment for the "old" offenses removed from

---

[157] By the Vagrancy Acts: 13 Geo II, c. 24 (1740), and 17 Geo II, c. 5 (1744).

clergy in the sixteenth century: murder, robbery, burglary, horse-theft, some forms of housebreaking. That disposition remained intact in the second quarter of the eighteenth century, despite the addition of numerous "new" crimes to the capital code since 1689, principally, it is clear, because the older offenses were not only regarded as more serious in themselves but were most often committed by "gangs" and by men who appeared to be old offenders, or at least men who were often strangers to the community in which their crimes were committed. In a total of nineteen years examined between 1722 and 1748, one hundred men and eleven women were hanged in Surrey (table 9.7). Of those, ninety-six (86.5 per cent) had been convicted of a property offense removed from clergy before 1660 (table 9.8). No fewer than sixty-two of the prisoners executed, well over half, had been prosecuted for robberies in the streets and on the highways, and another twenty-two had been convicted of burglary. No other property offense accounted for more than six. Seven of the 111 hanged in Surrey in these years had committed one of the forms of larceny removed from clergy and made capital since 1689. They were all men. The women accused of shoplifting or pilfering from houses and so on were mainly

TABLE 9.7

Pardons and Capital Punishment in Surrey, 1722–1748

(19 Sample Years)

		Pardoned and			
Period	Sentenced to Death	Transported	Imprisoned	Condition Unknown[a]	Executed
MEN					
1722–24	45	7	1	0	37
1732–34	20	11	0	1	8
1736–40	65	31	0	3	31
1741–48	56	20	0	12	24
Total	186	69	1	16	100
WOMEN					
1722–24	7	3	0	0	4
1732–34	1	1	0	0	0
1736–40	8	3	0	0	5
1741–48	5	1	0	2	2
Total	21	8	0	2	11

SOURCE: Hanged Count.

[a] Probably transported.

TABLE 9.8

Offenses for which Convicted Offenders Were Hanged
in Surrey, 1722–1748
(19 Sample Years)

Offense	Men	Women	Total	Percentage of Total Executions
PROPERTY OFFENSES				
"Old" capital				
Robbery	60	2	62	55.9
Burglary	19	3	22	19.8
Horse-theft	4	0	4	3.6
Housebreaking	2	0	2	1.8
Picking Pockets	2	4	6	5.4
Subtotal	87	9	96	86.5
"New" capital				
Theft from shop	2	0	2	1.8
Theft from warehouse	3	0	3	2.7
Sheep-stealing	2	0	2	1.8
Subtotal	7	0	7	6.3
Total (property)	94	9	103	92.8
MURDER	3	2	5	4.5
SODOMY	2	0	2	1.8
RETURNING FROM TRANSPORTATION	1	0	1	.9
Total	100	11	111	100.0

SOURCE: Hanged Count (1722–24, 1732–34, 1736–48).

convicted on the lesser charge of simple grand larceny or, failing that, were pardoned by the king. The remaining eight prisoners executed, six men and two women, had committed murder or, in the case of two men, sodomy; one man was condemned for returning from transportation before the expiration of his term.

The patterns of capital punishment were thus powerfully shaped by the prosecutions for robbery and burglary, and particularly by the prosecution of men in gangs. Such men could turn up in small knots in court at any time, and a year in which the criminal calendar was light might thus see an unusually large number of hangings. More commonly they responded to the same stimulants that encouraged less organized and less serious larceny, and when prosecutions for property crime increased and the court calendar became crowded it was normally the case that a large proportion of the prisoners were charged with the most serious offenses and were strong candidates to be selected to provide the "examples" the judges were anxious to find in moments of crisis. When crime seemed particularly threatening and more examples were needed to raise the level of terror, more suitable offenders were normally readily at hand.

One period in which a high level of prosecutions for these "old" capital offenses was met by an evident determination in the courts and in the administration to stamp out these crimes by the sternest of methods was 1722–24, the only years in the 1720s in which a complete run of data is available for the Surrey assizes. A total of fifty-two prisoners were convicted and sentenced to death in those three years, virtually all of them for the "old" capital offenses, and it is clear that both the judges and the king were reluctant to pardon many of them (table 9.9). There was great concern in the 1720s about crime in London, as we have seen, and particularly the violent crimes associated with gangs: but on top of that there were exaggerated fears in the government in these same years about threats to the stability of the Hanoverian regime. This combination of anxieties may explain why forty-one prisoners (including four women) were executed in 1722–24 in Surrey, why almost four-fifths of those convicted were in fact left to be hanged. That was the highest proportion of hangings to convictions by far in any period I have examined in Surrey between 1660 and 1800. The government and the judges, especially those who sat in the London courts and on the Home Circuit, were clearly anxious to present an uncompromisingly tough and unyielding face to the public in these years of apparently widespread violent crime and serious disorder. The

TABLE 9.9

Executions in Surrey, 1722–1748

(19 Sample Years)

Period	Sentenced to Death	Executed	
		Total	Average per Year
1722–24	52	41 = 78.9%	13.7
1732–34	21	8 = 38.1%	2.7
1736–40	73	36 = 49.3%	7.2
1741–48	61	26 = 42.6%	3.3

SOURCE: Hanged Count.

Recorder of London opposed an application for a pardon in 1726, for example, for an offender condemned to death at the Old Bailey, on the grounds that granting this man transportation instead of hanging him would be dangerously weak at a critical moment. Transportation, he said, was suitable only "for offenders of a lower kind." This man was a highwayman and pardoning him would

> prove of very dangerous consequence, especially at this juncture when so many notorious offenders are daily and nightly robbing the open streets in a most flagrant manner with violence and arms and terrifying His Majesty's innocent subjects.[158]

Another judge in 1725 recommended against the pardoning of a pickpocket "at this time" because it would "give encouragement to offenders who daily commit Robberies and other Disorders in the Streets."[159]

At another period in the second quarter of the century when crimes against property seemed to be running at an unusually high level, the gallows in Surrey were again very active. In 1738 two groups of Irishmen were convicted at the assizes for robbery. They made little defense and brought no character witnesses; eight were hanged, along with four other offenders in that year. In the following year eight more went to the gallows on Kennington Common, including three members of a gang who had been robbing for some months in Southwark. Twenty men and two women were hanged in two years. Many more prisoners were convicted at the Old Bailey across the river and hanged at Tyburn: at least fifty-two in 1738 alone, and as many as thirteen at once.[160] Still, a London newspaper could complain about the softness of the courts and about the easy availability of pardons. "It's no wonder there are so many Robberies," it was said in the *London Evening Post* in April 1738, "when so few are executed." Pardoning highwaymen and allowing them merely to be transported, it went on, "encourages others to set up the Trade."[161] Perhaps by this reckoning there could never be enough executions. But in practice the courts acted in the way that was being urged here, by hanging more offenders when violent property crimes increased, especially when it was clear they were being committed by the kind of men Fielding and others thought of as "banditti."

Examples of another kind were occasionally provided. The two men executed for sheep-stealing in 1742 in Surrey were the first to be charged under a recent statute that had removed the offense from clergy, and

[158] SP 35/61, f. 35.
[159] SP 35/61, f. 79.
[160] Based on *G. M.* 8 (1738), pp. 49, 162, 275, 379, 602, 659.
[161] *London Evening Post*, 18–20 Apr. 1738.

without doubt they were left to be hanged by the judge and the king both because it was thought that the level of sheep-stealing in the London area was unusually high (which led to the capital statute in the first place) and because such executions would make manifest the power of the new law. They were the only offenders hanged under it in Surrey in that decade.

On the other side, when the level of prosecutions fell off the level of capital punishment fell off too, both the simple numbers of offenders hanged and the proportion of the whole body charged. There was a significant difference, for example, between the experience in Surrey in the prewar years before 1740 and the years of war that followed. In the five years 1736–40, thirty-six men and women were hanged in the county, just under fifty per cent of those convicted of capital crimes; in 1738–39 alone, as we have seen, some twenty-two men and women were executed. During eight years of war, 1741–48, on the other hand, when the level of prosecutions fell off sharply, Surrey saw but three hangings a year on average; and indeed over a three-year period in the heart of the war, from the spring of 1744 to 1747, no one was hanged in Surrey at all.

Transportation thus did not make capital punishment unnecessary: nor was it intended to. There was no significant body of opinion in the second quarter of the century that doubted the need to counter outbursts of violent crime by demonstrations of the terrifying power of the law. But if there was any sentiment in the jury or on the bench or at court in favor of saving a particular offender, transportation encouraged it by providing an alternative substantial punishment that would prevent the offender from simply returning to society. Where it was particularly felt was in the administration of the statutes passed since the Revolution that had removed clergy from a number of common and relatively trivial offenses. Virtually every offender indicted under the statutes that made shoplifting and theft from houses and other minor forms of larceny capital offenses was transported (if found guilty), either because the jury convicted on a reduced charge or because the king pardoned them. Transportation undoubtedly eased those decisions. And despite there being some years of very high rates of hanging in the first half of the century and no simple, linear trend in the number or the proportion of prisoners executed, there was some small decrease in the level of executions, measured as a percentage of those sentenced to death by the judges. In the late seventeenth century that level had been roughly between fifty and sixty per cent. It was similarly around sixty per cent in 1714–15 before rising in those peculiarly vindictive years 1722–24 to almost eighty per cent. In the second quarter of the century (in sixteen years examined, years of both war and peace) the average was about forty-five per cent. It is not a massive or a decisive change, but it does confirm that pardons were being granted more routinely in this period, and it suggests that the establishment of transportation as a condition of pardon acceptable to the courts and the king had become a crucial aspect of the system of discretionary sentencing that so characterized the administration of justice.

Transportation to America for seven years, or in the case of a pardoned capital offender fourteen years, had introduced stability and flexibility into the administration of the law in the second quarter of the century. It had provided not only the secondary punishment that the courts had plainly sought for some time in their practice; it also made the discretionary application of the increasing capital statutes tolerable. At mid-century it had been a striking success for thirty years.

CHAPTER 10

PUNISHMENT, 1750–1800: THE EMERGENCE
OF IMPRISONMENT

The establishment of transportation had a profound effect on the punishment of convicted felons. It provided the courts with a welcome alternative to penal options that had seemed unsatisfactory for half a century and more before 1718. But the success of transportation was to fade relatively quickly, for only three decades after the Act was passed a series of crises of crime and disorder in London threw doubt on the wisdom of transporting convicts and brought the criminal law and its administration once more into public discussion. Thus even before the American Revolution closed the colonies to English convicts and brought transportation to a halt, the courts had been for some time increasingly sensitive to the value of alternative punishments. When transportation came suddenly to an end in 1776 the way had been prepared for the expedients that took its place, and in particular for the establishment of imprisonment as the main form of punishment in England.

HOUSE OF COMMONS COMMITTEE ON THE
CRIMINAL LAWS, 1751

It matters not at all for our present purposes whether the increase in indictments for crimes against property in the Surrey courts in the years immediately following the peace in 1748 reflects a reality of increasing crime or merely an increasing willingness to prosecute what crime there was (though I think the evidence points to the former). What is important is that contemporaries had no doubt that it was much more dangerous in 1750 to walk the streets of London or to travel into the capital by coach than it had been two years earlier. A significant number of men in the government and in parliament agreed with the commonly expressed view that things had gone badly wrong, that there must be some fundamental weakness in the law and the way it was administered. The responses to the "crime problem" in London were muddled and diverse. Nothing changed substantially in practice. But among the variety of responses to the evidence that social order and discipline were not as firmly based as propertied men would want were some that gradually encouraged a deeper and eventually more sustained criticism of the law and the means of its enforcement.

Perhaps the most significant response to the increase of violent crime was the appointment of a committee of the House of Commons in February 1751 to "revise and consider the laws in being, which relate to felonies, and other offences against the peace; and to report their opinion thereupon, from time to time, to the House, as to the defects, the repeal, or amendment of the said laws."[1] The appointment of a committee to consider the whole body of laws relating to felonies marks a significant departure from earlier parliamentary engagements with the law that had been largely confined to considering the penalties imposed in the case of a particular offense. It is likely that the instructions say more than was intended. Nevertheless, the fact that the committee could be asked to make a general investigation into the defects of the laws (if not yet the criminal law) and to offer suggestions about ways they might be made more effective marks a concern for policy-making in this area that has no previous parallels, at least since the Restoration. The investigation was almost certainly initiated by the government, which was encouraged to act by the alarm being expressed on all sides in 1750 and 1751 about the level and character of violent offenses, especially in the capital. The king's speech on 17 January 1751 called for measures to enforce "the execution of the laws" and to suppress the "outrages and violences" that were threatening lives and property in the metropolis.[2] Within two weeks the committee was formed. It included the prime minister, Henry Pelham, as well as William Pitt, then Paymaster General, and Henry Fox, Secretary of War; and many of those who took a lead in its work (Sir Richard Lloyd, for example) were men who acted as spokesmen for the government on legal matters on other occasions.[3] It also included all members of parliament for London and the counties of Middlesex and Surrey, a reflection of the concentration of the "crime wave" in the metropolis.

Over several months this committee brought down three batches of recommendations on a variety of matters, including the weakness of the watch and other preventative forces in London, possible ways of encouraging prosecutions, and ways of dealing with what was thought to be the

[1] *J.H.C.* 26 (1750–54), p. 27.
[2] Ibid., p. 3.
[3] The membership of the committee is at ibid., p. 27. For Lloyd see Romney Sedgwick, ed., *The History of Parliament: The House of Commons, 1715–1754*, 2 vols. (New York, 1970), vol. 2, pp. 220–21.

large disorderly population and the growing lawlessness of the capital.[4] These recommendations led to the introduction of no fewer than fourteen bills over the next two years.[5] This was not by any means a coherent program; not many of the bills were pushed through. But several of the committee's recommendations were embodied in a statute known as the Disorderly Houses Act,[6] and it is likely that the discussion of several other bills that arose from their work, such as a proposal to regulate pawnbrokers, had an influence on the development of opinion in penal matters.

Perhaps the most astonishing of the committee's recommendations was embodied in a bill "to change the Punishment of Felony in certain Cases . . . to Confinement, and hard Labour, in his Majesty's Dock Yards," introduced in January 1752 by Lord Barrington, a lord of the Admiralty.[7] There is a puzzle surrounding this bill in that it appears to have aimed to do one thing and actually does another. The resolution that it attempted to implement—it was not in the end accepted by the Lords—was among the second group introduced in April 1751. It stated cryptically that "it would be reasonable to exchange the Punishment of Death, which is now inflicted for some Sorts of Offences, into some other adequate Punishment."[8] This looks very much like an argument for wide-ranging penal reform, and it has been taken as such. Radzinowicz calls this recommendation "remarkably progressive" and takes it as proof that the committee realized "the need to revise the capital laws."[9] It was not in fact any such thing, for what the committee had in mind was not the revision of the capital laws—far from it. What they sought was a substitute for transportation.

The "adequate punishment" that the committee had in mind was hard labor, and the bill that emerged makes it clear that the target was not capital punishment but transportation, transportation ordered both by the courts directly and by the king as a condition of a pardon. The "certain cases" in which this new punishment would be enforced were those that led now to banishment, not death. "Whereas," the preamble begins,

> by the late Increase of Felonies, Robberies and other enormous Crimes . . . it is manifest that the Punishments inflicted by the

---

[4] For these see *J.H.C.* 26 (1750–54), pp. 159–60, 190, 289.

[5] Hugh Amory, "Henry Fielding and the Criminal Legislation of 1751–2," *Philological Quarterly* 50 (1971), p. 189.

[6] 25 Geo II, c. 36 (1752).

[7] *J.H.C.* 26 (1750–54), p. 400. The Bill is in the *Catalogue of Papers printed by order of the House of Commons, 1731–1800* (1807), vol. 2, no. 67, and in Lambert, *Sessional Papers*, I, vol. 9, pp. 357–67.

[8] *J.H.C.* 26 (1750–54), p. 190.

[9] Radzinowicz, *History*, vol. 1, p. 421.

Laws . . . are by no means effectual to suppress the same; and
that it is therefore requisite to appoint some other exemplary
Methods of punishment for those Crimes, in order more effectually to deter evil-disposed Persons from committing the like
Offences for the future; and to make such Offenders as shall not
be so deterred visible and lasting Examples of Justice to others,
and render them, by their Labour, in some degree useful to the
Publick:

    And whereas the Punishment of Transportation . . . hath
frequently been evaded by the Offenders returning from thence
before the Expiration of the Terms. . . .

    Be it therefore enacted . . . that . . . where any Male
Person shall be duly attainted of any Felony, Robbery or any
other Crime whatsoever, for which he shall be liable by Law to
suffer Death without the Benefit of Clergy; and his Majesty . . .
shall . . . pardon [him] . . . conditionally; and where any Male
Person or Persons shall be duly convicted of any Felony, Grand
or Petty Larceny . . . for which he or they shall be liable . . .
to be sent or transported . . . [such persons might now] be sent
to any of his Majesty's [dock] Yards, to be confined therein . . .
and to be constantly kept to work.[10]

The prisoners were to be kept in chains, to be distinguished from the
ordinary workers by special dress, and they were to be made to do the
most laborious work for the same period as their sentence of transportation.

    It is clear from the bill itself that it was not meant to signal an attack
on the fundamental bases of punishment as they had been well understood
for generations. Instead of being sent to America, convicts were to be put
on public display, chained in gangs, and marked out by their uniforms,
so that they would be "visible and lasting Examples of Justice" and deter
others from committing similar offenses. There was no expressed conviction
that such labor might *reform* the convict. Rather than being the first
attempt to undermine the great dependence on capital punishment, the
opening of a long campaign to reform the criminal law, the recommendations of the Committee of 1751 were intent on shoring up a penal system
that few people thought could work without frequent public displays of
the consequences of breaking the law. The very casualness of the committee's twenty-five-word reference to the reasonableness of exchanging
the punishment of death for some other penalty coming as it did between
a resolution dealing with disorderly houses and another concerned with

---

[10] *Catalogue of Papers printed by order of the House of Commons*, vol. 2, no. 67; Lambert, *Sessional Papers*, I, vol. 9, pp. 358–59.

houses of correction—was possible because no one assumed that they intended to restrict the death penalty in any way at all. Nor did they: their intention was rather to increase the pains and penalties inflicted on those who escaped the gallows, and the resolution to substitute some other punishment for death "in certain cases" was directed against those cases in which death was not in fact likely or intended.[11]

The committee's work was all of a piece, and it agreed with the spirit of other legislation passed in these years and indeed with the broader public reaction to the evident increase of violent crime in the metropolis. The instinct that was most clearly at work was an urge to enlarge and extend the terrors of punishment in order to frighten men into obedience. Far from abandoning capital punishment, parliament passed bills in this period on the well-established pattern of removing clergy from specific offenses that were thought by some to be increasing dangerously. The offense of stealing goods above forty shillings' value from a ship or wharf on a navigable river was removed from clergy in 1751, for example, at the urging of a group of London merchants who thought that pilfering from ships in the river had reached epidemic proportions.[12]

The clearest evidence of the continuing belief in exemplary and frightening punishments is the anxiety in this period to make public execution even more terrifying. It was widely agreed in London in 1750 and 1751 that the robberies and burglaries and thefts that were being reported with such frequency in the press demonstrated above all the failure of the law and the courts, the failure especially of capital punishment to deter offenders. The conclusions still most commonly drawn from this failure were not that hanging ought to be abandoned in favor of some milder punishment that might be applied with more certainty, but that if plain capital

[11] The committee's resolution shows the extent to which, as we shall see, transportation was coming by the middle of the century to seem weak and ineffectual. It is clear that mere incarceration was not thought to be an adequate substitute; the committee's reasoning on that point apparently followed that contained in the manuscript "Essay on the Punishment of Felony written in the year 1751" among the State Papers (SP 36/117, ff. 379–82). The argument here is that simple imprisonment is insufficiently exemplary to be an effective punishment. Imprisonment at hard labor might be acceptable, but what is really required, the author of this "Essay" argues, is a form of imprisonment "which makes example public and terrifies by an open enforcing of that labour and industry to avoid which the Common People are by degrees induced to commit the most atrocious crimes" (f. 379). Galley service and working in chains on the public roads fit some of the requirements but are difficult to organize. Work in the dockyards, on the other hand, answers every need. The convicts will be enclosed and thus will not pose a security problem; they will be seen by the public; they will work in chains and in a distinguishing uniform and will be in a position sufficiently ignominious that their punishment will work powerfully as example. In addition, dockyard labor will teach offenders good work habits, and it will be much less expensive than transportation to America as it was then organized.

[12] 24 Geo II, c. 45 (1751).

punishment failed to prevent crime, perhaps more aggravated forms of death would. And, unlike former periods in which such talk can be found, so intense was the sense of crisis in the middle of the century that parliament moved to give this notion some effect.

THE MURDER ACT, 1752

The view that England had the mildest criminal law in Europe, "the most void of Terror," as Fielding said,[13] was frequently expressed in this period. "The mildness of our Punishments," another man said in 1752, "are the chief reason why our weekly News-Papers are filled with such black Catalogues of horrid Crimes." The suggestion he goes on to make is that men convicted of particularly vicious crimes should not merely be executed but, as was common in Europe, also be subjected to additional public torments that would increase the agony of death and thus enlarge the exemplary effect of the execution.[14] Similar ideas had been advanced in the early years of the eighteenth century, as we have seen, and by George Ollyffe as recently as 1731.[15] But they were pressed forward with particular urgency in the middle years of the century and were frequently discussed in the press. One man thought that if convicted murderers were broken on the wheel, as serious offenders might be on the Continent, ordinary felons might finally be persuaded that dying was not pleasant—a notion it was widely assumed they needed to be convinced of. This man wanted all convicted felons brought out to witness the murderer broken on the wheel, so that "by seeing the Tortures of the Delinquents, they may be terrified into Obedience of the Law; for those Criminals are not sufficiently deterr'd from the Dread of Hanging, as they have imbib'd the Notion that it is an easy Death." Another man (repeating, though he could not have known it, a suggestion made in a petition to Charles II at the Restoration) urged castration as a substitute for hanging partly on the grounds that "intemperate lust is the most frequent cause of [capital]

[13] Fielding, *Increase of Robbers*, p. 2.

[14] Charles Jones, *Some Methods Proposed towards Putting a Stop to the Flagrant Crimes of Murder, Robbery and Perjury. . . .* (1752), p. 9. For European blood sanctions in the early modern period see, for example, Langbein's translation of the Carolina, the code of criminal procedure published in 1532 for the German Empire, in his *Prosecuting Crime in the Renaissance* (Cambridge, Mass., 1974), pp. 259–308, and the account of those sanctions in his *Torture and the Law of Proof*, pp. 27–28.

[15] In *An Essay Humbly Offer'd, for an Act of Parliament to prevent Capital Crimes, and the Loss of Many Lives, and to Promote a desirable Improvement and Blessing in the Nation* (1731). He urged more lingering and painful forms of death, including breaking on the wheel, in order to increase the deterrent power of the law.

crimes," and because it was "an operation not without a suitable degree of pain, sometimes danger" and thus would prove to be more frightening than mere execution. Another man thought that death brought on by the bite of a mad dog would both act as a deterrent and have the additional social value of offering valuable data for medical research.[16]

What so often lies behind such views of the inadequacy of mere hanging is the assumption that criminals could face death calmly because they were ignorant of religion and had no sense of the eternal punishment to come. The pain of the execution itself could safely be assumed to be as nothing by those who were not likely to have to experience it themselves; and of course the wretches who were brought to the gallows were not thought to have friends or families they would be pained to have hurt and regretful to leave. If there was no regret, no immediate pain, and no fear of eternal damnation the man on the gallows was not being made sufficiently miserable, not being sufficiently terrified, and the message that it was unwise to break the law was not being effectively broadcast. Instead, it was again said frequently in this period, offenders were allowed to go to the gallows in a spirit of carnival and as though in triumph. In his tract on the "great increase of robbers" published in 1751, Henry Fielding had a great deal to say about the failure of capital punishment to deter men from serious crime and the need for the authorities to assert control over the place of execution. He wanted executions carried out very soon after the sentence was pronounced to discourage petitions for pardons and to add terror to the sentencing process; and he wanted them to be carried out more privately and more solemnly so that the condemned man, unable to play to the crowd and to make light of his death, would suffer more intensely.

In time, some of these ideas were to be acted on: the gallows at Tyburn were removed to Newgate in 1783, for example, and the long parade of the condemned through the metropolis on the day of an execution came to an end. But in the middle years of the century the anxiety to get control over the scaffold and to restore to the punishment of death the shame and ignominy that the authorities thought were its natural and essential accompaniment took the form of adding aggravating circumstances to the execution, heightening the disgrace and the terror so as to reinforce the message. These turned out to be further attacks on the convict's body, not in the way the wheel-breaker or the castrator recommended, but by denying to the convict the comfort of a decent and Christian burial and denying to his family and friends the possibility of

[16] *Salisbury Journal*, 7 Jan. 1751, 17 Feb. 1752. I owe these references to Robert Malcolmson and Peter Munsche, respectively; for the earlier suggestion see SP 29/51, f. 44.

the customary forms of bereavement. These resulted from decisions to mutilate the convict's body after death by ordering it to be either hanged in chains or dissected by surgeons.

Neither of those assaults was new in the middle of the eighteenth century. Criminals' bodies had long been sought by surgeons for experimentation and teaching purposes. The demand for cadavers had indeed increased rapidly in the early decades of the eighteenth century as a consequence of advances in the teaching of anatomy and surgery.[17] Royal grants allowed the College of Physicians and the Company of Barber-Surgeons to claim up to ten bodies a year from Tyburn, but that was so far short of the numbers needed by the surgeons and the hospitals and private schools of London that they had to rely on what Peter Linebaugh has called "illegal and hazardous methods." These included persuading a condemned man in prison to sell his body in return for sufficient money to provide for his last necessities, including perhaps decent clothes for his hanging; and obtaining bodies at the gallows by stealth or by arrangement with the hangman or by main force.

The surgeons' agents were frequently resisted in what often turned into full-scale riots when the prisoner's friends, family, or work-mates or simply the crowd itself got word of what was afoot.[18] At an execution of two men in 1723, "the Populace was very riotous upon a Report that one or both were intended for Dissection and were not otherwise to be appeas'd than by Assurances that the same was groundless."[19] It was plainly taken to be a hideous fate. "Ordinary Wretches," a newspaper said loftily in 1738, when a crowd at Tyburn fought "to prevent several of the Bodies from falling into the Surgeon's hands," had "a terrible opinion of being Otamiz'd."[20] The anguish that it caused was made clear by the frantic efforts many convicts made to ensure it would not happen to them.[21] The added shame and disgrace that it heaped upon their families was among

---

[17] See Peter Linebaugh, "The Tyburn Riot against the Surgeons," in Hay, Linebaugh, and Thompson, eds., *Albion's Fatal Tree*, pp. 69–78, to which my account is greatly indebted.

[18] Ibid., pp. 79–88.

[19] *The Weekly Journal or British Gazeteer*, 10 Aug. 1723. The opposition to the surgeons' agents was most likely to come from those concerned with protecting a particular body. It seems clear that many bodies of the friendless were taken off without incident to be dissected. When four men and two women were hanged on Kennington Common in 1739 it was reported that "after hanging the usual time, they were cut down; the surgeons got John Hannah and Michael Lewis, the other four were taken away by their friends to be bury'd" (*A Genuine Account of the Lives . . . of the Six Malefactors. . . .* [1739], p. 18). It was alleged several times in the press in 1738 and 1739 that the crowds at the scaffold were mainly interested in rescuing bodies so that they could sell them themselves (*London Evening Post*, 7 Mar. and 25 May 1738; *G. M.* 9 [1739], p. 213).

[20] *London Evening Post*, 17 Jan. 1738.

[21] Linebaugh, "Tyburn Riot against the Surgeons," pp. 79–88.

the many reasons why, as a man said in 1750, "the Generality of Mankind have a very great Aversion to being anatomized" and why it was regarded as "more terrible than Death."[22]

Dissection was perhaps the greatest indignity that might befall a condemned man, but other aggravated forms of the death penalty were feared and resented almost as much. The most obviously shaming was being ordered to be gibbeted, suspended after death in a metal frame as a lasting warning and example. This "hanging in chains" could be ordered at the king's discretion, for the bodies of condemned men were thought to be at his disposal and it was not uncommon for murderers and robbers to be hanged in chains near where the offense took place or occasionally near their family's home. "The lower classes do not consider it a great disgrace to be simply hanged," the Swiss visitor Saussure believed (having heard it no doubt pronounced confidently in the circles he moved in in England), "but have a great horror of hanging in chains, and the shame of it is terrible for the relatives of the condemned."[23] It was not always welcomed either by those who lived near these temporary gibbets: a rotting body could become "a great Annoyance and a very great Prejudice," as two dozen inhabitants of St. George's parish in Southwark told the duke of Newcastle in a petition to get the bodies of two men hanging in chains removed from the bottom of their street.[24] "The carcass," another petitioner pointed out about a body gibbeted in warm weather a few years later, became "noisome and offensive." Hanging in chains was thought to enhance the deterrent power of the gallows by both prolonging the terror and intensifying the disgrace felt by the offender's family. A mother who petitioned to have her son "decently bury'd" after he had been executed at Kingston and ordered to be gibbeted said that it would "always be a blot in her family in being a public view to the world, and always fresh in memory if [he were] hanged in chains."[25]

Dissection and hanging in chains were practiced before the mid-eighteenth century. But they had never been within the court's discre-

---

[22] *General Evening Post*, 18 Sept. 1750.

[23] *A Foreign View of England in the Reigns of George I and George II. The Letters of Monsieur César de Saussure to his Family*, ed. Madame van Muyden (1902), pp. 126–27.

[24] SP 36/17, f. 156 (1729).

[25] SP 35/60, f. 75. The family of a man hanged in chains in Coventry petitioned the king to order the body and the gibbet removed because they labored "under inexpressible Grief, and frequently receive Reproaches from particular persons, on account of his hanging there, which hath almost drove them into despair, and rendered them incapable of transacting their necessary affairs." The reproaches were also occasioned by the crime itself, for the man had been convicted of murdering his aunt and her daughter—and on those grounds the petition was opposed by the mayor and aldermen of Coventry. But the family's despair was obviously heightened by the constant reminder provided by the gibbeted body (SP 36/32, ff. 115, 121–22).

tion—nor part of the sentence pronounced against the prisoner—but only as consequences of a subsequent executive decision. This was altered significantly in response to the apparent increase in violent crime in the years after 1748. In February 1752 a bill was introduced by two minor members of the administration who had been active over the previous months in organizing other aspects of the legislation aimed at strengthening the criminal law. It was passed as "an Act for better preventing the horrid crime of Murder,"[26] which, because the mere hanging of murderers had been found to be insufficiently frightening to act as a deterrent to others, authorized the courts to add "some further terror and peculiar mark of infamy" to their punishment. Henceforth the bodies of convicted murderers were to be delivered to surgeons to be "dissected and anatomized" or, at the judge's discretion, hanged in chains. In addition, the sentence was to be pronounced by the judge as soon as the jury reached its verdict—and the execution was to be carried out the next day but one unless it was a Sunday, and in that case the day following.[27]

All of this was intended "to impress a just horror in the mind of the offender, and on the minds of such as shall be present, of the heinous crime of murder." And its provisions applied only to that specific offense. It seems clear, however, that what lay behind it was not a fear that the kind of domestic or neighborhood quarrels that were the most common occasions of murder were increasing alarmingly, but rather the view that murders were being committed or certainly threatened every day with the increase of street and highway robberies in and around London. Few robbers as a matter of fact actually killed their victims. But beatings were common, especially during street muggings, and the possibility and the expectation that a robbery could turn violent was real enough for the equation of robbery and murder to seem entirely natural and for parliament to accept without question the proposition in the preamble of the Act that "the

---

[26] 25 Geo II, c. 37 (1752).

[27] The judges agreed that an order for dissection should be part of the sentence and that hanging in chains would follow upon a judge's order to the sheriff. See on that Foster, *Reports*, pp. 104–7; *Eng. Rep.*, vol. 168, pp. 52–53. That sentences should follow immediately upon verdicts and execution immediately upon sentence had been urged in the 1690s by the author of a set of proposals that remained, I believe, in manuscript, entitled, "An Effectual way to Ridd the Kingdom of Thieves, Robbers, Murderers and all other pernicious malefactors." It was mainly a plan to speed up trials, but he proposed, too, that sentences be carried out immediately. And, he added, "if the criminall bee a high-way man, let him bee executed near the place where hee committed the Robbery, and let his body being secured with chaines etc remaine on the Gibbet for a Terrour" (Add Mss. 42593, f. 5). In the first half of the eighteenth century there were usually two or three weeks between sentence and execution. The sheriff of Surrey was claiming compensation for supporting condemned convicts for such periods in the 1730s (T 90/147, pp. 127, 240, 274, 343).

horrid crime of murder has of late been more frequently perpetrated than formerly, and particularly in and near the metropolis. . . ." The Murder Act underlines the depth of anxiety that was felt in this postwar crisis, and confirms that the anxiety was aroused by fear for life as much as concern for property. It is thus of a piece with other solutions to the wave of violent crime in postwar London proposed by the Commons Committee of 1751 and embodied in other legislation in these years. Far from suggesting that capital punishment be restricted, the burden of this legislation was to reassert the centrality of hanging and of deterrence by terror at the heart of the English penal system.

CAPITAL PUNISHMENT, 1749–1775

Along with this insistence on the established principles of the system, a parallel argument was being made in these years that crime was being encouraged by the weakness of the courts and their anxiety to save offenders from the gallows. Henry Fielding, for example, thought that the criminal law was being crippled by jurors' eagerness to find partial verdicts and by the easy availability of pardons. If the consequences of committing crimes were not rigidly certain, he said, men would inevitably be tempted to take a chance:

> A single Pardon granted *ex mera gratia et favore*, is a Link broken in the Chain of Justice, and takes away the Concatenation and Strength of the whole. The Danger and Certainty of Destruction are very different Objects, and strike the Mind with different Degrees of Force. It is of the very Nature of Hope to be sanguine, and it will derive more Encouragement from one Pardon, than Diffidence from twenty Executions.[28]

This argument could lead to a conclusion that the law could not be fully enforced until punishments were more rationally distributed and capital punishment much restricted. Neither Fielding nor many others were ready to contemplate that in 1750. Fielding took the assumptions that had underlain the extension of capital punishment to their logical end (as others rarely did) and argued that if the law was put into effect and everyone convicted of a capital offense was hanged, the certainty of that fate and the terror of that example would discourage all but the most depraved of men from committing further crimes.

As a magistrate, Fielding was in no danger of having to put those

[28] Fielding, *Increase of Robbers*, p. 119.

ideas into practice himself. The juries and the judges of assize, who were in such a position, continued to administer the law as they had in the past: the juries found partial verdicts in the case of large numbers of minor offenders whose crimes had been removed from clergy; and judges reprieved many others. They also, however, continued to apply these discretionary powers flexibly so that more offenders would be hanged when crime increased, not simply because there were more at risk, but because the courts were more anxious to provide examples. In the years of crisis around the mid-century the judges were indeed being encouraged by the government to leave more convicted prisoners to be hanged, and the government (or the king himself) was anxious to be able to refuse pardons. Lord Chief Justice Willes complained in 1750 about the tightening up of the pardon process that required judges to submit detailed reports on those they reprieved rather than the customary vague justification listing "some favourable circumstances" that would lead automatically to a royal pardon. Willes objected that "the same Credit is not given to the present Judges, as hath been given to their Predecessors for many years last past."[29] Perhaps this encouraged some judges to leave more offenders to be hanged. But even if this new policy had been insisted on (which is far from clear) it must have altered only slightly the pattern of reprieves and pardons that would have resulted without it, for the judges required no encouragement to hang more offenders when crimes increased. They required no instruction in that tactic of judicial administration.

It was the habits established over decades (along with the increase of prosecutions) that accounts for the willingness of the courts in Surrey, and in London in general, to hang more offenders in these postwar years. As we have seen, during the war that ended in 1748 the level of executions had fallen in Surrey, and indeed for the three years 1744–47 no one was hanged in Surrey for any crime at all. By contrast, no session of the assizes ended without several men and women going to their deaths in the years 1749–56, during which forty offenders were hanged in Surrey for property crimes alone, almost all of which had been committed in the urban parishes within the metropolis (table 10.1). Thirty were men convicted of robbery. At Tyburn, across the river, the gallows were kept busy eight times a year

[29] SP 36/114, f. 49. When the judges were assembled at St. James's before going on their Lent circuits in 1754, Lord Chancellor Hardwicke told them to "make the rule laid down by the late Act of Parliament, for the better preventing the horrid crime of murder, as to staying the execution mentioned in that Act, the guide of their discretion in granting reprieves to offenders convicted of other capital felonies, (vizt.) to grant such reprieves only in cases where reasonable cause shall appear from the nature and circumstances of each particular case" (Add Mss. 35870, ff. 242–43). Hardwicke had added that passage in his own hand to an earlier draft of the speech (SP 36/147, f. 226).

TABLE 10.1
Capital Punishment in Surrey, 1749–1802

Period	Years	Sentenced to Death	Transported	Pardoned and				Granted Free Pardon	Executed		Number Executed per Year
				Sent to Hulks	Sent to Serve in Forces	Imprisoned	Unknown		No.	%	
MEN											
1749–1756	8	92	28	0	0	0	14	0	50	54.4	6.25
1757–1763	7	41	14	0	1	0	17	0	9	22.0	1.3
1764–1770	7	85	31	0	0	0	19	0	35	41.2	5.0
1771–1775	5	101	65	0	0	1	1	4	30	29.7	6.0
1776–1782	7	84	8	19	11	0	14	3	29	34.5	4.1
1783–1787	5	118	30	18	1	5	3	3	58	49.2	11.6
1788–1802	15	235	138	0	4	17	1	1	74	31.5	4.9
WOMEN											
1749–1756	8	7	5	0	0	0	2	0	0	0	0
1757–1763	7	3	2	0	0	0	0	0	1	33.3	.1
1764–1770	7	2	1	0	0	0	1	0	0	0	0
1771–1775	5	8	7	0	0	0	0	1	0	0	0
1776–1782	7	9	0	0	0	7	1	1	0	0	0
1783–1787	5	12	6	0	0	0	0	0	6	50.0	1.2
1788–1802	15	26	11	0	0	9	1	0	5	19.2	.3

TOTAL										
1749–1756	8	99	33	0	0	16	0	50	50.5	6.25
1757–1763	7	44	16	0	1	17	0	10	22.7	1.4
1764–1770	7	87	32	0	0	20	0	35	40.2	5.0
1771–1775	5	109	72	0	1	1	5	30	27.5	6.0
1776–1782	7	93	8	19	7	15	4	29	31.2	4.1
1783–1787	5	130	36	18	5	3	3	64	49.2	12.8
1788–1802	15	261	149	0	26	2	1	79	33.6	5.3

SOURCE: Hanged Count.
ª Between 1749 and 1775, most were undoubtedly transported.

as the judges at the Old Bailey raised the level of terror to stem the tide of robbery and burglary that engulfed the capital.

The same patterns were to be repeated over the next periods of war and peace. The number and the proportion of offenders executed fell in Surrey during the Seven Years' War (1756–63) and rose again in the period of peace that followed between 1763 and the mid-1770s (table 10.1).[30] In these peacetime years of relatively high prosecutions the judges again justified their decisions in court in terms of the needs of society. A laborer convicted of stealing from a dockyard in Portsmouth was not reprieved because it was an area that had suffered economic dislocation at the end of the war and the offender himself had no "extenuating plea of necessity." He was left to be hanged by a judge who thought that it was "of more consequence, by way of example (the end of punishment), that one man in good circumstances should suffer than twenty miserable wretches."[31] The need for examples was in other judges' minds as they pondered the fate of the men and women convicted before them for capital offenses.[32] And if there was some sign in the 1760s that hanging was coming to form a smaller proportion of all punishments administered by the quarter sessions and assize courts together, it was still clear that an offender who had not settled his fate by committing so vicious an offense that he would not be forgiven under any circumstances would be more likely to be hanged when offenses were common than when there was less anxiety about the safety of life and property.

Altogether, 339 men and women were convicted of capital offenses in Surrey over the third quarter of the eighteenth century; 125 were hanged. As in the years 1722–48 the overwhelming majority (ninety-five, or seventy-six per cent) had committed property offenses (table 10.2), though the domination of such offenses was not quite as massive as it had

---

[30] As during the previous war, there was a run of four years, beginning in 1759, without any hangings in the county for a crime against property. The same experience was reported in the press from around the Home Circuit and indeed from around the country (G. M. 30 [1760], p. 391; 32 [1762], p. 386). That latter report calculated that no more than eighteen had been condemned to death in the whole country (including four for murder); many of those may well have been subsequently pardoned.

[31] Cal. H. O. Papers, vol. 1, p. 487.

[32] Ibid., p. 486. A woman was convicted and sentenced to death at the Bristol assizes, Mr. Justice Foster reported, because she had picked a pocket during the time of the fair "when peoples occasions oblidge them to walk the streets with a greater charge of money than they usually carry about them," and she was thus condemned "for examples sake" (SP 36/106, f. 242). Another judge recommended against pardoning a man convicted at the Stratford assizes in 1766 of breaking into a house and stealing the few possessions of a laboring man and his wife while they were out at work. The law should take its course, he thought, "that an example should be made as a terror to others and to give a very valuable part of his Majesty's subjects (the laborious and industrious poor) that protection and security intended by the law" (SP 37/5, f. 99).

been in the previous period, when over ninety per cent of executions in the county had been for robbery, burglary, and theft. The reasons for this are not hard to find. There was a relatively sharp increase in the third quarter in prosecutions for murder, and a much greater likelihood after the Murder Act of 1752 that those convicted would be executed. This helps to explain why men and women hanged for murder accounted for fourteen per cent of those executed in 1749–76, compared with five per cent in the previous three decades. Another reason why the proportion of property offenses fell a little in the third quarter was that the Surrey courts virtually ceased in these years to execute men and women for crimes we have called the "new" capital offenses, those removed from clergy after 1689. Even when the general level of prosecutions rose, the juries and the judges combined to ensure that those charged with pilfering from houses, or stealing from ships or shops or warehouses, or even stealing sheep were transported if convicted. In 1749–75 only one man, a sheep-stealer, was hanged for an offense of this kind, although five men were executed for other offenses that were forms of property crime, three for forgery and two for coining. Again, as in the second quarter of the century, by far the largest number of offenders were hanged for robbery: more than half of those put to death in Surrey had been convicted of robbery in the streets or on the highways. Another twenty men were condemned for burglary and seven for horse-theft.

Perhaps the most striking aspect of the pattern of capital punishment in the third quarter of the century is the courts' treatment of women, for not only were few prosecuted, as in the past, but fewer than ever were convicted and of them very few indeed were left by the judges to be hanged. Not a single woman was hanged for a property offense (as against ninety-five men), and only one for murder. It is unclear whether another woman, convicted of infanticide, was hanged or pardoned, but by then a pardon was the usual outcome when the juries insisted on convicting under the infanticide statute. At most there were only two women among the prisoners who suffered death at the hands of the Surrey courts over the quarter century after 1749.

At the Sussex assizes some of these features of the Surrey experience in the third quarter of the eighteenth century were duplicated, though there were also some significant differences. Relatively high levels of property crime in the years of peace, 1749–56, were met by a high rate of execution, and, as in Surrey, both fell during the war that followed. But in Sussex property offenses did not increase sharply in the 1760s, and the level of convicted offenders left to be hanged continued at a low level after the peace of 1763. As in Surrey, few women were convicted of capital offenses in Sussex in the third quarter of the century: of the four who were

TABLE 10.2

Offenses for which Convicted Offenders Were Hanged in Surrey

Offense	1749–75				1776–87				1788–1802			
	Men	Women	Total	% of Total Executions	Men	Women	Total	% of Total Executions	Men	Women	Total	% of Total Executions
PROPERTY OFFENSES												
"Old" capital												
Robbery	65	0	65	52.0	37	4	41	44.1	21	0	21	26.6
Burglary	20	0	20	16.0	27	0	27	29.0	20	1	21	26.6
Housebreaking	1	0	1	.8	3	0	3	3.2	3	0	3	3.8
Horse-theft	7	0	7	5.6	5	0	5	5.4	8	0	8	10.1
Pocket-picking	1	0	1	.8	0	0	0	0	0	0	0	0
Subtotal	94	0	94	75.2	72	4	76	81.7	52	1	53	67.1
"New" capital												
Theft from house	0	0	0	0	5	0	5	5.4	2	0	2	2.5
Theft from shop	0	0	0	0	0	1	1	1.1	0	0	0	0
Theft from ship	0	0	0	0	0	0	0	0	1	0	1	1.3
Theft from manufactory	0	0	0	0	0	0	0	0	2	0	2	2.5
Sheep-stealing	1	0	1	.8	5	1	6	6.5	4	2	6	7.6
Subtotal	1	0	1	.8	5	1	6	6.5	9	2	11	13.9
Total (property)	95	0	95	76.0	77	5	82	88.2	61	3	64	81.0

MURDER	17	1	18	14.4	5	1	6	6.5	2	0	2	2.5
INFANTICIDE	0	0	0	0	0	0	0	0	0	1	1	1.3
RAPE	1	0	1	.8	0	0	0	0	1	0	1	1.3
SODOMY	1	0	1	.8	1	0	1	1.1	0	0	0	0
BLACK ACT	1	0	1	.8	1	0	1	1.1	2	0	2	2.5
ARSON	1	0	1	.8	0	0	0	0	0	0	0	0
COINING	2	0	2	1.6	2	0	2	2.2	4	1	5	6.3
FORGERY	3	0	3	2.4	1	0	1	1.1	1	0	1	1.3
RIOT	0	0	0	0	0	0	0	0	2	0	2	2.5
RETURNING FROM TRANSPORTATION	3	0	3	2.4	0	0	0	0	1	0	1	1.3
Total	124	1	125	100.0	87	6	93	100.2	74	5	79	100.0

SOURCE: Hanged Count.

threatened with death, two were pardoned. The two executed had been convicted of infanticide in one case and the murder of a husband in the other. Of the men hanged the largest number had been convicted of property offenses (sixty per cent), but a smaller proportion than in Surrey had committed the "old" and more serious offenses like robbery and burglary. Even more than in Surrey, murder convictions were strikingly prominent in the lists of those executed in the third quarter of the century, partly because more charges were laid, partly because of the increased reluctance in this period to pardon those convicted. Altogether, twelve men were executed for murder, and, along with the woman burned at the stake for killing her husband, they accounted for more than a third of the thirty-seven offenders put to death in Sussex between 1749 and 1770.[33]

NONCAPITAL PUNISHMENT, 1750–1775: TRANSPORTATION AND WHIPPING

Several aspects of the patterns of noncapital punishment in the third quarter of the century are also worth noting. There were some significant changes in transportation, for example. These are not immediately apparent in the broad pattern of punishments for noncapital offenses in this period (table 10.3), for sixty per cent of those so convicted in the third quarter of the century in Surrey were transported. If one adds the large number transported as a condition of pardon, it is clear that a very high proportion of all offenders punished for property crimes in the county had been sent to America. But the figures for the whole of the third quarter conceal a falling away of support for transportation that became apparent in the sentencing

---

[33] Sussex figures for offenders sentenced to death and subsequently hanged or pardoned are derived from ASSI 35 (Felony Files) and ASSI 31 (Agenda Books). Capital punishment in Sussex may be summarized as follows:

Period	Sentenced to Death (M & F)	Percentage Pardoned	Percentage Executed
1749–56	40	27.5	72.5
1757–62	11	63.6	36.4
1763–70	26	84.6	15.4

Offenses for which executions were carried out:

"Old" capital offenses against property	18,	or	48.6%
"New" capital offenses against property	4,	or	10.8%
Murder	13,	or	35.1%
Infanticide	1,	or	2.7%
Forgery	1,	or	2.7%
Total	37		

TABLE 10.3

Noncapital Punishments for Property Offenses in Surrey, 1749–1775

Offense Charged in Indictment	Allowed Clergy, Discharged	Transported	Whipped	Imprisoned	Other	Total
MEN						
Capital felony[a]	19	125	5	9	1	159
Simple grand larceny	47	332	140	58	6	583
Petty larceny	0	96	55	15	1	167
Total	66	553	200	82	8	909
WOMEN						
Capital felony[a]	10	36	4	3	1	54
Simple grand larceny	13	83	38	17	0	151
Petty larceny	0	31	33	0	2	66
Total	23	150	75	20	3	271
MEN	7.3%	60.8%	22.0%	9.0%	0.9%	100.0%
WOMEN	8.5%	55.4%	27.7%	7.4%	1.1%	100.1%

SOURCES: Sample and Count.

[a] Nonclergyable felonies mitigated by the trial juries' verdicts.

practices of the courts several years before war in America was to close the door to English convicts entirely.

In the 1750s and 1760s transportation was at its height. It was not, however, without its critics. Some people had always opposed sending men and women to America. Local authorities, as we have seen, frequently resisted the transportation of a petty offender if it meant that a family would be left in the care of the parish. More fundamental objections were raised by those who thought it an ineffectual way of punishing serious offenders, especially members of gangs, because they could simply buy their freedom on the other side of the Atlantic and return.[34] Within a few years of the Transportation Act magistrates in the metropolis were complaining that large numbers of "old offenders" sent to America were making their way back to England very quickly. The truth of that is hard to discover. But it was asserted as an explanation of the increase of serious crime in the capital. London magistrates were apprehensive about the return of transported convicts in the middle and later years of the 1720s, when there was a great deal of alarm about the high level of robberies in the streets of the metropolis and about the savagery of robbers. The connection with returned transportees was made directly. Nathaniel Blackerby, the Westminster magistrate, told the secretary of state in 1725 that robbery and housebreaking could be reduced in London if convicted felons were prevented from returning from transportation before their time was up; and a group of London magistrates petitioned Lord Townshend at about the same time on the same subject.[35] Both memorials made the point that the men who returned from transportation were not merely so many additional recruits to the street gangs. They were peculiarly attractive accomplices because, having been convicted of felony, they could not give evidence in court and so could be trusted like no other companion. But the magistrates' main concern was that men who arrived in England under such circumstances would not only fall to thieving again: they would be inevitably even more "desperate" than before, even more violent, for they would do anything to avoid being identified by their victims and to resist arrest. They had nothing to lose. Even the bounty-hunting thief-takers would not be likely to take them in since there was no reward for doing so, and Blackerby and his fellow London magistrates agreed that rewards would have to be paid if such men were going to be arrested in significant numbers.

This fatal weakness in transportation remained a sore point from then

[34] Poulter thought that numbers of transportees bought their freedom in America by paying the captain of the ship about ten pounds (*The Discoveries of John Poulter*. . . . [1753], p. 28).

[35] SP 35/61, ff. 121–22; SP 35/67, f. 14.

on, and it was always likely to be brought forward to explain outbreaks of violence in the London streets and on the highways around the capital. In the late 1730s, for example, when serious property offenses were at a high level, numerous reports like the following in a London paper in 1738 reinforced the widespread belief that large numbers of convicts were returning from America just as soon as they could find a ship:

> The celebrated Jane Webb, alias Jenny Diver, who was transported last April for picking of Pockets at St. Paul's, is returned from her Travels, as is Wreathock and others of the Gang, of whom only Bird is yet taken, who is now in Newgate. It's said that the Inducement to these People to return from Transportation, is, that Vaughan, Nick-nam'd Lord Vaughan, and several others that have return'd, are taken no Notice of, but appear publickly, as if they had never been Transported. . . .

"Transportation does not answer the End propos'd," that paper asserted on another occasion: only the gallows "can put a Stop to the great Number of Robbers."[36] The Commons Committee of 1751 clearly had similar doubts about transportation when they suggested hard labor in the dockyards as an alternative. They also resolved that a reward should be paid for the conviction of offenders who returned from America before their term was up and that prosecutions in those cases should be "more easy and less expensive."[37]

Part of the objection to transportation by the middle of the eighteenth century sprang from the undoubted truth that it no longer held the terror it had a hundred or even fifty years earlier. Ships were bigger and faster, and while the journey was no picnic, it was not as dangerous as it once had been; and certainly the country the convicts were going to was settled and prosperous. It came to seem that it might be doing some men a favor to transport them to a place where their prospects of employment and prosperity were better than those of the honest laborer at home, a positive inducement indeed to commit a crime, rather than a deterrent.[38]

By the 1750s and 1760s concerns about depopulation added another argument against sending young men to America when they might be profitably employed at home and serve in the army or navy. By the middle

[36] *London Evening Post*, 2 Nov., 21 Dec. 1738.

[37] *J.H.C.* 26 (1750–54), p. 190.

[38] This view was further entrenched by such cases as that of Elizabeth Martin, who was tried at the Old Bailey in 1766 for stealing a silver spoon from a public house and was at least alleged to have done it in order to get herself transported so she could join her husband in America. She was convicted and whipped (OBSP, Sept. 1766, p. 308–9; I owe this reference to John Langbein).

of the eighteenth century a perception was widely shared that the English population was declining, and that the consequent loss of labor and military manpower posed a serious threat to the national strength at a time when the country was locked in a struggle with France for commercial and imperial supremacy. A vigorous public debate arose on the depopulation question in the 1750s in which the causes were identified particularly in the debilitating effects of life in cities (and of course above all in London) and in the deleterious effects on the family and child-rearing of the immorality of large sections of the working population and of sexual irregularity in general.[39]

The concern and the convictions thus strengthened and elaborated can be seen clearly in the vigor of charitable activity in the middle decades of the century and in the striking innovations in the forms and the objectives of charitable giving.[40] There was a concentration of effort to encourage a large and healthy population, a population strong in numbers and in physical and moral health. It has been calculated that between 1740 and 1760 twelve voluntarily supported hospitals were founded in London, mainly devoted to the care of lying-in women, and including one, the Lock, established to treat venereal disease. A number of other charities were founded in this same period to care for orphaned and abandoned children and (in the Magdalen Hospital) to rescue and rehabilitate prostitutes. The Marine Society was founded in 1756 to prepare boys, the sons of the London poor who might otherwise be abandoned to a life of vagrancy, pilfering, and crime, to find places as sailors on merchant ships or in the navy. Altogether, there was an effort on the part, very largely, of the bourgeoisie of London—city merchants, financiers, members of the professions, who were always prominent among the subscribers of these charities, though peers and members of the gentry also gave valuable support to most of them—to create institutions that would encourage a larger and a healthier population by aiding women in childbirth, rescuing the abandoned young, girls as well as boys, rehabilitating prostitutes, and in general attacking some of the social conditions and the vice and immorality that were thought to explain the decline in numbers and in strength of the English population.

The policy and the practice of transportation were not directly threatened by this renewed emphasis on morality in society. But the broader national objectives that lie behind these hopes to enlarge the population were clearly not entirely in harmony with a punishment that in peacetime

[39] D. V. Glass, ed., *The Population Controversy* (1973).

[40] This paragraph is drawn largely from Donna T. Andrew, "London Charity in the Eighteenth Century" (Ph.D. thesis, University of Toronto, 1977), chap. 3.

saw several hundred mainly young and able-bodied men sent to America. There was at the least no support to be drawn from those concerned about national policy, as criticism of transportation as a penal weapon mounted in the middle decades of the century. Some men continued to regard it, in Sir John Fielding's phrase, as "the wisest punishment we have." By 1771, however, when William Eden thought of it as "often beneficial to the criminal, and always injurious to the community," the notion that transportation had some fatal weaknesses was widely shared.[41]

These apprehended weaknesses of transportation had implications for the punishment of all felonies, but particularly for those that were cler-gyable and for the large number of capital felonies that had come to be regarded as not serious enough to be often deserving of death. The need for an effective penalty for the vast majority of property crimes that could not be regularly punished by hanging was felt especially strongly in areas that were troubled not only by the violent robberies and burglaries that most seriously alarmed parliament, the courts, and the government but also by high levels of pilfering and minor theft. This was a notable problem in London, where a large segment of the bourgeoisie was deeply concerned about the extent of theft on the river, in warehouses, in shops, and at places of work. Such men were not unwilling in the middle of the century to use the threat of capital punishment to discourage thieves. It was in the midst of the postwar alarm that theft on the river was made a capital offense, and even before that Act was passed a committee of London merchants, who organized in 1750 "to unite in their endeavours to put a stop to [theft on the river] . . . by bringing some of the principals and their accessories to justice," had attempted to manipulate clergy in such a way as to threaten a number of convicted thieves with death and then offer them mercy in exchange for information about other offenders.[42]

It was among such men, however, that the insufficiency, the failure, of capital punishment registered soonest. By the 1760s and certainly over the later decades of the century and into the nineteenth the evidence of the patterns of prosecution and the more direct evidence gathered by parliamentary committees point to the conclusion that there was a strength-ening conviction among the pragmatic middle class of London that capital

---

[41] For Fielding see *Cal. H. O. Papers*, vol. 4, p. 11; William Eden, *Principles of Penal Law* (1771), p. 33.

[42] For this see SP 36/115, ff. 22, 24, 26; SP 36/117, ff. 90-92. The merchants' committee successfully opposed the granting of clergy to a convicted thief, Robert Davies, on the distinctly unusual grounds that he had had clergy once already and thereby got him condemned to death. They then quite deliberately used the threat of death to extort from him information about fourteen other offenses he had knowledge of—the men involved, the ships stolen from, and so on. The judge who sentenced this man clearly thought this an acceptable tactic.

punishment was ineffective in the face of massive waves of crime because, when it came to the point, individual merchants and shopkeepers and citizens were increasingly reluctant to bring charges for the more minor offenses that threatened the offender with the death penalty. The post-Revolution statutes had never been enforced with a will, but it would seem on the Surrey evidence that prosecutors, juries, and judges were even more reluctant by the middle of the century to send prisoners to the gallows for the crimes recently removed from clergy. There are suggestions by then, indeed, of a more general and more significant reluctance of victims of all property crimes to press charges that might send any offender to the gallows.[43] There were signs of a belief that capital punishment was unjustified and perhaps the beginning of an argument that it was ineffective because it was wrong; at the least it was coming to be regarded as wrong because it was ineffective.

The loss of faith in transportation as a deterrent was a matter of special consequence in London since it came at a time when reliance on the gallows to stem the tide of property crime did not command the easy assent it might once have. But it was the need for an effective punishment for more minor, noncapital offenses that was particularly pressing. A few offenders were still allowed clergy and were branded and discharged, but the main alternative to transportation in the third quarter of the century was whipping (table 10.3). This was especially the case when in the 1750s, suddenly and mysteriously, such corporal punishment was extended to grand larceny. Whipping had never previously been ordered for property offenses other than petty larceny; if the jury had wanted a prisoner charged with theft of more than a shilling to be subjected to corporal punishment they had to find him guilty of petty larceny. But in the middle years of the century, when, as we have seen, the Surrey quarter sessions took on the largest proportion of larcenies tried in the county simply by reducing the value of all thefts to ten pence, virtually all distinctions between grand and petty larceny disappeared in practice. Some of those convicted of petty larceny in this way were sentenced to be transported, others to be whipped in the way well established for petty larceny at the quarter sessions. And when after two or three years of this alchemy the justices began to deal with these cases more honestly as grand larceny, they continued to punish the convicted prisoners in these same ways, transporting most and ordering the rest to be whipped. For the first time in Surrey, men and women found guilty of theft of more than a shilling were being whipped, without

---

[43] A woman who had traveled thirty miles in 1765 to persuade a judge to reprieve a man condemned on her evidence told him that if the convict were hanged "the terrors of her mind would be inexpressible"; such views were being more commonly voiced I think in the 1760s than they would have been in the early decades of the century (*Cal. H. O. Papers*, vol. 1, p. 661).

first being negotiated into that punishment by the jury's verdict. The Transportation Act of 1718 appeared to provide authority for such a course, for it had made it lawful for the courts to transport for seven years those who had been convicted of "grand or petty larceny" and who were "liable only to the penalties of burning in the hand or whipping." This intended surely simply to state the law as it existed in 1718: that grand larceny was liable to burning in the hand and petty larceny to whipping. But by the j̶u̶r̶y̶, a̶f̶t̶e̶r̶ t̶h̶e̶ r̶u̶l̶e̶s̶ f̶o̶r̶ w̶h̶i̶c̶h̶ s̶o̶m̶e̶ o̶f̶ t̶h̶o̶s̶e̶ charged with grand larceny had been convicted of petty larceny and whipped, the apparent conflation of the punishments of the two offenses in the Transportation Act could be taken as providing authority for the whipping of those convicted of all forms of larceny.

The broadened scope of corporal punishment was apparently resisted at the Old Bailey. It was the opinion at that court, Chief Justice Ryder noted in 1754, "that one convicted of grand larceny cannot be whipped." And Ryder had serious doubts about the legality of the practice when he encountered it on the Home Circuit.[44] Whipping nonetheless became well established in Surrey as a punishment for both grand and petty larceny; it was used in both the assize courts and the quarter sessions in noncapital property cases when transportation or clergyable discharge seemed inappropriate. In both courts the judges and magistrates continued to specify when and how the whipping was to take place so as to ensure that many prisoners would suffer the maximum pain and humiliation. Sometimes the whipping was to take place at or near the scene of the offense; very often it was ordered to be carried out on a market day and at noon. The courts had previously instructed jailers and keepers of the houses of correction how they wanted such sentences carried out. But now that corporal punishment was being ordered for men and women convicted of grand larceny the magistrates seem to have paid even more attention at the sentencing stage to the form that the whipping would take and to make the conditions part of the sentence to ensure they would have the maximum effect.[45]

[44] Ryder noted these doubts in his "Assize Diary" when he ordered a man convicted of theft to the value of fourteen shillings at the Sussex assizes in 1754 to be whipped. In arriving at this sentence he had perhaps acted on the advice of the clerk of assize or of his brother judge, Foster. But he appended to his note of the sentence "query whether could be whipped" and later this explanation: "I doubt I was wrong in ordering [the sentence] . . . because that is punishment for [petty?] larceny at common law. . . ." He goes on to note that the Act 5 Anne, c. 6, which authorized imprisonment at hard labor, "don't empower inflicting whipping for grand larceny. And 4 Geo I c. 11 don't give power to inflict whipping for grand larceny, but only to inflict transportation for grand or petty larceny where the party is by law only to be burnt in the hand or whipped" (pp. 1, 12, 13).

[45] A man convicted of petty larceny at the assizes in 1773 for stealing plants from a nursery was ordered, for example, "to be openly whipped until his body is bloody from the turnpike in

Whipping was not, however, extended in this period to the most serious larcenies in which the losses amounted to significant sums, and there is no sign that it was thought to provide an adequate substitute for transportation. That was to become a matter of some importance as faith in transportation, the main noncapital punishment for several decades, began to wane in the 1750s and 1760s. And there is no doubt that it did begin to lose its dominance even before the American Revolution closed it off completely. It is unclear whether this was a result of the loss of faith in its efficacy as a punishment or the deliberate policy of the government to restrict such emigration to America as the colonial crisis became more serious. The Surrey evidence (which for this purpose is hardly sufficient to do more than suggest what the national pattern might have been) points to the latter, for the change in the county came very suddenly. Up to 1772 transportation continued to account for well over sixty per cent of noncapital sentences in the Surrey courts. In the four years before the Revolution, however, that fell to under forty per cent (table 10.4).

The sharpness of the change suggests that this was mainly a matter of policy. This impression is reinforced by alterations in the conditions being imposed for pardons in the late 1760s and in the early 1770s, for there is a strong suggestion in the way pardons were being granted that the government (or the king?) had indeed decided to restrict transportation.[46] Further, in 1772 the government stopped paying the bounty of

TABLE 10.4

Noncapital Punishments for Property
Offenses in Surrey Courts, 1763–1775

Period	Clergy/ Discharge %	Transportation %	Whipping %	Imprisonment %	Number of Sentences
1763–71	11.6	63.6	18.7	6.1	407
1772–75	13.8	37.2	22.9	26.2	218

SOURCES: Sample and Count.

Vauxhall to the nursery ground of Mr. Kitely, the prosecutor, next Thursday" (ASSI 35/213, Summer 1773, calendar). At the quarter sessions in the next year a man convicted of grand larceny was "to be whipped at the cart's tail till his back is bloody from the stockhouse round the market place at Kingston and back again" between noon and 2:00 p.m. on a market day (QS 3/5/9, p. 193).

[46] It appears that it became common in the 1760s and 1770s for men condemned to death to be pardoned on condition of service in the army or navy rather than transportation; and some of those originally sentenced to transportation were also being pardoned on this condition. This

five pounds a head to the merchants who took convicts to America. And while this was explained by a contemporary as the result of the demand for labor in America, which meant that merchants were willing to undertake the contract without a subsidy since the profits were so massive, it looks as though the government was not unwilling to see the trade run down.[47] It is also worth remembering that there was an American "problem" after 1763. The conflicts that had arisen over the Stamp Act and Townshend Duties and other commercial matters weakened any easy assumption that the American colonies were a fully reliable extension of England to which young Englishmen could be sent without their being lost entirely to the king and empire. The North administration that took office in 1770 was dominated by men whose political principles and ambitions had been defined to a considerable extent by that conflict, and they were both distrustful of the Americans and not unwilling to bend their energies to instruct them in their duty within the imperial system. Even before the more serious conflicts that led after 1773 to the Coercive Acts and the armed clashes and the Declaration of Independence, the North government was determined to keep America in its place, and a decision to restrict the flow of labor would not have been out of character.[48]

Sentiment and policy may well have worked together: if it had been widely believed that transportation had "almost ceased to be a punishment," as a judge said in 1766, a government decision to restrict it would not have been strenuously resisted.[49] The question was, what was the

---

apparent change was not applied often in Surrey, but it clearly did alter the sentences of a significant number of men tried at the Old Bailey and in other jurisdictions. For some examples of such conditions being imposed see *Cal. H. O. Papers*, vol. 2, pp. 468–69; vol. 3, pp. 75–76, 89, 221, 378–85. For the doubts and objections expressed by the Admiralty and commanding officers who received these men, see ibid., vol. 2, pp. 468–69; vol. 3, p. 228; Radzinowicz, *History*, vol. 1, pp. 124–25; A.G.L. Shaw, *Convicts and the Colonies* (1966), p. 34. This policy no doubt reflects problems in the recruitment of the army and navy, but it is also likely to reflect the dissatisfaction with transportation as a punishment being expressed in this period. It is possible that the practice differed from county to county, depending on the penal resources available at any particular time. There is some suggestion of this in April 1778, for example, when all the men pardoned from a sentence of hanging on the Western Circuit (following the Lent assizes) were sent to the armed forces as the condition of their pardon, while those pardoned on the Home Circuit were sent to the hulks, which were of course much more accessible to the counties of that circuit (SP 44/93, pp. 260–65). I have not investigated as systematically as the subject deserves the use of the armed forces as an alternative to punishment (as a condition of a pardon from hanging as well as an alternative to transportation or imprisonment) and the possibility that it was taken up as an alternative to prosecution, especially during wars.

[47] *J.H.C.* 37 (1778–80), p. 310; Lambert, *Sessional Papers*, II, vol. 31, p. 378. For evidence that the government might have been thinking of alternatives to transportation in the late 1760s and the early 1770s see Roger Ekirch's forthcoming study, *Bound for America: The Transportation of British Convicts to the Colonies, 1718–1775*.

[48] Bernard Donoughue, *British Politics and the American Revolution* (1964), pp. 16–20, 36–47.

[49] SP 37/5, f. 99.

alternative to transportation? It was plain that the administration of the law, in capital crimes as much as noncapital, depended on an effective secondary punishment. If transportation was losing favor, and whipping, though extended to grand larceny, continued to be regarded as appropriate only for minor offenses, what alternative was there? The answer was already being provided before the American Revolution stopped transportation entirely, for in the same period that transportation was being sharply diminished in Surrey, in the early 1770s, the courts began to substitute imprisonment. When transportation ended abruptly in 1776 the punishment that would take its place had already emerged in the practice of the courts. Why it was imprisonment that was turned to in this period, and why it became so quickly entrenched, apparently unshakeably at the heart of the penal system, are obviously complex questions. But there are a few clues worth following in the discussion of penal questions over the third quarter of the century and in the way imprisonment was established.

ARGUMENTS FOR IMPRISONMENT AT HARD LABOR

There have been a number of studies of English prisons in the century after the Restoration, before the reform effort of the 1770s and after.[50] Not a great deal is known in detail or in a systematic way, however, about the penal methods employed in jails or houses of correction in that period or about their inmate populations. Indeed we have hardly progressed beyond the evidence Howard collected, nor beyond the impression that that evidence and Howard's career inevitably created, that incarceration was first thought of as a punishment for felons when Howard began his tours and the American War brought transportation to a halt. Momentous changes did take place in the character of imprisonment after 1776. As we have seen, however, the developments of that period were foreshadowed early in the eighteenth century; and while that first impulse was diminished by the success of transportation, it had not been entirely lost, and it re-emerged in significant ways in the third quarter of the century. Well before the American colonies were closed to transportation imprisonment was again being discussed in England, out of the same conviction that had encouraged it earlier: that the regime of work and discipline that had been applied to the idle and disorderly poor would also provide an effective means of dealing with those who committed minor crimes.

After the establishment of transportation as a regular punishment in

[50] For some of the recent literature on prisons in the eighteenth century see above, chap. 6, n. 48.

1718, sentences of imprisonment became rare in the Surrey courts. Occasionally a judge seems to have remembered the possibility of ordering a term of hard labor, and having sentenced one offender to be imprisoned then ordered it in the cases of others roughly similar at the same session of the court. The Surrey assize records are incomplete in the 1720s, so one cannot be certain how common imprisonment was then. But there were no such sentences in the three years 1722–24, and it looks as though it was distinctly unusual that at the summer assizes in 1729 six convicts (five women and a man) were sentenced to be imprisoned for terms of six months to a year.[51] There were no imprisonments ordered in property cases in 1732–34 when the evidence is again complete, and very few in the late 1730s and 1740s. Indeed, there were a mere four or five altogether in that latter decade. It is clear that in the second quarter of the century the judges of assize did not look to a term of incarceration as a principal punishment in felonies.

Offenders convicted of a number of misdemeanors—especially fraudulence, cheating, unlawful entry, and a few convicted of assault—continued to be sentenced to terms of imprisonment with some regularity; but not felons. The merging of the poor law and the criminal law did not survive the rush to transport the crime problem. But the culture and behavior of the working population was so frequently identified by the respectable and comfortable classes as the main source of crime that there was a natural conjunction between these two systems of coercion. Whenever crime increased after 1718 and unemployment and poverty pressed, especially among the large concentration of people in London, the solutions that were put forward often attacked the inadequacy of both the poor law and the criminal law and offered some version of the idea that crime could be diminished if minor offenders were punished in such a way that their dissolute bad habits and unwillingness to work could be corrected. In 1735, to take one example, William Hay, a Sussex M.P. wrote a pamphlet in support of a campaign that he was to press in parliament over the next two years to make some fundamental changes in the administration of the poor laws, specifically to shift the responsibility for the employment of the able-bodied from the parish to a broader basis. Hay followed others, including Sir Matthew Hale, in wanting counties divided into districts, each with a workhouse in which the employable poor would be made to work. But he wanted in addition in each district a hospital for the genuinely "impotent" and a house of correction that would be reserved for the criminal poor, by which he meant those who refused to work and those convicted of minor crimes. Indeed he thought that many of the punish-

[51] S.A.P., Summer 1729, p. 4.

ments then in use, including hanging, might usefully be changed to some form of imprisonment: "It would be well," he said,

> to change the Sentence of the Law in Robbery, and other mixed Larcenies, from Death to Imprisonment for Life in these Houses. Felons within Benefit of Clergy might be confined here for seven Years; those guilty of Petty Larceny for a Twelve-month; which would be more effectual to reform them than either Burning in the Hand or Whipping, and at the same time make them useful to the Publick.[52]

The example not only of previous English experiments but also of Continental practice continued to have a good deal of influence on some of those who were writing in England in this period on poverty and crime and related questions. Thomas Robe, for example, took the Amsterdam Rasp House as a model in arguing in 1735 that criminals should be made to work, both as a punishment and as a means of training them to earn their living. "Thus Justice," Robe concluded, "managed as an Act of Mercy, by slow, and yet effectual Methods, will bring Criminals to a sense of their Crimes, and beget in them such a Habit of Industry, as in the end will make them useful, if not honest, Members of the Publick."[53]

[52] William Hay, *Remarks on the Laws relating to the Poor with Proposals for their Better Relief and Employment* (1751), preface.

[53] Eboranos [Thomas Robe], *Some Considerations for rendering the Punishment of Criminals more effectual. . . .* (1733), reprinted in his *Collection of Political Tracts* (1735), p. 47. Robe had clearly been influenced by Dutch models. He argued that convicts should be

> employed in Building a strong circular open Work-House, where they should be kept constantly at work in hewing and sawing of Stone, and in beating at the Anvil, in the same Manner as such kind of Offenders are in the Rasp-Houses at Amsterdam. And as the Time of their Servitude should be according to the Kind and Degree of their Crimes, so should the Nature of it too; for the greatest Offenders should be employed in digging and hewing of Stone in the Quarry, and in that sort of Work which is the most painful and labourious, while those whose crimes are but light and trivial, should be instructed by fit and able Workmen, to model the Stone, and to make and manufacture all sort of Iron-Work . . . by these Means, these lesser kind of Thieves and Felons, who now generally return to the same Course of Life again, will be enabled to get an honest Livelihood after their Time of Servitude is expired, which they will do with the greater Chearfulness and Spirit, as they will be so much the more inured to it. . . . Thus Justice, managed as an Act of Mercy, by slow, and yet effectual Methods, will bring Criminals to a sense of their Crimes, and beget in them such a Habit of Industry, as in the end will make them useful, if not honest, Members of the Publick. (Pp. 45–47)

He goes on to counter the objection, which he says one meets with in England, that "ill Consequences will happen (from inflicting any kind of Slavery on freeborn Subjecs) which in Time may affect our Liberties." He presents the argument that the Dutch had not found that imprisoning criminals at hard labor, which they had being doing since 1595, had "occasioned

Other men developed similar themes in the 1730s, both pointing out the weaknesses of the punishments then in use, including capital punishment applied indiscriminately, and arguing for labor that would, as Sollom Emlyn said, "reclaim and deter" offenders.[54] There thus remained into the 1730s an active belief in the value of incarceration and hard labor as a means of combating the idleness and the bad habits that led the poor down the road to the gallows.

There is no evidence in Surrey that judges or magistrates were much influenced by those arguments in the 1730s; in the next decade the falling away of prosecutions during the war laid the matter to some extent to rest. But the persuasions they rested on, the beliefs about the origins and nature of crime, did not disappear. On the contrary, they were deeply rooted and were likely to be restated and reworked whenever crime seemed to be particularly threatening. This was certainly the case after 1748, when crimes against property increased in the capital. In the public discussion that this stimulated, the view that much of this criminality arose fundamentally from the ill discipline and dissolute habits of the working poor once again found expression and once again led commentators to deal with the defects of both the poor laws and the penal system.

How closely related the two were assumed to be is nowhere more clearly revealed than in the work of the committee of the House of Commons appointed in 1751 "to consider the laws in being, which relate to felonies" and whose resolutions on the criminal law we noticed earlier. Within days of their appointment the House added the rider that they should also consider the laws relating to the poor, and that double charge to deal with the criminal laws and poor laws together, which obviously seemed entirely natural, guided their discussions and shaped many of their resolutions.[55] Compelling the disorderly poor to work and punishing convicted offenders more effectively were not separate issues in the committee's

the least Infringement upon the Liberties of their honest Subjects: Wherefore should we fear any worse Consequences from confining Felons to hard Labour at Home, in Respect to our Liberties, than we find at present from Transporting them Abroad to our Plantations?" (p. 48).

[54] Sollom Emlyn, ed., *Collection of State Trials*, 6 vols. (1730), vol. 1, preface. George Ollyffe similarly thought in 1731 that in some cases then being punished by hanging and transportation, work would be in the end more effective, partly because it would promote "the most sharp and lasting terror." He goes on to argue for new means to put a stop to begging and vagrancy, the nursery of thieves "with no edge for work" (*An Essay Humbly Offer'd*, pp. 11–13).

[55] *J.H.C.* 26 (1750–54), p. 123. The committee's second group of resolutions included recommendations that led to the passage in 1752 of the "Disorderly Houses Act," which aimed to control the places of public entertainment by bringing them under a licensing system and to encourage the prosecution of bawdy houses (25 Geo II, c. 36). The third group of resolutions deplored the inefficiency of the poor laws and proposed the abandonment of the parochial basis of poor relief in favor of a countywide system, the abolition of the Settlement Laws, and the grouping of parishes into units large enough to support an effective workhouse (*J.H.C.* 26 [1750–54], p. 289).

work, but two aspects of the same problem. This assumption was at the center of numerous other proposals advanced in the 1750s for solving various aspects of London's social ills. These make it clear that while it was still assumed that dangerous and violent felons deserved to be executed, it was increasingly believed that minor offenders ought actively to be rescued from the life and the habits that were leading them into serious trouble. And that persuasion led many to advocate some form of incarceration and labor as a punishment for convicted petty criminals as well as the poor.

Among these was Henry Fielding, whose stern advocacy of capital punishment we noticed above. But Fielding also wrote on the poor and on the forms of petty crime he confronted daily as a magistrate. In his *Proposal for Making an Effective Provision for the Poor* (1753) he supported the creation of a county workhouse in Middlesex to employ as many as five thousand able-bodied workers. Within this institution a house of correction would deal with vagrants, the idle, those convicted summarily by magistrates of embezzling materials from the workplace and similar offenses, and those "accused on oath" of petty larceny who were to serve a term of hard labor instead of being tried at the quarter sessions or assizes (where if convicted they might be sentenced to be transported). What he proposed in effect was making petty larceny a summary offense so that its punishment might be "proportionable" to the crime. He thought that a term in the house of correction would preserve the offender and his family "from utter ruin," because he would emerge chastised but nonetheless without having lost his character so entirely as to be "lost to the public." He would remain employable; indeed his training would render him more useful to the public than he was before. That training would take the form of periods of solitude, a fully structured work regime, and religious instruction that would act as a "correction of the mind" as much as "of the body."[56]

It was Fielding's view that the social problems of London stemmed from the weakness of controls over the lives of the poor and that political and legal weapons simply had not kept pace with the economic and social changes he broadly summarized as the growth of commerce. Others in the 1750s were similarly aware of the consequences of economic transformations over a long period. Joseph Massie, for example, recognized that problems like unemployment and poverty were more complex than they had been when the poor laws were formulated in the sixteenth century, and that London had special problems because it was a magnet for a large mobile population of laborers dislodged by changes in rural society, es-

---

[56] Henry Fielding, *A Proposal for Making an Effective Provision for the Poor* (1753), pp. 72, 153.

pecially agricultural specialization and enclosure. Massie believed that the higher levels of crime in the metropolis stemmed from the inability of large numbers of men and women in London to find work, especially the numerous immigrants, and from the failure of a poor law system that had been devised for a simpler society. He too urged the creation of houses of industry to serve more than one parish and in which the unemployed could be put to work and relief provided on terms that did not carry reproach. But behind all that Massie detected a deep "depravity of manners" in the working poor, and he also wanted a separate house of confinement and correction that would provide punishment in the form of "Hard Labour and Hard Fare" for idle and refractory poor people and for persons suspected of robbery.

Like Fielding, Massie urged the advantage of punishing petty offenders by means less serious than transportation and whipping. He thought that more moderate punishments would be less crippling to the character and that they would encourage prosecutions, for the penalties now laid down "are more severe than the generality of People desire to have inflicted on . . . pilfering thefts; and therefore they rather choose to put up with the loss of a few Fish and Fowls" than press charges even when they have caught the offender. Some men were thus encouraged to commit crimes that in time brought them to the gallows. If such men were caught at an early stage, he argued, and held in the house of correction "to beat Hemp or do other hard Work" for a month or more they would be put back on an "honest course of Life" and be saved from such an ignominious end.[57]

<hr>

[57] Joseph Massie, *A Plan for the Establishment of Charity Houses for exposed or deserted Women and Girls and for Penitent Prostitutes . . . Considerations relating to the Poor and the Poor's Law of England: wherein the great increase of unemployed Poor and of Thieves and Prostitutes, are shown to be immediately owing to the severity as well as the Defects of our Poor's Laws; and to be primarily caused by the Monopolizing of Farms and the Inclosure of Common Lands. . . .* (1758), pp. 53–54, 60ff., 118–19. There was renewed stress in the wake of rising prosecutions for property offenses in the 1750s on the linking of crime and immorality. William Romaine said, for example, that it was owing to the churches' neglect of their duty that "robberies and murders are becoming so common. Our people grow more corrupt in their morals, not for want of good statute laws, but for want of good gospel ministers" (*A Method of Preventing the Frequency of Robberies and Murders. . . .* [1754], p. 21). The government was also again pressed to encourage the "reformation of manners" by reissuing the proclamation against vice and immorality that George II had published at his accession in 1727. A meeting of the bishops urged such a course in 1754. The cabinet studied the proclamations issued by William and Anne and other precedents from that period before the king's proclamation was issued; and they revived from William's reign the practice of calling the judges before the king before they went on circuit in order to impress upon them the need for their own vigorous engagement and the need to encourage the magistrates, on whom the administration of the laws against vice and immorality actually depended. Such a meeting was held in February 1754 at which Hardwicke, the lord chancellor, delivered a charge to the judges before the king and the

THE IDEA OF PROPORTION IN PUNISHMENT

A number of solutions were thus advanced in the middle of the century to solve what was widely recognized as a serious problem of crime and social disorder in London; certainly there was no single dominating answer amid the babble of voices that led to massive changes in the law or in the practice of the courts. But a strong line of argument did emerge that minor offenses derived from the habits and way of life of the working population and that these habits should be corrected both before and after crimes were committed. Stronger measures of social defense were being called for, and there was forming in the parallel discussions of crime and the immoralities of the poor a view that the available punishments were not working because they were not touching some important aspects of the problem. There was clearly coming into being some predisposition to support the position expressed by Joshua Fitzsimmonds in 1751 that "such punishments as Branding, Whipping and even Transportation, might be very properly changed to hard Labour and Correction, suitable to the Nature of the Crime."[58]

One element of this argument had broad application: the notion that crime was being encouraged by the lack of proportion between offenses and punishments. The argument for a closer relationship between the act and its consequences was carried forward on the one hand by those who thought that adjustments were needed at the lower end of the scale, in the punishment of minor offenses. As we have seen, that had been part of an argument for some form of incarceration and compulsory labor for petty offenders. That case continued to be made in the 1760s, when London once again experienced a wave of crime following the Peace of Paris in 1763.[59] Disproportion in punishment was even more obvious at the other end of the scale, among capital offenses, and the point was being made

---

cabinet (PC 1/6/37, 5–6; SP 36/125, ff. 272–73; SP 36/147, ff. 275–76; for Hardwicke's speech see Add Mss. 35870, ff. 241–3). A copy made in 1753 of a collection of "Precedents in the Reigns of King William the 3rd, Queen Anne, and His late and present Majesty of Proclamations and Orders issued for punishing Prophaneness and Immorality, and for apprehending Street Robbers and Rioters etc." is at SP 37/15, ff. 491–98.

[58] Joshua Fitzsimmonds, *Free and Candid Disquisitions on the Nature and Execution of the Laws of England* (1751), p. 45.

[59] Two correspondents to a London paper in 1764, for example, repeated the argument made by Thomas Robe in the 1730s, among others, that the English houses of correction should adopt what they took to be the stricter forms of work and discipline carried on in Dutch institutions such as the Rasp House in Amsterdam, so that petty offenders would be punished in ways "proportionate to the crime" (*The Public Advertiser*, 1 Mar. [A.B.]; 28 Apr. [Meanwell]).

by the middle of the century that the indiscriminate harshness of a criminal law that ordered the same punishment for shoplifting or a servant's pilfering as for murder was more of a deterrent to prosecutors than criminals.[60]

There was little disposition to relax the capital laws; indeed the reverse. But over the 1750s and especially in the 1760s the failure of the law to deter offenders became increasingly evident in the long criminal calendars at all the courts in the metropolis (at least in peacetime) and perhaps more insistently in the columns of criminal news in the press. And whereas some men continued to argue that the fault lay with prosecutors and magistrates and courts too weak to put the law into effect, doubts were also being expressed about laws that encouraged duplicity and discretionary manipulation by juries and judges. There were undoubtedly much subtler shifts in sentiment behind the doubts that came to be expressed in the late eighteenth century about the justice of capital punishment on the scale the English law admitted. But its evident failure surely encouraged that loss of faith, and stimulated and focused those shifts in sentiment in the first place and gave the doubts about capital punishment room to bite. By the 1760s the older certainties were losing some of their hold, at least in some sections of the public. It was presumably those growing doubts that made Cesare Beccaria's *Of Crimes and Punishments* as influential as it was.

Beccaria's tract made a considerable impression and produced a violent debate in Europe, especially when a French translation was published in 1765, two years after the original Italian edition, and when in 1767 Voltaire's commentary appeared.[61] An English translation was also published in London in 1767. Beccaria's arguments against capital punishment—which he thought ought to be entirely abolished —undoubtedly became important reference points for reformist ideas in England: he provided support for conclusions already in process of formation. But the

---

[60] One man argued in 1754 that

> it is a kind of injustice, that the perpetrators of unequal crimes shou'd be equally punished. . . . In order to adapt penalties suitable to every offence, there ought to be in every well-govern'd state, an harmonical proportion regulated by distributive justice. For what can be more absurd, allowing there is a granted disparity in crimes, that one and the same sentence shou'd be appropriated for the punishment of the presumptuous villain that has butcher'd his own father; and the poor wretch, who by want and hunger (those great apologists for human frailty) has been goaded on to purloin a small trifle from the over grown opulency of his neighbour . . . (*Proposals to the Legislature for preventing the frequent Executions and Exportations of Convicts in a Letter to the Right Honourable Henry Pelham, Esq., By a student in Politics* [1754], p. 29).

[61] For Beccaria and the reception of his work see Coleman Phillipson, *Three Criminal Law Reformers* (1923); Radzinowicz, *History*, vol. 1, pp. 277–85; Franco Venturi, *Utopia and Reform in the Enlightenment* (Cambridge, 1971), pp. 100–16.

parallel argument more immediately influential in England was that punishments would only be effective when they were so proportioned to the crimes they were intended to prevent that they would be applied uniformly and with certainty by all courts without the interference of discretionary considerations. The brisk and uniform application of the law, Beccaria argued, would do more to deter crime than hit-and-miss severity that fell on a few selective victims, for a man about to commit a crime would know without any doubt that if caught he would pay a penalty. It was thus essential that punishments be rationally devised to fit crimes, and Beccaria offered the principle that they "should be chosen in due proportion to the crime, so as to make the most efficacious and most lasting impression on the minds of men, and the least painful of impressions on the body of the criminal." That meant simply that the "disadvantage of the punishment should exceed the advantage anticipated from the crime."[62]

Beccaria clearly had some immediate influence in England. Blackstone's ideas on punishment, for example, show evidence of it. In the fourth volume of his *Commentaries*, which dealt with "public wrongs" and which appeared two years after Beccaria's English edition, he addressed himself to general questions of punishment directly and in the first chapter—an indication perhaps of the liveliness of the subject in the late 1760s—and he was in fact very critical of some of the fundamental characteristics of the English criminal law.[63] He condemned the indiscriminate reliance on the gallows, and while he defended the death penalty in principle he confessed to finding it "difficult to justify the frequency of capital punishment . . . ; inflicted (perhaps inattentively) by a multitude of successive independent statutes, upon crimes very different in their natures."[64]

The mitigation that "so dreadful a list" compelled the courts to engage in weakened the law. In general, he concluded,

> punishments of unreasonable severity, especially where indiscriminately inflicted, have less effect in preventing crimes, and amending the manners of a people, than such as are more merciful in general, yet properly intermixed with due distinctions of severity.[65]

That passage continues with an approving reference to Beccaria's view that "crimes are more effectually prevented by the *certainty* than by the *severity*,

[62] Cesare Beccaria, *Of Crimes and Punishments*, trans. Jane Grigson (Oxford, 1964), pp. 42–43.

[63] Blackstone, *Commentaries*, vol. 4. On Blackstone's views of the value of certainty and proportionality in punishment, see the introductory essay by Thomas A. Green to the facsimile of the first edition published by the University of Chicago Press (vol. 4 [1979], pp. iii–xvi).

[64] Blackstone, *Commentaries*, vol. 4, p. 18.

[65] Ibid., pp. 16–17.

of punishment," and with an acceptance in broad terms of his argument that punishments ought to be proportioned to the crimes they seek to prevent.

> It is . . . absurd and impolitic to apply the same punishment
> to crimes of different malignity. A multitude of sanguinary laws
> . . . prove a manifest defect either in the wisdom of the leg-
> islature or the strength of the executive power. It is a kind of
> quackery in government, and argues a want of solid skill, to
> apply the same universal remedy, the *ultimum supplicium*, to every
> case of difficulty. It is, it must be owned, much *easier* to extirpate
> than to amend mankind: yet that magistrate must be esteemed
> both a weak and a cruel surgeon, who cuts off every limb, which
> through ignorance or indolence he will not attempt to cure.[66]

It is significant that Blackstone came to a view of the purposes of punishment that assigned weight not simply to incapacitating the offender and deterring others by the example of his execution but also to the "amendment of the offender himself." And while he does not discuss this in detail it seems clear that he was willing to contemplate reducing the scope of the death penalty and extending forms of punishment that would amend "the manners of the people" and "reform" prisoners convicted of offenses hitherto capital. Blackstone had thus already accepted in principle in 1769—long before John Howard's tours of the English prisons began— the views that led him ten years later to help draft the Penitentiary Act, and that appeared in subsequent editions of his *Commentaries*, that if imprisonment can be properly managed

> there is reason to hope that such a reformation may be effected
> in the lower classes of mankind, and such a gradual scale of
> punishment be affixed to all gradations of guilt, as may in time
> supersede the necessity of capital punishment, except for very
> atrocious crimes.[67]

The possibilities of new departures in punishment were thus being contemplated in English discussion of crime and its causes in the wake of the high levels of offenses in and around the metropolis in the early 1750s and in the 1760s. The failure of the established penalties to prevent either petty crime or the serious and violent offenses weakened the hold of the complex of assumptions on which they rested. A view was emerging that neither pilferers nor robbers could any longer be merely frightened into obedience, and a conviction was being voiced that punishment should not

[66] Ibid., pp. 17–18.
[67] Blackstone, *Commentaries*, 12th ed., ed. Edward Christian (1795), vol. 4, p. 370.

only attempt to save the petty offender from beginning on the road to the scaffold but also to reclaim men who were already deeply corrupted and committing more serious offenses.

How far positions shifted in the third quarter of the century is made clear by the work of another committee of the House of Commons set up in 1770 "to consider of so much of the criminal laws as relate to capital offences."[68] The inquiry was moved by Sir William Meredith, a Rockingham Whig of liberal political and religious views, who urged the need to revamp the criminal laws so that punishments might be made more moderate and thus be more uniformly applied, and who summed up what was becoming the conventional wisdom of critics of the law by urging the adoption of penalties that would render prisoners once again useful to the community. The committee recommended that eight capital statutes be repealed. The House agreed in the case of six, and that agreement was embodied in the Penal Laws Bill (1772); this was lost in the House of Lords by the prorogation of parliament, but it appears that there was support there too for abolition of the death penalty in at least five of the six statutes.[69]

By the early 1770s articles calling for the revision of the criminal law were common in the press, and such a program was suggested in a number of influential tracts. In 1771 Willliam Eden, the future Lord Auckland who was then at the beginning of his career as a lawyer, politician, diplomat, and reformer, published his *Principles of Penal Law* in which he advocated a sharp reduction of the scope of capital punishment, clearly much influenced by Beccaria. Like others in England he was not ready to abandon the gallows entirely, but he wanted to repeal the capital provisions of a large number of statutes—many of which he thought had been composed, as he said of the Black Act, with "vague, unfeeling, undistinguishing carelessness"—and he advocated a consolidation and codification of the law that would reduce the death penalty to a much narrower range of offenses. "It cannot be too strongly inculcated," he said, "that capital punishments, when unnecessary, are inhuman and immoral."[70] Other proposals in these years emphasized the failure and the rejection of terror as a penal weapon. "Death as a punishment for theft has been tried and found ineffectual," John Scott asserted in 1773; "perhaps no nation

---

[68] For the work of this committee see Radzinowicz, *History*, vol. 1, pp. 427–46.

[69] *Parliamentary History* 16 (1765–71), cols. 1124–27; Radzinowicz, *History*, vol. 1, pp. 427–46. The list of statutes to be abolished included the Infanticide Act (1624), but the remainder were essentially pieces of dormant legislation; none involved offenses against property. The House of Commons did not agree to the abolition of capital punishment for infanticide as the committee recommended, nor to the repeal of a Tudor statute dealing with forcible abduction.

[70] William Eden, *Principles of Penal Law* (1771), p. 263.

on earth is so prodigal of life as the English and no nation on earth is so
infested with thieves." And in wondering in an aside why so many offenses
had been made capital and yet so few offenders were hanged, "for small
crimes only," he concluded that the present system must have been intended from the beginning:

> Advantage may sometimes be taken of the commission of a small
> crime to hang a great villain, who would otherwise not have
> been capitally convicted, and possibly with a view to such ad-
> vantage, the penalty of death was appointed for so many venial
> transgressions, and, at the same time, a dispensing power of
> reprieve annexed to the office of a judge and of pardon to the
> prerogative of a king. Nor, on any other presumption than this,
> can I suppose, that the spirit of our laws meant to value life at
> a shilling.[71]

As yet in the early 1770s no alternative to capital punishment would
have received universal support. Many men were by then persuaded, as
we have seen, that transportation had ceased to have much efficacy as a
punishment. Similarly many would have agreed with Eden's strong opposition to mere incarceration in the county jail, which, he thought, "sinks
useful subjects into burdens on the community, and has always a bad
effect on their morals; nor can it communicate the benefit of example,
being in its nature secluded from the eye of the people."[72] Some common
ground was emerging, however, around the notion that the punishment
of all but the most serious offenses like treason, murder, robbery, rape,
and perhaps a few others not only should be noncapital but also should
be made to serve more rationally the interests of the community and of
the prisoner himself. Eden pursued this notion in respect to the punishment
for pocket-picking, which he thought should be removed from the capital
category. He suggested instead imprisonment at hard labor, the advantages
of which had by then been urged intermittently over several generations
as a punishment for minor offenders. It was a "mode of punishment,"
Eden said, "which by inducing a habit of industry, and by the effects of
that habit, would be equally beneficial to the criminal and the public.[73]

---

[71] John Scott, *Observations on the Present State of the Vagrant Poor* (1773), pp. 133–34. "Blood
undoubtedly requires blood," he conceded, "but for violations of property unaggravated by acts
of cruelty, the laws of God, of nature and of equity, certainly require a very different penalty."
For another proposal for a "revisal and reformation of our Criminal Codes" see Henry Dagge,
Considerations on Criminal Law, 3 vols. (1772, 2nd ed., 1774).

[72] Eden, *Principles of Penal Law*, p. 44.

[73] Ibid., p. 264.

THE END OF TRANSPORTATION TO AMERICA

The overlapping failure of the established system and the appeal of some form of incarceration had made enough converts among the judges (and perhaps in the administration) to have had an effect on the patterns of punishment even before the American Revolution threw the penal system into chaos. As we have seen, sentences of transportation diminished in Surrey as the American crisis deepened. They continued to be ordered at the assizes until 1775 and at the quarter sessions into 1776. But the pattern of noncapital punishment that had been established over several decades had already by then shifted substantially. Transportation accounted for less than forty per cent of sentences awarded in the Surrey courts in the five years before the American Revolution, compared with a level of close to two-thirds over the previous half century. Its place was taken by a modest revival of clergyable discharge and, most important, by forms of incarceration (table 10.4).

After the passage of the Transportation Act in 1718 the option of ordering that an offender who had successfully pleaded his clergy be branded on the thumb and discharged (or, as was possible, sent to a term in the house of correction) had faded noticeably in the Surrey courts. Felons convicted of clergyable offenses were either transported or whipped. But as transportation ran into difficulties in the years before the American war the branding and discharge of clergy came back into favor in the assize courts as a way of dealing with some of the more minor offenders (table 10.5). At the quarter sessions the magistrates also altered their pattern of sentencing in these same years, but rather than granting clergyable discharges they began in the middle of the 1760s to send a number of convicts to the county jail for a brief period. For the most part this sentence seems to have been conceived as a way of supplementing and extending a whipping sentence, for two-thirds of the prisoners incarcerated by the magistrates between 1766 and 1775 were ordered to be whipped as well as held in jail for a few weeks (table 10.6).

The patterns of sentencing were thus changing at both the assizes and the quarter sessions even before the government ended the transportation subsidy in 1772, although that clearly accelerated the changes going forward. At the assizes more prisoners were awarded benefit of clergy, but after 1773 with the significant difference that the judges began once again to take advantage of the Act of 1706 that authorized them to imprison such convicted offenders at hard labor in the house of correction. At the Lent assizes in 1773 five offenders were ordered to be burnt in the hand

TABLE 10.5

Noncapital Punishments for Property Offenses at the
Surrey Assizes and Quarter Sessions, 1763–1775

Year	Allowed Clergy, Discharged	Transported	Whipped	Imprisoned	Total
QUARTER SESSIONS					
1763	0	9	3	1	13
1764	0	26	5	0	31
1765	0	23	9	0	32
1766	0	16	6	2	24
1767	0	23	7	2	32
1768	0	18	16	6	40
1769	0	25	3	6	34
1770	0	11	7	5	23
1771	0	8	5	3	16
1772	0	11	10	14	35
1773	0	12	7	6	25
1774	0	13	6	7	26
1775	3	13	10	3	29
ASSIZES					
1763	2	11	0	0	13
1764	1	8	3	0	12
1765	2	7	6	0	15
1766	3	12	3	0	18
1767	7	11	1	0	19
1768	3	14	1	0	18
1769	8	9	0	0	17
1770	9	14	0	0	23
1771	12	14	1	0	27
1772	7	9	0	0	16
1773	7	8	1	12	28
1774	13	5	7	4	29
1775	0	10	9	11	30

SOURCES: Sample and Count.

TABLE 10.6

Imprisonment for Property Offenses at the Surrey Assizes and Quarter Sessions, 1766–1775

	Quarter Sessions	Assizes
PLACE AND CHARACTER OF IMPRISONMENT		
House of correction at hard labor	3	27
Jail	13	0
House of correction with whipping	2	0
Jail with whipping	40	0
Total	58	27
LENGTH OF TERM[a]		
House of correction		
One month	0	7
Two months	2	0
Three months	1	0
Four months	0	3
Six months	0	9
One year	0	4
Two years	0	4
Range	2–3 mos.	1–24 mos.
Average	2.3 mos.	8.0 mos.
Jail		
One week	2	
Two weeks	5	
Six weeks	1	
One month	6	
Three months	5	
Six months	8	
Range	1 wk.–6 mos.	
Average	2.7 mos.	

SOURCES: Sample and Count.

[a] For 1772–75 only.

and imprisoned for a month, and three others for four months. Such sentences had not been awarded in Surrey for more than half a century, and the judges who reinstituted them had clearly not looked up the statute that gave them their authority, for the Act of 1706 specified that the term in the house of correction (or workhouse) was to be not less than six months or more than two years. This was presumably pointed out to them (perhaps at one of their conferences at Serjeants' Inn), and in the next year the judges at the Surrey assizes got it right, to the disadvantage of several prisoners who were now granted clergy and sent to the house of correction for six months to a year, or in a few cases two years. In the three years before transportation was brought to an end by the fighting in America, imprisonment at hard labor accounted for about thirty-one per cent of the noncapital sentences at the Surrey assizes, while transportation fell to just over twenty-six per cent (table 10.5).

We are dealing here with very small numbers of cases, and with one county, and too much should not be made of these figures. Nevertheless, they do suggest that an important change was underway in penal matters before the American Revolution stopped transportation entirely: there was less reliance being placed on banishment and, at least at the assizes, a return to forms of imprisonment that had not been used extensively for several decades. At the quarter sessions, too, the magistrates diminished their reliance on transportation in 1772 and after. And they also increased substantially the number of sentences to incarceration. Unlike the assize judges, however, they did not (except in a few cases) order imprisonment at hard labor in the houses of correction; they continued to order imprisonment in the county jail mainly as a way of adding further pain to a sentence of whipping. They also imposed much briefer terms: even when they did not order an imprisonment with whipping they rarely imposed a term of more than three months. In the early 1770s, when there were not a large number of imprisonments from the quarter sessions, half were for no more than six weeks and they averaged about ten weeks. At the assizes in the same period twenty-seven prisoners convicted of clergyable felonies against property were sent to the house of correction for terms that averaged eight months (even counting the undoubtedly unlawful sentences to a few months in the first year); almost a third of the sentences were for a year or more.

Why the quarter sessions and assizes took two quite different paths is not entirely clear. It is possible that the magistrates were reluctant to sentence prisoners to long periods of incarceration because they were conscious of the costs (having to find the money to support these institutions). But that does not explain their use of the county jail rather than the house of correction. That seems to derive from their established patterns of sentencing and the habits of the past. Magistrates at the Surrey quarter sessions had not dealt with clergyable felonies when large numbers of prisoners were actually being granted clergy, burnt on the hand, and discharged. When they extended their criminal jurisdiction to include such offenses, clergyable discharges had been largely replaced by transportation, and the quarter sessions had no need in the 1750s to revive them. When transportation came to seem inappropriate in some cases, the magistrates in quarter sessions thus had no previous experience of the branding and discharge of clergy to fall back on, and they substituted instead a punishment they were familiar with—whipping—though they chose to make it more serious and more painful for some convicted offenders by tying it to a period of imprisonment in the county jail.

The divergence in the practice of the Surrey quarter sessions and assizes in the few years before the American war closed the colonies to transportation was striking both in the consequences for the prisoners and in the intentions being expressed. No one could pretend that a sentence to the county jail could be anything more than mere incarceration, whereas the commitment to a period of hard labor in the house of correction of six months or more that was invariably ordered by the assize judges was meant to be reformative and was in line with the new directions in punishment being urged in various quarters by the 1770s. Other benches in the London area—or at least some magistrates on those benches—apparently moved more vigorously than those in Surrey to accept the arguments being made in favor of imprisonment at hard labor. In 1772 the Middlesex magistrates were engaged in a fierce debate on this issue, with one group pushing hard for an extensive prison rebuilding program in the county so that they might substitute "actual hard labour as a punishment instead of transportation."[74] The Surrey magistrates in this period were also concerned about the condition of the jail and especially of the house of correction in Southwark (which a committee of justices recommended be entirely rebuilt in 1772 because it was too small to separate the inmates who ought to be kept apart and too small to provide adequate facilities to provide them with work).[75] But if there were those on the bench who wanted to impose sentences on quarter sessions prisoners of "actual hard labour" they did not make much headway against the majority.

Similar offenses were thus being punished in significantly different ways at the quarter sessions and the assizes by the first half of the 1770s. This underlines the absence of central direction in the administration of the criminal law (at least in the punishment of lesser offenses), and it is hardly surprising that when transportation was seriously curtailed in 1775 there was no national plan for dealing with the emergency. And although reliance on transportation had been reduced over the previous five years, the closing of the colonies did bring something of an emergency. In 1775 the government snatched at a number of expedients to deal with those already sentenced and awaiting passage to America. Most of the county jails were not yet seriously crowded when the sheriffs were asked in No-

74 *Cal. H. O. Papers*, vol. 3, pp. 560–61.
75 QS 2/6, Ep. 1772, 17.

vember 1775 to send in an account of the numbers of convicts in their care sentenced to transportation.[76] But Newgate was very full indeed, partly because it was the staging point for transportees brought from county jails, and because it received all the prisoners to be tried at the Old Bailey who were brought there from other London prisons on the eve of the sessions eight times a year.

When the reports on the prison populations were received in November 1775, it was decided that the prisoners still in Newgate waiting for ships should simply be put on board vessels in the Thames and kept there until something could be done with them. Many were subsequently freed on condition that they transport themselves—"serving and continuing to serve [His Majesty] out of Great Britain," as one order put it.[77] Whether any of them left, and whether anyone expected them to do so, is unclear.[78] That was only one of several forms of pardon cobbled together in the spring of 1776 as a way of diverting prisoners from America. Some men were sent to the army or navy; others who were too old or too infirm for the forces continued in the first half of 1776 to be allowed to transport themselves; still others and many women were simply allowed free pardons.[79] The government was clearly willing to accept any expedient to clear the jails when a man condemned to death at the Essex assizes in the summer of 1775 was pardoned on condition of his being bound as an apprentice for fourteen years to a coal dealer and grocer.[80]

THE HULKS, AND IMPRISONMENT AT HARD LABOR

It was no doubt thought in 1775 that transportation would only briefly be interrupted and that things would soon get back to normal. By the spring of 1776 that expectation must have been fading fast, and it was becoming certain that a longer-term stopgap would be necessary. It was

[76] SP 44/92, pp. 52–56.

[77] SP 44/93, p. 3.

[78] In November 1775, William Eden, then undersecretary of state, told the Recorder of London that the contractor who had dealt with transportees from the capital had been ordered to take all the prisoners waiting to be shipped to America "immediately aboard some proper vessel in the river in the usual manner, and as if in due course for transportation, after which the matter will, as soon as possible have every proper consideration, and such further steps be taken as may be thought expedient" (SP 44/91, p. 437). They were the ones turned loose in January 1776 to arrange their own exile. Another group of prisoners from the Old Bailey were pardoned on similar conditions in February, as were several from other courts, including a man convicted of highway robbery at the Surrey assizes (SP 44/91, pp. 23, 446).

[79] SP 44/93, pp. 126–27.

[80] SP 44/92, pp. 452–53.

then that an alternative that had been emerging in the practice of the courts in the previous few years—confinement at hard labor—was brought forward in legislation to serve the pressing needs of the moment. This decision was embodied in an Act "to authorize . . . the punishment by hard labour" of offenders who were liable to transportation.[81] The Act set out two alternatives to transportation. In the first place, male convicts could now be sentenced to be "kept to hard labour in the raising sand, soil, and gravel from and cleansing the river Thames, or any other service for the benefit of the navigation of the said river." The prisoners were to be placed under the direction of an overseer (to be appointed by the Middlesex magistrates) who would essentially enter into a contract to take convicts off the government's hands at so much per head, hire his own warders, and set up his own prisons on ships in the river. Noncapital offenders, who would earlier have been transported for seven years, were to be sentenced to this laborious confinement for a term of three to ten years at the judges' discretion. Those pardoned from a death sentence were to be set to work on the Thames for a period to be determined by the king in the grant of the pardon.

The Act said nothing about where the convicts were to be kept as they worked at improving the navigation of the Thames. That followed from the appointment of the first overseer. He was Duncan Campbell, a merchant who held the last contract for transporting prisoners from England and who had had a great deal of experience in organizing gangs of convicts and packing them into ships. He was authorized to anchor two ships in the river near Woolwich and to fit them out to receive something on the order of five hundred prisoners who would be taken every morning on lighters, in chains, to work at various tasks along the Thames. The *Justitia* and the *Censor* received their first convicts in August 1776.[82]

In the second place, the Act of 1776 made provision for women who would have been transported (for it was never intended that women would be sent to work on the Thames) and for men who were incapable of working on the river by reason of their age or health. They were to be confined in houses of correction, housed separately from the other inmates, and kept to hard labor (s. 18). The government wanted magistrates to build new houses of correction or to enlarge their present facilities in every town where the quarter sessions and assizes were held so that this program of separate confinement and hard labor for felons could be put into effect. A

[81] 16 Geo III, c. 43 (1776).
[82] *J.H.C.* 36 (1776–78), pp. 926ff.; W. Branch Johnson, *The English Prison Hulks* (1957), chaps. 1–2.

bill for that purpose was introduced by William Eden in May 1776, but it died at the end of the session.[83]

The hulks and house of correction Act of 1776 thus adopted and extended the practice of imprisoning noncapital convicts at hard labor that the assize judges had accepted for some offenders as the problems with transportation developed. Both expedients emerged out of the experience and discussion of the previous twenty years, and in some cases had been anticipated by much earlier practice, but the incarceration and labor now being undertaken were on a larger scale than ever before. The numbers involved were not enormous, at least not immediately, for as usual the level of offenses declined when the war with America began. Of those who received noncapital punishments in Surrey during the war, however, almost eighty-eight per cent sentenced at the assizes were sent to the hulks or houses of correction or (in very few cases) the county jail; at the quarter sessions the magistrates continued to prefer where possible to order whipping or whipping combined with a short term in jail, though more than a quarter of their sentences were for imprisonment at hard labor.

The establishment of incarceration in this way in turn encouraged the wider discussion and articulation of ideas and methods of punishment that had been merely implicit in previous practice. The hulks program was hardly imprisonment in a pure form; it had undoubtedly grown out of the experience of transportation of which it was conceived as a temporary substitute (a point underlined by the appointment of Duncan Campbell as overseer) as much as it had developed out of imprisonment schemes within England. Nevertheless it was a form of incarceration with hard labor, and many of the practices established to punish and manage the convicts on board the ships anticipated fundamental aspects of the penitentiary as it was to be conceived in both theory and practice within a few years. The convicts working on the river were to be punished and humiliated, for example, by being "fed and sustained with bread and any coarse and inferior food, and water or small beer" and by being made to wear a prison uniform.[84] Their overseer was authorized to punish misbehavior by "such whipping, or other moderate punishment . . . as may be inflicted by law on persons committed to a house of correction for hard labour" (s. 8). The Act also anticipated another technique of convict management in that it allowed inmates to earn early release if by their "industry and other good behaviour" they showed signs of reformation.[85]

---

[83] *J.H.C.* 35 (1774–76), pp. 796, 809. The text of the bill is in the *Catalogue of Papers printed by order of the House of Commons*, vol. 9, no. 286, and in Lambert, *Sessional Papers*, II, vol. 27, pp. 311–42.

[84] 16 Geo III, c. 43, s. 7.

[85] In sentencing three men to hard labor for ten years at the Sussex assizes in 1776, Mansfield

It is unclear how much the development of imprisonment over the 1770s was the result of a conviction that it was a valuable punishment in its own right, and how much it was simply the acceptable alternative to transportation when that lost favor and then was entirely interrupted. Perhaps it was mainly the latter. But it is significant that forms of incarceration were turned to rather than the clergyable discharge that transportation had itself replaced, or more whipping or more hanging. It is further significant that the forms adopted, at least at the assizes, were imprisonment in the house of correction and then in the hulks, for both provided in theory if not always in practice the possibility of incarceration involving hard labor. It was intended that the prisoners be put to work, so that, as the preamble of the 1776 Act declared, they might be "reclaimed from their evil courses" and with "proper care and correction" be turned away from the habits and behavior that had led them into crime. The bill that was introduced to encourage local authorities to increase the number of houses of correction expressed the hope that hard labor would not merely deter men from crime but "might also be the means of reforming many offenders, and of rendering them useful members of the community."

The acceptance of this program by the mid-1770s helps to explain the further rapid development of the *idea* of imprisonment over the next few years. It helps to explain the influence of men like Jonas Hanway and especially John Howard, who began making his tours of inspection of jails and houses of correction in 1773 and whose *State of the Prisons* was published in 1777. Howard provided a great deal of actual data about English prisons that no doubt helped to shape opinion. But Hanway and Howard did not so much convert men to the virtues of imprisonment as provide justifications and explanations for what had already been begun and provide a program of further development. They were influential because they spoke to a problem of immediate concern and helped to shape and lead opinion already in motion. But they also added elements that were to be of importance in making the idea of reformation a believable proposition. They outlined means and methods of regulating institutions that were known to be hellholes of disease and dirt and corruption; and they added an

---

is reported to have told them that if they behaved themselves their sentences "might be shortened according to the reports made to the K[ing] of their behaviour" (Philip C. Yorke, ed., *The Diary of John Baker* [1931], p. 361). Such provisions were indeed put into effect. When six men were discharged from the hulks in December 1776 before their terms were up, the overseer was reminded by the undersecretary who sent the pardon that "as these men have obtained his Majesty's mercy upon your representation of their having behaved particularly well during their confinement and hard labour, you will of course point out their example to the others in your custody." Campbell may well have wanted these men as warders, for he was further told that if they did not stay with him, he was to send them to the navy upon their release rather than "leave them at large" (SP 44/93, pp. 128–29).

important religious argument: the positive effects that could be anticipated from the teaching of the Christian faith to men and women whose education in this area had been neglected. To those who believed that the increase in immorality and thus in crime sprang fundamentally from the disintegration of the manners and habits of the working poor and of their neglect of their religious duty, such training in prison promised the most direct possibility of a real reformation. That religious instruction and hard labor were in fact difficult to combine in prisons was to become increasingly clear in the variety of reform schemes attempted in the first half of the nineteenth century.[86] That was not immediately apparent in the 1770s, however, when the harnessing of religious training and work held out the promise that imprisonment under the right conditions might not merely answer the problem of crime but, more broadly, offer a key to the preservation of social order.

THE IMPORTANCE OF HANWAY AND HOWARD

In both his writings and his active engagement in a variety of schemes in the middle decades of the eighteenth century, Jonas Hanway encouraged institutional solutions to social problems.[87] He was moved by the poverty and want so evident in London, and particularly by the social disintegration suggested by the numbers of abandoned children and prostitutes in the streets of the capital. He accepted the conventional wisdom that the root cause of these social problems and of the crime to which they led lay in the "dissoluteness which reigns among the lower classes of the people," to quote part of the title of a tract he published in 1772.[88] And he shared the renewed conviction that their solution could only come from the proper management of the poor and from schemes to educate and train them. Above all, Hanway believed in the primacy of religion. He strongly shared the view of those who argued (as men had for decades) that it was ignorance of the truths of the Christian faith that led men into the bad habits that brought them in the end to the gallows.

Hanway's writings and his schemes have a common vision and return again and again to a fundamental point: that the answer to the problems

[86] U.R.Q. Henriques, "The Rise and Decline of the Separate System of Prison Discipline," *Past and Present* 54 (1972), pp. 63–64.

[87] In this discussion of Hanway I am much indebted to Donna Andrew, "London Charity in the Eighteenth Century," chap. 3.

[88] *Observations on the causes of the dissoluteness which reigns among the lower classes of the people. The propensity of some to petty larceny. The danger of gaming, concubinage, and an excessive fondness for amusement. With a proposal to render Bridewell of service to the police* (1772).

caused by vice and immorality lay in the reformation and reclamation of the dissolute poor and of the individual offender. This could only be achieved, he concluded, when the individual was removed from the sources of contamination that made him what he was; thus his belief in institutions. In the 1750s Hanway founded or strongly supported several charities devoted to the "rescue and rehabilitation" of foundlings, deserted children, and prostitutes, and of others that gave help to pregnant women and trained boys for the sea service.[89] His views had not changed substantially when in the 1770s he wrote extensively on the problems of crime.

"I lay my foundation on the rock of *religion*," he said at the beginning of a tract published in 1775, "having every day fresh reason to believe, it is the only true basis of government; and that the national security and happiness must decay with the neglect of it." And, he went on, "there is no other means for a young man, or an old one, to *cleanse* his ways, than by ruling himself after the work of God; . . . whenever he goeth wrong, out of the commandments, it is because he has not been duly taught to *hide* them in his heart."[90] This was the work that Hanway thought the punishment of criminals ought to be accomplishing. It could be achieved, he argued, only by solitary confinement, by the total isolation of the prisoner from the bad influences of other inmates. Hanway thus offered a program and a justification for a form of punishment that was being adopted apparently without a clear purpose.

It was widely believed in the middle of the eighteenth century that prisons in England did as much to corrupt men as to reform them. The county jails and the houses of correction were commonly very small and were often overcrowded, dirty, and unhealthy. For at least half a century by the 1770s the magistrates of Surrey had been concerned from time to time with problems arising from the crumbling fabric of the jail they had built in the 1720s and the need to keep the county's three houses of correction in repair. They had been concerned with questions of security and in recent years particularly with questions of health, spurred on from time to time by the judges of assize, by doctors engaged to care for the prisoners, and, latterly, by parliament. The prisons had thus not been entirely neglected; they were in the 1770s in some significant ways rather different from the institutions of fifty or a hundred years earlier. Nonetheless, as John Howard was to confirm, they remained all too often noisome and unpleasant places.

The task of providing adequate accommodation and of keeping male prisoners separated from female, and felons from debtors, had been com-

[89] Andrew, "London Charity in the Eighteenth Century," chap. 3.
[90] *On the Defects of Police* (1775), pp. ii–iii.

plicated by the changing character of the prisons, and in particular by the fact that prisoners who would have been branded and discharged at the conclusion of their trial a hundred or fifty years earlier were now being returned to the jail to await transportation. Larger numbers of capital offenders were also being pardoned, also most commonly on condition of transportation. The jails were simply not being "delivered" as they would have been in the seventeenth century. In the 1760s and 1770s the prison populations were further enlarged by the terms of incarceration being ordered in increasing numbers by the courts.

Hanway addressed himself particularly to the question of how inmates were to be brought to repentance and rehabilitated in institutions. He offered a solution, albeit an expensive one (and that was a more important consideration than he was prepared to admit in 1775), because what he proposed was the building of "proper prisons" all over the country that would make it possible for every prisoner to be kept in "strict separation and solitude" for the duration of his sentence. He would be visited daily by a clergyman to be taught "what it is to be a man and a Christian." And he was to be kept away from all other influences. Such a regime, Hanway thought, would both strike offenders with terror and answer what seemed to him the central purpose of punishment, by serving to "break their ferocity of disposition, reform their illiterate infidelity and change their sensual enjoyments . . . for a manly, reasonable and religious conduct."[91]

Hanway was not the first to suggest that the separate confinement of prisoners would make imprisonment a more effective punishment, nor that it would be better to reform offenders than merely to punish them.[92] But his arguments in 1775 and 1776 were both extensive and timely. They were noticed favorably by John Howard, for example, and helped shape the ideas on how prisons ought to be run that he was to express in his remarkable report, published in 1777, on the condition of jails and houses of correction all over the country.[93] This influential document

---

[91] *Defects of Police*, pp. xii, 3, 210–22. And see his pamphlet of the following year: *Solitude in Imprisonment with proper profitable labour and a spare diet the most humane and effectual means to bring malefactors who had forfeited their lives or are subject to Transportation to a right sense of their condition . . .* (1776).

[92] The Reverend Samuel Denne had published some years before *A Letter to Sir Robert Ladbrooke, knt . . . with an attempt to show the good effects which may reasonably be expected from the Confinement of Criminals in separate Apartments* (1771); and it had been mentioned as a desirable objective by others in the 1760s (*The Public Advertiser*, 10 Jan. 1764). For earlier examples see Michael Ignatieff, *A Just Measure of Pain: The Penitentiary in the Industrial Revolution* (New York, 1978), pp. 53–54.

[93] *The State of the Prisons in England and Wales* (Warrington, 1777); 4th ed. (Warrington, 1792).

became a reference point and inspiration for men in parliament and in the government and for a number of active men in various parts of the country who were becoming anxious to see the English jails rebuilt and used more effectively as places of punishment and reformation.

Howard provided a program and an argument. He also provided systematic evidence about the physical condition and present state of all the jails and houses of correction in England and Wales. At his visits to each of these institutions he gathered information about the number and size of their rooms, the number of inmates, the conditions that affected the health of the prisoners, the arrangements for caring for the sick, the rules that governed their day-to-day management, the fees extracted from the prisoners, and so on. These reports were preceded by general remarks on the problems that arose from the jails being run as private businesses by men out to make a profit, from the lack of inspection, and from the "bad customs" he found wherever he went. And they were followed by his "proposed improvements." These put a great deal of emphasis on correcting the problems that had drawn Howard's attention to them in the first place when as sheriff of Bedfordshire he had seen the condition of the wretches brought to court to face their trials and had investigated for himself the horror of their existence in the county jail.

Howard's program for the physical reform and rebuilding of jails was strongly influenced by contemporary medical opinion of the causes of disease and aimed to incorporate into these institutions the best methods that science could devise for dealing with jail fever and similar endemic diseases. He was particularly convinced that stale and putrid air was a principal enemy, and he championed methods of ventilation that would bring fresh air into every part of the prison. But he was also concerned that the jails be kept clean and that the prisoners have running water, clean clothes, and nutritious if plain food. This healthy physical environment would make possible in turn a regime of work and meditation that was at the heart of Howard's program and that aimed at the spiritual health of the prisoners. He also acknowledged and accepted Hanway's argument for the separation of prisoners and for their physical isolation, at least at night. In the county jails Howard's plan called for enough cells to enable each prisoner to spend his nonworking hours "in solitude and silence," which would be "favourable to reflection and may possibly lead them to repentance." Such spiritual reformation was the central purpose. To encourage it, a chaplain would be engaged to visit the prisoners in their cells, to exhort and admonish them, and "to make known to the condemned, that mercy which is revealed in the Gospel." In the houses of correction Howard thought that there should be an even more insistent emphasis on the reform of manners and morals. He acknowledged that work was "indispensibly requisite" to this end, but it should not be allowed to overwhelm the spiritual function of the institution.[94]

THE PENITENTIARY ACT, 1779

Howard's investigations of the jails and houses of correction and his proposals for their improvement had an immediate influence. The hulks set up under the 1776 Act soon became controversial, for an (accurate) impression quickly got about that conditions on board were hideous and that the mortality rate was disgracefully high. Even more worrying (for those not on board) was the security problem. A number of battles were fought between the prisoners and their keepers, several men escaped and many others made attempts, and people in London became nervous about these cargoes of desperate men chained up so near the capital. A committee of the House of Commons established in 1778 under the chairmanship of Sir Charles Bunbury to look into the workings of the Act took evidence from Duncan Campbell, Howard, and other witnesses, and came to conclusions that confirmed many of the dismal rumors of life on board the hulks.

On the houses of correction, which the Act of 1776 directed to be enlarged and rebuilt for the separate confinement of felons, Howard himself informed the committee that he had found none in which the directions of the statute had been followed. Despite the efforts of the judges of assizes to remind magistrates of the provisions of the Act, "not the least Attention had been paid to it." In general, he reported, few inmates were doing hard labor in the houses of correction. Most of these institutions, he said, were like the Surrey bridewell in St. George's Fields in Southwark, which he took as an example, and simply failed to provide employment. The committee concluded that evidence provided by Campbell persuaded them that conditions on the hulks were improving and they ought to be retained, but they said nothing about the houses of correction.[95]

That question was being taken up in other quarters, however. The judges had already announced at the Summer assizes in 1777 that a bill was being prepared to authorize the establishment of houses of hard labor in each county, and grand juries and magistrates were being urged to

[94] Howard, *State of the Prisons*, 4th ed., pp. 22, 38, 40. For an excellent discussion of the complex inspirations and motives that lay behind Howard's program, and that moved him to spend the last sixteen years of his life traveling in England and over the Continent investigating the conditions and organization of jails, see Ignatieff, *A Just Measure of Pain*, pp. 47–79.

[95] *J.H.C.* 36 (1776–78), pp. 926–31.

consider the benefits of such an institution.[96] In the following year such
a bill was drawn up by Sir William Eden with help from Blackstone and
Howard. This put forward an elaborate plan to divide the country into
nineteen districts, each of which would have a "house of hard labour" in
which work, religious instruction, and solitary confinement at night would
combine to impose an entirely new regimen of discipline on prisoners.
This scheme, which was supported in its essentials by Jeremy Bentham,[97]
went no further. In 1779, however, another committee of the house, again
chaired by Bunbury, was charged to investigate the working of the 1776
Act, in particular the returns made to the house of the number of convicts
imprisoned in the hulks and in the jails and houses of correction in London
and the Home Circuit, and this committee recommended that the central
intentions of Eden's plan be adopted.

The 1779 committee ranged much more widely than the previous
year's. Their resolutions fell into three categories. In the first place, the
committee once again gave approval to the hulks, and indeed recommended
that they be extended to other rivers and ports. They thought that the
minimum sentence might be shortened to one year—that was subsequently
adopted—and they suggested a number of other minor changes. But in
essence they were content to leave the hulks as they were, at least until
transportation could be reestablished. In the second place, they heard a
good deal of evidence on the question of transportation and resolved that
it should be reestablished when a suitable place was found. But the committee focused particularly on the houses of correction that the 1776 Act
had intended would be enlarged in order to provide separate accommodation for the large numbers of offenders sentenced to hard labor outside
the hulks.

Witnesses again confirmed that nothing had been done by local
authorities to give this effect, and the committee concluded that

> the whole Arrangement of the Prisons, so far as they were
> informed, is, at the present, ill-suited, either to the Oeconomy
> of the State, or the Morality of the People, and seems to be
> chiefly calculated for the safe Custody of the Persons confined,
> without due Attention to their Health, Employment, or
> Reformation.

A suitable form of punishment was still required, they went on to say,
for those who would have been transported but who could not be sent to
the hulks—women, for example, and "such Males as from their Age,
Infirmities, or the slight Nature of their Crimes are improper Objects for

[96] G. M. 47 (1777), p. 250.
[97] Jeremy Bentham, A View of the Hard-Labour Bill (1778).

any severer Punishment." The "best corrective" remained solitary confinement, discipline, work, and religious instruction—the regime outlined
in Eden's hard labor bill—and the committee recommended a modified
version of that grand scheme by which parliament would encourage the
construction of institutions all over the country by building two "Houses"
(one for men, the other for women) to serve the metropolis and the counties
of the Home Circuit. If these were as successful as the committee anticipated as raising "a general spirit of reformation," magistrates everywhere,
they thought, would rush to copy them.[98]

These proposals were embodied in legislation passed in 1779, which
had been largely prepared by Eden.[99] The institutions to be built near
London were to be known as penitentiary houses (rather than "hard-labour
houses" as in the previous proposal), a name that emphasized the objective
and the intention at the heart of the life of discipline and labor they
intended to impose on inmates, a regime that would bring them to a sense
of shame and remorse so that they might be reclaimed and remade in the
image of the men whose institutions these were, and go back into society as productive and honest citizens. The Penitentiary Act expressed the
hope that

> if many offenders, convicted of crimes for which transportation
> hath been usually inflicted, were ordered to solitary imprison-
> ment, accompanied by well-regulated labour, and religious in-
> struction, it might be the means under providence, not only of
> deterring others from the commission of like crimes, but also
> of reforming the individuals, and inuring them to habits of
> industry. (s. 5)

And it set out in detail how that was to be achieved.

The convicts were to be given a uniform with badges (as marks of
humiliation); they were to be "fed and sustained with bread, and any coarse
meat, or other inferior food, and water, or small beer"; they were to be
punished for breaking the rules by whipping or confinement in a dungeon
on bread and water; and they were to be kept at work every day except
Sunday at

> labour of the hardest and most servile kind, in which drudgery
> is chiefly required . . . such as treading in a wheel, or drawing
> in a capstern, for turning a mill or other machine or engine,

---

[98] *J.H.C.* 37 (1778–80), pp. 313, 314; Lambert, *Sessional Papers*, II, vol. 31, pp. 25–26, 384, 389.

[99] 19 Geo III, c. 74. On the significance of this Act see Ignatieff, *A Just Measure of Pain*, pp. 93–99; Sean McConville, *A History of English Prison Administration, 1750–1877* (1981), chap. 5; Robin Evans, *The Fabrication of Virtue: English Prison Architecture, 1750–1840* (Cambridge, 1982), pp. 118–31.

sawing stone, polishing marble, beating hemp, rasping logwood, chopping rags, making cordage, or any other hard and
laborious service; and those of less health and ability, regard
being also had to age and sex, in picking oakum, weaving sacks,
spinning yarn, knitting nets, or other less laborious employment. (s. 32)

The convicts were also to be kept apart as much as was compatible with
this hard labor, being guarded closely by day to prevent unnecessary
communication and at night kept in separate cells. They were to be
rewarded for diligence and obedience with part of the profit of their work,
granted at their discharge, and with time off their sentence.[100]

NONCAPITAL PUNISHMENT DURING THE AMERICAN WAR

Thus did the penitentiary make its appearance in English law. Although
the Act was not put into effect—as is well known, the three-man committee established to oversee the buying of the land and the construction
of the buildings (of whom Howard was one) could not agree on a site,
and the initiative passed—it was nonetheless immensely influential. Not
only did it provide a model for a number of institutions built in various
parts of the country at the urging of local groups or simply of an active
and energetic man like the duke of Richmond in Sussex or Sir George
Paul in Gloucestershire,[101] but the language and the intention of the Act
also resonated through many subsequent penal experiments. More immediately important for those coming to trial in these years, the Acts of
1776 and 1779 considerably enlarged the sentencing powers of judges.
The term of three to ten years laid down in the 1776 legislation applied,
as we have seen, both to those working on the Thames and to those
convicts sent to the supposedly new houses of correction. The Penitentiary
Act changed these maximum terms to five years for a clergyable offense
(with a minimum of six months for a woman, twelve months for a man)
and two years for petty larceny.

[100] The Penitentiary Act touched on a number of other forms of punishment: it gave authority
to the courts to order transportation to a place other than America; it substituted for the branding
of clergy a small fine or whipping, the final stage of its transformation into a punishment in its
own right; and it reduced the minimum term in the hulks to one year and confirmed the authority of judges to continue to imprison offenders in the houses of correction for six months to
two years.

[101] For the new prisons see Ignatieff, *A Just Measure of Pain*, pp. 96–109; McConville, *English
Prison Administration*, pp. 88–104; Evans, *Fabrication of Virtue*, pp. 131–94; Esther Moir, "Sir
George Onesipherus Paul," in *Gloucestershire Studies*, ed. H.P.R. Finberg (1957), pp. 195–225.

Even with these reductions the courts were still empowered to sentence noncapital offenders for much longer terms than the two years that had been possible before 1776. This had a considerable effect on convicts sentenced to the houses of correction, for these new "penitentiary" terms were applied to them, the Act of 1779 laying it down that until the new institutions were built the houses of correction were "to be deemed and esteemed to be penitentiary houses" (s. 26). The distinction between the county jails and the houses of correction that had never been obliterated in the eighteenth century was thus of immense significance, for the bridewells became the vehicle for the development of the idea and the practice of reformative confinement even though few penitentiaries were built.

Henceforth the judges had a considerably enlarged range of noncapital penalties to choose among. They could continue to grant benefit of clergy and order such prisoners to be whipped or fined and, if they chose, have them placed in a house of correction for six months to two years; or, as a substitute for transportation, they could order a direct sentence of one to five years for a man, six months to five years for a woman; or they could order men to a period of hard labor in the hulks of one to seven years. Although the statutes of 1776 and 1779 were not much translated into bricks and mortar, they nonetheless had an important effect on the way convicted prisoners were treated. This was particularly noticeable at the assizes, where those suspected of crimes serious enough to make them candidates for a term in the hulks or for the new penitentiary discipline were mainly tried. The punishments handed out at the Surrey assizes over the war years 1776–82 show the impact of these changes, for almost ninety per cent of the prisoners convicted of noncapital property crimes were sentenced to some form of hard labor in the houses of correction or the hulks (table 10.7).

The more serious male offenders were most likely in these years to be sentenced to a term in the hulks, working at improving the navigation of the Thames—including those charged with a capital offense but convicted by the jury of a clergyable felony. Until the Penitentiary Act restricted this power to the assize judges, the quarter sessions also sent men to the prison ships. Over the years 1776–82 a sentence to the hulks accounted for about forty per cent of punishments ordered in property cases at the Surrey assizes and sixteen per cent at the quarter sessions.[102] Before they became crowded and the full horror of life on board was

[102] At the Sussex assizes in roughly the same period (1776–84) only thirty-two offenders were convicted of noncapital property crimes, but of these twenty (62.5 per cent) were sent to the hulks. The Sussex quarter sessions sent only a handful of men to the hulks.

TABLE 10.7

Noncapital Punishments for Property Offenses at the Surrey
Assizes and Quarter Sessions, 1776–1782

Court	Clergy/ Discharge %	Transportation %	Imprisonment with Hard Labor %	Imprisonment with Whipping %	Hulks %	Whipping %	Service in Forces %	Other %	Number of Sentences
Assizes	1.8	0	47.8	6.3	40.5	2.7	0	.9	111
Quarter sessions	0	6.4ᵃ	16.4	22.7	16.4	35.5	2.7	0	110

SOURCES: Sample and Count.

ᵃ Seven sentences to transportation in 1776.

revealed, the courts sentenced some prisoners to terms of six or seven years (as the Act authorized), making them serve out the full period of transportation.[103] Most were sent for three or four years, however, and the common term shortened further when the 1779 Act reduced the minimum to one year. Nonetheless, the average period of incarceration on the hulks during the American war for prisoners from the Surrey courts was about three and a half years (table 10.8). One might presume that judges paid some attention to the physical condition of the prisoners they were contemplating sending to the hulks, and that they might have been reluctant to sentence very young boys to a term of such hard labor on the chain gangs under the brutal conditions that developed in the prison ships. That they were not invariably disposed in these directions is clear from the reports of young prisoners and cripples being in the hulks only a year or two after they were founded.[104] The presumption of such a bias seems not unreasonable, however.

In applying their considerably enlarged discretion in sentencing, the judges clearly differed in their views of what constituted a reasonable and effective punishment, for sentences at one session of the assize court were often quite different from those at the next. The court record in these years gives the distinct impression that reasonably fine judgments were being made on the bench.[105] We will examine these sentencing patterns in more detail later in an effort to uncover the considerations that were most influential. But whatever reasons might have inclined the judges and magistrates to impose one sentence in one case and another, only slightly different, in the next (six months in the house of correction, then nine

[103] Four of the first men sent to the hulks from Surrey in the summer of 1776 went for the maximum term of ten years; they were in jail awaiting transportation to America for fourteen years or life as a condition of pardon, and they were ordered to the hulks by the government in accordance with the Act that had just been passed. At the same time, four women were sent to the Surrey houses of correction also for ten years.

[104] *J.H.C.* 36 (1776–78), p. 928.

[105] To give some examples: Catherine Floyd, aged thirty-nine, the wife of a laborer in Southwark, was convicted at the Lent assizes in 1780 of stealing goods to the value of fourteen shillings, sentenced to be fined a shilling (that is, the consequence of a grant of clergy after 1779), and kept to hard labor in the house of correction in Kingston for nine months. In the next case to be tried, two women, nineteen and twenty-two, also of Southwark, were charged with stealing goods worth five pounds from a house (a capital offense), and were found guilty by the jury of stealing "but not in the dwelling house" (a noncapital offense) and sentenced to hard labor in the Kingston house of correction for a year each (ASSI 31/12, p. 220). At the Summer assizes in 1780 convictions for offenses involving small amounts of money and no complicating violence all brought sentences on both men and women of a private whipping and hard labor in the house of correction for six months. At the following session of the Surrey assizes, in the spring of 1781, the pattern of sentences was different again, and men were being sent to the house of correction for a variety of terms from six to eighteen months (ASSI 31/13, pp. 25–26).

TABLE 10.8

Imprisonment for Property Offenses in Surrey, 1776–1782

	Quarter Sessions	Assizes
PLACE AND CHARACTER OF IMPRISONMENT		
House of correction at hard labor	8	51
Jail	10	2
House of correction with whipping	10	5
Jail with whipping	15	2
Hulks	18	45
Total	61	105
LENGTH OF TERM		
House of correction		
Under six months	7	1
Six to nine months	2	20
One to two years	0	27
Three years	2	7
Range	2 wks.–3 yrs.	4 mos.–3 yrs.
Average	7.4 mos.	13.2 mos.
Jail		
Under six months	26	1
Six months	3	0
Range	2 wks.–6 mos.	1 mo.
Average	2 mos.	1 mo.
Hulks		
One year	0	2
Two years	0	7
Three years	11	20
Four years	0	8
Five years	3	0
Six years	0	2
Seven years	4	2
Average	4.2 yrs.	3.3 yrs.

SOURCES: Sample and Count.

months, then six months with a whipping, three months without), they clearly took advantage of the flexibility inherent in imprisonment, an advantage its proponents frequently emphasized. Whether prison terms were being parceled out according to "the different degrees of malignity in different offences," in Bentham's phrase, there is no doubt that the judges availed themselves of what he called its "superior divisibility."[106]

[106] A View of the Hard-Labour Bill, p. 108.

The results during the war years may be seen in table 10.8. In noncapital property cases the prisoners were ordered to serve varying terms of hard labor in the house of correction or they were sent to jail or to the hulks, or they were ordered to be whipped and discharged. The periods of incarceration ranged from a matter of weeks to six months in the county jail, up to three years in the house of correction and up to seven on the Thames.

The differences that had characterized the sentencing patterns at the quarter sessions and assizes before the war continued into this period. The judges sent almost half the assize prisoners to the Surrey bridewells, most commonly for a year; the average sentence during the American war was over thirteen months. At the quarter sessions, on the other hand, the magistrates were much more sparing of long terms of incarceration, and they were much more likely to order corporal punishment. This was, no doubt, partly because they dealt with more minor offenders than typically came before the assizes, and because whipping had for long been well established at the quarter sessions as the punishment for petty theft. But the main difference continued to be that even when they wanted to imprison an offender, the magistrates were more likely to sentence him to a brief period in the county jail than in the house of correction, and to order him to be whipped as part of his punishment. The average sentence at the quarter sessions was between three and four months.

These differences in sentencing apparently did not derive from the magistrates' distaste for long terms of incarceration as such, or for imposing hard labor on the prisoners.[107] During the three years in which they had authority to send men to the hulks the Surrey magistrates were happy to do so, and for periods well above the established minumum. They might have been discouraged from ordering terms in the houses of correction by the burning down of the Southwark bridewell in the Gordon Riots in June 1780. But, as earlier, the main consideration may have been that the justices in quarter sessions were more conscious than the judges of assize of the pressures on the available accommodation in the county jail and houses of correction and of the expenses that long-term incarceration would require. They did not grasp the opportunities provided by the new legislation presumably because that would have meant assigning minimum terms of six months and in some cases a year. Thus while the assizes judges put into practice the new emphasis in punishment embodied in the recent

---

[107] Work was being done at the Kingston house of correction in 1782—mainly beating hair for saddles, though the magistrates thought that beating hemp and picking oakum were more appropriate tasks. A committee of magistrates suggested that the new house of corrections being built to replace the structure destroyed during the Gordon Riots in 1780 have installed a number of iron places for the purpose of pounding brill for the use of soap makers "to keep the prisoners constantly employed" (QS 2/6, Mids. 1782, 22, 23, 25).

legislation, the magistrates, upon whom the implementation of that policy ultimately depended since they would have to build the new and enlarged houses of correction it required, were not yet as a body prepared to accept it. Their sentencing policies make that clear. They were just as calculating as the judges in assigning punishments, and as apparently as anxious to make the punishment fit the crime and the criminal. But they operated with different assumptions and from different bases.

Despite the legislation that sought to replace transportation with hard labor, the double system that had developed as transportation had been gradually abandoned before the American war was thus perpetuated in Surrey. Just as the magistrates were left to build penitentiaries if they chose, so they were left to sentence as they chose, within the law. The same lack of political means and political will made the national government impotent in the face of local opinion in both cases. There took root in this period a form of "national" system that sprang from the sentencing policies of the assize judges, who dealt with the more serious offenders and who responded to the changes introduced by recent legislation, and a "local" system that dealt with more minor cases and that was shaped by the magistrates' concern for the implications of that legislation for their community.

CAPITAL PUNISHMENT, 1776–1800

The desirability of reforming convicts by a discipline of hard labor, solitary confinement, and religious instruction was established in legislation during the American war but made little headway in practice, at least not in the form of two national penitentiaries in the London area and the stimulation of others locally, as its proponents had hoped. The scheme outlined in the Penitentiary Act did not make progress. At the end of the American war the state of the jails and the question of the effectiveness of punishment in general once again pressed forward as matters of public discussion, for the courts and the prisons were once again overtaken after 1782 by another crisis of violent crime in London and, to a greater extent than ever before, throughout the country. There followed another period of panic and alarm at what appeared to be a serious threat to social order and to life and property.

During the war, prosecutions for property offenses and serious violence had again fallen away from peacetime levels, though not nearly as substantially as in previous wars in the century—a reflection in part perhaps of the growth in population in the 1770s and 1780s. Between 1776 and 1782, ninety-three men and women had been convicted of capital offenses in Surrey, of whom sixty-four had been pardoned and twenty-nine, just under a third (and all of them men), had been hanged (table 10.1). If the contrast between these war years and the peace that followed was not as stark as it had often been earlier, the anxiety at the level of reported and prosecuted offenses in 1783 and the next several years was perhaps more deeply felt than ever. The press was full of reports of robberies and burglaries, and prescriptions were offered on every side. The sense of alarm that this fed, as well as the number and the character of cases to be dealt with, had an effect on the verdicts reached by the juries and particularly on the levels of pardons granted to those condemned to death. This latter was a matter of deliberate policy, part of the means adopted to enlarge the deterrent power of the gallows. The government made it known that pardons would be difficult to obtain if the judge did not reprieve the convicted offender and recommend him. A correspondent to Lord Shelburne in September 1782 expressed satisfaction that the king had "determined to put a restraint on the mercifulness of his disposition, and will not, in future, grant pardons or respites to any who shall be convicted of . . . atrocious crimes."[108] A few years later a secretary of state was attempting to maintain this policy by letting it be known that in making recommendations for pardons to the king he would rely entirely on the judges' opinions and that any solicitations would have to be addressed to the trial judge.[109] Petitions on behalf of the condemned continued to pour into the Home Office and continued to be addressed to the king. But there is no doubt that attempts were made in these years to put the law more stringently into effect because, as was said of an earlier such period, "the spirit of the times [required] severity."[110]

Other efforts were made in these years to heighten the severity of punishment. The judges were instructed, for example, to order that some condemned prisoners be hanged within a few days of their conviction (on the model of the Murder Act of 1752), since rapid execution would both forestall petitions for pardons and serve to make the sentence more frightening. Judges issued such orders at the Surrey assizes at least until 1785, when two men convicted of highway robbery were sentenced to be hanged three days hence.[111] The courts also resorted frequently to the other familiar forms of the aggravated death penalty, ordering that the bodies of some of those executed be taken for dissection and that others be hanged in chains near the scene of the crime.[112]

---

[108] HO 42/1, f. 344. On the restriction of pardons in this period and a similar policy in the 1750s see Hay, "Crime, Authority and the Criminal Law," pp. 583–85.

[109] HO 13/3, p. 184.

[110] SP 37/15, f. 612.

[111] ASSI 35/225/7/15.

[112] Three of the women executed in this period had taken part in a brutal robbery in Southwark and were ordered to be hanged in chains in Kent Street, where the crime had taken place, along

584 ADMINISTRATION OF JUSTICE

The result of the increased prosecutions and a tougher attitude in the courts was that 118 men were sentenced to death in Surrey in the five years following the peace, almost half of whom, fifty-eight, were actually hanged (table 10.1). This was a much higher rate of executions to convictions than in any comparable period since the great panic of the early 1750s. The treatment of women was perhaps even more striking. Since the middle of the century only one woman had been put to death in the county; indeed, at the end of the American war no woman had been executed in Surrey for more than twenty years. In the five years 1783–87, by contrast, twelve women were convicted of capital offenses, of whom eight appear to have been executed.

The courts clearly remained persuaded in the 1780s that the gallows provided the most effective deterrent against serious offenses. As robberies and burglaries mounted in the postwar years, executions mounted with them. In 1785 alone, twenty-two offenders were hanged in Surrey, more by far than in any other year in the second half of the century. Large numbers of executions were also reported from other places. A total of sixty-four prisoners were hanged in the five counties of the Home Circuit in that same year, for example, compared with an average during the previous thirty years of thirteen.[113] At the Old Bailey, where most of the London cases were tried, the eight annual sessions ended relentlessly through these years in long lists of prisoners sentenced to death, as many as thirty or forty in some sessions. "Nothing could be more affecting," the *Gentleman's Magazine* allowed in describing one such session after several years of this, "than to hear judgement of death pronounced against a little army of fellow creatures, to be hanged like dogs."[114] Despite the reprieves and pardons that some of them would be granted after this sentencing ceremony was completed, it is clear that hundreds of offenders must have been executed at Tyburn and in front of Newgate when the gallows were moved there in 1783; on several occasions a dozen or more were hanged together.[115] As great as the carnage was in London and its

with the four men who also suffered for the same offense. Three men were hanged at Hindhead, though that was thirty miles from Kingston, where they were tried, and it added considerably to the expense to get them there and to build the gibbet. Others who were thought to be members of a gang in Chertsey were taken there to be executed, as a "good example" to deter others. Severity of this kind was applauded. The sight of fifteen or twenty men and women being executed together on the new machine in front of Newgate was as likely as not to be seen in these years as "indispensably necessary . . . as a means of securing the safety, peace and good order of society," as was said of one such occasion (*G. M.* 55 [1785], pp. 151, 662; QS 2/6, Mids. 1789, 48; HO 13/3, p. 185).

[113] *Report on Criminal Laws* (1819), app. 7.
[114] *G. M.* 56 (1786), p. 990.
[115] *G. M.* 53 (1783), pp. 891, 973–74; 54 (1784), p. 955; 56 (1786), p. 990. The gallows

neighboring counties, high levels of prosecutions and executions were also reported from all over the country. After the Lent assizes in 1784 it was said that there were so many condemned men in so many jails that "were they all to be executed, England would soon be marked among the nations as the *Bloody Country*."[116]

The case for the strictest possible severity in the administration of capital laws as they stood—and against the flexible use of partial verdicts and pardons—was stated once again in this period with force and clarity in a pamphlet that received a good deal of attention. This was Martin Madan's *Thoughts on Executive Justice* (1785), which made with uncompromising logic the familiar argument that certainty of punishment provided the greatest deterrent, and the equally familiar case, made often in earlier moments of crisis, that the discretionary application of the law weakened it. The result of strict application of the law would be harsh for a while, no doubt; but, like others who pursued this line of argument, Madan of course believed that this harshness would diminish serious and violent crime and thus save lives in the end. Criminals were capable of making choices, the argument ran, and when they realized that if they committed an offense and were caught death awaited them with absolute certainty, they would choose not to break the law.

Madan (who was a Surrey magistrate) dedicated his pamphlet to the judges of assize and sent each of them a copy.[117] It is possible, as Romilly later claimed, that its influence accounts for the very large number of offenders hanged in 1785.[118] But that seems unlikely. Pardons had been more difficult to obtain, and the level of executions had been high in the previous two or three years. Madan's pamphlet may have stiffened the

---

were moved from Tyburn to the front of Newgate in December 1783 to eliminate the parade to the scaffold, which had been for so long a part of the festive calendar of the metropolis, and which was being criticized by the eighteenth century—by Mandeville and Henry Fielding, among others—because it allowed some convicts to put on a brave front and die defiantly and thus undermine the terror that the gallows was intended to create. The long journey through the streets of London from Newgate to Tyburn came to seem a positive encouragement to crime rather than a deterrent. Moving the scaffold, according to the *Gentleman's Magazine*, was intended "to strike a serious awe into the hearts of the more obdurate." At the same time, a new type of gallows was to be used, one with a drop, designed to break the prisoner's neck when the platform on which he was standing was removed. By the previous method, which had involved the prisoner's being launched merely by drawing the cart away on which he had been standing with the rope around his neck, death had been by strangulation. Dr. Johnson denounced both the move to Newgate and the new gallows as products of an age "mad after innovation." For the Tyburn procession and the move to Newgate see Radzinowicz, *History*, vol. 1, chap. 6; and for Tyburn generally, Linebaugh, "The Tyburn Riot against the Surgeons," pp. 65–118.

[116] *G. M.* 55 (1785), p. 379.

[117] Radzinowicz, *History*, vol. 1, p. 243, n. 43.

[118] *Memoirs of the Life of Sir Samuel Romilly*, edited by his sons, 3 vols. (1840), vol. 1, p. 89.

judges' resolve and may have encouraged severity in one or two cases. In their actual practice, however, the judges plainly rejected his central argument, as one, Mr. Justice Perryn, rejected it in so many words in his charges on the Home Circuit that year.[119]

The practice of the courts was in any case also given its clearest and most coherent defense in that same year by Archdeacon Paley.[120] Paley was not concerned with the particular circumstances of the mid-1780s, for much of his book was based on lectures he had given in Cambridge between 1768 and 1776.[121] The chapter "Of Crimes and Punishments" shows the influence of Beccaria and Blackstone, whom he no doubt read then. Paley's chapter is a description and a justification of the way the courts administered the law in practice, and since it so clearly reported and explained the system familiar to everyone involved with it, and not only explained it but made it seem humane and wise, his work had a great public success.[122] His central point—which had been made by others in the same period, and which was a better description of present practice than it was sound history—was that parliament had never intended the dozens of capital statutes to be put strictly into effect, but rather had wanted to create a category of offenses that "sweeps into the net every crime, which under any possible circumstances may merit the punishment of death" and that then would be administered with lenity by "the executive magistrate, whose discretion will operate upon those numerous, unforeseen, mutable, and indefinite circumstances, both of the crime and the criminal, which constitute or qualify the malignity of each offence."[123] Paley thought that there were some offenses in the capital category that should not under any circumstances bring an offender to the gallows (picking pockets, for example, as Eden also had suggested), but principally he made the system in being appear to be brilliantly conceived, and he fully justified those who were inclined to carry on as usual.

The value of a flexible and discretionary application of the law was that harsh punishments could be mitigated, sanctions could be tailored to some extent to fit the offense and the offender, and the level of terror, of deterrence, could be adjusted to meet the circumstances of the moment. The judges had required no instruction from Madan to tighten the screw

[119] Sir Richard Perryn, A Charge given to the Grand Jury for the county of Sussex at the Lent Assizes (1785).
[120] William Paley, Principles of Moral and Political Philosophy (1785).
[121] M. L. Clarke, Paley: Evidences for the Man (Toronto, 1974), pp. 14ff.
[122] Radzinowicz, History, vol. 1, pp. 248–59. For the broader significance of Paley's arguments see Douglas Hay, "Property, Authority and the Criminal Law," in Hay, Linebaugh, and Thompson, eds., Albion's Fatal Tree, pp. 25–26.
[123] Paley, Principles, pp. 532–33.

as prosecutions increased after the war; and as prosecutions diminished in the late 1780s and particularly in the years of renewed warfare in the 1790s, the juries and judges (and the king) combined to relax the stern application of the capital laws that had characterized the five years following the American war. The result was that just over five men and women were executed every year on average in Surrey in the period 1788–1802, compared with the more than twelve brought to the gallows between 1783 and 1787 (table III.1). In Sussex, too, though the levels were considerably lower, the postwar years had brought an unusually high level of prosecutions and executions for that county. There was also a substantial decline of prosecutions in the late 1780s and through the 1790s in Sussex and a sharp decline in the level of hangings, until the turn of the new century, when prosecutions for capital offenses rose again (particularly in the years of very high food prices) and there was a brief increase in the number of executions.[124]

At the end of the eighteenth century and into the nineteenth, capital punishment thus continued to fluctuate with the levels of serious offenses— not merely because when more accused were at risk of being hanged more were hanged, but also because (in the face of the more threatening crimes at least) the courts continued to believe that one function of punishment was to provide vivid and terrifying examples of the consequences of breaking the law. So long as that belief remained secure, the capital laws continued to be administered with some concern for the broad effect that executions would have on society at large, and from a conviction that while too much leniency might encourage crime, too many executions might both weaken the law's acceptance and harden further the hearts of those whom exemplary punishments were designed to reach and control.

As Douglas Hay has pointed out, that view of punishment meant that where offenses increased over time (as they did, for example, in London in the second half of the eighteenth century) the tendency was for the level of pardons to increase as a proportion of the whole body of those condemned to death. But the apparent softening of attitudes toward capital punishment that this might suggest at first glance did not in fact result in any diminution of the actual numbers of offenders hanged, since the numbers of

[124] Capital punishment at the Sussex assizes, 1783–1802 (from ASSI 35 [Felony Files] and ASSI 31 [Agenda Books]):

Period	Years	Sentenced	Pardoned	Executed	Executed per Year	Percentage Executed
1783–1787	5	50	21	29	3.0	58.0
1788–1792	5	14	8	6	1.2	42.9
1795–1799	5	25	20	5	1.0	20.0
1800–1802	3	32	23	9	3.0	28.1

prosecutions and convictions was broadly increasing over time. Outside London, the provincial assizes also maintained executions at a roughly stable level over the second half of the century, but because of the different pattern of prosecutions in those courts they did so by maintaining pardons at a roughly stable level too. Hay has demonstrated from the data on capital punishment collected by the parliamentary committee in 1819 that the number of executions remained undiminished in all parts of the country into the second decade of the nineteenth century.[125]

That was clearly the experience of Surrey and Sussex. In Surrey, the number of executions fluctuated over the 140 years we have been dealing with, without establishing a trend in either direction. In figure 10.1 the proportion of offenders sentenced to death who were executed and the actual number of executions are set out by decade. The pattern established follows that of the courts of the metropolis as described by Hay: the proportion of condemned offenders who were hanged and the actual numbers hanged both rose noticeably in the first decades of the eighteenth century; after 1740 the proportion hanged fell away (i.e., the level of pardons rose), but the average number of offenders hanged every year was not diminished. More men were hanged in the 1790s in Surrey than in the 1690s. In Sussex, the numbers hanged were consistently lower than in Surrey, but there too the levels of executions were if anything higher at the end of the eighteenth century than they had been in the middle.[126]

Paley identified the characteristics of an offense and an offender that should determine the selection of men to be hanged as "repetition, cruelty, combination." They should be old offenders who had threatened violence and operated in gangs.[127] These were indeed overwhelmingly the kinds of men hanged in Surrey over the last two decades of the eighteenth century, as they had been earlier. Three-quarters of the men hanged in the county

---

[125] Hay, "Crime, Authority and the Criminal Law," pp. 511–26.

[126] Capital punishment at the Sussex assizes by decades (from ASSI 35 and ASSI 31):

Period	Years	Sentenced	Executed	Executed per Year	Percentage Executed
1750–1759	10	35	19	1.9	54.3
1760–1769	10	26	5	.5	19.2
1770–1779	4	9	2	.5	22.2
1780–1789	10	67	34	3.4	50.8
1790–1799	7	31	5	.7	16.1
1800–1802	3	32	9	3.0	28.1

[127] Sir John Fielding made the same point. "When it is necessary to make public examples by executions," he advised a secretary of state, "wisdom, policy, and humanity dictate that the most abandoned, dangerous, and incorrigible offenders should be pointed out for this melancholy purpose" (*Cal H. O. Papers*, vol. 4, p. 10).

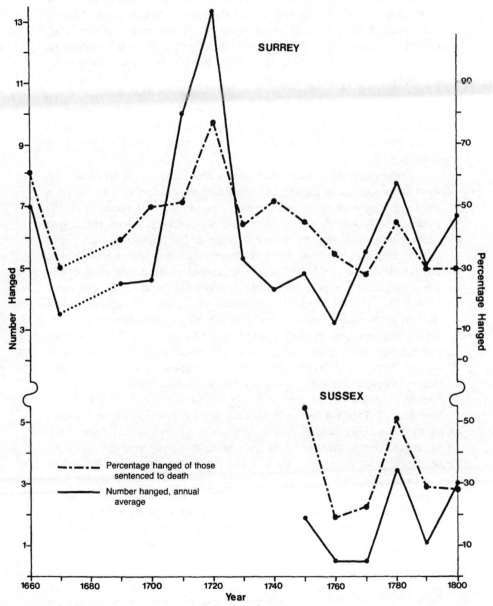

Figure 10.1 Capital Punishment in Surrey.

in 1783–87 had been convicted of either robbery or burglary; and if violent property offenses accounted for fewer of those hanged in the last decade of the century, they were still by far the most common single offenses that brought men (though not women) to the gallows, and the "old" capital property crimes continued to account for two-thirds of the offenders executed in the county (table 10.2).[128] When one adds those hanged for the more trivial property crimes made capital since 1689 (of whom there were a relatively large number in the last decade of the century) crimes against property in general can be seen to have retained at the end of our period the dominant place they had occupied in the lists of those brought to the gallows in Surrey over the entire century and a half we have been dealing with.

Crimes against property did not of course account for all those who were hanged either in the last two decades of the century or over the years since the Restoration, though one could be forgiven for thinking on the evidence of this book (so narrowly have we concentrated on the largest group of offenders) that there were no other capital offenses in eighteenth-century England. A broad range of other crimes had been removed from clergy or had been established by statute as nonclergyable. The most serious offenses against the person—murder, infanticide, rape—had been made capital in the sixteenth and seventeenth centuries; a large number of statutes appointed the death penalty for offenses concerned with counterfeiting the coinage, or clipping and diminishing it; in the eighteenth century especially, numerous statutes were passed as trade and commerce and credit facilities expanded to make the forging of an ever enlarging number of paper instruments capital crimes. Further capital offenses were created to protect other aspects of life and property and the security of the state.[129] This vast array of statutes did not result in large numbers of offenders being hanged. Taken together, they accounted for the death of one convicted offender a year on average in Surrey over the last years of the eighteenth century, about a fifth of the executions carried out in the county. Of the 518 men and women executed in the years we have examined in Surrey between 1663 and 1802, sixteen per cent went to the gallows for an offense other than burglary, robbery, or theft (table 10.9). Just about half of that number had been convicted of murder, and the next largest group were the thirteen men and women condemned for

---

[128] The courts' attitude toward burglary was especially striking in this period. There seem to have been more complaints about breaking and entering even than robbery, and this no doubt explains why the judges and the king were especially severe on men convicted of burglary, more than three-quarters of whom were hanged. For comments on the prevalence of burglary see G. M. 55 (1785), p. 662; HO 42/1, p. 344.

[129] For a survey of the capital statutes in force in the eighteenth century see Radzinowicz, History, vol. 1, app. 1, pp. 611–59.

TABLE 10.9

Capital Punishment in Surrey, 1663–1802

Offense	Men	Women	Total	Percentage of Total Executions
Property offenses	409	27	436	84.2
Murder	37	5	42	8.1
Infanticide	0	4	4	.8
Rape	2	0	2	.4
Arson	1	0	1	.2
Black Act	4	0	4	.8
Coining	12	1	13	2.5
Forgery	5	0	5	1.0
Sodomy	4	0	4	.8
Returning from transportation	5	0	5	1.0
Riot	2	0	2	.4
Total Executions	481	37	518	100.2

SOURCE: Hanged Count.

offenses against the coinage. Five men suffered for forgery and another five for returning from transportation before the expiration of their term; four men were hanged for sodomy and two for rape. Women went to the gallows for fewer offenses than men, for apart from those condemned for crimes against property and one woman executed for coining, only murder and infanticide claimed women victims in the ninety-six years examined.

The significance of the capital code does not reside of course simply in the number of prisoners who suffered death under it. The value and the broad significance of the sanguinary laws as ideology and as a support for the established social and political order has been persuasively argued.[130] As in the case of so many property offenses from which clergy was removed after 1689, the "effectiveness" of a capital statute is not revealed simply by the number of times it resulted in an execution. This has been shown most clearly in the case of what was surely the most notorious capital statute of the century, the Black Act, which added a fearful list of acts often associated with rural protests to the capital category. It was not often invoked (though four men were hanged under it in Surrey for "shooting at" someone), but it added powerfully to the threat that the authorities or a prosecutor could bring against an individual or a group of protesters. It was a weapon that could be brought to bear, as Edward Thompson has

[130] Hay, "Property, Authority and the Criminal Law," pp. 17–63.

said, "where an offence appeared to be especially aggravated, where the state wished to make an example of terror, or where a private prosecutor was particularly vindictive. . . ."[131]

The Black Act did not have to be invoked very often to retain this capacity. The mere incidence of hanging is thus not in itself necessarily very revealing of the usefulness to somebody of a capital statute. It is nonetheless significant that many of the capital statutes on the books rarely resulted in an execution. In Sussex, where many fewer prosecutions took place and many fewer offenders were condemned than in Surrey, murder accounted for a much larger proportion of executions in the second half of the eighteenth century, and other nonproperty offenses occupied an even less prominent place in the list of offenders put to death.[132]

THE RE-ESTABLISHMENT OF TRANSPORTATION

Capital punishment was required in England, Paley had said, because of "a defect in the laws, in not being provided with any other punishment than that of death sufficiently terrible to keep offenders in awe." Like many others, he thought that transportation was inadequate partly because "exile is in reality a slight punishment to those who have neither property, nor friends, nor reputation, nor regular means of subsistence at home," partly because even if the transported convict did feel some pain in his exile "his sufferings are removed from the view of his countrymen" and do not serve as a warning and an admonition to others.[133] These were commonplaces of the late 1760s and the early 1770s, when Paley composed his lectures, but not of 1785 when they were published. By then the attraction of transportation, and the need for transportation, were as powerful as they had ever been, precisely because Paley was right about the way the system of criminal justice worked. Large numbers of men and women who had committed offenses that might have brought them to the gallows were saved by the mitigating powers of the courts and the king. But the relatively smooth functioning of these devices depended on there being an alternative that would at the least punish and incapacitate prisoners who were regarded as serious offenders. When the crisis of numbers came at the end of the American war it was clear that neither the hulks

---

[131] Thompson, *Whigs and Hunters*, p. 247.

[132] In forty-six years examined in Sussex between 1749 and 1802, eighty-eight men and three women were executed. They had been convicted of the following offenses: "old" property crimes, sixty-three (69.2 per cent); "new" property crimes, five (5.5 per cent); homicide, sixteen (17.6 per cent); infanticide, two (2.2 per cent); forgery, one (1.1 per cent); rape, four (4.4 per cent).

[133] Paley, *Principles*, p. 543.

nor hard labor (in the houses of correction or in the penitentiaries that
were yet to be built) provided that alternative. And after losing favor when
America was the destination, transportation emerged again as an attractive
penal option because the need for it was deeply felt. In addition, of course,
some of the terror that had once surrounded a journey across the Atlantic
might be restored if the right depository could be found.

The hulks did not provide a permanent solution. Committees of the
House of Commons in 1778 and 1779 heard evidence of their heavy
mortality rates: something on the order of one in three of all convicts sent
in those years died on board, hardly surprising among men brought from
prisons in which jail fever was endemic and then jammed together, closely
chained, and forced to live in such proximity.[134] There remained always,
too, the problem of security, the fear that this large group of desperate
men (more than five hundred by the end of 1779) would escape and go
on a rampage. Even if they did not escape they would eventually be released
legally, and the prospect of these men returning to society became increasingly alarming to many commentators as prosecutions for serious and
violent offenses mounted in the postwar years. Such men, a witness was
to tell a parliamentary committee in 1785, were "too dangerous to remain
in this country."[135] Nor were the hulks cheap to run. Duncan Campbell
was paid about thirty-eight pounds a year for each prisoner on board his
ships. The government got the benefit of their labor, but it came nowhere
near that figure in value.[136] Besides all that, the hulks were simply not
able to handle the numbers of convicts to be dealt with. Even during the
war they were frequently crowded, despite their being increased in number
and established at Portsmouth and Plymouth as well as in the Thames.[137]
After 1782, when prosecutions and convictions skyrocketed, the inadequacy of the hulks was plain on every ground.

In an effort to ease some of the problems, a House of Commons
committee recommended in 1779 that the minimum term be reduced to
a year and that they be restricted to the more "serious" offenders, those
tried at the assizes. But that same committee also recommended that
transportation be reestablished. Since the usual destinations had been
closed, and since they were assured by Duncan Campbell that no other
North American colony could take many English convicts, the committee
cast about for alternatives and took evidence from merchants and others
with knowledge of various parts of the world. Joseph Banks, who had

[134] *J.H.C.* 36 (1776–78), pp. 926–32; 37 (1778–80), pp. 306–15; Lambert, *Sessional Papers*,
II, vol. 31, pp. 363–91.
[135] *J.H.C.* 40 (1784–85), p. 955; Lambert, *Sessional Papers*, II, vol. 49, p. 20.
[136] Johnson, *English Prison Hulks*, p. 9.
[137] Ibid., pp. 29–31.

been with Captain Cook, made a strong case for establishing a penal colony at Botany Bay in Australia, and a number of witnesses gave evidence about the climate and other conditions along the west coast of Africa. The committee came to no conclusion but recommended that the authority granted by statute for transportation to America be enlarged to include "any other Part of the Globe that may be found expedient." Such authority was granted in 1779.[138]

The question after 1782 was not so much whether transportation as where. The Surrey magistrates returned to sentencing prisoners to periods of transportation as soon as it seemed possible to do so. Eight men were sentenced to periods of three to fourteen years' banishment to Africa in the early months of 1783, but beginning in February the sentence was normally established as transportation to "one of his majesties colonies in America." That remained properly ambivalent, though it seems clear that there was some expectation, even in the administration, that the new United States might return to normalcy in this particular and once again accept England's unwanted convicts. Several attempts were made to land convicts there. While not everyone could have been as out of touch as the king, who saw it as a favor to the Americans ("the permitting them to obtain men unworthy to remain in this Island, I shall certainly consent to"),[139] it was obviously a surprise to many when the Americans refused to resume the old relationship.[140] One shipload was apparently landed in 1783, but the merchant who had arranged it was unsuccessful at a second attempt, and it was clear by the following year that there was going to be little possibility of disposing of any of England's convicts in the new nation in America. Some were sent in small numbers to Nova Scotia, but the remaining British colonies made it clear that they were not willing to accept convicts either, and in any case the population of places like Cape Breton was simply too small to absorb large numbers.[141]

In the meantime, there was confusion in England about how "serious" offenders convicted of simple larcenies or pardoned from a capital sentence should be dealt with. The hulks had been a temporary solution during the war. But in some important ways both the hulks and the new sentence of hard labor in the house of correction had if anything increased the need

---

[138] J.H.C. 37 (1778–80), p. 314; Lambert, Sessional Papers, II, vol. 31, p. 391. A number of convicts sentenced to be transported or pardoned on such a condition before 1787 were sent to Africa and other places on the authority of the 1779 statute (19 Geo III, c. 74).

[139] Sir John Fortescue, ed., Correspondence of George III, 6 vols. (1928), vol. 6, p. 416.

[140] In Surrey, at least two prisoners were sentenced to be transported to America at the assizes in 1784, but by the Summer assizes most sentences of transportation did not include a destination: the Privy Council was given statutory authority to arrange for the convicts' disposal. The magistrates in quarter sessions either did not hear about that or did not care to; they sentenced one man as late as January 1785 to seven years' transportation to America for fraud (QS 3/5/9).

[141] J.H.C. 40 (1784–85), p. 956; Lambert, Sessional Papers, II, vol. 49, p. 22.

for transportation. It was not simply a matter of numbers, important as that was in these postwar years. The anxiety about crime was enlarged by the way that serious offenders were now dealt with and particularly by the inadequacies of imprisonment. Men who had been in the hulks or the prisons were so stigmatized by it that they found it difficult to find work when they were released. They had lost what character they had had and were in greater danger than other offenders of being shut out from society. The notion of there being a group in society whose habits and way of life led them and their children into minor offenses and then into greater crimes had long been recognized. But here was a much more clearly defined and more dangerous group of men who would be let loose after serving their terms of imprisonment, and who would almost certainly turn to robbery and pillage—perhaps even be forced to do so.

The experience of incarceration in the hulks and houses of correction thus in a sense created and identified a group among the disorderly poor as particularly troublesome and dangerous. Of course, some men believed strongly that if only the new penal institutions were properly managed they would both deter offenders and so reform their inmates that they would leave as new men and be able to withstand any temptation to return to their old life, whatever difficulties they might face. But more immediately, there was stronger support for getting rid of such offenders entirely, to Africa if necessary (even though it was clear that that was tantamount to a death sentence), or anywhere else. A Middlesex magistrate, John Bindley, put this point in writing to the Home Office about the current crisis in September 1782:

> It is a common saying, that there is a livelihood to be got honestly if people are inclined to work. I hope it is true with respect to those who have not forfeited their character. But it is false with respect to the pardoned, the discharged whether from gaols or from lighters, and with respect to those who are or were the[ir] associates. Sir Sampson Wright told me lately that he could apprehend dangerous and suspected persons enough, if afterwards any good could be made of them.
>
> I wish therefore to submit it to your consideration whether some spot of this globe at present uninhabited and uncultivated might not be found, for the reception of those whose crimes and misconduct have made it impossible to earn their bread upon these islands.[142]

Sampson Wright, the Bow Street magistrate mentioned by Bindley, had been engaged with this question himself, and in the previous months

[142] HO 42/1, f. 334.

had been in correspondence with the Home Office about the government's authority under the Penitentiary Act to transport some of the prisoners then serving a term on the hulks to "places beyond the seas." He was unsure, he said, about the legality of that, "but this I will venture to affirm that the public will be happy to get rid of them at any rate." Failing that, he thought it would be "a very easy matter" to get such men taken on board ships at their discharge to prevent them from "mixing with the community."[143]

The argument for transportation was very strong, the pressure intense. After some years in which the courts had not passed such sentences they began to do so again in 1783, as we have seen, naming such destinations as Africa or "his majesty's colonies in America," without having any assurance that they would be carried out. In the following year their authority to do so was confirmed in a statute that re-established transportation as a punishment available to the courts. The destination was to be left to the king in council to decide; and in the meantime the prisoners under such orders could be moved to the hulks to serve there the time established in their sentences, or until some place could be found to send them.[144]

The Surrey assizes as well as quarter sessions began to sentence to transportation, and once again pardons were granted to some convicted capital offenders on that condition. Over the next five years some 112 men and women were ordered transported by the courts—more than a quarter of the noncapital sentences at both the assizes and quarter sessions (table 10.10)—and another thirty-four as a condition of pardon. It is not entirely clear how many of the men involved were actually sent to the hulks, but at least a dozen or so of the forty ordered transported at the assizes in the two years after the Act was passed were sent to the prison ships (according to the assize calendar), which brought some relief to the press of bodies in the county jail and houses of correction.

That problem of crowded prisons was being felt all over the country by 1784 and 1785, not merely in London and the counties of the Home Circuit. The government was clearly under a great deal of pressure to help local benches dispose especially of the more serious prisoners. A Lancashire magistrate told a Commons committee in 1785 that the quarter sessions there had been sentencing convicted prisoners who would earlier have been transported to terms of imprisonment, and that the consequence was serious overcrowding in the county jail and the houses of correction. This was problem enough, but it is clear that it was in addition an important

[143] Ibid., f. 290.
[144] 24 Geo III, c. 56 (1784).

TABLE 10.10

Noncapital Punishment for Property Offenses at the Surrey
Assizes and Quarter Sessions, 1783–1802

Court and Period	Clergy/ Discharge %	Transportation %	Imprisonment %	Imprisonment with Whipping %	Hulks %	Whipping %	Other %	Number of Sentences
1783–1787								
Assizes	1.8	31.0	35.7	20.8	8.3	1.8	.6	168
Quarter sessions	0	25.5	11.9	23.4	0	38.3	.9	235
1788–1798								
Assizes	.4	46.9	40.2	3.2	0	3.9	5.6	286
Quarter sessions	0	24.1	37.2	13.3	0	23.1	2.2	580
1799–1802								
Assizes	0	41.0	52.5	1.4	0	4.3	.7	139
Quarter sessions	0	21.4	62.2	12.9	0	3.4	0	294
1783–1802								
Both courts	.2	29.7	39.7	12.7	.8	14.9	1.9	1,702

SOURCES: Sample and Court.

consideration that these prisoners were being maintained out of county rates at great expense and that they brought little in return, for, "being closely ironed," they could not work.[145] Requests for help poured into the Home Office from around the country. In a typical letter the sheriff of Shropshire told a familiar story of the county jail being full, in part because they were still holding convicts sentenced to transportation as long as two years before. The prisoners, he said, were becoming desperate in their cramped and crowded conditions, and some had escaped. The county had agreed to build a new jail, but in the meantime he wanted the government to remove the transports and do something with them.[146]

The government's response was the Act of 1784 that allowed convicts under sentence of transportation to be sent to the hulks. They also remitted some sentences and granted some free pardons. And for other more serious offenders they tried to make more room available on the prison ships. The Treasury agreed to pay Duncan Campbell to establish another vessel in the Thames in January 1783. A year later, having received "representations from the several Counties" about their crowded jails, the Home Secretary contracted with Campbell for two hundred more places. Within a few months another ship was moored in the Thames, and in 1785 another was established in Portsmouth harbor.[147]

This might have relieved the problem for some benches (though how equally they had access to the hulks is unclear). But it did not touch the long-term problem; indeed, as we have seen, some men perceived that putting convicts into the hulks or the houses of correction and jails made more intractable the difficulty of absorbing them back into society. And it was the accumulation of dangerous offenders that finally pushed the government to act more decisively to find a place to which convicts might actually be transported. As had been the case in the past, it was perhaps pressure from the City of London that focused the administration's attention on the problem. Early in 1786 the mayor and aldermen of the city presented the king a petition in which they pointed to the "rapid and alarming increase of crimes and depredations in this city and its neighbourhood, especially within the last three years," and the greatly extended sessions at the Old Bailey that had resulted. What particularly concerned them were the problems caused by the ending of transportation. Crimes having increased and "few opportunities [having been] found by the Government of sending convicts abroad—and these only in small numbers," they concluded

[145] J.H.C. 40 (1784–85), p. 954; Lambert, *Sessional Papers*, II, vol. 49, p. 28.
[146] HO 2/6, f. 245.
[147] HO 13/3, pp. 118, 262.

that it necessarily follows that after making an allowance for the small number sent abroad, and for the convicts who may have died during that period, there must now remain within the kingdom, either at large or in the different prisons, at least four thousand persons who, in the judgement of the law, were proper to have been sent out of it.

That your petitioners humbly conceive that this dreadful accumulation alone is sufficient to account for all the evils that are so heartily felt and so justly complained of, both as to the overcrowded state of the gaols and the increase of crimes and of offenders.

To what extent the mischiefs that are so severely felt already, and the fatal consequences so justly apprehended, may be carried by a longer continuance of so rapid and alarming an accumulation of convicts within the kingdom, no human wisdom can foresee. . . . [148]

It seems likely that it was the argument of both short- and long-term necessity—and the pressure from as influential a source as this—that pushed the government to act to find a place to which a large number of convicts might be sent. The story of that search has recently been told in detail. The evidence about Africa was discouraging, and the government's consideration of Canada and the West Indies in 1786 gave no firm promise of a satisfactory solution from those directions, any more than did the numerous schemes suggested by correspondents in the newspapers and magazines, ranging from the purchase of Greenland to the creation of a convict colony on Tristan da Cunha, to the employment of prisoners in the herring fishery or coal mines or lead mines.

In the end, and despite serious objections, the cabinet agreed in August 1786 that a colony should be founded at Botany Bay in New South Wales for the reception of England's transported convicts. The decision was condemned by some as "wild and extravagant" because of the hazards of the journey and the considerable costs involved in taking men half way around the world. Others objected because such a colony promised few commercial benefits for England. But the need to dispose of hundreds of men and women whose release from the jails and hulks of England was contemplated by nobody with equanimity overcame all objections and difficulties, including the heavy costs to the Treasury. The first fleet sailed in the early months of 1787. Perhaps there was some hope in the administration that those ships carried with them the promise of

[148] Quoted by Margaret Weidenhofer, *The Convict Years: Transportation and the Penal System, 1788–1868* (Melbourne, 1973), p. 21.

enhanced British naval supremacy. What mainly delighted magistrates and judges and no doubt large numbers of people who feared for their safety and for their property was that they carried almost a thousand dangerous prisoners. Getting rid of people who had put themselves outside the bounds of society had always been the main argument for transportation: it continued to be so in the 1780s, and indeed transportation was thought for that reason to be more necessary than ever.[149]

Transportation emerged once more as the most important noncapital punishment available to the courts. It was immediately welcomed in practice. The first several fleets cleared some of the backlog of men and women in the hulks and jails who had been originally sentenced to transportation, without regard for the length of time they had already served. Twenty men and eight women from Surrey sailed in the first fleet to Australia. Most had been convicted in 1784 and 1785, though one man had been in jail since 1782 and could reasonably have expected to have been freed in a little over a year when he was marched off to the ship.[150] But little thought was given to niceties of that kind. If prisoners had been condemned to transportation and were still in jail or the hulks they were likely to be sent.[151]

With the backlog reduced and the convict settlement firmly established, the courts sentenced offenders to transportation even more readily after 1787. In the years 1788–1802, for example, about a third of the men convicted of noncapital offenses in Surrey were ordered to be sent to Australia. A similar proportion of offenders were transported from the Sussex courts between 1795 and 1802.[152] Banishment for a term of years also emerged again as the most common condition of a pardon from capital punishment. Direct sentences to the hulks virtually ceased when the convict colony was opened, although convicts awaiting transportation were

[149] Shaw, *Convicts and the Colonies*, pp. 44–57. The reasons for the re-establishment of transportation and the choice of Botany Bay as the destination have been the subject of recent debate. The view that the motive was mainly penal has been challenged, for example, by Alan Frost, *Convicts and Empire: A Naval Question, 1776–1811* (Melbourne, 1980), who argues that the decision to colonize Australia was taken to establish a naval port in the East as one aspect of a larger naval and imperial policy developed by the Pitt administration in the mid-1780s. That has been effectively answered by Mollie Gillen, "The Botany Bay Decision, 1786: Convicts, Not Empire," *English Historical Review* 97 (1982), pp. 740–66, who provides a guide to other contributions to the recent debate about the origins of Australia and reaffirms the view that the disposal of convicts was the primary motive and that "Botany Bay was chosen because all other destinations considered suitable for the felons had been closed or discarded" (p. 766).

[150] John Cobley, *The Crimes of the First Fleet Convicts* (Sydney, 1970), passim.

[151] The backlog was cleared over several years in Surrey. At least three men convicted before 1787 were sent in July 1789, and the fleet that sailed in the following December included twenty-seven others, some convicted as early as 1783 (HO 11/1, pp. 23ff.).

[152] In 1795–1802, for example, 184 noncapital sentences were handed down in the Sussex courts for property offenses. Of those, 53 (28.8 per cent) were for transportation to Australia.

still sent there.[153] The re-establishment of transportation also provided the courts with what must have been a welcome option in the case of the few women convicted of serious offenses or pardoned from a capital conviction, for the hulks had always seemed an inappropriate place to send women. In the last decade of the century twenty per cent of women convicted of property offenses in Surrey were also ordered to be transported; they too were kept at hard labor, though in houses of correction, while waiting to be shipped to New South Wales.[154]

IMPRISONMENT AT THE END OF THE EIGHTEENTH CENTURY

The importance of transportation may be measured in the fact that more than a quarter of the men and women convicted of noncapital property crimes at the Surrey and Sussex quarter sessions and assizes in the last decade of the eighteenth century were sent to Australia. It was particularly valued as a means of diverting those thought to be the most threatening offenders. But transportation to Australia never came to account for as large a proportion of convicted offenders as had been sent to America at the height of transportation to Maryland and Virginia. This was partly a matter of the costs involved in sending convicts across the world to a colony that had to be supported and maintained. It was also a matter of the sheer number of convicts to be dealt with as the population of England increased. The population of Surrey more than doubled in the second half of the eighteenth century, for example; the Borough of Southwark and its neighboring urban parishes included more than 175,000 people by 1800. The growing numbers of men and women being convicted of theft in this period, and particularly in the first half of the nineteenth century, simply could not have been sent to Australia as they might at an earlier time have been sent to America. For the vast numbers of noncapital offenders the sanction of imprisonment remained essential, even as the ships were carrying off hundreds of prisoners regularly to Australia. By the 1790s incarceration was the common punishment for offenses against property that did not involve some particularly heinous aggravation, and imprisonment under the right conditions carried the hopes of many for a punishment that would not only penalize the offender and deter him and others but also reform and rehabilitate him in such a way as to make possible his return to society and to honest employment.

[153] Colquhoun, *Police of the Metropolis*, pp. 328–29. The man who remembered a generation later that "the system of the hulks was found so entirely to have failed, that the judges avoided as much as possible sending any prisoners there" was certainly right as far as the Surrey courts were concerned (*Report on Criminal Laws* [1819], p. 33).
[154] See, for example, the sessions roll for Ep. 1801 (QS 2/7).

Certainly the need for an effort to "reform" the manners of the poor was even more intensely felt over the last two decades of the century than ever before. There was an anxious and urgent concern about the health and stability of the social order in the wake of the postwar violence in the mid-1780s and the shocking reliance on the gallows all over the country. The rapid escalation of payments under the poor law was further evidence of fundamental problems in society.[155] The most common explanation of immoral criminal behavior continued in the late eighteenth century to reflect views that had long been persuasive and that located the main fault in the habits of life of the poor. The urge to reform their "manners" had not arisen merely from a desire to preserve social order, but there is no doubt that it was evidence of disorder, of immorality, and particularly of crime that focused attention over several generations on the personal and social consequences of sabbath-breaking and drunkenness and the other vices that blinded men to their duty.

The war on immorality had proceeded in phases over the century. It had not continued into the second quarter of the eighteenth century at the level of intensity reached in the 1690s, but nor had it disappeared entirely. Zealous individuals and small groups of men continued through the middle decades of the century to bring prosecutions under the statutes, and when the campaign against immorality was resumed on a large scale in the 1780s in the wake of the American war, it was a broadened and more intense phase of a struggle that had never entirely ceased. It was both broadened and more intense in part because of the renewed engagement and passionate concern of groups of men whose primary motivations were religious, especially from among the enlarging congregations of Dissenters and perhaps most importantly among Evangelicals in the Church of England. By the 1780s another powerful movement of such opinion was again organizing to root out vice, to suppress crime and disorder, and to purify literature. As in earlier campaigns in the reigns of William and Anne to which many leaders like William Wilberforce consciously looked for guidance, these forces were galvanized and legitimized by a royal proclamation calling on the authorities to put the laws against vice into effect. The so-called Proclamation Society (otherwise the Society for the Suppression of Vice and Prophaneness), founded in 1787 by Wilberforce, focused the efforts of the late eighteenth century as the Societies for the Reformation of Manners had done on the earlier occasion.[156]

Whether the inspiration of those who offered solutions to the social

[155] E. J. Hobsbawm and George Rudé, *Captain Swing* (1969), chap. 2.

[156] G.F.A. Best, *Temporal Pillars: Queen Anne's Bounty, the Ecclesiastical Commissioners, and the Church of England* (Cambridge, 1964), chap. 4; Radzinowicz, *History*, vol. 3, pt. 3. For the attack on aspects of popular culture by this "reformist" movement see Robert Malcolmson, *Popular Recreations in English Society, 1700–1850* (Cambridge, 1973), chap. 7.

problems of the late eighteenth century derived from broadly secular concerns or from a more immediately religious argument, they all tended to see such problems in moral terms.[157] What was by then a very old cause continued to provide common ground: what one man called in 1784 "the only radical cure . . . A REFORMATION OF MANNERS."[158] The central strand of the Yorkshire magistrate Henry Zouch's explanation of why poverty and crime were increasing so rapidly emphasized the evil effects of the customs and culture of the poor.[159] On all sides, small groups of magistrates, acting from those same convictions, mobilized constables and the rest of the machinery of local control to bring prosecutions against unlicensed alehouses and against men conducting business unlawfully on Sundays, against drunkenness and other debilitating habits. A group of Surrey magistrates announced the beginning of such a campaign in a proclamation issued in 1787.[160] Little of this was new in its essentials, although the concern and the campaign seems clearly to have been more widespread, more broadly based than ever before.

One indication of this wider base lies in the character and the success of the Sunday Schools that were being founded in such numbers by the mid-1780s to teach the children of the poor to read the Bible and to educate them in the religious principles they were so clearly not acquiring at home.[161] Sunday Schools were not simply crude instruments of social control, but many of their supporters, certainly of their publicists, shared a fundamental belief that social order and harmony could only rest securely on a religious foundation; and the connection between the work of the

[157] Best, *Temporal Pillars*, pp. 143–45.

[158] *G. M.* 54 (1784), pp. 18–20.

[159] Henry Zouch, *Hints Respecting Public Police* (1786), pp. 4–7. For Zouch, the clerical chairman of the West Riding quarter sessions and a powerful influence in the antivice campaign of the 1780s, see Webb and Webb, *The Parish and the County*, pp. 356–57.

[160] William Man Godschall, *A General Plan of Parochial and Provincial Police* (1787).

[161] Such schools recreated and reflected the strong impulse in the late seventeenth-century charity schools to rescue children, especially of the urban poor, and to shore up the foundation of social order by a religious education that would save their souls and at the same time provide a means for the regeneration of society. It was an impulse that had not entirely died out, for Sunday Schools were being founded in the 1750s and 1760s. But there is no doubt that they multiplied rapidly in the years after the American war, when Wesley said (in 1784) that he found "these schools springing up wherever I go," and a national Sunday School Society was formed (1785) as a philanthropic stimulus to their growth, to provide advice and encouragement to local groups and individuals who wanted to begin to teach the children of the poor on Sundays. The pace of growth and the geographical distribution of the schools is not entirely clear before the nineteenth century (and the reasons for both are surely very complex), though it can at least be said that they flourished mainly outside the capital and were perhaps especially strong in the Midlands and the industrializing north. On this subject see Thomas Walter Laqueur, *Religion and Respectability: Sunday Schools and Working Class Culture, 1780–1850* (New Haven, 1976), chap. 2.

Sunday Schools and other institutions in society working for the suppression of vice, disorder, and crime was frequently made. "If these institutions should become established throughout the kingdom," Henry Zouch concluded in 1786, "there is good reason to hope, that they will produce an happy change in the general morals of the people, and thereby render the execution of criminal justice less frequently necessary."[162]

The increasing emphasis in the 1770s and especially in the 1780s on religious means to reform was reflected also in penal thought. Both Howard and Hanway wanted prisons that would have mainly encouraged penitence and a religious awakening in the prisoners, and both favored a regime of separation and solitude that was to some extent in conflict with another pattern of management that aimed primarily at the reformation of prisoners through labor, instilling habits of work that would encourage and enable them to earn their living on their release. Despite Howard's influence, the Penitentiary Act put the greatest reformative emphasis on labor, as did some of the local institutions constructed under its influence in the 1780s. But there was also then a reassertion of emphasis on solitary confinement and religious instruction and on spiritual training over the discipline of labor. The system introduced into the Gloucestershire county jail by Sir George Paul in 1791 aimed to create such a regime.[163] In Sussex, the county jail had been rebuilt as early as 1775 on a cellular plan inspired by Howard's recommendations and pushed through by the interest and the immense influence of the duke of Richmond.[164]

There were no such massive changes in the prisons of Surrey in the 1770s and 1780s. But in Surrey, as in Sussex and elsewhere, there were significant alterations in the patterns of sentences, and a period of incarceration became the most common penalty imposed on prisoners convicted of property offenses over the last two decades of the century (table 10.10). And the magistrates in Surrey were not entirely indifferent to the injunction in the Penitentiary Act of 1779, and in subsequent legislation in 1782 and 1784 that the new carceral discipline be imposed on offenders sentenced to hard labor in the bridewells and that they be subjected to work "of the hardest and most servile kind, in which drudgery is chiefly required."[165] In 1785 they ordered the keeper of the Southwark house of correction to

---

[162] Zouch, *Hints Respecting Public Police*, p. 23. For similar comments see *G. M.* 54 (1784), p. 177; and see also M. W. Flinn, "Social Theory and the Industrial Revolution," in Tom Burns and S. B. Saul, eds., *Social Theory and Economic Change* (1967), p. 15.

[163] Henriques, "The Rise and Decline of the Separate System of Prison Discipline," pp. 68–69; Moir, "Sir George Onesiphorus Paul," pp. 195–225; Evans, *Fabrication of Virtue*, chap. 4; Ignatieff, *A Just Measure of Pain*, pp. 93–113; McConville, *English Prison Administration*, chaps. 4–5.

[164] Evans, *Fabrication of Virtue*, p. 132.

[165] The statute of 1782 (22 Geo III, c. 64) provided a set of "rules, orders, and regulations to be observed and enforced" in the houses of correction.

acquire large quantities of sand and gravel that his prisoners might move around from one part of the prison to another—the idea having come presumably from the work being done by the men on the hulks, though that work had some point to it. The keeper had complained that he had difficulty finding work for the inmates to do, in particular because he could not get a sufficient supply of hemp to keep them busy. This make-work would not only require their physical labor but would eminently conform to another requirement of the Penitentiary Act, that prisoners be given materials that were "little liable to be spoiled by ignorance, neglect, or obstinacy."

The magistrates also moved in a more fundamental way in the last decade of the century to embrace the new views of imprisonment by building a new county jail at Newington, replacing the old building in Southwark with a prison in which prisoners could be more effectively classified and separated, in which some forms of solitary confinement might be imposed, and in which hard labor would be a central element of discipline. A variety of improvements had been made in the old jail in the 1780s (improvements in the arrangements for housing sick prisoners, for example), and a committee of magistrates was clearly by then paying more attention to the internal management of the jail and the condition of the prisoners than would have been the case earlier in the century.[166] By 1790 the quarter sessions accepted that there was a need for a new building (and a new sessions house to go with it), and an Act of Parliament was procured to authorize the building of a new jail in Newington.[167] Before this new jail was opened in the last years of the century a committee of magistrates drew up the rules and orders under which it would function.[168] The prisoners were to be brought together during the day to work, though kept apart even then "as far as the nature of the employment will admit." And at night they were each to have a separate cell and be held "as far as possible, in solitary confinement." It was the magistrates' hope that the prison labor would return a profit. When that proved in the first year to be impossible, it was nonetheless commended by another committee of magistrates, "upon the broad scale of public utility," because it would bring the convicts "into habits of honest industry, which, when they regain their liberty, it is hoped they will pursue, and thereby retrieve their Character by supporting themselves and families with comfort and respect."[169]

---

[166] QS 2/6, Ea. 1785, 26, 29; Ea. 1787, 3.

[167] 31 Geo III, c. 22: "An Act for building a new Common Gaol and Sessions House . . . for the County of Surrey" (1791). The Account Books and Minute Books of the magistrates' committee that oversaw the building of the new jail are at QS 5/4/1–3.

[168] QS 2/6, Mids. 1798, 7a–c.

[169] QS 2/6, Mids. 1799, 39.

TABLE 10.11

Imprisonment for Property Offenses at the Surrey Assizes and Quarter Sessions, 1783–1802

Court	House of Correction %	Jail %	House of Correction with Whipping %	Jail with Whipping %	Number of Sentences
Assizes	70.8	13.2	12.5	3.5	288
Quarter sessions	34.2	37.4	12.9	15.6	597

SOURCES: Sample and Count.

By the end of the century one of the sharp differences between the county jail and the houses of correction had thus been removed—at least on paper—and sentences of hard labor could be served in either institution. Indeed, the Southwark house of correction was absorbed into the new prison at Newington, and the old building sold.[170] Not surprisingly, sentences at the quarter sessions began to reflect the magistrates' conversion to the new discipline. Until the end of the century the Surrey magistrates had not only consistently ordered much briefer terms of imprisonment than the assize judges (a reflection in part of the fact that the more minor offenders came before the quarter sessions), but they had also been much more likely to send prisoners to the old county jail and order that they be whipped in the course of their imprisonment. The assize judges, on the other hand, were much more likely to send prisoners to one of the three houses of correction in the county to serve at hard labor.

Such differences in sentencing between the judges of the assize courts and the magistrates at quarter sessions had emerged when imprisonment developed in the 1760s and during the American war, and they continued into the last two decades of the century (tables 10.11, 10.12). But when the new Surrey jail was opened, the magistrates almost matched the level of hard labor sentences imposed by the assize courts: in 1800–02 they sent almost twenty per cent of the offenders they imprisoned to the new county jail under that order, and another forty-six per cent to the houses of correction. In common with the assize judges, they also began to impose longer terms of incarceration than had been usual earlier. By the beginning of the nineteenth century fully seventy per cent of the prisoners incarcerated by the Surrey courts were being ordered to serve at hard labor, and many were being sent for as long as two or three years. The average term of imprisonment rose to about four and a half months at the quarter sessions and close to a year at the assizes (table 10.13).

[170] QS 2/6, Ep. 1800, 78; Mids. 1800, 17; Ep. 1801, 94.

TABLE 10.12

Imprisonment for Property Offenses in Surrey, 1783–1794: Length of Sentences

	Quarter Sessions	*Assizes*
HOUSE OF CORRECTION AT HARD LABOR		
Under six months	111	76
Six to nine months	15	72
One to two years	4	54
Range	1 wk.–1 yr.	1 mo.–2 yrs.
Average	2.3 mos.	8.4 mos.
JAIL		
Under six months	110	21
Six to nine months	9	0
One to two years	10	0
Range	1 wk.–1 yr.	2 wks.–9 mos.
Average	2.8 mos.	2.9 mos.
AVERAGE TERM	2.5 mos.	7.5 mos.

SOURCES: Sample and Count.

In Sussex, imprisonment had come to play as large a role in noncapital punishment as it had in Surrey, but the distinctly less serious nature of property crime in Sussex made for some significant differences in the patterns of sentences imposed by the courts in that county. It is particularly striking, for example, that a large proportion of noncapital property cases were dealt with at the quarter sessions. It would seem that only the worst cases were reserved for the assize judges, and that is presumably why in the years 1795–1802 only ten convicted offenders were sentenced at the assizes to a term of imprisonment, as against thirty-three ordered for transportation. At the same time, the magistrates sentenced 141 men and women convicted of property crimes at the quarter sessions, the overwhelming majority of whom (eighty-four per cent) they sent to a term of imprisonment. As in Surrey, the judges favored longer prison terms for the handful of offenders they sentenced than did the magistrates, and they favored sentences to the houses of correction at hard labor.[171]

[171] There was also some difference in the patterns of sentencing at the East and West Sussex quarter sessions. In West Sussex, the bench was more inclined than were the justices in East Sussex to order imprisonment in the house of correction with a whipping. Seventy per cent of the imprisonment sentences ordered between 1795 and 1802 in West Sussex took that form, whereas in the eastern part of the county only thirty-seven per cent did so. In East Sussex twenty-one per cent of imprisoned offenders were sent to a house of correction at hard labor and the remaining forty-two per cent were described simply as being "committed." The East Sussex

TABLE 10.13

Imprisonment for Property Offenses in Surrey, 1800–1802: Length of Sentences

	Quarter Sessions	Assizes
HOUSE OF CORRECTION AT HARD LABOR		
Number	88	51
Range	1 wk.–3 yrs.	6–24 mos.
Average	6.0 mos.	12.3 mos.
JAIL		
Number	35	8
Range	1 day–1 yr.	1–12 mos.
Average	3.1 mos.	4.4 mos.
JAIL AT HARD LABOR		
Number	35	0
Range	1 wk.–2 yrs.	
Average	3.5 mos.	
HOUSE OF CORRECTION WITH WHIPPING		
Number	14	0
Range	1–6 mos.	
Average	2.5 mos.	
JAIL WITH WHIPPING		
Number	20	0
Range	1 wk.–6 mos.	
Average	1.8 mos.	
AVERAGE TERM	4.6 mos.	11.2 mos.

SOURCES: Sample and Count.

The great advantage of imprisonment, its proponents had argued, was that it allowed fine gradations of punishment to be assigned to each offense and offender. That was an advantage that magistrates and judges welcomed in dealing with offenses other than the property crimes we have been so concerned with, particularly offenses against the person. The apparent desire to punish some offenses of that kind more seriously appears to have been encouraged by the increasing availability of a punishment

magistrates also favored longer hard labor sentences: none in West Sussex in these years was for more than six months, while several offenders in East Sussex were incarcerated for as long as three years. On the other hand, other sentences—not imposing hard labor—were longer in West Sussex, and the average term of imprisonment (3.6 months) was the same in both parts of the county.

that allowed distinctions to be drawn among degrees of culpability. In the case of manslaughter, for example, the finding by a jury in a homicide that the victim's death came by way of accident led most often to a clergyable discharge until the 1780s. In the last two decades of the century the courts were more inclined to punish such offenders by a term of imprisonment, especially in cases in which their recklessness or imprudence had caused the accident. This is perhaps an aspect of a shift in attitudes toward violent behavior, but that shift was more easily registered in the courts by the increasing acceptance of a form of punishment that allowed judges to make a reasonably precise calculation of the penalty to be paid for a particular form of irresponsibility.

Precisely the same enlargements of punishment can be observed with regard to the range of acts prosecuted as assault or assault and battery. During the century after the Restoration convictions for assault invariably brought a fine, and often a minimal fine that was as much a recognition of the conclusion of a personal conflict as a sanction imposed by the State on a man who had broken its laws. Not all assault cases had this character, as we have seen, and not all fines were mere tokens. Some were large enough to hurt all but the reasonably affluent, though crippling fines were not common in ordinary assault cases. Two trends in the punishment of assault are noticeable in the second half of the eighteenth century. One is that fines tended to get larger.[172] The second is that the courts were increasingly willing to order a term in jail as a punishment in cases in which the violence charged was real enough. There are a few examples of imprisonment in the 1740s, but such orders began in a serious way in the third quarter of the century, and by the last two decades seventeen per cent of those convicted of assault in the Surrey courts were sentenced to a term in jail or the house of correction. In addition, a handful of prisoners were sentenced to transportation and at least two men were sent to the hulks for particularly vicious attacks. Such sentences surely derive from a deepening conviction that public violence was harmful to society, that it was more than merely a private matter, especially perhaps when an incident threatened to create a disturbance and undermine public order. It seems reasonable to think that behind these sentences there lies an urge for a more disciplined society and a persuasion that violent behavior ought

---

[172] At the Surrey quarter sessions in 1795–98, for example, seventy-six fines were imposed in sentences for assault. As had been the case a hundred years earlier, most were modest. In forty-five per cent of the cases the fine was a shilling. But in the 1790s a significant number were substantially larger than the court had imposed in the late seventeenth century, when only a fifth of the fines for assault convictions were five shillings or more. In 1795–98 forty-five per cent were over that amount, and twenty-nine per cent were two pounds or more (QS 3/5/10, pp. 224–411).

to be prevented. But as in the case of manslaughter, the availability of a punishment that was capable of infinite gradations allowed the desire to impose more serious sanctions in assault cases to develop in practice.

SENTENCING DECISIONS

Magistrates and judges could call upon a wide range of noncapital penalties in the late eighteenth century. They could order transportation, imprisonment, imprisonment at hard labor (under which the prisoner was meant to be subjected to a particular regime that included classification and isolation), or corporal punishment in association with a term in jail or followed by immediate discharge. In a few cases in the last decades of the century judges were fining felons, a development that might well have been encouraged by the substitution of a fine (usually a shilling) for the branding of clergy in 1779. The range of punishments was further extended, particularly during wars, by the forced recruitment of men for the army or navy by means of sentences that offered service in the forces as an alternative to a term in prison.[173] The flexibility that this widened range of secondary punishment provided may be seen in other conditions imposed on prisoners, forcing some to return to their masters in exchange for an abbreviated term of imprisonment, in some cases of days or even hours.

The patterns of punishments imposed in the Surrey courts in the last two decades of the eighteenth century suggest that the magistrates and judges took their sentencing duties seriously, that they believed it made some difference what penalty they chose for particular prisoners. Not uncommonly two prisoners convicted together for the same offense at the assizes were punished in different ways: in a case of larceny at the Lent assizes in 1783, for example, one man was sentenced to the house of correction at Kingston for two years, another convicted with him for the same offense, to the house of correction at Southwark for one year. Similarly prisoners convicted of what appear to have been virtually identical offenses were given quite different sentences, varying in the duration of imprisonment, the institution it was to be served in, the addition or not of corporal punishment. At the Summer assizes of 1785, to take that simply by way of illustration, of eleven men convicted of simple larceny five were ordered to be transported, one was fined and discharged, one was granted

---

[173] For pardons from imprisonment upon condition of serving in the forces see, for example, SP 37/15, f. 590; SP 44/92, p. 488; ASSI 31/12, p. 166. In the last two decades of the eighteenth century a number of young men convicted at the Surrey and Sussex quarter sessions were offered the choice at the sentencing stage of joining the forces as an alternative to several months in jail.

a clergied discharge, one was sent to the hulks for two years, and three were fined and sent to the house of correction to hard labor, one for a year, two for six months, though one was also ordered to be publicly whipped. The same apparent care in sentencing is evident at the quarter sessions. At the Epiphany sessions in 1795 nine different sentences were pronounced against eleven men and women convicted of simple larceny; at another session five years later twenty-seven prisoners were sentenced in ways that produced fifteen slightly different judgments.[174] In selecting from the range of punishments available to the courts the magistrates at one session of the court or a judge at one assize session could easily produce a pattern of sentences very different indeed from that of the immediately preceding and following meetings of the courts.

Without having more than the indictment and the session calendar to go on, without knowing what kind of character witnesses prisoners were able to bring forward and what impression they themselves made on the judges, it is impossible to discover why particular sentences were ordered and to explain the variety of sentences pronounced. It is a fair presumption that much depended on such considerations: whether the prisoner was thought to be an old offender, for example, or whether he had an employer willing to take him back, and so on. The nature of the offense was also undoubtedly of crucial importance, and the decision to transport a man or woman or to send them to hard labor (and for how long) would most likely have been determined by the impressions gained by the bench during the trial of the prisoner and of the offense charged, supplemented undoubtedly in some cases by information supplied by magistrates and other men whose opinions counted.

Given the courts' interest in the character of the offender, it is not surprising that the sex and age of the prisoner made some difference to the sentences pronounced. Men and women convicted of property offenses were treated rather differently by the Surrey courts over the last two decades of the century, though the differences were narrowing by 1800. The problems with transportation before the opening of the Australian penal colony introduced a certain distortion into the courts' treatment of women because they could not be sent to the hulks. This seems likely to explain why a much smaller proportion of women than men were sentenced to be transported in the five years between the end of the American war and the establishment of Botany Bay, though even after 1788, when the courts were less inhibited, women were transported at a lower rate than men because their offenses were on the whole less serious (table 10.14). Men

---

[174] Based on the sessions rolls for Ep. 1795 and Ep. 1800, and the summaries in the Process Book (QS 3/5/10, pp. 224–31, 350–61).

TABLE 10.14

Noncapital Punishments for Property Offenses in Surrey, 1783–1802

| Period | Transportation % | Imprisonment | | Imprisonment with Whipping | | Whipping % | Hulks % | Other % | Number of Sentences |
		H.C. %	Jail %	H.C. %	Jail %				
MEN									
1783–1787	30.5	15.0	2.5	18.2	3.5	24.9	4.1	1.8	341
1788–1798	34.0	17.6	16.1	5.0	4.8	18.6	0	3.9	715
1799–1802	29.9	34.9	19.6	2.5	8.7	3.9	0	.6	358
WOMEN									
1783–1787	13.1	44.3	3.2	26.2	0	13.1	0	0	61
1788–1798	22.3	43.9	14.2	5.4	5.4	7.4	0	1.4	148
1799–1802	17.1	42.7	35.4	0	1.2	2.4	0	1.2	82

SOURCES: Sample and Count.

were more likely to be transported and also more likely to be whipped— and certainly to be simply whipped and discharged. Women, on the other hand, were much more likely than men to be sent to the house of correction to serve a term of hard labor until the end of the century, when the Surrey magistrates became persuaded with the opening of the new county jail that incarceration at hard labor was an appropriate penalty for others besides the most minor offenders.

The evidence concerning the influence of age on sentencing decisions is more difficult to interpret, since it is impossible to separate and isolate the factor of age from several others that might have determined the judgment that was to be delivered. In addition, the ages of prisoners are available only at the assizes and for a few years at the end of the century. But this fragmentary evidence does suggest in a general way that age played some part in the sentences arrived at: at least the term of years to be served in both the hulks and the houses of correction and jails increased a little with the age of the prisoner until they reached a peak with prisoners in their late twenties and thirties, after which they moderated slightly.[175]

THE TRANSFORMATION OF PUNISHMENT

By 1800 a term of imprisonment was the most common sentence in noncapital property cases. At the turn of the century close to sixty per cent of convicted offenders in Surrey and forty-three per cent in Sussex were subjected to such a sanction—some of them for very brief periods, of course.[176] Another nine per cent in Surrey and twenty-six per cent in

[175] At the Surrey assizes in 1782–88, the average terms of the sentences imposed on men convicted of noncapital property offenses were as follows (from ASSI 31/12–15):

Age	Hulks (Years)	House of Correction and Jail (Months)	Number of Sentences
Under 25	2.2	6.8	34
25–39	2.6	9.6	23
40 and over	2.3	9.3	16

For further evidence about age as a factor in sentencing see Peter King, "Decision-Makers and Decision-Making in the English Criminal Law, 1750–1800," *Historical Journal* 27 (1984), pp. 34–43.

[176] Noncapital punishments for property offenses at the Sussex assizes and East and West Sussex quarter sessions, 1795–1802, were distributed as follows: transportation, 28.7 per cent; imprisonment, 36.8 per cent; imprisonment with whipping, 29.2 per cent; whipping, 1.0 per cent; other sentences, 4.3 per cent; total number of sentences, 185 (from the Sample). In the Surrey courts in the same period a total of 440 sentences were distributed as follows: transportation, 27.7 per cent; imprisonment, 59.3 per cent; imprisonment with whipping, 9.4 per cent; whipping, 3.7 per cent (calculated from table 10.14).

ADMINISTRATION OF JUSTICE

Sussex were sentenced to a term in the county jail or a house of correction with the additional order that they be whipped in the course of serving that sentence. By then, however, corporal punishment was clearly falling into disfavor. Public whippings did not disappear entirely by 1800, but they were strongly in decline in the last years of the century.

The falling away of corporal punishment, and particularly corporal punishment carried out in public, marks the emergence of a new penal order. Throughout the century whipping at the cart's tail before as large a crowd as could be assembled had been the main sanction employed by the magistrates in quarter sessions against those convicted of petty theft. As late as 1783–87, out of every ten offenders convicted of theft at the Surrey quarter sessions four had been whipped and discharged and another two whipped and held for a brief prison term. By the end of the century corporal punishment on this scale had been rejected. In 1799–1802 only fourteen men and two women were ordered to be whipped and immediately discharged—out of more than four hundred convicted property offenders. And even in conjunction with a term of imprisonment, whipping had been curtailed, for that penalty was imposed on only forty others (table 10.13).

It seems reasonable to think that the decline of physical violence as a penal weapon proceeded from the persuasion on the one hand that imprisonment under the right conditions would be a more effective means of encouraging law-abiding behavior than scourging offenders in public, and on the other from a rejection of physical violence as an acceptable means of punishment, a rejection that reflects a larger change in sentiment in society regarding the legitimacy and acceptability of violence itself. The penal consequences of this larger change in attitude and outlook marked a crucial stage in the fundamental transformation of punishment that was taking place over the late eighteenth century and in the early decades of the nineteenth, in the course of which punishment ceased to be mounted with an eye to those who watched, and was concentrated (at least in intention) single-mindedly on the prisoner in order to reform and rehabilitate him and send him back to the world a new man. This transformation is perhaps seen at its clearest in the way the pillory fell into disfavor, the punishment that might stand as a paradigm of the old penal order.

The essential characteristic of the pillory was the participation of the community in the denunciation of the offender and his deed. As we have seen, the experience was often very serious for the prisoner, even fatal. Following several notorious cases in London in which men had been killed in the pillory under circumstances that smacked of collusion on the part of the local authorities, opposition was being voiced by the middle of the eighteenth century to a punishment that encouraged the fury of the crowd and allowed them in effect to impose on the prisoner a sentence the law had not intended.[177] And while the pillory continued to be employed in Surrey for offenses involving fraud, attempted rape, sexual relations with a child, homosexuality, and perjury,[178] the Southwark authorities seem to have made more of an effort in the third quarter of the century to protect some of the men and women on public display and at the mercy of the crowd. A man pilloried in Southwark in 1764 for a sexual attack on a child was saved, it was reported, "from the usual cruel behaviour of the populace" by the prudent conduct and personal attendance of several justices of the peace.[179] And it was becoming common in the metropolis by the 1760s for large bodies of constables to be assembled at the pillory to keep the crowd some distance from the prisoner.

This may have been as much a concern for public order in a city that at several points in that decade saw massive demonstrations by "Wilkes and Liberty" crowds and violent clashes arising from industrial disputes[180] as for the fate of the prisoner. Whatever the deeper reason, a fundamental uneasiness is apparent over the last decades of the century about the validity of a punishment that licensed brutality. The number of sentences declined in Surrey after 1770, and in the last two decades of the century there was barely one every two years. The violent treatment of men in the pillory did not disappear overnight.[181] But if Francis Place is to be believed and if the scenes that he describes around the pillory at Charing Cross are typical of events elsewhere at the end of the century, it would appear that the authorities got control over the crowds at pillories at the price of allowing a kind of ritualized stoning and dishonoring of the offender (when the crowd was hostile to him). Place describes occasions on which the

[177] *Evening Advertiser*, 20 Mar. 1756; G. M. 26 (1756), p. 166. For earlier criticism of the violence allowed at the pillory see Sollom Emlyn's preface to his edition of the *State Trials*, vol. 1, p. xl.

[178] There was indeed a modest increase in the number of sentences to the pillory in Surrey after the mid-century. In fourteen years sampled between 1750 and 1770, twenty-four men and three women were set on the pillory in Southwark. That was to fall away sharply, as we will see, after 1770. The Surrey sample does not include any cases of women pilloried for deviant sexual practices, but there were occasional examples in London north of the river. And such women were treated as roughly as men convicted of sexual deviancy. In 1777, for example, Anne Marrow was put on the pillory at Charing Cross for "marrying three wives." She was so severely dealt with by the crowd that she lost her eyesight (G. M. 47 [1777], pp. 348, 402).

[179] *The Public Advertiser*, 27 Jan., 7 Feb. 1764.

[180] George Rudé, *Wilkes and Liberty: A Social Study of 1763 to 1774* (Oxford, 1962); Walter James Shelton, *English Hunger and Industrial Disorders* (1973), pt. 2.

[181] See, for example, Burke's speech in the House of Commons in 1780 about the death of a man in the London pillory (*Parliamentary History* 21, pp. 388–91), and his letter to the attorney general on the same occasion (John A. Woods, ed., *The Correspondence of Edmund Burke*, vol. 4 [1963], pp. 230–31).

constables maintained a ring around the pillory to keep the crowd away from the prisoner, but allowed a number of women to break through to act as appointed tormentors, taking successive handfuls of filth from the watching crowd and covering the offender with it until the constables called them off.[182] There was clearly a deep ambivalence about the pillory at that point, and by the end of the century it was going the way of public whipping.

No doubt the restrictions on the use of the pillory were further encouraged by several examples in the first decade of the nineteenth century of men whom the government wanted to expose as traitors and libelers being honored by the crowd rather than despised.[183] But of course the courts were not obliged to order any particular offender to the pillory, and it seems reasonable to think that it fell into disfavor for the same reasons as had whipping and other physical punishments carried out in public—that is, from a fundamental rejection of punishments that were violent in themselves or that encouraged public violence. The use of the pillory was seriously restricted by statute in 1816 and entirely abolished in 1837.[184]

CONCLUSION

The fundamental impression that emerges from these changes in punishment over the last decades of the eighteenth century is that the consequences of conviction had become more serious. A smaller proportion of convicted offenders were hanged by the end of the eighteenth century than had been common over most of the period we have been concerned with, and that proportion diminished further in the early decades of the nineteenth century. But in property crimes convicted offenders were being imprisoned or transported by the end of the eighteenth century, when they would have been branded or whipped and released a hundred years earlier. And after 1750 some of those convicted of offenses against the person were being similarly subjected to more stringent penalties. The

---

[182] Add Mss. 27826, pp. 173–75.

[183] Such miscalculations had happened before, but the crowd's honoring the radical printer Daniel Isaac Eaton when he was ordered to stand on the pillory at Charing Cross in 1813 perhaps hastened the end of so unreliable a form of punishment at a time when Jacobinism was thought by the propertied to be pervasive in England and the bloody overthrow of the government actively plotted. According to Place, Eaton would not have been pilloried if it had not been Lord Ellenborough's pigheaded belief that he would be dishonored if he were exposed in public, despite the popularity of his cause (Add Mss. 27826, p. 176).

[184] 56 Geo III, c. 138 (1816); 1 Vict, c. 23 (1837).

ambitions of the courts by the end of the eighteenth century were quite clearly to bring the greatest unhappiness to the greatest number of convicts. And this had encouraged fundamental changes in the character and the function of punishment.

The transformation was not completed for many years, for there remained in 1800 a broadly shared conviction that public executions—and in the case of particular malignancy, hanging in chains—remained an essential weapon against the most serious and dangerous offenders, especially murderers.[185] But by the end of the eighteenth century one penal regime was rapidly giving way to another. The older forms of punishment were public and violent. They attacked the body. The more private forms of punishment inside prisons were not necessarily less cruel, nor indeed less violent, for at least as they were to develop in the nineteenth century the disciplines of many penitentiaries could only be maintained by vicious and frequently administered corporal punishments.[186] The intentions of the courts in sentencing men to periods of imprisonment, certainly the intentions of the reformers and publicists who urged incarceration at hard labor in the late eighteenth century, were not, however, primarily to create a frightening deterrent but to reduce crime by bringing about a change in the prisoner himself. The essence of the new cause was to attack not the prisoner's body, but his mind and soul. Sir George Paul sought a regime in which the convict would feel his utter degradation and humiliation and in which he would be punished "by corroding reflections on his crimes, and the denial of his accustomed habits" so that he might be "so reformed in mind as to become an useful member of the community."[187] Not all reformers believed in the forms of absolute solitude favored by Paul. But all would have agreed with the fundamentals of his prescription: to transform men, to break their spirit, to curb their luxurious habits and appetites, to force them to reflect on the shame of their present situation, so that by labor and religious instruction they might be reformed.

All of this required larger economic resources and more concentrated and activist political power and the greater participation of the state in the administration of justice than could then be delivered. With the failure

[185] It was also believed by some that public hangings provided a necessary check on the royal prerogative (the character and scope of which had been made an issue by the Whigs in the 1780s), permitting as they did a check to be made on the pardoning power and preventing the king from translating this source of favor into parliamentary votes and in other ways extending the power of the Crown. See, for example, *G. M.* 58 (1788), p. 316.

[186] Ignatieff, *A Just Measure of Pain*, p. 178.

[187] Sir G. O. Paul, *Proceedings of the Grand Juries, Magistrates and other Noblemen and Gentlemen of the County of Gloucester on designing and executing a general reform in the construction and regulation of the Prisons for the said County*, 3rd ed. (Gloucester, 1808), p. 60, quoting a speech of 1783.

to mobilize such support, the move to build penitentiaries foundered. Such reform was as yet a minority interest (as were the parallel ambitions to reform the law and to create a more effective police), an interest of men of the middling classes—professional men, manufacturers, and a "small constituency of reform-minded magistrates on the county benches."[188] But the failure to reconstruct the prisons in a massive way should not obscure the extent to which penal practice had in fact changed in England by 1800. The old regime in penal matters had long since passed, even as it had existed in 1750, let alone 1660. The sentencing practices of the courts were the practices of the world coming into being, for a system that had relied on the participation of the crowd and on terror and example had given way to one in which correction was administered largely out of the public eye and at least in some minds for purposes beyond mere punishment and deterrence. The buildings and the discipline of the total institution had not yet materialized, but the sentiments and convictions upon which they would be built were already in place.

[188] Ignatieff, A Just Measure of Pain, p. 97.

CHAPTER 11

CONCLUSION

Over the century and a half from the Restoration to the early nineteenth century significant changes took place in the criminal law, in criminal procedure, in prisons, and in punishment, changes that together transformed the system of judicial administration. The introduction of lawyers into the courtroom as both prosecuting and defense counsel, to take merely one element of the changing institutions and practice, had led by 1800 to the beginning of fundamental alterations in the character of criminal trials and in the way that suspects were dealt with at the first stage of the judicial process, the enquiry before a magistrate. By the end of the century, too, the establishment of stipendiary magistrates at "public offices" in London and other large cities had made for other significant changes in the work of the magistracy and in the character of policing.

Perhaps the most striking change in the period we have been dealing with had been in the punishments that convicted offenders were subjected to. In 1660 the courts had little choice between hanging convicted felons or releasing them back into the community with a branded thumb. If the jury convicted a prisoner of the less serious charge of petty larceny the courts might order that he be whipped before being released. But that was the only real punishment other than hanging the judges had at their disposal, and it was in any case rarely resorted to in the 1660s. By 1800 the vast majority of those convicted of a felony to which capital punishment did not apply, or who had been pardoned from a capital sentence, were either transported or incarcerated for periods that might vary from a few weeks to several years. The penal system was more humane by the early years of the nineteenth century than it had been at the Restoration in that a growing public abhorrence of physical cruelty was undermining belief in the justice and efficacy of capital punishment, at least for the broad range of offenses to which it had applied, and had led in addition to the virtual abolition of public whipping and the use of the pillory. But the particularly notable change over the previous century had been the creation of secondary punishments. These had derived as much from a concern for effectiveness in penal matters as for fairness and humanity.

The broad character of these changes in the sanctions available to the courts is illustrated in rather schematic form in figure 11.1, in which the

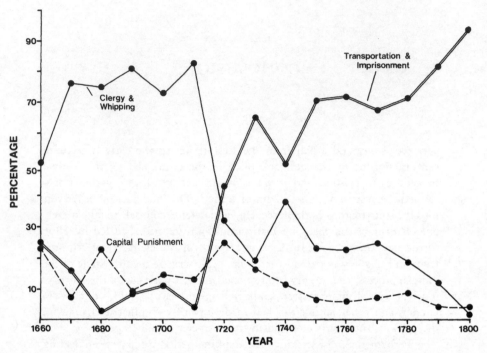

Figure 11.1   Patterns of Punishment in Surrey Courts: Crimes against Property.

proportion of three categories of punishments inflicted on convicted property offenders in Surrey are shown as they changed by decades over this
period. These are: capital punishment; the punishments that led to immediate discharge, that is, whipping and the branding on the thumb of
clergy, which though not strictly intended as a punishment had become
one in effect; and transportation and imprisonment, brought together
because they involved longer-term consequences in that they removed the
offender from the community. Combining these punishments in this way
is intended to do no more than to illustrate and summarize the changes
we have been dealing with over this period and to underline the transformation they wrought in the penal system. It is intended particularly
to emphasize a point that bears repeating, that the fundamental break
with the penal practices and penal intentions of the past came with the
introduction of transportation in 1718 as much as with the establishment
of imprisonment in the last decades of the century.

Transportation provided the secondary punishment that the courts
had sought—and that some men in parliament, in London, and elsewhere
had sought—at least since the Restoration. As transportation became

established it encouraged a reduction in the proportion (though, as we have seen, not the actual number) of convicted property offenders who were hanged, that proportion falling away after the fluctuating and occasionally high levels of the late seventeenth and early eighteenth centuries. Even more immediately, transportation led to a sharp reduction in the number of convicted felons who left the court virtually as soon as the session ended and returned to society. These two trends were established after the Act of 1718 put transportation on a firm footing, and they were accelerated and enlarged when imprisonment was introduced in the 1760s and over the last decades of the century.

The chronology and the character of change in penal practice that is suggested by this way of looking at the transformation of punishment bears directly on the question of how changes in law and administration are to be explained, if only because in pushing back their beginnings to the late seventeenth century (at least) we will have to search for explanations that do not depend on the immediate influence of Enlightenment rationality or on the social consequences of the Industrial Revolution. Changes in punishment are likely to be explained by the anxieties and concerns about the state of crime and social disorder expressed by the landed and mercantile elites, and by those broad classes of men of property and respectability who dominated their neighborhoods, served in local offices, and helped to run the courts. The changes in punishment and in other aspects of criminal administration—in the process of prosecution and policing, and in the watch, trials, and prisons—clearly did not all derive from a simple and single set of motives and concerns. But all aspects of the system of judicial administration were to some extent interrelated: changes in one area were likely to be felt in others, even if those changes had been inspired by autonomous or "external" factors. To follow the pattern of punishment over the period we have been dealing with helps to bring some of those interconnections into clearer focus and to explain the substantial changes that were taking place in all aspects of the criminal law and administration.

The criminal law in the eighteenth century served several purposes. It acted broadly to sustain and legitimize the established social and economic and political arrangements of the society, and in some crucial areas it was enlisted in the effort to effect changes that powerful groups in society wanted. In addition, the opportunities for the exercise of discretion at all stages of criminal administration provided occasions on which men of the propertied elite could exercise and demonstrate their influence and thus enhance the bases upon which their local reputation and local authority rested. Whether that was intended when the capital statutes were drawn up or whether it had emerged as a natural consequence of the way the harsh laws had to be administered—which seems more likely—the use-fulness of the distinctly personal nature of criminal administration cannot be doubted. But if the criminal law had served only the interests of the propertied classes it would hardly have attracted the widespread approval that was clearly bestowed upon it; nor, as Edward Thompson has said, would it have worked as effectively as ideology. To be seen to be serving the interests of the broader community in a fair manner it had indeed to be doing so. However constrained in practice access to the courts was for the working population, the law appears to have been widely accepted in society as a means of settling disputes and ameliorating public grievances. The courts offered a wide range of individual victims of theft or violence some sense of satisfaction.[1]

The law may have served interests well beyond the mere maintenance of order and the restraining of criminals, but that was plainly its most immediate and obvious task, and criticism of both its substance and its administration arose when crime appeared to grow beyond acceptable limits. What those limits were was itself coming to be a matter of disa-greement by the late seventeenth century, or at least the experience of crime was such that some sections of the community were often anxious about the institutions that were meant to preserve order. Those concerns gave rise to the push for secondary punishments that is evident in the late seventeenth century and into the eighteenth. But, as we have seen, that did not imply any fundamental criticism of the established system. In 1660 and for long afterwards there was broad agreement about the nature of crime and how it should be dealt with. It remained widely agreed that some offenses and offenders were particularly deserving of capital punish-ment and that in the course of a criminal career men reached a point of moral collapse from which they were unlikely to be reclaimable. Their execution rid society of dangerous individuals and at the same time served as a frightening example to others who might still pull back from that moral abyss. It was also agreed that some men might be reformed by proper punishment, but over much of the period we are concerned with that ambition was reserved for the most minor offenders: vagrants, drunk-ards, prostitutes, and perhaps petty thieves.

So long as there were not large numbers of offenders and so long as informal means of coercion and control worked reasonably effectively, the

---

[1] For these themes see Douglas Hay, "Property, Authority and the Criminal Law," in Hay, Linebaugh, and Thompson, eds., *Albion's Fatal Tree*; Thompson, *Whigs and Hunters*, chap. 10; Brewer and Styles, *An Ungovernable People*, introduction; Peter King, "Decision-Makers and Decision-Making in the English Criminal Law, 1750–1800," *Historical Journal* 27 (1984), pp. 25–58. John Langbein has questioned the bases of Hay's conception of the law as ideology in "Albion's Fatal Flaws," *Past and Present* 98 (1983), pp. 96–120.

lack of an intermediate punishment was not widely felt as a serious deficiency. Over most of the country in 1660 informal authority—in the family and the wider community—still worked to constrain much wayward behavior. The few who were obdurate or independent and who persisted in putting themselves outside the moral boundaries of the society could be left to the courts, deserving of whatever treatment they received. The institutions by which they would be judged were shaped by a society in which character and reputation were supremely important. The criminal trial was as much devoted to establishing the circumstances of the offender as it was to searching out the more abstract truth of his guilt or innocence. In exercising the broad discretion available to them in verdicts and sentencing, both judges and jurors were swayed by the personal characteristics of defendants and prosecutors. In reaching their decisions they were also often influenced by the general state of criminality as indicated in part by the number of offenders before the court. Most often, and in most parts of the country, the level of crime was such that an occasional terrifying reminder on the gallows of the consequences of falling into bad habits was found to be sufficient demonstration of the power of the law. Since the trial selected the prisoners whose deaths would send this message to the laboring population and cast the rest aside, the jails in which they waited for trial could continue as small and nonspecialized holding pens, for they typically would not have held large numbers of inmates, and even if the numbers did increase substantially before an assize session the visit of the judges would result in their being largely cleared by the discharge or the execution of the prisoners.

The established systems of law and administration and punishment and the assumptions that lay behind them not only survived the Restoration but were extended and enlarged over much of the period we are concerned with. That is particularly clear in the dependence on capital punishment. The dozens of statutes that over the course of the eighteenth century either created offenses without benefit of clergy or removed clergy from offenses that had been within the scope of the privilege significantly increased the number of offenders at risk of being hanged and thus reaffirmed some of the fundamental characteristics of the established system, particularly the necessity of discretionary decision-making. The need to select men to be hanged increased rather than diminished over this period. For a century and more after the Restoration there was little sign of opposition to the principles and assumptions upon which the law and its administration rested. Few objections were raised in parliament (as far as one can tell) or in addresses to the king or elsewhere to the narrowing scope of benefit of clergy and the consequent broadening of capital punishment, until humanitarian concern and doubts about the effectiveness of the law began to converge toward the end of the eighteenth century. But at least until the 1780s the system worked reasonably well in the rural and small-scale communities in which most Englishmen lived. Serious crime was rare, and informal controls in conjunction with the threat of the royal courts served sufficiently to restrain more minor offenders.

A system that suited a society in which men were known—or were at least known to be strangers—and in which their dispositions and characters could easily be enquired into was less satisfactory, however, for those who had to deal with crime and disorder in the metropolis of London. Conditions there were different in 1660, and if anything the contrasts widened as immigration from the countryside increased and the population grew, and with it the number of workers dependent on wages in an economy with highly fluctuating employment opportunities. If mayors and aldermen or grand jurors of London did not object in principle to capital punishment or benefit of clergy or other aspects of judicial administration, by the late seventeenth century they and the propertied classes they represented were prominent among those who thought the lack of secondary punishments intolerable. It was at the urging of the London authorities that judges were authorized in 1706 to sentence clergied offenders to a term of up to two years at hard labor in the house of correction. Behind this is surely the conviction that minor thefts in London were committed by men and women who would be most effectively treated by methods long established for the punishment of vagrants and the disorderly poor. The point was not to dismantle the system in being—far from it— but to add punishments for those whose offenses were too petty to deserve the death penalty and who were sufficiently independent to be beyond informal means of control.

The urge for new measures by which the poor could be restrained arose not only as the commercial and financial opportunities of the capital were expanding rapidly but also, in the generation after the Revolution of 1689, as the deepest concerns were being expressed about the immorality and lack of religious knowledge and experience of the working population. It was this anxiety about the spiritual health as well as the behavior of the working population that engaged the energies of the Societies for the Reformation of Manners in the last decade of the seventeenth century. Concern about crime and the immorality of the poor arose at a time when another parallel strand of opinion was stressing the crucial role of the laborer in the national economy of a mercantilist state and the need to harness the labor of the unemployed in workhouses and similar institutions. The management of the poor, the imposition of social discipline and morality, and the prevention of crime were all related concerns to the propertied classes of London, where the concentration and size of problems posed to the health of the social order seemed to require more active measures of coercion than might continue to serve adequately in the world of the village and town.

The Transportation Act of 1718 was passed by a government anxious about the security of the new Hanoverian regime as well as the high levels of violent crime in London after the peace signed at Utrecht and the demobilization of Marlborough's armies. Transportation answered a long-felt need. It was a need felt largely at home and not in the colonies or among those thinking about the sinews of empire. It is of course striking that it served the commercial interests of the mother country and arose at a time when colonies were highly valued as markets for English manufactures and as sources of raw materials and the products of semitropical agriculture. But transportation to America emerged because the empire provided the opportunity for the development of a sanction that would ensure domestic tranquillity, not because of the requirements for imperial expansion.

Transportation served the interests of the established penal system while helping to shift its bases. It added considerable flexibility to the administration of the law by enabling juries more readily to reduce by their verdicts capital to noncapital charges, even against serious offenders, and it enabled the king more readily to pardon men condemned to be hanged, since in both cases the prisoner would be banished and not simply discharged back into the community. Thus the capital laws could remain enforceable even as support for hanging eroded. Transportation introduced an acceptable secondary punishment and brought a period of stability to the penal system that was in marked contrast to the experimentation and anxiety that had characterized penal matters during the previous half century.

As transportation began to effect a significant transformation of penal practice in the middle decades of the eighteenth century other elements in the administration of justice began to shift significantly, and to some degree at least in response to those changes. The concern about the country's prisons evident in Surrey in the late seventeenth century that resulted in the building of a new jail in the 1720s was also perhaps encouraged in part by anxieties about immorality and crime. But changes in punishment particularly forced the question of the prisons on the attention of the magistrates, for the establishment of transportation meant that the jails were not being cleared as effectively as they had been earlier. Men who would once have been branded and discharged were now returned to prison to await transportation, along with those who had been reprieved from a death sentence and who were also waiting to be sent to the colonies. The result was occasional overcrowding, which brought the questions of jail security and the health of the prisoners (and the danger that jail fever posed for the community outside, not least for those who would meet the prisoners in the courtroom) before the quarter sessions as frequent topics of discussion.

Magistrates and grand jurors and others engaged in the administration of justice were forced to concern themselves with institutions that earlier had been more taken for granted. Their engagement remained occasional, and their responses piecemeal, stop-gap, pragmatic. Nevertheless, the result over the first half of the eighteenth century was that a new relationship emerged between the prisons and the local authorities. By 1750 the magistrates were giving attention to the need to provide cleaner air and water in the prisons, to provide medical attention and nourishing food for prisoners who were ill. Much remains to be explained about why that happened, why the response to problems in the jails took the form it did, and why men became persuaded of the need to improve the sanitary arrangements and ventilation of prisons—why, in general, scientific and especially medical knowledge played an increasing part in shaping their responses. But it seems clear that overcrowding presented the problems, and that that was a product (particularly in the London area) of moments of high levels of prosecutions compounded by the changing functions of the jails that followed the establishment of transportation.

Anxiety about theft and violence in the metropolis, and more broadly about the indiscipline and immoral behavior of the working population, encouraged several other changes over the first half of the century in aspects of the administration of justice. Some attempts were made to bolster the night watch and to discourage street crime by improving lighting. At the same time, a more public style of magistracy was emerging in London, both in the city, where the institution of the sitting alderman made for a preliminary enquiry at least partially open to the public, and in Westminster, where magistrates like de Veil and the Fieldings responded to high levels of violent street offenses by examining suspects in a way that would encourage victims to come forward to identify and accuse them. By the 1760s several "public offices" were operating in London in which business that once would have been conducted entirely behind closed doors was being done in the open.

One result was to make it possible for accused offenders to engage lawyers on their behalf when they were taken before the examining magistrate—at least they were doing so well before the end of the century—and that helps to explain the development of the notion that an accused man ought to be granted certain rights at this stage of the investigation, rights that had certainly not been envisaged in the Marian legislation creating the preliminary hearing. The claim began to be made in the course of the century, for example, that the accused man ought to know the precise charges brought against him and that he had the right to challenge the evidence upon which his commitment to trial would be based. The notion of prisoners' rights was particularly enlarged by the participation of lawyers as defense counsel at the trial itself, a role they began to play in the second quarter of the century. Why they had done so is not entirely clear, but it is possible that lawyers were encouraged to think at least of prosecuting in the criminal courts by the concern of the government after 1714 about public order and the security of the Hanoverian regime. The emergence of the defense lawyer (as a consequence, possibly, of the increasing engagement of prosecuting counsel) transformed the criminal trial. It altered the dynamics of the courtroom and the relationship of judge, jury, and accused. Even more important, the engagement of a trained advocate for the prisoner brought the factual basis of the charge forward for examination, created a more fully developed law of evidence, and changed the form and even the function of the trial in profound ways.

Anxieties about the level and character of property crime, especially in London, help to explain changes in the law, in punishment, and in several aspects of the judicial process in the first half of the eighteenth century. Such concerns were even more clearly at work after 1750, when waves of prolonged and enlarging crime were experienced in the metropolis (and by the 1780s well beyond). The evident failure of the law and other agencies of control to restrain the common people and to prevent them from falling into habits that led them to crime, the failure particularly to combat the effects of commerce and the growth of luxury in society, encouraged a wave of criticism. One characteristic of the administration of the law that came under strong attack by the middle of the century was the wide discretion with which capital statutes were administered, discretion that had undoubtedly broadened over the previous thirty years as a result of the introduction of transportation. The balance between the terror of the gallows and banishment for a term of years that had brought a great measure of stability to sentencing in the courts was undermined by the evidence of failure so clear in the bulging jails and the long calendars of prisoners to be tried in the 1750s and 1760s.

Several elements that made up this balance came in for criticism: the apparent laxity in the application of the death penalty; inconsistencies in verdicts and sentences; and the failure of transportation to deter potential offenders. A number of solutions were pressed forward. What seemed the fundamental problem to men like Henry Fielding in the middle of the century and to Martin Madan in the 1780s was that offenders were being encouraged to think that even if they were caught and convicted they would almost certainly not be punished harshly. Their solution was to enforce the capital laws strictly by limiting the "pious perjury" of juries and the granting of pardons. The bloodbath that would ensue would not only be the most effective way of dissuading men from choosing to commit crimes, this argument ran, but also the most humane, for it would make the consequences of crime clear where they were now confused. This argument was also usually linked to the notion that policing ought to be improved and victims encouraged to prosecute so as to leave the potential robber or burglar in no doubt that he would be pursued, brought to trial, and severely punished.

At the same time, others were concerned about the failure of transportation to discourage less serious offenders and to prevent a burgeoning of immorality in London in the 1750s and 1760s, of which property offenses were merely one result. By the middle of the eighteenth century transportation to America was losing its sting—in the minds of those who were in no danger of being sent—and the persuasion that the crisis that overcame the capital was as much one of immorality as crime encouraged a renewal of ideas about the management of the poor that had emerged in Anne's reign and had been put aside in the triumph of transportation. The important notion was that not only was it possible and necessary to reform those who refused to work, to train them in habits of mind and body that would enable them to support themselves, but that such intervention would also provide an effective way of dealing with the large numbers of offenders at the lower end of the crime/immorality spectrum in the capital. The failure of transportation to restrain such petty offenders was plain in the aftermath of wars in the middle decades of the century, and there was a return then to the arguments that had underlain the earlier experiment with imprisonment at hard labor, a return made all the more necessary by what appeared to be the sheer size of the problem of crime and immorality.

The impulse behind the reemergence of imprisonment by the 1760s was more complicated than that, as we have seen, but the usefulness of a punishment that promised to reform and train as well as chastise the large numbers of offenders who were thought to have emerged from the corrupt urban environment and were unmoved by the prospect of transportation was what made it increasingly attractive. In any event, the courts were persuaded of its value even before the American Revolution brought transportation to an end. The Penitentiary Act of 1779 reveals how fully converted men had become over the previous twenty-five years to the value of the certain, moderate, and reformative punishment that imprisonment at hard labor promised. A program advocated in the writings of Beccaria and Howard was quickly adopted after 1776, on paper at least, and it seems likely that these men had been avidly read because they justified courses of action that a significant number of men in positions of authority in the localities as well as in parliament had come to believe in.

For more than a century by the 1770s two modes of administration and punishment had been developing in parallel and largely in harmony within the criminal justice system. On the one hand, what one might call the "established" view depended on a conception of crime and criminals that derived essentially from rural experience in which serious property crimes were rare and in which informal means effectively restrained many minor offenders. At the same time another view of crime took shape after the Restoration. It can be seen emerging in London, though it is likely that it was shared by men who dealt with the poor and vagrants and crime in other cities and in other areas in which the problems of social order were different from those normally prevailing in the countryside. Particularly in London by the late seventeenth century the authorities confronted problems that seemed to derive not simply from the waywardness of a few individual offenders or that inconvenienced a few victims, but from a broad threat to social order from the immorality of large numbers of offenders. If those who Defoe called "troops of human devils" were not yet identified in the early eighteenth century as the "criminal" or "dangerous" classes, the periodic alarm at moments of pervasive crime gave rise to the same sense of the unmanageability of the urban poor that was to underlie such conceptions at the end of the eighteenth century. It was the persuasion that problems of social order in the capital derived from the isolation and independence of the poor, from the failure of the church to instruct them and of the magistracy to bring the laws against immorality to bear on them, that had encouraged some men to think of imprisonment at hard labor as an effective means of dealing with minor criminals because it promised to attack the source of the problem.

That promise made imprisonment even more attractive after 1776. It was not merely that there was a need then for a substitute for transportation, but that there was a need for punishment that would attack the root causes of crime. That view was more widely shared as the growth of population and the expansion of manufacturing and the economic and social changes that accompanied it, produced replications in other parts of the country of the kinds of problems that had been largely confined to the capital over the previous century, problems that derived from the circumstances of life in an urban environment.[2] That was particularly true

---

[2] As against the dislocating effects of the *process* of urbanization. For this distinction, a discussion of "structural" vs. "tension" analyses of crime, and the bearing of nineteenth-century French data, see Charles Tilly and Abdul Qaiyum Lodhi, "Urbanization, Crime and Collective Violence in Nineteenth-Century France," *American Journal of Sociology* 79 (1973), pp. 296–318.

in the 1780s, when crime on a new scale was being reported from many parts of the country, and new means of social defense and a new campaign to reform the manners of the poor were being called for from others besides the beleaguered authorities of the capital.

The size and character of the problem of crime after the American war was met by a vigorous enforcement of the law, and large numbers of offenders were hanged throughout the country. By the mid-1780s, however, it was clear to many that capital punishment could hardly touch the problem when so much crime seemed to derive from a spreading immorality and a brutalized population. Significant numbers of men had come by then to doubt not only the utility but the justice and the legitimacy of capital punishment for many of the offenses to which it then applied. A correspondent to the *Gentleman's Magazine* put clearly what had come by the late eighteenth century to be a position held not merely by a few writers or by a handful of men in parliament. "The laws of England," he said, "have long been esteemed, by the generality of men, the most equitable and merciful in the world; and in some respects they certainly are so." But, he went on,

> for the most part, they are cruel, unjust and useless. The number of our fellow-mortals hung up so frequently like the vilest animal is a terrible proof of their cruelty; the same punishment inflicted on the parricide and the man who takes the value of three shillings (or less) on the highway is a proof that they are unjust; and the frequency and multiplicity of crimes is a proof that they are useless. England, which contains some of the most philosophic, humane, and liberal minded men in the world, is disgraced with a code of laws which even the most barbarous savage would be ashamed of.[3]

The fundamental change in sentiment that represents over positions that would have been taken on capital punishment a generation earlier is also reflected in a growing reluctance of victims of minor but capital property crimes to prosecute those offenses. More directly, it can be seen in the evidence given to a parliamentary committee in 1819 by members of the London bourgeoisie who declared themselves unwilling to bring charges against shoplifters and pilfering servants and similar offenders so long as there was a chance they might be hanged.[4]

There is no doubt that capital punishment was perceived by the end of the century in some segments of the community as cruel and unjust

[3] *G. M.* 60 (1790), p. 1185.
[4] *Report on the Criminal Laws* (1819); Radzinowicz, *History*, vol. 1, pp. 526–66.

for all but the most serious offenses. The withering of support for a penal system that depended fundamentally on the threat of execution is to be explained by the merging of several strands of opinion and sentiment. To some degree it resulted from a broader movement of opinion in Europe and in England that came increasingly to abhor physical violence and cruelty to men and animals, and that can be seen at work in campaigns to abolish blood sports and other violent customary recreations, as well as in the movement of opinion against physical punishments of all kinds.[5] That is perhaps the mental sea-change lying behind the opposition to capital punishment. But it was also coming to seem unjust, as the *Gentleman's Magazine* correspondent said in 1790, that men were hanged for offenses of such wide disparity. It had not shocked the sensibilities of men in 1723 that the Black Act could appoint the death penalty for the offense of breaking down the head of a fish pond or for setting fire to a handful of straw. It did by the last two decades of the century. By 1800 a significant body of opinion was ready to condemn cruelty and disproportion in punishment as fundamentally unjust and unacceptable in a civilized society, and to support penal measures that more nearly reflected a sense of the equality of men, of the worth of the individual and the rights of all men to fair and equal treatment before the courts.[6]

These sentiments were focused and the changes they encouraged given urgency by another factor that the correspondent of 1790 alluded to and that clearly helps to explain some of the disenchantment with capital punishment, that is, its ineffectiveness. It didn't work. At least it was clear in the 1780s in the face of the pervasiveness of crime in the middle years of the decade that it had utterly failed to deter the very large number of offenders who crowded the jails and filled out the court dockets in many parts of the country. In some sense the loss of faith in hanging was a more national recognition of a truth apparent in London a century earlier: that minor offenders could not be deterred by fear, and that the problem of crime was not merely a matter of one or two individuals going wrong. The increasingly widespread acceptance of the notion that crime was the product of a class of offenders who were beyond the reach of normal controls and whose immorality and pleasure-seeking self-indulgence was like a disease, infecting all who came into contact with them, undermined the belief in capital punishment as it encouraged the view that such offenders needed to be treated and reformed. The promise of the penitentiary was

[5] Robert Malcolmson, *Popular Recreations in English Society, 1700–1850* (Cambridge, 1973), pp. 89–157; Keith Thomas, *Man and the Natural World: Changing Attitudes in England, 1500–1800* (1983), pp. 143–91.

[6] Randall McGowen, "The Image of Justice and Reform of the Criminal Law in Early Nineteenth-Century England," *Buffalo Law Review* 32 (1983), pp. 89–125.

that it would isolate men and women from the environment in which they had been corrupted and check what the solicitor general in 1810 called "the contagion of vice."[7] This view of crime as the product of a "criminal" population, which came to be so deeply entrenched by the early nineteenth century, was antithetical to extensive capital punishment, for it held that the corrupted minds and hearts of the "dangerous classes" would not be deterred by the sight of dozens of men executed in public. Indeed the reverse, for, as another correspondent to the *Gentleman's Magazine* observed in 1791, "instead of damping the feelings of the lower orders of people . . . [public hangings] only served to heighten their wickedness."[8]

Such sentiments lie behind the crumbling of support for a system of punishment that depended fundamentally on hanging. The old world was not transformed without protest, however. Douglas Hay has emphasized the reluctance of especially landed men to see the penal system dismantled because of their sense of the egalitarian implications of the new emphasis on uniformity of treatment and their anxiety not to lose the opportunities discretionary justice afforded to enhance the authority and personal power upon which their local preeminence rested.[9] But it seems to me that that protest was essentially perfunctory and the struggle short-lived. It is true that more than half a century elapsed between the publication of Beccaria in England (which elicited some response among people willing to consider a reduction of capital punishment) and Peel's statutes of the 1820s that swept away so many of the capital provisions in the criminal law. But it is striking how rapid and decisive the rejection of the old system was once the issue was fully engaged. It is also true that arguments were being made in parliament against the further extension of capital punishment in the 1770s and that in the next decade Sir Samuel Romilly and others set out much of the case that would eventually underpin the attack on the central elements of the established system.[10] But there were no serious threats in parliament in these years to overthrow the dozens of capital statutes passed since the sixteenth century. While a Penal Laws Bill did pass the House of Commons in 1772 (though it was lost in the Lords because of the dissolution of parliament), that had merely proposed the abolition of six obsolete statutes, none of which dealt with property offenses. Fifteen years elapsed before a direct and more general attack was made on

---

[7] *Parliamentary Debates* 16 (1810), col. 774.

[8] *G. M.* 61 (1791), pp. 510–11.

[9] Hay, "Property, Authority and the Criminal Law," pp. 17–63. For a broad view of the debate over the reform of the criminal law as a conflict between opposing conceptions of criminal justice deriving from differing views of class relations and state power see McGowen, "The Image of Justice," pp. 96–99.

[10] Radzinowicz, *History*, vol. 1, chaps. 10, 15.

the criminal code. In 1787, an M.P. moved the appointment of a non-parliamentary commission to consider a reform of the law, but that was turned back without difficulty by the prime minister, William Pitt, whose observation that "it would be extremely dangerous to take any step which might have the smallest tendency to discredit the present existing system, before proper data and principles should be established whereon to found another" induced the mover to withdraw his motion.[11]

It was not essentially until 1808 that the parliamentary battle began in earnest between proponents of reform and the defenders of the established system. It was then that the effort began to repeal some of the statutes that had made numerous forms of larceny capital offenses and that were by then only rarely put into effect. The resistance in the House of Commons—where landed men retained a decisive majority—was not formidable. Romilly's bill to repeal the Elizabethan statute making pocket-picking a capital offense passed without great opposition and was accepted by the Lords. Further bills in 1810 to repeal the more recent statutes that had removed clergy from shoplifting and from theft from houses and ships met with stiffer resistance; even so, the shoplifting bill passed the House of Commons, and in the next year three such reform bills were adopted by the House. Despite the opposition of those who continued to believe in the immense value to the maintenance of order and authority of the wide areas of discretion created at all stages of the criminal process by capital statutes, the battle to preserve the law as it stood had clearly been conceded in the House of Commons by 1811. The repeal of the shoplifting Act passed not only in 1810 and 1811, but on three further occasions over the next seven years.[12]

Neither they nor other bills that passed the Commons became law, because on each occasion they were thrown out by the House of Lords. That was where the center of the opposition lay. It was organized and led not by aristocrats of large acres (who might have defended the current arrangements for the opportunities they afforded for the exercise of interest and influence) but by the lord chancellor and the lord chief justice. The case they presented was straightforward and by then very familiar, and it carried considerable weight coming from the leaders of the legal profession. Lord Ellenborough, the lord chief justice, said in opposition to the repeal of the shoplifting Act in 1810 that "terror alone could prevent the commission of that crime. . . . Although the law as it stood, was but seldom carried into execution, yet the terror was precisely the same; and such were the minds of those upon whom it operated, that he believed the

[11] *Parliamentary History* 26 (1786–88), col. 1059.
[12] Radzinowicz, *History*, vol. 1, chap. 16.

apprehension of no milder punishment would produce any thing like safety to the public interest."[13] He also claimed that the repeal of capital punishment for pocket-picking had led to many more offenses (confusing, so the proponents of reform said, the increased willingness of victims to prosecute with the incidence of the offense).

Ellenborough went on to present what was by then a familiar argument for the value of judicial discretion in fixing an appropriate sentence, as against the new ambition to make all punishments certain and equal for the same offense. "There were always circumstances," he said, "which aggravated or mitigated the crime, but it would be impossible to make them the subject to an act of parliament." In the debate in 1810 and again in the following year Ellenborough and Lord Eldon, the lord chancellor, rested their successful opposition to the repeal of capital punishment for shoplifting on the twin propositions that only "the apprehension of death" deterred offenders, and since that and other offenses varied enormously in seriousness it was essential to vest "a very large share of discretion in the judges."[14]

When the lord chief justice was able to say, as he did in 1810, that "he had consulted with the other judges, and they were unanimously of opinion it would not be expedient to remit the severity of this part of the criminal law," it made a strong impression in the House of Lords. These same judges knew full well that a shrinking proportion of those charged with capital offenses, particularly under statutes passed since the Revolution, were actually being hanged in the early years of the new century. But they continued to insist on the necessity of discretion—especially their own discretion at the sentencing stage—and in general to exalt the importance of their role in the trial. The unanimous agreement of the judges that only the gallows held back hordes of potential offenders perhaps inevitably carried weight in a chamber that was much less open than the Commons to the influence of public opinion.

This formidable professional and institutional barrier to change continued to operate long after the fundamental argument for reform had been accepted in the lower House. But even the Lords could not resist the demands for more effective laws and a more effective system of judicial administration that arose in the deluge of crime, protest, and disorder in the years after 1815, when recession and the demobilization of the vast army and navy that had fought against Napoleon brought men and women all over the country into the greatest difficulties. The rate of prosecutions rose to levels never before experienced and made increasingly irresistible

[13] *Parliamentary Debates* 17 (1810), col. 197.
[14] Ibid., 20 (1811), cols. 300–1.

the argument that if propertied men would not prosecute thieves because they objected to capital punishment (even though everyone knew that there was no longer any realistic danger of a shoplifter or other petty offender actually being hanged), then the law was preventing society from defending itself. Within a few years, on the strength of evidence collected by a Commons committee in 1819 and finally under the lead of the government in the person of the Home Secretary, Sir Robert Peel, majorities were found in both Houses for bills in 1823 and 1827 that repealed dozens of capital statutes, consolidated offenses, and in several other ways (including the abolition of benefit of clergy) brought the criminal law more into harmony with the practice of the courts.[15] When one considers that hundreds of men and women had been hanged throughout England in the 1780s, a mere generation earlier, the overthrow of the assumptions upon which the law had been based for centuries was accomplished in a remarkably brief period of time.

Some of the opposition to change had arisen from the sense that the uniformity of treatment being advocated for all offenders (and the bureaucratic order and regularity it implied) threatened to eliminate personal distinctions throughout society and to attack the privileges that men of rank believed were essential to the maintenance of a stable social order. And indeed it is undoubtedly true that opposition to the harshness of the capital laws and to the arbitrariness of criminal procedure had arisen in part from a belief in the justice of a fairer and more equitable treatment of prisoners. Greater protection of the rights of the individual before the courts had been emerging in practice over the eighteenth century, as we have seen, with the fuller engagement of lawyers as defense counsel, for even though only a minority of defendants had the services of such counsel their influence was clearly felt in trial procedure and particularly in the developing law of evidence. Thus the practice of the courts was moving independently in the century toward a position that sprang from more general beliefs that men should be treated equally and fairly and that they ought to have a full opportunity to defend themselves against the charges alleged in their indictment. The notion that a man ought to be regarded as innocent until he is proven guilty beyond doubt had been emerging over a long period and was fully established in the accelerating changes at the end of the eighteenth century and the early years of the nineteenth.

Over the same period in which the repeal of the capital statutes had been proposed and resisted, an even more powerful opposition had arisen to face another novelty that posed what seemed to many men in the late

[15] For Peel and the beginnings of criminal law reform in the 1820s see Radzinowicz, *History*, vol. 1, chap. 18; Norman Gash, *Mr. Secretary Peel* (1961), chap. 9.

eighteenth century the greatest danger to the liberties of all Englishmen, that is, the proposal to replace the old system of parish constables by centralized and paid police forces. The resistance to that threat of arbitrary and uncontrolled centralized authority was powerful and tenacious. It drew on a deep and widely shared inheritance of libertarian thinking. To some extent the situation in London had been altered by the work of the Fieldings and the establishment of the "public" magistrates' offices, which had encouraged the organization of small numbers of full-time, more "professional" police constables. But the full establishment of police on a new footing was successfully resisted until, after 1815, the sheer size of the problems of crime and public disorder began to undermine the fundamental objections that had prevailed for so long. The new order was also encouraged by the changes in the criminal law, for the arguments made in favor of the unpaid and amateur parish constable had always been tied to the character of the old law: since the death penalty worked to terrorize men into obedience there was no need for an organized and powerful police. When the criminal law came to depend on moderate punishments and their effectiveness (it could be argued) required certainty of detection and prosecution, much of that argument was undermined. Peel's Metropolitan Police Act of 1829 established the first force of paid and full-time and uniformed policemen and added another element to the remodeled system of judicial administration.[16]

The criminal law and the machinery of its administration had been transformed by the third decade of the nineteenth century. A system of justice that had been intensely personal and concerned with the particular attributes of offenders and that had conceived of punishment as a means of deterring others by bloody example was giving way to a system of administration that came to emphasize equality and uniformity of treatment as ideals and that thought of punishment as reformative. Violent punishments that attacked the body, carried out in public, were replaced by incarceration and punishments that aimed to reconstruct the prisoner's mind and heart. Undoubtedly the earlier system had served reasonably effectively the needs of rural communities, maintaining serious offenses at an acceptable level while supporting and enhancing the authority of local men of property and influence. But it had become clear at least as early as the second half of the seventeenth century that it did not serve as adequately the needs of an urban society in which vast amounts of movable property provided targets and temptations for a large population of men

---

[16] David Philips, " 'A New Engine of Power and Authority': The Institutionalization of Law-Enforcement in England, 1780–1830," in Gatrell, Lenman, and Parker, eds., *Crime and the Law*, pp. 155–89.

and women who were both more independent of authority and more liable to suffer from extreme and sudden deprivation. The commercial and propertied class of the capital made it clear that they required a criminal administration that would intervene more actively against thieves and robbers, that would actually encourage prosecution and relieve the private prosecutor of some of the burden of bringing a charge, and that would punish those convicted in a way that might prevent or discourage them and others from offending again. The particular problems and interests of the propertied men of the metropolis of London encouraged the search for effective ways of preventing crimes against property over much of the period we have been dealing with—until in the last decades of the eighteenth century the problem of unacceptably high levels of theft engaged the attention of local authorities well beyond the capital.

It was the reality of crime that acted as the catalyst of this change—violence of various kinds, but particularly crimes against property that harmed the interests both of individuals and of society by interrupting the flow of goods and in other ways weakening the foundations of the nation's prosperity. And beyond the harm caused by individual acts of theft and violence, crime stimulated reform ambitions because it signaled much deeper and more serious social ills. As offenses became widespread at certain times over the second half of the eighteenth century and appeared to arise from a detached and threatening "criminal class," new measures of social defense were called for. The proponents of these reforms and those who resisted them were not seriously divided in the objectives they sought or in their views of the ultimate purpose of the criminal law. They both sought to preserve society from the corrosive forces from below. They differed about the measures that ought to be taken, in part because they differed in their assessment of the problem and the justice and efficacy of the established system. But they were both concerned about the threat to social order posed by crime and what it signified. The offenses they were concerned about were real enough, because they derived from the circumstances in which the working population lived. Crime acted over this period as the motor of change in the law and criminal justice system, for both the behavior of those who broke the law and the response of the authorities sprang from changes in society that were already underway at the Restoration and that were accelerating rapidly a hundred and fifty years later.

A wide range of judicial and other data has been drawn on in this book, but the central core of evidence and the basis of most of the tables and the other quantitative statements about the offenders prosecuted and the way they were dealt with by the courts is that derived from the assize files of the Home Circuit and the quarter sessions rolls of Surrey and of East and West Sussex. The data reported in the tables are mainly based on the indictments in those judicial records. That document was the indispensable source, though the evidence it contains about the defendant, the offense charged, and the outcome of the trial was supplemented, where these records were available, by the calendars of indictments, the minute books, and other records of the courts' business kept by the clerks of the peace and the clerks of assize.

The analysis was confined to years in which complete indictment evidence was available, that is, years for which the indictments survive for the two annual sittings of the assizes and the four annual meetings of the quarter sessions so that all the criminal business in the country could be brought together and one year could be compared with others. In addition, I tried to restrict the analysis to groups of at least three contiguous years to avoid the possibly distorted results of an isolated single year, though in the end I was not consistent about that. The decision to select only years in which the indictment data were complete for both assize sittings and all four quarter sessions had the effect of emphasizing the unevenness of coverage over the period 1660 to 1800 that was in some degree inevitable because of the pattern of survival of the Home Circuit assize records.

Before about 1730 the files of the Home Circuit assizes are very patchy. Many individual files in that period are either badly damaged or have disappeared entirely. These records are being gradually cleaned and repaired, which will make them more accessible than they have been, but the spottiness of their survival will continue to make it impossible to get a complete record of the annual business of the assize courts in Surrey and Sussex for more than about half the years between 1660 and 1730. From 1730 on, the main assize records of the Home Circuit are virtually complete; in Surrey and Sussex, certainly, the files put together by the clerks when the circuit was concluded—a "felony" file for each county and a "general" or "misdemeanor" file for the circuit as a whole—have not only survived but are also in good repair. The quarter sessions records of greatest importance to my work—the sessions rolls—are largely complete over the entire period 1660 to 1800. The situation is thus that over the 140 years

I was dealing with, from the Restoration to the end of the eighteenth century, complete indictment evidence is available from the Surrey and Sussex assizes and quarter sessions together in about a hundred years. It is from those years that the four bodies of evidence I have described as the "Sample," the "Count," the "Homicide Count," and the "Hanged Count" have been derived, as follows:

Sample: In dealing with the indictments in the assize files and the quarter sessions rolls, I decided initially to collect virtually all the evidence they contained for every offense brought before the courts other than those that concerned administrative and economic irregularities, though in the end I concentrated on property crime and serious violence. This meant that some form of sampling was necessary, and I began with five groups of five consecutive years (or before 1730 as close to five years as was possible), equally spaced over the period. The full indictment information was coded and entered onto tape to be analyzed by computer. That original data base was, however, gradually enlarged over the years as the focus of the work and the questions being addressed changed, in particular as the administration of the criminal law and the history of punishment emerged as increasingly important themes in my work. Twenty-five years turned out to be an inadequate sample for many purposes because it excluded years and whole periods that came to be particularly interesting. The sample grew, therefore, not out of a concern for its accuracy as a sample, but from a desire to include periods that had been ignored. The data base was broadened in this way until it included the following sixty-one years in Surrey (and only slightly different years in Sussex): 1663–65, 1674–77, 1690–94, 1708, 1710, 1714–15, 1722–24, 1736–43, 1747–58, 1762–70, 1780–84, 1795–1802. All the evidence that could be gathered about each indictment laid before the quarter sessions and assizes in these years was brought together under a separate case number, and the indictment (or case) was made the unit of analysis.

Count: The data included in the "Sample" were the main quantitative evidence used in the book. That evidence has been supplemented, however, for a number of specific purposes. For example, in order to get as full a sense as possible of the changing levels of prosecutions over time of the main offenses dealt with, I have added a simple count of the number of indictments in most of the other years for which complete annual data are available, noting some of the major characteristics of each case—the offense charged, the sex of the accused, the place of the crime, the jury's verdict, and so on—but not collecting the evidence in detail. When those years were added to those in the Sample the changing levels of a number of categories of offenses could be established in ninety-eight years in Surrey between 1660 and 1802. This body of evidence, the "Count" and "Sample" together, includes the following years: 1663–65, 1674–77, 1687–88, 1690–1701, 1708, 1710, 1714–15, 1722–24, 1732–34, 1736–1802.

Homicide Count: The "Homicide Count" also supplements the evidence of the Sample for Surrey. Because there were so few charges each year it was feasible to take a full record of the additional homicide cases, and the result was a file of evidence on the homicide charges brought to the Surrey assizes, in this case in ninety-five years: 1663–65, 1674–77, 1687–88, 1690–1701, 1708, 1710, 1714–15, 1722–24, 1732–34, 1736–43, 1747–1802.

Hanged Count: It is impossible to be certain how many of those convicted of capital offenses at the assizes and sentenced to death were actually hanged because pardons were common and are not easy to trace in every period. The "Hanged Count" is the result of my investigation into the granting of pardons, and thus the level of capital punishment, in Surrey in the following ninety-six years: 1663–65, 1674–77, 1690–1701, 1708, 1710, 1714–15, 1722–24, 1736–1802.

As we have seen, a large number of condemned prisoners were re-prieved by the judge at the conclusion of the court session and recom-mended for a royal pardon; others, overlooked by him and left to be hanged, were subsequently saved as the result of a direct petition to the king or a secretary of state. The problems involved in discovering who was pardoned in these ways are very different on the Home Circuit before and after 1748, for in that year the clerks of assize began to keep an "Agenda Book" (ASSI 31) in which they recorded the daily business of the court and in which they attempted to keep a record not only of the judges' reprieves but also of pardons granted by the king as the result of a later private petition. It was no doubt impossible for the clerks to record all pardons: as the clerk of assize said in 1819 (when asked by the parliamentary committee looking into the criminal law in that year to provide them with the Home Circuit statistics on capital punishment over the previous century and more), condemned men and women were sometimes pardoned at the last moment and that information was not always sent back to the court.[1] A check of the Agenda Books in the years 1771–74 and 1780–86 against the warrants and correspondence of the secretaries of state con-cerning the granting of pardons reveals that some pardons were in fact not recorded. But they were very few. The clerks were clearly in the habit

[1] ASSI 39/7, miscellaneous correspondence.

of keeping track of pardons granted after the conclusion of a session and of recording them months or even years after the prisoner had been condemned in their court. One can thus take the record of the pardons in the Agenda Books as being reasonably complete. They certainly provide a consistent record of the minimum number of pardons granted, and therefore a reliable account of the maximum number of prisoners hanged.

The difficulties of discovering who was hanged and who pardoned are much greater on the Home Circuit before 1748, when the Agenda Book begins. The indictments sometimes note when a condemned prisoner had been reprieved after sentence, but not invariably. Similarly, the assize calendar—what might be called the punishment calendar—which the clerks made up at the conclusion of the session as the offical record of what had taken place, of verdicts reached, and sentences pronounced, also records reprieves granted by the judges before they left town. Before 1730, however, these calendars survive erratically; and because they were often the outside wrapper of the file, they are frequently badly damaged and incomplete even when they have not disappeared. They provide some foundation, but one would miss a great deal if one relied only on them or the indictments.

In the late seventeenth century perhaps the best supplementary source is provided by several classes of records in the Chancery, records surrounding the issuing of the pardon itself. The index volumes to the patent rolls (C 66) include some of the pardons granted (entered under "pardons" or "Home Circuit pardons"), but they are mysteriously incomplete and in the eighteenth century disappear entirely, though pardons for other circuits continue to be entered. A more consistent recovery of names of those pardoned in the last few decades of the seventeenth century seems to be possible by following the process by which the pardon was granted, particularly in the warrants for the great seal (C 83 [series II, to Anne's reign] and C 83 [series III, from George I]). These are filed monthly; to use them it is first necessary to discover the month in which the pardon was issued in the Crown Office docket books (C 231). But the Chancery records also begin to thin out considerably by the first decade of the eighteenth century, at least with respect to pardons on the Home Circuit. The chase can be taken up then, however, in the correspondence between the secretaries of state and judges about reprieves and pardons in the State Papers, Domestic. The judges' circuit pardons (as well as their correspondence) are also increasingly common in the State Papers in the eighteenth century and are especially numerous by the reign of George II (SP 36). Copies of the correspondence with the judges and of warrants relating to pardons are also to be found in a set of letterbooks dealing with criminal matters in the period 1704 to 1782 (SP 44/77–96). Judges' reports and correspondence and other relevant material continue after 1782 in the Home Office papers (HO 13 and HO 47).

I might say that I also investigated the possibility of using sheriffs' cravings to establish who was in fact hanged, since the sheriff would have paid the hangman's fee and various other charges connected with executions and then presumably made a claim for these costs. I did not pursue this in great detail. But my sense is that, apart from the fact that the surviving sheriffs' cravings are not complete, sheriffs did not enter execution expenses consistently in the eighteenth century, and that even when they are available their records could not be relied on to provide a dependable account of the men and women executed in the country.

In the end, one cannot be certain that these rather fragmentary records will provide a reliable account of the pardons granted to condemned prisoners in Surrey between 1660 and the middle of the eighteenth century, and thus of the real levels of capital punishment in that period. It is possible that apparently heavy concentrations of executions in some years may be the result of poor recording of pardons or my failure to find the pardon evidence. But while one could not claim absolute accuracy or certainty, it seems likely that the court records and the evidence from the Chancery and the State Papers, Domestic, and after 1748 the Agenda Books, taken together pick up most of the pardons that were granted, and that the account of those left to be hanged (the "Hanged Count") is not so inaccurate as grossly to distort the level of capital punishment in Surrey over the period 1660 to 1800.

BIBLIOGRAPHY OF MANUSCRIPT SOURCES
AND SURREY ASSIZE PROCEEDINGS

I. MANUSCRIPT SOURCES

A. *Public Record Office (London)*

   1. *Clerks of Assize (Home Circuit Records)*

ASSI 31/2–19	Agenda books, 1748–1802
ASSI 34/32	Clerk's cash books of receipts and payments, 1792–1815
ASSI 34/43–48	Entry book of indictments, witnesses, and costs (criminal proceedings), 1783–1806
ASSI 34/54–56	Precedent books
ASSI 34/68	Presentment book, grand jury, 1768–1812
ASSI 34/69–70	Process books, criminal proceedings, 1773–79, 1786–1812
ASSI 35/101–242	Indictment files, 1660–1802
ASSI 38/1	Estreats, 1770–1870
ASSI 39/7	Correspondence, 1770–1890
ASSI 39/8	Law papers, 1730–1890

   2. *Secretaries of State*

SP 29–37	State Papers, Domestic, 1660–1782
SP 43	State Papers, Regencies, 1716–1755
SP 44/77–96	Entry books, criminal, 1704–82
SP 44/97–145	Secretaries' letter books, 1688–1782
SP 44/146–49	Undersecretaries' letter books, 1684–1771

   3. *Home Office*

HO 7/1	Minutes of the committee respecting transportation of convicts to the West Coast of Africa (1785)

HO 11/1   Convict transportation registers,
                     1782–1809
HO 13   Entry books of letters, warrants,
                     and pardons, 1782–
HO 42   Letters and papers, 1782–
HO 43   Domestic letter books, 1782–
HO 47   Judges' reports and correspond-
                     ence, 1784–

4. *Privy Council*

PC 1   Unbound papers
PC 2   Registers
PC 4   Minutes

5. *Chancery*

C 66   Patent rolls
C 82–83   Warrants for the Great Seal: Hen
                     VIII–Geo IV
C 189   Circuit fiats
C 231   Crown office doquet books
C 234   Fiats for justices of the peace

6. *Treasury*

T 53   Warrants relating to money
T 90/146–170   Sheriffs' cravings, 1733–1822

B. *Surrey Record Office (Kingston upon Thames)*

1. *Quarter Sessions Records*

QS 1/1–4   Commissions of the Peace, 1767–
                     77
QS 2/1/1–31   Order books, 1659–1802
QS 2/2/1–20   Minute books, 1694–1802
QS 2/5   Sessions rolls, 1661–
QS 2/6   Quarter sessions papers, 1701–
QS 2/7   Indictment files 1759– (the indict-
                     ments are included in the ses-
                     sions rolls, 1661–1758)
QS 3/1/1–4   Estreat books, 1689–1800 (bro-
                     ken series)

QS 3/5/1–10	Process books, 1671–1803
QS 5/1/1	Minute books of committees, 1766–79
QS 5/4/1	New Gaol and Sessions House account book, 1791–1805
QS 5/4/2–3	New Gaol and Sessions House minute books, 1791–1824
QS 7/3/1–6	Freeholders books, 1696–1763, 1762–1807

2. *Other Records*

PS 2/1/1	Petty sessions notebook, Hundreds of Copthorne and Effingham, 1784–93
PS 3/1/1	Petty sessions notebook, Hundreds of Kingston and Elmbridge, 1752–93
KS 2/1/1	Petty sessions notebook, Hundreds of Kingston and Elmbridge, 1723–51
2253/15/1	Proceedings of the Godalming Society for the Prosecution of Felons, 1796–1844
2414/8/1–22	Papers of the Mortlake Society for the Prosecution of Felons, 1784–1804

C. *Guildford Muniment Room*

LM 987–2026	Loseley Mss.
Ms. 85/2/4/1	Resolutions of the justices at quarter sessions, 26 July 1785, *re* recent increases in crime; proposals for a county-wide society for the prosecution of felons.
Ms. 85/2/4/166	Society for the Prosecution of Felons, Hundred of Blackheath (n.d.)
Ms. 129/29/40	Guildford Society for the Prosecution of Felons, rules and orders, 1800

Ms. 77/3/1   Godalming Society for the Prosecu-
                              tion of Felons, 1807

D. *East Sussex Record Office (Lewes)*

    Quarter Sessions Records

    QI/EW 2–9   Indictment books, 1652–1789
    QM/EW 1–16   Minute books, 1673–1805
    QO/EW 4–34   Order books, 1660–1802
    QR/E & EW
        127–693   Sessions rolls, East Sussex (E), with
                              the joint session with West
                              Sussex at Midsummer (EW)
    QZ/EW 1–9   Recognizance books, 1660–1809

E. *West Sussex Record Office (Chichester)*

    Quarter Sessions Records

    QR/W 96–639   Sessions rolls, 1660–1802

F. *British Library (London)*

    Add Mss. 27825–30 Place Mss.
    Add Mss. 35600–04 Hardwicke Mss.
             35870   Hardwicke Mss.
             35875–78 Hardwicke Mss.
    Add Mss. 33052   Newcastle Mss.
    Add Mss. 42593   Brockman Mss.

G. *Corporation of London Record Office (Guildhall, London)*

    Southwark Sessions Records

    Box 12.1   Rough minute books and papers
    223 f   Sessions books, 1666–1791 (bro-
                              ken series)
    224 A–B   Files of indictments, recognizances,
                              jury panels, etc., 1667–1870
                              (broken series)

H. *University of Chicago Law Library*

    Ryder Notebook   A copy of the typescript on deposit
                              at Lincoln's Inn of the notes

on cases at the Old Bailey, 1754–56, made by Dudley Ryder as lord chief justice, transcribed from the original shorthand by K. L. Perrin. It is identified as "Law Notes of Sir Dudley Ryder," and numbered Document 14. I follow Langbein in referring to this as the "Ryder Notebook."

Ryder Assize Diary   Ryder's notes on cases at the Home Circuit assizes, 1754–55, a transcription as above of the "Legal Notebook of Sir Dudley Ryder, 1754/55," numbered as Document 19(f). Again, I follow Langbein in citing this as "Ryder Assize Diary."

II. SURREY ASSIZE PROCEEDINGS (S.A.P.)

The titles of the pamphlet accounts of the trials at the Surrey assizes, abbreviated in the notes as S.A.P., vary slightly from one to the other. The publishers of the Proceedings tended to change frequently: the complete run of ten pamphlets over the years 1738 to 1742, for example, were produced under four different imprints. But even the same publisher might alter the title in a minor way from one session to the next. After the first few years, however, the titles were generally similar to that of the account of the session held in March 1749, which ran as follows: *The Proceedings of the King's Commission of the Peace, Oyer and Terminer, and General Gaol Delivery, for the County of Surrey, held at Kingston-upon-Thames, in and for the said County, on Thursday the 16th, Friday the 17th, Saturday the 18th, Monday the 20th, Tuesday the 21st, and Wednesday the 22nd Day of March, 1748–9. . . .* Occasionally, the title is simplified to *The Proceedings of the Assizes for the County of Surrey, held at Kingston upon Thames*, followed by the dates of the session; or to *The Proceedings at the Assizes of Oyer and Terminer and General Gaol Delivery*. The eighteenth-century pamphlets also often add the names of the judges and of the sheriff. (Two of the pamphlets—those for the Summer 1688 and Lent 1739 sessions—contain accounts of the trials at all five counties of the Home Circuit.) None of these variations seems so crucial that I have thought it necessary or worthwhile to list each title separately. On the other hand, because the sessions for which the assize Proceedings have survived are identified in the notes simply as "Lent" or "Summer" sittings, I have given in the list below the dates of the sessions as they appear on the title pages, and I have added in the notes the few titles that do not begin with *The Proceedings*. I have also added at least one location where each pamphlet can be found, abbreviated as follows: BL, British Library; Bod, Bodleian Library (Oxford); GL, Guildhall Library (London); HLGLRO, History Library at the Greater London Record Office; LI, Lincoln's Inn; ML, Minet Library (Lambeth Public Library, Archives Department).

Lent 1678	21–26 March 1678 (ML)
Lent 1679	begun 24 March 1679 (ML)[1]
Lent 1680	12–13, 15–17 March 1680 (Bod; LI)[2]
Summer 1680	19–22 July 1680 (Bod; LI)[3]
Lent 1683	13–15 March 1683 (BL; LI)[4]
Lent 1688	13–14 March 1688 (BL; Bod)
Summer 1688	30 July–1 August 1688 (Bod)[5]
Summer 1711	25–28 July 1711 (GL)
Lent 1715	9–12 March 1715 (GL)
Summer 1718	5–8 August 1718 (GL)
Lent 1726	30 March–4 April 1726 (BL)
Summer 1729	30 July–4 August 1729 (BL)
Lent 1732	23–28 March 1732 (BL)
Lent 1737	begun 16 March 1737 (HLGLRO)
Lent 1738	16-21 March 1738 (BL; ML; HLGLRO)
Summer 1738	3–7 August 1738 (BL; HLGLRO)
Lent 1739	22–24 March 1739 (BL; ML)[6]
Summer 1739	22–25 August 1739 (GL; HLGLRO)
Lent 1740	27–29 March 1740 (BL)
Summer 1740	30 July–2 August 1740 (BL; GL)

[1] *A Narrative of the Proceedings at the Assizes holden in Southwark at the Marshalsea for the County of Surrey, begun on 24 March 1679* (1679).

[2] *The True Narrative of the Proceedings at the Assizes holden for the County of Surry: which began on Fryday the 12th of this instant March 1679/{80} and ended on the Wednesday following. . . .* (1680).

[3] *The True Narrative of the Proceedings at the Surry Assizes holden at Kingston upon Thames, 19–22 July 1680* (1680).

[4] *A True Account of the Proceedings on the Crown-Side at the Lent Assize held for the County of Surrey in the Burrough of Southwark, 13–15 March. . . .* (1683).

[5] *The Proceedings of the Home Circuit on the King's Commission on the Crown side at the several Assizes (viz) Hertford, Brentford, Croydon, East-Grensted, and Rochester* (1688).

[6] *The Genuine Proceedings at the Assizes on the Home Circuit held in March 1739. . . .* (1739).

Lent 1741	20–24 March 1741 (BL)
Summer 1741	22–25 July 1741 (BL)
Lent 1742	26–29 March 1742 (BL)
Summer 1742	13–16 August 1742 (BL)
Summer 1743	5–9 August 1743 (BL)
Lent 1745	22–27 March 1745 (BL)
Lent 1749	16–22 March 1749 (BL)
Summer 1751	15–22 August 1751 (BL)
Lent 1752	31 March–3 April 1752 (BL; ML)
Lent 1753	2–6 April 1753 (BL; GL)
Summer 1756	20–24 August 1756 (GL)
Lent 1759	28 March–3 April 1759 (BL; GL)
Summer 1759	9–11 August 1759 (BL)
Summer 1764	23–25 August 1764 (GL)
Lent 1774	23–28 March 1774 (GL)
Summer 1780	10 July 1780 (BL)[7]

[7] *The Proceedings of the King's Special Commission of Oyer and Terminer for the County of Surrey held . . . on Monday the 10th of July, 1780. . . .* (1780; trials arising out of the Gordon Riots).

INDEX

Lightning Source UK Ltd.
Milton Keynes UK
UKOW042248050412

190200UK00001B/1/A